Africa and the World

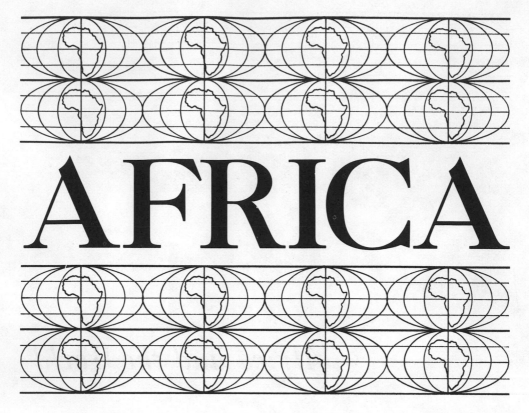

AFRICA

*An Introduction to
the History of Sub-Saharan Africa
from Antiquity to 1840*

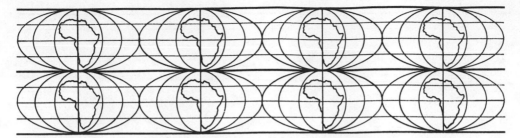

AND THE
WORLD

Lewis H. Gann
and Peter Duignan

WITHDRAWN

CHANDLER PUBLISHING COMPANY
An Intext Publisher
SAN FRANCISCO • SCRANTON • LONDON • TORONTO

Cartography by Vincent Kotschar. Maps in this book include several specially prepared, several from Mr. Kotschar's forthcoming atlas of Africa, and several redrawn as acknowledged from other publications.

Previously published and copyrighted materials are reprinted with the permission of authors, publishers, or copyright owners as listed below:

John Pepper Clark's "Night Rain," Ellis Ayitey Komey's "The Change," and David Rubadiri's "An African Thunderstorm" from *Modern Poetry From Africa*, eds. Gerald Moore and Ulli Beier (Harmondsworth Middlesex, England: Penguin Books, Ltd., 1964). Reprinted by permission of the publishers and authors.

O. G. S. Crawford, ed., *Ethiopian Itineraries Circa 1400–1524* (Hakluyt Society, Second Series, No. CIX, Cambridge, 1958) reprinted by permission of the Cambridge University Press, publishers on behalf of the Hakluyt Society.

Elspeth Huxley, *Four Guineas: A Journey Through West Africa* (London: Chatto and Windus Ltd., 1954) reprinted by permission of the publisher.

Daniel Kunene, "Deculturation: The African Writer's Response," from *Africa Today*, August-September, 1966. Reprinted by permission of *Africa Today*.

A. W. Lawrence, *Trade Castles and Forts of West Africa* (Stanford: Stanford University Press, 1964) reprinted by permission of Jonathan Cape Ltd., 30 Bedford Square, London WC 1, England.

Eric Williams, *Capitalism and Slavery* (Chapel Hill: University of North Carolina Press, 1944; New York: Russell & Russell, 1961; London: Andre Deutsch Ltd., 1966) reprinted by permission of the publishers.

Contents

Illustrations

Maps

5

Preface

Some seventy years ago, Sir Harry Johnston, a great British empire builder, published a general history of Africa.[1] His was a pioneer study which, for the first time, dealt with the whole continent. But the very title of the book showed the limited nature of its approach. To Johnston, the annals of Africa contained but a succession of invasions that dated from antiquity to his own times. In these dramatic events, alien intruders played all the star roles; indigenous Africans appeared only as a supporting cast. About half a century later, Diedrich Westermann, a German missionary and scholar, compiled a very different work. This chronicled the story of the indigenous African kingdoms before the imperial conquest.[2] When Westermann put pen to paper, the study of African history had progressed. Nevertheless, much of his work is now dated. Not only was his knowledge necessarily limited, but he was interested mainly in political history and paid little heed to social and economic factors.

Since Westermann, scholars have made many advances. There are now great numbers of monographs covering subjects that range all the way from Yoruba warfare in the nineteenth century to the spread of manioc.[3]

In addition, a number of important works have appeared which consist of essays

[1] Sir Harry H. Johnston, *History of the Colonization of Africa by Alien Races* (Cambridge, 1899).

[2] Diedrich Westermann, *Geschichte Afrikas: Staatenbildungen südlich der Sahara* (Cologne, 1952).

[3] See for example: J. F. A. Ajayi and Robert S. Smith, *Yoruba Warfare in the Nineteenth Century* (Cambridge, 1964). William O. Jones, *Manioc in Africa* (Stanford, 1959).

contributed by experts. Some of these studies cover particular areas such as eastern or southern Africa.[4] Others deal with specific issues such as the formation of plural societies in precolonial Africa.[5] These books are designed primarily, though by no means solely for specialists. There are likewise excellent books suitable for college students and general readers on, individual African countries such as J. D. Fage's brief but fascinating introduction to Ghanaian history.[6]

But there are not many books which cover Africa—or even sub-Saharan Africa—as a whole. The best of these is surely a paperback written by R. Oliver and J. D. Fage, a pioneer study on the bookshelves of every Africanist.[7] This "Penguin" is, however, brief, and some of the theories put forward by its authors no longer meet with the unanimous consent of Africanists. Donald L. Wiedner's textbook, the first to be compiled in America to assist college students, devotes more time to the colonial than to the precolonial period.[8] Robert W. July's learned and readable study concentrates above all on the more modern period.[9] Robin Hallett's thoroughly documented work will be found useful,[10] especially the chapter on "suggested readings." Hallett's volume is mainly organized by geographical divisions. Teachers making use of his textbook will have to emphasize the importance of synoptic chronology, lest students lose a sense of what was and what was not historically contemporaneous.

In our own teaching experience, we have found the need for an introductory history which specifically links the African past with the history of the wider world, while at the same time providing more geographical and ethnographic information than most history texts offer.

We hope that this book will prove useful to undergraduates working on the precolonial and early colonial history of sub-Saharan Africa. We believe that this volume will also help students and general readers who wish to find out more about African history within the wider context of world events. It is also designed for students who wish to study the impact of Europe on the non-Western world, the history of the Atlantic basin, or who wish to emphasize interdisciplinary studies with an African content. We have necessarily been selective. A brief glance at an ethnic map of Africa reveals a mosaic of incredible complexity. It would have been quite impossible to trace the history of each separate ethnic group, however interesting for its own sake. But we have endeavored to take account of major economic and social factors as well as of some more recent studies in anthropology, archaeology and history and art.

We are fully aware of the debate concerning academic bias that exercises so many minds in Black studies today. Complete impartiality is unattainable. The only perfectly objective book is a telephone directory—but no one in his right mind reads

[4]See Roland Oliver and Gervase Mathew, eds., *History of East Africa*, vol. 1, (Oxford, 1963) and Monica Wilson and Leonard Thompson, eds., *The Oxford History of South Africa vol. 1, South Africa to 1870.* (Oxford, 1969).

[5]Leo Kuper and M. G. Smith, *Pluralism in Africa* (Berkeley and Los Angeles, 1969).

[6]John D. Fage, *Ghana: A Historical Interpretation* (Madison, 1959).

[7]Roland Oliver and John D. Fage, *A Short History of Africa* (Baltimore, 1962).

[8]Donald L. Wiedner, *A History of Africa South of the Sahara* (New York, 1962).

[9]Robert W. July, *A History of the African People* (New York, 1970).

[10]Robin Hallett, *Africa to 1875: A Modern History* (New York, 1970).

telephone directories for instruction or pleasure. Historians are not omniscient; their conclusions stand in need of constant revision, like any other kind of human knowledge. They can only strive for some measure of informed and judicious fairness. They should also attempt to become conscious of their own preconceptions, which—in our case—derive from our background as middle and working class Westerners. We strongly reject the view, still upheld by distinguished historians like Professor Hugh Trevor-Roper, that the developments among Africa's indigenous peoples were of no significance for mankind at large. We likewise have no patience with romantic historians who see the precolonial era as a golden age where men lived in the state of primordial innocence and harmony.

Writing, as we do, in the United States during the early 1970s, we must also take account of objections that may be put forward with regard to our racial descent. Only black men—some argue—can write Black history in an impartial fashion; only black men have the required empathy for the task. We do not share this view. We do not consider that the Republic of Letters can be split into cantons of color. A Hausa's view concerning the Ibo is not necessarily freer from prejudice than an Irishman's. A Hutu does not necessarily have more empathy for a Tutsi than has a German. Historical comprehension transcends racial boundary. Otherwise world history could not be written, and would disappear from our university syllabuses.

In choosing our terms when referring to the people of Africa, we are aware that the very choice of words raises some highly emotion-laden issues. A hundred years ago, ethnographers writing about the black-skinned peoples of Southern Africa referred to "Kafirs." The word "Kafir" in due course became little better than a swear-word; educated people then began to speak of "natives" instead. During the present century, this term also became unacceptable; black people now want to be known as Africans. We have used all these expressions as synonyms. The descendants of Dutch immigrants in South Africa have become equally conscious of their national identity. Fifty years ago, British South Africans referred to their Afrikaans-speaking neighbors as Dutchmen or Boers. The term "Dutchmen" is no longer regarded as polite in South African society. Boers want to be known as Afrikaners, as people of Africa, and they will refer to European Dutchmen as Hollanders. Again, we have used these terms according to the customs of the time.

Many Africanists also object to the use of the term "tribe." They point out that some of the so-called tribes identified during the colonial period were not really traditional communities. They also feel that the use of the term "tribe" implies condescension or contempt. Some scholars have suggested a variety of alternative terms, ranging from "ethny" to "nation." We do not, however, accept their reasoning. The term "ethny" strikes us as artificial. The term "people" is useful, but often too general in its meaning. The term "nation" is sometimes most apposite. The Amhara, a people with a well-defined territory, a language of their own, a historical tradition that goes back to antiquity, and a great literary tradition are certainly a nation. The Lala and the Lamba of Zambia, on the other hand, are not nations, and no Zambian would describe them as such; a Zambian patriot would prefer to weld such smaller local communities into a Zambian nation. The term "nation" indeed raises as many questions as it answers. Is there or is there not a Biafran nation? At the time of writing (in 1970), black Nigerians would answer this question in many different ways. Nigerian soldiers fought a bloody war over the issue, and we do not feel competent to adjudicate between them. Neither can we accept the contention that the use of the term "tribe" implies a measure of conservative condescension or of racialist contempt for black people. White-skinned Jews proudly refer to their ancestral Twelve Tribes. Germans talk of Swabians, Bavarians, and Saxons as *Stämme* or tribes. Neither is the use of the word "tribe" confined to the adherents of any particular political persuasion. Militant African radicals like Kwame Nkrumah, or the leaders of the revolutionary Movimento Popular de Libertacão de Angola warn their countrymen against the perils of tribalism. Hence the word "tribe" seems to us appropriate within certain contexts. We do not consider all Africans to have been members of a tribe; some of the ancients were indeed city-folk. We use the word "tribe" to signify a community—large or small, weak or powerful, white or black— whose members all depend on a fairly simple system of technology, who are mostly or entirely non-literate, and who make their living primarily from the soil. They speak the same language, obey the same rules of political and social conduct, and observe the same religion. They acknowledge extensive obligations to a wide circle of kins- men, both living and dead. Above all, the members of a tribal community—whether the subjects of an ancient Teutonic duke, an erstwhile Montenegrin prince-bishop, or a Zulu king—all have specific land rights. These vary a good deal in their nature; there was no universal system of tribal land law, either in Africa or anywhere else. But in most parts of precolonial Africa land was plentiful. Members of the same community were linked to the land through membership in the social group. Leaders might or might not have the right to allocate farming sites, to levy tribute, or to impose some other kind of impost. But no one could become a landed magnate; there was no room for private ownership of land.

We likewise make no apologies for dealing at some length with the affairs of Portuguese, Afrikaners, the French and English, as well as with those of Zulu, Amhara, and Fulani, since we feel that Africa's past cannot be understood in isolation. For instance, Africa was profoundly influenced by the New World, which supplied the continent with a variety of new food crops; on the other hand, Africa deeply influenced the West Indies and the America's which, in part, were half-Africanized by the slave trade.

In putting together this work, we have set some limits on the scope. We have concentrated on Africa south of the Sahara. Geographically the Maghrib forms part of the African landmass. But historically and culturally, it is linked to the Mediter- ranean and the Middle East. Such divisions can, of course, never be absolute. The Mediterranean countries helped indirectly to shape history in the desert, savannah, and forest belts to the south. But North Africa is now primarily part of the Arabic- speaking world, and may one day belong to an Arab political union. We have touched upon Madagascar, but we have not followed up its history, as Madagascar is in some ways a little world of its own, belonging to the Indian Ocean community as much as to Africa.

We have taken our story to about 1840—but no further. The impact of European imperialism of Africa deserves a book of its own. We have already put forward our own personal interpretation of this more recent era.[11] We have also been able to draw on the help of many distinguished scholars in a multi-volume study that is now being published in England.[12]

In giving references, we have made no attempt to provide students with complete bibliographical information. There are numerous detailed annotated guides available. In giving source references, we have tried to direct students to works that are not only scholarly but also readable, avoiding books and articles that will appeal to specialists rather than beginners.

We are aware than in an age of exploding knowledge, texts such as these are out of date before they even go into galley proofs. Scholars in many different disciplines are constantly broadening the range of knowledge, and it is physically impossible to read all the books and articles that have been and that are being published on the immense subject of Africa's past. We are therefore all the more grateful to the many specialists who have given advice, or who have kindly read sections of our book. They include Professors R. O. Collins, E. Colson, J. Desmond Clark, B. M. Fagan, J. Greenberg, W. A. Hance, G. W. Johnson, G. W. Irwin, R. K. Kent, S. Ottenberg, W. F. Lye, L. Spitzer, D. L. Wiedner, D. L. Wheeler, and F. Willett. We are much indebted to all these scholars, but take full responsibility for any errors or misconceptions that may have crept into this book despite their help. To Frances, Kathy and Patty Duignan our thanks for their care and energy in checking footnotes and typing the manuscript.

L. H. Gann
Peter Duignan

Hoover Institution, Stanford University
1971

---

[11]L. H. Gann and Peter Duignan, *Burden of Empire: An Appraisal of Western Colonialism in Africa South of the Sahara* (New York, 1967).

[12]Peter Duignan and L. H. Gann, eds., *Colonialism in Africa 1870–1960*, 5 vols., (Cambridge, 1969–).

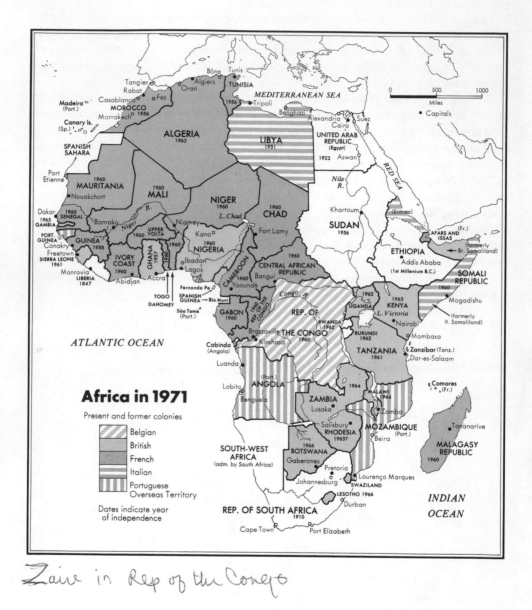

Africa in 1971

Zaire in Rep of the Congo

Africa and the World

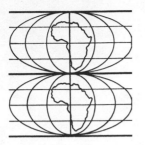

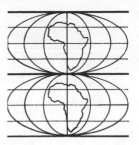

PART I

THE GEOGRAPHY OF AFRICA SOUTH OF THE SAHARA

Chapter 1

Introduction

THE STEREOTYPE OF AFRICA

An old-fashioned steamer slowly chugs up the river. The captain, a red-faced Englishman, takes off his sun-helmet and wipes his brow as he anxiously watches his course. There is a hum of mosquitoes in the air. The water is sluggish; the flow of the current cannot be discerned; the reflections are glassy and mirrorlike, except that the water in the foreground is strewn with lotus leaves. Overarching branches frame in the scene from an island on the opposite bank. On the mainland shore stand tall acacia trees with smooth trunks and whitish-green branches. Their foliage is spangled with tiny, golden-stemmed flowers. These exhale a penetrating scent that wafts far across the water.

The small vessel slowly negotiates a concealed sandbank and passes a magnificent palm grove and a tropical forest of rich green with purple shadows, lovely in their warm tints under the rays of the late afternoon sun. Over the waterside hang thick bushes overgrown with convolvulus creepers that almost hide the foliage of the bush. The green lacework is lit up by mauve flowers. Tiny kingfishers of purple-blue and orange flit through the network of gnarled trunks. Deep in this recess of shade, night herons and bitterns stand bolt upright, so confident in their assumed invisibility against the background of brown and grey that they do not move, even when the ship brushes against the tangle of undergrowth.[1]

Such is the conventional picture of Africa, a continent of steaming jungles and hidden creeks where crocodiles lie in wait for the unwary. Africa is so described in the Bible as the mysterious land of Ophir from where King Solomon's navy brought "gold, and silver, ivory, and apes, and peacocks."[2]

3

But a very small part of the continent conforms to this image. Geographers reckon that only some eight percent of the African landmass has a tropical rainy climate. Indeed, Africa comprises about a third of the dry lands of the world, and has "the highest percentage of arid wastes (60%) of any continent except Australia."[3] In over half of Africa, water is man's principal problem, and the lack of regular rainfall is the main physical obstacle to progress. The continent as a whole is an enormous plateau with terraced table lands, going up one above the other. They rise and fall, tilt and dip, fold and fracture; and a traveler in, say the Eastern Highlands of Rhodesia, will see sights very different from those of the Malawi River course described above.

A tourist motoring southeast from Salisbury, the Rhodesian capital, passes Rusape, a small settlement, and follows the route to Inyanga. The road starts rising gradually over a series of detached plateaus, connected by warped saddles. The visitor is unaware of gaining much height, until he happens to catch a glimpse of the valleys on either side of the road. He looks at a mass of ancient hillocks that range from a few feet to several hundred. Practically all of them have exposed their hard, silver-gray granite cores. The naked stones take on the most fantastic shapes—sugar loaves, convex cones, rectangular blocs, all piled up on one another. Some enormous boulders balance precariously one on the other. Others have a more stable appearance and look like weathered medieval castles, heaped up by some forgotten race of giants. The *kopje* (small hill) country gradually falls away, and the scenery opens into rolling plateaus, elevated downs covered with short grass and ferns, and broken with cliffs and waterfalls. Much of the area is clothed in man-made forests whose trees are almost as cosmopolitan as the peoples of Rhodesia. There are pines from Mexico and the Himalayas, black wattle, eucalyptus, and gum imported from Australia, cypresses, poplars breaking into new leaf by the banks of streams. And brooding over the scene is Inyangani, Rhodesia's highest point, over 8,500 feet above sea level. A traveler who has looked at the massive Table Mountain in Cape Town at the extreme southern tip of Africa knows that he is still on the same continent when he sees Inyangani.

A stranger who makes his way into Rhodesia's northern lowlands (or veld) again sees a different kind of scenery. The country is dry. The bush is studded with sinister-looking "fever trees"; their bark has a pale greenish-white sheen. Euphorbias stand out like great candelabras, resembling Arizona cactuses, ideally suited to stand prolonged droughts. There are enormous baobab trees with massive trunks, which Africans say God, in a fit of anger, stuck upside down in the ground because He did not like His handiwork. The country looks dry and grim under a sky of bright-burnished blue, stretching out towards a distant horizon, hazed by smoke from veld fires. Down in the lower Zambezi Valley there is coarse elephant grass, upwards of twelve feet high. In the dry season great fires sweep over the land and turn the bush into a flaming inferno. The thick grass stems burn with loud, crackling sounds, and in a few minutes a compact column of smoke rises high in the air, like the trail of a rocket that has been launched into space.

But there are many other Africas: the Africa of snow-tipped mountains; the Africa of low shores, lined with coconut palms and pale green mangrove swamps. There is the Africa of the desert, yellow, sandy, seemingly limitless; the Africa of highland forests where the morning mists merge into the mountains, and where an unsuspecting traveler might imagine himself stranded in some forlorn part of Central Europe. There is the Africa of the Cape, with its pleasant vineyards and Mediterranean scenery; or the Africa of great river cataracts, where white swirling walls of water hurl down with unimaginable fury. It is a continent of monotony and variety, a land where few generalizations hold true and where most comparisons break down.

Above all, Africa is of tremendous size. Its area, including Madagascar and other adjacent islands, amounts to something like 11,700,000 square miles. The United States fits into this great land mass 3.32 times for the fifty states and 3.9 times for the forty-eight contiguous states. A major European country like Great Britain occupies less than 1 percent of Africa's acreage. The area of Belgium, an important ex-colonial power, would have to be enlarged nearly a thousand times before it equaled Africa's size. Africa's length—from north to south—is approximately 5000 miles; this is only about 200 miles less than the distance from New York to Suez. Africa's extreme breadth exceeds 4600 miles, slightly more than the distance from San Francisco to Yokohama in Japan. Judged by these standards, even American proportions dwindle, and the observer remains overwhelmed by the sheer immensity of the continent.

EARTH SCIENCE AND THE STUDY OF MAN

In the past some philosophers have made the most extravagant claims for the study of geography. The configuration of lands and climates supposedly could explain all the vagaries of man's fate. Hard climates—the argument went—would breed tough and warlike men. Soft climates would create soft and languid people. Civilizations would flourish only in temperate zones, especially in countries with jagged coastlines, indented peninsulas and surrounding rings of islands, where man would easily learn the arts of trade and navigation.

Such theories have some plausibility at first. But they explain too much by too little. The Eskimos had to contend with the world's harshest climate; they have always been famed as a peaceful race. The Masai of Kenya dwell near the equator in the tropical sun. They are, however, intrepid warriors. Southeast Asia has developed great civilizations in tropical conditions. Even the "indented coastline" theory will not hold. The ancient Greeks, living in a country cut up by bays and inlets, richly endowed with natural ports, developed a great maritime and mercantile civilization. The West Indian aborigines, on the face of it, enjoyed similar geographical advantages. But no settlement on the Great Antilles ever reproduced the glory that was Athens. The English-speaking colonists of New England became great seafarers and traders. Their Amero-Indian predecessors, living in an identical environment, never developed a similar way of life.

Geography, in other words, greatly influences man's history. Primitive man could do little about his environment. Modern engineers can create artificial ports on shores where none existed before; they bore tunnels through mountains; they can dam up rivers and create artificial lakes. Geography nevertheless remains important. The physical framework of the earth is rather like a great arena in which mankind plays his various parts. The stage does not make the plot. It can, however, impose considerable limits on the playwright's ingenuity. A vast open air theatre is not suitable for small intimate scenes. A tiny platform precludes mass spectacles of the Hollywood variety. Historians, who untangle the processes of history, also have to study its stage —its size, acoustics and light effects. But they must never forget that many different plays can be enacted upon an identical stage, or in the glare of the same footlights.

THE SHAPE OF AFRICA

The Phoenicians, a Semitic-speaking people from the Near East, were the greatest seamen of antiquity. Ships from Tyre, with their blue and purple sails, their masts of Lebanese cedar wood, and their great oars fashioned from the oaks of Bashan, were a familiar sight in every Mediterranean port. The Phoenicians also traded in African produce. "The men of Dedan were thy merchants," says Ezekiel, "many isles were the merchandise of thine hand: they brought thee for a present horns of ivory and ebony." The very benches of some rich men's vessels were inlaid with elephant's or rhino's tusks.[4] So great was the Phoenicians' interest in Africa that some time in the seventh century B.C. a Phoenician fleet is reputed to have sailed around Africa.

Some historians, however, doubt whether this journey ever took place. For Africa is the world's second-largest continent. Its coastline measures about 16,000 miles, so that these ancient mariners would have had to cover a distance equivalent to more than six separate journeys from New York to San Francisco. This great land mass has relatively few natural ports, such as Freetown, Luanda, Table Bay, and Delagoa Bay. Ships often experience great difficulties in approaching the coast on account of sandbars deposited by currents flowing along the shore, or by rivers in their lower course. The sailors would have really found themselves at home only on the Barbary littoral of northwest Africa, where there are a number of good harbors and where the Phoenicians had founded the great overseas colony of Carthage.

The shape of Africa can be drawn fairly simply. The continent is an irregular triangle with its base at the Mediterranean and its apex at the southern Cape. The equator runs more or less through the middle of the great African landmass, which is disposed at a nearly equal distance on either side of this imaginary dividing line. The northern portion looks like a big ellipsoid, with the great Sahara-Sudanic middle belt as its axis. On the northeast there is a massive triangular projection which juts out into the Indian Ocean. This is the Somali Peninsula; the area is sometimes called "the Horn of Africa." The southern portion of the continent resembles a triangle whose landmass stretches all the way from the northern interior of the Congo to the Cape of Good Hope, where the waters of the Indian and Atlantic oceans mingle.

CONTINENT IN ISOLATION

Africa as a whole faces enormous problems of access and occupies a position of partial isolation. In this respect the northern portion of the continent is better off than the lands beyond the Sahara. The North African landmass is connected to the Near East by a narrow land bridge crossed by countless invaders, from ancient Egyptian footmen and charioteers to modern British soldiers in khaki. It was only in 1869 that the narrow land connection was cut by the completion of the Suez Canal, and French engineers thereby turned Africa into a continental "island." The Red Sea, a relatively narrow corridor, forms a means of communication as well as a water barrier. From times immemorial, navigators from the Yemen and adjacent lands in Saudi Arabia have made their way across the Red Sea to the African mainland. Northwest Africa, however, looks out towards Mediterranean Europe. The Straits of Gibraltar—at their narrowest—interpose only nine miles of salt water between southern Spain and Morocco.

The bulk of Africa is to some extent cut off from the Mediterranean coastlands by the Sahara, the world's largest wasteland. This is a land of wind-worked sands and dunes, of gravel plain, of grotesquely eroded rock, of granite strewn surfaces, of great tracts covered with stones and waterworn pebbles. The Sahara supposedly covers some 3,500,000 square miles of North Africa, from the Mediterranean to the Sudan. It is by no means an impassable barrier. Oases occur whenever there is water; considerable areas are utilized by wandering herdsmen, and caravans have passed across this portion of Africa for many centuries. Over the last milennium or more the Sahara has become, however, increasingly arid. Ancient water courses dried up, and the process of desiccation continues. The Sahara thus increasingly hindered communications and played a considerable part in imposing relative isolation from the developing world on vast portions of the African continent.

Sub-Saharan Africa, surrounded as it is by deserts and oceans, lacks any particular orientation towards other continents. There is one exception. The bulge of West Africa looks towards the Atlantic and to Latin America. There is, indeed, a theory that Africa and South America were once joined together, but later slowly drifted apart, leaving a widening oceanic gap between them. The great right-angled bulge of Brazil would fit well into the West African indentation formed by the Biafra Bight. Geologists and biologists have adduced additional evidence in support of Wegener's theory of continental displacement. Africa and parts of Latin America now share certain geological features; these similarities have made for some interesting historical parallels between the world's two great southern land masses.[5] But sailing and rowing ships and boats could not master the great distances involved, and modern links between Africa and America date only from the age of the European discoveries.

Nature likewise placed enormous obstacles in the way of maritime contacts between West Africa and the Mediterranean. The ships of Phoenician, ancient Greek and Roman mariners were of a simple pattern. Their sails were square; the boats lacked rudders; they could not therefore travel against the direction of the wind, unless propelled by oars. Vessels of such a kind would have been capable of making the journey from the Mediterranean shore of North Africa to West Africa, but they would not have been able to come back because of the unfavorable winds and currents of the coastal region now comprised within Spanish Sahara and Mauritania. European ships of a more efficient pattern, equipped with lateen sails (triangular sails attached to a long yard suspended from the mast), and provided with rudders, date only from

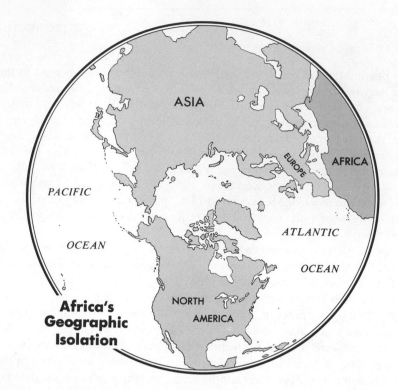

Africa's Geographic Isolation

the twelfth century. These medieval vessels could now tack, that is to say they could laboriously sail against the wind in a zigzag pattern, and they could thereby ultimately conquer the perils of the West African shore.

The East African coast, on the other hand, was much more favorably situated from the navigator's point of view. The regime of the Indian Ocean monsoons allowed sailing ships of a very simple kind to travel all the way from India to East Africa, wait for the shift in winds, and come back again. East Africa's coastlands were therefore less isolated than those of West Africa, and East Africans were able to establish early contacts with other countries on the littoral of the Indian Ocean.

Sub-Saharan Africa not only looks away from the ancient centers of civilization in the Mediterranean and the Near East, but is also deficient in good natural harbors. Again there are exceptions. Freetown, the capital of Sierra Leone in West Africa, has one of the world's finest natural anchorages. There are protected bays in Angola, Mozambique and other parts of Africa. But for accessibility from the sea, the subcontinent compares unfavorably with, say, the northeastern states of the United States or Western Europe. Even a major maritime center like Cape Town, at the southern tip of the continent—a great seaport somewhat resembling San Francisco in climate, character and natural beauty—lacks first-rate natural port facilities. Table Bay has a splendid scenic entrance, an unforgettable sight for immigrants. But the Bay is exposed to fierce oceanic gales, and its great modern harbor owes more to the art of the engineer than to the provisions of nature.

Africa has put additional obstacles in the way of inland explorers or traders. Africa is a plateau continent. The coastal zone is often only twenty miles in breadth; this low-lying belt is commonly backed by steep scarps (cliffs) which make road and railway construction a costly undertaking. The profiles of many African railroads reflect this difficult pattern. On the first sixty miles of the line from Djibouti to Addis Ababa, for instance, the train has to go up 2,300 feet; in the final 180 miles it rises 4,625 feet. The track winds and turns, passing over no less than 1,426 bridges; it also has to go through numerous tunnels and over many viaducts. Transport firms calculate that shipping an automobile from Djibouti to Addis Abada costs as much as sending the same car from Detroit to Djibouti.

The plateaus of the continent create a special stream profile, and many African rivers have rapids near the coast and inland. Cataracts afford a magnificent spectacle to tourists and vast opportunities to hydroelectrical engineers. From the transportation point of view, however, their existence is an unmitigated disaster. With some exceptions like the Niger and the Senegal in West Africa, most African rivers have not provided natural roadways for transportation and communications, and in this respect Africa's geographical pattern greatly differs from that of Europe or North America.[6]

The history of river navigation on the Zambezi in Central Africa illustrates these difficulties in graphic fashion. The great water course is navigable for about 120 miles from its mouth on the coast of Mozambique—though with difficulty in the dry season. Subsequently, a river captain encounters some of the world's most dangerous rapids. In the last century, David Livingstone, the famous Scottish missionary-explorer, tried to go up the Zambezi in a steam vessel, but for all his courage and dogged energy the Scotsman had to give in to the river. In the closing years of the last century, a group of British officers led by Major St. H. Gibbons embarked on yet another attempt. The major, a resourceful man, tried to avoid the mistakes which had frustrated Livingstone's attempt. He used two launches and a barge, all made of aluminum, light, and skillfully fashioned into portable sections. The party grimly pushed inland from the Indian Ocean and got to the foot of the Kebrabasa rapids. Here everything was taken apart, packed, and carried up river on the backs of sweating carriers who took their loads to Chicoa, on the south bank of the river. Again the boats were put together and refloated, but the ensuing journey proved a nightmare. After unremitting toil and setbacks of the most harassing kind, the British decided to abandon the Zambezi route.

Many water courses also suffer from a markedly seasonal flow, to say nothing of having shoals, shifting sandbars, and cataracts. Road builders have to contend with heavy seasonal downpours. A storm may wash away a piece of road in a night. A rapidly rising stream may make a low bridge impassable. Even today many an outlying community finds itself isolated when the rains start coming down. In the savannah country motorists must reckon with alternating seasons of mud and dust, fine red dust that can make the life of a person afflicted with sinus trouble an aching misery. Rain forests present transport engineers with even greater problems. In steppe or desert country the scarcity of water is another challenge, requiring the use of special condensors or expensive supply installations. In most parts of Africa locomotives cannot get local coal; trains either have to run on wood or they require expenditure of foreign exchange to pay for imported diesel oil.

Other difficulties included diseases like the one transmitted by the tsetse fly, which restricted or prevented the employment of draft animals. Horses and camels could only be used north of the great West African forest belt. For centuries Arab and Berber horsemen and camel drivers carried on trade with the Sudanic peoples. White pioneers introduced horses into the uplands of South Africa, but elsewhere precolonial Africa largely depended on porters who could bear something like fifty to sixty pounds on the heads or their backs. Carriers, however, could not walk fast. They also needed food for their own sustenance, so that caravans could move only with relatively small payloads. Africans also made good use of river canoes; indigenous people like the Lozi of the Upper Zambezi became some of the world's most intrepid inland navigators. But river like carrier-borne transport depended on human muscle power, an expensive commodity, so that transport remained an ever-present challenge to human endeavor on the African continent.[6]

THE PLAGUES OF AFRICA

The first account of the natural afflictions besetting Africa is found in the Book of Exodus. Seven terrible calamities struck down the land of Egypt before Pharaoh consented to let the Children of Israel depart. These plagues still stalk the land, and perhaps the greatest curse of all are mosquito-borne diseases. "And there came a grievous swarm of flies into the house of Pharaoh and into the servants' houses, and into all the land of Egypt: the land was corrupted by reason of the swarm of flies."[7] Annoying and painful as mosquito bites may be, they are not of themselves dangerous. But mosquitoes unfortunately act as carriers of malaria and yellow fever, which in the past formed an invisible but deadly barrier against newcomers—white or black, who had not acquired at least a partial resistance to the parasites. Malaria is endemic in most parts of sub-Saharan Africa. It seriously weakens even those who have some degree of immunity. It struck down with deadly effect strangers who came into the malarial regions (only late in the nineteenth century did man learn how to protect himself by drugs and other prophylactic means). Malaria is caused by a minute parasite transferred by the anopheles mosquito to man. Blackwater fever, a consequence of poor treatment of repeated malaria infections, is also a potent killer.

Another terrible disease is yellow fever, which is endemic throughout the middle belt of Africa. It is caused by an ultra-microscopic virus transmitted from man to man by the mosquito *Aedes aegypti*. If a victim survives his first attack, he is safe for life, and many Africans probably have acquired immunity in their youth. But if the disease strikes severely, the patient usually dies. Other sicknesses transmitted by mosquitoes include elephantiasis, which produces enormous swelling of the legs and sometimes other limbs, and sleeping sickness (carried by the tsetse fly).

In addition there are water-borne plagues. They comprise, among others, bilharziasis or schistosomiasis. This is caught through contact with water contaminated by the bilharzia parasite, with a water snail acting as its intermediate host. Modern medical men can cure the disease, but they do not as yet know of any satisfactory way of clearing infected streams, and far from dying out, the disease is even spreading through new parts of Africa. The Guinea threadworm is another culprit. It lives in a minute freshwater crustacean and then makes its way under the human skin, where it may reach a yard or more in length and cause terrible ulceration.

Lice and fleas also form a threat to human health because of the infections which they carry. Relapsing fever, for instance, is spread through a blood parasite borne by a louse or tick. The murine plague is transmitted to man through fleas from rats, and there are many other sicknesses. In addition, Africans have had to cope with killers familiar to northern continents. They suffered from tuberculosis, pneumonia, small-pox, influenza, syphilis, and a host of other diseases. The pharmacopoeia of the medicine man, with its assortment of herbs, entrails and charms had no answer for the more severe of these afflictions. Up to the second part of the nineteenth, and the beginning of the twentieth century, Europeans were almost as helpless in dealing with these diseases. The great revolution that opened up the tropics only began from the end of the 1890s, and disease therefore played, and is still playing a major role in holding back the development of Africa.[8]

Africa's medical adversities are matched by its veterinary tribulations. Here we shall mention only a few of the more destructive diseases. These include rinderpest or cattle plague, which is caused by a virus, and has periodically swept through large portions of the continent. Contagious pleuropneumonia or lung plague persists in many parts of the land mass; so do sicknesses more familiar to American ranchers like foot-and-mouth disease or tuberculosis of cattle. Horses suffer from a host of illnesses and, as we have seen in the previous sections, could be used only in restricted areas of Africa. Finally, farmers had to cope with plant diseases of all kinds and with destructive insects. Among others were the locust, that disastrous plague, whose impact is hard for northerners to imagine and whose terrors only Biblical language can do justice to. "And they shall cover the face of the earth, that one cannot be able to see the earth: and they shall eat the residue of that which is escaped, which remaineth unto you from the hail, and shall eat every tree which groweth for you out of the field."[9]

Only scientific research of a comparatively recent vintage has been able to make some impression on these age-old problems. Throughout its recorded history, Africa has been exposed to these and other natural calamities, more severe than those which have afflicted the more favored northern latitudes. The great landmass of Africa has been, and to a considerable extent still is, enthralled to diseases of every kind.

NOTES

1. This is the Shire River in what is now Malawi, as seen in the late 1890s by Sir Harry Johnston, *British Central Africa* (New York, 1897), pp. 2–3.

2. 1 Kings 10:22.

3. William A. Hance, *The Geography of Modern Africa* (New York, 1964), p. 15. One of the basic limitations of the continent is that almost 92 percent of Africa suffers from some climatic disability.

4. Ezekiel 27:15 and 16.

5. Hance, pp. 4–6.

6. Relative lack of accessibility to other peoples and to other cultures lessened Africa's

cultural contacts—the usual source of new ideas, crops, and techniques for man. This was an especially important factor when Europe began its great technological leap forward in the sixteenth century and left Africa far behind.

7. Exodus 8:24.

8. For a more detailed account see Lawrence Dudley Stamp, *Africa: A Study in Tropical Development* (New York, 1964), pp. 164–181.

9. Exodus, 10:5.

Chapter 2

Africa's Relief Map and Political Boundaries

THE GREAT RIFT VALLEY

In 1896 a caravan commanded by Lord Delamere, later one of Kenya's most outstanding British pioneers, slowly made its way southwards from Berbera in Somaliland towards the interior. The long column of camels, each tied by the jaw to the tail of the beast in front, traversed stony, barren desert country. Gradually the dry waste gave way to bush, with a little grazing and reasonably frequent water holes. In the middle of 1897 they reached Furoli, on what is now the Kenya-Ethiopia boundary, and then advanced across a waterless plain towards Lake Rudolf. As they drew nearer to this lake, they encountered more and more evidence of great volcanic eruptions which once devastated this region in prehistoric times. They marched across flat, rhino-infested land, strewn with great boulders of basalt. Scattered flat-topped hills rose here and there out of the bush, but the vegetation remained scanty. Camels and ponies had to lumber warily across big blocks of sharp-edged lava under a blazing sun. The heat was scorching, for the altitude of the lake was only 1200 feet, and a southeasterly wind blew in heat and dust from the desert. The caravan rounded Mount Kulal, an extinct crater rising suddenly out of the plain—split clean in two from top to bottom as if cloven by some gigantic axe. They trekked along the sandy shores of the lake, dotted here and there with hippo skulls, and peopled by cormorants and beautiful, long-necked flamingoes.[1]

They were inside one of the most forlorn portions of the Great Rift Valley. This enormous depression stretches all the way from the River Jordan and the Dead Sea in Israel to Lake Nyasa in Malawi. The Red Sea itself forms part of this huge rift,

13

which continues across Somaliland and Ethiopia. It goes on to Lake Rudolf where it divides. One portion extends southwards, further into Kenya, Tanzania and Malawi. Another branch sweeps westwards, and then southwards to Lakes Kivu and Tanganyika uniting with the eastern portion at Lake Nyasa—a body of deep water 360 miles long and only some fifteen to twenty miles wide. The hot Luangwa trough and central Zambezi Valley also form part of the Rift system.

These valleys are tremendous cracks in the earth's crust. At some points the rifts are thirty to fifty miles in width, and anywhere from a few hundred feet to several miles in depth. At its deepest Lake Tanganyika goes down nearly 5000 feet. The flanking walls, at their highest, rise to 5000 feet above water level. From end to end the main rift valley is more than 3000 miles long.[2]

No one knows exactly how the Great Rift Valley system came into being. Wegener's theory of continental displacement asserts that tensional forces produced great ocean rifts and caused the present isolation of the southern continents. The African

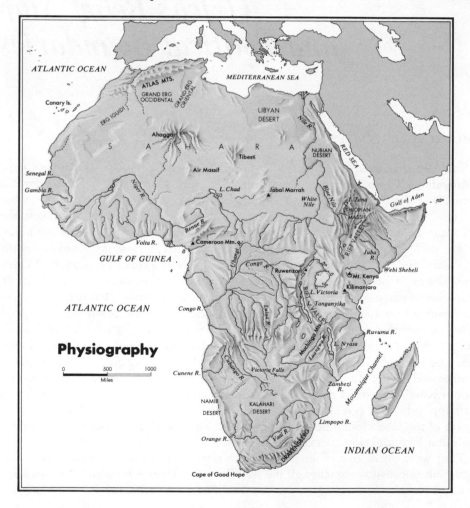

Rift Valley, according to this interpretation, was made when the East African plateau tore apart. If Wegener is right, this gigantic fissure will ultimately widen and thereby complete the disruption of East Africa.

Gregory, another geographer, has come to a different conclusion. He points out that the Rift Valley cuts across the highest land along its course. He believes that some time in the Cretaceous and Early Tertiary period, the earth underwent an enormous compression. A crustal arch gradually upfolded along a north-south axis. This movement rather resembled the motion of two hands pressing together a flat tablecloth and thereby producing a large ridge. But this process went with the formation of a submerged syncline or trough, which separated the island of Madagascar from the mainland. Then the floor of the Indian Ocean gradually foundered. This vast dislocation reacted upon the East African arch, whose supports weakened, resulting in the slow collapse of the keystone. The foundering of the Indian Ocean floor, and the formation of the Great Rift Valley were accompanied by tremendous volcanic breaks. Molten lava poured out from the bowels of the earth. These eruptions ranged all the way from Ethiopia to Malawi, and raised the plateau level here and there by successive outflows of fiery, molten rock. African's two loftiest summits, Mount Kilimanjaro and Mount Kenya, are both ancient volcanoes, and one day there may yet be further geological disturbances in this part of Africa.[3]

ETHIOPIA AND ITS BORDERLANDS

The Great Rift splits Ethiopia into two large massifs of unequal size. The northern rampart commonly rises to about 8000 or 9000 feet, but some of the higher peaks go up to between 12,000 to 15,000 feet. The mountains are somewhat lower in the south. These two huge highland areas are usually called plateaus, but the word gives a somewhat misleading impression. Both are broken by hills and peaks; the mountain ranges may display fantastic forms and are often cut by enormous fissures resulting from erosion. The complex and rugged pattern of these two massifs makes them among the most isolated parts of Africa; between them they form the most extensive upland zone of the continent.

To the south there is a sparsely populated region which projects both northwestwards and southeastwards from Lake Rudolf. It extends between the basin of the River Sobat and the Jubaland coast; its average width considerably exceeds one hundred miles. This belt has therefore acted as a "march" area that has cut off Ethiopia from the south. The hot arid zone has not entirely excluded immigration from the south; but newcomers could filter into the country in small numbers only; the arid depression between the East African plateau and the Abyssinian massifs have therefore become a clearly marked ethnological divide. The drought zone, which encircles Ethiopia to the west and south, continues to the Somali coastlands, and also to the north, so that the Abyssinian "heartland" resembles an enormous double fortress, protected by outer rings of dry country, but with its main approaches looking towards Southern Arabia.

The northern uplands usually slope towards the northwest, and most of the rivers

Tizizat Falls on the Blue Nile, Ethiopia. (De Wys, Inc.)

drain into the Nile. They include the Abbai or Blue Nile, whose waters join with the White Nile near Khartoum in the Sudan. The Blue Nile is essential to the prosperity of both the Sudan and Egypt; control of the river has often therefore been subject to bitter disputes.

The chief eastward-flowing river is the Awash, which rises in the Shoan uplands and reaches the Danakil lowlands through a broad breach in the eastern escarpment of the plateau. The river, however, fails to reach the coast, and after a long and winding course, loses itself in Lake Abbé. Going southwest from Shoa towards Lake Rudolf, a traveler passes a chain of upland lakes, some fresh, some brackish, some completely closed, some linked by channels.

The chief rivers of Somalia are the Juba and the Webi-Shebeli; these rise on the southeastern slope of the Abyssinian highlands and flow generally southward toward the Indian Ocean. Most of their course goes through Ethiopian territory. The bulk of Somalia itself is a low plateau, averaging about 3000 feet in height, and rising fairly gradually from the Indian Ocean. In the north, an extension of the Harar Plateau runs in two ranges parallel with the Gulf of Aden to Cape Guardafui, which is situated on the entrance to the Gulf, and forms Africa's easternmost point.

Politically this region comprises the empire of Ethiopia, Africa's oldest independent state which, in more recent times, has also absorbed the formerly Italian colony of Eritrea. Former French Somaliland, on Ethiopia's eastern border, continues as a French enclave (now called territory of the Afars and Issas). The Somali Republic (composed of the former colonies of British and Italian Somaliland) mainly occupies the southeastern portion of this area.

EAST AFRICA

A modern political map of East Africa shows five different-colored patches; each of these indicates an independent state: Kenya, Uganda, Tanzania (pronounced Tan-zan-ée-a, all formerly British), Rwanda and Burundi (formerly Belgian trust territories). As in most other parts of Africa, political boundaries do not, however, reveal much correspondence with geographical regions; a physical map of East Africa, therefore, gives a very different arrangement.

The Great Rift System, mentioned in the previous section, continues southwards. The Western Rift includes the hot dry lowlands of Lake Albert in Uganda; it also comprises Lake George, Lake Edward, and further south, Lake Tanganyika. The Ruwenzori Mountains, a huge uplifted block, lie within the rift and rise to a height of 16,794 feet.

The Eastern Rift Valley runs through Kenya and is flanked by imposing mountains or plateau blocks. Volcanic cones are scattered on adjacent plateaus, or stand at some distance as outliers of this system. The most famous of these is Mount Kilimanjaro, Africa's highest mountain at 19,565 feet. This great mass, situated on the borders of northern Tanzania, is so high that a mountain climber on his ascent will traverse most of Africa's vegetation zones, from bushland to forests and grasslands, to glaciers and snow.

The Kenya Highlands of southwestern Kenya are equally spectacular. The floor of the Rift Valley, which goes up to only 1280 feet at Lake Rudolf, rises to 7000 feet near Naivasha. The valley is studded with volcanoes, but all of these are now extinct. East of the Rift Valley lies the Aberdare Range rising to about 13,000 feet. Beyond the Aberdares is Mount Kenya, 17,058 feet. Much of this country is breathtakingly beautiful. But the Rift system with its escarpments imposes formidable problems to transportation and communication. Yet this area also contains a great deal of fertile land, some of it of volcanic origin. Large portions have a pleasant, salubrious climate that in the past attracted European settlers to the country.

The region between the Eastern Highlands and the Western Rift zone is occupied by a huge unlifted basin. Much of this is unsuited for cultivation. The regions adjoining Lake Victoria, however, contain better watered soil, and some parts are densely populated. Lake Victoria, or Victoria Nyanza, is itself Africa's largest inland body of water; as a freshwater lake it is inferior in size only to Lake Superior. The portion of the lake basin now situated in Uganda contains some of the finest land in Africa. Much of the scenery is characterized by a seemingly endless succession of low, flat-topped hills, often with deep, rich, red and chocolate loam soils on the slopes. These areas can support a relatively dense population and have thus become the focus of an agricultural inland civilization owing little, if anything, to the remote coastlands.

The great highland and Rift Valley system is divided from the coastal plain of the Indian Ocean by a series of low-lying plateaus. These vary in elevation from about 300 to 2000 feet and rise from the littoral belt by a series of steep slopes or scarps. The American geographer William A. Hance has likened this plateau system to a gigantic hour glass. Its upper part rests in northern Kenya, where it includes the arid volcanic desert of the northern frontier province. Much of this is an arid thorn bush plain supporting only a small nomadic population. In southeastern Kenya the region is somewhat better watered, but rainfall is still scanty and unreliable. The waist of the "hour glass' lies near the borders of Kenya and Uganda, and its southern portion in Tanzania. Much of the widening low plateau of that territory is covered by woodland and thicket; most of it has tsetse fly and therefore is sparsely populated. There are some exceptions such as the Makonde plateau where artificial irrigation helps to sustain more people on the land.

The coastal belt is very different. Most of it forms a relatively narrow plain, except where it broadens into the Tana lowlands of eastern Kenya and the Rufiji lowlands of central Tanzania. The rainfall varies enormously. In eastern Kenya precipitation is small, and the plain merges into the arid Jubaland low country of Somalia. Conditions inprove a good deal in southern Kenya and northern Tanzania, and the precipitation declines once more, as the traveler passes to the southern Tanzanian coast. Monsoons play a major part in the climate of the region, which has traditionally looked towards the Indian Ocean, and which has from ancient times sustained close contacts with Arabia, the Near East, and India. Many of the coastal lands are formed of coral rock, and light sandy soils are also frequent. Coconut woodland and bush are common; light green mangrove swamps line the coastal creeks and river valleys, while dense forests occur but rarely.[4]

SOUTH CENTRAL AFRICA

Geographical classifications have no pure existence outside of textbooks. Just as one set of historical events flows into another, without taking heed of such artificial compartments as "the Renaissance" or "the Industrial Revolution," so one landscape merges into the next, without regard to partition lines drawn by map makers. The coastal plain carries on along the Indian Ocean to Mozambique. But geographers like to break up reality into manageable fragments.

This section will, therefore, treat of Southeast Central Africa as a unit. Politically it comprises the Republic of Malawi (formerly Nyasaland), the Republic of Zambia (formerly Northern Rhodesia), and the self-governing colony of Rhodesia (formerly Southern Rhodesia). The region also embraces the Portuguese Overseas Territories of Mozambique (often spelt Moçambique), and Angola, which are bounded respectively by the shores of the Indian and the Atlantic Oceans.

Much of this land is characterized by plateaus, set at different levels, and traversed sometimes by rivers that have bitten deep into the bedrock to form spectacular gorges, falls and cataracts. The lower plateaus do not easily attract and husband rainfall. Some lack surface drainage. Others are full of seasonal swamps and streams, which often run out of water in the dry season. The higher plateaus are cooler and more pleasant; they are also better watered, and often show developed drainage systems and deeply gouged surfaces. In the Eastern Highlands of Rhodesia the plateaus rise to over 8000 feet and have table-like hills, bizarrely-shaped bosses of granite and other hard-wearing rock.[5] Lake Nyasa and its borderlands form the southern extension of the Great Rift Valley. This large lake, some 360 miles long, is flanked by scarped highlands that, in places, rise to more than 8000 feet and often display great scenic beauty. These highland masses encircling the lake, together with the unusually narrow lacustrine shore, form a distinct physical unit. The political divisions are Malawi, Tanzania, and Mozambique.

Mozambique, broadly speaking, divides into three zones. There is a huge, monotonous coastal belt. It is narrow in the north, but keeps widening to the south, and extends far inland into the Zambezi Valley, and further south again, towards the borders of the Transvaal. Going inland, the traveler sees a transitional zone of hills and low plateaus. Further in the interior there is a high plateau and mountain region between the lower Zambezi and Lake Nyasa; in addition the colony shares in the eastern extension of the mountain country flanking part of Rhodesia's eastern frontier.

The landlocked state of Zambia separates the Portuguese possessions on the East and West Coasts of Africa. The greater part of Zambia forms a huge plateau 3000 to 5000 feet above sea level. Usually the surface is flat; but it is broken by small hills, the results of countless ages of erosion that wore away the underlying crystalline rock containing the bulk of Zambia's great mineral wealth. Southwards from the great divide between the Congo and the Zambezi rivers, the plateau is cut by the valleys of the Zambezi and its tributaries. In the country's mountainous northeastern corner the land rises in places to over 7000 feet, overlooking the western corner of the Great Rift Valley. Zambia just touches on the southern tip of Lake Tanganyika, and it is difficult to imagine a more delightful sight than the blue expanse of this inland water seen from the shore. The highlands are largely isolated by the low-lying, hot and unhealthy Luangwa Valley. West of the Muchinga Mountains, which border the Luangwa rift, there lies a plateau containing the shallow Lake Bangweulu and its interminable swamplands.

Zambia takes its name from the Zambezi River, one of the great waterways of Africa, which winds its way from northwestern Zambia to the Indian Ocean over a distance of some 1700 miles. The course of the river is broken by great gorges and rapids. The biggest drop of all is formed by the Victoria Falls, one of the wonders of the world, and more imposing even than Niagara Falls.[6] Natural obstacles, however, render most of the Zambezi useless for large-scale navigation; the lack of good natural communications indeed forms one of Zambia's greatest problems.

Rhodesia lies south of the Zambezi, and extends as far as the Limpopo River, the northernmost boundary of the Republic of South Africa. Rhodesia is essentially an "island" of high veld, generally about 4000 to 5000 feet above sea level. The people of Salisbury, the capital, live at an elevation greater than that of Ben Nevis, the highest mountain in Great Britain. Tourists who make their way to the Eastern Highlands can admire scenery reminiscent sometimes of the Scottish highlands or of Central European mountain country. The high veld continues from the neighborhood of Bulawayo to Salisbury and beyond, following a northeasterly direction, with two narrow extensions, the lesser sinking into the low veld of the Zambezi, the greater leading eastward to the Portuguese border of the colony of Mozambique. The central plateau corridor rarely exceeds 50 miles in length, and its configuration has helped to determine the boundaries of European settlement. The transverse ridge of the high veld forms a great watershed. To the north a series of roughly parallel streams run into the Zambezi; other streams flow southwards into the Sabi and the Limpopo rivers. The central area is surrounded by an outer rim of low-lying, hot country that stretches along the Zambezi and the Limpopo. The areas below 4000 feet occupy the greater part of the colony; they have a strange attraction of their own, but have generally been avoided by white farmers in search of land.

Angola occupies the western portion of this artificial territorial grouping. Along the Atlantic is a coastal plain, which varies in width from about 12 to 100 miles in the lower valley to the Cuanza River. Going inland, the tourist makes his way through transitional escarpment country. In the north the rise to the main plateau is gradual; in the central and southern sections it is quite abrupt. The plateau goes up to between 3300 and 5000 feet; but as in Rhodesia there are elevations of 7000 to 8000 feet, with the highest summits in the country's west-central portion. This region forms a huge watershed, and rivers radiate in many directions. The Cunene and Cuanza flow to the Atlantic, the former in a northwesterly, the latter in a southwesterly direction. Others go northwards to the Congo, or to the south, or directly east, into the Zambezi.

MADAGASCAR

Madagascar (formerly a French colony, now the independent Malagasy Republic) is one of the world's four greatest islands, comparable in extent with Borneo, and about three and a half times the size of New England. It is a world of its own, with great variations in climate and vegetation. La Grande Île, as it is known to the French, was cut off from the African mainland at an early stage of geological development and developed a flora and fauna distinct from that of the mother continent. Its people are of mixed origin, but mostly speak Malayo-Polynesian, not African tongues. Historians might dispute whether the "Great Island" should not rather be classed with the lands of the South Seas from where its people had drawn so much cultural inspiration. But from a geographer's and a politician's point of view, the island clearly belongs to Africa. As Hance puts it, Madagascar stretches like a gigantic breakwater for nearly a thousand miles along the Mozambique coast; it is separated from the mainland by the Mozambique Channel, a broad expanse of water which varies between 250 and 500 miles in extent. The island has an elongated shape, and no part of it lies more than 150 miles away from the sea.

Madagascar's main axis runs roughly parallel to the shore line of Southeast Africa; it passes for the greater part through a great central upland rising to a mean of about

4000 feet above sea level. This elevated region is often called a plateau; it is, however, cut by deep valleys, and "high-based hill-land." Three great mountain masses tower high above the rest of the country. Tsaratanana in the north has a summit of volcanic rock rising to 9449 feet. Ankaratra, an enormous volcanic massif, dominates the center of the country. Andingitra, a huge bloc of denuded granite, goes up south of Ambalavao. The highlands are usually higher in the east, where they drop abruptly in one or two steps to the coastal zone, which is itself only about 10 to 15 miles broad. The western side of the island has a broader belt of plains and low plateaus, with an average width of 60 to 120 miles.

Transport engineers in Madagascar face problems of great magnitude. The highlands are difficult to penetrate; the coast line lacks good natural ports in convenient locations. The topographic features of both plain and mountain lands have thus played a major share in dividing the country into many subregions, whose contact with each other often remains slight, and whose divisions have played an important part in determining the country's history.[7]

SOUTHERN AFRICA

Southern Africa includes the Republic of South Africa, South-West Africa—a United Nations Trusteeship Territory under South African administration—Lesotho (Basutoland) and Swaziland, mountainous enclaves within the Republic, and Botswana (Bechuanaland) to the north of South Africa.

The shore of Southern Africa is bounded on the west, south, and east by a narrow coastal belt. This region, like most of Africa, is ill-favored with harbors; the relative absence of secluded bays and sheltering headlands is a serious disadvantage to shipping; river estuaries are usually blocked by sand bars, and first-class ports are few and far between.

The coast of Southwest Africa is largely barren and contains some of the world's most forbidding and desolate country; its only good natural port is situated at Walvis Bay, the "Bay of the Whale." To the south the country becomes more pleasant and hospitable; from the scenic point of view the Cape Coast has a good deal in common with northwestern California. Cape Town, a great maritime city, lies on Table Bay, and looks out to the southern Atlantic. Table Mountain, flat-topped and cloud-girt, towers above the Bay to a height of 3582 feet. After doubling the Cape of Good Hope, a coastal steamer enters False Bay, which captains of East Indiamen in days gone by often mistook for Table Bay. Here lies Simonstown, the country's naval port. Going on to the east, a vessel passes Danger Point, whose very name stands as a reminder to past perils of coastal navigation. The boat then doubles Cape Agulhas, the "Cape of Needles," and comes to Mossel Bay, one of the first sights known to early Portuguese seamen in this area. The journey continues to the sandy shore of Algoa Bay, the site of Port Elizabeth. Durban, the main commercial center of the Province of Natal, lies in a landlocked tidal bay, and has a splendid enclosed harbor, which helps to make it one of the great commercial centers of the Indian Ocean.

South Africa's narrow coastal belt rises sharply inland to a great interior plateau,

The Drakensberg (Dragon's Mountains), South
Africa.

which varies in height from about 3000 to 6000 feet. The plateau is bounded by a
chain of mountains. Towards the east, the Drakensberg (Dragon Mountains) run
parallel to the coast; their seaward slopes are precipitous; their landward fall is more
gradual and forms part of the tableland of the interior. The portion of the chain lying
between Natal and Lesotho, South Africa's Switzerland, contains the highest points,
including the Mont-aux-Sources, which rises to 10,822 feet.

A section drawn through the southern mountain system looks almost like the plan
of some great defensive system. The coastal plan forms the moat. Then there are steep
outworks, prominent folds which enclose the so-called "Little Karroo." Beyond the
Swartberg range lies the "Great Karroo," the foreland of the interior plateau. Towards the west, flat-topped hills and plateaus stand above a level floor, indicating the
former elevation of the Karroo platform before erosion. Eastward the Karroo is
lower, and rainfall increases; but even so, this is still dry country, particularly suitable
for sheep. To the north, the tableland gently falls to the valley of the Orange River.

The Orange itself rises in the Mont-aux-Sources and then flows westward until it
finally reaches the Atlantic. Much of the country it traverses is wasteland, and sand
bars, shallows, and falls make navigation impossible along its course.

Beyond the Orange there are grassy plains and plateaus, sloping towards the north
from the Drakensberg; to the east, on the Lesotho border, the country becomes
hillier. Generally speaking, the country lies at an altitude of 4000 to 5000 feet above
sea level, and cattle farmers can make a good living. The high veld continues into

the Transvaal. Johannesburg, South Africa's greatest industrial and mining city, lies at an altitude of nearly 6000 feet and thus enjoys a clear and bracing climate. The vast plateau surface puts no great obstacle in the way of inland movement, and immigrants, white or black, who had once made their way into this great upland could always trek on. But South Africa lacks great navigable rivers, while the country's character as a great, uplifted basin restricts the area of desirable coastal land available for intensive farming.

Botswana, west of the Transvaal, is a huge, semiarid plateau averaging about 3000 feet in height. It is hilly and broken in the east, but otherwise has mostly an undulating or flat surface. Beyond lies South-West Africa, which likewise forms part of the great South African plateau. The table land rises towards the center of the country, but subsides into an alluvial plain in the extreme north. A 1000-mile coastal belt—with an average width of 60 to 100 miles—extends along the entire coast of the country and fringes the Atlantic Ocean.

THE CONGO BASIN

The Congo is one of the world's greatest rivers, longer than the Niger or the Volga. Its drainage basin extends over something like 1,400,000 square miles, over a region larger than the immense area comprised within the Republic of India. Put in North American terms, the Congo basin stretches from north to south along a line equal in length to the distance from Ontario in northeastern Canada, to the Gulf of Mexico.

From the political point of view, this immense region takes in most of the Republic of Congo (Kinshasa), formerly known as the Belgian Congo, and the Republic of Congo (Brazzaville), formerly part of French Equatorial Africa, and Cabinda, a small Portuguese enclave on the shore of the Atlantic. The Ubangi, a great northern tributary of the Congo, flows through the Central African Republic (formerly the French colony of Ubangi-Shari), and thereby links much of this area to the Congo drainage basin.

The Congo basin has been graphically described as a shallow saucer of mammoth size set into the table top of tropical Africa.[8] At its center, the saucer is only about 1000 feet high. From there it rises slowly and often imperceptibly to between 3000 to 4000 feet at the rim. The alluvial floor of the basin is almost dead flat. The river has plenty of room to stretch; it is usually wide and much given to inundation. Great permanent marshes, swamps and lakes form an unduly large proportion of the total drainage area.

The highlands on the rim of the saucer vary in character from smooth table lands to deeply cut in, sierralike ridges. In the western segment of the rim, the unending action of equatorial rain-fed streams cuts intensely into rock and soil. The Congo has cut a tortuous channel through the impeding Crystal Mountains to reach the sea. It finally enters the Atlantic through a true river estuary, the bottom being a great canyon extending far out into the ocean.

The peripheral area of highlands and plateaus is lowest on the west and north, but

Rapids on the Congo. (De Wys, Inc.)

rises progressively towards Katanga in the extreme south of the country. In the east the region shares in the Great Rift Valley, which is bordered on both sides by uplifted mountains. There are also volcanic formations particularly near Lake Kivu. Distances are enormous. A journey from Kinshasa on the Congo to Lubumbashi, the great mining and commercial center of the south, is longer than the distance between London and Warsaw. Communications from Katanga to the main river basin are mainly by rail and then down the Kasai River, which flows in a northwesterly direction into the Congo. In addition, use is made of the Upper Congo (or Lualaba River), which is navigable along part of its huge course.

The Congo basin, with its multitude of tributaries, forms one of Africa's most important systems of inland waterways, and has greatly facilitated inland trade. Ocean-going vessels can cruise some 80 miles from the Atlantic to the river port of Matadi on the Congo. Traffic up the next 250 miles inland is impeded by rapids. From then onwards, ships can travel more than 1000 miles along a great riverine artery to Kisangani. Navigable stretches on the Congo total something like 1700 miles, but the total mileage of usable waterways in the Congo basin is about 7200.[9]

Kinshasa, formerly Léopoldville, the capital of the Republic of Congo, enjoys a strategic position on the vital converging point of the river on its lower reaches. The Congo forms an equally important communication artery for the Republic of Congo (Brazzaville). Brazzaville is likewise a great river port, and is situated on the northern bank of the Congo, opposite Kinshasa. Ships can also travel along the Ubangi, a right-bent tributary of the Congo. Traffic continues northward to Bangui, the capital of the Central African Republic.

WEST AND WESTERN EQUATORIAL AFRICA

West Africa has no claims to physiographic unity. Its conventional boundaries are set by the Senegal River in the west and by the Niger delta in the east. For purposes of classification, Cameroun and Gabon are, however, also included in this area. Cameroun and Gabon, like their western neighbors, are bounded by the shores of the Atlantic. They lie for the most part outside the Congo drainage basin; they also have climatic problems similar to those of other West African territories. Inland this region becomes more arid, and ultimately merges into the Sahara. A somewhat arbitrary northern border might therefore be drawn, separating the Atlantic seaboard states from the landlocked countries of the dry interior.

The Gulf of Guinea has been accessible to European navigators for a long period. Cultural, commercial, and political crisscrossing between different white and black groups occasioned a complex power-pattern, which, in the end, resulted in today's somewhat involved political boundary lines. The Atlantic coast is now ringed by a chain of independent African states. These include Senegal and Guinea (formerly French), Gambia and Sierra Leone (formerly British), Liberia (the earliest African state set up on Western lines and strongly influenced by American ideas), the Ivory Coast (formerly French), Ghana, previously known as the Gold Coast (formerly British), Togo (formerly a French trusteeship territory), Cameroun (formerly a trusteeship territory mainly under French administration), and Gabon (formerly French). The area also comprises small colonial enclaves: Portuguese Guinea in the west and Spanish Guinea in the east, just above the equator.

The seaman coming in from the Atlantic sees a low-lying plain which is often encumbered by sandbanks, lagoons, creeks, and mangrove swamps. This is the Africa of story books and mariners' tales, and unfortunately there are few natural ports. The single exception is Freetown, the capital of Sierra Leone, where at one time in the Second World War 250 ships rode at anchor on one day. Dakar, a great French-built port in Senegal, is an artificial creation; so is Monrovia in Liberia and Takoradi in Ghana. The port of Abidjan on the Ivory Coast was fashioned by cutting a channel through a coastal bar, thereby affording access to a well-protected lagoon. Lagos in Nigeria is likewise a lagoon harbor.

Behind the coast stretches a sedimentary plain of varying depth. In Senegal the lowland stretches deeply inland over several hundred miles, following the valley of the Senegal; Gambia also lies in a riverine plain. The lowland contracts at the coast of Guinea, but there are deeper "bulges" at Sierra Leone, on the Ivory Coast and Ghana. The deepest penetration occurs in the Niger-Benue region, where an immense alluvial plain stretches far inland for nearly 700 miles.

The plain rises gradually to more or less well marked escarpments inland, and then on up to the great West African plateau. This elevated region lies at a much lower height than the corresponding highland belts of East Africa. There are only a few

At the edge of an equatorial rain forest, Gabon.
(De Wys, Inc.)

areas high above water level. These include the Fouta Jallon Plateau of Guinea and the Jos Plateau of Northern Nigeria. Cameroun, to the east, has wide topographic variations, ranging from coastal mangrove swamps to great uplands. The larger part of Cameroun is a plateau; north and west there are rugged mountains which stretch across the country in the form of an arc. The highest elevation is Mount Cameroun (13,352 feet), an active volcano situated at the western end of the arclike mountain range. It is Africa's only mountain by the sea and, especially from the ocean, presents an unforgettable spectacle to any voyager. "Certainly it is most striking when you see it . . . as I first saw it, after coasting for weeks along the low shores and mangrove-fringed rivers of the Niger Delta. Suddenly, right up out of the seas, rises the great mountain. . . . But every time you pass it by its beauty grows on you with greater and greater force, though it is never twice the same. Sometimes it is wreathed with indigo-black tornado clouds, sometimes crested with snow, sometimes softly gorgeous with gold, green and rose-colored vapours tinted by the setting sun, sometimes completely swathed in dense cloud. . . ."[10]

West Africa's most remarkable geographical feature is its magnificent river systems, which connect part of the inland with the Atlantic coast. Going from west to east, the first important water course is the Senegal, with a total of some 890 miles, of which about half is navigable. To the south lies the Gambia River, which discharges its waters into the Atlantic at Bathurst through a magnificent deep estuary. Lighter craft can go up the river for several hundred miles. In the olden days, the area between these two rivers used to be called Senegambia, a term now in disuse but one which well expresses the region's geographic unity.

The Volta River, with its two upper branches—the White and the Black Volta— plays a major part in Ghana's topography. The Volta's use as a waterway is restricted by numerous rapids and by obstructions at its mouth. The Volta has, however, a great hydroelectrical potential and will in future supply Ghana with great quantities of "white gold," in the shape of falling water harnessed to industrial use.

West Africa's greatest river is the Niger, whose total length amounts to something like 2600 miles and whose basin probably extends over about 600,000 square miles. On the African continent the Niger ranks next in length to the Nile, followed by the Congo. In the past the river's course was a riddle to European geographers who assumed that, like most streams in this area, its course must go from east to west or from northeast to southwest. But the Niger does the very opposite. It rises in the west, in the highlands of Fouta Djalon, about 150 miles from the coast. It continues through Guinea, and carries on in a northwesterly direction through Mali. It then turns in an enormous bend and flows towards the southeast through the Republic of Niger towards Nigeria.

Long stretches of the river are navigable down to Niamey in Niger. Below, the waters are obstructed by a series of rapids down to near the Nigerian border. Ships can then proceed further, but Jebba, nearer the southeast, marks the head of navigation from the sea for shallow boats.

The Niger joins the Benue (originating in Cameroun), which is also navigable for part of its course. The Niger finally reaches the Bight of Benin by way of an enormous delta with an area of something like 14,000 square miles. This huge region is broken by an intricate network of channels, which divide and cross, both with each other and with branches of other streams. A vast area in southeastern Nigeria is thus covered with waterways accessible to canoe men, and this great natural communication system played a major part in the country's past. Today the delta is still a great highway. But rivermen encounter a host of difficulties owing to seasonal fluctuations in the water volume, and this "riverine rhythm" considerably influenced earlier patterns in Nigeria's commercial and political history. Other important rivers discharge their waters into the Bight of Biafra further east. These include the Cross River, which flows through southeastern Nigeria, and the Ogooué in Gabon.

THE SUDAN

From ancient days Berber and Arab merchants from North Africa traded with the lands beyond the Sahara. The vast southern interior was known to the Arabs as *Bilad-al-Sudan,* the land of the blacks. It was vaguely bounded by the Atlantic in the west, the maritime regions stretched out along the Gulf of Guinea, the Congo basin and, in the east, by the mountains of Ethiopia and the Red Sea. Some have defined the Sudan in a wide fashion, so as to include the whole of "black Africa" away from the Indian Ocean, but under Mohammedan cultural, religious or political influence.

Old maps print the word "Sudan" across the whole of West Africa, so as to comprise all lands beyond the great coastal forest belt within its borders; even portions of the former French and the former Belgian Congo were said to lie within its borders. (Today the name is usually applied only to the Republic of the Sudan, Africa's largest state, situated south of Egypt.) There is something arbitrary about all these divisions. Cultural boundary lines are never easy to draw; physiographic features do not quite correspond to modern political frontiers. For our purposes, we shall include within the Sudan all the formerly French "middle belt" territories, that is to say Mauritania, and the landlocked countries of Mali, Upper Volta, Niger, and Chad, as well as the Republic of Sudan, formerly under Anglo-Egyptian condominium, but administered in effect under British supervision.[11]

The eastern portion of the Sudan is lined by a belt of sandy country which runs along the Red Sea. Journeying inland, the traveler comes through the Nubian desert, a rocky waste traversed occasionally by river courses which fill up only in the rainy season.

Westward lies the valley of the Nile and Africa's greatest river. The Nile has a total length of over 4000 miles; its drainage basin covers more than 1,000,000 miles and includes Uganda, parts of Ethiopia, the cultivated portion of the United Arab Republic (Egypt) and most of the Republic of Sudan. The mainstream of the White Nile has its origins on the lake plateau of East Africa; below Lake Albert, the river is known as the Albert Nile or *Bahr al-Jabal,* the "River of the Mountain." It ceases to be navigable near the Uganda-Sudan boundary, where it descends from the plateau into the Sudanese lowland. It continues on its northward course and passes through great swamps where it divides into numerous branches, winding its way through papyrus, reeds, water lilies, and elephant grass, called *sudd,* where much of the land is but floating vegetation. The permanent swamp land ends near its junction with the *Bahr al-Ghazal,* the "Gazelle River," which comes in from the west. Thence, the river continues northward, meeting the Blue Nile at Khartoum.

The Blue Nile probably has its main source in Lake Tana in northern Ethiopia. It describes a great semicircle, and then comes down into the Sudan. On its lower course stands the Sennar dam, which irrigates a huge fertile area, the Gezira, lying between the Blue and the White Nile. From Khartoum the main Nile flows northward through desert country, with a narrow green strip of vegetation on each side. On the drier margins of the basin, the monotony of the landscape is relieved by occasional hills and, towards the desert, by dunes. The Nile subsequently receives the Atbara, which comes in from the southeast and is the last tributary of the Nile on its course to the Mediterranean. In flood the Atbara is a great muddy water river and in the dry season a string of pools. The main Nile then trances an "S" on the map and at the same time hurls its way down a series of great cataracts. These are numbered from south to north; the Sixth Cataract lies just north of Khartoum and the First Cataract is situated at Aswan in the United Arab Republic. Between the Fourth and Third Cataracts lies Meroë, an ancient city, once the capital of Cush and the seat of a great civilization. After having completed its wide bend, the river once again flows northward and leaves Sudanese territory below Wadi Halfa, the northernmost frontier town near the Egyptian border.

River traffic on the Nile, Sudan. (De Wys, Inc.)

The Nile traverses an immense area, but cultivation along the 1000 mile stretch of the Nile from Khartoum to the Egyptian frontier is restricted to a narrow, disconnected belt; communications between north and south remain extremely difficult, and from a transportation point of view the country mainly looks west, towards the Red Sea.

To the southwest of Khartoum, the land goes up in height; there are several mountain massifs overtopping the flat terrain, with Jabal Gimbala in the province of Darfur rising to 10,073 feet. Beyond the Sudan's western boundary lies the Republic of Chad, and the traveler enters into a distinct region of its own. From the map maker's point of view, there are no obvious distinctions. Climatically, the "Sudanic" lands of former French West Africa resemble the Republic of Sudan in containing different belts ranging from rain forest or savannah to steppe and finally to desert. Culturally and linguistically, these regions also occupy the border zone between the Islamized north, and a south where Christian and pagan influence is more pronounced. But whereas in the Republic of Sudan it is the Muslim northerners who are politically and economically dominant, the position is reversed in Chad. Here the balance of power rests with the south. As in the rest of former French Africa, French cultural influence is supreme, and the region looks to the west and south, rather than to the east and north.

Chad lies in the middle of Africa's northern bloc and, like its western neighbors, suffers severely from isolation. The country's center of gravity lies in the southwest;

Fort Lamy, the capital, is situated in the Shari-Lagone basin and has little connection with the north. The Shari River flows into Lake Chad, a vast watery expanse, where the political boundaries of Chad, Cameroun, Nigeria and Niger all converge. Lake Chad, with its varying water level, is subject to long-term desiccation; it used to be much bigger, but still covers a vast area, varying from 5000 to 9000 square miles according to season. It has no outlets; its shoreline is broken by bays, peninsulas, and on the east side especially, by lagoons. It is studded by islands, and the region comprises vast swamp areas.

The Sudan's third main hydrographic system centers on the northern bend of the Niger (which has already been mentioned in the previous section). Between Bamako, the capital of Mali, and the region south of Timbuktu, the river annually floods a large inland delta, a "potential Egypt." The most extensive floods occur downstream from the junction of the Niger and the River Bani. The waters seep through a maze of channels and shallow lakes. In some places inundations cover areas more than eighty miles wide; in some years the total expanse of water spreads over 30,000 square miles. Southwest from Timbuktu, there are a series of vast but shallow depressions, including Lake Debec, which are temporarily filled by the overflow of the Niger, and gradually desiccate as the level of the river falls again.[12] Northward, the country's rainfall steadily diminishes, and the traveler finally comes into the true desert, an immense belt stretching from Mauretania all the way to the Republic of Sudan.

NOTES

1. Elspeth Huxley, *White Man's Country: Lord Delamere and the Making of Kenya* (London, 1953), vol. 1, pp. 43–48.

2. George H. T. Kimble, *Tropical Africa: Land and Livelihood* (New York, 1962), vol. 1, pp. 41–43. A flat map on the pages of an atlas does not give the student a true idea of this enormous divide. The best thing is to stand before a relief map and slide one's fingertips across its outlines. The hand traces vast corridors with subsidiary divides, all of which probably played an important role in channeling human migrations in the past.

3. Walter Fitzgerald, *Africa: A Social, Economic and Political Geography of its Major Regions* (London, 1950), pp. 4–7.

4. See Hance, pp. 397–422.

5. Kimble, vol. 1, pp. 43–44.

6. The strength of the river has now been harnessed by the Kariba Dam, where British, French, and Italian engineers have constructed one of the world's greatest man-made lake, extending about 180 miles upstream.

7. Hance, pp. 586–588.

8. Kimble, vol. 1, p. 45.

9. Hance, p. 310.

10. Mary Kingsley, *Travels in West Africa: Congo Français, Corisco and Cameroons* (London, 1897), p. 550.

11. The confusion of nomenclature is made worse by the fact that the French at one time defined the French Sudan as the area bounded by Algeria, Mauritania, French Guinea, the Upper Volta, and the Niger colony.

12. Fitzgerald, pp. 335–336.

Chapter 3

Climate and Vegetation

WHAT MAKES THE WEATHER?

Generations of Hollywood script writers and popular authors have produced a stereotype of Africa which remains hard to dislodge. Millions of people imagine Africa as a land of limitless forest, where the rains pour down without end, and where heroic white explorers made their way boldly through hot, steamy swamps—followed as often as not by a faithful black gunbearer and a beautiful blonde! But Africa, as we have stressed before, produces almost every conceivable kind of climate. The study of its climatic variations is extremely complex, but there are a few simple underlying principles that present no difficulties to the layman. A Californian who visits the Cape will often be reminded of his native land. Tropical Africa, on the other hand, is totally different, and often experiences a tremendous amount of precipitation. Just what these rains mean is best conveyed by a Nigerian poet who recalls his childhood days in a peasant's hut:

> What time of night it is
> I do not know
> Except like some fish
> Doped out of the deep
> I have bobbed up bellywise
> From streams of sleep
> And no cocks crow.
> It is drumming hard here

31

And I suppose everywhere
Droning with insistent ardour upon
Our roof-thatch and shed
And through sheaves slit open
To lightning and rafters
I cannot make out overhead
Great water drops are dribbling
Falling like orange or mango
Fruits showered forth in the wind
Or perhaps I should say so
Much like beads I could in prayer tell
Them on strings as they break
In wooden bowls and earthenware
Mother is busy now deploying
About our roomlet and floor.
Although it is so dark
I know her practiced step as
She moves her bins, bags and vats
Out of the run of water . . .[1]

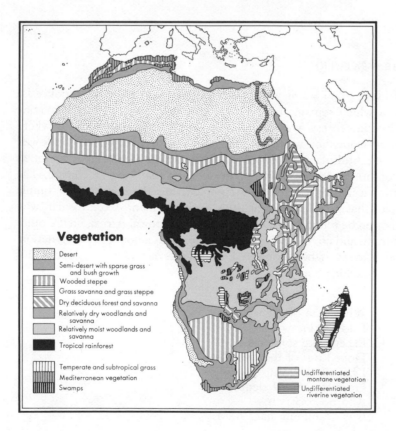

Vegetation

Desert

Semi-desert with sparse grass and bush growth

Wooded steppe

Grass savanna and grass steppe

Dry deciduous forest and savanna

Relatively dry woodlands and savanna

Relatively moist woodlands and savanna

Tropical rainforest

Temperate and subtropical grass

Mediterranean vegetation

Swamps

Undifferentiated montane vegetation

Undifferentiated riverine vegetation

To the north of the convergence zone, the winds are dry and dusty, since they have their origins in the Sahara and the desert. As the zone moves southwards at the end of the northern summer, these hot air currents sweep down the Guinea coast, and cities like Accra often suffer from alternating rains and heavy droughts. In West Africa when the hot, rainless *harmattan* blows in from the Sahara, the diurnal range may be as much as 45°F; people suffer acute discomfort, and farmers fear crop loss.

> . . . In harmattan the locusts filled the sky
> Destroying the sweat put into the field
> And restless seas shattered canoes
> The fisher-folk put to sail by noon . . .[2]

The lands east of the Rift Valley are influenced mainly by the Indian Ocean and the Arabian desert. Even in the northern summer, most of the rainy spells that occur north of the equator are probably associated with the incursion of moist tropical air from the Indian Ocean. In the southern summer, the Indian Ocean is without rival as rainmaker of East Africa.

Africa thus experiences regional variations both in the timing and the amount of its rainfall. Even in the wettest regions the monthly rainfall graphs may show considerable variations. As the country gets drier, these fluctuations increase, and farmers and stockbreeders may face problems of even greater magnitude. Even when the rains arrive in time, they may create all sorts of other headaches. Tropical precipitation all too often comes down "by the bucket full." Frequently the earth cannot absorb these sudden downpours. Much water is lost; precious top soil may be leached out or washed away; low-lying land may get flooded, so that tropical Africa suffers from climatic difficulties on a vaster scale than those experienced in the more temperate regions of Europe (about 92 per cent of the continent has major climatic disabilities).

Africa's most characteristic vegetation zones comprise tropical rain forest, savannah and desert. All of these have prolonged periods of heat as a common factor, though their rainfall differs immensely. The vegetation and rainfall maps of Africa show a curiously symmetrical arrangement. The humid Congo basin in the center and most of the coastal lands on the West Coast are covered by tropical rain forest. Great belts of savannah country stretch to the north and south respectively, until they merge into dry steppe and finally into desert. The extreme south and the extreme northwest experience Mediterranean climate. The symmetry is, however, far from complete. The extent of the desert in North Africa is immensely greater than in southern Africa, where the continental landmass is narrower. The savannah regions of South Central and East Africa are generally broader than those of the Sudan. The Mediterranean belt of North Africa is much more extensive than that of the Cape, and this factor has played its part in making North West Africa such an important part of the Mediterranean world. The symmetry is further thrown out of balance by the Ethiopian Highlands in the northeast, the Great Rift Valley in the east, and by the massive Atlas ranges in northwest Africa; their topography considerably affects the local climates. Climatic and vegetation maps in school atlases can easily give a false impression of the country's climatic configuration, for they tend to overaccentuate the borders between the different zones. In Africa there are comparatively few great mountain barriers; most of the continent consists of plateau country. Hence there is a tendency for the various climatic zones to merge imperceptibly into one another, and a somewhat arbitrary element must always enter into classification schemes.

THE RAIN FORESTS OF GUINEA, THE CONGO, AND MADAGASCAR

The Guinea coast experiences heat, with heavy summer rainfall and high atmospheric humidity throughout much of the year. The rains are followed by a brief period of low precipitation or even drought, but there are wide regional variations. The sun, moreover, is by no means unendurable. Freetown in Sierra Leone has a mean temperature of 81°F and a mean annual temperature range of only 3°F, so that an American from, say, central Georgia, might indeed find a trip to the African west coast a pleasant change from his own summer. The northern half of the Congo basin experiences constant heat. Rains fall throughout the year, and the high moisture content of the air makes life trying for those not accustomed to these conditions. Soil and climate usually favor luxuriant plant growth. Many coastal regions thus are lined with great mangrove swamps that have a peculiar fascination of their own:

There is an uniformity in the habits of West Coast rivers, from the Volta to the Coanza, which is, when you get used to it, very taking. Excepting the Congo, the really great river comes out to sea with as much mystery as possible; lounging lazily along among its mangrove swamps in a what's-it-matter-when-one-comes-out and where's-the-hurry style, through quantities of channels intercommunicating with each

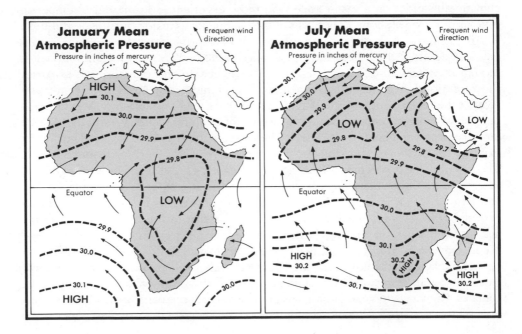

A forest trail in West Africa. (De Wys, Inc.)

other. Each channel, at first sight as like the other as peas in a pod, is bordered on either side by green-black walls of mangroves, which Captain Lugard graphically described as seeming 'as if they had lost all count of the vegetable proprieties, and were standing on stilts with their branches tucked up out of the wet, leaving their gaunt roots exposed in mid-air.' High-tide or low-tide, there is little difference in the water; the river, be it broad or narrow, deep or shallow, looks like a pathway of polished metal; for it is as heavy weighted with stinking mud as water e'er can be, ebb or flow, year out and year in. But the difference in the banks, though an unending alternation between two appearances, is weird.

At high-water you do not see the mangroves displaying their ankles. . . . They look most respectable, their foliage rising densely in a wall irregularly striped here and there by the white line of an aërial root, coming straight down into the water from some upper branch as straight as a plummet, in the strange, knowing way an aërial root of a mangrove does, keeping the hard straight line until it gets some two feet above water-level, and then spreading out into blunt fingers with which to dip into the water and grasp the mud. Banks indeed at high water can hardly be said to exist, the water stretching away into the mangrove swamps for miles and miles, and you can then go, in a suitable small canoe, away among these swamps as far as you please.[3]

Inland there are extensive jungles. Map makers used to mark simply "rain forest," but this term cannot convey the immense variety of plant life found in these regions. Westerners usually have a very unfavorable stereotype of these great forests. But they can indeed afford magnificent sights. This is the way Mary Kingsley, the famous nineteenth century West African traveler described a road newly cut through the forest country of Cameroun:

I, with my crew, keep on up the grand new road the government is making, which when finished is to go from Ambas Bay to Buea, 3,000 feet up on the mountain's side. This road is quite the most magnificent of roads, as regards breadth and general intention, that I have seen anywhere in West Africa, and it runs through a superbly beautiful country. It is, I should say, as broad as Oxford Street; on either side of it are deep drains to carry off the surface waters, with banks of varied beautiful tropical shrubs and ferns, behind which rise, 100 to 200 feet high, walls of grand forest, the column-like tree-stems either hung with flowering, climbing plants and ferns, or showing soft red and soft grey shafts sixty to seventy feet high without an interrupting branch. Behind this again rise the lovely foothills of Mungo, high up against the sky, coloured the most perfect soft dark blue.

The whole scheme of color is indescribably rich and full in tone. The very earth is a velvety red brown, and the butterflies—which abound—show themselves off in the sunlight, in their canary-coloured, crimson, and peacock-blue liveries, to perfection.[4]

Toward the drier margins of these forest belts, the variety of species of plants and trees gets less; the canopy becomes more open, so that the undergrowth has a better

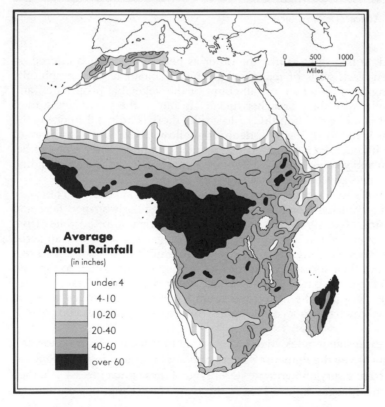

Average
Annual Rainfall
(in inches)

	under 4
	4-10
	10-20
	20-40
	40-60
	over 60

0   500   1000
Miles

chance to grow. In many parts of Africa indigenous farmers or foreign plantation companies have made deep dents into the deeply wooded zones, and most of the primary growth has now disappeared. Much cultivation has taken place in the Guinean and Nigerian forest belts, for instance; the equatorial jungles remain the largest and the least disturbed.

East Madagascar likewise experiences a hot, steamy climate, with heavy rainfall throughout the year. There are dense rain forests with some valuable trees, including rosewood and ebony much prized by cabinet-makers. Again, farmers and lumbermen have cut heavily into the woodland, though great areas of dense forests still survive, especially in the narrow eastern plain and on the flanking escarpment, while mangroves grow to profusion on the lagoon-fringed coast.

THE FORESTS OF EASTERN AND SOUTHERN AFRICA

East Africa is on the whole much drier than West Africa, and therefore lacks the enormous, compact masses of evergreen forests found on the Atlantic watershed. There are patches of dense woodland on the coast, where the rainfall is heaviest, and also on the upper slopes of the higher mountains, which intercept the trade winds. In East Africa, a series of uplands, running generally from north to south, succeed one another all the way from Ethiopia to the cliffs of the Drakensberg mountains in South Africa. Mountain forests luxuriate on many of the slopes and escarpments exposed to the wet winds of the Indian Ocean. Where the mountains are isolated, like Kenya, Kilimanjaro, and Meru, forests encircle bare or glacier-clad summits. Tree life differs to an enormous extent. The woodland of the coastal belts is usually less dense than the forest country of Guinea, and is very dissimilar in composition. The rain forests of Uganda have some affinity with those of the equatorial Congo region.[5] On the higher altitudes, new species make their appearance, and the scenery undergoes vast changes. The deep forests of the Mau in Kenya, for instance, contain junipers, locally known as cedars. Their trunks are straight and tall; gray-green lichens droop from their crown of dark foliage. The forest rises and falls in ridges. From the summit of one ridge, a mountaineer can look down on the treetops below, and distinguish two shades of color, the deep sea green of cedars and the spring green of olives, splashed with the racing shadows of clouds that merge into a restless pattern, like a leafy ocean. All through the forest the traveler suddenly stumbles on natural glades, where brilliant sunlight shines through the cold gloom of the woods. Brilliantly colored orange and turquoise blue butterflies dart in and out of the shadows and hover over the tall grass. The Mau itself rises to over 10,000 feet, and the plateau on the top looks like a piece of Scotland. There is bracken and peat; icy streams trickle over brown stones. There is a kind of heather too, a giant species standing as tall as a man. A chilly tang lies in the air, and at night ice crusts over the swampy puddles.[6]

There are many other kinds of forest country. The wooded regions of Ethiopia alone show great variations. Many upland areas are covered with mimosas, wild olives, giant sycamores and junipers. Others are famed for the natal yellow pine, a magnificent conifer which resists the attacks of white ants. South Africa, at the bottom of the continent, can boast of an equal variety in its forest vegetation. The South African "south coast and montane forests" are evergreen, with a rather uniform type of leaf. The canopy is in two strata; the upper one is discontinuous, and this gives the forest a characteristically irregular outline. There are also "wet forests," where the ground layer is usually composed of ferns. North of Cape Town there are some splendid forests covered with Kingwilliam cedar; some of these have a diameter of four feet and a height of fifty to sixty feet. The forests of the southeastern coastal belt occur at low altitudes in a climate characterized by summer rainfall and dry winters. They are for the most part confined to steep-sided river gorges, where the effect of the dry season is somewhat mitigated. On the narrow, low-lying coastal strip of Natal, from the northern border southwards to the neighborhood of Port St. John there is a good deal of dense woodland resembling to some extent the tropical forests of east central Africa. The canopy is usually bound together by a large number of climbers; palms and large monocotyledons are of frequent occurrence. Many of these forests have been cut down to make way for sugar plantations or to be burnt as fuel in the sugar mill. Here, as elsewhere in Africa, woodland which has been cut but not cleared raises serious problems for the forester. The forests rapidly became an impenetrable tangle of bushes, bound together by climbers.[7] Under such conditions, the growth of tree seedlings is inhibited by competition and by lack of light, so that the woodland quickly degenerates.

SAVANNAH, BUSH, AND MOUNTAIN LANDS

The geography of Africa has no agreed terminology, and classifiers soon run into numerous difficulties. North of the West African forest belt, the rainfall diminishes. Dense forest is succeeded by open woodland, which in turn gives way to orchardlike bush. The parkland changes into desert country. The transition between these, and related climatic and vegetational zones are, however, seldom sharp, and geographers use the most variegated kinds of description. Some refer to dry forests when others talk of savannah forest; some speak of dry savannahs where others mean bush veld.

Climatologists can nevertheless agree, roughly speaking, on the following main divisions. The "Sudan climate," north of the equatorial belt, is marked by considerable heat with a considerable temperature range, amounting to something like 15° to 20°F. Diurnal ranges are also great, and night frosts may occur in the coolest season. The thermometer normally rises to its highest point in the late spring, when the mean temperature at many stations exceeds 90°F. In summer the southwest monsoon is drawn towards the North African "low," and rain-bearing currents penetrate into the Sudan from the Guinea coast. From the northern limit of the equatorial forest to the borders of the Sahara, precipitation steadily diminishes; so does the duration of the rains, which become increasingly less reliable. In addition, the swing of the equatorial convectional rainfall belt from south to north and back again, may bring additional precipitation, and thereby occasion a "double maximum." There are wide areas in the Sudan where the amount of rain, on paper, seems adequate to sustain arable farming. Yet cultivation may be out of the question without irrigation. This is occa-

Savannah grasslands in the Transvaal. (Foto Hegelman, from De Wys, Inc.)

sioned by the intensity of evaporation. The dry lands, moreover, may well be increasing in their geographical extent; there are indications that the desert is spreading southwards. In all probability, this is a long-term process, and in earlier times the Sudan was almost certainly much better watered than it is now. There is evidence that the basin of Lake Chad, has long been filling in.[8]

The lands extending southward from the southern districts of the Congo and the southern parts of Tanganyika enjoy what has been called a "modified Sudan climate." The subcontinental peninsula between the Indian Ocean and the South Atlantic is relatively narrow when compared with the northern half of the continent. The poleward coast also opens out to the sea. Oceanic influences are thus more strongly marked than in the Sudan. In addition the plateau rises on an average to a height of no less than 3000 feet, often more. Except for the river valleys, or low-lying areas such as in the Great Rift and the basin of Lake Nyasa, temperatures are rarely excessive. The mean of the hottest month immediately preceding the summer rains, rarely goes above 82°F. The midwinter mean, on the other hand, does not often drop to less than 60°F. During the southern winter, from about June to August, the sun shines bright, the air is dry, the nights are cold and clear. Subsequently the thermometer goes up, and then the rains come. These may be "convectional" in character, occasioned by the anticyclonic system over the subcontinent (that is to say by an atmospheric system marked by high barometric pressure, which causes heated air currents to rise). Or there may be "orographical" rains, born in by the southeast winds from the Indian Ocean.

> From the west
> Clouds come hurrying with the wind
> Turning
> Sharply
> Here and there
> Like a plague of locusts
> Whirling
> Tossing up things on its tail
> Like a madman chasing nothing
>
> Pregnant clouds
> Ride stately on its back
> Gathering to perch on hills
> Like dark sinister wings;
> The Wind whistles by
> And trees bend to let it pass.[9]

There are very considerable variations in the rainfall, and hence in the vegetational regimes of these areas. Zambia and Malawi, for instance, lie beyond the reach of the equatorial low-pressure rainbelt. But the southeast brings in abundant rain, especially to Malawi. Further east, on the coast of Mozambique and in the lower valleys of the Zambezi, temperatures are higher, and the climate becomes oppressive.

The nature of the rainfall regime profoundly affects the character of the tree life. The savannah has several months of drought; many rivers run empty in the summer, and the trees have to find some means of getting by in dry weather. The strangely shaped baobabs can store up considerable quantities of water. Many trees reduce transpiration by shedding their leaves. But there are great variations in the vegetation of the savannah. In the southern portion of the Congo (Kinshasa), in adjacent parts of Angola, and northern Zambia, there are endless acres of dry forest. Southward, in Zambia and Rhodesia, the forest usually opens out, and the scenery commonly assumes a parkland appearance. The tree canopy is not continuous; high grass grows on the ground. In many regions the landscape is scattered over with great termite mounds, overgrown with thickets of bush, small trees, and lianas (woody vines). The bush stretches into the distance like a never-ending sea of brown and russet that bursts out into green after the rains and sweeps on against a background of translucent blue sky. During the brief spells of dawn and dusk, the land is plunged into gold and purple, but becomes grim and oppressive under the white glare of the midday sun. At first sight the veld frightens and oppresses by its monotony, but as people get accustomed to its appearance they often find a strange fascination in this kind of country; the different kinds of trees and shrubs acquire an individuality of their own.

The savannah is subject to great bush fires in the summer. During the drought all herbaceous growth stops. The grass becomes brown and dry; the midday heat is intolerable; there is a smell of dust in the air, and the northerner who has made his home in these latitudes at last understands the psalmist's allusion to the "destruction that wasteth at noonday."[10] This is the time when great fires sweep through the bush. The fire of course does not destroy all the trees, for some are protected by their thick or corklike bark. The woody species, moreover, have great powers of regeneration through stump shoots and suckers. Nevertheless, millions of seedlings are destroyed every year, and it therefore seems that "the dry lands of tropical Africa are condemned to go on living, at least for many years to come, below their botanical par."[11]

In the less favored areas the trees get fewer and smaller. Treeland in turn gives way to stunted bush and scrub. In places like central Tanzania (Tanganyika) this tangle may form an impenetrable *maquis* of bushes and small, spiny, twisted trees. As the country gets drier still, the bush gives way to thornland. The East African savannah proper has many features of its own. Nairobi, the capital of Kenya, lies at an altitude of 5500 feet. The city is only a few degrees away from the equator, but at this elevation height tempers heat. The highest monthly mean amounts to no more than 66°F; the climate might be likened to one of eternal spring, and recalls the regime of countries such as the high Andean plateau of Colombia.

The annual rainfall shows the characteristic double maximum of equatorial latitudes, and the periods of most intense precipitation usually occur a few weeks after the equinoxes of March and September.[12] The plateau as a whole does not get a great deal of rain, though there are considerable differences. The mean for the plateau amounts to no more than 45 inches, though well watered districts like the region on the western and northern shores of Lake Victoria get as much as 60 to 70 inches.

The relatively low temperature and the diversity of soil, relief, and rainfall result in great variations of plant life. Savannah, with rank coarse grass sometimes as high as twelve feet, usually predominates. At its richest the country takes on the character of tropical parkland; at its poorest it is arid grassland scattered with thornbush. A journey to the top of Mount Kenya is itself a lesson in plant geography. To the north and east, the traveler comes into gentle, fertile country, creased by streams. There are splendid views all around, up to the forest that still clothes the mountain and toward the white peak above, or down across green pastures, over African plantations and round thatched huts towards the baked plains in the distance. It is from this part of the mountain that the trail begins. The tourist first makes his way through rain forest, next through a belt of arched and feathered bamboos; then he comes out on bleak moorland with mountain vegetation. As he scrambles up, the grass thins out and then disappears. There is more climbing—slowly now, for he has reached the thin air and gasps for breath—and then he comes to the outposts of the glaciers, somewhere about 15,000 feet. After this it is a matter of climbing with ice-axe, rope, and all the rest of such paraphernalia. The summit is guarded by glaciers of such formidable nature that the final ascent to Batian, the highest peak, represents a major achievement of mountaineering.

GRASSLAND AND DESERT

Most of the grasslands of tropical Africa occur in association with bush, scrub, or trees; hence the cartographer's neatly drawn boundary lines between different vegetational zones always have more of an approximate than a definitive value and can give little idea to the uninitiated of the vast range of local conditions. In North Africa the transition from savannah to desert is made through a belt, roughly varying in width from 200 to 300 miles, and extending all the way from north of the Senegal to the Republic of the Sudan. Some geographers speak of the "acacia desert," but there are many variations in the vegetational character of this great middle zone. Great portions of the Lake Chad basin, for instance, are covered with marshland. The swamps by the confluence of the *Bahr al-Jabal* and the *Bahr al-Ghazal,* with their tangle of tall reeds, bear some similarity to the Chad marshes. On the Abyssinian plateau, the regional distinctions between various rainfall and altitudinal zones likewise produce great contrasts in vegetation. The plateau levels of the interior, lying at an average about 6000 feet above sea level, are commonly covered with treeless steppe. At elevations exceeding 6000 feet, the country sometimes changes into parkland. In the Sudan proper vast expanses are covered by stunted plants; there is little rain, but water is found in wells and waterholes. This advantage, added to the absence of densely growing vegetation, enables the indigenous people to lead a nomadic life whose rhythm is determined by the availability of water and pasturage. From times immemorial, sheepherders and, later, cattle and camel men have driven their beasts across these expanses, and the North African middle belt has played an important part in the history of migration and culture contacts.[13]

To the north of the transitional zone lies the Sahara, the world's greatest wasteland. Readers of adventure stories usually associate the word "Sahara" with endless sand dunes, where mounted Bedouins lurk in ambush. Sandy wastes, known as *erg,* do indeed extend over vast regions, especially in southern Algeria and Libya. But in addition to desert of this kind, there are also great pebble and gravel deserts, as well as rocky wastelands known as *hamada.* This is the "dry and thirsty land where no water is"; the camels' feet, and it is hard to imagine a more desolate scenery. Yet large areas are by no means bare of vegetation. There are considerable differences in day and night temperatures; the rock alternatively expands and contracts; great cracks appear in the stone, and shrubs of different varieties may gain a lodging in the clefts. Where rain is available, or ground water appears in sufficient quantities, the desert may spring to life with a rich growth of annual greenery, and there are oases where date palms may be cultivated in great quantities. The date palm thrives best in almost rainless districts, where the roots can go down to ground water. The palm groves and the intensive cultivation areas of the Saharan oases do not, however, find a parallel in the deserts of the southern portion of the continent.

The drier regions south of the equator show the same range of vegetational differences occurring in the more northerly latitudes. In the higher parts of Malawi and Rhodesia, for instance, there are great "alpine" grassland regions where the traveler is more likely to suffer from cold than from heat. Further south, in the Republic of South Africa, the huge areas of the interior are covered with tall grass

Sand dunes and an oasis in the Sahara. (Afrique Photo, from De Wys, Inc.)

that offers magnificent pasture to cattle. To the west, towards Botswana, the land gets drier, and the country becomes more inhospitable. But, as David Livingstone put it with the explorer's practiced eye for nature, "The so-called Desert . . . is by no means a useless tract of country."[14] Making his way across the grim-looking Kalahari, Livingstone found a surprising quantity of grasses, as well as watermelons and other kinds of edible plant. The grass "usually rises in tufts with bare spaces between, or the intervals are occupied by creeping plants, which, having their root buried far beneath the soil, feel little the effects of the scorching sun. The number of these which have tuberous roots is very great; and their structure intended to supply nutriment and moisture when during the long droughts they can be obtained nowhere else." The drier parts offer a desolate and sometimes frightening appearance. "All around Serotli," for instance, "the country is perfectly flat, and composed of soft white sand. There is a peculiar glare of bright sunlight from a cloudless sky over the whole scene; and one clump of trees and bushes, with open spaces between, look so exactly like another, that if you leave the wells, and walk a quarter of a mile in any direction, it is difficult to return." Perhaps the driest and most forlorn region in the world is the Namib desert, further west, on the coast of South-West Africa, where the average rainfall amounts to less than one inch every year. Inland the annual precipitation increases a little, varying from three to six inches in Namaqualand to about twenty-two inches further north. Ranchers can sometimes tap underground water, or they construct dams to hold surface runoff. In the more favored regions, water is also obtained from rivers, or by tapping water flowing beneath the sandy beds of seasonal streams, so that it is difficult to generalize about the potentialities of such areas as a whole.

THE FRINGE LANDS OF "MEDITERRANEAN" TYPE

A tourist flying from Salisbury in Rhodesia to Cape Town, on the southern tip of South Africa, only has a few hours to go. But from an ecologist's point of view, he might just as well be in another world, and the visitor newly arrived from the north sometimes feels that he is no longer in Africa. The magnificent motor ways, skirting the sea outside Cape Town, are reminiscent of drives along the French Riviera. A short trip by train takes the stranger to places like Paarl, the "Pearl," or Worcester, great centers of the wine industry with magnificent vineyards that can make even a Rhinelander feel envious.

In this part of the world the sea shapes the climate. During the winter, the stormy and rainy westerly wind belt swings northwards, and affects the country up to a distance about 150 miles away from Table Bay. From then onwards the Mediterranean regime gradually merges with that of hotter, drier, and more inhospitable lands. To the east of Cape Town, along the coast, the winter rains and summer droughts characteristic of this climatic zone, persist some distance beyond Cape Agulhas, but towards Port Elizabeth there is an increasing proportion of summer rainfall. Directly inland from Cape Town, towards the northeast, the Mediterranean belt is shut off, less than 100 miles away, by the border ranges, beyond which extends the first step of the South African Plateau, the arid lands of the Karroo.

The climate here is greatly influenced by oceanic wind and water currents. On the western shore of the Cape Province a cold equator-bound stream, known as the Benguella, lowers summer temperatures through the medium of onshore breezes. In addition, the southeast Trades of the summer season exert a seaward drag on the surface water, so that there is an upswelling from the colder depths: sea bathers in Cape Town are well familiar with the astonishing differences in temperature that are found in the waters of the Atlantic and the Indian Ocean sides of their shores. Cape Town is exposed to strong sea breezes and the midsummer (January) mean is below 70°F, which is unusually cool for a "Mediterranean" station. Winters in Cape Town (which in the southern latitude occur in July) are generally mild; the July mean is 55 °F, and the region as a whole thus enjoys a genial and temperate climate.

Conditions in the mountainous Cape are thus similar to those of the Mediterranean basin, some 5000 miles away on the other end of the continent. In the past, the highlands within the regime of abundant winter rains used to be clothed with cedars and cypresses similar to those of the Syrian Lebanon and the Maritime Atlas, but within historical times there has been much deforestation. Considerable areas of woodland are still found in the narrow belt of well-distributed rainfall west of Port Elizabeth, and on the southern slopes of the Outeniekwa and Tsitsikama Mountains. These remnants largely consist of broad-leafed evergreens, though the yellowwood, which was once common, is not of this type. Thicket growth, similar to the Corsican *maquis,* represents a typical form of vegetation in the Cape, and the narrow, well-watered highlands of the Cape Peninsula have a variety of shrubs. Evergreen and hard-leaved bush and shrub usually grow to a height of no more than six feet; there are also many varieties of protea, including the *suikerbos,* the sugar bush, which is so frequently mentioned in Afrikaans folk songs.

NOTES

1. Quoted from John Pepper Clark, "Olokun," in Gerald Moore and Ulli Beier, *Modern Poetry From Africa* (Harmondsworth, Middlesex, England, 1964), p. 86.

2. Quoted from Ellis Ayitey Komey "The Change," in *Modern Poetry From Africa*, p. 77.

3. Kingsley, *Travels in West Africa*, pp. 87–88.

4. Kingsley, pp. 552–553.

5. Andre M. A. Aubréville, "Tropical Africa," in Stephen Haden-Guest, John K. Wright, and Eileen M. Teclaff, eds., *A World Geography of Forest Resources* (New York, 1956), pp. 375–378.

6. For a description of the Mau see Huxley, *White Man's Country*, pp. 135–136.

7. Robert S. Adamson, "South Africa" in *A World Geography of Forest Resources*, pp. 385–391.

8. For the whole of this section see Fitzgerald, *Africa: A Social, Economic and Political Geography*.

9. Quoted from David Rubadiri, "An African Thunderstorm," in *Modern Poetry from Africa*, p. 159.

10. Psalm 91:6.

11. Kimble, *Tropical Africa*, vol. 1, p. 73.

12. Equinox is derived from the Latin *aequus,* meaning equal, and *nox,* meaning night. The equinoxes are the two days in the year when the days are equal to the nights all over the world.

13. Fitzgerald, pp. 53–61.

14. David Livingstone, *Missionary Travels and Researches in South Africa, Including a Sketch of Sixteen Years' Residence in the Interior of Africa* (London, 1857), p. 51. For the subsequent quotations see pp. 47 and 57.

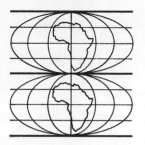  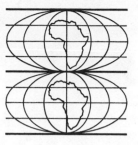

PART II

THE PEOPLE OF AFRICA

Chapter 4

Introduction

BASIC POPULATION FIGURES

From times immemorial censuses have been apt to excite superstitious dread in the minds of peasant peoples. The Old Testament speaks of David's first attempt at a national enumeration as a calamity. "And again the anger of the Lord was kindled against Israel, and he moved David against them to say, Go, number Israel and Judah. For the king said to Joab the captain of the host, which was with him, Go now through all the tribes of Israel, from Dan even to Beersheba, and number ye the people, that I may know the number of the people." The commander-in-chief diplomatically tried to avoid this unpopular task. "And Joab said unto the king, Now the Lord thy God add unto the people, how many soever they be, an hundredfold . . . but why doth my lord the king delight in this thing?" But David persisted, and a great pestilence smote Israel to punish the king for what his people regarded as a very wicked design.[1] David's census, moreover, was almost certainly highly inaccurate, and modern governments in Africa have encountered problems very similar to those encountered by the Jewish king. Some Africans believe, like the ancient Hebrews, that it is unlucky or sacrilegious to count the people. Many dislike furnishing information about themselves to the government. Many more suspect that the census taker only wants to gather figures so as to facilitate the imposition of additional taxes. Even where information is given willingly, the nature of the replies may preclude accurate results. At one census at Brazzaville, for instance, a certain man claimed to be 430 years old; another stated that he was thirty-five years of age, and had a son of thirty![2] One ethnic group would not allow its data to be recorded on forms of a particular color; in

49

another location, 2000 people bore the same name and could not therefore be easily identified. Sometimes one particular regional or ethnic group may deliberately try to exaggerate its own numbers so as to gain political advantages for themselves. Alternatively, numbers may be underplayed for corresponding reasons.

But above all, census takers face enormous administrative obstacles. Distances are great; available funds are small. Census taking, moreover, is a highly skilled task, requiring a complex and reliable administrative machine, as well as expert knowledge. Throughout many parts of Africa, these desiderata hardly exist even at the present time; in the past they did not exist at all. Instead of skilled demographers, David had to employ "the captains of the host" to count his people. Modern governments in Africa have used overworked policemen, district commissioners or treasury officials to gather local data, which were then often evaluated in the crudest possible fashion by some unqualified man working in the capital. Even relatively closely administered territories have thus been traditionally deficient in accurate statistical information concerning the people within their borders. In the beginning of the present century, for instance, responsibility for Southern Rhodesia's first census was entrusted to the Director of Education who, being an intellectual, was expected to add his sums with precision! A quarter of a century later, the Southern Rhodesian Director of Census, a senior civil servant of proven merit, frankly prefaced his report by pointing to his national stocktaking as a venture resting on amateur productions, assembled by a scratch team without previous experience in such work.[3] Yet Southern Rhodesia was still in a relatively fortunate position. In 1934 the authorities at Salisbury at last appointed a trained government statistician, and his department subsequently acquired a high reputation among professionals.

Most other African countries were, or in some cases still are, badly provided with statistical data. The bulk of African statistics, especially those compiled in earlier days, represents little more than enlightened guesswork. Even modern experts have been apt to underestimate the real figures of the indigenous races, the margin of error sometimes amounting to as much as one-fourth or even one-third of the total population. By and large it is true to say that the older the statistical information the more unreliable it is. In addition, it has always been easier to compile figures concerning immigrants—be they Europeans, Indians or Lebanese. The majority of newcomers live in cities; they make their living in a cash economy, which requires an enormous amount of documentation to function. African villagers, dwelling in small settlements, dispersed over wide areas, are a more difficult case. Peasants mainly engaged in subsistence farming do not require many written documents; they are further away from the government's watchful eye, and except for selective surveys on a small scale, good statistics are hard to come by. In Africa the studies of historical demography or of economic history are as yet in their infancy; and all generalizations about population growth and population movements, about alleged increases or decreases in the gross national product, or what have you, must be treated with great caution.

No one knows exactly how many people live in Africa. No one can be certain about growth rates in the past. In all probability Africa has witnessed, during the last two generations or so, the swiftest demographic expansion in its history. Improved communications, advances in agriculture and medical services have occasioned a swift, though uneven growth of population; sub-Saharan Africa as a whole may well now be doubling the number of its people every generation. A recent figure given by the United Nations Statistical Offices assesses the population of the continent at 269,294,000.[4] If the UN's estimate is anything like correct, the overall density of Africa's population is less than 23 per square mile. The figures for sub-Saharan Africa are smaller still. Probably something like 42,000,000 dwell in North Africa, in the great belt of Islamic countries, which stretches out on the Mediterranean shore, and which includes Morocco, Algeria, Tunisia, Libya, and the United Arab Republic. If these figures are accurate, the vast regions between the Cape and the Sahara would contain only some 227,000,000, that is to say slightly more than the United Kingdom of Great Britain and Northern Ireland and the six member states of the European Economic Community between them. The number of Africa's inhabitants is, however, increasing. Admittedly, it is a mistake to speak of a universal population explosion throughout the continent. In the past, administrators have, in fact, worried that certain communities, like the Ila in what is now Zambia, may have actually diminished rather than increased in numbers. Birth rates may be high, but so are death rates. Nevertheless, in many parts of Africa the population probably now doubles itself every twenty-five or thirty years. On paper, all these newly-born babies ought to have plenty of living space when they grow to manhood. But Africa's population is, in fact, very unequally distributed, both as between one country and another, and very commonly also within each country.[5] Some experts, therefore, fear that certain portions of Africa are severely overcrowded in relation to their existing resources and modes of production. Hance estimates that as much as 28 percent of the continent has too many people, and that 38 percent of Africa's inhabitants live in what he calls overpopulated regions.[6] Not all would concur with this pessimistic assessment. But there is no doubt that a large proportion of Africans are concentrated in a few relatively limited areas. These include the coastal belt along the Mediterranean in northwest Africa, the Nile delta, the lands adjoining the northern and northeastern shore of Lake Victoria, Ruanda, Burundi, southern Nigeria, southern Ghana, parts of Sierra Leone, as well as of the Congo, South Africa, Lesotho, and other countries.

CRITERIA OF ETHNIC CLASSIFICATION

The ancient Egyptian neatly divided the human race into four: Asiatics, Libyans, Nubians, and Men. It is hardly necessary to point out that in this scheme only the Egyptians themselves figured as "men."[7] Many modern theories of race have about the same degree of objectivity, and Africa especially has been one of the myth makers' special hunting grounds. The business of ethnic classification is, unfortunately, a complicated one. The first criterion that comes to mind is skin color. Most of us group the peoples of the world into brown men, black men, or white. This threefold division of humanity not only seems to correspond to common sense observation; it can also look down upon an ancient intellectual pedigree, to Biblical accounts which traced the descent of mankind to Ham, Shem and Japheth, the three sons of Noah. This textbook follows the established pattern in using this color classification; but we do so only as a literary device, not as a scientific description. The so-called "black" peoples of Africa are not all black; some are brown, some are reddish-brown; others again have skins of rich yellow. Neither are the "white" races really white. Some Europeans have pink or ruddy faces; others are sallow—darker even than some Indians.

There are different theories to account for the variations in human skin color. One school of thought holds that the ancestors of modern man originated in a hot climate, probably in east or southeast Central Africa. Starting with a chance mutation (that is to say, a random change in the elaborate chemistry of human chromosomes governing man's biological makeup), these early beings may have taken on a dark pigment. The dark color protected their skins against harmful radiation from the sun. Dark pigmentation, by filtering solar radiation, may also have had the additional effect of impeding the synthesis of vitamin D, a substance manufactured by the human body from the rays of the sun. Vitamin D has the peculiar characteristic of preventing rickets. As early man moved from the tropical into the temperate zone, where solar radiation was less intense, a dark skin may have become something of a biological handicap. Light skin, on the other hand, conceivably became something of an advantage by admitting more vitamin D-producing sunlight into the human body. It is therefore possible that, as time went on, climatic factors may have produced appropriate genetic changes.

But whatever the reasons for the differences in human skin color, pigmentation alone is an unsatisfactory criterion for grouping people. Hence physical anthropologists have tried many others. They have recorded the color and texture of hair, the shape and color of eyes, the height of people's build, the shape of their skulls, lips and noses. These indices, however, do not provide a good basis for dividing mankind into groups, whose members all have certain distinguishing traits in common. From times immemorial, Africa has been a great racial melting pot. Hence, the different criteria mentioned above do not always go together. Within each population there is usually a wide range of variation, so that two people from the same group may differ more widely from each other than they would from individuals of another group. To take just one example, the average height of the Dinka in the southern Sudan is among the tallest in the world. But there are some Dinka who are shorter than tall Pygmies.

Theories based on the shape of skulls have proved equally fallacious. More satisfactory results may perhaps be attained through the measurement of blood groups. Investigators have claimed for instance that Africa south of the Sahara shows a preponderance of a particular chromosome (c De) of the Rh group, which is said to be unique. No substantial component of the Rh blood group extends from Egypt or the Mediterranean southwards beyond Abyssinia. This conclusion suggests that the Pygmies or allied stocks may constitute a major component of many African tribes. But though results obtained through such means are interesting, they do not as yet provide material for the complete classification of the Africans on the basis of their blood groups.[8]

Certain scholars have drawn attention to a condition known as sickle frequency. This is a peculiar condition of certain red blood corpuscles, which assume sickle shape when deprived of oxygen. The incidence of sickle frequency varies, but it is difficult to arrive at hard and fast conclusions, as there may be a peculiar disposition to the sickle gene in populations exposed to endemic malaria.

Some investigators have tried to measure the distribution of intelligence through the administration of standardized tests; others have assumed that there must be innate differences in the mental capacity of persons belonging to different groups. But this basic-intelligence approach is also open to serious criticism. It is difficult to establish how much man owes to nature and how much to nurture; how far intelligence is a hereditary endowment and how far it is influenced by our environment. Many have criticized the tools of inquiry themselves. Just what exactly does an intelligence test measure? Ability to cope with a wide range of generalized problems, say the designers! Nothing but ability to pass intelligence tests, argue the skeptics! For instance, town-bred youngsters commonly do better in intelligence tests than country-bred youngsters. But this result may simply reveal the hidden bias contained in intelligence tests that are thought up by city people. In any case, even convinced believers in the thesis that intelligence is unevenly spread among different human groups do not necessarily try to establish hard and fast divisions between different stocks. The more moderate adherents of the school only talk about the *average* distribution of intelligence. In other words, even the supposedly less well-endowed groups can turn out geniuses, and the more favored ones may produce duds.

The most fanciful classification schemes try to correlate differences in culture with differences in personality types. There is a whole school of what might be called nursemaid psychology, whose adherents put forward arguments that the long periods of suckling habitual in many parts of Africa create a state of emotional dependence, which makes it difficult for black people to adapt themselves to the competitive conditions of modern life.[9] Such theories are on a par with views that account for quirks in the Russian folk soul through the tight swaddling of Russian infants or for German authoritarianism in terms of early beatings administered by angry German fathers to their offspring. These theories all have one thing in common—a complete lack of historical perspective. Chinese mothers in the past also used to suckle their infants for lengthy periods, without, however, necessarily condemning them to a life of future economic backwardness. Strong-minded, domineering Germans like Karl Marx enjoyed the advantage of having been brought up by a very permissive father; yet Marx as a man always lusted after authority.

We are left with language as the most convenient means of classification. This method too entails many difficulties. Language is something learned. There is no necessary correspondence between a man's mother tongue and his motherland. There are Basuto in Johannesburg who speak nothing but English; there are Algerians of French descent who can talk only Arabic. Many people, moreover, are bilingual or multilingual. A Zambian clergyman of Malawi descent living on the upper Zambezi may well be as proficient in Chinyanja and Silosi as he is in English. In Europe it is just as "natural" for an educated Alsatian to converse in German and French with equal facility, as it is "natural" for the average Parisian to know nothing but French. The picture is further confused by the development of *linguae francae* that are widely used among different ethnic groups for purposes of trade and communication. These may be of indigenous or European origin, and include a great variety of tongues such as the upcountry Swahili of Kenya, Uganda, Tanzania and the Congo, Hausa in parts of the sub-Saharan borderland, Sango in portions of Central Africa, Umbundu in Angola, "Kitchen Kaffir" (a modified form of basic Zulu) in South Africa and Rhodesia, various forms of Africanized English, French, Portuguese, and so forth.

Most people, however, do fall into one specific language group. There are also objective criteria for the construction of linguistic systems. This does not mean that all scholars agree or that students of language are necessarily free from bias. But on the whole, linguistic methodology transcends political conflicts. Language and culture are, moreover, closely interwoven. It is only through language that men communicate. It is only through language that communities of different kinds, with their intricate network of social institutions, their differing ways of life, their poetry and ritual, can be fully understood. Hence, the following divisions will stress linguistic rather than racial descent.

NOTES

  1. II Samuel, 24:1–3 and ff.
  2. Hance, *The Geography of Modern Africa,* p. 51.
  3. Southern Rhodesia: *Report of the Director of Census Regarding the Census Taken on 4th May 1926: Part III* (Salisbury, Government Printer, 1927), p. 28, (CSR 6–1928).
  4. United Nations Statistical Office, *Demographic Year Book: 1963* (New York, 1964), p. 4.
  5. The following census figures or estimates are given for the population of the main sub-Saharan countries by the United Nations Statistical Office, *Statistical Yearbook: 1968* (New York, 1969) pp. 84–89. The figures given represent recent estimates of growth from earlier census figures.

COUNTRY	LATEST CENSUS	MOST RECENT POPULATION ESTIMATES
Angola (Portuguese)	(1960)	5,362,000
Botswana (Bechuanaland)	(1964)	611,000
Burundi	(1965)	3,406,000
Cameroun	(1965)	5,562,000
Central African Republic	(1959/60)	1,488,000
Chad	(1964)	3,460,000
Congo (Brazzaville)	(1960)	870,000
Congo (Kinshasa)	(1958)	16,730,000
Dahomey	(1961)	2,571,000
Equatorial Guinea	(1960)	281,000
Ethiopia	(1962)	23,900,000
Gabon	(1961)	480,000
Gambia	(1963)	350,000
Ghana	(1960)	8,376,000
Guinea	(1955)	3,795,000
Ivory Coast	(1958)	4,100,000
Kenya	(1962)	10,209,000
Lesotho (Basutoland)	(1966)	910,000

Liberia	(1962)	1,130,000
Malagasy Republic (Madagascar)	(1966)	6,500,000
Malawi (Nyasaland)	(1966)	4,285,000
Mali (Soudan)	(1961)	4,787,000
Mauritania	(1965)	1,120,000
Mozambique (Portuguese)	(1960)	7,274,000
Namibia (South-West Africa)	(1960)	605,000
Niger	(1960)	3,806,000
Nigeria	(1963)	62,650,000
Portuguese Guinea	(1960)	529,000
Rhodesia	(1964)	4,670,000
Rwanda	(1952)	3,405,000
Senegal	(1961)	3,685,000
Sierra Leone	(1963)	2,475,000
Somalia	(1962)	2,745,000
South Africa	(1960)	19,167,000
Sudan	(1962)	14,770,000
Swaziland	(1966)	395,000
Tanzania	(1967)	12,590,000
Togo	(1960)	1,772,000
Uganda	(1962)	8,133,000
Upper Volta	(1962)	5,175,000
Zambia	(1963)	4,080,000

6. Hance, p. 52.

7. H. W. Fairman, "Ancient Egypt and Africa," *African Affairs*, (Spring 1965), p. 69.

8. See Lord Hailey, *An African Survey: Revised 1956* (London, 1957), pp. 28–50, for a summary of these various theories.

9. J. F. Ritchie, *The African as Suckling and as Adult*, Rhodes-Livingstone Institute Paper No. 9 (London, 1943).

Chapter 5

The Languages of Africa

THE "CLICK" LANGUAGES (BUSHMEN AND HOTTENTOTS AND OTHERS)

Probably the most ancient race now living in Africa is the Bushmen, hunters and food gatherers of exceptionally small physical stature. At an early stage in African history, people akin to the modern Bushmen may have roamed over most of the continent. Subsequently, more technologically and agriculturally advanced immigrants occupied most of the Bushmen's traditional hunting grounds, and intermarried with the various aboriginal people, driving the remaining bands into the more barren and inaccessible areas. Today the Bushmen are mainly found in the most arid parts of South-West Africa, Botswana and southern Angola.[1] The various Bushman languages are diverse, but are all characterized by the copious use of "click" sounds of a type not known anywhere outside Africa. The Hottentots,[2] another South African people, speak a similar language, and it is probable that the Hottentots in the past have intermarried to a considerable extent with the Bushmen. The Hottentots, a nomadic people, knew the arts of herding cattle and of smelting iron, and were in this respect technologically more advanced than the Bushmen. They did not, however, develop any skill in cave paintings, and, unlike the Bushmen, did not leave any such pictorial relics to posterity. There are not many Hottentots left today. The majority have been absorbed into the Cape Colored people, a South African mulatto population, who speak Afrikaans as their native tongue. The Hottentots call themselves *Khoi;* their name for the Bushmen is *San;* and the people speaking these various "click" tongues are often grouped under the compound term Khoisan. In East Africa, on the mainland of Tanzania, there are small linguistic islands where Sandawe and

56

Hatsa are spoken; both bear some resemblance to Khoisan.[3] The Sandawe live by hunting, and to some extent by agriculture. The Hatsa make a scanty living as hunters and food gatherers, but many of these people face the likelihood of linguistic and cultural absorption by their more advanced neighbors.

NIGER-CONGO, NIGER-KORDOFANIAN, AND NILO-SAHARAN LANGUAGES

The classification of African languages poses intricate problems. For most parts of Africa scholars as yet have not developed large-scale linguistic genealogies that can pretend to any degree of certitude. There is, however, one exception. The Bantu group of families, spoken throughout most parts of Africa south of an imaginary line from the southern Camerouns to southern Uganda, Tanganyika and southern Kenya, shows clear similarities among its various members. Many experts believe that the Bantu languages can all be traced down to one common ancestor; this hypothetical progenitor may not have been very different from what we now think of as Bantu tongues, although the original culture of the Bantu speakers must have been very different. Linguistic and other evidence seems to indicate that the people using proto-Bantu tongues engaged in hunting and agriculture, that they kept some domes-

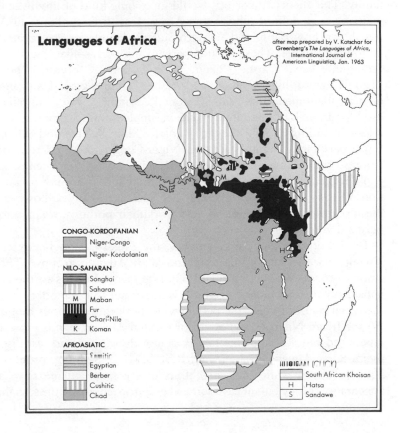

Languages of Africa

after map prepared by V. Kotschar for Greenberg's *The Languages of Africa*, International Journal of American Linguistics, Jan. 1963

CONGO-KORDOFANIAN
Niger-Congo
Niger-Kordofanian

NILO-SAHARAN
Songhai
Saharan
M Maban
Fur
Chari-Nile
K Koman

AFROASIATIC
Semitic
Egyptian
Berber
Cushitic
Chad

KHOISAN (CLICK)
South African Khoisan
H Hatsa
S Sandawe

tic animals, and that they knew how to smelt iron. They apparently lived in an area where there was both forest and savannah. Some say that they probably came from the southern edge of the equatorial forest, roughly mid-way between the Atlantic and the Indian Ocean.[4] Others postulate a more northerly point of departure, on the bend of the Niger and Benue river basins. But for untold centuries succeeding waves pushed outwards; all available evidence suggests that this *Völkerwanderung* must have begun sometime during the first millenium before Christ. By the tenth or eleventh century of our era, the Shona, a Bantu-speaking people probably reached what is now known as Rhodesia (Southern Rhodesia).[5] By the sixteenth century, Bantu-speaking tribesmen seem to have penetrated down to where the modern city of East London now stands in the Eastern Cape.[6] The Bantu-speaking peoples are now one of the most numerous linguistic groups in Africa. Their total number has been estimated at about 60,000,000 people.

The unity of the Bantu languages is obvious. But their relationship to the great cluster of diverse tongues—spoken all the way from the Senegal, to Ghana, Dahomey, southern Nigeria, and southern Cameroun, the Central African Republic and beyond—is still being disputed. The task of classifying these multifarious tongues is more complex than that of grouping the Bantu languages. But some experts now believe that they should all be regarded as different branches of one great "Niger-Congo" family. This theory, if correct, would give some kind of linguistic unity to the great majority of people in sub-Saharan Africa. Joseph Greenberg, an American scholar, has shown how Bantu and Western Sudanic languages use related terms for words of common usage. These include parts of the body—like "head," "ear," "mouth," "tongue," "jaw," "arm," "hand," "leg," "knee," "breast," "belly" and so forth. "Family" words like "mother" and "father" are designated with similar terms; so are natural phenomena like "sun," "stone," "wind," "water." Similar expressions are used for animals of great importance in simple hunting, farming, and pastoral economies—including "fowl," "egg," "goat," "dog."[7] This and other evidence makes Greenberg into a champion of the "Niger-Congo" theory. Critics of his thesis argue, among other things, that his concepts have not as yet been substantiated by the application of comparative procedures, and that they are not backed by any formulations of laws of sound shift. To laymen such as ourselves, however, the Greenberg thesis seems to carry conviction. As a working hypothesis, we therefore accept Greenberg's division.

In addition to the Bantu tongues, the Niger-Congo family comprises Mande, Voltaic, Kwa, Adamawa-Eastern, and West Atlantic groups.[8] The latter embrace, among others, Wolof and Fulani. Despite many theories to the contrary, Fulani is apparently not of Hamitic origin. It is important to remember, moreover, that from the racial point of view, the people who speak these various tongues are all mixed. West African Negroes and South or Central African Bantu show a great variety of types, and physical anthropologists cannot draw hard and fast distinctions between them. Some Malawi Africans may have heavily "Semitic" profiles, with prominent aquiline noses, while their neighbors in the same village have a more Negroid appearance. Many Fulani have somewhat Europeanate features, so that theorists in the past even came to suggest a probably somewhat fanciful hypothesis, which considered the Fulani to have been descended from Judaeo-Syrians.

Linked to the Niger-Congo group are the people who speak Kordofanian languages, and who dwell in the Nuba hills of Kordofan. The Kordofanian tongues divide into a number of subgroups, each with its own particularities. Racially, however, Kordofan was also a melting pot, so that these distinctions are of interest to the linguist rather than to the student of physical features.

North of the East and Central African "Bantu belt" there is another distinct linguistic zone, which covers much of northern Tanzania, Kenya, the southern Sudan, the Central African Republic, and Chad. The so-called Chari-Nile languages, spoken in this area, fall into several branches. The Eastern Sudanic family includes the Nubian, Barea, Ingassana (Tabi), Nyima, Temain, Merarit, Dagu, Nilotic, and other groups. This classification conflicts with that of more traditional scholars, who used to class the Great Lakes and related languages under a more general category known as "Nilo-Hamitic."

Greenberg's researches, however, show that what used to be called the Nilo-Hamitic and the Nilotic languages form part of a single Nilotic sub-family and are therefore of common origin. This Nilotic sub-family in turn forms part of yet a greater language group, Eastern Sudanic. Such tongues are spoken by a great variety of peoples. These cannot all be listed here without turning this account into a wearisome catalogue. But communities are varied as the war-like Masai herdsmen of Kenya, and the Nuer, pastoralists who practice transhumance in the swamp country of the White Nile, all understand languages which have distinct similarities. Related to these groups are Central Sudanic languages such as Efe and Lendu, as well as Berta and Kunama. These display a general kinship with northwest and north-Central African languages such as Songhai, Saharan, and Maban, all of which Greenberg groups under a general category called Nilo-Saharan.

AFRO-ASIATIC (HAMITO-SEMITIC) LANGUAGES

The classification of the Hamito-Semitic languages poses many linguistic problems and has led to sharp academic controversy. In many of the older theories the sons of Ham played a decisive part. Conquering Hamitic pastoralists, supposedly representing a higher type of civilization and speaking a language related to Hamitic, pushed into East Africa. The newcomers—the argument continues—were more quickwitted and better armed than the sedentary Bantu farmers in their way; the Hamite herdsmen therefore vanquished these so-called inferior populations, taught the use of iron to their subordinates, but gradually mingled with their subjects.[9] The Fulani of West Africa were similarly classed as Hamites, and so were the Hausa of Northern Nigeria, who combine agricultural skills and ancient traditions of trade, soldiering, and craftsmanship, and whose tongue has become a *lingua franca* over much of West Africa. The "Hamitic" interpretation is now, however, under strong attack.[10] Critics point out that there is no necessary connection at all between social attributes such as a pastoral way of life and military superiority, or the use of a particular tongue. Not all pastoral peoples are better at fighting than sedentary communities. In the Old Testament, for instance, Cain, a "tiller of the ground," commits the aboriginal murder when he slays his brother Abel, a "keeper of sheep," in a dread deed which may well symbolize the age-old encroachment of the farmer on the herdsmen's grazing grounds. Again not all conquering pastoral peoples in Africa were Hamitic. Above all, as we have seen, race and language do not necessarily go together. What is more, even the linguistic use of the word "Hamitic" is open to question. As Greenberg puts it "the non-Semitic languages of the Hamito-Semitic family do not form a linguistic unity as against Semitic. Therefore, the term Hamitic . . . does not refer to any valid linguistic entity."[11] Greenberg's classification scheme thus avoids the older "Hamitic" interpretation. He postulates an "Afro-Asiatic" group of languages, which falls into five major subdivisions. The first is ancient Egyptian, an extinct tongue which is preserved only in hieroglyphics. The second group is Berber, spoken extensively throughout northwestern Africa. The third is Cushite, which again has several branches. They include Somali, Galla and other related tongues spoken around the "Horn of Africa" and beyond. Going westwards, to the area of Lake Chad, linguists can trace yet another great bloc in the Lake Chad region. This comprises Hausa and other West-Central African forms of speech.

There are certain linguistic connections between the Semitic and the "Hamitic" tongues. The Hebrews call heaven *sh'maym,* the Arabs *sama.* The Hausa use the word *sama* to mean above and in Logone it stands for "rain." Of the Semitic languages in Africa, by far the most important is Arabic. The links between Arabia and Northeast Africa are very ancient, and this is not the time to go into the details concerning the diffusion of Arabic into North Africa. There is, however, one convenient key date. In A.D. 639 Caliph Omar sent an army to take Egypt. Omar defeated his enemies in 640, and from then onwards Arabic rapidly spread. By the beginning of the following centuries, the Muslims had overrun all Africa north of the Sahara, and Arabic was the *lingua franca* throughout the southern littoral of the Mediterranean. Arabic subsequently spread southward by land. Additional maritime contacts between the Near East and the shores of the Indian Ocean also gave Arabic a footing in East Africa. Arabic gained tremendous importance as the language of trade, religion, literature, warfare, and administration, and therefore made enormous peaceful, as well as warlike conquests. It provided many indigenous African peoples with a written language, and continues as a powerful cultural influence in modern Africa.

Arabic—unlike the languages of Latin derivation—has essentially kept its unity. There are differences in pronunciation and vocabulary between the Arabic spoken, say in Syria, Egypt, and Algeria; but these are not essentially greater than those between British, American, or South African English. The people who speak Arabic as their native tongue, moreover, are just as heterogeneous in their ethnic composition as those who employ English. There is a stereotype of the Arab as a tall, dark man, with a hawk-beak nose, wearing a white burnoose and a bejeweled scimitar, and riding through the desert on a magnificent steed. Such people exist; but they form a very small minority among the people speaking Arabic. A traveler's first impression in a country like Egypt may well center on the great variety of physical types. Some people look like the conventional idea of a German peasant; others might be Sicilian; others again have dark, Negroid features, so that, as always, Semitic language and racial descent should never be confused.

The same generalization applies to the people who speak Swahili. There is no Swahili race; Swahili, indeed, is not the speech of any particular tribe or ethnic community. It grew up among the descendants of Arab and Persian settlers on the coast, who had intermarried with Bantu women and who had enslaved a group of people. In the nineteenth century it was carried by Arab trade caravans to the Great Lakes to the eastern portion of the Congo, becoming the accepted *lingua franca* over much of East Africa. Swahili is closely related to various Bantu tongues such as Nyika. Swahili has, however, absorbed many Arabic words. All kinds of Bantu particularities have been sloughed off; the language has extensively borrowed prepositions and adverbs, and has thereby acquired considerable flexibility. Classical Swahili was written in the Arabic alphabet and has a literature of considerable antiquity. Modern Swahili has been reduced to Latin script and has widely spread through various parts of East Africa. Tanzania and Kenya have selected Swahili as a national language. But except for the Somali Republic, they are the only newly independent African states who have chosen an African tongue for the purpose. Swahili fundamentally belongs to the Bantu family, but by reason of the historical and cultural associations Swahili maintained with the Arab world, we shall group Swahili with the Afro-Asiatic languages of Africa.

Another important language is Amharic, the speech of the politically dominant group in Ethiopia. Amharic is used mainly in the central portion of Ethiopia. It is basically a Semitic tongue, but it has a script of its own; the Amhara are Christians, and they have a literary tradition dating back many centuries. Amharic is now the official language of Ethiopia, but not all Ethiopians can speak it (indeed half the country's population today are Muslims). Amharic, like Swahili and Arabic, moreover, has to contend with strong competition from English, which is better equipped to deal with modern scientific and technological concepts.

INDIC AND POLYNESIAN LANGUAGES

The greatest concentration of Indian people on the African continent is found in the Republic of South Africa, which has some 550,000 citizens of Asian origin. In the nineteenth century many Indians came to Natal as plantation workers; many of their descendants subsequently entered other professions, especially trade, and they now live mainly in the cities. East and Central Africa formerly had a total of some 400,000 settlers of Indian or Pakistani descent, including at one time about 180,000 in Kenya, more than 100,000 in Tanzania, and substantial communities in Zambia, Malawi, Uganda, and other parts of Africa. The East African coast had ancient links with India, and Indian merchants played an important part in both local and maritime commerce. During the nineteenth and early twentieth century, many more Indians came to East Africa as railway construction workers, traders, minor government employees, artisans, soldiers, and in other "middle-level" jobs. Indian village traders played an important part in advancing the money economy into the backwoods, but today Indians in East Africa are mainly town dwellers. They were prominent in commerce, but also in the administration, the professions, in handicraft, and industry. Never having held political power, Indians and Pakistanis could not impose their language on other subordinate groups, as the Arabs had been able to do for a time. Many Indians in Natal speak English, while most Goanese use Portuguese as their native tongue. The Indian immigrants include people from many parts of the subcontinent, but settlers from the northwestern corner of India are particularly numerous, and Gujarati is one of the most widely understood tongues among the Indians of East and Central Africa.

From early days onward, Madagascar and southeast Africa attracted immigrants from what is now Indonesia. Some scholars believe that Malagasy colonists settled as far afield as Natal and the Mozambique coast, but that about the year A.D. 800 they were cut off from their former contacts with Indonesia and were finally submerged among the indigenous people. In addition, the Dutch settlers in South Africa used to import slaves from the East Indies. Today, the descendants of these laborers are classed with the Coloreds, though the so-called "Malays" still practice Islam and maintain certain cultural traditions of their own. The Southeast Asian impact proved much more important in Madagascar. The Merina, one of the most advanced peoples of the *Grande Ile,* probably originated in Indonesia, and made their way by sea to Madagascar, where they intermarried with indigenous black peoples. The Merina, and related communities like the Betsileo (sometimes called the Southern Hova), and the Betsimisaraka make up about half the people of Madagascar, and differ considerably from the less developed coastal tribes. Malagache is itself divided into numerous dialects.

INDO-EUROPEAN LANGUAGES

AFRIKAANS

Africa's most numerous white community lives in the Republic of South Africa which, in 1970, comprised some 3,779,000 people of European descent. Nearly sixty percent of white South Africans speak Afrikaans as their native language, but the great majority of white people in South Africa are bilingual in Afrikaans and English. The Republic of South Africa also embraces a total of about 1,996,000 Colored (mulatto) people, of whom over 1,000,000 speak Afrikaans as their mother tongue. South African emigrants have carried Afrikaans further afield, to parts of Rhodesia, the Zambian "Railway Belt," and Kenya. Afrikaans is now the most widely spoken Indo-European language in southern Africa and appears to be gaining at the expense of English.

Afrikaans is the product of the South African frontier. It began its career as a trekkers' patois, and in time diverged more and more from the High Dutch spoken by the first white settlers at the Cape. Its vocabulary remains essentially High Dutch, with some additional loan words from other languages. But in the course of time, Afrikaans shed many of the original Dutch inflections; the Dutch genders were reduced to one; from the linguistic standpoint Afrikaans, in many ways, evolved rather like English towards greater simplicity and increasing linguistic flexibility. From the end of the last century onwards, Afrikaans began to develop a vigorous literature of its own. Afrikaans, therefore, increasingly supplanted High Dutch, not merely as a medium of daily intercourse, but also as the language of Afrikaner churches and universities, while High Dutch fell into desuetude. In 1925 Afrikaans was recognized as an official language of what was then the Union of South Africa; the publication of an Afrikaans Bible in 1933 marked the final step in the ecclesiastical emancipation from European Dutch.

The Afrikaners were originally a rural people. Indeed the very word "Boer," an older term for Afrikaner, means "farmer." The growth of cities and of industry caused more and more Afrikaners to move into the cities, where they became workmen, and later supervisors in mines and factories. Today Afrikaners are found in every conceivable urban profession, though the Afrikaner people still have a very much larger rural component than any other white community in Africa. The majority of Colored people are farm laborers, employees in industry, though the Coloreds too are beginning to create a middle class of their own. In the Western Cape, Afrikaners and Coloreds between them form the majority of the labor force, and the vast majority speak Afrikaans.

ENGLISH

English serves as the official language for most parts of Africa that were once under the Union Jack. It is the official language of Liberia, and one of the official languages in the Republic of South Africa. It plays a vital part as a means of communication for Africans with different native tongues; it has an outstanding role as a language of trade, education, science, literature, and administration, and serves as an indispensable link between Africa and the outside world. English, as well as French and Portuguese, was the language of imperialism, of Africa's white conquerors. But English, like French, also became the language of antiimperialism, of protest, and has become part of the political heritage taken over by the emergent nations. English, together with other European tongues like French, may well in the end remain the most important cultural legacy of empire.

In South Africa, English is the second most widely spoken language among the country's 3,779,000 white citizens. It is employed most extensively in the big cities, and also in Natal and the Eastern Cape, which in the nineteenth century, attracted the bulk of British settlers to South Africa. English is also the native tongue for the great majority of the 300,000 Europeans in Rhodesia and Zambia, and for most of the smaller groups of white expatriates in Tanzania, Kenya, and other parts of Anglophone Africa. In southern Africa, many of the original British immigrants came as mineworkers, railwaymen and artisans; others came to farm or to work in trade and the professions. Today English-speaking South Africans live mainly in the cities, where they make their living as skilled workers, commercial employees, as managers of factories and other enterprises, and in similar capacities. There are also English-speaking farmers and planters scattered as far afield as Natal, Rhodesia, Zambia, and

Kenya, but in a country like Rhodesia, farmers form only something like nine percent of the employed population.

Africa has produced many new English derivatives. South African English has acquired a peculiar accent of its own, influenced variously by Cockney, Scottish, and Afrikaans. South African speech is characterized, among other things, by sound shifts which turn "park" into "pork," car" into "cor," and "pin" into "p'nn," producing a rather clipped way of talking. Everyday speech in southern Africa has acquired a number of loan words from Afrikaans and from Bantu tongues; but there has been no essential change, and South African English literature remains part of the wider English world of letters.

In the nineteenth century, transatlantic forms of English were carried into Liberia and Sierra Leone by Negro settlers from the New World. Modified kinds of English, known as Pidgin, spread far afield as a trader's *lingua franca*. The impact of English has given rise to several different kinds of Creole, which blend a simplified variety of English with African speech patterns in varying proportions. Roughly speaking, the longer Creole has been established in any particular part of West Africa, the further it is likely to have diverged from the original. The process of transformation is likely to continue, as most of the English teachers in African schools do not talk English as their native tongue, and therefore willy-nilly teach a modified form of English to their pupils.[12] Modern English is now being widely employed as a literary language by African writers. This is true both in South Africa, where most African intellectuals use English rather than Afrikaans, and in the remaining parts of Anglophone Africa, where English is also a compulsory subject in schools. Some African writers have also composed works in Nigerian Creole or other types, and there is a popular Nigerian English literature which finds expression in chapbooks, broadsheets, and similar publications.

FRENCH, PORTUGUESE, AND OTHER TONGUES

French is the official language of all states once comprised within the French colonial empire and of what was once the Belgian Congo, Rwanda, and Burundi. It plays the same cultural role that English does in Anglophone Africa; it is widely used by the indigenous elites of these various countries, and is also being used as a literary medium, the means of expression for a new kind of Franco-African literature. French is also the native language of numerous white expatriates in former French Africa and the Congo. Estimates of their numbers vary, but they are likely to exceed 100,000 people, and they still play an important part as technicians, soldiers, administrators, as businessmen, as professional people, and sometimes as planters. In West Africa there are also various forms of French Creole, which show local variations.

Portugese remains the official tongue in Portugal's overseas provinces in Africa, including Angola, Mozambique, Portuguese Guinea, and a few minor possessions. In Angola there are something like 330,000 European settlers; Mozambique comprises about 220,000 white people—the overwhelming majority of them Portuguese—and immigration continues. Portuguese people make their living as government employees, as traders, artisans, and workmen; others engage in peasant farming or work as planters, but by and large the Portuguese middle class is appreciably smaller than that of any other group of settlers from Europe. Portuguese is also spoken as a native tongue by most *assimilados* (Portuguese of African, Asian, or mixed descent or by educated indigenous people) while the island of Saõ Thomé, off Gabon, has produced a Portuguese Creole of its own. An incipient Portuguese-African tradition is now being created by Portuguese-speaking Black intellectuals.

Spanish continues to be widely spoken in Equatorial Guinea, Spanish Sahara, and the island of Fernando Po, west of Cameroun. Italian is still widely used in Somalia and Eritrea, where the Italian tricolor once used to fly. There are numerous Italian expatriates in many parts of Africa, especially in Somalia and Ethiopia. Germans have settled in South-West Africa, South Africa, Tanzania, and elsewhere; Greeks have likewise made their homes in many parts of South, East and Central Africa. Other European languages heard in different parts of the continent include Dutch, Yiddish, Danish, Polish, and many others.

NOTES

1. There are probably only 50,000 Bushmen in Africa. In addition, there are perhaps 100,000 Pygmies in the Congo, a small-statured people who live in small bands and make their living from hunting and the collection of roots and berries.

2. The Hottentots today probably number no more than 24,000. These and the other figures have been taken from Paul Fordham, *The Geography of African Affairs* (Baltimore, 1965), pp. 41–46.

3. These sections on African languages are based mainly on the work of Joseph H. Greenberg. His important book, *Studies in African Linguistic Classification* (Branford, Conn., Compass Publishing Company, 1955), was revised and extended in *The Languages of Africa* (Indiana University Research Center, 1963), and in *Anthropology, Folklore and Linguistics,* Publication no. 25, (1963).

4. Malcom Guthrie, "Language Classification and African Studies," *African Affairs* (Spring 1965), pp. 29–33.

5. Roger Summers, "A Tentative History of the Bantu Movements in the Federation and Adjoining Countries," in William Vernon Brelsford, ed., *Handbook to the Federation of Rhodesia and Nyasaland* (London, 1960), p. 52.

6. Monica Wilson, "The Early History of the Transkei and Ciskei," *African Studies,* XVIII (1959), pp. 167–179.

7. Greenberg, *Studies in African Linguistic Classification,* p. 34.

8. The total number of West African Negroes has been estimated at about 60,000,000.

9. For a classical statement of the Hamitic theory see Charles G. Seligman, *Races of Africa* (London, 1957).

10. See for instance Philip D. Curtin, *The Image of Africa: British Ideas and Action 1780–1850* (Madison, 1964).

11. Greenberg, p. 54.

12. Guy Butler, "The Future of English in Africa," *Optima* (June 1964), pp. 88–97.

Chapter 6

Traditional Methods of Subsistence

CHARACTERISTICS OF AFRICAN AGRICULTURE

Today, most American and British people dwell in cities and get weekly or monthly paychecks. However much they may worry about their jobs, the majority assume as a matter of course that there will be enough to eat on their tables today, tomorrow, and next week. The realities for other times and places—say the early American settlement colonies in the past, or most sub-Saharan countries in the past or at present—are very different. In tropical Africa something like three-quarters of the population or more still makes its living from agriculture. Some are subsistence farmers, and others make a scanty living from their fields. A smaller proportion lives comfortably and employs improved systems of cultivation. But throughout Africa's history, hunger or malnutrition has been a present reality in the lives of many villagers, especially during certain times of the year. In this respect the ordinary Bantu tiller is more like our ancestors in Europe, whose lives were determined by the rhythm of the crops.

The position of the tiller, of course, has always varied a great deal from one part of Africa to another. The rainfall climates along the Guinea coast, suitable for the production of palm oil, bananas, and similar crops, provided much more favorable conditions than, say, the low-rainfall regimes of Somalia, whose inhabitants had to eke out an existence by grazing camels and other beasts. The tropical highland "islands" stood yet in another category. Their importance derived from a variety of natural phenomena, which might or might not all be present at the same time. Some had rich volcanic soils, favorable rainfalls, a relatively low incidence of human, animal or plant

66

Terraced farming among the peoples of Central Nigeria.
(De Wys, Inc.)

disease, a cool and pleasant climate. River valleys subject to periodic floods, such as the fertile plain of the upper Zambezi, faced farmers with problems very different from those of the arid savannahs of the northern Sudan. Africans therefore had to adapt their methods to an enormous variety of conditions, and generalizations about Africa's early farming conditions are hard to make. Economic historians, however, are probably on safe grounds when they stress the "island" pattern of Africa's agricultural and mining activities, a pattern which characterizes economic development on the continent to this day.[1]

The "islands" are uneven in size, distribution, and fertility; individual "nodes" are either separated from one another, or joined only by tenuous economic links. Today the coastal "islands" play a predominant part (geographers estimate that in 1957 nearly half the agricultural exports of tropical Africa came from within 100 miles of the coast, and the same may also have been true of earlier periods about which, however, we can only speculate). There are also irrigation "islands," where artificially installed water supplies allow intensive production. At present, such "islands" exist in the Gezira region of the Sudan, in parts of the Rhodesian low veld and elsewhere, but some ancient peoples also managed to irrigate land, and remnants of great works still survive in many parts of the East and East-Central African highlands.

It is therefore almost impossible to speak of "traditional" African agriculture. The

expression itself begs the question. The term conjures up a romantic image of un-
changing folkways, of a life in which each man did exactly what his ancestors did and
in which each community was wrapped in an unbreakable cocoon of custom. Such
concepts, however, belong to the realm of fairy tales. Of some 136 East African food
crops whose history has been investigated, only some 30 are believed to be of African
origin. Of the others, nearly 60 have probably been imported from Asia. The rest
—including most of the present-day staples like maize—have come to Africa from the
New World and from Europe.[2] The manner in which these plants spread through
Africa raises fascinating problems. The career of each could become the subject of
intricate detective work of the kind that has gone into the story of manioc (better
known as cassava.)[3] American Indians first developed basic crops like cassava
(manioc), maize, tobacco, and cocoa, which now play a major part in Africa's
economy; Mediterranean peoples have contributed sugar cane and citrus fruit; the list
could be extended almost indefinitely. Africans throughout the ages have "naturalized" these and other plants, so that the economic history of Africa has been one of
unceasing agricultural adaptation.

African farmers, however, faced many obstacles. Traditionally, manpower and
capital were scarce, but land was plentiful. People tried to make the most of this
resource of open bush and developed a great variety of extensive farming methods.
These usually involved stumping or pollarding trees, firing the bush, planting gardens, and moving on when the ground was exhausted. There are hundreds of variations on this basic technique. In Sierra Leone, for instance, the farmer starts to prepare
his rice farm about February. His grandfather was able to choose high forest for his
farm. Nowadays there is hardly any well-timbered land left; but the farmer still tries
to pick "strong" bush for his gardens. He cuts down small trees and bushes with the
help of his neighbors. When the dead vegetation is dry, the workmen burn it to kill
the weeds and insects and to make plenty of ash to feed the soil.

When the first rains come, they plant cassava. Shallow holes are dug with a hoe.
The cassava cuttings are put into the ground, and the holes are filled in. In early June
it is time to sow the rice. The seed, probably saved from last year's crop, is scattered
on the soil. Mixed with the rice may be bulrush millet, guinea corn, cotton, pigeon
pea, and other crops. Only a part of the farm can be sown at a time, for the seeds
must be hoed in before the birds eat them. Bird-scaring is important until the seeds
have begun to grow and the shoots are strong. Weeding is necessary until the rice
harvest in October or November, so the farmer's family has plenty of work to do.
The other crops are picked as they ripen. The cassava and pigeon pea are left for
another year when the bush is growing over the land again. That piece of land is now
allowed to rest for between four and ten years. The cassava will be used only if the
rice fails, or if there is a "hungry season," when last year's rice runs out and the new
crop has not yet ripened. A peasant and his wives usually manage to work about four
acres, but far more ground is required for the purpose of letting the bush lie fallow.[4]

Systems of this kind have many advantages. They do not require much physical
capital. They provide cultivators with a natural supply of fertilizers. They carry their
own insurance against soil erosion, provided the acreage available for farming remains plentiful. Forest or bush clearings are seldom "clean" enough or big enough

to present raging tropical rainstorms with an opportunity of washing off the exposed top soil. These systems, moreover, help to preserve the balance of nature by which the soil succeeds in maintaining itself in the difficult circumstances imposed by a tropical climate. Such methods, however, cannot feed many people. They do not provide much of a marketable surplus, and they need a great deal of land for their successful operation.

WEALTH FROM LAND AND WATER

One of the most important crops of Africa is millet, of which there are many varieties. Before the introduction of maize (corn), millet formed one of the principal kinds of food in tropical Africa, and by the mid-1950s the total area under this crop still amounted perhaps to almost three times that of maize. The yield is seldom large, but millet can make do with less rainfall and a less fertile soil than maize. It is also less liable to total failure when times are bad. The great millet or sorghum, also known as Kaffir corn or Guinea corn, is the usual variety, but in the more arid regions, bulrush millet or finger millet are widely grown both as pure or mixed crops.

Cassava is another staple crop grown almost entirely by Africans. Cassava is comparatively free from pests; it also plays an important part as a reserve in times of scarcity. The villagers consume their cassava mainly at home, but some territories, such as Togo, have also built up a valuable export trade in products made from the cassava roots. The wetter regions of Africa, including the coastal regions and the middle belt of Africa, produce yams, an edible tuberous root that often serves as a staple food. Expert farmers can grow huge tubers weighing fifty to sixty pounds. In South Africa and in most parts of East Africa the rainfall is insufficient for yam cultivation.

In addition, Africans adapted maize, a transatlantic crop brought in by the Portuguese. Where conditions are favorable, maize nowadays is rapidly gaining on other food crops. Rice was another important plant. Some varieties may have been indigenous to Sierra Leone and Senegal. Others are said to have been imported by Muslims. Today it plays a valuable part in the economy of Madagascar and in some West African countries like Sierra Leone. Rice, however, requires a great deal of moisture, and only limited areas are suitable for its cultivation. Africans also produced a number of cash crops. Kola nuts, obtained from a tropical tree, contain caffeine; from ancient times they have been chewed as a stimulant, and have been traded across the Sahara. Long before the Europeans made their appearance, African weavers in the northern savannah belt knew how to make cloth, and indigenous farmers cultivated the required cotton.

From ancient times, Africans were also familiar with the art of domesticating animals. Today there are still groups who rely wholly or largely on herding for their livelihood. These include people as varied as the Masai of Kenya and the Somali in the "Horn of Africa." Other farmers combined pastoralism with agriculture, and cattle, pigs and other beasts represented a considerable economic resource. Herdsmen unfortunately faced—and still face—a host of obstacles. The tsetse fly, for instance, transmits a dangerous parasite which causes sleeping sickness in human beings and fly disease (nagana) in cattle and other beasts, leading to great loss of domesticated animals in many parts of tropical Africa. The fly therefore keeps vast areas out of cultivation, and its prevalence is a major economic problem. In addition, pastoral farmers have to contend with tick-borne diseases, the irregularity of rainfall over most of Africa's grazing lands, locusts and other plagues, and antiquated methods of cattle breeding adhered to by many indigenous herdsmen who, all too often, prefer quantity to quality.

Wood formed another essential component in Africa's traditional economy. Forests, for one thing, play an essential role in maintaining the delicate balance of soil and climate; they conserve rain-water and sustain soil fertility. Woodland suffers less from either dry spells or torrential rains than unforested areas. Woods prevent soil erosion, and fulfill a major part in replenishing the well and spring water on which forest dwellers chiefly depend in the dry season.[5] Without forests the majority of indigenous cultivators would starve. The burning of bushland and forests provides cultivators with fertilizers. The dry forest zones afford pasture for animals who, in many areas, would never survive drought seasons but for the dried foliage of bushes and trees. Forests are also an essential source of food. From tropical rain forests come oil palms, "wine" palms, and kola nuts. Dry forests produce the fruits of the tamarind, the locust bean, the mango, and the shea tree. Even the very dry forests have their uses, and shrubs such as *Salvadora persica* are often the only means whereby tribesmen can obtain salt, that most precious of commodities. Forests likewise play an essential part in the production of commercial crops by giving shade and shelter. Cocoa and tea and—to a lesser extent—coffee and bananas need varying degrees of protection from wind or sun, which only trees can provide. Carpenters and furniture makers rely on wood, and African forests are specially rich in hardwoods like mahogany and ebony. Craftsmen fashion softer wood into domestic wares such as mortars, pestles, and spoons. The villagers build their huts and their canoes out of wood. The list could be extended almost indefinitely, for wood is the most versatile of all crops.

Africans also derived a great deal of wealth from their rivers and streams. Indeed the capture of fish for food was probably one of man's earliest economic enterprises. For people who live near a stream, it is much easier to catch fish than to shoot buck, and for thousands of years fish have formed an important part of the human diet: they are good to eat, valuable as a source of protein, and easy to store when properly preserved.

Tropical Africa is probably almost as rich in the number of its fish as in its tree species. Fish constitutes a great, but as yet relatively scantily used, source of food. There are many reasons for this comparative neglect. Many parts of the continent are either remote from the sea or poorly provided with rivers and lakes. Alternatively, many inland waterways are subject to severe fluctuations that would jeopardize an economy based on catching fish. Fish would quickly rot in the hot climate, and the art of smoking or dry-salting requires special skill. People, moreover, do not like to change their food habits, if they can help it. Many pastoralists, for instance, will eat fish only if they are too poor or miserable to consume anything else. Some will not eat fish at all. They may have religious taboos, which either prohibit the consumption of fish altogether, or rule out certain species in the manner of Leviticus, insisting that "whatsoever hath no fins nor scales in the waters, that shall be an abomination unto you." Nevertheless, fish became a staple food for most African coast and lakeshore dwellers. Many other Africans buy fish as a seasonal or occasional item, and fish probably play and have played a significant part in the traditional diet of at least one-third of the peoples in tropical Africa.[6]

WEALTH FROM THE SUBSOIL

In 1663 King Charles II of England struck a new coin, known as the guinea. The piece was originally made from gold obtained at the Guinea Coast. Early issues bore an elephant on one side, and the great beast engraved on these pieces symbolized in a picturesque fashion the connection between Africa and the gold trade.[7] From antiquity onward many African communities appreciated the economic importance of gold, and one of Africa's first major contributions to the world's commerce was to be found in the export of the yellow metal. Old European maps are full of names like the "Gold Coast," and "Gulph of Gold" or the "River of Gold." African gold stimulated in turn the imagination of Egyptian, Phoenician, Arab, and European adventurers.

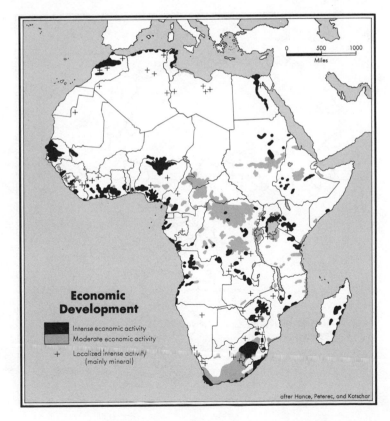

Economic Development

■ Intense economic activity
▨ Moderate economic activity
+ Localized intense activity (mainly mineral)

after Hance, Peterec, and Kotschar

Gold was exported from many parts of Africa: from the forest belt of the West Coast, from various parts of East Africa, and from what is now Rhodesia. No one knows exactly just how this trade was distributed throughout the continent and how much was taken out of the soil. In 1896 a British authority estimated that some £60,000,000 worth of gold had been extracted from Southern Rhodesia by "the Ancients."[8] But no geologist can feel certain about the Rhodesian figures, and it is even more difficult to compile the most tentative statistics for Africa as a whole.

Africans also worked basic metals, above all iron. Precolonial Africa passed straight from the stone age to the iron age without going through an intermediary era of bronze, as did most of early Europe. Skilled smiths knew how to make hoes, arrow heads, lance heads, and similar implements that determined African methods of food production. Africans also mined copper. The red metal formed a significant part of pre-European commerce in south Central Africa, and Katanga was a copper-mining center of some importance, long before Europeans set foot in the country. Salt was another valued item of commerce, and many precolonial communities were skilled in commerce.

African producers nevertheless labored under many serious limitations. Black miners had neither dynamite nor pumps; hence they could not mine to any great depths, and much of Africa's potential wealth remained inaccessible to them. By far

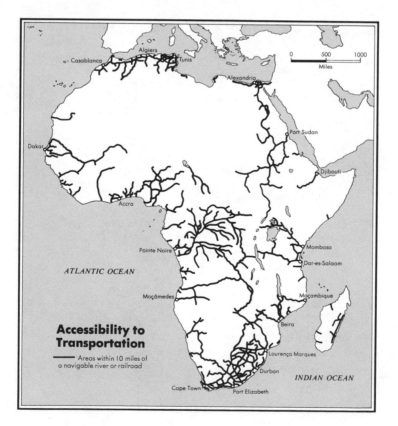

Accessibility to Transportation

—— Areas within 10 miles of a navigable river or railroad

the greatest part of Africa's long-distance trade hinged on commodities like ivory, salt, gold—goods of small bulk and great value that could more easily stand the enormous cost of transportation than bulkier items. In precolonial days the regions north of the equator accounted for the greatest part of Africa's international commerce in precious metals. But from the second part of the nineteenth century, Africa experienced a great mining revolution. European and American entrepreneurs introduced new methods, new scientific and technological devices, new forms of transport, power, and a host of other innovations. The production of metals increased in a spectacular fashion. There was also an enormous increase in the output of base minerals like copper and iron, which primitive miners had been able to work only in small quantities. The whites also made use of resources like coal, uranium, and potash, which indigenous tribal economies had not been in a position to utilize. Base minerals thus steadily gained in importance, and now play a far more significant part in Africa's total economy than gold. Africa's economic axis shifted to the south. Today the mineralized areas that stretch from the Republic of South Africa northward into the Katanga province are of much greater significance than the "Guinea Coast," from whence Charles II obtained the gold to mint his coins.

NOTES

1. See Hance, pp. 46–50.
2. Kimble, *Tropical Africa,* vol. 1, p. 121.
3. See William O. Jones, *Manioc in Africa* (Stanford, 1959).
4. K. G. Dalton, *A Geography of Sierra Leone* (Cambridge, 1965), pp. 30–31.
5. See Kimble, vol. 1, pp. 184–204.
6. Kimble, vol. 1, p. 238.
7. The elephant was the emblem of the Company of the Royal Adventurers into Africa, later succeeded by the Royal African Company.
8. *Southern Rhodesia: Notes on the Mining Industry of Southern Rhodesia,* compiled by N. H. Wilson (Salisbury, Southern Rhodesia, ca. 1934).

Chapter 7

Lives and Livelihoods

Africa has many peoples, and over the centuries the various groups have intermingled as a result of migrations and conquests. The different communities of Africa also had to adapt their way of life to different natural conditions. Hence variety is the keynote of African ethnography. Throughout Africa's history, most of its people have depended on the soil in some fashion or other. In the greater part of Africa there was no lack of useable land; labor and capital might be short, but the bushland seemed inexhaustible. Under such conditions, private landownership of the kind familiar to the Western world was unknown. Individuals owned their tools and weapons. Families reaped their own crops. But, generally speaking, every recognized member of the community had a right to be allocated sufficient land for his needs and those of his followers. The details concerning indigenous land rights differed a good deal from one people to another. By and large, however, the chiefs in agricultural communities acted as trustees for their respective people. They could exclude strangers; they could allocate land, subject to local rules of inheritance, and the degree to which particular lineages were able to assert claims to particular stretches of the countryside. This text cannot give anything like a complete account of the many different ways in which Africans made their living and ordered their communities. We can only pick out a few representative groups, each of which practiced one particular mode of production.

HUNTERS AND FOOD GATHERERS

The most ancient way of making a living was by hunting game and gathering food. The Bushmen never passed beyond this stage, and we may take them as characteristic representatives of one of mankind's oldest cultures. The Bushmen are small-statured folk, rarely more than five feet in height, with yellowish-brown skin, broad noses, prominent cheek bones, and broad foreheads. Their existence was harsh; most of their time was spent in getting enough to eat. Their very lives depended on the tight organization of their bands, for only mutual support assured survival in a harsh environment. History has known many Bushman cultures, adjusted to varying habitats, and generalizations from a specific instance are therefore dangerous. It is a mistake, in other words, to assume that the ancestors of modern Bushmen all lived the kind of life forced on their modern descendants whom stronger races have now pushed into the barren lands of the Kalahari Desert in Botswana and South-West Africa. Nevertheless, we can still learn a good deal from the observations of present-day anthropologists, and as a characteristic example of a surviving Bushman society we shall describe the !Kung, who still roam through the arid lands of the Nyae Nyae region in South-West Africa.[1]

The !Kung have no agriculture. They subsist mainly on wild plant food (referred to subsequently by the convenient Afrikaans name *veldkos*). This comprises many species of berries, fruit, edible leaves, and morsels of gum from certain trees, tsama melons, and wild cucumbers, as well as underground roots, tubers, seeds, and nuts. Each band roams a territory with vaguely defined boundaries. In the interior of the Nyae Nyae region, where water is scant, there are about seventeen bands with no more than 447 persons. The ground itself does not belong to any group, but the scattered patches of *veldkos* within each territory are clearly owned and jealously guarded against outsiders from other bands. Social convention and the dreaded deterrent of poisoned arrows (against whose toxin there is no known antidote) prevent robbers from raiding other peoples' *veldkos* patches. Bushmen have developed their powers of observation to such an astonishing extent that they know everyone's footprint as well as his face. It is difficult therefore to steal *veldkos* without being discovered. In theory, thieves may rightly be killed by the band they have injured, but punishment might involve hostility or even war between two communities, a situation to be assiduously avoided; hence breaches of convention are rare.

Life throughout the seasons revolves round the gathering of *veldkos*. !Kung know how much each patch will yield, whether the rains have been good or poor. The !Kung consume their *veldkos* in a certain order, taking good care to leave some beds of roots and tubers until the dry season has advanced so that there will be food in the ground all the year round. The headman of each band plans the movement of his people or of separate parties. Accurate "staff work" is a matter of life or death, lest a band travel for days on end only to find at the end of their trek that another segment of the band had already consumed the available *veldkos*. The logistics of the !Kung are determined by the presence of water. During the big rains, and for several weeks after, the pans and *vleis* (low-lying meadows) become shallow ponds; there is plenty to drink, and people can move with relative ease. When the dry season sets

A Bushman hunter.

in the people have to solve the difficult problem of carrying enough water in ostrich-shell containers from a waterhole to a *veldkos* area, and life becomes one of ceaseless labor. The !Kung may have to travel anything from a few miles to twenty or thirty miles between their water and fertile patches. In the rainy season they may cover as much as seventy-five miles to reach a *mangetti* forest with its nuts. As a result the !Kung have developed extraordinary physical stamina.

Water is not owned as exclusively as are *veldkos*. Two or more bands may share the ownership of a waterhole, and the !Kung apparently feel that the precious liquid belongs to the whole of mankind. The ownership of waterholes thus relates more to the management than to the withholding of supplies. The headmen control the water, but rainwater which collects in hollow *mangetti* trees belongs to individuals. So does the food which each woman gathers with her digging stick and then cooks for her family and invited guests. Custom does not require the woman to share her *veldkos* with other families, and the !Kungs are not truly communistic.

Game, however, stands in a different category. Hunting, unlike food gathering, is a cooperative venture, for a man cannot effectively pursue game on his own, so he gathers in parties to stalk wild animals. The kill is distributed according to a strict, though complicated, system, which depends on membership in the hunting group and kinship. The !Kung go after all kinds of animals—eland, kudu, gemsbok, wildebeest, even buffalo, or occasionally a giraffe. The hunter's arrow slowly kills the prey by poison, and when an animal is shot, several days may elapse until it dies of the toxin. Hunting is a difficult art. The !Kung must track their prey, shoot it, and find the carcass before lions, leopards, hyenas, or vultures can devour the meat. Thus, according to Lorna Marshall's calculation, a !Kung band gets on an average no more than between fifteen and eighteen large beasts a year and mainly subsists on plants. But although hunters supply only one-fifth, and the women four-fifths of the peoples' food, the men rule in society, and women play a dependent role.

The !Kung construct temporary dwellings of reed and grass, but the fire, not the shelter, is the visible symbol of home for a !Kung family. The !Kung are no longer a Stone Age people, but nowadays use metal for knives, axes, spear blades, drills, and arrow points, employing stone only for sharpening blades, stretching carrying nets, and pounding food. Wood is fashioned into bows and quivers, into sticks for making fires, for digging, carrying, and stirring, as well as into handles for knives, axes and spears, into bowls, spoons, mortars and pestles, and into musical instruments—the five-stringed *guashi* and a one-stringed violin. Reeds and bones are available in plenty for arrow shafts. There are abundant supplies of fiber and sinews for cordage. Tortoise shells are turned into dippers and cosmetic boxes. Ostrich shells are used for water containers, and some women make ostrich shell beads. The !Kung, though skillful craftsmen, do not accumulate artifacts as wealth, and their possession does not confer high status. Any man can make what he needs when he wants it. Most of the materials are abundant and free for all to take. In a society in which people must move so much, and have to carry all they have, there is no point in multiplying material objects. Instead of acquiring status by accumulating possessions, the !Kung seek honor in precisely the opposite fashion. As Lorna Marshall puts it (and her statement applies to many other preliterate societies) "they practise a custom of gift giving to such an extent that their belongings all move in a slow flowing current among them and no one keeps anything of particular value very long. !Kung society requires that gifts be made in return, and the custom serves as a means to mitigate jealousy, to express friendly intent, and to weave people together in mutual obligation."[2]

HERDSMEN

Africa has known many pastoral societies; some ethnographers have spoken of "cattle complexes," in which the herdsmen's needs dominated the life of the tribe. In the Victorian era, cultural historians tried to construct ascending ladders, on whose rungs humanity was supposed to have climbed from hunting to herding and thence to hoe farming—or the other way round. Modern anthropologists have become skeptical of such designs. They regard man's multifarious economic activities as adaptations to many different challenges. They also take pains to show the infinite number of gradations that exist between different cultures. The Jie, for instance, a Nilotic people dwelling in northeastern Uganda, are commonly classed as a pastoral people—yet though the Jie value cattle for ritual, aesthetic, and social as well as economic reasons, arable farming provides the bulk of their staple food. The pastoral

Fulani of northern Nigeria derive their subsistence from cattle, but many other Fulani groups practice mixed types of agriculture, and many have become townsmen. Even "pure" cattle keepers have evolved a great range of economic methods, depending on their natural environment, the kinds of animals they breed, and the social constitution of their respective communities. A full account of Africa's pastoral peoples would thus require many volumes. Again we can only pick out an illustrative example—in this case, the northern pastoral Somali, who live in what is now the Somali Republic.[3]

The Somali speak a Cushitic tongue that belongs to what Greenberg styles the Afro-Asiatic family. In appearance they are generally tall, with long narrow heads and frizzy hair. Their skin color ranges from light brown, with a reddish or copper tinge, to extreme brown. Some Somali have Arab blood in their veins; others show Negroid features, their ancestors having intermarried with dark-skinned peoples whom they encountered many hundreds of years ago. The Somali Republic is poorly endowed with natural wealth, and the northern pastoralists have to contend with a peculiarly harsh environment. The herdsmen themselves distinguish three main topographical zones. The coastal plain is a sun-scorched land where the annual rainfall rarely exceeds four inches, though water is relatively easily available below the sandy topsoil. The highlands, rising behind the coastal plain, are somewhat more favored by nature; but there are no permanent streams, and the people have to sink wells, often in dry river beds. To the south, the highlands descend into rolling plains, often covered with red topsoil. After the rains cattle find rich covering of tall graze, interrupted in spots by thick scrub. There is no permanent water, but beasts—especially camels—nevertheless can find excellent pasture. In many places the plain dips into natural basins which the rain turns into ephemeral lakes. Here less hardy stock—sheep, donkeys, horses, and cattle—find water, and merchants may gather in semi-permanent trading settlements.

The Somali nomads subsist on milk and meat. Donkeys serve as beasts of burden; horses are sometimes ridden in battle, but more generally serve as a means of rapidly getting about the country and as a mark of social distinction. Somali life revolves round the needs of their beasts and the vagaries of the climate. Throughout the three zones, there are four main seasons—two wet and two dry—and these impose a rigid system of seasonal migration on the clansmen. In spring, about April or May, the shore lands become unbearably hot, and the coastal pastoralists move into the cooler highlands. These in turn have by now been largely deserted by those communities whose home wells lie on the plateau, and who have moved into the southern plains. During the rains of September or October, the northernmost lineages[4] return to the coast, which by this time offers fresh grazing. During December and January, the principal dry season sets in. This is the grimmest time of the year, when beasts and even men may die of thirst and debilitation, and the people that wander through the southern plains now withdraw to their home wells in the highlands.

Movement is also affected by other factors, such as the prevalence of disease, the availability of salt for stock, or lineage competition for access to the same pastures. The seasons, moreover, are by no means constant, for annual rainfall varies considerably. There is accordingly no strict localization of the various pastoral groups. Grazing land is regarded as a gift of God—not something to be specifically parcelled out

Masai cattle keepers, Kenya.

among specific communities. Men of different lineages and clans move where pasture and water is available for their animals. Hence there are many quarrels over access to water and pasture; these may spark bloody feuds that may smolder on for generations.

Most Somali pride themselves on their prowess as herdsmen and warriors. Crafts such as leather and metal working are mainly left to specialist class groups, bondsmen who were traditionally attached to Somali families and were debarred from marrying into the ruling class. For the Somali—as for the Bushmen—a nomadic existence, however, precluded the accumulation of material objects. The principal exception was stock, which could move on its own four feet and therefore presented no transport problems. The Somali thus have few possessions and are able to get by on a relatively small range of local raw materials. Wood is worked into cooking utensils and spoons, vessels for milk and water, and water bottles. Bark is fashioned into water storage containers that are strapped to pack animals. Bark and aloe fiber is used for ropes; wall mats are made from bark, grass or palm fiber, for the women are skilled weavers. Nowadays the Somali—like the Bushmen—are beginning to take a tenuous share in the world market; imported metal ware has begun to replace traditional utensils; rifles have commonly replaced buckler and lance. But despite extending contacts with the outside world and many modern developments in trade, education, social services, and politics, the age-old northern pastoral system is well adapted to the natural environment and continues in full vigor.

The Somali way of life breeds warlike men, full of poetry and pride, and the Somali are among the world's best irregular cavalry. Like so many other mounted nomads

—the Bedouin Arabs and the Fulani for instances—the Somali enjoyed a natural military superiority over their more sedentary neighbors, who perforce had to fight as infantry. They have accordingly played an important part in the military history of Africa, and have always been a hard people to subdue. Their mode of existence has stood in the way of a hierarchical system of governance; the Somali are a highly egalitarian people, and political leadership generally lies with the elders of the lineage segments. Only at the level of the clan is there sometimes to be found a special political office, that of clan head.

HOE FARMERS

Africa's main implement of tillage has been the hoe, and hoe farming remains Africa's principal economic occupation. Hoe farming, however, may take a thousand different shapes, depending on the nature of the country, the crops, and the people. The Ganda of Uganda have as their staple food the banana, which can be raised on the same plot for several decades without exhausting the fertility of the soil. Thus the laborious bush fallowing and shifting cultivation, practiced by so many African farmers, is not found in Uganda, where agriculturists do not have to reserve a large proportion of their land for fallow. The Ganda can therefore utilize their land in fairly intensive fashion. The land can sustain a dense population and an elaborate, centralized political hierarchy. There is no need to clear the bush continually and break new grounds; hence the role of men in farming is reduced, and women assume a larger share of the work. Ganda men had more time for administration, politics, and war and evolved a highly complicated political structure. The Ganda, however, are unusually fortunate. The mode of livelihood, for example, of the Suku of the southwestern Congo is historically more characteristic of the agricultural Bantu at large.[5]

The Suku speak a Bantu tongue belonging to the Niger-Congo group of languages. In physical appearance they differ little from the general population of Central Africa, with their frizzy hair and flattened noses. They tend to be lighter in complexion than the Africans of the Central African forest, but they are usually rather short in stature. They dwell in rolling savannah country, with occasional stretches of light woods. The soil is sandy and relatively poor, but until recent times the land abounded in game. There are several swift-flowing rivers with numerous cataracts; the waters are usually fringed by a heavy gallery of forests and swamps. There are two main seasons. The dry, cool spell begins in May and ends in September. At this time the sky is grey; dusty winds blow during the day, and the nights are uncomfortably cold. The land turns yellow, with dark stretches of burned grass. When the rains set in during September, the dust vanishes from the air, the sky becomes blue, and tall green grass springs forth from the soil.

The yearly work cycle depends on this alteration between the wet and dry seasons. During the rains every adult woman plants three and sometimes four fields in succession, so that crops are available while a new field is being prepared. The agricultural staple is cassava, but in addition the women plant sweet potatoes, pumpkins, beans, and peas, which are interspersed between the main crop. Peanuts are cultivated in separate gardens—usually on the site of abandoned villages, where the soil is more fertile. When the rains end, the people no longer prepare new fields, and by the middle of the dry season there is a shortage of vegetables, though not of cassava. Cultivation is of the shifting kind which we have described in previous sections. The soil, once used, needs fifteen or twenty years to recover its fertility, and the Suku, like most other Bantu, thus have required a great deal of land to sustain their traditional mode of life. In the past, population density was low and land was plentiful, so land was available to all members of the community.

In addition to their fields, the Suku have tiny gardens where they grow bananas, tobacco, tomatoes, and other plants. The men also tap palms and certain bamboo

(Left) **Two brass hoers cast for the Dahomean king at Abomey. 3½ inches high. (Below) Birom hoe farmers in Nigeria.** (Both courtesy of the Lowie Museum of Anthropology, University of California, Berkeley.)

stalks for "wine." Cultivated crops are also supplemented by wild fruit, berries, mushrooms, wild honey, and such delicacies as caterpillars and flying ants. The chase is man's work, and when the dry season sets in the men stage large cooperative hunts, stalking various kinds of antelopes, wild hogs, leopards, and many other beasts. Domesticated animals include dogs, goats, pigs, and chicken, and since the arrival of the white man, pigeons, ducks, guinea pigs, turkeys, and rabbits. The Suku could rightly be described as "mixed farmers," but cassava provides them with something like 90 percent of the total calories they consume, so that the hoe rules supreme on the land.

The Suku also engage in crafts, and here the division of labor between the sexes is also clearly pronounced. The women make pottery. The men weave baskets, mats, raffia cloth, fishing nets, and so forth; they also carve in wood. To some extent all men are artisans, for all can build a house, make a bow, weave a mat, or hammer out a crudely made arrow point. There is, however, some specialization, even though the more highly skilled craftsmen cannot live off their peculiar skills alone but also engage in ordinary activities like hunting and fishing. Blacksmiths practice a highly respected occupation, surrounded among the Suku—as among so many other preliterate people —with special taboos and initiation ceremonies. Others acquire renown in the making of certain objects, or as traveling healers, dancers, and musicians. The Suku do most of their work in an individualistic fashion. Women farm individually; houses are individually built; fishing weirs are individually exploited; trade, crafts, and animal breeding are carried out on an individual basis.

But individuals cannot accumulate great wealth. The Suku regard land as a commodity which is free to all, even though hunting rights over specific stretches of bush may be vested in specific lineages, so that there is incipient economic differentiation on a kinship line. Lineages may also exercise control over fishing sites or palm and bamboo groves. The Suku believe that a man can acquire property only because of the supernatural and physical protection received from his kin group. Thus all individual domestic property is, in a sense, viewed as belonging to the lineage as a whole, and there is a continuous circulation of household goods and money among members. Such sharing is especially pronounced when the lineage is faced with special needs, for instance when a member must find goods to pay bridewealth for a wife or to pay a fine. Conversely, when legal compensation or bridewealth is received from another lineage, every adult member can claim an apportioned share. Some people do manage to accumulate more wealth than their neighbors, but no Suku questions the assumption of the right of the lineage to draw on such property in times of need. In such a society there are no class divisions of the kind known in more advanced societies. To be sure, some lineages own hunting lands, whereas others do not. A few lineages control the offices of regional chief and profit from tribute collected in the name of the Suku king. But the resulting differences of wealth are comparatively slight and do not make for profound social conflicts.

Even the institution of slavery did not at first introduce great social cleavages, for slavery resembled a form of adoption more than servitude. Slaves became, for all practical purposes, fully fledged members of their lineage. Slaves accordingly did not become a class in Suku society, which was split vertically between different lineages rather than horizontally between different classes.

On these relatively simple foundations, the Suku were nevertheless able to build up a fairly complicated system of political authority; supreme lordship rested with the king, residing in a large village of his own, accommodating most members of the royal lineage. Royal powers were delegated to a considerable extent to regional heads, who in turn controlled local chiefs with authority over groups of villages, a system of governance found in different forms among many Bantu people in Africa.

MIXED FARMERS

Africans have evolved a great variety of agricultural systems; some of these depend on hoe farming, some center on pastoral pursuits, and others again combine tillage with the herding of large animals. Nothing would be more mistaken, however, than to arrange these systems in a simple ascending graph to indicate economic "progress." The Yoruba of Nigeria, for instance, dwelling in the savannahs and forests that lie between the lower Niger and the Gulf of Guinea, prepare their gardens in the age-old manner, by clearing the bush, lopping the branches of smaller trees and burning them. They depend on a few uncomplicated instruments—the short-handled hoe, which farmers use over most parts of tropical Africa, the ax, and (nowadays) the imported machete. But Yoruba agriculture yields a relatively large surplus. Yoruba farmers grow maize, yams, peanuts, beans, cowpeas, cassava, and other crops, and the tillers have a good knowledge of how to rotate their crops, the Yoruba keep poultry and a few sheep and goats; they are not cattle herders; yet in the past they were able to sustain an elaborate political organization and even to maintain cities. The Yoruba were perhaps the most urbanized people of precolonial Africa south of the Sahara, even though their towns were primarily aggregations of farmers. In this chapter we are not concerned with the relative productivity of different African farming systems, but with the way people adapted their lives and modes of livelihood to differing economic habitats. For purposes of illustration we therefore turn to a Bantu people, the Barotse (Lozi) in what is now western Zambia. The Lozi were once a prosperous people and their agricultural system was a model of what could be achieved with simple methods of production. Now, unfortunately, they face all kinds of serious agricultural problems by reason of the deleterious ecological changes affecting the upper Zambezi plain. The present account, however, remains relevant for historical purposes.[6] It also seems to show that local shortages of good land may have stimulated tillers to devise more intensive systems of cultivating the soil.

The Barotse dwelled in the plain of the upper Zambezi River. Every year, about December, the plain began to flood and between February and March became a vast lake. The Barotse built their villages on mounds in the plain standing to some extent above the flood water. The inhabitable plain sites were accordingly limited in number and size. Only a restricted number of people could reside on a single mound and use the garden lands and fishing sites that went with it. Barotse gardens were small, but the soil in the lower parts of the plain was enriched by the alluvium carried in by each innundation. Certain fertile mounds were periodically refreshed by putting cattle on them. The plain provided luscious pastures for large herds of cattle at low seasons of the year: in winter, after the floods had fallen between May and July, until the grass shrivelled during the hot, dry months of August to October; and in spring, when the rains brought on new grass during November to January. During the flood months, that is to say between January and May, the cattle moved out to the plain to graze in the bush or in the small plain and river valleys that were interspersed in the woodland stretching east and west of the flood plain itself.

The Barotse also cultivated gardens on the plain margins. These gardens were made where there was underground seepage under the steeper slopes in the marshy grassland drained by artificial canals. The Barotse planted root crops in heaps of soil raised above the water. Further out toward the margin there was sometimes a belt of humic soil watered by underground seepage but naturally drained; this land could be cultivated in perpetuity. Beyond this, up the slope, there was a belt having some underground seepage, but requiring artificial fertilization. Then came a zone of dry soil that may be cultivated when manured. Beyond lay the bush, which was worked on a cycle of cropping and regeneration, with clearing and burning to provide a first enrichment with ash. The Barotse as a whole thus cultivated some eight different kinds of gardens, spreading from the Zambezi to the sand scarp, and their farming methods showed considerable variety. They had to work their various lands all the months of the year; but in return for their labors they could produce many different kinds of crops. The plain provided pasture for cattle and rich fishing sites. Farmers also grew sorghum, maize, and root crops. From the woodland regions came tobacco, cassava, millet, groundnuts, and honey. The woods also yielded the raw materials for dugouts, mats, baskets, fishing nets, wooden utensils, drums, iron implements, as well as bees wax and other commodities. The plain gardens were worked in perpetuity, and the riverine economy of the Barotse thus differed considerably from the systems of other tribes in the region who had to subsist on slash-and-burn agriculture and who constantly moved their villages.

The flood, in other words, dominated Barotse life. "It covers and uncovers gardens, fertilizing and watering them; it fixes the pasturing of the cattle; it conditions the methods of fishing. All life in the Plain moves with the flood: people, fish, cattle, game, wild-fowl, snakes, rodents, and insects."[7] The Barotse calendar was largely defined by the state of the flood. The two great national events of the year were the moves of the king, carried out with great ceremony and splendor, between his capital in the plain and his capital on the margin of the plain. The Barotse system of transhumance also profoundly influenced the political structure of the country, to which further reference will be made in a later section. Suffice it to say at this point that the Barotse, with their developed agriculture, worked out an intricate system of political checks and balances, as well as an elaborate mode of distributing goods through their kingdom, whereby specialized commodities were paid to the court from outlying provinces in the form of tribute and then redistributed to some extent to other regions in the shape of royal gifts.

The riverine situation influenced the Barotse military system; the Barotse acquired great skill as canoemen, and Barotse war vessels dominated large stretches of the Zambezi. Barotse administration also reflected to some extent the peculiar conditions of their plain. The characteristic feature of the Barotse policy was that the Barotse heartland was not divided into territorial provinces (like most Bantu kingdoms), but into a series of nonterritorial political "sectors," which were more fitted to cope with the needs of Zambezi transhumance. (The territorial system, on the other hand, was applied to conquered provinces away from the plain. These were governed by an intricate system of "indirect rule," under their own chiefs, guided or bullied, as the case might be, by Barotse residents.)

TOWNSMEN IN OLD AFRICA

Logistics are the lifeblood of economic development. During the last two generations, more has been done to develop communications in Africa than ever before in its history; but the continental transport grid still presents a broken appearance, and many of the connecting crossbars are still missing. As we have seen in the previous chapter, nature all too often works against man. Africa has great rivers, but these great waterways are commonly interrupted by falls and rapids. Floating vegetation presents serious problems to captains navigating the Nile or the Congo. Many African rivers have only a seasonal flow, so that riverine transport can play only a limited part in the development of Africa. There are, nevertheless, a number of important water arteries. The Atlantic side of the continent, with its heavier rain, is more amply provided for than the drier Indian Ocean side. The Niger plays a significant part in carrying bulk shipments; the Senegal has considerable local importance, and the Gambia River is lined with wharf towns, which enjoy direct connection with Bathurst, the capital. The large estuary of the Sierra Leone River affords one of the most commodious deep water ports in Africa, while the huge inland water system of the Congo handles traffic on a vast scale, providing the country with more than 7000 miles of navigable waterways. In addition, the great lakes of East and Central Africa play their part in getting men and goods to their destination. Lakes Kivu, Albert, Nyasa, Kyoga, Tanganyika, and Victoria all carry regular freight and passenger businesses.[8] But lake transport has many limitations. On a large-scale map, the long, narrow water bodies of the Rift Valley look as if they could form part of a huge, integrated transport system. Appearances are unfortunately deceptive, and lakes all too often are more an impediment than an aid to overland transport. Africa, as we have previously noted, is also deficient in good natural harbors; in most parts of Africa, therefore, urban life developed but slowly; even to this day, well over four-fifths of Africa's population lives in the country. (The only great exception is South Africa, where something like one-third of the population is urbanized.)

Most African cities are of recent origin, but the more favored parts of precolonial Africa had developed some important aggregations of people. Most of these probably began as great agricultural settlements, where people drew together in fertile spots for purposes of defense. The Lunda of northeastern Zambia, for instance, built a great, stockaded agro-town in the rich Luapula Valley, where crops grew abundantly and where people could catch plenty of fish in the river. Kazembe, the Lunda paramount chief, used to rule from a settlement, which at the end of the last century contained a population of over 20,000.[9] Kazembe's people were mainly farmers who cultivated manioc, millet, maize, and beans. But Kazembe also traded in slaves, ivory, and salt; he imported oxen, guns, cloth, and other commodities, so that this early agro-town already knew some specialization of labor.

Even more important was the *kibuga* of Buganda, a great tribal capital, the royal, administrative, and ritual center of the kingdom, where the sacred fire and the national drums were kept, and where matters under dispute were brought before a court of appeal. The *kibuga* formed an impressive agglomeration of buildings, constructed of cane and rattan, divided by well-maintained streets, and centering on the royal palace. From the economic point of view, the *kibuga* was neither quite a village or a town. It may have contained some 40,000 inhabitants, but the bulk of its people depended on agriculture. The retainers of great chiefs cultivated gardens within the settlement, but the urban crop had to be supplemented by food brought in from country estates.[10]

In parts of West Africa, this rudimentary division of labor was carried considerably further. From ancient days, cities like Timbuktu became great entrepôts in the trans-Saharan trade, exchanging goods from the southern forest region—gold, slaves, kola nuts—for commodities like cloth, salt, figs, dates, beads, and horses from North Africa. The towns of the northern Sudan developed, as it were, into commercial "ports," receiving regular convoys of "ships" (that is to say, horse and camel caravans) which had left equivalent "ports" on the northern shore of the desert sea, and called at various "islands" (oases) for food and fresh water on their voyage to the distant south.[11]

A further step in the specialization of labor came in the rise of crafts; the Hausa settlements of West Africa developed into important handicraft centers, which sold the products of local smiths, metalworkers, dyers, tanners, and shoemakers all over the Western Sudan and as far afield as North Africa. Further south, in what is now the Western Region of Nigeria, the Yoruba people likewise developed a semi-urban civilization. Today the cities of Yorubaland, red in appearance, with red clay houses behind red clay walls, spaced out on roads thick with red dust, are still important settlements. Ibadan, the greatest of them all, and the biggest existing city created by Africans, for Africans, without European intervention, now probably has more than 600,000 people, and is still growing mightily, in contrast to Timbuktu, whose former glory has departed. Ibadan looks best at night:

By the door of every close-packed dwelling, at every booth lining the streets, glows a candle or home-made oil lamp, each throwing its little nimbus of light into the warm air. The whole center of the town is aglow, as if the Milky Way had floated down to earth. All ugliness and dirt are hidden. A gentle light flickers on bronze cheekbones, shadowed eyes, on slim wrists and fingers. The women's heads are swathed in folds of cloth and they sit beside their stalls like crowned princesses waiting for suitors. Noon or midnight, every woman trades. . . . In the dark, soft streets—there is no paving—the men pad quietly to and fro in their native dress of baggy trousers and full tunic, greeting, smoking gossiping. Far into the night—all night perhaps— lamps burn, footsteps shuffle, tongues wag. Trade and talk, talk and trade, night and day, late and early—that is Ibadan.[12]

The people of Ibadan also do a great deal more. The impact of a modern cash economy has transformed the city; Ibadan is now a major center of the cocoa industry, with mercantile houses, brokers, and insurance offices, and with a processing plant; it is a center of government and the seat of an important university; and all these activities in turn attract more service industries, so that Ibadan stands out among the relatively small number of traditional African communities, that have successfully adjusted themselves to the rhythm of modern urban existence, and have expanded into huge centers of population.

In addition sub-Saharan Africa developed a number of important seaports. The subcontinent as a whole is not, as we have seen, well-provided with natural harbors; maritime cities were never numerous; but there have been some exceptions. Whydah (in Dahomey) in the early eighteenth century, for instance, was an important African settlement that practiced a system of free trade, then almost unique in the Gulf of Guinea. The port was open to ships of any flag, and the forts of three European nations stood in close proximity, each enclosed by a wall, which, according to a later African ordinance, was not allowed to exceed three feet in height.[13]

From very early days onwards, the eastern shore of Africa developed an important maritime civilization, blended of Bantu and Near Eastern and Indian components, and linked to the world of Islam. Communities like Kilwa, Mombasa, and Zanzibar traded as far afield as Persia, Arabia, and India, selling gold, slaves, ivory, and (in the case of Zanzibar) cloves in exchange for cloth, beads, and other commodities. Today Zanzibar, for instance, is still a city of small, winding, narrow streets, with high houses and shuttered windows. Memories of its ancient splendor survive in old Arab buildings with magnificent carved doors. The lanes were thronged with people of every conceivable nationality, Africans, Indians, Pakistanis, Arabs; it is still a substantial port and a big center of the clove and copra industry. But by and large these towns of ancient provenance do not compare with cities of more recent origins; their former importance rested on agriculture or trade in precious metals, ivory, or slaves.

AFRICAN KINSHIP SYSTEMS, RELIGIONS, AND ART

From ancient times, Africa has been a cultural as well as an ethnic melting pot. African ways of life were extremely varied, and so were African religious beliefs. Many Sudanic communities, as we have seen, converted to Islam. The Amhara preserved an eastern form of Christianity that became adapted to the conditions of an Ethiopian highland community. Judaism influenced the folkways of the Falasha, an Ethiopian people who adopted the tenets of Moses, blended with pagan beliefs. The Portuguese impact on the Congo produced syncretic religions such as the Antonine heresy, which will be mentioned in a subsequent chapter. The vast majority of Negroid peoples, however, held on to their more ancient religions. African worshippers never held a single set of dogmas—indeed they probably lacked the very concept of dogma; hence present day scholars remain inadequately informed on the subject of African religion.

The reasons for our relative ignorance are not hard to find. In our own century

European colonial officials have studied indigenous customs, but they were primarily interested in customs and beliefs that bore on court cases or on general administrative problems. Many anthropologists have, until recently, been more concerned with questions of social structure than with religion. Their approach has often been encouraged by the agnostic and rationalist convictions that numerous social scientists have brought to their work. Missionaries, on the other hand, have frequently fought shy of a subject that they felt to be so incompatible with Christianity. Christian preachers, moreover, have often been regarded with suspicion by African animists who were convinced that the white strangers hated the black men's faith.

If we remain ignorant of many African religions practiced today, we know even less about what Africans believed in the past. There are no sacred texts or theological treatises to enlighten the investigator. The records of European traders and clergymen or of Arab travelers are only of limited help, for none of these foreigners was much interested in what they considered to be heathen superstitions. Even the most open-minded among them were liable to misinterpret what they saw. Historians must take recourse to reconstructions based on inadequate or biased eyewitness accounts and to the surmises of modern observers. Such proceedings do not lend themselves to accuracy, and our own account must necessarily be based on guesswork more than exact knowledge.

Nevertheless, we may perhaps arrive at certain tentative generalizations. Throughout recorded history the bulk of the African peoples lived their daily lives as members of small communities. No matter whether an African might be subject to a great Bantu king or whether he belonged to a stateless society, his entire way of life was usually bound up with that of a hamlet or a village. Villages were commonly composed of kinsmen and their followers, so that Africans relied upon their relatives in a way that white men now find hard to understand.

Tribal organization varied immensely, in accordance with the degree of economic specialization attained by each given community, with their geographical habitat and their history. But broadly speaking there were two major patterns of kinship. The so-called patrilineal peoples—many though not all of them, cattle keepers—traced their descent through their fathers and grandfathers. Their village commonly consisted of kinsmen related to a common ancestor. A man and his several wives sometimes lived in one homestead or each wife had her own residence. Close to him might be the huts of his full and half brothers and those of his paternal uncles. These communities helped one another in peace and war. They commonly venerated the same ancestral spirits and accepted some responsibility for each others' acts. Intermarriage within such a descent group was forbidden for fear of terrible supernatural consequences. If a man wanted a wife he had to bring her in from outside. Traditionally, there were two ways of doing this. A powerful and warlike community might acquire wives as the Romans had supposedly got the Sabine women—by abduction. The other (and more customary) means was to pay a "bride price" to a woman's kinsmen, who then agreed to let their female relative leave their village. Among pastoral peoples payment was normally made by means of cattle; patrilineal communities who kept no stock offered weapons, tools, and ornaments, a practice familiar also to the ancient Teutons in the days of Tacitus. There were also some groups where a man could acquire a wife by working for her, as Jacob had done for Leah and Rachel in Biblical times. Once the bridewealth had been paid, the husband's kinfolk could lay claim to his wife's children and to her labor. At first the young bride did not count for much among her in-laws, but the more babies she bore, the more highly respected she became, and a Bantu matron, whose sons had grown up and married in turn, was a person of consequence.

In addition to this form of social organization there was a second, known as the matrilineal kind. The matrilineal tribes traced their descent not through men, but through women, villages being generally composed for the most part of people who had sprung from one common ancestress. In some communities wives came in from another group to live in their husband's homestead, but their children returned to their mother's villages as soon as they became of age.

But whether a people were matrilineal or patrilineal, the farmers' way of life had generally much in common. There was, for instance, always a clear-cut division of labor between the sexes. The men went out hunting, deliberated on public affairs, and fought as members of their local levies. In pastoral societies it was normally the men who were expected to perform tasks requiring great physical strength, like felling trees or lopping off big branches to make ash beds. The women did the domestic chores, looked after the small children, and performed many jobs in the fields, such as hoeing and weeding. Men associated with men in their work and women with women. Children were looked after, not merely by their mothers, but by a host of aunts, cousins, and other relatives. The tribesmen felt themselves members of a closely-knit community that supported its members in sickness and in health, in peace or war, through a complicated network of kinship and other obligations.

Social organizations of this kind offered many advantages to their members. But tribal life also knew much unhappiness. Polygamy, while it may relieve some psychological or even physiological stresses, creates new tensions of its own, especially between wives who competed for the favors of the same husband. The Bantu, for instance, had to devise codes of family duties much more onerous and elaborate than any that exist in European families. They also faced vast natural forces they could neither understand nor control. Drought and famine were an ever present danger. Life was usually insecure.

There were few labor-saving devices, neither windmills, watermills, wagons, or plows. No tribal community possessed sufficient resources to tide itself over prolonged periods of want, and yet want always lurked around the corner. The rains might not fall; locusts might destroy the crops; cattle plagues might strike down the herds; hostile war parties might carry off the women and empty the granaries. Life, accordingly, was much more precarious than among modern men who can accumulate capital reserves, partially control their natural environment, and ensure economic co-operation on an intercontinental scale.

Africans, like everyone else, needed a system of thought to help them explain the universe and its purpose, to satisfy their sense of the numinous, and to provide them with a code of ethical conduct fit for rational men. African thinkers seem to have arrived at different solutions to these problems. But as far as we know all African communities postulate a Supreme Being who created all things. The Ashanti of

Ghana, for instance, have a proverb "no one shows the sky to the child." The sky in this context symbolizes the abode of the Supreme Deity. The Ashanti, in other words, consider that all human beings have a natural propensity to conceive of God, and other African communities endorse this belief.

The human mind, Africans believed, was incapable of fully understanding God or of reaching the Divine Presence. There is an Ashanti myth, similar to the story about the tower of Babel, which warns mankind against its overweening pride. Long ago, God lived near to men. But there was an old woman who used to pound her grain in a wooden mortar. Whenever she did so, her pestle hit the abode of God, which was the sky. So one day God said, "I will take myself away where men can no longer reach me." God disappeared in the heavens. Then the old woman told her children to collect all the mortars they could find and pile them on top of one another. They did so, and at last only one mortar was needed to make the tower reach God. But they could not find another mortar. The old woman then told her children, "Take the mortar from the bottom and put it on the top." The children obeyed her command, but as they did so the great pile of mortars collapsed; the mortars fell to the ground and killed many people.

Man, in other words, required intermediaries between himself and the Divine Creator, for God did not communicate directly with the world of ordinary men. African religions conceived of a great host of subordinate deities. Africans also had complicated concepts of the human soul. The people of Dahomey in West Africa, for instance, believed in four souls for an adult male; the Ashanti believed that man received at birth both his peculiar ego, which perished with him, and the life force, which was a part of the Creator and returned to God after a person died.[14] African societies without exception, therefore, attached great importance to the world of spirits.

For a specific example, we may take the Shona, a patrilineal people in what is now Rhodesia. The Shona, like all Bantu tribes, believed in a Supreme Being. But God was not concerned with the problems of the individual. A Shona would not pray to God directly, unlike a Christian, who may seek divine guidance however insignificant his station in life. The individual depended on his ancestors, and on the tribe; the fortunes of the tribe were guided by the tribal and ancestral spirits. The spirits looked after a great variety of matters affecting the community as a whole, such as rain, which was a collective and not an individual matter. The tribal spirits in turn were graded in importance. At the head of the Shona spiritual organization stood Chaminuka, the greatest rain spirit of all. Below him were provincial deities who in turn were helped by district spirits. Below these were spirits who looked after family groups. All these beings, whatever their importance in the hierarchy, played a part in community affairs.

The problems of individuals were looked after by ancestral spirits. No man could find a better or more faithful friend than his parents or grandparents. Therefore no spirit could be trusted more than the departed spirits of one's own family, who would provide help in trouble. The ancestral spirits, however, can also be roused to anger. Woe to the man who offended them by impious deeds, for his ancestral spirits would punish him. The forefathers' spirits, in other words, were guardians of tribal and individual ethics, for the laws of right and wrong were not regarded as being linked to the will of God, as they are in the Judeo-Christian tradition, but were associated with the custom of the people and enforced by the customs and sanctions of the departed.

Of evil-doers, unfortunately, there were only too many, and many Shona, like other Africans, lived in constant dread of those who might hurt them. The point is worth stressing, for the tribesman is all too often imagined by those who do not know him as a happy savage who lives in a spiritual paradise, "a world which we have long since forgotten, in which the whole of nature was filled with the divine breath of life,"[15] a world from which we have now supposedly been driven out by the neuroses and inhibitions of industrial society. Tribal societies, however, had their own kind of tensions, fears, and terrors. Many tribesmen feared twins as harbingers of misfortune and killed them at birth. Some tried to appease the angered divinities by sacrificing not only cattle but human beings—a custom widely adopted by many ancient peoples, including the Teutons of early Germany. Others tried to acquire magic powers by eating human flesh or by dismembering corpses in order to use certain parts for occult purposes.

African art embodied both these concepts—grim and grand alike. It also tried perhaps to transcend them. This makes it extremely difficult to explain the modes and meaning of African art, especially for Westerners such as ourselves. At this point we shall leave out Ethiopian art, which, with all its diversity and splendor, essentially represents a branch of Christian art, linked to the ancient traditions of Byzantium. Instead we shall concern ourselves with the art of preliterate societies.

The earliest known art was produced by stone-age hunters who left a great number of rock paintings and engravings in various parts of the Sahara and East, Central, and southern Africa. The rock art in Africa south of the Sahara was created by Bushmen and Hottentots, by hunting and food-gathering cultures, dating from about 8000 B.C. to modern times.

Some of this rock art is nonrepresentational in character. But many paintings left in caves, rock shelters, and rock outcroppings tell us a great deal of the Bushman way of life and of incidents in their history. Ancient artists recorded the appearance of the animals hunted by their fellow-tribesmen, or objects worshipped by the people. Some paintings seem to provide evidence concerning invaders from North Africa and the Nile Valley and of invaders on chariots or of herdsmen driving their cattle before them. The migration of cattle-keeping people (probably Bantu-speakers), for example, is vividly depicted on rock paintings in Central Africa.

Although much of this rock art looks alike, experts argue against any continuity or connection between the Saharan style and the pictures in southern Africa. Nevertheless, two major themes characterize all naturalistic African rock paintings: large pictures of animals and small human figures.

The function of rock art has been variously explained. Some scholars see it as a form of sympathetic magic to help people catch the game the artist sketched. Others see rock paintings as serving religious or instructional purposes. In any case, rock painting has artistic and historical value. The beauty of these representations moves us today even though we can only see photographs of them. And if we cannot comprehend fully the meaning of the art, we can certainly be impressed by the skill, the vivid beauty and poignancy of the rock paintings of these ancient artists.

The Negroid peoples of West and Central Africa created artistic traditions of a different kind. Their artists knew how to work in bronze, brass, copper and iron, as well as in wood and ivory. The technological resources of metal using, agricultural societies were much greater than those of the most advanced Stone Age or early Neolithic cultures. Hence the new artists of West and Central Africa produced artifacts of astonishing diversity.

Negro African art is characterized by stylization, diversity, and consistency. Realism was not a necessary skill of the African artists: he felt no compulsion to make mirror images of reality. So African artists have varied the dimensions of the body; they have simplified some features, exaggerated others, and blended the supernatural and the mythical with the human and the animal. The great majority of black sculptors did not portray nature realistically; hence African art forms were not appreciated in Europe until early in the twentieth century. To the artists of Western Europe trying to free themselves from the competition of the camera and from the canons of naturalism, the style of African artists was a liberating vision. Vlaminck, Derain, Picasso, and Matisse all were moved by the pure lines and strangeness of the few masks and statuettes brought back to Paris and Berlin after 1900. The influence of African art was revolutionary and had a deep impact on cubism, impressionism, and surrealism—in fact on most of the postimpressionist movements of Western art.

The artists of Europe were not alone, however, nor were they the first to appreciate African art. Missionaries, colonial officials, explorers, and scholars had brought back art objects that caused wonder and awe. In 1899 Leo Frobenius, the German scholar, had published *Die Masken und Geheimbünde Afrikas.* Many books and articles had appeared on the Benin bronzes and ivories—the first African art to gain public recognition. In 1897 British troops sacked the city of Benin, and looted Benin bronzes soon found their way into the museums of England, Germany, and the United States.

The variety of African styles (or tribality, to use Fagg's term) is at first bewildering to students, but exposure to African sculpture enables critics to distinguish a Yoruba carving from a Dogon mask, a Fang work from a Baluba. While stylistic diversity lends excitement to African art, stylistic consistency provides a guide to the recognition of recurring themes or motifs. As William Bascom, the anthropologist and Lowie Museum curator has noted: "One's ability to distinguish one art style from another depends upon the recognition of this adaptive repetition and upon consistency in body proportions, in the rendering of the face, or in such details as treatment of the ear or mouth as well as upon a knowledge of the inventory of genres produced in a given society."

We do not know enough about the meaning of much African sculpture. But if we survey African religion, we can understand a great deal about the purposes, functions, and modes of African art. African religions, as we have stated earlier, hinge on reverence for the ancestors, for nature, for spirits or gods, for magic, and divinations (to control evil spirits, and to bring peace and plenty to the community.) The ancestors or spirits supposedly controlled the life forces to ensure that the community had enough of the vital forces of nature to guarantee health and well being. These spirits were often represented by statues or reliquaries. Some groups, like the Yoruba, had separate cults for each god, for Shango, the god of thunder, and Ogun, the god of iron, for example. These spirits could be represented in sculptured objects or ornamented pieces and were placated by dance, ritual, and song at annual festivals. Masks were especially important in fertility ceremonies, magic and divination rituals, initiation ceremonies, and the rites of passage to mark puberty and death.

Most African art was basically religious in inspiration. It grew out of the beliefs and customs of the people and represented their efforts to portray graphically the moral and religious doctrines of the community. Each people had a particular view of the world and their place in it; African art was thus marked by incredible variety. Art was supposed to represent traditional ideals and concepts. Hence the African artist had to conform to the conventions of the people; he was not free to pursue art for art's sake or to express his own particular vision.

The special qualities of African art have been assessed many different ways. Until recently, Western observers imagined that African art was primitive and undisciplined, the work of unskilled men, the product of emotion. The discovery of the art of Nok and Benin forced Westerners to reappraise African art. Concerned as it is with religion, the representation of the spirit and the vital forces that animate all living things, African art is the opposite of primitive—for its essence is to give physical forms to abstractions. The symbolism and the content of the art are products of the religion —the long, traditional communal process embodying the essence of the spiritual vision of the people. Thus sculptured figures were meant to capture and hold the spirits of the religious pantheon: ancestral figures, fertility figures, rain gods, animals.

Present-day critics see African art in perspectives very different from those of the Victorians. African statues are said to manipulate reality in a way attempted by European artists only in the twentieth century. African music depends on the beat of the drum more than on melody and harmony. Above all, African artists commonly merge different art forms for specific religious purposes. As Léopold Senghor, the Senegalese poet and statesman put it:

The arts in the general sense of the word are . . . linked together. Thus sculpture only fully realizes its object by the grace of the dance and the sung poem. Look at the man who incarnates Nyamié, the Sun-Genie of Baoulé, under the mask of the Ram. Watch him dancing the action of a ram to the rhythm of the orchestra, while the chorus sings the poem of the deeds of the genie. In both cases we have a functional art. In this last example the masked dancer must identify himself with the Genie- Sun- Ram, and like the sacrificer, communicate his force to the audience which takes part in the drama.[16]

In viewing African art in books or in exhibits, the observer should realize that the African art objects are torn out of their context, which encompasses costume, dance, human beings, and the fabric of belief into which they are woven in their native environment. Bereft of motion and the drama of the rituals in which they were employed, they lie lifeless on the printed page and hang silently in the exhibit case.

Since many rituals were performed after dark, the masks were meant to be seen in the shadows and by the flickering light of oil lamps.''[17]

In this respect there are of course certain parallels to older European traditions. The wooden statue of a Rhenish madonna, splendidly adorned and solemnly carried through a city in a procession, fulfilled a religious even more than an aesthetic purpose. (The same carving, put into a millionaire's showcase or placed on exhibition in a museum, has lost something of its essential quality.) The cantatas of Johann Sebastian Bach, to give another instance, were designed to form part of a Lutheran church service—not of a musical program offered in the auditorium of a college campus.

Nevertheless, the traditions of African art were singular and distinct. Unfortunately, however, a complete history of African art will never be written, for much has been lost. The splendid bronze works of Ife and Benin in West Africa, produced to glorify chiefs and kings, survive to astound the beholder. So do other artifacts made of metal, of bronze and brass, of lead and of gold. Bronze and brass casting was a peculiarly popular form of art, practised in West Africa from the Senegal to the Cameroons. In the so-called lost wax process a wax model is coated with clay, and one or more wax stems are left projecting from the wax form. After the clay has dried the mold is heated and the melted wax runs out through the stems. Molten metal is then poured into the hollow form left by the melted wax. Many of these artifacts survive in our museums, as do various forms of secular art such as stools, drums, brass weights to measure gold dust, personal objects, and household goods. But wood carvings and colored mats are made of perishable substances, and a good deal of Africa's older visual art has disappeared.

Other forms of African art centered on dancing, drumming, or storytelling, much of which is now irrecoverable. Yet these art forms were of tremendous importance (indeed, they may have been more important art forms to Africans than sculpture). Dances could unite the people and express religious feelings in rhythmic representation of the group's life and ceremonies.

Dances could be ceremonial (to signify the start of the hunt or the time of planting), ritual (to mark a birth, marriage, or a death), festive (to celebrate feast days of gods), or recreational (to entertain the villagers). Usually everyone took part in dancing, but on special occasions trained artists did the dancing with masks enriching the form and drama, the ritual and spirituality of the dance.

African artists also produced many different musical cultures. Unfortunately the history of African music will never be written, except in the crudest outlines. Scholars may be able to reconstruct certain features in the development of Africa's musical technology, the way in which the hunter's bow developed into a stringed instrument, for example, and the manner in which African craftsmen developed fairly complex means of production, instruments that included all manner of pipes, drums, xylophones, and such. But traditional African music, like traditional African poems and epics, were the products of nonliterate cultures. The art of musical notation was a Western invention, taught to Africans in the first place by white mission teachers and military bandmasters. Notation allows the artist to exercise an exact and lasting form of control over his inventions. Notation permits composers to be known as individual creators. Notation helps them to build on elaborate structures created by their prede-cessors, and facilitates the quest for deliberate innovation. Notation also allows artists to perfect a whole variety of technical devices such as counterpoint, which remained unknown to African music. African musical development, for its part, necessarily depended on the collective memory of artists and their audiences. It remained subject to a variety of technical limitations, but retained that element of spontaneity which is characteristic of all good folk music. African music, on the other hand, developed a great variety of styles, distinguished by a peculiar sense of rhythm, harmony and depth of expression, which have begun to exercise a growing influence on Western music.

African music in turn was closely linked to the art of the singer and the story teller; indeed the very notion of introducing a rigid distinction between different art forms was remote to the African genius. The ancient *griots* (bards) of Senegal, or the Zulu "praise singers" at a king's court could not record their music in printed scores or their stories or poetry in books. Their work passed on from generation to generation by word of mouth. Their task was to preserve the traditions of the community, to instruct the young and remind adults of past glories, to reiterate in striking forms the rules and obligations of the society, and of course also to entertain the people.

In stressing the unique features of African art, it is all too easy to forget the similarities of human experience in many fields, or, on a lower plane, the impact of material modes of production upon art forms. The drum, for instance, is a relatively easy instrument to make. It does not require the intricate craftsmanship needed to make a harpsicord. White Macedonian highlanders could make drums as easily as could Africans from a Nigerian rain forest. It is perhaps for this reason that Macedonian folk dances depend on the rhythm of the drum in a way that displays some interesting parallels to African music.

All we can say with certainty is that African artistic heritages were tremendously varied. The indigenous peoples of Africa produced elaborate cosmologies, striking ritual, and elaborate forms of music that differed greatly from one part of Africa to another. The Mbuti (Pygmies) of the Ituri forest combine yodelling and the use of head voice in a peculiar manner. The Bemba of Zambia round their voices and give them a characteristically palatal quality. The Akan singers of Ghana may choose a nasal head voice. There are many other variations in technique. In combining several parts, the Kotokoli of Togo use parallel thirds. The Lundi Kalimba players accompany their singing with parallel fourths most of the way. The Lobi xylophonists of Ghana use a reticulate multipart style in which some notes are confluent to two distinct pitch lines. The Gonja of Ghana have a heterophonic style in which thirds, sixths, fourths, fifths, and sevenths occur in a yet unclassified order.[18]

The difference between European and African art derive from many sources. They were influenced by variations in methods of production and in manners of social life. But above all, these differences owe a great deal to different religious or philosophical interpretations of the world, which affect African beliefs on other topics. The tradi-tional African firmly believed in a world of spirits, and to a considerable extent Africans hold comparable convictions to this day. The Shona of Rhodesia, for exam-ple, commonly dread witches—malignant persons who have supposedly inherited or acquired a peculiar capacity for doing evil to their fellow men. These beliefs purport to give an answer to the universal problem of evil. At one time or another, every man and every society must try to answer Job's question of why misfortune befalls the just. Some modern philosophers explain this predicament by the workings of an inscrutable Providence. Others talk about the statistical laws of chance. The Bantu, and indeed most African communities not affected by Christianity or Islam, tended to see this question in terms of human personality. Villagers know no privacy; everyone knows everyone else. Most traditional Africans therefore tended to explain real or apparent evil in terms of personal relations. If an unskillful hunter was trampled to death by an enraged elephant, his friends would mourn him, but, as Professor Max Gluckman, a modern British anthropologist, points out, they would not talk of witchcraft. They talked in terms of natural causation; they knew that the victim's death had been occasioned by his lack of skill.

But if an elephant should kill a veteran huntsman with many tuskers to his credit, no such simple explanation would suffice. The hunter's death could not have been caused by insufficient experience. His misfortune is therefore ascribed to some occult evil-doing. His death was not to be blamed on the workings of nature, but on direct human intervention. Some person or other must have encompassed the victim's death by magic means. The tribesmen arrived at this conclusion not because they were incapable of rational observation or because they had a "pre-logical mentality." Their logic was perfectly sound.[19]

It was their religious or philosophical explanations that were different from ours. They explained the unknown in personal terms. Misfortunes were brought about by envy, malice, and greed translated into witchcraft. Hence they looked for the supposed malefactor through skilled diviners. The "witch doctors"—of popular European parlance—has gained an undeservedly bad reputation among whites, who often mix him up with a witch or evil magician. In reality the Shona *nganga* was a good man, a helper and healer, who would protect his clients from occult threat and who had a high standard of professional ethics and etiquette. The *nganga* usually determined the cause of an illness that was always supposed to be spiritual in character. He did this through a guiding spirit of his own, the spirit of a dead relative who then got in touch with the patient's ancestral spirits. There were also doctors who give only medicines, special roots, or herbs. A man of such a kind among the Shona was known as an herbalist *(murapi)*; he stood in a distinctly lower category than the *nganga*, for he merely treated the symptoms while leaving the deeper causes of evil to be discovered by the *nganga*. Most *nganga*, however practised both as herbalists and as diviners. (In modern times the European physician is looked upon as an herbalist whose remedies may be worth trying but who has no deeper, occult insight.)

The Shona spirit world also had many other inhabitants. Among these were the angered spirits of the dead. If a man had been murdered, and his assassin escaped punishment, the spirit of the victim would return to the world and avenge himself on the person or the clan of the person who had wronged him. Then there were the wandering or alien spirits, usually those of foreigners who had died in the country and had not received a proper burial. Such a spirit would choose a particular person as a medium and in return confer special favors upon him in exchange for his burden.

The inspiration received from such a supernatural benefactor might be concerned with many things, but usually related to dancing, hunting, or healing. The belief in spirits was shared by all our ancestors and is perhaps man's oldest form of religion.

When advice on a tribal matter had to be sought, the Shona sought help of a different kind. The tribal, regional, district, and family spirits all spoke through a medium. The medium had to be consulted on all matters affecting the community as a whole, such as rain, relations with the whites, and other political and social matters.[20] (There is a certain similarity between the religion of the Shona and that of some modern white spritualist churches.)

The belief in a supernatural world and in the ability of mediums to give voice to the spirit of the departed in turn helped to shape Shona ethics; so did the physical requirements of a society where wealth was scanty, where the margin of survival was narrow, and where a man necessarily depended on the goodwill of kinsmen and neighbors. Shona philosophy thus valued above all the notions of brotherhood and solidarity. Of brotherhood there were two forms. The first stemmed from kinship links to the common ancestor of a clan. The Shona were divided into different clans, each of whose members was entitled to sufficient land for his needs. Clan members were expected to live in harmony with one another. Harmony, however, became impossible if any individual were to accumulate an excessive amount of wealth. The second type of brotherhood emphasized the links between a man and his more immediate relatives in a smaller family unit. The members of a family group were expected to share their resources, so that each member might have his proper chance of happiness.

Felicity in Shona life was in turn bound up with the possession of many children. In a society where life was precarious, and manpower always in short supply, whether for work or war, the childless earned pity, and the fathers of many offspring merited respect. Children were essential to defend their parents, to help them at work, to look after them in old age, to honor their spirits when they died. The highest personal quality in Shona life was *unhu,* the possession of a fine personality, kindly, measured, balanced, reasonable, in harmony with one's self, one's kinsmen and one's community.[21]

Religious beliefs of this kind helped to serve as a moral cement holding society together. For woe to the man who offended the ancestral spirits by offending the moral laws set forth by ancestors. Such creeds were, however, apt to have other far-reaching social and economic consequences. Witches or wizards were liable to be severely punished; they might be ostracized, banished, or put to death. In many societies, moreover, the man who "got on" by means other than those sanctioned by custom was liable to be accused of using magic. "If there is any one among them who is more diligent and a better husbandman, and therefore reaps a fresh crop of millet and has a larger store of provisions," a Portuguese priest wrote four centuries ago about the Bantu of South East Africa, "they immediately falsely accuse him of all kinds of crimes, as excuse to take it from him and eat it . . ."[22]

Remarks such as Monclaro's should not be taken too far. Africans were capable of making a great many economic innovations. As we shall see in later sections of this book, many African communities developed an extensive long distance trade; they perfected the craft of working in iron. They managed to adapt to their use a large number of foreign crops such as maize, cassava, and tobacco. But in most cases economic readjustment was a lengthy process. Innovation usually required the approval of entire groups and thus seldom cases left little room for individual initiative. The economic conservatism that distinguished many, though not all, African communities probably derived reinforcement from the ethos of religions that placed a special emphasis upon the spirit world and upon traditions, morals, and accustomed ways of doing things.

There are obvious limits to generalizations of this kind. The Ibo of eastern Nigeria, for instance, were organized in village democracies where individuals were permitted to exercise a great deal of initiative, once trade developed. The Ibo, like various other West African communities, had secret societies that played an important role in the life of the community. Among the Ibo, a man could make his way up the various grades of a society, but he could not pass on his position to his heirs, who again had to start climbing the greasy pole on their own.

African creeds—the point bears repeating—differed a great deal from place to place, from period to period, from people to people. African religions were not static; they developed through the ages. Not all Africans, for instance, worshipped their ancestors. Many Africans who were subject to powerful monarchs gave divine honors only to the spirits of departed rulers, who had to be approached in a special way by the reigning king. The sphere of spirits was conceived in many different fashions. There were likewise all kinds of ways in which the supernatural world was to be reached, or in which its occult powers might be manipulated.

In conclusion, however, we may say that all Africans had some notion of a Supreme, all-pervading, all-sustaining Deity. All had faith in a spirit world; many dreaded witchcraft. Their belief in witchcraft rested on a specific system of moral philosophy. These tenets seemed to explain the mysteries of the universe to those who held them. The cults designed to put man in touch with the spirit world provided an element of high religious drama. They also emphasized the values of the community against the aspirations of individuals. Within the framework of the African village, they seemed to work. They also possessed tremendous resilience. Foreign deities like Jesus could be assimilated into the African pantheon. Hence Christianity and Islam encountered tremendous obstacles when their evangelists tried to convert the peoples of Africa, and the battle between the old gods and the new remains far from being decided even today.

NOTES

1. This account is taken from Lorna Marshall, "The !Kung Bushmen of the Kalahari Desert," in James L. Gibbs, Jr., ed., *Peoples of Africa* (New York, 1965), pp. 241–278. Gibbs' book is an excellent collection of essays on selected African peoples, illustrating different forms of traditional life.

2. Gibbs, p. 258.

3. The following account is taken from I. M. Lewis, "The Northern Pastoral Somali of the Horn," in Gibbs, pp. 319–362.

4. "Lineage" means a group of people directly descended from a common ancestor. The

exact composition of lineages may vary considerably between different tribal communities.

5. The following account is taken from Igor Kopytoff, "The Suku of Southwestern Congo," in Gibbs, pp. 443–477.

6. It derives from Max Gluckman, "The Lozi of Barotseland in Northwestern Rhodesia," in Elizabeth Colson and Max Gluckman, eds., *Seven Tribes of British Central Africa* (London, 1951), pp. 1–93. All articles in this book are worthy of study.

7. Colson and Gluckman, p. 11.

8. Kimble, vol. 1, p. 367.

9. Deputy Administrator Codrington to Chief Secretary, British South Africa Company: 19 September 1889, British South Africa Company Minutes 13 December 1899, annexure 13, LO 1/2/1, National Archives of Rhodesia.

10. Peter C. W. Gutkind, *The Royal Capital of Buganda: A Study of Internal Conflict and External Ambiguity* (The Hague, 1963), pp. 9–21.

11. John Donnelly Fage, *An Introduction to the History of West Africa* (Cambridge, 1962), p. 10.

12. Elspeth Huxley, *Four Guineas: A Journey Through West Africa,* (London, 1954), p. 180.

13. A. W. Lawrence, *Trade Castles and Forts of West Africa* (Stanford, 1964), p. 40.

14. K. A. Busia, *Africa in Search of Democracy* (New York, 1967), has an excellent chapter on the African religious heritage.

15. C. G. Jung, *Essays on Contemporary Events* (London, 1947), p. 65.

16. Léopold Sédar Senghor, "The Spirit of Civilization, or the Laws of African Negro Culture," cited in Hans Kohn and Wallace Sokolsky, *African Nationalism in the Twentieth Century* (Princeton, 1965), p. 158.

17. William Bascom, *African Arts: An Exhibition at the Robert H. Lowie Museum of Anthropology at the University of California, Berkeley, April 6 to October 22, 1967* (Berkeley, 1967), p. 9.

18. Atta Annan Mensah, "Learning to View African Music," *Bulletin, University of Zambia Institute for Social Research,* no. 3, (1968), pp. 111–112.

19. For a detailed discussion of these and related questions, see Max Gluckman, *Custom and Conflict in Africa* (Oxford, 1955).

20. See Michael Gelfand, *Medicine and Witchcraft Among the Mashona* (Cape Town, 1955) and Michael Gelfand, *Shona Ritual: With Special Reference to the Chaminuka Cult* (Cape Town, 1959).

21. For a more detailed though somewhat controversial discussion, see Michael Gelfand, *African Crucible: An Ethico-Religious Study with Special Reference to the Shona-Speaking People* (Cape Town, 1960).

22. Fr. Monclaro, "Account of the Journey made . . . with Francisco Barreto in the Conquest of Monomotapa in the Year 1569," in G. M. Theal, ed., *Records of South-eastern Africa . . .* (Cape Town, 1896–1905), vol. 3, p. 231.

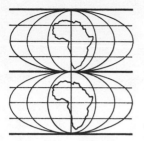

PART
III

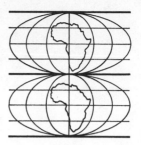

THE
PREHISTORY OF AFRICA

Chapter 8

Problems
of African Historiography

TOOLS OF HISTORY

Historians throughout the ages have been beset by many pitfalls in their attempts to write history. For an illustration we can do no better than to quote a passage from G. G. Coulton, a great English historian, who recorded the way in which Bishop Agnellus of Ravenna approached his task. Agnellus, a medieval churchman, was writing the history of his predecessors. But he found the going hard, and thus honestly explained in his preface, "Where I have not found any history of any of these bishops and have not been able—by conversation with aged men, or by inspection of the monuments, or from any other authentic source, to obtain information concerning them, in such case, in order that there might not be a break in the series, I have composed the life myself with the help of God and the prayers of the brethren."[1]

Modern historians of Africa face problems very similar to those of the venerable bishop. In many instances they are in a worse predicament. An Italian medieval scholar lived in a world of written documents, or he could look for inscriptions in permanent stone buildings and stone tablets. He could draw on the rich lore of Latin, Greek, and even of Arabic and Hebrew scholarship. Most Africans south of the Sahara, however, lacked the alphabet, and there was insufficient specialization among most communities to sustain a literate intelligentsia. African written languages were mainly confined to Ethiopia, to the Sudan, and to the maritime cities of the East Coast. Early Greek, Roman, Arab, Amharic, Fulani, and Swahili texts still survive to give us some idea of bygone days. Future collectors will almost certainly find additional records when they search for documents in North Africa and in faraway countries like Persia and Saudi Arabia (or even in the dusty corners of various European archives).

In tropical countries, however, old papers are preserved only with great difficulty, for white ants and atmospheric humidity pose serious problems even to modern archivists. Early record-keepers were even less equal to their task, and much material has been lost or destroyed.

The lack of written material means that we shall never be able to read, for example, the memoirs of a Luba king in the eighteenth century. Worse still, we cannot draw on administrative archives. Dull as they look, administrative files have a peculiar value denied to other written records. They are composed of documents drawn up or used in the course of an administrative or executive transaction of which they had formed a part.[2] This does not necessarily make official memoranda, communiqués, and such more reliable, for officials often enough lied to their inferiors and superiors alike. But —unlike the authors of so many autobiographies—they hardly ever wrote in order to deceive posterity; hence archival evidence has an unusual degree of authenticity. The lack of such material makes the historian's job hard indeed. For where there is no writing, there are large areas of human behavior that cannot be accurately described, except by speculative extrapolations from literate cultures, or by conjectures determined to a large extent by our own cultural preconceptions.

Some historians, therefore, try to supplement their sources with information from indigenous traditions and folklore, heroic legends, genealogical tables, and personal reminiscences. The use of oral history, however, again presents many difficulties. A historian can look at the same document again and again; so can his successor. An artifact can be preserved in a museum, and different conclusions can be arrived at by going over the same evidence again and again. But two or three people cannot interview the same aged informant twice; even should they do so, they will not necessarily elicit the same information, for the interviewer himself helps to impose a subjective pattern on the answers that he obtains. A human witness, moreover, will remember previous interviews; his memory can never be erased like a magnetic tape in such a way that he can be questioned over and over again without changing his answers at least to some degree.

Admittedly, it is easy to underestimate the value of material elicited by oral historians who investigate preliterate societies. Professional bards may faithfully record the same lay or the same genealogical table for many generations, for their memory is sure, and augurs usually sanctify accuracy for ritual reasons. Nevertheless, oral tradition is always subject to change. The Lunda people, who dwell on the Luapula River, are, for instance, very interested in their own past. But as Ian Cunnison, a British anthropologist observes, "this is not . . . history as we know it. It is the handing on of what is already known or believed, and it does not involve the asking of questions about the past, and the search for the answer to them."[3] As regards the supernatural, Cunnison adds, "Mythological and possible, old histories and new histories are received with the same degree of credulity. Mythical happenings may be greeted with a gasp of astonishment but that is simply because of the things which people of old could do. . . . History is no more open to European logical analysis by the African than is witchcraft. History, in fact, is caught up in the wider mystical circle, and belief in mythical events both attest to and is strengthened by the beliefs in magic, witchcraft and other mystical forces."[4]

Meyer Fortes, another British anthropologist, writes in a similar vein concerning the historical traditions of the Tallensi in West Africa. "The Tallensi . . . have no history in the sense of a body of authentic records of past events. The memories and reminiscences of the old men are part of their biographies and never contribute to the building up of a body of socially-preserved history. . . . Myths and legends counterfeit history; they do not document it. They are a part of . . . social philosophy, projected into the past because the people think of their social order as continuous and persistent. A myth or a legend postulates a beginning for what has existed thus ever since."[5]

This does not mean that oral traditions are without value to historians. They enlarge his imagination, they help him to pose new questions, and they tell him a great deal concerning a people's culture; they also provide a substratum of fact. They are, however, difficult to interpret, and the conventional historian's intellectual tools may often prove inadequate for the task. Oral traditions, moreover, like all other forms of evidence, always stand in need of corroboration and can never be accepted on the basis of their own authority.

This is how Thucydides, greatest of ancient Greek historians, criticized annals that were based on nothing but oral tradition. "Men do not discriminate, and are too ready to receive ancient traditions about their own as well as other countries. . . . He (the historian) must not be misled by the exaggerated fancies of the poets, or by the tales of chroniclers who seek to please the ear rather than speak the truth. Their accounts cannot be tested by him, and most of the facts in the lapse of ages have passed into the region of romance. At such a distance of time he must make up his mind to be satisfied with conclusions resting upon the clearest evidence which can be had."[6]

Historians of early Africa are therefore dependent on help given to them by archaeologists. Many African societies, however, lived by slash-and-burn agriculture. The tillers built their huts of wood and sun-dried mud, or of sun-baked brick; their villages shifted as the land became exhausted, and few permanent constructions survived. There are some exceptions, such as the tremendous ruins of Zimbabwe in what is now Rhodesia. Nevertheless, archaeologists in sub-Saharan Africa cannot find anything like the same number of great temples, of stone tables, of grave stones, and such as they do, say, in Egypt or in Ethiopia. The work of termites and the acidity of the soil, moreover, commonly destroy every object made of wood, cloth, or leather in most parts of Africa. Pottery survives more easily than any other kind of artifact, and archaeologists often have to cope with a peculiar kind of bias that depends on natural forces.

Archaeologists face other obstacles. Skilled men can disinter ancient skulls, but even the most brilliant scholar can never know what went on in those skulls. Archaeologists may, therefore, be tempted to place too much emphasis on certain kinds of evidence, on physiological peculiarities revealed by the bone structure of surviving skeletons, or on tools that may have happened to survive the ravages of time. They may thus place too much stress on the technological as against the ideological aspects of a vanished culture.

Historians and archaeologists alike may have to supplement their information by means of other forms of evidence, by the findings of linguists, of medical men interested in blood groups, by plant biologists, or of experts in the selective breeding of animals. The conclusions of such scientists are often hard to handle for laymen and may easily be misinterpreted even by specialists.

History based on sources of this kind will always contain a considerable element of uncertainty. Generations of English historians have made exhaustive inquiries into the details of early Anglo-Saxon migrations into the British Isles. In doing so, some have used the most advanced means of investigation. Yet much remains unexplained. (A recent monograph has put forward a good deal of evidence showing that parts of England must have been settled by Franks rather than Anglo-Saxons.) If an old country with an ancient historical tradition runs into troubles of this kind, the early history of technologically backward countries remains subject to even greater limitations for the available data have—in all probability—as yet hardly been scratched.

Still history based on archaeological sources, on folklore, on our knowledge concerning the movement of plants or of cattle can provide a great deal of information about the annals of whole groups, of migrations, of development in technology, and so forth. It cannot, however, provide us with reliable information concerning distinguished individuals. The ancient Bantu who migrated into central and southern Africa must have contained among them men like Alexander the Great or Napoleon. But we shall never know much about them. Early history—and this includes the history of many a European *Völkerwanderung* in the Dark Ages—necessarily has a faceless anonymity, where we know nothing about personalities and about considered policies. To cover up our ignorance, we vaguely speak about "impersonal forces" and "long-term trends." But these "forces" comprised rational decisions by councillors and leaders, men with strengths and foibles like our own, which must remain hidden in an impenetrable shroud.

Inquirers into the African past can also draw on the researches of anthropologists. The study of primitive societies was originally the preserve of armchair scholars who laboriously pieced together accounts from sea captains, missionaries, and travelers who told of the strange customs practiced by "outlandish tribes." Gradually the scissor-and-paste students gave way to men who were prepared to study preliterate societies at first hand. From the beginning of the present century, a small band of scholars spent long periods among the tribes they wished to study; often they became almost naturalized citizens of "their people," to whom they referred with a proprietary kind of pride. The new approach resulted in major contributions to scholarship, and few African historians can practice without some background of anthropological knowledge.

Anthropologists, like anyone else, have their biases or their specialized interests, and anthropologists seldom give identical accounts of the same society. American scholars interested in the Indians usually displayed more interest in the past of vanishing societies than British social anthropologists who investigated what they considered to be autonomous working systems in tropical Africa. Some anthropologists were all too much inclined to study "their" people as a self-sufficient entity in time and space. According to a British anthropologist, the inquirer thus studies "the customary modes of activity, clusters of ideas and institutionalised patterns of social relations, in communities or social aggregates sufficiently small in scale and simple in organisation to be comprehended as, and analysed as total working systems."[7] But what exactly is "a total working system"? Even the most isolated villages may for centuries have been influenced by outside contacts of some kind, so that they can no longer be understood as self-sufficient communities. The more civilization advances, the greater the importance of commerce and communications. Anthropological evidence is not, therefore, the same as historical evidence. The tribal groups studied, say, in the 1920s are just as much the product of an age-old transformation as our own. The rate of change may have been much slower. But the members of a Bantu group living in some remote area of a modern African country cannot simply be identified with their ancestors who lived there many centuries ago.

The study of tribes, or of "micro-nationalities," as they are often called nowadays, also poses other problems. An ethnic map of Africa reveals a bewildering variety of ethnic groups. Something over 1500 or more dialects and languages are spoken in Africa. No precolonial history can, therefore, ever be complete. None can attempt to comprise every known tribal group, or it would soon have to grow into encyclopedic size. African history covers an enormous region and great time spans; any account of it is bound to be selective to an unusual degree.

From anthropology we go on to the more orthodox methods of historiography, which center on the study of documents. Right from the start, however, the African historian has to face two major questions: the uneven nature of his material and the question of bias. The earliest sources on Africa commonly served utilitarian purposes. Medieval Arab sailors, for instance, were not particularly interested in the structure of African society. They primarily accumulated information useful for their job. They would report, for instance, on navigational problems. Their reports were often fanciful. Sea captains would tell the most marvelous stories of seas of boiling lead surrounding the remote portions of Africa, of giant birds that destroyed the ship of Sinbad the Sailor, and so forth. Such tales reflected the very real perils of maritime pioneers. Some may even have been put into circulation to deter potential competitors. Accordingly, they need sifting with a great deal of care.

Traders and officials were likewise concerned above all with information of a utilitarian kind. The bulk of the early records relating to Mozambique from the early sixteenth century on are prosaic. There are bills of lading, receipts, returns of weapons and stores that read much like entries in a modern quartermaster's office. Most chronicles of Africa appear in written records created during the modern colonial period, during the nineteenth and the twentieth centuries. Much information can be gleaned from government files, from letters of private provenance and similar sources. Unfortunately, this evidence has many gaps or is liable to distortion. Official records are of particular value, but the early period of colonial enterprise is usually poorly covered by documents derived from firsthand experience. In the early days of imperial administration, there were not many civil servants, and the men in charge were more concerned with immediate tasks than with writing reports. White ants, omnivorous rats, and careless filing clerks have destroyed a good deal of material. Much has been misfiled, burned, or lost.

BIAS IN HISTORY

Historians also have to cope with the problem of bias. Just how much credence should we give to the white man and the brown man, or—for that matter—the black man's writing about black men. A great deal of traditional information about Africa must be taken with a grain of salt. The early Arabs and Portuguese were often inclined to draw oversharp contrasts between the heathen and the converted. Muslims and Christians alike despised the infidel. Pagans often appeared as the unredeemed villains of a morality play. Proselytes, by contrast, got an exceptionally good press. In the seventeenth century, for instance, Monomotapa, the head of a great tribal confederacy in what is now Rhodesia, concluded an alliance with the Portuguese and became converted to Christianity, with the result that contemporary best sellers endowed the Karanga monarch with fantastic splendor.

More often, however, distortion went the other way round. For many centuries Europeans, Americans, and—to a lesser extent—Muslims purchased Africans as slaves. The institution of slavery was sometimes rationalized by an elaborate mythology asserting that blacks were racially inferior, or that heathen were peculiarly vile. The accelerating pace of industrial development in the West further widened the gap between the most advanced European and preindustrial societies. An east-coast *dhow* could stand comparison with a small Mediterranean galley of the type familiar to the Portuguese in the fifteenth century. The same *dhow,* not to speak of an African war canoe, looked infinitely less impressive when compared to an eighteenth-century East Indiaman. The *dhow* and the canoe alike appeared utterly puny when laid alongside a steam-driven armored vessel of the nineteenth-century kind. The Europeans developed a host of explanations, some sound, some fanciful, to account for their claimed superiority, and all these ideologies played some part in besmirching the image of the black man in the minds of the white.

From the sixteenth century on stereotypes of African inferiority were developed to justify the slave trade. During the late eighteenth and nineteenth century, the white man's image of Africa was further modified by missionary and humanitarian accounts. Missionaries and humanitarians alike wished to destroy the evils of the slave trade and help Africans to improve their moral condition. The white paternalist, unlike the profit-seeking white slave-trader, did not, however, deal with black potentates on a basis of equality. Whether he put his trust in physical force or moral persuasion, the humanitarian wished to change African society from something he regarded as lower to something higher, something nearer to the reformer's own preconceptions of what was right and what was wrong. The Christian evangelists who wished to convert Africans had similar assumptions. They believed Africans capable of redemption, but most preachers generally considered African creeds no better than the superstitions of Moabites, Edomites, and other accursed races in the Old Testament. The lugubrious accounts of evangelists concerning the real and assumed iniquities of African society were not corrected by equally fanciful speculations concerning the "noble savage" who supposedly lived a life of simple virtue.

As Africa was gradually colonized, unfavorable impressions were reinforced by the accounts of other Europeans. Many—though not all—late nineteenth-century soldiers and colonial administrators joined in criticizing Africa. These servants of empire were after all faced, not with the academic task of reconstructing a preliterate society from the safety of their arm chairs. Instead they had to police huge areas with tiny forces. They had to run territories as large as a principality on budgets fit only for a parish. They had to cope with slave traders, with tough war lords, with hardy adventurers in search of easy money. They had lost their own stereotypes regarding blacks and their preconceptions concerning themselves. Nothing could better illustrate the spirit of these paternalistic autocrats than a half-facetious jingle written by a late nineteenth-century British administrator in praise of a subordinate running a remote station in the interior:

> On Luapula's bank by rock and pool
> Bwana Kijana exercises rule.
> Around his boma [station] turmoil ceases not,
> Belgians intrigue and missionaries plot,
> Witch doctors brew concoctions to destroy him:
> But all these things are powerless to annoy him:
> Unmoved, undaunted, undismayed he still
> Will bend or break them to his iron will.[8]

Men like the writer of these lines were not necessarily insensitive to African achievements. Some of them wrote valuable accounts concerning the history and customs of their temporary subjects. Nevertheless, historians must always remember the bias of these travellers, traders, and colonial officials and treat their work with the caution required in any scholarly enterprise.

Victorian and Edwardian literature of the "Tales that Won the Empire" variety often produced a distorted picture of Africa. But after World War I the pendulum began to swing the other way. New schools of psychology and sociology subjected Victorian codes to a scathing analysis. The ills of Europe and America were denounced; the virtues of Africa seemed to gain by comparison. In America there was a craze for Harlem and for jazz, for the supposedly happy, uninhibited, and lusty denizens of black slums. Theoreticians on the Left produced a faddish *Proletkult,* a cult of the strong-armed proletarian. Theoreticians on the Right produced an equally unrealistic literature extolling the virtues of supposedly simple, unspoilt peasants, whom the literati had rarely met in real life.

The reaction against Victorian values in turn affected Western attitudes toward Africa. Many Victorians had identified Africans in some ways with the "lower orders" of metropolitan society. Now the African gained from this assumed likeness, for peasants and proletarians suddenly became praiseworthy. Some writers began to popularize a rosy picture of Africa's past that bore no more resemblance to ancient reality than the "rivers of blood and mountains of skulls" school of thought. A whole new school of writers used ancient Africa as a foil to set off the real and assumed evils of their own society, much as Tacitus had exaggerated the valor and virtues of ancient Teutons to embarass his Roman countrymen or as Madame de Staël had praised the simple virtues of Germany so as to censure the French of the Napoleonic era.

After the Second World War the African colonial empires largely disintegrated; a host of new independent countries appeared on the international scene. Many scholars felt obliged to create new national histories on the ground that "every self-conscious nation looks back upon its past to revive former glories, to discover its origins, to relate its history to that of other parts of the world . . . The coming of independence to so many African states has accordingly brought history . . . to the foreground."[9] The use of history as a means of cementing national consciousness is familiar alike to Europeans and Americans. It has, however, many pitfalls. This is how Macaulay, one of the greatest of English historians, describes the Gaelic revival in Scotland during the nineteenth century: "The Gaelic monuments, the Gaelic usages, the Gaelic superstitions, the Gaelic verses, disdainfully neglected during many ages, began to attract the attention of the learned from the moment at which the peculiarities of the Gaelic race began to disappear. So strong was this impulse that, where the Highlands were concerned, men of sense gave credence to stories without evidence, and men of taste gave rapturous applause to compositions without merit . . . Whatever was repulsive (in ancient Highland life) was softened down: whatever was graceful and noble was brought prominently forward . . ."[10]

Historians of Scotland, Macaulay continued, were apt to contrast the assumed and real miseries of the present with the supposed virtues of vanished tribal polities. As long as the Highland tribes raided the Lowlanders for their cattle, the Highlander was an object of hatred to his more civilized neighbor, and when the Englishman deigned to consider Highlanders at all "they considered him a filthy abject savage, a slave, a Papist, a cutthroat and a thief."[11] But once the traditional Highland tribes had disappeared, the popular and the learned writers quickly changed their mind concerning the ancient clan. "As they had formerly seen only the odious side of that polity, they could now see only the pleasing side. The old tie, they said, had been parental: the new tie was purely commercial . . . As long as there were Gaelic marauders, they had been regarded by the Saxon population as hateful vermin . . . As soon as cattle were as safe in the Perthshire passes as in Smithfield market (in London), the freebooter was exalted into a hero of romance . . ."[12]

The follies of neotraditionalism went even further. The old and new were strangely blended into an ideological mishmash that oddly blended past and present realities. To continue with Macaulay regarding the Gaelic revival in late eighteenth and nineteenth century Scotland: "Soon the vulgar imagination was so completely occupied by plaids, targets, and claymores, that, by most Englishmen, Scotchman and Highlander were regarded as synonymous words. Few people seemed to be aware that, at no remote period, a Macdonald or a Macgregor in his tartan was to a citizen of Edinburgh or Glasgow what an Indian hunter in his war paint is to an inhabitant of Philadelphia or Boston. Artists and actors represented Bruce and Douglas [two ancient Scottish national heroes] in striped petticoats. They might as well have represented Washington brandishing a tomahawk, and girt with a string of scalps . . ."[13]

Neotraditionalism in the African and Afro-American field is apt to produce movements similar to those created in Scotland, Ireland, Germany, and so many other European countries. The colonialist bias is apt to be replaced by an anticolonialist one. One set of prejudices may simply give away to another.

And yet African history has an essential part to play in our understanding of man. The study of other continents should broaden the imagination, widen our time perspective, do away with encrusted prejudices, and contribute to our understanding of what the human race has achieved in the past—often under the most desperately difficult circumstances. For all its uncertainties, for all the provisional nature of its findings, the study of African history is as critical to an understanding of modern Africa as a knowledge of medieval history is desirable for a comprehension of modern European civilization. But African history need not, and indeed cannot, be wholly Afro-centric. From times immemorial, Africa was linked to foreign shores. It is the object of this study to show ancient Africa within the wider framework of world history.

NOTES

1. G. G. Coulton, *Medieval Panorama,* vol. 2, *The Horizon of Thought* (London, 1961), pp. 66–67.

2. See H. Jenkinson, *A Manual of Archive Administration* (Oxford, 1922), p. 11.

3. Ian Cunnison, *History on the Luapula,* Rhodes-Livingstone Paper No. 21 (London, 1951), p. 4.

4. Cunnison, p. 21.

5. Meyer Fortes, *The Dynamics of Clanship Among the Tallensi: Being the First Part of an Analysis of the Social Structure of a Trans Volta Tribe* (London, 1945), p. 26.

6. See Thucydides, *History of the Peloponnesian War* (Chicago, n.d.), Book 1, Chap. 1, pp. 13–14.

7. Daryll Forde, "Social Anthropology in African Studies," *African Affairs* (Spring, 1965), p. 15.

8. Cited by L. H. Gann in "The 'Northern Rhodesia Journal' as an Historical Source Book," *Rhodes-Livingstone Journal,* 23 (1959), p. 51.

9. J. Vansina, R. Mauny, and L. V. Thomas, eds., *The Historian in Tropical Africa: Studies Presented and Discussed at the Fourth International Seminar at the University of Dakar, Senegal, 1961* (London, 1964), p. 59.

10. Thomas Babington Macaulay, *The History of England from the Accession of James the Second* (Chicago, 1888), vol. 3, p. 284.

11. Macaulay, p. 282.

12. Macaulay, pp. 283–84.

13. Macaulay, pp. 284–85.

Chapter 9

*From Hominids
to Stone Age Man*

THE PREDECESSORS OF MAN

In the middle of the seventeenth century, Archbishop James Ussher, an Irish divine, wrote a monumental Latin work called *Annales Veteris et Novi Testamenti (Annals of the Old and New Testament)*. This magnum opus set the creation of the world at exactly 4004 B.C., and such authority did the compilation command that for many years Ussher's chronology was printed in the margins of certain reference editions of the King James Bible. The eighteenth and nineteenth centuries, however, saw a great change in man's perception of his own past. The combined labors of naturalists and antiquaries, geologists and students of archaeology lengthened the known span of history, and brought about a Copernican revolution in our awareness of time. Where Ussher had reckoned in millennia, modern scholars think in billions of years. Ussher's picture of the earth's remote antiquity produces a curiously flat effect; our own has a stereoscopic effect and possesses immense depth.

Geologists nowadays estimate the age of the earth at about 4,500 million years; the higher mammals are only a comparatively recent creation. The earliest known fossil apes come from Oligocene beds in Fayum, Egypt, and are about forty million years old.[1] Some time in the Miocene period, about thirty million years ago, there developed a creature known to archaeologists as *Proconsul*. *Proconsul* was an apelike creature with large canine teeth and a relatively good-sized brain. His limbs show that he was in part a ground dweller, and the forelimbs do not show the later specialization for woodland seen in those of the existing great apes. *Proconsul* lived in East Africa, in country that was a mosaic of forest and more open savannah. The fossil remains

112

are found often on the slopes of old volcanoes that provided a wide altitudinal range in vegetation zones.

Our knowledge concerning the social organization of these beings largely derives from guesswork, or from what we can ascertain about the behavior of more highly developed mammals who live in groups. Contrary to what many laymen believe, wild beasts do not roam through the countryside at random. In fact, they have their own territories, with their homes and refuges, their drinking and watering places, their food stores and feeding areas. Herds are usually patterned according to definite social hierarchies. A definite ceremonial is accorded to each grade. Infringement of the ceremonial leads to rebuke or fighting. The popular idea concerning the "golden freedom" that supposedly prevails in nature derives from poetic imagination. Monkeys, for instance, are subject to rigid social restraints. Only the very young, those who do not as yet count for anything, are excused from conforming to the behavior pattern of the group. Mating is likewise accompanied by an elaborate ceremonial; this may be so strict that pairing cannot take place at all if the ceremonial is disturbed. But wild animals are concerned above all with the need for safety. Flight is the be-all and end-all of existence. Hunger and love take secondary place, for the satisfaction of hunger and of sexual needs can be postponed, while flight from a dangerous enemy cannot. Lastly, we know that some wild animals are quite adaptable regarding their diet. They are often less choosy than we suppose. Even among the carnivores, pure flesh eaters are rare; so are pure plant eaters among the ungulates.[2]

We may assume that early beings like *Proconsul* lived in socially organized groups, that these groups were strictly organized according to some hierarchical principle, and that they may have occupied specific territories. Life must have been determined by the need for security and food. It seems likely that band members adhered to quite specific behavior patterns, both with regard to mating and to rules of dominance. In reconstructing their lives, we must forget all about ill-considered musings concerning "nature red in tooth and claw," and we must think in terms of much more complex relationships. *Proconsul* and his like were capable of physical and mental adaptions, and of further development.

The later Miocene and subsequent Pliocene age (ca. fourteen to ten million years ago) saw the evolution of forms more specifically related to man. These were known as Hominids. Archaeologists now postulate that these Hominids used their lower limbs for bipedal locomotion, and their forelimbs for manipulating various implements. The Hominids were living in the savannah, which provided them with a fairly favorable environment. Hominid evolution during the Pliocene age may have continued for some eight million years. During this period the Hominids learned how to use their lower limbs more effectively for walking and how to employ their arms and hands for the manufacture and use of simple tools. It appears that by the beginning of the Pleistocene age (about three and a half million years ago) the Hominids had experienced a considerable degree of biological development. This evolution was influenced by changes in the way of life followed by the various bands, by modifications in their diet, and by the use of tools which constituted the beginning of culture. The more highly developed Hominids are known as *Australopithecinae*, which simply means "southern apes." They are definitely known only to date in Africa and represented a considerable step forwards in the evolution of man. Their bodies and limbs were generally slender and essentially close to those of modern man. The size of the skull shows that they were possessed of a brain that was surely intellectually superior to that of the African apes. They walked upright, and they could use their arms and legs—essentially human in appearance—for purposes other than locomotion. In the beginning, they probably lived on shoots and leaves, on berries, bulbs, and fruits. Later, the savannah climate probably deteriorated. There was less rain; the dry season lengthened; vegetable food became scarcer, and the man-apes began to supplement their diet with meat. In all likelihood they stalked game as a group, like wild dogs. No doubt they made capital out of the way in which thirsty beasts had to congregate at specified water holes in the arid months of the year. Their mental capacity was sufficient to allow their collaboration in small bands for the purpose of ambushing other creatures and chasing carnivores away from their kills. A meat diet may well have enforced a greater degree of social cooperation than was required for the collection of wild plants. In addition, nature now placed a premium on the use of tools. The ape-men lacked sharp canines to remove skin and fur from a captured carcass. Some East African *Australopithecinae* therefore began to pick up sharp stones for the purpose of tearing the skin off dead buck and antelopes. Bashing instruments were employed to break open large bones or the shell of a tortoise. Pointed sticks

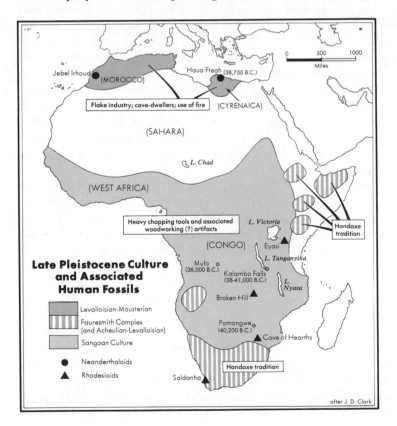

served for digging roots. The *Australopithecinae* thereby managed to overcome the challenge of a changing environment and roamed further afield. Their remains have been found in South and East Africa, Chad, and perhaps even the Far East, so that tool using and rudimentary forms of toolmaking spread across parts of the Old World with remarkable speed.[3]

THE ORIGINS OF MANKIND

Archaeologists have made extraordinary progress in untangling the origins of our species. Yet great gaps still remain in our knowledge of man's childhood. Biologists who trace human evolution must consider a multitude of different factors. These include. among others, natural selection favoring new adaptions, though not exaggerated specialization. They also have to reckon with mutations, whereby genes undergo permanent change—often deleterious in their nature. Mutant genes sometimes manage to survive in small isolated pockets (this is known to specialists as "genetic drift"). In addition there is hybridization, or the crossing of individuals with a different genetic makeup. Archaeologists who attempt to reconstruct a genealogical table for the early human race thus face a tremendously difficult task, and absolute certitude as yet remains an unattainable ideal. A good deal of research has, however, been accomplished, and it seems likely that the cradle of mankind stood in Africa.

The Olduvai Gorge in East Africa is an archaeological treasure house of the utmost importance for the study of man's origins. It yields evidence of early breeds, and also of another kind that may have represented a different species. This is known as *Homo habilis.* Some specialists claim that only *Homo habilis* could actually *make* tools, as distinct from simply picking up sharp stones that lay conveniently at hand. Others doubt whether *Homo habilis* was indeed a new species, and suggest that he may simply have been another *Australopithecine.* Only additional evidence, preferably from outside East Africa, can solve the riddle of man's subsequent evolution. But it seems that some time between a million and 500,000 years ago, the reciprocal relationship between biological and cultural evolution gave rise to a more advanced form known as *Homo erectus,* whose mental life must have been basically much superior to that of earlier beings. Toolmaking bands of hunters spread out further afield. Remains of a more advanced stone tool equipment, known as Lower Acheulian (or Abbevilian in Europe), have been found in France, Algeria, Morocco, and Kenya.

In East Africa the later and more advanced stage of this culture is probably less than half a million years old. Man's tool kit expanded and so did his capacity for group organization. The population increased, and early hunters made their way into areas hitherto unoccupied. At certain periods during this age, Africa experienced a more temperate environment than it does today, and the climate was favorable to the development of man. New species of antelopes, pigs, and other mammals proliferated; the hunting bands grew more numerous and more skillful. They must have been capable of performing great feats of strength and courage, for most of their prey were of gigantic proportions. There were pigs as big as rhinoceroses, baboons as large as chimpanzees, and sheep of buffalo size; these great beasts were driven into swamps, slaughtered, and devoured; their bones were split open, and the marrow was sucked out as a final delicacy.[4]

The aboriginal bands still had to choose their ground with much care, and Africa's human population remained infinitesimally small. Tropical forests in all likelihood remained inaccessible. The bands remained confined to savannah and steppes where water was available and game was plentiful. They could strike camp only in the immediate neighborhood of a stream or a lake, presumably because they had not yet found a way of carrying liquid over any distance.

Within these limits, man acquired somewhat greater mastery over his environment. The art of chasing large animals implied a higher degree of social cooperation, and bands acquired the cohesion displayed by packs of wild dogs. Acheulian man was also better equipped from the technological standpoint than his predecessors. Aboriginal craftsmen learned how to select their materials. The tougher, harder rocks were used for heavy cutting and chopping tools, while fine-grained, homogeneous rock, capable of making small brittle edges, was fashioned into smaller implements. The hand axes surviving from this period stand out as fine examples of the early stone worker's craft. They were made by what is known as the "cylinder hammer technique," which allowed axe makers to remove thinner and flatter flakes; this method resulted in shapely tools with straight cutting edges. The tools, however, all tended to follow a similar pattern. There is little difference between the artifacts found at the Cape, in Zambia, East Africa, the Sahara, Egypt, or India, except in the raw materials used. The reason for this is not as yet fully understood. It may result from the fact that the hand axe people were confined largely to one type of country—the savannah—and to the enormous length of time (about one million years) involved in this development.

As to Acheulian man's physical appearance, we can as yet only speculate. It seems that responses to changes in environment and adaptations produced several different forms, and it is from one of these that modern man derives.

Our ideas of man's early social institutions are even more uncertain. Skeletons and skewers survive, to be classified and evaluated by museum curators—but ideas do not. We can identify skulls, but not the thoughts that once passed within. Hence all our reconstructions of early man are perhaps bound to place undue stress on physiological and technological factors alone. Again we can look at the behavior of modern Bushmen and draw inferences concerning the habits of our remote ancestors. But we are apt to forget that contemporary Bushmen are as far in time from primeval men as we ourselves. Lack of evidence has thus left the field clear for the most extraordinary speculations concerning the customs of early bands.

Nineteenth- and early twentieth-century writers, enamored of evolutionary theories, especially delighted in formulating unproven and unprovable theories. The ancient hordes, according to some, were ruled by autocratic old males who governed with an iron fist and monopolized all the females in the tribe until they were slain by their younger and stronger sons. Freud, for instance, deduced from psychological investigations conducted among the well-to-do bourgeois of imperial Vienna that at some point in time the primitive bullies were stricken with remorse; the sons instituted an incest taboo denying the kinswomen to themselves. This Oedipal conflict supposedly played an essential part in developing human culture.

Others tried to prove that the higher apes lived in pairs. From this original condition early man fell into group marriage, or a man took several wives, or more rarely, one woman several husbands. Some scholars formulated theories of mother–right, according to which authority over the children originally rested with the mother and her elder brother. This theory was justified on the *a priori* assumption that mankind was originally promiscuous; therefore no one knew who the father of a child was; only the mother was definitely known. Others insisted that authority first rested with the father, and that mother-right, where it existed, was a subsequent development.

We simply do not know what occurred. All we can say is that the observed behavior of baboon bands in contemporary Africa lends no support whatever to the Freudian theory, even if we could assume—as we cannot—that the customs of baboons are in any way relevant to those of Bushmen. Abstract thought-spinning of this kind adds nothing to our real knowledge. As Max Gluckman, a modern anthropologist, has so aptly put the matter:

Arguments can be worked out to support all these schemes, and if one varies one's definition of what has survived from an earlier stage, the facts can be marshalled to support each argument. When one has worked out one's scheme, one places each tribe on the right rung of the ladder: if in a society with mother-right, customs of father-right are found, they indicate the beginnings of the assertion of father's power; if in a society with father-right, customs giving some power to the mother's family are found, these are survivals from the stage of mother-right—or the other way round. Aside from their inherent weakness, the theories are sterile, for they pose no further problems.[5]

All we can say as a common-sense inference is that the demands of more complex hunting economies must have imposed a good deal of voluntary coöperation in communities where the leader's physical powers of coercion were small, where even the strongest male would have been no match for any two or three of his followers. Early man must have evolved some rules for regulating his group behavior, and must have embarked on his career as a social animal.

We shall never know what his rules were like or how they developed. But we do know that among modern Stone Age communities—however backward technologically—there are neither "primitive" customs nor "primitive" languages. Savages depicted in comic strips woo their mates by knocking them on the head with a club, and dragging them into caves. Real live hunting peoples, be they Eskimos or Pygmies, conduct themselves in a very different fashion. They all have elaborate rules of conduct and of etiquette. Tarzan and his like talk in broken English, punctuated by "ughs" and "aughs." Real Bushmen, people who have so little worldly wealth that they can carry all their possessions on their persons, speak tongues of great complexity. The economic foundations of their respective cultures are of the simplest. But their rules of grammar are so difficult that they may defy the efforts of highly skilled linguists to understand them. We may assume therefore that primitive man stepped into history, not merely as a tool maker, but as a unique creature, capable both of speech and thought.

FIRE FROM HEAVEN

Greek legend tells of Prometheus, the demigod who first stole fire from heaven, and became mankind's teacher and benefactor. The Prometheus of myth was the son of a Titan. The real Prometheus was probably a half ape-like creature; he belonged to a subspecies of *Homo erectus* called Peking man, who lived at the furthest end of Asia and may have learned how to employ fire something like half a million years ago. In addition there were fire users in other parts of the world, in Hungary and presumably elsewhere.

No one knows exactly when fire was first used in Africa, though evidence for the employment of fire suggests a much more recent date than in Eurasia. It seems, however, that some 50,000 or 60,000 years ago the world experienced a great climatic change. More rain fell on the African continent; the days and nights became colder. Forest plants suited to a greater height replaced lowland forests down to some 600 to 900 meters below their present altitude range. Mediterranean flora spread southward to what are now the southern parts of the Sahara. Most of the gigantic fauna of earlier days became extinct and was largely replaced by species living today. The earth saw further movements and volcanic eruptions that significantly altered the topography of East Africa and gave the Rift Valley something like its present form.

During this period aboriginal man in Africa must have hit on the idea of capturing the flames. One day, perhaps, lightning struck a tree and caused a great bushfire. A roaring conflagration swept over the land, driving men and beasts before it. When it had burnt itself out and the first terror had passed, a band of hunters may have returned and stumbled upon the smoldering remains. Overcoming their fears, they began to feed the flame and learned how to control the blaze. Scavengers could also have found the half-charred carcass of an animal trapped in the inferno; they tried the meat and decided that it was better to eat broiled meat than raw. The hunters at first could not make a fire at will, but they kept the coals alive, and woe betide the man or woman who let it go out. The religious history of mankind is full of cults where priestesses, like the Vestal Virgins of Rome, had to maintain an eternal fire and suffered terrible punishment if they allowed the sacred flame to go out.

The use of fire is very ancient and represented a great step forward in technology. Much more difficult still was the discovery of how to make fire at will. There are several ways early man may have achieved this extraordinary advance, but whatever the first method of lighting fire, the controlled use of combustion was infinitely greater in its impact on humanity than the discovery of nuclear energy. Bands became less restricted in their movements and spread out into upland and forest regions. Hunters occupied favorably situated, but densely wooded, regions of Equatorial Africa. The migration routes into the Congo basin and the West African rain forest probably led along grass-covered interfluves, and man became more skilled at using the opportunities provided by savannah land and forest galleries in adjacent river valleys.[6] Rock shelters could be turned into habitations where men could warm themselves by their fireside and seek protection from cold and storms. Fire enabled man to clear bush and fell trees. The invention of deadfall traps may well have originated in savannah country when hunters saw trees crash through veld fires, and then hit on the idea of deliberately making trunks of branches fall down on game. Man also learned how to start controlled blazes for the purpose of driving game into a swamp or over a cliff. The use of fire in the chase must have greatly increased the number of beasts that might be killed; it is possible, therefore, that the progressive extinction of the larger forms of horses, hartebeest, and buffalo in this part of Africa was accelerated by man.

Changing methods of game killing in turn influenced man's social organization. The early hunters must have wandered widely in search of food. During the rains they presumably banded together for community hunting. In the dry season, when water was scarce, they probably split into smaller groups that camped near permanent water. Improved equipment and the invention of traps may have enabled man to survive in smaller bands, while hunting assumed a more individual aspect. Instead of sleeping near his kill, man began to carry chunks of meat to the shelter of overhanging rocks that provided more comfort than rude windbreaks on the open veld. The use of semipermanent camps, warmed and protected by fire against the attentions of wild beasts, must also have contributed to increasing specialization of labor and perhaps to a more exact division of activities between the sexes. Tools became more adapted to different regional environments. In addition, men may have begun to develop their aesthetic sense. Charred sticks and lumps of coloring matter served as body paint, for the decoration of weapons and utensils and perhaps also for magical purposes. Man was now able to communicate more complicated ideas to his fellow man. The evolution of more highly specialized implements, the use of pigment, the similarity of industrial patterns within regional varieties, all point to a degree of group cohesion requiring a common tongue. We have no idea what these languages were like or what thoughts they could express. They may well have been "click languages," like those of the modern Bushman; but however constructed, they represented an enormous step forward in the intellectual and moral progress of man. It seems probable that *Homo erectus* could communicate ideas by means of language. It is also likely that the success attained by Homo sapiens something like 35,000 years ago in supplanting all other forms of man was brought about by his developed linguistic ability as much as by his technology. All we know for certain is that the evolution of language played a vital part in human development. There is a profound symbolical truth in the Biblical account that tells how God led every beast to Adam "to see what he would call them: and whatsoever Adam called every living creature, that was the name thereof."[7]

NOTES

1. Sonia Cole, *The Prehistory of East Africa* (Penguin Books, 1954), p. 65. In addition to this work, the subsequent account draws heavily on John Desmond Clark, *The Prehistory of Southern*

Africa (Penguin Books, 1959), and Henriette Alimen, *The Prehistory of Africa,* trans., Alan Houghton Brodrick (London, 1957).

2. H. Hediger, *Wild Animals in Captivity* (New York, 1964), pp. 4–26.

3. John Desmond Clark, "The Prehistoric Origins of African Culture," *Journal of African History,* vol. 5, no. 2 (1964), pp. 162–183.

4. Sonia Cole, "The Stone Age of East Africa," in Roland Oliver and Gervase Mathew, eds., *History of East Africa* (Oxford, 1963), vol. 1, p. 27.

5. Max Gluckman, *Politics, Law and Ritual in Tribal Society* Oxford, 1965), p. 13.

6. Clark, "The Prehistoric Origins of African Culture," p. 172.

7. Genesis 2:19.

Chapter 10

Stone Age Hunters

THE EARLY STONE AGE: LATER PHASE

Man's advance about 60,000 years ago into different kinds of geographical environment, into savannahs, dry steppes, mountain and lowland forest fringes, imposed some degree of regional specialization upon the scattered communities. In Europe the last of several Ice Ages drew to its close. The glaciers began to recede, and cave-dwelling hunters of the Neanderthal type trekked northward in pursuit of mammoth and reindeer. Neanderthal man had a stocky build, a protruding brow, and a low, sloping forehead. Yet some authorities consider that he belonged to a subcategory of *Homo sapiens,* our own species. Perhaps an ordinary commuter, sitting next to a normally dressed Neanderthaler in a subway train, might notice nothing very peculiar about his neighbor. However this may be, the cranial capacity of Neanderthal man was equivalent to our own, and we have no means of knowing whether his inborn intellectual ability was less. In Africa his kind was also widely represented. Rhodesian man, whose remains were found at Broken Hill in Zambia, must have looked rather like his European contemporaries, though he was taller and possessed a more beetling brow. In North Africa people of another Neanderthal stock developed a specialized culture based on the manufacture of light cutting, scraping, and piercing tools from thin, fine flakes. This culture, known to archaeologists as the Mousterian and Levallois-Mousterian, replaced the Acheulian, with its heavier and more unwieldy implements, and the tools bear a strong resemblance to similar varieties found in the Levant, where they date between 50,000 and 60,000 years B.C. No one is quite certain whether the new way of working stone came about as an indigenous evolution

121

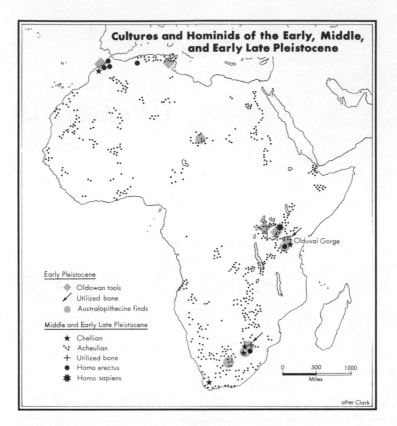

Cultures and Hominids of the Early, Middle, and Early Late Pleistocene

Olduvai Gorge

Early Pleistocene
◆ Oldowan tools
/ Utilized bone
● Australopithecine finds

Middle and Early Late Pleistocene
★ Chellian
⋰ Acheulian
+ Utilized bone
● Homo erectus
✳ Homo sapiens

0   500   1000
Miles

after Clark

from the Acheulian, or whether it resulted from immigration into Africa from Europe or the Middle East. The latter alternative appears more likely; but whatever the answer may be, it seems that from then onwards the culture of North Africa became increasingly differentiated from cultures in the rest of the continent. The desert was now increasingly encroaching upon more fertile lands, and even though cultural interchange between North and Central Africa never ceased, the people of the Maghrib, for instance, developed a specialized way of working stone, perfecting the use of flakes and points, while further east, and as far south as the Horn, the more generalized Levallois-Mousterian pattern continued.

In other parts of Africa there was also progress. The more heavily forested parts of the continent saw the development of a woodland culture, between 45,000 and 35,000 years ago, known as the Sangoan, which centered on lakes, on river valleys, on the margins of tropical forests, on bush and thicket country. The Sangoan spread through the Congo, through West Africa, into East Africa west of the Rift Valley, and into southern Africa down as far as Natal. Sangoan toolmakers designed heavy chopping implements and also smaller denticulated artifacts that were probably used for working wood. Timber could have served to make all kinds of traps, game stakes, and concealed spikes; bark rope was employed as string for trip lines, and the hunters supplemented their diet of meat, fruit, berries, and bulbs with wild honey. Stone Age craftsmen, having discovered how to make rope and string, also found ways of hafting stone on wood and thereby greatly increased man's technological potential. A few rare lance-heads date from the Middle Sangoan. During the Upper Sangoan the manufacture of spearheads greatly improved. Wooden lances with fire-hardened points could only pierce the hunter's quarry. Stone-headed spears could cut as well as penetrate the skin. Stricken animals therefore weakened much more quickly from loss of blood; their spoor became easier to follow, and hunters secured more kills. In addition, aboriginal hunters—like the more recent Hottentots—must have developed skill in hitting game on the run with throwing sticks and stone missles.

Elsewhere in southern and eastern Africa, the old hand axe tradition lingered on in modified forms. Communities whose culture is known as the Fauresmith complex flourished in grasslands where hoofed animals lived in profusion and where hunting bands perfected the art of communal stalking and driving. Fauresmith features have been identified in the Orange Free State, in Botswana, in Kenya and Ethiopia. Fauresmith toolmakers made small hand axes and cleavers of a peculiar pattern, but their equipment does not appear to have included picks or lance heads.[1]

THE MIDDLE STONE AGE AND THE EMERGENCE OF *HOMO SAPIENS*

Archaeologists and prehistorians have a difficult assignment: methodical excavation; the investigation of tools, pots, cave paintings, human and animal remains; the study of strata; the use of sophisticated dating devices such as the "Carbon 14" method;[2] research into plants; inquiries into the ways of life followed by primitive communities still in existence. These techniques enable scholars to build up some kind of factual framework about the past. A great deal of the more specialized archaeological literature consists in accounts of digs and of the problems encountered in evaluating their evidence. Laymen usually have great difficulty in following these highly technical reports. But the collection of factual evidence is only a first step. The finds have to be put into a wider setting, and research is finally cast into the form of a narrative. The verisimilitude of a story, however, depends to some extent on the teller's ability to convey to his audience a sense of time. This is exceedingly hard when a historian has to describe processes that extend over long periods. By compressing

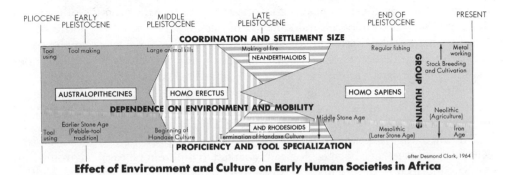

Effect of Environment and Culture on Early Human Societies in Africa

huge timespans into a short section, a chapter, or even a book, the narrator acts—as it were—like a film projectionist, who lets a long reel run off at tremendous speed and thereby accelerates the action to an extraordinary degree. Our projectionist, by playing back a film with unwonted rapidity, can create the illusion, say, of a flower growing out of the soil before our very eyes, though this phenomenon extended over a much longer period. Historical reality is further twisted out of shape by what might be called the illusion of foreshortened time perspective. Generally speaking, we know much more about the recent than the remote past. Short time spans of a recent vintage are infinitely better documented than long time spans of ill-defined antiquity. There is no way of avoiding distortion. All we can do is to make mental allowances for our inevitably biased sense of chronological perspective.

To recapitulate from previous sections, the first evidence for the regular use of fire in Africa dates from the end of the Acheulian (hand axe) culture, about 60,000 years ago. The more limited period of cultural diversification into Sangoan, Fauresmith, and related cultures probably extended from about 50,000 to 35,000 years ago, that is to say, over a duration nearly three times the length of mankind's recorded past, or seventy-five times the duration of United States history from the Declaration of Independence to the present day. These 15,000 years or so witnessed great accumulative changes, but the adaptations made extended over many millennia. Even so, the various cultures man evolved on the African continent were specialized only in a very general sense. It was not until something like 35,000 years ago that they branched out on an essentially regional basis. This new step in human development probably coincided with the emergence of *Homo sapiens,* that is to say, man as we know him today.

The origins of *Homo sapiens* are in dispute. Archaeologists formerly imagined that *Homo sapiens* evolved out of an unspecialized type of Neanderthal man in the Levant. Recent findings show that the history of mankind cannot be so easily determined. Early sapient forms coexisted with more specialized forms of Neanderthal breeds, but more work remains to be done to arrive at a greater degree of certainty. *Homo sapiens,* wherever he originated, spread rapidly to other parts of the world. The ancestors of the modern Europeans in all likelihood made their way to the European continent in several waves, presumably coming from the direction of Palestine. In Europe the earliest stock predating modern man is associated with a peculiar type of stone industry known as "blade and burin," which rather abruptly replaced the Mousterian culture and its Neanderthal makers about 35,000 B.C. In Africa, on the other hand, there was no such rapid cultural shift. Stone techniques resembling those of the Neanderthal people continued for another 25,000 years, and were employed by people of very different racial stock. The reason for the survival of these older traditions is not apparently to be sought in technical backwardness. The older forms of tools were the most suitable for making the specialized equipment needed by hunters in tropical and subtropical environments, as against the very different tools required in the cold forests and icy tundras of a northern latitude.

The ancestral *Homo sapiens* stock of Africa, perhaps represented by recent finds in Kenya, appears to have been ecologically adapted to different physical environments. Archaeologists now differentiate between several main types. At Singa, on the Blue

Nile in the Sudan, diggers have found remains of a person resembling a Bushman. He had a short flattened face and nose bridge, but he was much more robust than a South African Bushman of the twentieth century. Skulls of a similar type derive also from South Africa. They are known as Boskop (after the place in the Transvaal where the first of these fossils were discovered in 1913). In Kenya S. B. Leakey, a celebrated scholar, excavated five skeletons dating immediately after the end of the Pleistocene. These belong to what has been called an Afro-Mediterranean type. These were tall people, over 5 foot 10 inches in height, with long, fairly wide noses and well-developed chins. Their stone industry was based on blades and resembles that of a later Upper Paleolithic industry on the Eurasian landmass. The origin of these people is still disputed. Leakey thinks that they reached East Africa from Palestine, via Arabia and a land bridge over the southern part of the Red Sea, and that they subsequently spread to North Africa, where they appeared much later than in Kenya. There is in fact good reason to believe that Palestine may have been a racial melting pot. Emigrants from the Near East, taking their blade and burin (Upper Paleolithic) culture with them, may well have pushed both southward into Africa and westward along the northern shores of the Mediterranean. If this theory is correct, it would lend some support to the poetical tradition of Genesis, which described Noah as the ancestor of modern man and his sons Shem, Ham, and Japheth, "and of them was the whole earth overspread."[3] But it is equally possible that this longheaded stock may be an evolutionary adaptation to the conditions of the desert and grassland; hence we need not perhaps look outside the continent for its origins.

The Negro stock appears about the same time as the "Afro-Mediterranean" breed and may likewise have evolved from proto-Bushmanoid ancestors. An ancient representative of Negroid stock comes from a Mesolithic site at Khartoum. Only one skull from this find was sufficiently well preserved for restoration, but it tells us a good deal. It is long and narrow, with a wide, long face and a wide, flattened nose. These and other Negroid characteristics are said to mark its owner as one of the earliest recognizable Negroes in Africa.[4] A number of fossils supposedly deriving from Negro people have also been found as far afield as the Sahara and other parts of Africa; existing conclusions on the early history of *Homo sapiens* are thus necessarily tentative in character. Future archaeologists will probably come across new finds that are likely to modify further existing conclusions. We do know, however, that there is no such thing as a pure race. The various stocks migrated widely and merged with each other in different proportions. The climate of Africa was relatively favorable at the time, and hunting bands spread out widely into many previously uninhabited parts of the continent.

STONE AGE REVOLUTIONS

Stone Age technologists began with fairly simple tools, but gradually their artifacts became increasingly specialized. Toolmakers in the savannah and grasslands of East and southern Africa, where rain was comparatively plentiful, thus learned how to fashion light cutting, piercing, and throwing implements made of stone. A contemporary culture, native to the Congo forests and known as the Lupemban, specialized in the manufacture of axes and other chopping implements, magnificent lanceolate knives or stabbing points, gouges and boat-shaped planing tools. (Lupemban finds from Kalambo Falls in what is now Zambia date from between ca. 25,000 to 27,000 B.C. Late Lupemban industries have been discovered in northeast Angola; they derive from about 12,600 B.C.)

In time, however, the process of change speeded up, and from about 10,000 or 12,000 years ago, there was an even more fundamental change in toolmaking techniques. Craftsmen in various parts of Africa gradually worked out new ways of making composite implements, fashioned by hafting small stone blades or flakes into wood or bone. This method produced more effective spearheads and knives than those previously known to mankind. Toolmakers now required only small pieces; they could therefore select finer and more suitable stones. Their finely grained raw material permitted better workmanship, greatly increased the killing potential of primitive weapons, and thereby considerably added to the community's food supply. The most important individual invention was unquestionably the barb. Missiles with barbed heads stick in the wound much longer than those without barbs. Not only will a barbed spear hinder a quarry in its flight, but a barbed spearhead, smeared with poison, will also make sure that the toxin will disperse and kill the prey. Light arrowheads also facilitated the use of bows and gave greater range and striking power to roving archers in search of game. Archery spread widely after ca. 8500 B.C.

The new technology had many regional variants, and several different ethnic stocks must have had a share in its creation. The close of the Pleistocene about 8000 B.C. was preceded by a cooler and wetter climatic period of about 2000 years' duration. This age saw two new waves of immigrants who made their way into North Africa. One group settled in the Maghrib, the other in Cyrenaica, bringing their own cultures to the new country.

During the fifth millenium B.C. another culture grew up in the valley of the upper Nile, in the Sudan. This was created by Negro peoples, who may have originated in the northern forest margins and then pushed into country previously occupied by Bushmen. These Negroid communities lived by the waterside and, in addition to being hunters and collectors, became fishermen of outstanding skill. They learned how to make stone knives and arrowheads, fashioned from small stones, carefully worked. They speared game and fish with barbed spears, and thereby acquired a relatively secure livelihood. They delighted in the use of red ochre and gained some artistic skill. The rivermen lived a semisedentary existence, and built themselves shelters made of wattle and daub. In addition they became proficient in the manufacture of pots, developing a craft that is obviously of much greater use to a semisedentary than to a nomadic community.[5]

The Middle Stone Age people seem to have developed more complex kinds of religion than their predecessors. This may be inferred from the careful way in which they buried their dead. In Kenya, for instance, archaeologists have come across a burial ground in a spot known as Gamble's Cave, used by people of Caucasoid stock. The mourners carefully laid their dead on the right side; the corpses had their knees drawn up to their chins, with the face turned towards the opening of the rock shelter.

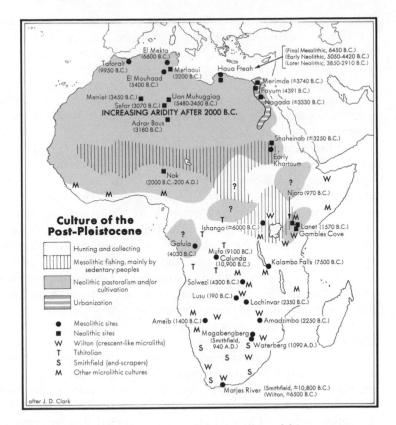

Culture of the Post-Pleistocene

(Final Mesolithic, 6450 B.C.)
(Early Neolithic, 5050-4420 B.C.)
(Later Neolithic, 3850-2910 B.C.)

El Mekta (6600 B.C.)
Taforalt (9950 B.C.)
Metlaoui (3200 B.C.)
El Mouhaad (5400 B.C.)
Haua Fteah
Meniet (3450 B.C.)
Uan Muhuggiag (5480-3450 B.C.)
Sefar (3070 B.C.)
Merimde (±3740 B.C.)
Fayum (4391 B.C.)
Nagada (±3330 B.C.)

INCREASING ARIDITY AFTER 2000 B.C.

Adrar Bous (3180 B.C.)
Shaheinab (±3250 B.C.)
Early Khartoum
Nok (2000 B.C.-200 A.D.)
Njoro (970 B.C.)
Ishango (±6000 B.C.)
Lanet (1570 B.C.)
Gambles Cove
Gafula (4030 B.C.)
Mufo (9100 B.C.)
Calunda (10,900 B.C.)
Kalambo Falls (7500 B.C.)
Solwezi (4300 B.C.)
Lusu (190 B.C.)
Lochinvar (2350 B.C.)
Ameib (1400 B.C.)
Amadzimba (2250 B.C.)
Magabengberg (Smithfield, 940 A.D.)
Waterberg (1090 A.D.)
Matjes River (Smithfield, ±10,800 B.C.)
(Wilton, ±6500 B.C.)

Hunting and collecting
Mesolithic fishing, mainly by sedentary peoples
Neolithic pastoralism and/or cultivation
Urbanization

● Mesolithic sites
■ Neolithic sites
W Wilton (crescent-like microliths)
T Tshitolian
S Smithfield (end-scrapers)
M Other microlithic cultures

after J. D. Clark

The bodies were pushed with their backs up against the wall, and big stones were placed over and around them. Traces of red ochre were found in the surrounding earth, having evidently been used to decorate the dead and prepare them, perhaps, for their journey into the next world.

Technologically, these Kenyan cave dwellers seem to have been exceptionally advanced. Their toolmakers fashioned highly serviceable implements from obsidian, a black volcanic glass that is easily flaked and gives a razor-sharp edge. Craftsmen worked in bone, leather, and wood. The people "mined" obsidian, and probably traded the precious stone over long distances. They were great fishermen and hunters, and they may have been among the first to use bows and arrows. Living a fairly stable life in the vicinity of Lakes Naivasha and Nakuru, they could also make good use of pottery. They had sufficient artistic taste and leisure to adorn their persons with ochre, beads, and pendants. (This so-called Upper Kenya Capsian culture dates from about 7000 years ago.)

In the meantime, hunting communities scattered over the Congo, Rhodesia, Zambia, western Kenya, Uganda, and also South Africa had acquired a tool kit known as Magosian, after a site in northeastern Uganda. Magosian artifacts date from ca. 15,000 to 8000 B.C., and their makers blended the newer stoneworking techniques with older traditions. The Magosian was not, however, as widespread as the Middle

Stone Age cultures proper. There was a period at the end of the Pleistocene when the climate appears to have deteriorated over vast parts of Africa. Hunting bands seem to have concentrated in the better-watered parts, such as large river valleys, and some migratory movements may have ensued. It is possible that settlers seeking new homes for themselves in the south may have spread cultural elements from the Kenya Capsian further afield and thereby helped to produce an economic revolution in the more backward areas, as well as introduce new ethnic strains to the Bush people of central and southern Africa.

The Later Stone Age witnessed the evolution of several more specialized cultures. Perhaps 7000 years ago the Magosian of eastern and southern Africa was succeeded by a number of regional variants. East, Central, and parts of South Africa witnessed the emergence of an industry known as Wilton. The Wilton people of what is now Rhodesia produced a magnificent rock art, with splendid lifelike paintings that are generally associated with grassland and open bush country. These representations tell us much more about the daily life of the people than one can normally infer from tools and skulls. There are paintings of masked dancers, of hunters disguised as animals, of ceremonies that conceivably depict rain rituals, marriage scenes, or burials of important people. Other pictures indicate that friendly meetings must have taken place between different bands, where arms and sandals were put down at some distance from the gathering place. There was probably some trade in salt, ornaments, obsidian, ochre, and similar commodities of small bulk and high value. Artists frequently illustrated tribesmen engaged in the chase of wild animals, bow and poisoned arrow now having become the Bushman's weapon par excellence. In addition, there are many scenes of war, which may have followed trespasses on hunting preserves, the abduction of women, murder, and other disputes. Some of this art probably had a magical purpose. Hunters may have imagined that by representing animals and using the right ritual they would catch the beasts; but whatever the object of this art, it stands out among the great aesthetic achievements of early mankind, and could have been produced only by people of considerable intelligence and taste, favored with a reasonable degree of leisure.

Again we must stress the speculative nature of this evidence. We can classify and analyze cave paintings, but we can never be certain of what they really meant. We cannot think like primitive hunters; we do not know what concepts they formulated about the universe. We can argue by process, by analogy, and by looking at the beliefs, say, of modern Australian aborigines, reasoning that like economic circumstances must have produced like ideological effects. Australian Bushman myths are certainly instructive; they reveal a considerable capacity for imaginative thought. "Black Fellows" have a complicated cosmology. According to their creed, there is an ordered universe including both the natural and the social order, which alike came into existence at a remote time called the "World Dawn." The order of nature and of society resulted from the doings and adventures of sacred "Dawn Beings," whose past activities explain present-day phenomena as diverse as their country's topographical features, the natural species, the social laws, customs, and usages. The cosmos is ruled by law. But whereas we think of natural laws as statements of what invariably happens, and of moral law as what ought to happen but is sometimes broken, the

Australian Bushman does not make this distinction. For him, men and women ought to observe the rules of behavior that were fixed for all times at the "World Dawn." The beliefs, myths, and rituals involved in the concept of these beings are very complex. The Australian aborigine's attitude is found among many other peoples, among Pueblo Indians in the American Southwest, Trobriand Islanders in the South Seas, Andamanese in the Bay of Bengal, Dogon tribesmen in West Africa, and so forth. They all affirm, in various ways, the age-old warranty of the natural and social order; they all insist on the importance of ritual to keep this order working.[6]

The ancient Bush folk of southern Africa may well have had similar beliefs. We can identify their technology and their hunting techniques. We can even argue that these formed the material "base" which required a given ideological "superstructure" to maintain their society. But even if we adopt the superstructure theory, we shall never be sure of what it was like, or of how and why it was raised upon the original base. Even today peoples with comparable ways of life may develop many different artistic or mythological superstructures, some simple, some highly elaborate. All these superstructures were obviously influenced by the realities of social life; but no one can say with confidence why they should differ so much from each other.

Already in prehistoric times, people with related economic techniques, for instance, would develop very dissimilar superstructures in the realm of art. The denser forests north of the Zambezi produced a culture where wood was probably used more extensively than among the Wilton peoples. This culture was named after the Nachikufu caves in Zambia, but also extended into Tanzania. Racially, the Nachikufu culture bearers may have been somewhat different from the Bush people to the south as they also sometimes show East African and Negro characteristics.[7] The Nachikufu people were also hunters and collectors; similarly they had fine painters; but these

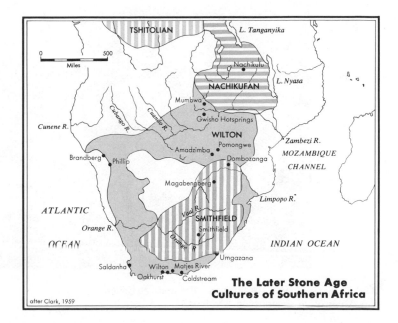

The Later Stone Age Cultures of Southern Africa

after Clark, 1959

expressed themselves in a totally different style, making extensive use of a schematic and non-naturalistic rock art, whose full meaning is now beyond our understanding.

Fortunately, however, we can sum up this chapter on a somewhat more certain note. During the enormous period under review, the various cultures of Africa began to undergo major changes. Generally speaking, the northern portion of the continent began to assume a decisive lead over the southern parts. River banks, sea coasts, and lake shores attained greater economic significance. Fishing provided man with a more reliable means of sustenance than he had been able to obtain by hunting and collecting alone, and allowed him to become a semi-permanent resident in regions where he had previously been no more than a casual visitor. A subsequent wet climatic phase, known in East Africa as the Makalian, which lasted from about 5500 B.C. to 2500 B.C., changed man's habitat over wide regions; the use of bone harpoons and similar implements spread throughout much of the southern Sahara, the Nile, and the central African lake area; the economic advances entailed by this revolution played their part in later enabling man to change from a stone-using to a metal-working economy.[8] Central, southern, and many parts of eastern Africa perfected existing hunting economies. Bushmen and related bands relied on the abundant vegetable and game resources of the tropical savannah and carried their stone age cultures to the utmost limits of perfection attainable with the existing means of production. For the first time in African history there was outstanding representational art. To the untutored observer, the Bushman paintings are still the products of "faceless men." We cannot distinguish one particular human countenance from any other on these rockside engravings. But the new art already displayed a character all of its own, and for the first time in the annals of Africa particular craftsmen were able to impose a recognizable individuality on some of their work.

Rock painting near Bulawayo, Rhodesia. (Courtesy the Ministry of Information, Rhodesia.)

NOTES

1. Clark, *The Prehistory of Southern Africa,* pp. 131–153; and Cole, *The Prehistory of East Africa,* pp. 15–182.

2. This method was worked out by American atomic scientists. It is based on making a count of the disintegration undergone by the radioactive isotopes of a carbon known as "Carbon 14." A regular percentage of "Carbon 14" is assimilated by living matter—say a tree trunk. But this assimilation ceases as soon as a specimen dies. At death, the radioactive carbon is broken down by the emission of radiation that proceeds at a known and constant rate. By this means, scientists can date with some accuracy the organic matter found in an archaeological deposit.

3. Genesis 9:12.

4. Cole, pp. 82–104, 183.

5. For the early history of the Sudan see Anthony J. Arkell, *A History of the Sudan from the Earliest Times to 1821* (London, 1955), pp. 22–29.

6. Gluckman, pp. 268–270.

7. Clark, *The Prehistory of Southern Africa,* pp. 217–280.

8. Clark, "Prehistoric Origins of African Culture," p. 178.

PART
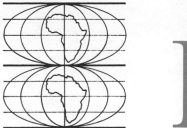## IV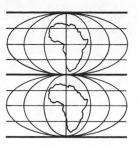

AFRICA
IN ANCIENT TIMES

Chapter 11

The Emergence of Agricultural Civilizations

THE FIRST FARMERS' FRONTIER

The world's first civilizations usually had their origins in the fertile valleys of great rivers and depended on flood control. The Yellow River basin was the cradle of Chinese thought and civility; the Sumerian city states of the Near East grew up round the Tigris and Euphrates; the Indus plain became the focus of the earliest great culture on the Indian subcontinent. In Africa, civilization first began on the banks of the Nile. The long, deep, narrow trench that forms the Nile Valley was created partly by geological action and partly by the river itself. The Nile indeed performed a double action. The waters first eroded the land; subsequently they deposited a rich layer of alluvium, thereby forming one of the most fertile land strips on our globe. Perhaps something like 7000 years ago this process caused large, continuous areas of land to emerge from oozing swamps and marshes, and thereby enabled man to occupy the valley floor.

One of the earliest cultural pioneers in the Nile Valley were the Negroid people of the Sudan, to whom we have referred in the previous chapter. Negro fishermen and hunters adopted sophisticated methods of working in stone. They also began to domesticate a few animals, including a species of dwarf goat still common in the southern Sudan today. There were, however, also other communities that were more technically advanced. An early settlement, for instance, disinterred at some distance south of Cairo, belonged to a people known to archaeologists as Badarians. Their culture was likewise basically "African," and they probably entered the country from the south and west, presumably because the Sahara was steadily drying up, and advancing sand drifts presented them with a new challenge. Physically, the Badarians appear to have been short, slender, delicately built men, with narrow heads, brown skins, and a trace of Negroid in their racial makeup. They fashioned arrowheads from stone, similiar to those found further south. They also manufactured finely made pots with characteristic rippling patterns, having possibly learned this art from the Negroid peoples of early Khartoum. Another characteristic object of early Egyptian culture was a mace head made of stone, developed perhaps from the sandstone grinders fashioned by the Khartoum folk for the purpose of working up red ochre. These grinders were eventually perforated, attached to sticks, and used as maces to crack enemy skulls in battle. The Badarians adorned their bodies with copper beads, the earliest metal objects found in Egypt. Their culture partly overlapped with, and was finally succeeded by, another, known as Nagada 1, whose remains have been found between Assiut and the First Cataract. This culture too was primarily "African," but, like its predecessor, must have been influenced by the Near East, where civilization was already in bloom.

Food production and the domestication of animals perhaps began in Egypt during the latter half of the sixth or during the early fifth millenium B.C. By this time, many Near Eastern communities were familiar with agriculture. There is little doubt that these skills were transmitted to the Nile Valley from beyond the Sinai Peninsula, which in turn may have been influenced by Sumerian civilization. Threatened by the encroaching desert, the Egyptians made the most of their ecological opportunities. They kept goats, pigs, sheep, and cattle. They grew wheat and barley; they learned how to store their grain and transport the surplus in boats along the river. The rich alluvial Nile soils, whose fertility was replenished by perennial floods, provided them with more food than their ancestors had ever known. The agricultural revolution resulted in an astonishing population explosion, and Africa's demographic balance of power turned decisively in Egypt's favor. The Mediterranean peoples of the northern Nile Valley—short, rather lightly built, with brown or red-brown skins and straight noses, speaking a Hamito-Semitic tongue related to modern Cushite—probably grew to be the most numerous ethnic group on the African continent.

Once having been introduced to the Nile Valley, the new agricultural economy spread with considerable speed. Egypt became the "funnel" transmitting most of the crops originating in southwest Asia to other parts of Africa, including crops such as lucerne, chick-pea, and onions, as well as tree fruits like apples, date palms, figs, mulberries, and many other plants of Middle Eastern, Mediterranean, or local Egyptian provenance.[1] By about 5000 B.C. the new economy had established a foothold in Cyrenaica, and perhaps between 3500 B.C. and 3000 B.C. it had penetrated into the great oases of the central Sahara. It spread along the Nile Valley, into Egypt's "southern frontier," and everywhere man's way of life was profoundly affected.[2] Barley and wheat, however, are winter rainfall crops and can rarely be grown in the tropics without irrigation. Few Negroid communities in the Sudan, therefore, adopted either wheat or barley, the staples of ancient Egypt, and neither crop ever occupied a place in the local economy comparable in importance to that of indigenous Sudanic cereals.[3]

The agricultural history of sub-Saharan Africa therefore took a different course, and scholars have arrived at several different explanations. One school of thought, represented by archaeologists such as Raymond Mauny, considers that agriculture may have spread to West Africa from the valley of the Nile some time during the second millenium before Christ. The basic discovery did not originate in West Africa. But once having understood the possibilities of *growing* rather than *gathering* food, Africans skilfully began to adapt new crops to new conditions. Botanists do not know when crops indigenous to West Africa, such as the various varieties of wild rice, sorghum and fonio began to be grown. But the knowledge of agriculture may have spread from Nubia and triggered off a local neolithic revolution when food production replaced hunting and food gathering.[4]

Other scholars put forward a more "Afro-centric" interpretation. They posit a culture lag between northern and sub-Saharan Africa. The abundant resources of the tropical savannah, according to this view, provided the small-scale neolithic hunting communities with all the food they needed, and gave them about the same living standards as did the crops and herds of settled farmers—and perhaps with less effort. Cereals and domestic flocks, in other words, were not essential to sustain life in the more favorable environment of tropical Africa as they were in Egypt. Hence there was a time lag in agricultural advance.

In due course, however, the peoples of the Sahara had to meet a new climatic challenge. The Sahara used to be a well-watered land, and geologists can prove the existence of great lakes where there is now desert. Between 7000 and 3000 B.C. parts of the Sahara began to dry out. This process may have been linked with the retreat of the northern European icecap and a general climatic shift throughout the Northern Hemisphere. Saharan stockmen may have contributed to the desiccation of their pastures by firing the steppe and by sporadic overgrazing. Whatever the reason, the lakes started to diminish in size. Many wells yielded less water or none at all. Game moved southward and there was less to eat. Hence many neolithic bands, and perhaps later on iron-using communities, began to trek into the Sudanic belt, where rains were more plentiful, and thereby initiated a great migration, which will be discussed in greater detail in a subsequent section. By the second millenium B.C., many communities had probably worked out simple kinds of "vegeculture" under conditions where the distinction between collecting vegetable food and gardening may have been tenuous. For instance, the Guinea forest yams may have supplemented the diet of more specialized hunter-food gatherers, used to prising open roots with weighted digging sticks. The techniques involved in cultivating yams may likewise have been more a continuation of the methods involved in the food collecting economies of the Later Stone Age.[5] We should not, therefore, think in terms of a single "revolution," but of a series of complex processes that entailed great regional variations. But whatever the details, cultivators developed a considerable number of crops: rice in Guinea, sorghum and pennisetum in the Sudan, teff and eleusine in those parts of Ethiopia where rice and barley would not grow. Experimentation may also have stimulated the cultivation on the forest fringes of the indigenous *Dioscoreas* and ensete. From about 2000 B.C. onwards, neolithic tool kits appear in West Africa, and their owners probably made their living as cultivators. Some of these people made their homes in northern Nigeria where their descendants, in the second half of the first millenium B.C., created an outstanding artistic tradition, known to archaeologists as the Nok culture. Neolithic industries penetrated into the Congo Basin, though this movement probably occurred during a more recent period.[6]

A third school of thought refuses to accept the concept of a time-lag. According to this school, West Africa was itself one of the world's four cradles of agriculture, as important in its way as the southwest Asian, the Middle Eastern, and the Middle American complexes to which mankind has owed its main agricultural innovations. The invention of agriculture is credited to the Mande, a Negroid people, who dwelt in the extreme western part of the Sudan, less than a thousand miles away from the shores of the Atlantic. The West African agricultural revolution, according to this interpretation, began some time between 5000 B.C. and 4000 B.C. During the following millenium, the knowledge of farming spread through the western Sudan to Ethiopia and Nubia, where the Sudanic and Egyptian streams of culture mingled.[7] Other scholars, arguing either from a botanical or a historical standpoint, agree that West Africans must have invented agriculture independently, but they date this great economic change much later, say about 1500 B.C., and favor the coastal or middle-Niger Negroes rather than the Mande.[8]

The subject remains highly speculative, and controversy is certain to continue for a long time. We may take it that the West African Negroes at some early date developed, borrowed, or adapted several cereals, including several types of millet, yams, an indigenous form of groundnut, oil palms, rice, and other plants.

In addition there were perhaps also a number of secondary centers of development, including possibly highland Ethiopia. Africa later benefited from agricultural innovations brought in from southeast Asia, including the banana and yams and other crops more suited to humid and forested areas. These were so important that they will be dealt with in a separate chapter concerned with the Indonesian impact.

The southern portion of Africa, on the other hand, continued in the old hunting and food gathering stage. There was probably enough wild food and game to support scattered bands in the accustomed fashion. Neolithic hunters were not well equipped for the task of clearing dense forests. His numbers remained small; his needs were slight. Southern Africa continued to use traditional methods of production until new immigrants arrived from the north and east and west, carrying improved techniques to wring a better living from the soil.

EGYPT AND THE SOUTHERN BORDER

Agriculture for the first time gave to the people of the Nile Valley a food surplus sufficiently large to maintain craftsmen, warriors, scribes, and traders—classes of men who had no need to labor in the field under the blazing sun, but who could devote themselves to their respective professions the year round. Artisans manufactured a distinctive pottery with red and white designs. Shipwrights built river boats with cabins, capable of long journeys down the Nile. Smiths learned how to work in copper, and even though stone tools continued in use for the commoner purposes for many centuries, the Egyptian economy had already passed far beyond the neolithic village farming phase by 3000 B.C. Merchants imported turquoise, obsidian, lapis lazuli, gold, and copper from far afield, and built up an exchange network that presumably extended into the Aegean, Palestine, and down to the Dead Sea. The introduction of these raw materials must in turn have given a stimulus to technical development in a country deficient in ores.

The Nile Valley also became a racial melting pot. Contacts with the Near East led to the diffusion of many new skills. Priests pondered over the meaning of the world, the will of the gods, and the life hereafter. The Nile Valley as a whole became more prosperous; its economy ceased to be based on villages alone, but grew to sufficient complexity to support country towns, with houses built of sun-dried brick.

Egypt was at first divided into numerous independent lordships. These coagulated into two principal kingdoms, but in about 3200 B.C. the country was unified under a common crown. According to Greek lore, King Menes became the first monarch of united Egypt and founded Memphis, near Cairo, as the capital of his empire. Memphis was a great, white-walled city, with large cemeteries, and royal burials became important matters of state. Craftsmen developed the arts of making stone bowls, furniture, jewelry, and copper tools to unsurpassed heights, and the king and great noblemen lived in magnificent luxury. The kingdom developed a highly controlled system of river irrigation that depended on a servile peasantry and on centralized political control over the Nile Valley. The state was administered in an autocratic fashion by officials who used hieroglyphs to keep their records. The monarch himself was regarded as godlike; an elaborate court ceremonial proclaimed his splendor in life; tombs and monuments spoke of his glory in death. The technical and administrative problems arising from the need to run this highly organized "hydraulic" economy probably gave a great impetus to sciences like astronomy and mathematics. Egyptian priests learned how to divide time into solar years, how to trace the course of the stars, and how to calculate the onset of the river floods. They solved complicated geometrical problems of a kind required in land surveys and related tasks. Above all, they applied the art of mathematics to large-scale buildings, and Egyptian engineers subsequently astonished posterity by the construction of great pyramids, erected by forced labor to serve as royal tombs.

Egyptian cultural influence extended southward into Nubia, where a brown-skinned or Mediterranean people, known to archaeologists as the "A Group," sustained a civilization based on copper. The A Group people, whose graves north and south of Wadi Halfa date from about 3100 B.C., imported pottery and tools from Egypt, and must have been contemporary with the First Dynasty.[9] The southern lands, far removed from the main centers of civilization, never paralleled the might of Egypt, however, and some time between 3100 and 3000 B.C. King Jer, the third monarch of the First Dynasty, conquered the country. A pictorial record survives to commemorate this early feat of Egyptian imperialism. It shows a boat with the high prow and vertical stem characteristic of the period; the corpses of the vanquished float on the river, and a captured chief, with his hands bound at his back, still holds a peculiarly curved bow popular among the Nubians.

Egypt's southern frontier acquired considerable economic importance as an exporter of gold, diorite, frankincense, ebony, leopard skins, and ivory. Nubia was also

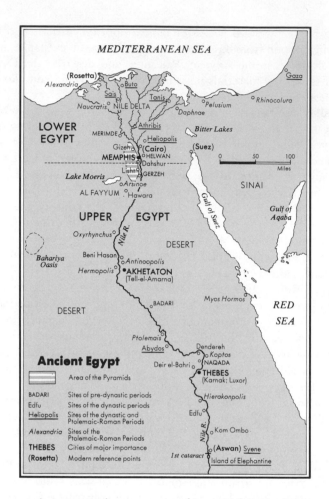

important as a transit route to the treasures of inner Africa and as a supply center of slaves, servants, and soldiers. Egyptian power in the south rested on a great fortified base at Elephantine, an island opposite the modern Aswan. Here a powerful Egyptian garrison held watch over the land, controlled immigration, guarded the local granite quarries, and protected the storehouses, where merchandise from the south accumulated. Later on, during the period of the Sixth Dynasty, the Egyptians managed to open the First Cataract to navigation, and trade—conducted both by boats and by donkey trains—probably reached considerable proportions. About 2235 B.C., Harkhuf, an Egyptian commander, even succeeded in bringing home, to the delight of his monarch, a "dancing dwarf," a Pygmy, having presumably managed to penetrate to the upper reaches of the Nile in Central Africa, where these little people dwelt.

The Egyptians appear to have exploited the conquered territory with considerable ruthlessness. Their own inscriptions boast of the number of prisoners captured and the great herds of cattle led away. No one knows how far this was the conventionally mendacious language of military communiqués, but the later graves of the A Group people seem to show evidence of impoverishment. Not surprisingly, therefore, when the Old Kingdom weakened, the Egyptian grip on Nubia was temporarily lost. Egypt, like so many other great riverine kingdoms, appears to have been subject to a long-term rhythm, where internal growth provided resources to be used for foreign conquest; prosperity in turn was succeeded by disorders. Perhaps the population outgrew the means of subsistence. There was social strife; powerful district governors made themselves independent of central control; foreign invaders made their way into the fertile valley, and the country's power contracted. Border provinces like Nubia were lost until a strong central authority once more unified the country, prosperity returned, and the cycle of growth and decay was repeated. The Kingdom again began to weaken; in Lower Egypt the aristocracy was dispossessed, and the delta was overrun by Semitic intruders.

After a long period of internal disorder, Egypt, however, recovered. By about 2060 B.C. the kingdom was once more united, and under the twelfth Dynasty the country re-embarked upon a vigorous policy of southward expansion and advanced the borders of the kingdom to the Second Cataract. The frontier was held with powerful fortifications of sun-dried mud bricks, whose military sophistication is equal to that of the most advanced creations of the European Middle Ages.[10]

But the Middle Kingdom in turn decayed; Egypt broke up into a number of smaller states, and in the end pastoral conquerors of Semitic origin, known as the Hyksos, invaded the country. By about 1730 B.C. the Hyksos, who introduced the horse and the two-wheeled fighting chariot into Egypt, had acquired control over the whole of the country. But during the preceding disorders, Egyptian control over Nubia once more disintegrated. The fortresses were abandoned, though Egyptian cultural influence continued, and Nubian princes adopted many cultural features from their northern neighbors. When the Egyptians of the reunited New Kingdom returned to the counterattack many generations later, they found a country which had already been conquered from the cultural point of view. The first kings of the eighteenth Dynasty occupied Nubia as far as the Second Cataract. Their successors completed their work by fixing the Egyptian border at Napata, just below the Fourth Cataract (about 1530 B.C.), and Nubia was thoroughly integrated with the rest of Egypt. The country was graced by walled cities, with splendid temples and tombs. River boats shipped the treasures of Nubia—ivory and ebony, carneole and turquoise, amethyst and ostrich feathers, monkeys, giraffes, and other luxury goods—back to Egypt. Above all, Nubia was also a gold producer, and the southern gold probably played a major part in establishing Egypt's position as a great power.

THE ANCIENT KINGDOM OF CUSH

The glory of Egypt did not last; by the beginning of the first millenium the country was once again in turmoil. The southern lands, known to the ancients as Cush, correspondingly increased in power, and by the eighth century B.C. the colonized conquered the colonizers. About 730 B.C. a combined Cushite military and naval force assaulted Memphis from the river, forced its way into the city, and then "Memphis was taken as [by] a flood of water, a multitude of people were slain therein, and brought as living captives to the place where his majesty was."[11]

The northerners, however, looked upon the Cushites as provincials rather than barbarians. The Cushites, often referred to as Ethiopians by ancient writers, had nothing to do with the people of modern Ethiopia. Their culture was blended of Egyptian and indigenous Sudanese elements. Racially the Cushites must have been very mixed, containing both the light-skinned stocks—comprising the Egyptians, the Berbers, Lybians, and other kindred Mediterranean races—and Negro people of a much darker hue. Egyptian artists carefully distinguished on their tomb and temple frescoes between their own ruddy or light brown people and the black or dark brown folk from the "Deep South"; the truly Negroid people in those days do not seem to have lived north of the Fifth or Sixth Cataract.

The new Cushite rulers of Egypt surrounded themselves with all the pomp and adoration traditionally due to the rulers of the land and controlled an empire stretching all the way from the Mediterranean to the borders of Ethiopia. They attempted to maintain the age-old Egyptian interest in the Near East, and intervened in Palestine for the purpose of checking the overweening might of Assyria. Egyptian power, however, was not sufficient for the purpose. Egypt was not truly united, and it was in vain that Isaiah warned the Jews against an Egyptian alliance. "And I will set the Egyptians against the Egyptians: and they shall fight every one against his brother, and every one against his neighbour; city against city, and kingdom against kingdom."[12] Egypt, the seer foretold, would crash into dust, and "so shall the king of Assyria lead away the Egyptian prisoners, and the Ethiopian captives, young and old, naked and barefoot, even with their buttocks uncovered, to the shame of Egypt."[13] The prophet proved right, and Assyria gained a series of overwhelming victories. The Egyptians were still in the bronze age. The Assyrians, on the other hand, knew how to smelt iron, and their military equipment was superior to the Egyptians'. The Assyrian armies possessed formidable discipline and cohesion; the Assyrian combination of weapons, mobility, and shock tactics proved invincible in open battle. Assyrian valor was backed by excellent siege techniques and a fine system of logistics. The victorious Assyrians crossed the Sinai desert with the help of a camel train, and in 671 B.C. they captured Memphis. In 666 the Assyrians drove the Cushites out of lower Egypt, pursued them up the Nile, and sacked Thebes. This, the last and most terrible of Assyrian visitations, did away with Cush's pretensions to be a great power. The existing Cushite dynasty continued to style themselves Kings of Upper and Lower Egypt in a grandiloquent fashion, but protocol no longer corresponded to power, and the days were gone when Cushite rulers could determine the fortunes of the Near East.

The kingdom nevertheless displayed remarkable longevity and remained in existence for nearly a millenium after the loss of Egypt. The capital at first remained at Napata where the Cushite rulers upheld the Egyptian heritage, complete with splendid architecture, an elaborate court ceremonial, and the worship of Egyptian gods. Massive pyramids continued to be built; but as time went on the country's luxury industries slowly began to decline. Masons, sculptors, jewelers, and faïence makers went on pursuing their respective crafts, but modern archaeological excavations seem to show a gradual degeneration of the craftsmen's skills. The people of Napata must also have faced the problem of soil erosion. They presumably accumulated huge herds of cattle, sheep, and goats; but pastoral farming on such a large scale would have caused overgrazing on both sides of the river; the soil would have lost its plant cover, so that the desert must have steadily encroached upon the fertile land. Some time in the sixth century B.C. the Cushites transferred their capital from Napata to Meroë in the south, thereby shifting their main center further towards Negro land.

The exact extent of the Cushitic kingdom is not known. Recent excavations suggest that it must have included what is now the central Sudan. It may have stretched south of the sudd (floating masses of weeds and reeds) near the mouth of the River Sobat, so that the Negroid element would have steadily increased in importance. The Assyrian military challenge at the same time probably stimulated technological progress, and in this respect the south was well-placed. Egypt proper had little iron, except in the vicinity of the First Cataract, and there was not enough wood to feed the furnaces. At Meroë, on the other hand, iron and timber were plentiful. After 500 B.C. the people of Meroë were renowned as iron workers, and became "the Birmingham of the ancient world."[14]

Meroë also has other advantages. It lies at the northern edge of the annual rainfall belt, and receives much more precipitation than the drier regions to the north. In addition, the so-called "island of Meroë" benefits from the floods of the Nile River to the west, and the Atbara, a tributary of the Nile to the east, so that farmers found better land and pastures. Meroë stood on the river bank near a crossing point on the

The ruins of Meroë: general view of the central temple. (Courtesy of the Oriental Institute, University of Chicago.)

Nile; caravans were able to carry trade both to the west and to the east, following the Atbara River into the Abyssinian highlands and thence to the Indian Ocean.[15]

For many centuries Meroë continued in great splendor, and its magnificent Sun Temple, adorned with glazed tiles and magnificent representations of Meroitic military victories, was famous throughout the ancient world. Meroë did business with Egypt, with the other lands adjoining the Red Sea, and, indirectly, even with India. The people developed a cursive script of their own, in place of the Egyptian hieroglyphs, and probably exerted a profound cultural influence on their less advanced neighbors. According to some scholars, whose theories will be discussed in a subsequent section, it was from Meroë that the art of working iron was diffused to the Negroid communities of the south and west.

But whatever the precise relationship between Meroë and other African states, Meroitic civilization was syncretic in character, blending Egyptian and Negroid strains. Scholars are not yet able to decipher the inscriptions found at Meroë, and until they do much of the country's history is bound to remain obscure. But the inhabitants of Meroë were (in all probability) essentially an African people. Their styles, walls, carvings, and paintings were strongly influenced by Egyptian artists, but they represented African more than Mediterranean strains. The Egyptians depicted the Cushites with dark skins, and sometimes drew the Cushites' hair in a fashion different from that used for their own Egyptian fellow citizens. The Cushites, for their part, showed their queens as plump ladies, quite different from the slender women portrayed by the Egyptians. The great statues of the kings found at Jebel Barkal, although Egyptian in style, display African features. Their language is believed to have been an African tongue, and scholars are trying to find a modern African idiom which might be a key to the understanding of Meroitic.

The ruins of Meroë cover a wide area, and at the height of its prosperity it must have been a town of great size. It lies close to the Nile, and scholars have found the ruins of a stone quay where barges plying their trade along the river were once tied up. To the east of the town a ridge of low sandstone hills encircles the plain, and on its slopes a row of pyramids stands out sharply against the blown sand. Only a small part of Meroë has been excavated, but archaeologists have dug out temples, two palaces, and an elaborate, if rather rough, copy of a Roman swimming bath.

The ordinary houses were all built in a style that still survives, for instance, in the northern part of the Sudan. The home centers on an open courtyard surrounded by a series of rooms. Entrance to the house is by a single door set in the outside wall. The two palaces were built in the same fashion, but the plan of the chambers was, of course, much more complicated, and one of them had a big veranda.

Scholars have found a great deal of ordinary household wares—grindstones, pottery, baskets, simple stone tools and metal knives, axeheads, swords, and razors. The housewife's cooking pots, beer pots, bowls, and basins were heavy and often handmade—perhaps by the women of the house. Pots of this kind are still in use with much the same type of decoration and finish, and they are typically African.

The finer pottery was of a high standard, wheelmade, of a fine, hard paste, and decorated with a variety of designs. The wealthier citizens of Meroë imported luxury wares from abroad, and Meroitic art was subsequently influenced by Greek and

The ruins of Meroë: Temple A from the northwest.
(Courtesy of the Oriental Institute, University of Chicago.)

Roman models. The Meroites were themselves famed as metal workers; their artifacts show all the craft of the Mediterranean world, but their designs bear the character of Africa.

One of the most interesting features of Cushite culture is the way in which the people took what they found useful from other civilizations, yet never submerged their own character. The Cushites may have learned the art of building tanks and reservoirs from the Arabs, though there is no direct evidence that this was so. Indian influence is seen perhaps in the three-headed lion god, Apedemak, and in the picture of a Meroitic king riding an elephant. Egyptian thought shaped Cushite religion, and the Cushites built their temples and pyramids in the Egyptian style.[16]

As the centuries passed, the civilization of Cush benefited from extensive riverine flooding, whereas the Nubians had to employ much ingenuity in making do with more restricted water supplies. There is much evidence that from about 100 B.C. onward, rainfall and the Nile floods may have diminished. Meroë may also have experienced that deadly cycle familiar to so many pastoral civilizations. Prosperity occasioned a great increase in cattle and goats, for wealth in the Sudan meant flocks and herds. Overgrazing led to the destruction of the tree and grass cover, and soil was washed or blown away. Excavations indicate that erosion of ancient settlement sites seems to have become serious from about A.D. 100. Relations with the outside world became fewer, and this retrogression must have been further influenced by the decline of Egypt. The prosperity experienced in the Nile Valley in the first century of Roman rule began to wane from the second century A.D. The corn tributes paid to Rome speeded the general impoverishment. Depopulation of villages became widespread in the third century: irrigation canals fell into disrepair; starving peasants took to brigandage. There were riots, especially in Alexandria, and tribesmen raided Upper Egypt. The greatness of Meroë crumbled; wealth decayed, and the last kings of Meroë were buried under miserable little red-brick copies of the splendid stone pyramids of earlier times, fitting symbols of the new Sudanic "dark age."[17]

NOTES

1. For a more complete list see George Peter Murdock, *Africa: Its Peoples and Their Culture History* (New York, 1959), pp. 102–103.

2. See John Desmond Clark, "The Spread of Food Production in Sub-Saharan Africa," *Journal of African History,* vol. 3, no. 2 (1962), pp. 211–228.

3. Murdock, p. 67.

4. Merrick Posnansky, "The Origins of Agriculture and Iron-Working in Southern Africa," in Merrick Posnansky, ed., *Prelude to East African History: A Collection of Papers given at the First East African Vacation School in Pre-European African History and Archaeology in December 1962* (London, 1966), pp. 82–94.

5. Posnansky, p. 84.

6. John Desmond Clark, "The Prehistoric Origins of African Culture," *Journal of African History,* vol. 5, no. 2 (1964), p. 181.

7. Murdock, pp. 64–71.

8. John Donnelly Fage, "Anthropology, Botany and the History of Africa," *Journal of African History,* vol. 2, no. 2 (1961), pp. 302–304.

9. Anthony J. Arkell, *A History of the Sudan from the Earliest Times to 1821* (London, 1955), p. 37.

10. Georg Gerster, *Nubien: Goldland am Nil* (Zurich, 1964), pp. 41–44.

11. Quoted by Basil Davidson, *The African Past: Chronicles from Antiquity to Modern Times* (London, 1964), p. 52, from J. H. Breasted, *Ancient Records of Egypt* (Chicago, 1906), vol. 4, para. 861.

12. Isaiah 19:2.

13. Isaiah 20:4.

14. Arkell, pp. 138–173.

15. Margaret Shinnie, *Ancient African Kingdoms* (New York, 1965), pp. 26–27.

16. See Shinnie, pp. 23–42.

17. Arkell, pp. 136, 166–168.

Chapter 12

Cultural Syncretism
in North and East Africa

EARLY SEMITIC CONTACTS: SABAEANS, PHOENICIANS, AND CARTHAGINIANS

The Red Sea splits Arabia from Africa, but from ancient times the long, narrow water moat has been more a link than a divide between the two land masses. Southern Arabia is favored with terraces, hills, and mountains that attract the monsoon rains and thereby lighten the farmer's lot. The southern part of the peninsula, known to the ancients as Arabia Felix or "Happy Arabia," developed into an important center of civilization from the end of the second millenium B.C. There were reservoirs and irrigation works; there were prosperous towns, and merchants conducted an extensive overseas trade in frankincense, gold, spices, precious stones, and similar commodities. Southern Arabia became an emporium for the far-flung commerce between the Mediterranean, East Africa, and Western India. The famous Queen of Sheba who visited King Solomon "with a very great train, with camels that bore spices, and very much gold, and precious stones,"[1] probably came from this part of Arabia.

The peoples of this region, known as the Sabaeans, soon gained a foothold on the other side of the Red Sea, where the country in many ways resembled their own. The newcomers first established themselves on the arid coast, then ascended the foothills, and finally gained the inland plateau, where the monsoons brought rain, the soil was fertile, and land plentiful. Immigration across the Red Sea may have begun some time from the seventh century B.C. onward. It continued for generations, and left a profound mark on the new country. The settlers imported camels; they brought improved techniques of building houses and reservoirs, new crops like wheat and barley; it may also have been the new settlers who introduced to Ethiopia the practice

147

of milking animals. The colonists also introduced more elaborate handicrafts as well as the art of writing, and they left numerous stone inscriptions in their native Sabaean, a Semitic tongue. In time they intermingled with the local Cushitic population, who were probably themselves partly of Caucasian stock. Political ties with the Arabian motherland weakened, and by the last two centuries B.C. the African settlements seem to have attained independence. The people of Axum apparently gained predominance over those of Akkele Gyzay, and by the first century A.D. the Axumite kingdom (situated in the northern portion of what is now Ethiopia) stood out as a substantial power.[2]

The Semitic peoples of the Mediterranean also had links with northeast Africa. Solomon (ca. 970–931 B.C.) had an outlet to the Red Sea, and made judicious use of his geographical opportunities by a partnership with Hiram, ruler of Tyre, the great Phoenician maritime center in what is now southern Lebanon. "And King Solomon made a navy of ships in Ezion-geber, which is beside Eloth, on the shore of the Red Sea, in the land of Edom. And Hiram sent in the navy his servants, shipmen that had knowledge of the sea, with the servants of Solomon. And they came to Ophir [situated probably in the southern portion of the Red Sea], and fetched from thence gold, four hundred and twenty talents, and brought it to King Solomon."[3] Many Jews settled in Southern Arabia, and Jewish colonists probably made their way from there to northeast Africa, in company with non-Jewish emigrants. It is not clear whether they established separate Jewish colonies on Ethiopian soil, or whether they dispersed over a wider area, intermingling with their Arabian neighbors. The widespread character of Hebraic influence and practice in Abyssinia, however, favors the latter alternative.[4] In addition, Jewish pioneers may also have made their way southward, by land from Egypt. Egypt had an important Jewish diaspora; from there Jews penetrated into Upper Egypt, Nubia, and possibly beyond, for there is reference in the Bible to exiles "from beyond the rivers of Ethiopia."[5]

The foremost traders and navigators of antiquity, however, were the Phoenicians living on the coast of the country now known as Lebanon. Their vessels, with boards fashioned from fir trees, masts made of Lebanon cedars, and magnificent sails dyed in blue and purple, were a familiar sight throughout the Mediterranean, the Red Sea, and beyond. Herodotus, the father of historiography, records that about 600 B.C. Necho, the king of Egypt, sent out a fleet manned by Phoenicians to explore the southern ocean. The ships skirted the coast of the Red Sea, and when autumn came the sailors went ashore, sowed a tract of land, and waited until the grain became ripe. Then they slowly continued on their way in this fashion, and after the third year they passed through the Strait of Gibraltar and made good the return to Egypt by way of the Mediterranean. Herodotus' account may well be based on fact. The historian states with much scepticism that the sailors claimed to have had the sun on their right hand in sailing around "Libya." But if the voyagers had doubled the Cape of Good Hope, they would indeed have had the sun on their right hand as they proceeded westward round the southern shore.[6] The Phoenicians would thus have been the first to circumnavigate Africa, proving thereby that the huge landmass did not stretch on without limit to the ends of the world, but only formed a vast continental "island."[7] Whether the story is true or not, the Phoenicians apparently never tried to repeat the exploit, for the Stone Age peoples of southern Africa were too scanty in number and too backward in technology to participate in international trade and thereby justify the outlay involved in such an expedition.

Carthage, the great Phoenician colony situated on the northern shore of what is now Tunisia, subsequently became the heir to Phoenician seapower and built up a great maritime empire. Carthaginians set up commerical posts on the Atlantic shore of Morocco. Some time between 500 and 470 B.C. Hanno, a Carthaginian admiral, supposedly sailed southward with a great fleet and continued on his way until his provisions gave out. No one is quite certain how far he got. Some say that he reached the Senegal River or even the Gulf of Guinea. But more recent authorities maintain that he is unlikely to have got beyond Cape Yubi, off the Canary Islands, if his journey took place at all.[8] The Carthaginians did, however, do a certain amount of business with the people of the Atlantic coast. Herodotus gives a convincing description of the "silent trade," a method that avoided personal contact. The Carthaginians would go ashore, unload their goods, and arrange them in neat little piles. Then they would return to their boats and make smoke signals. The indigenous people then came to the beach and put a certain quantity of gold on the ground. They would then retreat and give the Carthaginians a chance to inspect the gold. If the sailors were satisfied with the deposit, they would collect the precious metal and hoist anchor. If not, they left the gold on the ground and waited until the local people had brought some more. There seemed to be trust and honesty between the two partners.[9] Neither side apparently attempted to cheat, for that would have smashed the foundations of this trade in precious metals.

Finally there were some tenuous links between the middle portion of North Africa and the lands beyond the Sahara. According to Herodotus, a wild crew of high-born young Nasamonians (originating probably from the Siwa oasis in the Libyan Desert) indulged in all manner of daredeviltry and cast lots for five of their number to explore the southern desert and to travel further than any man before them. They made their way through the inhabited parts of Libya, penetrated the Sahara, and apparently reached the savannah belt. Here the party was captured by black-skinned, small-statured people who spoke an unintelligible language. The prisoners were led across extensive marshes and finally to a town situated by a great river running from east to west and containing many crocodiles. The Nasamonians finally got away, avowing that their captors belonged to a nation of sorcerers. Ancient geographers assumed that the young explorers must have reached the Nile. But in all probability the water course flowing from east to west would have been the Niger, and the Nasamonians may have been the first recorded travelers to surmount the Sahara. But the savannah people probably had not yet reached a sufficient level of economic development to build up a major export industry overland.

Merchants, moreover, still faced enormous transport difficulties. Long-distance traffic at first depended on the strong backs of men and donkeys. A major innovation came with the introduction of the camel, which could carry greater loads and could travel much further through thirsty country than porters or jackasses.[10] Camels may have come to North Africa from Arabia via Egypt; the evidence is not clear. The beasts were first mentioned in literature in an account of a battle at Thapsus in 46 B.C.,

when the Romans captured twenty-two of these valuable animals from a local potentate.[11] The use of the camel spread widely throughout North Africa, and played an
important part in facilitating inland commerce by putting the desert into more effective touch with the main centers of civilization. But communications with the lands
beyond the Sahara remained most tenuous. Pliny the Elder, a Roman writer who died
about A.D. 79, had some vague notions about West African geography, but to him
the inhabitants of these distant regions remained a mysterious people, fit subjects for
the Latin equivalent of science fiction. The Troglodytae supposedly lived in holes in
the ground, ate snakes, and uttered only squeaking noises. The Atlantes were described as having lost every semblance of humanity, and were said to hurl the most
dreadful imprecations against the rising and the setting sun. The Himantopodes
walked like serpents; the Blemmyae had no heads.[12]

Communications between the Mediterranean and the savannah lands were probably slight. We do not know when relations between the peoples of North Africa and
those of the Sudan began. Some believe that Berbers from North Africa were in touch
with the inland people across the Sahara between 3000 and 2000 B.C., and that the
Carthaginians later imported ivory, ostrich feathers, gold, and slaves from Negro
land. Others date regular commerce between North Africa and the African "middle
belt" much later, perhaps from the tenth century B.C. onward.[13] But whatever the
extent and origin of the earliest trans-Saharan trade, it could not have been very
extensive. The Romans themselves knew little about the more distant "Ethiopians,"
and for centuries to come the impact of the Mediterranean world on the Sudanic belt
probably had but small significance.

ROME, AXUM, AND THE FALL OF MEROË

Carthage broke against the might of Rome in 146 B.C. when the great city was
captured and wiped out. Latin-speaking colonists settled in North Africa, and the
southern littoral of the Mediterranean became one of the most flourishing portions
of the empire. Roman settlement was most dense in the province known as *Africa
Proconsularis,* now largely coextensive with the northern portion of Tunisia. (In
subsequent ages the word "Africa" came to denote the continent as a whole.) In
addition, many Roman settlers made their homes in the northeastern portion of what
is now Algeria. To the west, Berber tribesmen held their own in isolated mountain
strongholds, and Roman colonization was largely confined to the coastal plain. Further to the east lay Cyrenaica, a valuable possession initially occupied by Greek
immigrants, but again effective Roman occupation was largely confined to the regions
adjacent to the Mediterranean shore. In addition, Egypt fell under Roman sway and
became one of the most important dependencies of the empire, vital to Rome for its
grain exports. Roman might extended to the First Cataract at Aswan and beyond; the
province of Dodekaschinus formed a buffer zone against the fierce tribes of the
interior. In 61 A.D. the Emperor Nero dispatched an expedition southward to find
the sources of the Nile. The Roman explorers got to the sudd on the White Nile but
could not pass the swampy wilderness. Their venture marked Rome's southernmost

penetration into the African interior; another eighteen hundred years were to pass until Europeans once again managed to reach the papyrus thickets of the upper Nile. The Romans held on to their southern marches for something like two centuries, but in the course of the third century A.D. their grip began to relax.

Egypt was in a state of chronic unrest. The southerners, known to the Romans as Blemmyae, acquired dromedaries, and thereby greatly added to the striking power and mobility of their forces. In addition, climatic changes may have reduced the fertility of the nomads' pasture lands and made the attractions of the Nile Valley irresistible. Shortly after 270 A.D., Blemmyae raiders wasted much of upper Egypt, and after much fighting the Romans were forced to withdraw from the extreme south.

The Romans also occupied a powerful position in the northern portion of the Red Sea. Graeco-Roman vessels traded far to the south, and the *Periplus of the Erythrean Sea,* a commercial handbook dating from the first or early second century A.D., still provides an interesting description of contemporary conditions on the East African coast. The ship captains of antiquity were familiar with Somaliland, whose shores were lined with "emporia," apparently maritime stations with a fixed commercial organization and regular customs dues. Down the Red Sea came Graeco-Roman vessels loaded with dyed cloth and tunics, copper, tin, worked silver, wine, drinking cups, and other luxury goods. On their return journey they carried cinnamon, incense, fragrant gums, tortoise shells, ivory, and slaves. The emporia also handled trade from Western India, including cotton cloth and girdles, grain, oil, sugar, and ghee (butter).

Greek merchants also traded with the coasts of what are now Kenya and Tanzania. Rhapta, a port somewhere on the Tanzania coast, imported iron weapons and metal implements in exchange for ivory. Business here was apparently organized by Arab merchants, subject to a southern Arabian king, who farmed out the commerce to the men of Mocha. The people of Rhapta were probably of mixed origin, blended of Mediterranean and other racial elements. They were ruled by their own chiefs,

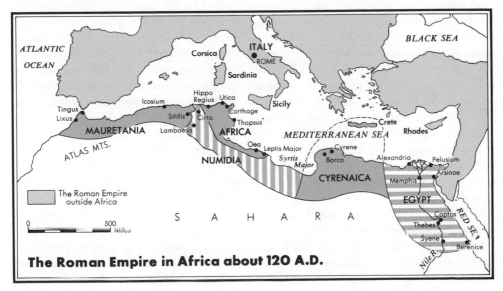

The Roman Empire in Africa about 120 A.D.

subject to Charibael, a Southern Arabian potentate, and they had a reputation as seafarers and pirates.

Graeco-Roman trade with the south continued to expand. Gervase Mathew, an authority on the East African coast, hazards that Greek vessels, having first pressed round Cape Guardafui into the Indian Ocean during the second century B.C., made further progress in the first century A.D. Greek navigators now began to understand and utilize the monsoon winds and were able to make regular trips to India. Until the coming of steam power, the monsoon conditioned the maritime trade of East Africa, and from the first to the early nineteenth century the East African coast shared in each changing rhythm of the Indian Ocean trade.

In addition, Graeco-Roman merchants strengthened their hold on the East African commerce, and by the second century A.D. the economically developed northern zone stretched continuously south toward the Kenya border. Rhapta developed into an independent state of considerable importance, maintaining contacts with less civilized people far to the south and far inland. Graeco-Roman sailors believed that further to the south there lived "man-eating Ethiopians." They also described a great snow mountain lying inland from Rhapta; this surely was Mount Kilimanjaro.[14]

One of the main beneficiaries of Graeco-Roman trade was the kingdom of Axum, which we have mentioned in the previous section. By the first century A.D., Axum was exporting ivory to the Roman Empire, and was ruled—according to the *Periplus of the Erythrean Sea*—by Zoscales, "a covetous and grasping man, but otherwise noble and imbued with a Greek education."[15] About 328 A.D. Constantine the Great made the momentous decision to transfer the Roman capital from Rome to Constantinople. The move symbolized the shift of power and prosperity from the western to the eastern half of the Mediterranean, and Byzantium continued its profitable trade relations with the east. Axum's prestige grew to such an extent that in 336 the Emperor decreed that Axumities should be treated as if they were Roman subjects. The alliance between Rome and Axum was sealed by the Axumites' acceptance of Christianity. According to ancient sources, Frumentius, a young Roman, attained high office in the Axumite kingdom. "While . . . Frumentius held the reins of government in his hands, God stirred up his heart and he began to search out with care those of the Roman merchants who were Christians and to give them great influence and to urge them to establish in various places conventicles to which they might resort for prayer in the Roman manner. He himself, moreover, did the same and so encouraged the others, attracting them with his favor and his benefits, providing them with whatever was needed, supplying sites for buildings and other necessaries, and in every way promoting the growth of the seeds of Christianity in the country. . . . "[16] About the middle of the fourth century Christianity in its Monophysite[17] form became the state religion in Axum. As it already was in the Roman Empire, commercial contacts between the two states were strengthened by religious and cultural links. The Axumite Church centered on a great number of monasteries, which played a vital role in the development of Ethiopian civilization. Monks served the king as scribes, scholars, and political advisers; monks converted the pagans and thereby helped to extend and unify the kingdom. Monks developed the Ge'ez language as the essential vehicle of ancient Ethiopian literature and ecclesiastical culture. The monasteries originally depended on neighboring villages for food and drink. But as the monasteries grew in numbers, and as they attracted more inmates, the local resources became inadequate. Hence the Church received many great estates, including numerous villages. The Church thus became a powerful landowner; it enjoyed all manner of privileges, and its favored position was liable to occasion clashes with the secular authorities. The Church, on the other hand, not only supplied the kingdom with indispensable spiritual and intellectual support, but also provided charity to the poor and a haven for those who wished to retire from the ordinary cares of the world.[18]

Axum prospered mightily, and during the fourth century its wealth grew to such an extent that the kingdom was able to put a gold coinage into circulation. The kingdom's military power matched its commercial wealth, and the country considerably extended its borders.

The ancient kingdom of Meroë by this time was no longer a match for its Abyssinian rival. Egypt, Meroë's economic hinterland, had long been in economic and political decay. Meroë seems to have shared in the ruin of its main trading partner, and by the fourth century Meroë was but a shadow of its former self. In the end the rulers of Axum delivered the death blow. About 325 A.D. an Axumite army took the field. According to Azana, the Axumite king, his forces burned the enemy's towns, destroyed the Meroitic granaries, and brought back great quantities of booty, including food, copper, and iron. The royal family of Meroë probably fled west of the Nile to northern Kordofan and thence to northern Darfur, where the influence of Cush remained strong and in all likelihood exerted a profound cultural influence on many communities dwelling further to the west. The Nubians beyond the Nile continued to call themselves "people of Cush," and it is possible that the institution of divine kingship at Darfur may have owed its origins to Meroitic precepts.[19]

AXUM AND NUBIA

During the fourth century Axum stood at the height of its power. The country was a cultural melting pot where Byzantine, Coptic Egyptian, Jewish, Southern Arabian, and Syrian elements all blended with indigenous traditions. This cultural syncretism is reflected in the nature of the inscriptions dating from this period. Some are in the Ethiopian language and characters; others are in Ethiopian written in South Arabian letters, or again in Greek language and Greek script. Out of these influences, the Axumites fashioned a characteristic civilization of their own. This found expression in the indigenous development of writing, which incorporated vowels into the main body of consonants.

The foremost literary achievement of the Axumite period was the translation of the Bible. The work owed its completion to Syrian monks who had come to Axum in order to escape the Byzantine persecution of followers of the Monophysite creed. The Syrian scholars used Ge'ez, an indigenous tongue, but the Syrian imprint became a characteristic part of Ethiopia's cultural heritage. The translation of the Bible comprised not only the canonical and apocryphal books but also an additional body of literature that was accepted as genuine in Abyssinia and that still remains of great interest to Biblical scholars. The Christian religion became the focus of all literary creation, and Biblical writing left a profound imprint on the nation's thought.

Ethiopian literature also absorbed other Greek productions of this period, including a monastic book of rules that was expanded to cover the special contingencies of monastic life in Ethiopia, a collection of Christological writings, and the *Physiologus,* a handbook on natural history liberally spiced with homiletics. These literary works were translations, but they were also more than that. Foreign works were transformed by the spirit of Christian Abyssinia in such a way as to achieve an intellectual autonomy of their own. Some of them, such as the *Fetha Nagast* ("Legislation of Kings"), was subject to so much local rethinking that the final results bore little resemblance to the original.

The monarchs of Axum wielded considerable power. In the heyday of their power they would have looked down with contempt on the Anglo-Saxon princelings who governed England in the sixth century A.D. Axum traded with Byzantium, Persia, India, and Ceylon. Her markets, stocked with gems, gold, spices, and ivory, attracted merchants from many different countries who publicized Axum's splendor abroad. Abyssinian builders constructed a magnificent royal palace, strengthened by four corner towers and adorned with statues in the form of unicorns. They also put up impressive obelisks, some of them more than 100 feet in height. Such enterprises must have required large numbers of workmen and also considerable technical and administrative resources. In addition, the Axumites were famed for their martial prowess. In the sixth century an Axumite expeditionary force crushed a Judaized kingdom in Southern Arabia, and the Ethiopians for a time extended their influence to the Arabian shores of the Red Sea.

Axum, however, was not strong enough to hold on to a far-flung empire beyond the sea. The Axumite governor in Southern Arabia apparently made himself independent of his sovereign, and Christian rule in the area came to an end when the Persians occupied the country at the close of the sixth century. The Persian conquest probably disrupted maritime communications between Axum, Southern Arabia, and Byzantium, and the subsequent expansion of Islam—to which we shall refer in another section—deepened the isolation of Axum. Trade with Arabia and Byzantium declined. The Axumites were increasingly thrown on their own resources. Repulsed from the Red Sea, they turned southward and carried their speech, culture, and religion to the central and southern portions of the Abyssinian highlands. The country's political center of gravity shifted towards Amhara, Lasta, and finally Shoa. Semitic influence weakened; Cushite elements reasserted themselves, and Axum—like Meroë before it—became increasingly African in complexion.[20]

Greek clergymen, architects, administrators, and artists also exercised a profound influence on the northern Sudan. In the sixth century, Nobatia, a kingdom situated probably between the Second and Third Cataract, was converted to Christianity in its Monophysite form. To the south lay Mukurra or Makuria, which in 569 A.D. adopted Orthodox Christianity. A third Christian kingdom, known as Alodia, with its capital at Soba near Khartoum, stretched southwards into the valleys of the Blue and the White Nile.

These countries maintained a syncretic civilization, blending Byzantine with Me-

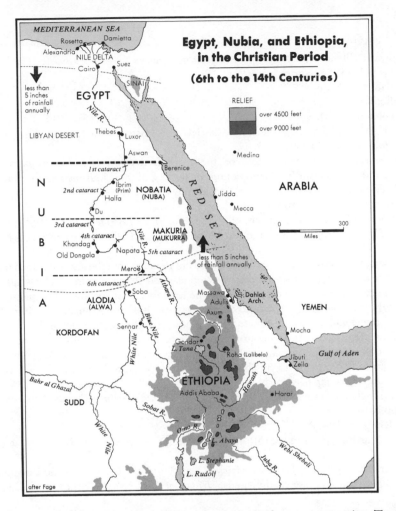

roitic traditions, and for a time experienced a period of great prosperity. Towns and villages lined the banks of the Nile. A city such as Ikhmindi, now in ruins, still affords evidence of impressive town planning; there were mighty fortifications, covered streets, and a splendid basilica that owed its inspiration to Byzantine precepts. Administration was patterned on the Byzantine example; senior civil servants bore Byzantine titles. There was a vigorous ecclesiastical life, and many pagan temples were turned into monasteries. Architects used sun-baked bricks, which were whitewashed and adorned with colorful murals.[21]

The Nubians, moreover, traded not only with Egypt and Byzantium, but also westward. Their commerce may have extended through the Sudan as far as West Africa, which seems indicated by the way in which Byzantine bronze objects from Egypt found indigenous imitators as far away as Ghana.[22] Nubia and Ethiopia, in other words, may have become important centers of cultural diffusion, and thereby exercised a considerable influence on the far interior in Negro Africa.

NOTES

1. I Kings 10:1.

2. Edward Ullendorf, *The Ethiopians: An Introduction to the Country and the People* (London, 1960), pp. 47–53. See also Murdock, p. 183.

3. I Kings 9:26–28.

4. Ullendorf, p. 52.

5. Zephaniah 3:10.

6. C. K. Meek, "The Niger and the Classics: The History of a Name," *Journal of African History,* vol. 1, no. 1 (1960), p. 3.

7. Some scholars doubt the story on the grounds that winds and currents would have prevented the Phoenicians from completing the last leg of their journey with the ships at their disposal. The seafarers could, however, conceivably have completed the journey through what is now Mauritania and Morocco by land.

8. Catherine Coquery-Vidrovitch, ed., *La Découverte de l'Afrique* (Paris, 1965), pp. 24–28.

9. *The History of Herodotus,* George Rawlinson, trans., and Manuel Komroff, ed. (New York, 1934), p. 259.

10. The camel was used by Assyrians, Arabs, and Persians, but the ancient Egyptians disliked these beasts so much that they hardly ever represented them in paintings or sculpture. The camel was acclimatized in Egypt long before the time of Christ and was subsequently adopted by the Berbers of the desert, who used camel cavalry to fight the Romans. The Berbers spread the use of the camel across the Sahara. The camel proved more adaptable than the horse or any form of wheeled transport, because camels could go wherever wells were found. Neither camels, horses, or carts, however, could make their way into tropical forest beyond the savannah. The horse first came to Egypt about 1500 B.C. It spread to Libya sometime around 1200 B.C., and later to other parts of North Africa.

11. Diedrich Westermann, *Geschichte Afrikas: Staatenbildungen südlich der Sahara* (Cologne, 1952), pp. 61–62.

12. Meek, pp. 10–12.

13. See Murdock, p. 44 and p. 150; and Fage, *An Introduction to the History of West Africa,* p. 6.

14. Gervase Mathew, "The East African Coast Until the Coming of the Portuguese," in Roland Oliver and Gervase Mathew, eds., *History of East Africa* (Oxford, 1963), vol. 1, pp. 94–98.

15. A. H. M. Jones and Elizabeth Monroe, *A History of Ethiopia* (Oxford, 1955), p. 22.

16. Quoted from Rufinus by Jones and Monroe, pp. 26–27.

17. The Monophysites taught that Jesus had but one divine nature (not a human and a divine nature), a heresy of the fourth, fifth, and sixth centuries. Its doctrines dominated the Coptic Church of Egypt and of Ethiopia.

18. Bairu Tafla, "The Establishment of the Ethiopian Church," *Tarikh,* vol. 2, no. 1 (1967), pp. 28–42.

19. Arkell, pp. 170–173.

20. Ullendorf, pp. 54–59.

21. Gerster, pp. 122–126.

22. Arkell, pp. 180–185.

Chapter 13

West Africa
and the Savannah

THE EARLY WEST AFRICAN NEGROES

In a previous chapter, we have referred to the forward movement of the farmer's frontier into West Africa. We have spoken of the part played by Negro agriculturists in the economic history of this region, and we have mentioned their early contacts with North Africa and the civilizations of the Nile.

Meroë's most important legacy to its African neighbors was probably the use of iron. Our knowledge of the way in which iron working spread in Africa is mostly circumstantial. But many consider that the knowledge of iron working methods was carried from Meroë westward through the Sahara to the Chad region and then to West Africa. By the third century B.C., for instance, the people responsible for the Nok culture in northern Nigeria had learned how to work iron. Some time during the latter half of the first millenium their ancestors had created a striking artistic tradition, based on a developed form of neolithic farming. They produced clay figurines of great beauty, and Nok traditions may have exerted a considerable influence on the lands between the Niger and the Benue.

The use of iron now provided these and other Sudanic communities with better weapons and better tools. Farmers using hoes and axes with iron blades could penetrate woodland much more easily than neolithic cultivators. The employment of iron must therefore have given a general impetus to the art of tilling and to the opening of the southern forest frontier. It is possible, though as yet only speculative, that the crafts of the miner and the smith were diffused also from the middle Nile to the Nile-Congo watershed and thence perhaps via the headwaters of the Congo to the

157

Zambezi. This process probably took place some time from the beginning of the present era. Iron working skills may then have spread further southward into what is now Zambia, where the first Iron Age wares have been dated to around 100 A.D. to 500 A.D.[1]

In all probability, however, the art of working iron—like similar technical revolutions—did not have a single center of diffusion. Iron working skills may also have reached parts of West Africa from the north across the Sahara. Alternatively, some West African communities may have begun to smelt iron by a process of independent discovery. The peoples of Rhodesia and Zambia may have acquired a knowledge of iron from southeast Asia via Madagascar and the Zambezi Valley, though the evidence for such theories still is uncertain. The archaeological evidence remains deficient, but the widespread use of the bowl and furnace indicate an originally Sudanic source area.

All we can say with some certainty is that the vast majority of all Negroid communities adopted the use of iron at some early period, and that the new techniques spread relatively quickly. The bulk of the African continent passed straight from the Stone Age into the Iron Age, omitting the intermediate Bronze Age phase that characterized the development of so many early European cultures. Africans also exploited wealth from water and the woods; they knew how to hunt, fish, and gather forest fruit. Their main occupation, however, was agriculture. Land was cleared with fire, axes, and hoes around the village. When the soil was exhausted, old gardens were left fallow and new land was cleared. Farmers also kept small livestock, such as goats and poultry, and their mode of life may not have differed a great deal from the ways still followed by the more backward communities in West Africa, whose agricultural practice we have referred to in a previous section.

The lands lying between the forest and the desert, in other words, supported a semisedentary economy for many centuries, but no one knows exactly how many. There is also evidence that the farmers gradually hacked and burned their way into the great forest belt; but again we cannot tell for sure how this process began and how quickly it went on. The Sahara in Roman times was more fertile than it is now, but wasteland began to encroach on the more fertile soil, and Negroes were probably pushed both southward and eastward. Some explain the progressive desiccation of the desert by climatic factors. Others blame the influx of pastoral people from North Africa, whose predatory habits and sheep, goats, and camels may have destroyed the scrub. Evaporation of moisture from the soil, they argue, became more rapid; the land dried out. Erosion by wind and water speeded up the process of soil degeneration as the herdsmen's beasts encroached upon the farmer's acres.

However this may be, from the first millenium B.C. onward Negro tribesmen pushed southward and westward, developing and adapting new crops to wring a living from the soil. The forward march of the pioneers into the forest frontier may have been facilitated by the spread of additional crops, which supplemented existing agricultural resources. There is a stimulating theory linking the Negroes' southward expansion to the introduction of new food crops from southeast Asia. According to this thesis, Indonesian settlers from Borneo learned how to make use of the monsoons to sail their craft to Madagascar and thence to the coast of southeast Africa. Sometime from 400 B.C. to 200 A.D. The newcomers brought bananas, coconuts, taro, and yams, which spread from east to west across "an uninterrupted corridor of agricultural peoples, running, at around the time of Christ, across the Bushmanoid territory and north of the Pigmy country to the Guinea coast."[2] An alternate theory has the crops from southeast Asia traveling up the east coast and through the Zambezi Valley. Others criticize this interpretation. They agree that Indonesian colonists played an important part in the history of Madagascar, but they argue that emigration from Indonesia got under way much later, an observation that fits in with the known fact of increased maritime activity in Indonesia during the fifth and sixth centuries. The banana and certain kinds of yams, for instance, are hardly a staple crop in present-day West Africa, as they are in East Africa. Around the area of the Ivory Coast, West Africans had their own yams. West of the Ivory Coast they may have had their own rice. Indeed it may have been the needs of increased rice cultivation that provided the main incentive for venturing into uncleared forests.[3]

No early solution to these and related problems lies in sight. No written records survive to elucidate these remote periods, while archaeologists have in all likelihood not even scratched the evidence that may still remain undiscovered beneath savannah and jungle. Historians can, of course, use oral traditions, but these are difficult to evaluate. Africans, especially those traditionally organized into large states, have recorded genealogies of chiefs, accounts of migrations, or tales about divine ancestors. They tell stories about mythical culture heroes, comparable to Noah, the patriarch of mankind, who supposedly built the Ark, salvaged "of every living thing of all flesh two of every sort" from the Flood, and later benefited the human race by the invention of wine and viticulture.[4]

But the further such accounts extend back into time, the more condensed they become, and the more time is telescoped. Among less highly organized communities, folk memory may be limited to the span of a few generations; the most advanced groups probably record no more than a few centuries. Tribal communities, in any case, interpret history in a fashion very different from our own. Meyer Fortes, a modern anthropologist who has studied the Tallensi of West Africa, thus doubts whether the Tallensi have a history in the sense of authentic records of past events. The memories and reminiscences of aged Tallensi are part of their biographies and never contribute to a body of socially preserved history. Their myths and legends are a means of rationalizing and defining the relationships of group to group or the pattern of their institutions. Some of these tales may refer to actual people, but there is no objective evidence. Tallensi traditions, according to Fortes, are a part of their social philosophy, projected into the past, because people think of their social order as continuous and persistent, handed down from generation to generation. Tallensi myths and legends, in other words, counterfeit, but do not document, history.[5]

This does not mean that sagas and such are useless for the historian. They may well throw an interesting light on other ways of thought. The *Nibelungenlied* ("The Song of the Nibelung"), a famous Germanic epic, for instance, completely discards chronology by placing Dietrich von Bern (Theoderic the Great), a king of the Goths, at the court of Attila, where Theoderic could not possibly have been. But the work is enlightening for other reasons. Attila, the dreaded Hunnish monarch whom churchmen described as the Scourge of God, is pictured as a good but weak king! Historians may well infer that Attila, a monster to cultured Roman priests, appeared in a very different light to his Germanic camp followers and allies. But no historian would use the lay of the Nibelung as historical evidence for the *Völkerwanderung,* unless supported and elucidated by other sources, documentary, archaeological, and so forth. The same criterion applies to the study of African history, and speculations built solely on oral traditions are probably not more than stimulating intellectual exercises.

We cannot, therefore, give an exact account of early Africa, and much of its early prehistory must remain a mystery. The best we can do is to present an expert summary of the scanty knowledge concerning West Africa as it may have looked by the seventh century, that is to say, before the West African Negroes had come under alien influence to any great extent.[6]

North of the forest in the west, in Futa and along both banks of the Senegal, lived the Tukulor, Serer, and Wolof. In the east, along the left bank of the Niger, lived the Songhai, divided perhaps into clans of farmers and fishermen. Between the Songhai and the Tuculor, between the upper Senegal in the west, the Niger lakes in the east, and the forest of the south, were the peoples of a great Mande-speaking group, including the Malinke in the south and the Soninke in the north. East of the Mandingo, between the Songhai in the north and the forest in the south, were the ancestors of the people who now speak Voltaic or Gur languages. Of the peoples east of the Songhai and in the forest from the Gambia to the Niger Delta, we know little. The peoples of North Africa do not seem to have made permanent contact with the former before about the tenth century A.D., and they never penetrated into the forest. It is, however, possible that the people dwelling in the area between the Niger in the west, Lake Chad in the east, and near the Benue in the south, may have been subject to influence from immigrants originating in the Nile Valley, Ethiopia, or even southwestern Arabia. These communities probably lived in descent groups, often small enough to claim kinship with a common ancestor. They probably believed in a world of spirits, who spoke through human mediums and maintained a never-ending interest in the affairs of the living community. Farming was their principal occupation; the axe and the hoe, the spear and the fishing pole shaped the pattern of their lives.

THE MEDITERRANEAN AND THE WEST AFRICAN TRADE

The Negro communities of West Africa dwelt in relative isolation and produced most of their necessities at home. Their isolation, however, was not absolute. From times immemorial there was probably some exchange between hunters, fishermen, herdsmen, and cultivators. We know that even by the end of the nineteenth century, when communications had greatly improved, the bulk of West African trade centered on food, which was exchanged by petty middlemen, operating with tiny amounts of capital and infinitesimal profits. The more spectacular commerce in precious metals and slaves, to which we shall refer in subsequent sections, was meant only for the rich. But there was one exceptional merchandise, small in bulk, easily carried, but vital for human sustenance. Even the humblest farmer needed some salt, but salt was often hard to get. The villagers living by the shore of the Atlantic Ocean experienced no difficulty in extracting salt from the sea. But many of the inland peoples had no such ready source; traders must have found great obstacles for long distances through the forest barrier that separated the savannah from the Atlantic. The Negro communities of the interior, therefore, secured the bulk of their salt from rock deposits in the Sahara. These mines were controlled by Berbers, light-skinned people from North Africa and the desert, who were willing to barter salt for gold and other commodities from the forest belt. The Berbers in turn traded with the ports of North Africa, so that the forest belt was gradually linked to the wider economy of the Mediterranean.

No one knows when the trans-Saharan commerce first began. Some experts believe that it may have commenced as early as 3000 or 2000 B.C. Others date the regular traffic between North Africa and the African "middle belt" from a later period. It seems clear, however, that by 1000 B.C. chariots travelled across the Sahara along two main routes: one from Morocco to the banks of the Senegal and the Niger, the other from Tripoli through Ghadames to Gao on the Niger. By the fifth century B.C. the desert traffic in luxury products such as exotic animals, precious stones, and slaves may have flourished to such an extent that the Carthaginians tried to explore the Sahara directly. Three centuries later, the Saharan trade centered on the Tripoli-Fezzan-Bornu route; this traffic constituted an important source of wealth for Carthage.

In all likelihood the desert trade expanded in a dramatic fashion when Roman conquerors introduced the camel into Tripolitania, probably in the first century A.D. Arabs and Berber tribesmen subsequently spread the use of the camel throughout Barbary and into the Sahara, thereby providing a tremendous boon for merchants. J. D. Fage has graphically likened the navigators of the desert, using camels, to those of the sea using ships. Cities like Fez and Marrakesh in Morocco, Constantine in Algeria, Tunis and Kairouan (Kairwan) in Tunisia, and Tripoli in Libya, developed —so to speak—into the northern desert ports, sending convoys of ships (the caravans) southward. These convoys called in at various desert "islands" (the oases) for fresh water and food, until they finally reached their destination on the southern "shore" of the desert sea. The merchants' itineraries varied in accordance with the changing fortunes of mounted men of the desert, both in trade and in war, and control over the inland trade remained with Berber middlemen, who probably kept their knowl-edge to themselves. The Romans knew little about the distant "Ethiopians." The Romans had hardly any contacts with the Africans of the Sudan, and the direct impact of the Mediterranean world on West Africa presumably remained slight.

The indirect effects of the trade, were, however, considerable. The merchants of the Sahara gradually built up a complex network of caravan routes, and in the course of time the trans-Saharan trade expanded greatly. Gold, ivory, ostrich feathers, kola nuts, and other products of the forest region traveled northward on the backs of camels. In addition many slaves were compelled to undertake the grim journey accross the desert. The West Africans received salt, copper, cowrie shells, cloth, figs, dates, beads, and perhaps also horses and cattle in payment.[7] Many West African and Sudanic economies became increasingly complex; commerce also had a profound influence on local politics. In time three principal routes came to dominate the

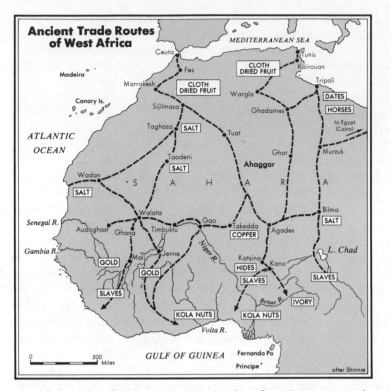

trans-Saharan trade: a western one, leading from Morocco to the great northern bend of the Niger and to the country west of it; a central route from Tunisia to the region between the Niger and Lake Chad; and an eastern route from Tripoli to the lands adjoining Lake Chad. All three played an indirect part in the solidification of great new empires in the savannah.

The importation of gold in turn exercized a considerable influence on the economic history of Europe. Until European explorers opened up the mines of South and North America, Australia, and the Transvaal, Europe largely depended on Africa for its gold supplies. The Carthaginians, the Romans, and other European peoples all used African gold as a means of internal exchange, as currency to purchase luxury goods from the east, and as a raw material for the creation of artistic works, so that the fortunes of West Africa became linked indirectly in some measure to Europe's, especially to that of the Mediterranean basin.

EUROPE AND THE IMAGE OF TROPICAL AFRICA

The African migrations were paralleled to some extent by massive movements of population in Europe. In 330 A.D., as we have seen, the Emperor Constantine dedicated Constantinople as the new capital of the Roman Empire. His decision was symptomatic of the economic and political decline of the Roman empire in the west;

this great polity slowly crumbled into pieces while Constantinople continued as the center of a great Byzantine and Greek Orthodox civilization for more than a millenium to come. In 407 the Roman legions evacuated Britain; the island was subsequently invaded by Saxon settlers from across the North Sea, one of the many tribal groups now in motion in Northern Europe. In 410 Gothic warriors sacked Rome itself. In 439 the Vandals, another Germanic people, by now firmly established in North Africa, captured the Roman city of Carthage. In 476 the last Roman emperor of the West lost his throne. The West Roman crown became a matter of historical memory until in 800 when Charlemagne, the greatest of Frankish rulers, had himself crowned Roman emperor once more. He reigned as the head of a great feudal and Catholic confederacy embracing France, western Germany, Bohemia, Carinthia, and northern Italy; all part of a loosely associated kingdom with a mainly agrarian economy, that had nothing but the name in common with the ancient Roman dominion centering on the Mediterranean.

Western Christendom gradually lost command of the seas. Viking vessels for many generations dominated most of Europe's northern shore. Muslim sailors—as we shall see in a subsequent chapter—gained almost complete supremacy in the Mediterranean. In Western Europe the Church became almost the sole repository of culture and learning. Its cultural legacy, including geographical scholarship, depended largely on the Graeco-Roman heritage, subsequently enriched by the Arabs. Insofar as Western Europeans thought about Africa at all, they did so in terms set by the ancients and the Muslims. Western Europe's image of Africa, created largely by Greek and Roman writers, persisted for more than a millenium, until the great Portuguese journeys of discovery at the end of the fifteenth century.

A glance backward into ancient history will give some indication of how Europe's geographical image of Africa first came into existence.[8] The world of Homer, about 1000 B.C., centered on the eastern and central Mediterranean. For Homer's contemporaries the world was flat, with an oceanic rim. Eastern Africa was supposedly linked to Phoenicia in the west. A land bridge connected Morocco to Spain, making the Mediterranean a self-contained lake and center of the world. The Phoenicians, as we have seen, acquired a vastly greater degree of geographical knowledge. So did Greek sailors of a subsequent period who discovered the Pillars of Hercules (the modern Strait of Gibraltar) in the seventh century B.C.

Herodotus (ca. 484–425 B.C.), postulated an Africa shaped as an irregular rectangle, bordered in the east by the Red Sea, in the west by the Pillars of Hercules, and in the south by an enormous expanse of water which merged into the Indian Ocean. Herodotus had no real idea of Africa's huge extent. The southern coast of Africa, in his view, lay somewhere south of Meroë. The Nile, according to his calculations, started somewhere in West Africa, flowed inland through the whole continent, and then turned northward in a sharp bend, until it emptied its waters into the Mediterranean.

North Africa was absorbed into the Graeco-Roman world, but the ancients knew little about the far interior. By the first century B.C. Arab, and perhaps even Indian and Indonesian, mariners knew much more about tropical Africa than their colleagues in the west. Once Rome acquired control of Egypt, however, the sea route to India

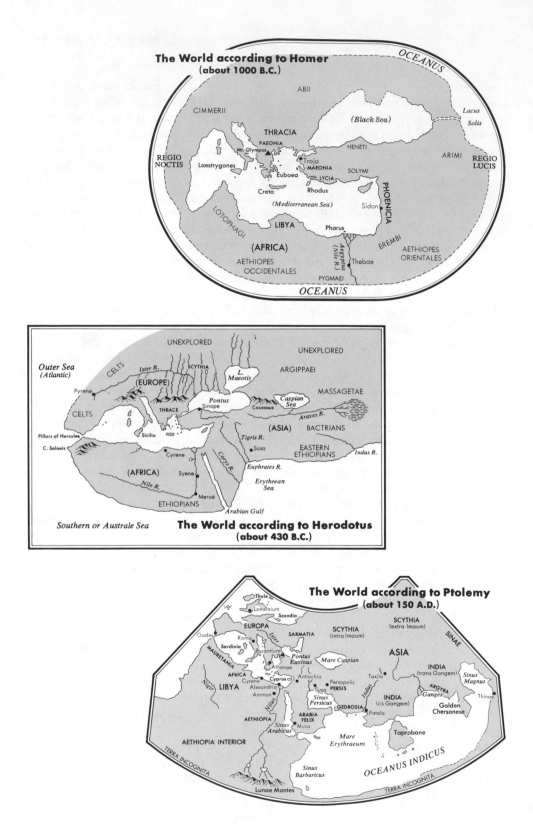

The World according to Homer
(about 1000 B.C.)

OCEANUS

ABII

CIMMERII

(Black Sea)

Lacus
Solis

THRACIA
PAEONIA
Mt. Olympus
Troja
MAEONIA
LYCIA
Euboea
HENETI

ARIMI

REGIO
NOCTIS

Laestrygones

REGIO
LUCIS

SOLYMI

Creta
Rhodus

(Mediterranean Sea)

Sidon

PHOENICIA

LOTOPHAGI

LIBYA

Pharus

EREMBI

(AFRICA)

Aegyptus
(Nile R.)

Thebae

AETHIOPES
ORIENTALES

AETHIOPES
OCCIDENTALES

PYGMAEI

OCEANUS

Outer Sea
(Atlantic)

UNEXPLORED

UNEXPLORED

CELTS

Ister R.

SCYTHIA

ARGIPPAEI

Pyrene

(EUROPE)

L.
Maeotis

MASSAGETAE

CELTS

THRACE

Pontus
Sinope

Caucasus

Caspian
Sea

Pillars of Hercules

Sicilia

Araxes R.

C. Soloeis

(ASIA)

BACTRIANS

Cyrene

Tigris R.

Susa

EASTERN
ETHIOPIANS

Indus R.

(AFRICA)

Syene

Corys R.

Euphrates R.

Nile R.

Erythrean
Sea

Meroë

ETHIOPIANS

Arabian Gulf

Southern or Australe Sea

The World according to Herodotus
(about 430 B.C.)

The World according to Ptolemy
(about 150 A.D.)

Thule

Londinium

Scandia

SCYTHIA
(extra Imaum)

EUROPA

SARMATIA

SCYTHIA
(intra Imaum)

SINAE

Gades

Roma

Ister

ASIA

MAURETANIA

Sardinia

Byzantium

Pontus
Euxinus

Mare Caspian

INDIA
(trans Gangem)

Sinus
Magnus

AFRICA

Athenae

Cyprus

Antiochia

Taxila

Cyrene

Alexandria

Persepolis

Susa

PERSIS

ARGYRA

LIBYA

Ammon

Sinus
Persicus

GEDROSIA

Indus

Ganges

Thinae

Niger

INDIA
(cis Gangem)

Golden
Chersonese

AETHIOPIA

ARABIA
FELIX

Patala

Nilus

Musa

TERRA INCOGNITA

Sinus
Arabicus

Mare
Erythraeum

Taprobane

AETHIOPIA INTERIOR

OCEANUS INDICUS

Sinus
Barbaricus

TERRA INCOGNITA

Lunae Montes

assumed new importance, and Graeco-Roman sailors accumulated a good deal of information concerning East Africa, Arabia, and western India. A considerable amount of geographical literature was published, and by collating and comparing details from travelers' reports and other sources, Ptolemy, an Alexandrian astronomer, mathematician, and geographer, compiled his famous *Geography* about 150 A.D. This endured as a standard work until the fifteenth century, and many of Ptolemy's views concerning the interior continued to influence European thinking until the Victorian era.

Ptolemy, in the scientific fashion of his age, envisaged the earth as a sphere at the center of the universe, with the heavenly bodies moving in circles around our globe. Ptolemy drew a reasonably accurate outline of Europe and the Mediterranean basin. He also had a more realistic appreciation of Africa's size than did earlier scholars like Herodotus. In many other ways, however, his concept of Africa lacked accuracy. According to Ptolemy, Africa formed a vast rectangle. The African West coast stretched southwards in an almost unbroken straight line. The shores of northeast Africa were delineated with greater fidelity. But Ptolemy postulated Prason (probably Cape Delgado) as the southernmost limit of the continent. The African landmass, in his view, then merged into a vast *terra incognita* which continued eastward and ultimately joined China, leaving the Indian Ocean as an inland sea. Ptolemy had heard of the Niger River which—in his interpretation—flowed from lakes to swamps, without an outlet to the sea.

The eastern interior, in Ptolemy's view, contained Mounts Pylae and Maste (which may or may not have been identical with Mounts Kenya and Kilimanjaro). Ptolemy also postulated a mysterious mountain range, the Mountains of the Moon, which stretched from east to west. From there rivers wound into two great lakes from whence issued the Nile and its principal tributary. The Nile supposedly traversed nearly the whole of Africa, from south to north, and the theory that the great river issued from one or two great lakes inland continued to influence mapmakers until relatively modern times. In the far south of Ptolemy's Africa lay the land of the Agisymba, which the geographer probably placed much further south than the Agysimba region (perhaps Chad) that a Roman officer named Julius Maternus had visited during the early part of the second century.

Ptolemy's account, though masterful for his period, contained a strangely fanciful element. Cannibals and white elephants abounded; the far interior appeared as a land of mystery. This air of imaginative and fantastic romance, enriched by many subsequent accretions, continued to pervade European thinking on Africa for many centuries to come. Sailors like Shakespeare's Othello told terrible tales

> . . . of antres vast, and deserts idle,
> rough quarries, rocks, and hills whose heads touch heaven,
> And of the Cannibals, that each other eat,
> The Anthropophagi; and men whose heads
> Do grow beneath their shoulders . . .

Some elements of this atmosphere pervaded Western travelogues until the days of Victorian empire building.

NOTES

1. For this and the following see the excellent summary by Merrick Posnansky, "The Origins of Agriculture and Iron Working in Southern Africa," in Posnansky, pp. 82–94.

2. Murdock, p. 223.

3. Fage, "Anthropology, Botany and History," *Journal of African History*, vol. 2, no. 2 (1961), pp. 307–308.

4. Genesis 6:19 and 9:20.

5. Meyer Fortes, *The Dynamics of Clanship among the Tallensi* (London, 1945), p. 26.

6. Fage, *An Introduction to the History of West Africa*, pp. 6–8.

7. Fage, pp. 9–10.

8. Based on the excellent summary in Robert I. Rotberg, *A Political History of Tropical Africa* (New York, 1965), pp. 13–30.

Chapter 14

The Great Migrations

THE SPREAD OF CROPS

In a previous section we discussed the origins of African farming. In subsequent sections we propose to make further reference to the importation of new plants into the African continent. Here our aim is to summarize this information so that the reader may conveniently find this material in one spot, even though we do some violence to a strictly chronological approach.

The present agricultural staples of Africa come from three continents.[1] Wheat and barley came to Egypt from western Asia. By about 6000 to 5000 B.C. these grains had spread to the middle and lower reaches of the Nile, where they made a profound impact on the life of the people. Wheat and barley are, however, winter-rain crops; they cannot be grown in the tropics without irrigation, and they did not lend themselves to adoption by the cultivators of sub-Saharan Africa. Wheat and barley, as well as other west Asian crops such as the lucerne, the chick pea, and fruit trees like the date palm and the mulberry tree, could easily be grown on the northern shore of Africa. It seems that by about 5000 B.C. the new economy may have gained a foothold in the Cyrenaica west of Egypt. Later on these plants probably penetrated into the Maghrib and into the great oases of the central Sahara.

Scholars still dispute the exact origins of West African agriculture. But it seems likely that certain crops of vital importance to modern cultivators probably came from Africa. These comprise sorghum (Indian millet or kafir corn), a hardy grain crop of which there are now many varieties and which is resistant to drought and heat. Other African-descended grains include pearl or bulrush millet (pennisetum) and finger

167

millet (eleusine); these likewise can be grown on soils of relatively low fertility and require less moisture than many other food crops. In addition fonio (hungry grass), certain species of rice (especially *Oryza glaberrima*), and various other plants may well have come from West Africa.

Historians as yet do not agree how these plants first came to be cultivated in West Africa. Some believe that a knowledge of agriculture spread westward from the Nile Valley into the western Sudan via Lake Chad at a time when the climate in these regions was wetter and warmer than today and when the Sahara was much less of a barrier. Others hold that West Africans developed their own forms of agriculture, independent of foreign influence. The fact that wild rice is cultivated in a different fashion from the Nile Valley crops favors the theory of independent discovery. Certainly the Niger delta—the region best suited to rice growing—was not in contact with the Nile region until much later. The Guinea forest yams, an indigenous root crop, may originally have been garnered in its wild state by hunters and food gatherers, who first of all prised up the roots with weighted digging sticks, but subsequently turned to more regular kinds of farming.

The details of this agricultural revolution are thus disputed. All we can say with certainty is that the great cultural transformation involved in the growing of crops did not come about by one sudden innovation, but by a series of complex processes with great regional variations. The vexed question of diffusion versus independent invention need not concern us at this point, for the two interpretations are not mutually exclusive. Some more advanced communities in West Africa may well have invented local forms of farming; these may have been subsequently enriched by foreign importations. Alternatively, certain farmers may have learned from their neighbors and then started to experiment on their own. We may conclude, as a rough guess, that the neolithic revolution in African agriculture probably took place at some time between 3000 to 1000 B.C., though no one can be quite certain about the exact dates.

In addition, Africa probably derived certain plants, including bananas and other species, from southeast Asia. The details of this migration are discussed in a subsequent chapter. All we need to repeat here is that these crops appear to have hailed from what is now Indonesia, that they were brought to Madagascar by adventurous navigators, and that this diffusion may have occurred some time between 200 B.C. and 400 A.D. These plants are well suited to humid and forested regions, and they spread to many different parts of Africa, though the details of this process also remain far from clear. The Indonesian impact was probably of great importance. The banana, for instance, a palatable and nourishing plant, was developed in many different varieties; it can be eaten raw, dried or cooked, and today forms a staple crop in various parts of Africa.

Africa also benefited from contact with Muslim settlers from the Near East who brought new crops and new methods of cultivation to the African East Coast. When Portuguese navigators first reached the shores of East Africa at the start of the sixteenth century, they found much to admire: for instance, the civilization of Kilwa, a Muslim port "around [which] are many tanks of water, and orchards, and gardens with much fresh water."[2] Muslim colonists probably introduced limes, oranges, various kinds of vegetables, and possibly sugar cane to Africa; certainly they played their

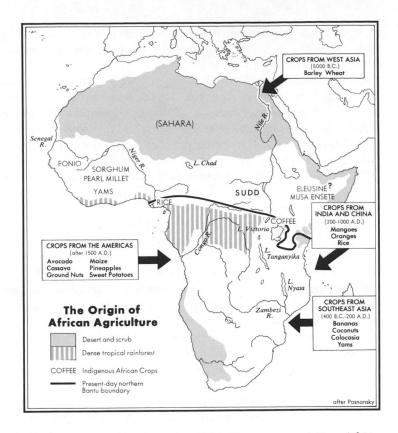

The Origin of African Agriculture

CROPS FROM WEST ASIA
(5000 B.C.)
Barley Wheat

(SAHARA)

Senegal R.

FONIO

SORGHUM
PEARL MILLET

YAMS

RICE

L. Chad

SUDD

ELEUSINE?
MUSA ENSETE

COFFEE

CROPS FROM INDIA AND CHINA
(200-1000 A.D.)
Mangoes
Oranges
Rice

CROPS FROM THE AMERICAS
(after 1500 A.D.)
Avocado   Maize
Cassava   Pineapples
Ground Nuts Sweet Potatoes

L. Victoria

L. Tanganyika

L. Nyasa

Zambezi R.

CROPS FROM SOUTHEAST ASIA
(400 B.C.-200 A.D.)
Bananas
Coconuts
Colocasia
Yams

Desert and scrub

Dense tropical rainforest

COFFEE Indigenous African Crops

Present-day northern Bantu boundary

after Posnansky

share in diffusing all sorts of Mediterranean and Middle Eastern crops to East Africa.

Much to the foregoing is speculation. We are, however, sure that by the sixteenth century Africans had elaborated many agricultural systems, that they had become familiar with all sorts of plants, one of the chief staple crops being millet. According to contemporary descriptions, the "Kaffirs" (Bantu-speaking peoples) of southeast Africa cultivated millet as a staple crop. "Of this millet, ground between two stones or in wooden mortars, they make flour, and of this they make cakes which they cook among embers. Of the same grain they make wine [or rather beer] which, when it has fermented in a vessel of clay and has cooled and turned sour, they drink with great enjoyment."[3] Other food resources known to the people of southeast Africa included "rice, many vegetables, large and small cattle, and many hens,"[4] so that in good years the tribesmen must have eaten quite well.

The diet of the indigenous people was further enriched by plants brought to West Africa by European, especially Portuguese gardeners, who were employed to supply local European forts with more varied foods than were locally available. The Portuguese, for instance, brought lemons and sugar cane to West Africa from the Mediterranean. Oranges, tamarinds, and coconut palms derived from the Indian Ocean, and European navigators, especially the Portuguese and Dutch, probably played their part in acclimatizing such food in West Africa.

Even more outstanding, however, was the contribution made to African agriculture and to world civilization at large by the ingenuity of American Indians. Africans obtained an immense boon from Indian corn, which was brought to Africa by Portuguese navigators and possibly also by seamen of other European nations. The peanut (groundnut) is of American origin; today it is also a major food crop in many parts of Africa. Cassava (manioc), whose roots resemble sweet potatoes, derives from Brazil. It appears to have been carried to Angola some time about 1600 and then spread further afield. The prickly pear (Indian fig) hails from America; so do tobacco, cocoa, and other tropical crops of major economic importance. Their diffusion to Africa was occasioned by the worldwide system of maritime trade built up by Europeans and, to a lesser extent, by Muslim merchants as the result of the sixteenth century period of "Great Discoveries."

An immense amount of historical and biological detection work remains to be done in order to resolve how and when these various crops spread through the different parts of Africa. But historians can—with a good conscience—arrive at certain broad generalizations. African farmers obtained incalculable benefits from the contacts established between Africa and other continents by foreign intermediaries. Africans skillfully adapted a large number of new crops to local usage; in addition they developed or ennobled many plants of their own. By the second part of the eighteenth century, tribesmen in even a remote region like Delagoa Bay (in what is now Mozambique), then little visited by foreign traders, were familiar with a host of crops deriving from many parts of the globe. "The Country [wrote a contemporary explorer] produces good Rice, Sweet Potatoes in abundance, Indian Corn and Tobacco: the latter does not grow to any perfection from the Inhabitants not understanding the proper mode of culture, Onions, Saffrons, Chillies, Calabashes, Sugar Cane and Pine Apple, but the latter is not plentiful. They also raise a sort of grain called by them Mahabar [probably *durra*] which bears some resemblance in growth to Caffre Corn and from which they make a very pleasant and wholesome beverage . . ."[5]

THE DIFFUSION OF DOMESTIC ANIMALS

For untold millenia the indigenous peoples of Africa depended on hunting and food gathering. In southern Africa these primordial ways probably survived longer than in most other parts of the continent. But as time went on the Stone Age people of the southern veld encountered strangers from the north who lived in a very different fashion. Bushmen artists in Mashonaland in Rhodesia, for instance, have recorded this invasion. Their rock paintings show how tall men came into the country, driving cattle or fat-tailed sheep before them.

This herdsmen's invasion in turn raises the question of how these beasts spread through Africa and requires a brief explanation. The evidence is unclear. But cattle in Africa may have come from the Nile Valley around 5500 B.C. According to Professor Posnansky's summary,[6] longhorn humpless cattle (Hamitic longhorn) of western Asia came from Egypt through North Africa to West Africa. It is also conceivable that Africa's modern cattle derive at least in part from wild species that flourished in North Africa and the northern Sahara. In addition, shorthorn cattle of Asian origin may have come to Africa from Asia via the horn of Africa.

The next newcomer was the Zebu, a shorthorned humped cow. The Zebu is of Indian origin and may have migrated along the east coast into the Ethiopian highlands, and possibly also via the Nile-Congo watershed to the Lake Chad area and down into East Africa. Thirdly there was a process of hybridization between the Zebu and the humpless stock. This probably began in the Ethiopian highlands and resulted in a hardy crossbreed known as the Sanga. The Sanga also traveled southward into what is now Rhodesia and South Africa. The details of this process are not well documented, but we know that the Hottentots encountered by the first Dutch settlers at the Cape in the seventeenth century, had a form of the Sanga cow—usually said to be the longhorned Zebu—which accompanied them sometime during the first half of the millenium in a great southward trek.

The spread of cattle profoundly affected the course of African history. Of course there were, and there still are, many parts of the continent where cattle cannot live because of animal diseases. But fortunately extensive areas remained free of the dreaded tsetse fly, and pastoralists could make a good living, especially in the higher and drier zones where grazing was adequate. There were also many "corridors" of uncontaminated land, and these played an important part in channelling pastoral migrations. Cattle made an important contribution to the herdsman's diet. Pastoralists now had a steady supply of protein. Cattle also helped to make its possessors more mobile, for herdsmen, so to speak, now commanded a four-legged commissariat. The introduction of cattle enriched many of Africa's existing arable economies. It also permitted some races, such as the Somali and the Masai, to embark upon a course of pastoral specialization and led to a way of life that centered to a greater or lesser extent upon horned beasts.

Conditions were peculiarly favorable in parts of East and Central Africa, so that some anthropologists formerly spoke of "cattle complexes" to denote such cultures. The newcomers to Rhodesia probably participated in such a cattle-centered economy and kept extensive herds. They also had iron tools and they may have picked up their metallurgical knowledge from Cushitic peoples in East Africa. They may have spoken a Khoisan tongue, full of clicks, though archaeologists and anthropologists still dispute their origins. All we can say is that their material culture and social organization were probably comparable to those of the Hottentots whom John Maxwell, an English traveller at the Cape Province in South Africa, described much later, at the beginning of the eighteenth century. "They besmear their faces and bodies all over with suet or other oleaginous stuff, which together with exposing their bodies to the warm sun, makes their skin of a tawny colour, . . . They adorn their hair . . . with shells, pieces of copper etc. Both sexes are clad with the skin commonly of sheep . . . the hairy side outward in summer but inward in winter. . . . They go barefooted, except when they travel they wear a piece of skin fasten'd about their feet. Their weapons are javelins . . . and bows with poisoned arrows. . . . Their houses are hemispherical, made of mats supported with stakes . . ."[7]

Maxwell's unflattering description helps to explain the contemporary white man's aversion to the Hottentots, but cannot give modern readers any idea of the tremendous advance Hottentot and kindred cultures represented over the Bushman way of life. Hottentot herds provided their owners with milk, their staple diet, and represented a more reliable source of food than hunting and food gathering alone. The Hottentots used copper and iron. In addition to bows and arrows, they carried clubs, small shields made of hide, and sometimes even breastplates fashioned of animal skin. Their clans were apparently not bound by any larger loyalties. Each was ruled by a chieftain of feeble authority, but pastoralism could presumably sustain larger communities than an economy dependent solely on the chase and collection of wild fruits and plants.

In addition to cattle, newcomers also brought other animals to Africa. We have previously mentioned the advent of horses and camels to Africa in ancient times, and we have discussed the impact made by the application of their muscle power to transport and war. The use of camels and horses remained confined largely to North Africa and the Sudan owing to climatic, ecological and epidemiological conditions. The humble pig, however, spread very much further afield. Muslims and Jews are not allowed to eat pork. The Christian religion, however, contains no such dietary restriction. In all probability, pigs were first brought to Africa on Portuguese vessels, though the available evidence allows for differing interpretations.

Pigs can live in regions where the tsetse fly prevents farmers from raising cattle;

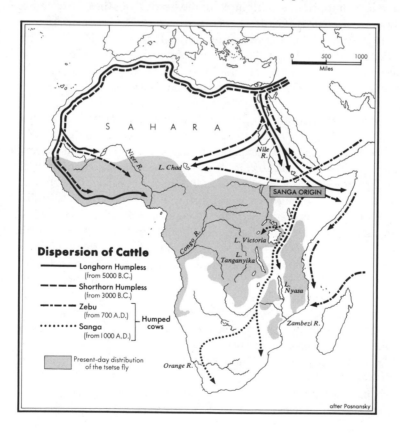

pork therefore formed a valuable addition to the protein supplies available to forest dwellers, and the pig, like the sheep and the goat, spread far afield. The details of its migration remain little known. But there is documentary evidence that by the second part of the eighteenth century the people dwelling near Delagoa Bay, set great value on pork and that goats were plentiful in the country.[8]

The African villagers' inability to cope with wide-spread animal diseases and their ignorance of breeding methods and other refinements of agricultural science continued to place many obstacles in the path of progress. But Africans did manage to adapt many different animals, large and small, to their use and black farmers played a major part in safeguarding and expanding the food supply available to their continent.

THE BANTU DISPERSION

The cattle-owning immigrants who settled in southern Africa were only one of many groups who helped to diffuse the art of smelting iron and herding cattle. More important than the Khoisan speakers were the Bantu, who now occupy a large portion of sub-Saharan Africa. The word "Bantu" is an omnibus term. It does not denote a race but a group of people speaking related languages. Today the Bantu speakers all show Negroid characteristics in varying degrees, but they do not all look alike. Some have yellow skins and others are black; some have strikingly Negroid features and others look more like Bushmen. Some reckon their descent through the father's line. They are known as "patrilineal," and they comprise many cattle-owning peoples. Others trace their ancestry through the mother's line; anthropologists call them "matrilineal." Some make their living by keeping herds. Others practice only arable farming or mixed forms of agriculture. Nearly all Bantu-speakers, however, learned the art of smelting and working metal, and these iron-users made a profound impact on the history of Africa.

Their exact origin remains a matter of dispute. The ancestral Bantu apparently came from an area where there was both forest and savannah and where there were cool winds at certain times of the year. Unfortunately from the historian's point of view, there are many regions in the northern portion of Africa that could fit this description. Malcolm Guthrie, a British scholar, thinks that the progenitors of the Bantu must have come from the southern edge of the equatorial forest, roughly midway between the Atlantic and the Indian Ocean.[9] If this theory is correct, the Bantu may have originated somewhere in the Shari basin. From there, some traveled west to the Niger region where they fused with existing communities. Others moved south, down the rivers of the Congo rain forest to the savannahs of Central Africa. Supporters of Guthrie's thesis trace the use of iron hoe and of the drum bellows used for metal working to the Shari basin. From there the Bantu carried their technology to other parts of Africa. Joseph H. Greenberg, an American linguist and anthropologist, puts the original Bantu nucleus much further to the north and west, somewhere in the central Benue Valley near the present boundary of Nigeria and Cameroun.

These two intepretations might conceivably be merged into a "two stream" theory.

It is possible that the forerunners of the present Bantu-speaking peoples may have migrated from West Africa eastward, along the northern fringe of the equatorial forest belt. Subsequently they may have reached the interlacustrine area of East Africa. Avoiding the great African rain forests, Bantu pioneers then possibly pushed southward along the Great Rift Valley, a much used natural migration route. Some drifted into what is now southern Tanzania. Others moved past Lakes Tanganyika and Nyasa, and subsequently dispersed in various directions.

In addition a few groups may have used the shorter but much harder route that led from West Africa through the Congo forests into the southern savannah belt. At some point the peoples who had passed along the western route made contact with those who had avoided the jungle barrier by passing to the north, east, and south of it. Hence there may not be any fundamental conflict between the evidence adduced respectively by Guthrie and Greenberg.[10]

The two stream theory necessarily presents a highly simplified account. The two main southward movements were broken by many cross currents. Certain scholars suggest that some Bantu-speaking peoples, having penetrated parts of the Congo forest and beyond, made their way into East Africa. They may indeed have entered East Africa from the south, moving from the southwest to the northeast. They ultimately occupied most of the East African littoral, and by the beginning of the Middle Ages a great Negroid belt probably spread all the way from north of Mogadishu or the southern coast of Somalia down to the coastal area of Sofala (situated south of the modern city of Beira) in what is now Mozambique.[11] This vast area of settlement may have roughly corresponded to the "land of Zanj" mentioned by contemporary Arab geographers. Bantu-speaking communities likewise spread out from the Congo basin, which became a base for further southward expansion and a nursery of new Bantu states.

Other Bantu-speaking immigrants made their way into Central and southern Africa. The details and chronology of these migrations also remain a matter of dispute. It seems likely that sometime during the first century A.D. Bantu-speaking agriculturists made their way down the Great Rift Valley into what is now Malawi. From there, some trickled westward into Zambia, where archaeologists now distinguish several different Iron Age cultures, named respectively after finds in Dambwa, Kalomo and elsewhere. (Further reference to these will be made in the following chapter.)

In addition, Iron Age communities settled in Mashonaland, in what is now Rhodesia, where the first of many Bantu-speaking invaders may have arrived some time during the fourth century A.D., though these dates remain subject to dispute. According to one interpretation, the other Bantu-speaking groups gradually filtered into Mozambique. Others may have gone to southwest Matabeleland, and from there into Botswana and the western Transvaal. Further south, Bantu-speaking peoples migrated into Natal, which they may have occupied sometime during the fifteenth or sixteenth century. From there, the Bantu pushed southward until they encountered European colonists in the Eastern Cape during the course of the eighteenth century.

We know little concerning the impact of the immigrants on the indigenous people. The newcomers at first came presumably in small numbers. There was probably plenty of land for everyone; hence the invaders may not have seriously pressed on the Bushmen's hunting grounds. In time, however, more pioneers made their way southward, where their arrival may well have resulted in local scrambles for land, causing the Bush people to retreat into the remoter and less desirable areas.

Over the course of many centuries, Bantu-speaking communities spread over most of East, Central, and southern Africa. The Bantu dispersion made a decisive change in the history of the continent. Wherever they went, they carried the arts of smelting and working metal; hence the Bantu migration made a major contribution to the cultural history of mankind. The settlers had to adapt themselves to all kinds of ecological circumstances, to forests and savannahs, to dry bush and mountain country; and these changing conditions of life must have occasioned considerable changes in their social structure. The Bantu wanderings must also have involved a great deal of hybridization with other stocks—Bushman, Pygmy, Hottentot, and so forth, so that the ethnographic pattern of Africa became even more variegated and complex than before.

THE DIFFUSION OF METAL WORKING CULTURES

The history of the Bantu dispersion will always involve a good deal of speculation, for the Bantu left no written records, and the remaining evidence will always remain subject to different interpretations. There seems, however, little doubt that the Bantu migrations occasioned the spread of metallurgy throughout wide areas of eastern and southern Africa. The use of iron probably enabled the proto-Bantu and Bantu people to produce tools suitable for practicing slash-and-burn agriculture in the forest. Iron tools may have enabled the Bantu to break the forest barrier. Iron weapons gave them a great military superiority over their opponents. The history of iron working therefore merits some additional discussion.

The introduction of iron played a major part in the rise of civilization at Meroë. Clearly, iron was worked at Meroë before the fourth century B.C. The use of iron may have spread westward; the art of smelting was certainly known to the people of Nok in the fourth century B.C. The smith's craft may then have spread southeastward into Bantu Africa; in all probability the Bantu used iron-tipped tools when they pioneered new land. The widespread nature of the Bantu stem form *uma,* for iron, and the present day use, in the northern part of East Africa, at least, of the bowl and bellows, indicate in all likelihood a Sudanic source. Other Africans may have learned a different technique involving the use of bag bellows and dome furnaces from craftsmen originating in lands adjoining the Indian Ocean, perhaps Indonesia. In the coastal regions and in large parts of southern Africa the bag bellows and dome furnace may indeed have overlaid an earlier use of Sudanic forms.[12] In southern Africa one of the earliest instances of actual iron working is found at Gokomere in Rhodesia, dating from the sixth century A.D. The use of iron was widely associated with peoples manufacturing a peculiar kind of channeled pottery, and finds of such channeled ware have been dated to around 100 B.C. to 900 A.D. in parts of what is now Zambia. These dates are astonishingly early and they suggest perhaps a southeastern rather than a northern cultural impact.

Another large Iron Age site has been disinterred at Dambwa, north of Livingstone

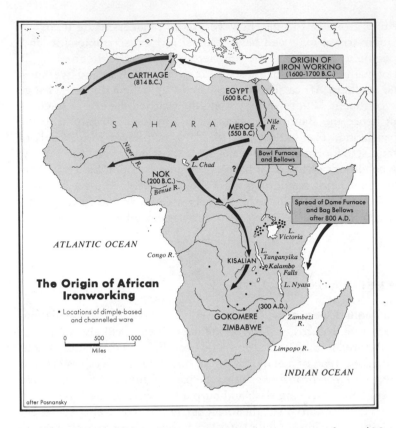

The Origin of African Ironworking

• Locations of dimple-based and channelled ware

in present day Zambia. This settlement dates perhaps from 400 A.D. and the varied nature of such finds makes it likely that there were several Iron Ages in Zambia. At Dambwa archaeologists have found a great deal of iron slag, indicating that iron working must have been an important activity. The villagers must have lived in a large settlement, for discolored soil and pottery occur over an area of about 100 yards in diameter. Piles of wall rubble and patches of mud floors are scattered in the deposits. The huts at Dambwa resembled those found in African villages today. The inhabitants dug storage pits into the sand; these were probably lined to protect the contents from termites. The dead were buried in small grave pits, and surviving burial sites show a mixture of Negro and Bushman features. The Iron Age peoples of the Zambian plateau must have lived in comparative isolation from the outside world. Copper was traded from village to village, but only rarely did the agents of coastal merchants come into these remote settlements away from the Zambezi Valley. It was not until the rise of great Kongo kingdoms at the beginning of the second millenium A.D. that the rich mineral resources were exploited to any great extent by their owners.[13]

In addition Iron Age communities settled in Mashonaland, in what is now Rhodesia, where they may have arrived some time by the fourth century A.D. and crossed the Limpopo River some time later into what is now South Africa. A proportion of this population was of Negroid ancestry, but their features were somewhat changed by intermarriage with the Bushmen who were already settled in the country. The Stone Age hunters and food-gatherers seem to have lived in peaceful association with Iron Age farmers until recent times. The influence of the new immigrants may have led many Bushmen to abandon their traditional way of life and turn to food-producing; this could have resulted from a gradual process of acculturation benefitting both partners, for the new immigrants also adopted economic practices from the Stone Age people, and much of the botanical knowledge of the present tribes in southern Africa may have derived from Stone Age sources.[14]

Subsequently, Bantu-speaking herdsmen made their way to Rhodesia. It is not quite certain where these cattle-keepers originated; they may have come from the Congo or Ethiopia. They appear to have journeyed through East Africa, past the shores of Lake Nyasa, reaching Rhodesia about the tenth or eleventh century A.D.[15] According to another theory, elaborated by D. P. Abraham, the Bantu invasion of Rhodesia may have occurred even somewhat earlier. According to his interpretation, the ancestors of the modern Karanga or Shona entered the country about 850 A.D. They gradually increased in number, and spread toward the south and southeast, toward the Limpopo Valley. They came into contact with Bushmen and the indigenous Iron Age communities of the country and enriched their material culture through knowledge picked up from their neighbors. The proto-Karanga located copper and gold deposits; they produced finely wrought ornaments for their own use and also developed more elegant styles of pottery than their predecessors. In the tenth century they began to trade with Arab pioneers from the coast; gold became a marketable merchandise, and the Rhodesian mining industry supplied the east coast towns with much of their wealth.

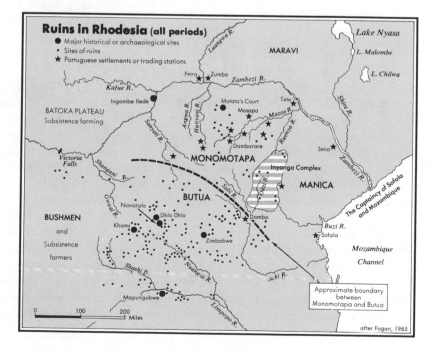

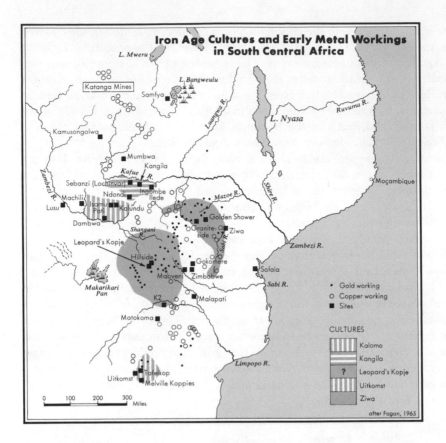

Iron Age Cultures and Early Metal Workings in South Central Africa

• Gold working
○ Copper working
■ Sites

CULTURES

Kalomo
Kangila
Leopard's Kopje
Uitkomst
Ziwa

after Fagan, 1965

The Bantu of the interior thus created an important African civilization. They participated in the commercial life of the Indian Ocean, but not to the extent of that taken by the West African forest communities in the trading systems of the savannah and North Africa. Trade helped to advance the Bantu in the arts of civilization; trade may also have played a part in developing a more tightly organized state. The Karanga also advanced in the arts of stone building, and archaeologists have discovered a great number of ruins, extending far afield, into Rhodesia, Botswana, the northern Transvaal and Mozambique. Their structure was of two basic types. Platform walls were made for retaining daga (mud) structures. In addition, the early builders erected free-standing walls, sometimes of impressive size. They consisted of dry, dressed stone, and no mortar was employed. In Mashonaland the early architects made use of a type of granite that exfoliates in natural layers. Walls were almost invariably circular, and entrances were gently rounded, with few right angles, resulting in simple, but impressive structures.[16] Stone served for the construction of military defenses, perhaps for cattle kraals, and also for religious purposes. The Karanga, like the remaining Bantu-speaking peoples, worshipped the spirits of their ancestors who, according to Bantu beliefs, maintained a never-ending interest in the affairs of the living and who linked humanity with Mwari, the Supreme Being, the creator of the world and of man. The Karanga built many sacred shrines, the principal one on a hill called *mhanwa*. This was called Dzimba dzembabwe (or Zimbabwe, the house of stone), and became the focal point of the nation. By astute maneuvering, the Karanga leaders established an overlordship over a loose confederacy of tribal chiefs who paid tribute in ivory and gold dust, so that political power and trade went hand in hand. In time the Karanga, like many other Bantu or Negroid peoples, built up a stronger monarchy. According to Abraham, consolidation was assisted by outside pressure. During the thirteenth century the Karanga had to contend with immigrants from Botswana, who sought new land because of the progressive desiccation of the Kalahari desert. The Karanga met this threat by organizing their nation on a more military basis. The Karanga kings ruled by means of a council of prominent men, by strategically placed regiments of warriors, and also by maintaining tight control over the cult of Mwari.

In conclusion we may say that over a period of centuries, Bantu-speaking tribes thus spread over something like one-third of Africa, and their dispersion made a decisive change in the history of the continent. They carried with them the art of smelting and working metal, so that the Bantu migrations made a major contribution to the cultural history of mankind. Their wanderings must have involved a great deal of hybridization with other stocks—Bushman, Pygmy, Hottentot, Cushite, and so forth, so that the ethnographic pattern of Africa became even more variegated than before. The settlers had to adapt themselves to all kinds of ecological circumstances —to forests and savannah, to dry bushland and well-watered coastal plains, to mountain country and low-lying lacustrine swamps. They accordingly developed many different forms of agriculture, different political systems, and different kinship organizations, which greatly added to the richness and diversity of Africa's cultural traditions. Generally speaking, however, the Bantu *Völkerwanderung* involved a southward shift of population. The Bantu, in other words, were moving *away* from the main centers of civilization in the Near East, the Mediterranean, and the northern savannahs of Africa. For many Bantu groups migration, to some extent, therefore entailed a considerable degree of cultural isolation, so that in the long run the Bantu-speaking peoples had to pay a substantial price for their achievement in peopling such a huge slice of the African continent.

THE INDONESIAN IMPACT

The Bantu were essentially landsmen. Their technology was adapted to the conditions of the African veld and precluded large-scale expansion by sea. There were exceptions. Arab records, for instance, attest that black people dwelling in the region of Zanzibar used canoes, and some Africans may have ventured into the Indian Ocean. The dugout canoe without an outrigger is not, however, suitable for long journeys by sea, and Madagascar probably remained as inaccessible to the early Bantu as it did to the Bushmen. Archaeological evidence favors the assumption that throughout the prehistoric period Madagascar remained uninhabited. The island was settled only in more recent times, and the first colonizers were probably seamen from Indonesia, familiar with more advanced navigational techniques and also with the use of iron. This hypothesis is strengthened by what we know of the Malgache language. The dialects of Madagascar all belong to the Indonesian branch of the Malayo-Polynesian group. They are similar in character: their likeness suggests original immigration by people with a uniform linguistic and cultural inheritance.

Scholars still dispute when and how the first Indonesians came to the island. The colonists are unlikely to have arrived before iron was commonly used in Indonesia, but even this hypothesis provides an uncertain starting point. Estimates for the date of the introduction of iron to the Indonesian archipelago vary from 300 B.C. to 200 A.D., so that there is room for a good deal of speculation. The first transoceanic migrations, on the other hand, presumably occurred before Indonesia adopted Hindu culture, for the proto-Malagasys seem to have conserved the original Indonesian ways without later admixtures. This theory derives strong support from the small number of Sanskrit words from India found in the Madagascar languages. Malagasy civilization is still, in a certain sense, a cultural museum, which preserves certain material objects characteristic of earlier periods in Indonesian history. But again there is room for many different interpretations. The Hinduization of Indonesia extended over a long span of time; it did not proceed in a uniform fashion (and has not been completed to this day). Hindu culture appears to have been established on the east coast of Sumatra, in Malaya, in Java, and in some parts of Borneo some time between the second and the fifth centuries A.D. But many other portions of the archipelago remained pagan, or succumbed to Hindu civilization at a later period, so that the settlement of Madagascar could have occurred as late as the eighth century A.D. The exact period thus remains difficult to determine, but the fifth or sixth centuries A.D. would be a reasonable guess.

Long-distance navigation across the Indian Ocean was made possible by the outrig-

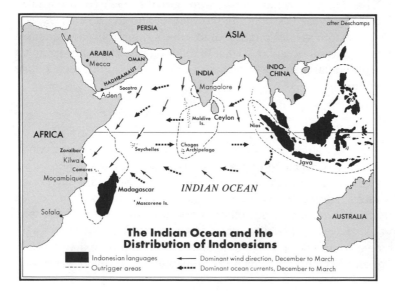

The Indian Ocean and the Distribution of Indonesians

████ Indonesian languages   ⟵ Dominant wind direction, December to March
------ Outrigger areas   ⟵▪▪▪▪ Dominant ocean currents, December to March

ger canoe, whose invention represented one of the great advances made by mankind in the art of shipbuilding. The outrigger vessel with sails was a highly seaworthy and dependable craft, which enabled South Seas navigators to accomplish feats greater than those of the Phoenicians and the Vikings. Indonesians apparently first learned to master the sea lanes of their own enormous archipelago; later they ventured far into the Pacific and established regular trade routes linking Malaya, Sumatra, and Java with the Philippines, and then with the southeast coast of China and with Formosa. In addition, Indonesian sailors journeyed westward to the Nicobar Islands and Ceylon, to the Laccadives, to the west coast of India, to Southern Arabia, and finally to East Africa and Madagascar, making skillful use of the favorable winds and currents on the way.

There are several possible hypotheses to explain the route taken for the colonization of Madagascar from the east. The most likely one postulates Indonesian settlements on the African east coast. Some of the newcomers may have stayed on and intermarried with the indigenous population. Others went further afield and—making use of the peculiar navigational conditions of the Mozambique Channel—reached northeast Madagascar, from where they penetrated further inland.[17] The topography of the "Great Island"—a landmass so large that it might almost rank as a small subcontinent—with its vast differences in climate, altitude and vegetation, made for settlement in "penny pockets" on the part of relatively small groups, organized as independent clans. The geographical remoteness of Madagascar gave a considerable degree of natural protection to the newcomers. Beset by the sea, the scattered colonists were able to maintain a considerable measure of cultural unity, even though the original Indonesian stock must have been further enriched by Negroid admixtures.

The importance of Indonesia's cultural contribution appears to have been considerable. The pioneers apparently brought all manner of new goods, including sewn boats, outrigger canoes, musical instruments such as the xylophone and the zither, as well as new fishing methods. Above all, they brought various food crops, including rice, taro, yams the Polynesian arrowroot, and bananas. The banana may conceivably have spread from the Mozambique coast via the mouth of the Zambezi and the great lakes of East Africa as similar varieties of the cultivated plant and similar names for the cooked food are found all along this route. The banana must be planted and carried in the form of suckers and corms, as it cannot be grown from seed. Though these corms can survive for short periods, they are not suitable for migratory peoples and involve a settled kind of agriculture of the kind now found in the vicinity of Lake Victoria. The banana may also have reached Africa by other routes, via South Arabia and Ethiopia, but southeast Asia seems the most probable region of origin. In addition settlers from southeast Asia may have brought Asian coco-yams and other crops. These became acclimatized in the mainland of Africa, though the details of this process remain a matter of dispute. These crops were, however, well-suited to the humid forest regions that cover great parts of Africa, much more so than grains like wheat or rye. The proto-Bantu and Bantu settlers who became familiar with the use of yams and bananas thus acquired an asset of enormous value; the additional crops imported from southeast Asia probably gave them a great advantage in colonizing the tropical zones of east and parts of central Africa.

The Indonesian settlers in Madagascar also acted, as it were, as cultural middlemen for African products, importing chicken, sheep, and cattle from the mainland to Madagascar and developing a relatively diversified and productive form of agriculture. They constructed well-built houses of a rectangular structure, with thatched gable roofs and walls of bamboo, reeds, or mats. They were skilled potters and wood carvers; they knew how to work iron and weave cotton; they were expert fishermen, and apparently developed a more complex technology than the early Bantu peoples. Malagasy society also took over many religious institutions from ancient Indonesia; these may possibly have been blended with African beliefs so that the island became a melting pot of Indonesian and mainland traditions.

NOTES

1. Posnansky, "The Origins of Agriculture and Iron Working in Southern Africa," in Posnansky, ed., *Prelude to East African History.* This excellent collection of essays has been used extensively in this section.

2. "Extracts from the Book written by Duarte Barbosa [1513]," in George McCall Theal, ed., *Records of South-eastern Africa* (Cape Town, 1898), vol. 1, p. 98.

3. "Wreck of the Ship Saint Albert at the Rock of the Fountains, in the year 1593," in Theal, vol. 2, p. 293.

4. "Extracts from the Decade written by Antonio Bocarro [1959]," in Theal, vol. 3, p. 355.

5. "Delagoa Bay by Mr. Fynn," in Theal, vol. 2, p. 480.

6. Posnansky, pp. 86–89.

7. Quoted by Eric A. Walker, *A History of Southern Africa* (London, 1957), p. 35.

8. "Delagoa Bay by Mr. Fynn," in Theal, vol. 2, p. 480.

9. Malcolm Guthrie, "Language Classification and African Studies," *African Affairs* (Spring 1965), p. 33.

10. Aidan Southall, "The Peopling of Africa—The Linguistic and Sociological Evidence," in Posnansky, pp. 60–81.

11. Gervase Mathew, "The East African Coast until the Coming of the Portuguese," in Oliver and Mathew, vol. 1, p. 101.

12. Posnansky, p. 89.

13. Brian M. Fagan, *Southern Africa During the Iron Age* (New York, 1965).

14. Fagan, p. 64.

15. Roger Summers, "The Iron Age Cultures and Early Bantu Movements," in William Vernon Brelsford, ed., *Handbook to the Federation of Rhodesia and Nyasaland* (London, 1960), pp. 43–56.

16. Fagan, pp. 100–102.

17. Hubert Deschamps, *Histoire de Madagascar* (Paris, 1960), pp. 13–38.

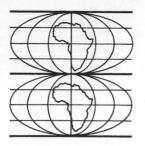
PART

V
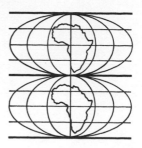

ISLAMIC AND INDIGENOUS EMPIRES: AFRICA'S MIDDLE AGES

Chapter 15

Cross and Crescent in Northeastern Africa

THE ARAB INVASIONS

In 622 A.D. a group of earnest believers of the prophet Mohammed slipped away from the city of Mecca in Arabia where Islam, their new religion, had failed to find much of a welcome. The fugitives found a new home in Medina, some 250 miles away, and their migration *(hegira)* is accounted the beginning of the Muslim era to this day. Mohammed considered himself to be the greatest and last of the prophets, the successor both of Moses and of Jesus. Islam absorbed Jewish and Christian, as well as indigenous Arab, elements, and came to rest on what Muslims regard as the five pillars of the faith—the belief in one God and His prophet, regular daily prayer, alms giving, a pilgrimage to Mecca, and fasting in the month of Ramadan. Islam provided rules for the whole life of man, from ritual purity, the prohibition of usury and of alcoholic liquors, the regulation of polygamous marriages, the punishment of crimes, down to the right way of trimming one's beard. Mohammed also had the qualities of a statesman; he embarked on the unification of the Arabian Peninsula, and when he died in 632, Arabia—for the first time in its history—had become a power of considerable consequence.

Arabia had to contend with two powerful, but mutually hostile blocs, the Byzantine and the Persian empires. Neither Greek nor Persian, however, could prevail against Muslim arms. Arab forces, small but highly mobile and brilliantly led, embarked on a series of extraordinary campaigns that, in time, carried Islam to the borders of China in the east and to the shores of the Atlantic Ocean in the west. In 641 the Persians suffered a crushing defeat at Nehavend; the last king of Persia's Sassanid Dynasty sought salvation in flight, and Persia, with its rich civilization, passed under Arab rule. The Byzantines did only a little better. In 639 Jerusalem fell to the Muslims, and the Byzantines subsequently lost nearly all their possessions in the Middle East outside Anatolia.

In 640 the Arabs invaded Egypt and subsequently penetrated into Tripolitania and what is now Tunisia. In the second half of the seventh century the Arabs resumed their attacks, and the Arab forces finally reached the Atlantic. The invaders both fought and cooperated with the Berbers of North Africa. Many Berber communities, some of which had leanings towards Judaism, subsequently rebelled, but could not stem the tide. The Arabs held their positions, conquered most of Morocco, and largely converted the country to Islam. In 711 a Muslim army, composed largely of Berbers under Arab leadership, invaded the Iberian Peninsula. The Visigothic rulers of Spain failed to hold out; the Muslims conquered the country and crossed the Pyrenees into France: their advance was brought to a halt in 732 near Tours, some 250 miles away from the shores of England.

In the East, the core of the Byzantine empire held out successfully, becoming essentially a Greek rather than a Graeco-Roman power, but the Byzantines had to accept territorial losses of great magnitude. Arab fleets secured control over the better part of the Mediterranean, and Crete, Sicily, and other Mediterranean islands subsequently fell under the Crescent's sway.

Arab warriors and their allies thus conquered the greatest empire which the world had seen hitherto—an aggregation of land compared with which the dominions of Ashurbanipal, Alexander, and Augustus seemed small. Arab might, moreover, did not depend on arms alone. Islamic law, based on the Koran and the traditions of the Prophet, proved extremely flexible and was modified by skillful exegesis and ingenious analogies to suit many different social circumstances. Political unification speeded up the flow of ideas and of goods all the way from the frontiers of China to the Middle East, the Mediterranean, and the shores of the Atlantic. Muslim merchants came to control a considerable share of the world's trade; Muslim vessels sailed far afield, into the Tyrrhenian and the Red Sea, the Atlantic and the Indian Ocean.

Arabic, the sacred language of the Koran, became the accepted *lingua franca* for much of the civilized world. Arab scholars learned from Byzantines, Jews, and Persians, and in turn passed new ideas on to their neighbors. Arab-derived words, like "admiral" in naval usage, "algebra" in mathematics, "nadir" and "zenith" in astronomy, "alcohol" in chemistry, are living reminders in our own tongue of the military and intellectual supremacy the Arabs once attained.

The Muslim conquests brought about a decisive shift in the cultural configuration of Europe. The Muslims overran a large share of the former Graeco-Roman world. Only a portion, including the Iberian Peninsula and Sicily, was ever permanently recovered for the Cross. North Africa and the Middle East, once part of the Christian world, remained firmly in Muslim hands, and none of the many subsequent European counterattacks was ever able to re-Christianize any substantial part of the areas thus lost. The success of Arab colonization depended on an astonishing capacity for cultural assimilation. In the conquered lands of North Africa, for instance, there was an Arab ruling class. This, however, soon came to consist of persons with mixed ancestry, Berber, Greek, Vandal, or other stocks, and many of the so-called "Arabs" soon had little in common with the original invaders. The Spanish orientalist Julian Ribera has thus worked out mathematically that the percentage of Arab ancestry in Abd al Rahman III (912–961), a Muslim monarch in Spain, was only 0.39 percent.[1]

Intermarriage and large-scale conversions to Islam thus produced a civilization whose level depended to a considerable extent on the contributions made by the original inhabitants. In Tunisia, where there was an old, established cultural tradition, a highly developed Islamic way of life came into being almost at once, whereas in Morocco, a relatively backward country in the seventh century, the flowering of civilization took much longer. In addition to the ruling class of Arab or Arabized landowners, civil servants, soldiers, and merchants, conquest also brought in its wake whole Arab tribal communities, who found new land for themselves in various parts of North Africa. These newcomers sometimes amalgamated with the existing population; but sometimes they remained a compact mass and a backward element. The Arab occupation soon turned the whole region into the "Maghrib" ("the West"), giving it that typically Arabo-Berber aspect which it has retained ever since. Within a century or so the process of cultural assimilation was often so complete that Arab rule was no longer felt as foreign domination. In time logistic difficulties, Arab and Berber dislike of central control, and social, political, and economic tensions in the Islamic world itself led to political fragmentation. Local dynasties assumed command and a new political balance of power came into being.

Roughly speaking, Arab culture came to radiate from three main centers. Egypt in time became an independent realm as well as a major power, famed for the skill of its artists, the learning of its scholars, and the prowess of its warriors. The rulers of Tunisia assumed control over much of eastern Algeria and Tripolitania. (For a time they even dominated the European island of Sicily.) There was also a great Islamic center in the west which drew its main strength first from southern Spain, later from Morocco. Muslims and Jews from Spain came to exercise a peculiarly profound influence on the development of science and philosophy in Europe. Morocco played an important role in Spanish history. Moroccan missionaries and travelers, merchants and conquerors also had a major part in shaping the destinies of Morocco's distant southern frontier, in the lands of the desert.

CHRISTIAN ENCLAVES: THE NORTHERN SUDAN

In a previous chapter, we have alluded to the development of a vigorous Christian, half-Byzantine civilization in the northern Sudan. The Islamic conquest of Egypt largely cut off Nubia from the world of Greek Orthodoxy, and the country suffered several invasions from Egypt. But the Nubians as a whole seem to have been willing to resist the Muslim advance—unlike the Christian Copts of Egypt, who had welcomed the Arab warriors as deliverers from the yoke of Byzantium. In the face of common danger from the north, Nobatia and Mukurra fused—though possibly the union may have first been occasioned by Mukurran conquest. The united kingdom, known as Dongola, stretched from the First Cataract to the borders of Alodia (somewhere between the Fourth Cataract and the confluence of the Nile and the Atbara) and constituted a state of considerable power. Nubian archers—wont to aim for their opponents' eyes—acquired a deadly reputation as marksmen, and for many centuries the Muslims failed to make much headway. Admittedly the Nubians (that is to say the Dongolans) sometimes had to deliver a tribute in slaves and other commodities to their northern neighbors, but this tenuous relationship may have corresponded to a commercial treaty, with the Nubians receiving grain, wine, and horses in exchange.

The Islamic presence in Egypt also seems to have facilitated a shift from Greek Orthodox to Monophysite Christianity in the interior. This change may have both reflected and accentuated Nubia's relative isolation from the Byzantine world. The Monophysite patriarch of Alexandria apparently made good use of his opportunities to gain more influence in Nubia, and the country largely adopted his creed. This ecclesiastical transformation seems to have begun at the beginning of the eighth century under King Mercurios, who became known to his Monophysite adherents as the "New Constantine." Copts accordingly played a considerable part in the civilization of the northern Sudan. Coptic clergymen occupied high religious offices; Coptic refugees found new homes for themselves in the country; Coptic monks established numerous communities; Coptic became the recognized language of trade in Lower Nubia.

But the region was never fully Copticized. The administration continued to operate on the Byzantine pattern. Art and architecture still owed a great deal to Greek, Syrian, and even Mesopotamian inspiration. Greek, sometimes in a barbarously garbled version, remained the language of devotional literature and of the liturgy. The Nubians also began to commit their own language to writing, using mainly the Coptic form of the Greek alphabet. Some of their inscriptions in archaic Nubian survive to the present day.

Dongola for a long time was able to conduct an active foreign policy, and occasionally even threatened the southern portion of Egypt. In 745 King Cyriacos of Dongola marched northward with a powerful army composed of horsemen and camel riders, penetrating deep into Egypt. The kings of Nubia were briefly able to assume a kind of protectorate over their patriarch in Egypt. In the tenth century Nubian forces raided the oases of Kharga and Aswan. In addition Dongola seems to have exercised considerable influence beyond its southern and western borders. The kings of Dongola dominated a part of Darfur, and Christian monks, we are told, introduced the cultivation of the date palm to this distant region. The uplands of Ennedi and Tibesti may also have formed part of the Nubian sphere of influence. Medieval Nubia, in other words, seems to have formed an inner-African bridgehead of Christian-Byzantine civilization, playing perhaps a part similar to that of Meroë, which once represented an outpost of Egyptian civilization in the far south. This Christian civilization seems to have shared many features with European medieval civilizations. Church and state were separated, but Christianity exercised a profound cultural effect. There was a vigorous legal tradition; there was outstanding art that owed its creative impulse to ecclesiastical inspiration.

We cannot tell for certain how far, or in what form, Nubian cultural influence extended beyond the borders of Dongola. Some believe that Nubian political institutions and symbols may have found imitators in lands as far away as the Niger bend. Indigenous traditions of the ancient Hausa, Songhai, Nupe, and Yoruba states all point to ancient links with the east, and there were certainly some commercial contacts between the eastern and the western Sudan. But the details are hard to make out. A tradition from Benin thus tells of a priest king who governed a country twenty months of travel east of Benin; this potentate supposedly invested the Benin rulers with a pilgrim's staff, helmet, and Cross upon the succession of the Benin monarch. This tale may refer to some kind of a political relationship between Benin and Dongola. But the story could also reflect contacts between Benin and Ethiopia or Benin and Christian North Africa; we simply cannot say for sure.

In the long run, however, Christian Nubia could not hold out against the Islamic tide. Geographically, Dongola formed part of the Nile Valley; the country depended on its northward communications and lacked those natural mountain bastions which helped to assure Ethiopia's independence. Muslims gradually infiltrated into the region south of Aswan and acquired more and more landed property. In the ninth century the gold mines of the eastern desert attracted numerous Muslim adventurers, and Islamic pressure on Dongola increased. In the late twelfth century, Sultan Saladin of Egypt inflicted a smashing defeat upon Dongola which, by this time, seems to have completely lost its ancient splendor. According to an Egyptian report of the period, Dongola was by then a poverty-stricken country where, except for the king's palace, people dwelt only in huts. The king of Dongola appeared in public in a silken dress and rode his horse bareback. The Muslims made steady gains, and by the end of the thirteenth century they controlled Dongola up to about the Second Cataract. The remainder of the country was torn by dynastic disputes. Muslim armies devastated large areas, extorted hostages and tribute, and installed their own kinglets. In 1316 Muslim invaders carried off Kerenbes, the last Christian ruler of Dongola; his successor bore the Arab name of Abdullah, and Christian rule became a matter of history.[2]

The Christian religion in Dongola did not for long survive the end of the dynasty. We can as yet only speculate as to the reasons for the rapid disappearance of the Monophysite creed. Perhaps Christianity had made the mistake of identifying itself too closely with the state instead of the people. Christianity, after all, had not been able to hold out against Islam even in North Africa. Possibly the relatively close doctrinal relationship between the Monophysite creed and Islam facilitated conversion to the faith of the conquerors. Perhaps the powers of Nubia as a whole, threatened as it was both from the north and by primitive tribal communities on other borders, had been severely overtaxed. About all we can say with certainty is that Dongola was rapidly Islamized. The isolated kingdom of Alodia held out longer, but finally succumbed to Muslim invaders in 1504. Nubia's syncretic Christian civilization, one of the longest-lived in Africa, finally collapsed, leaving Islam in a position of unchallenged supremacy throughout the Sudan.[3]

THE CHRISTIAN ENCLAVES: ABYSSINIA

In the meantime, Christianity had also become solidly established in a great mountain bastion in the highlands of northeastern Ethiopia. In the fourth century A.D., Axum was a powerful kingdom, in touch with the Byzantine civilization of the eastern Mediterranean, with southern Arabia, with Egypt, and with India. Archaeological evidence suggests that sometime around the year 330 A.D. Ezana, king of Axum, decided to adopt Christianity, and replaced the old pagan systems of crescent and disk on his coins by the sign of the Cross. The apostle of the Axumites was Frumentius, a learned Syrian, who adhered to the Monophysite form of Christianity adopted by the Copts of Egypt. Frumentius found the soil well prepared. Merchants, scholars, and craftsmen from the eastern Mediterranean were probably a fairly familiar sight at Axum. Many Monophysites (that is to say, Christians who rejected the official religion of the Byzantine or East Roman Empire, and who held that in the person of the Incarnate Christ there was but a single divine nature) had sought refuge in Egypt, Arabia, and different parts of Ethiopia. Their influence helped to spread Christianity throughout much of the Axumite kingdom. They found numerous monasteries, which became the main centers of learning, mission work, and worship. They translated the Bible into the indigenous tongue. They gave an inspiration to the arts. They helped to establish new links between Ethiopia and the eastern Mediterranean; at the same time they also played their part in keeping Ethiopia distinct in religion and culture from Byzantium, which continued to look upon the Monophysites as heretics.

By the time Frumentius came to Axum, the kingdom was already a melting pot of different cultures—indigenous African, Byzantine, Coptic, Syrian, and Indian. Axumites traded with southern Arabia (from whence much of their culture had come), with Persia, and the countries beyond. Axum's physical wealth found expression in the use of a gold currency. The country's artistic tradition gave rise to a syncretic art of great power. As early as the pre-Christian era, the Axumites had made their name as carvers in wood and rock and as stone masons. They put up huge steles (stone pillars), which served as grave stones and memorials to the great of the kingdom. Modern engineers still puzzle over the means by which the ancients quarried, moved, and finally raised the giant stone slabs that went into the making of these steles. The greatest of them rose to a height of 110 feet—today it lies shattered in pieces, perhaps the greatest monolith of antiquity. All we can say for certain is that the Axumites not only possessed great technical skills, but also must have been able to mobilize, feed, and discipline a great labor force that provided the muscle power for these great enterprises.

When the Axumites became Christians, their builders and their carvers in wood and stone turned their skill to the construction of churches on a truly impressive scale. Initially, the Axumites built their churches in wood and masonry, with monumental doors, and latticed windows. They employed a peculiar form of constructing walls by means of alternative layers of wood and stone. In addition, Axumite builders began to carve their churches into solid rock. These incredible churches, with their vaults, arches and domes, reveal something of Axum's Byzantine heritage. But in addition, these buildings, with their splendidly painted walls and ceilings, their shrines hewn out of great monoliths, their air of dark splendor, have a genius of their own that renders them uniquely African.

The Axumites also excelled in the art of war. Axumite warriors campaigned successfully in Southern Arabia and spread their country's influence beyond the Red Sea. But the Axumites could not hold on to their scattered conquests. Towards the end of the century, the Persians, sworn enemies of Byzantium and Christianity, occupied Southern Arabia and disrupted the seaborne communications between the Axumite state and Byzantium. The rise of Islam left an even deeper mark on the development of Abyssinia. Hitherto, the country had formed part of a semicontiguous Christian frontier, in touch with the Mediterranean world. The Muslim conquest of Egypt and Southern Arabia, did not by any means destroy all links between Abyssinia and the Christian world, but it helped to accentuate the country's cultural isolation and forced Abyssinia ever more on its own resources, with the result that its energies were diverted southwards. Colonization in the Yemen and in the Nile-Atbara, to the east and north respectively, generally gave way to expansion into the central and southern highlands. There was also a gradual shift of political power away from the Akkele Guzay and the Tigrai towards Amhara, Lasta, and finally Shoa. The Cushitic elements reasserted themselves, and Axumite civilization probably became increasingly "African" in composition. Yet, as a long–term policy, the concentration on the large and homogeneous plateau was sound, for undoubtedly the collapse of the empire had been facilitated by its far-flung commitments and geographical decentralization. As Edward Ullendorf, a noted authority, puts it, the virtual imprisonment of the people within its great mountain massif, whatever its consequences in terms of civilization may have been, at least molded all those diverse elements into a nation that in times of external danger could abandon its centrifugal proclivities and become conscious of its essential unity.[4]

Historians are not well acquainted with the details of Abyssinia's Dark Age, but the main lines of the story appear to be the following. During the eighth century the Abyssinian state was assaulted by warlike communities from the north, the Beja, who occupied the coast and the foothills of the Eritrean plateau. In addition, Islam spread among the peoples of the littoral. There was probably a considerable influx of Arabs or Arabized invaders, and despite occasional reversals of fortune, when the Abyssinians managed to establish temporary footholds on the Red Sea, the Muslims could never be permanently dislodged from the coastal plain, where the climate was too hot and conditions too unfamiliar to attract Abyssinian settlers from the mountains. Muslim seafarers dominated the Red Sea, and the Dahlak Archipelago northeast of Massawa (now a little-known group of islands in the Red Sea) became a powerful and civilized maritime state doing extensive traffic in slaves. The commerce in human beings itself became an important agent in the Islamization of the coastal plain, strengthening the links between the Arab world and Africa and sustaining the prosperity of far-flung ports such as Zeila and Mogadishu. Slave raids also accelerated the diffusion of Islam among the pagan tribes of the interior, as conversion was the easiest way of escaping the depredations of alien dealers. The traffic created Muslim bridgeheads far inland, and what had begun as a commercial expedition might end in the establishment of petty Muslim sultanates. Islam in time spread far inland, gaining ground among the nomadic communities who dwelt between the sea and the eastern shores of the escarpment. Finally Islam began to encroach even upon eastern Shoa, in the center of what is now Ethiopia, and Sidamo in the southeast, engulfing something like half the area now included within the Ethiopian state.

For a time, the very existence of the Christian kingdom was threatened by a combination of foreign pressure and internal revolts of conquered people, including bitter resistance from the Agaw dwelling in the north, who, like many other Abyssinian groups, had been influenced by Judaic traditions imported at an earlier stage by Jewish settlers from Southern Arabia. The Abyssinians, however, managed to survive the desperate crisis that shook their country at the end of the tenth century. There was a revival of Christianity, which received fresh vigor by the arrival of Dan'el, the new Abuna (or Catholicos), as head of the Abyssinian Church. Dan'el, like all the other Abunas, owed his appointment to the Coptic patriarch of Alexandria, and Coptic influence was paramount in keeping the flame of civilization alive in the remote mountain enclave. The Agaw were converted and effectively brought within the orbit of Monophysite Christianity. The Christianization of these fierce fighters greatly strengthened the Abyssinian state, and brought about "a further installment in the 'indigenization' of monophysitism which, charged more and more with the residue of Judaic and pagan practices and beliefs, assumed a truly national and peculiarly Abyssinian form."[5]

The cultural and religious conquest of the Agaw also changed the country's political balance of power. Between 1137 and 1270, an Agaw dynasty, regarded by orthodox Abyssinian historians as "usurpers," seized the throne. Among the Agaw rulers, however, were men of considerable ability who defended the faith, built new churches and monasteries, and engaged in extensive missionary activity among pagan communities. The Agaw monarchs also maintained some contact with Egypt and Jerusalem, and Lalibela, the greatest of the dynasty, constructed a series of magnificent rock churches. Today these buildings, which took generations to complete, still offer an incredible sight. Ethiopian craftsmen carved out a great complex of churches and chapels into a bank of pink tuff on the shoulder of a mountain. They freed massive blocks of stone by trenching straight down into the stone. Artists then sculptured the blocks into churches, each fashioned of a single chunk of rock, each with its own character. Despite these achievements, the Agaw line, however, could not maintain itself in permanent power, and in 1270 the last king was murdered. Yekuno Amlak, the leader of the dissident party, was proclaimed king, and with him the rightful Solomonic dynasty, which claimed direct descent from Solomon and the Queen of Sheba, was said to have been "restored." Political power now centered upon Amhara, the true geographical heart of the country, and it was from here that the kingdom was stabilized. The restoration of the Solomonic kings was accompanied by a great literary renascence, and from then onward Abyssinia entered upon a more modern era for which better documentation at last became available.

THE AFRICAN EAST COAST FROM THE SIXTH TO THE THIRTEENTH CENTURY

The prosperity of Axum had depended to some extent on the African gold trade, and by the sixth century Axum's commercial contacts may have extended to the auriferous regions of Kenya. Axumites' communication lines to the south probably ran parallel to the coast from which they were often divided by great areas of impenetrable bush. Echoes of Axumite influence occur perhaps as far as Rhodesia. The medieval custom of erecting stone pillars, frequently phallic in shape, seems to have had its origin in Sidamo, in southern Ethiopia, and subsequently spread far to the south. There is, however, no evidence for any Axumite political control of the coast. Neither do the Persians seem to have established authority in these distant lands —subsequent traditions to the contrary. There were, however, many commercial contacts..Persian as well as Indian merchants dealt in soft ivory, gold, tortoise shells, and slaves from Africa. In addition Arab seafarers and merchants gained footholds on the coast and established trading posts, including centers like Kilwa and Zanzibar.

The origins of these various coastal cities are still in dispute. According to one interpretation, they began as Persian or Arab colonies, but according to Gervase Mathew, a noted authority on whose work this section is based, there is no conclusive archaeological or documentary evidence to support this assumption.[6] A second hypothesis holds that trade occasioned a gradual development of town life among the Negroid population of the coast before these cities became Islamized. Indigenous African rulers then profited by their contacts with Arab, Persian, and Indian Muslim traders, and slowly adopted the techniques and organization of Islamic states. A third theory argues that the cities may have been created by a conjunction of two factors. Muslim sailors first of all established temporary settlements where ships were beached between the monsoons; these posts in time became permanent "factories" with storage rooms for slaves and ivory. The appearance of foreign seamen created seasonal African settlements, where tribesmen gathered year by year to barter, and gradually these aggregations attained permanence. All three interpretations may well have proved true in different cases; but whatever the origin of these cities they must soon have become cultural melting pots.

The Muslim immigrants comprised men of very different backgrounds. East Africa, for instance, attracted many religious refugees. Some time in the eighth century, for instance, a group of Arab Muslims, followers of the fourth Islamic Caliph 'Ali, escaped from the ruling dynasty, the Umayyads (whose capital was in Damascus). These immigrants became known as the Zayadiyah and became a self-contained community designated by their opponents as heretics, or Shia. In the tenth century many orthodox Muslims, known as Sunni, settled in East Africa. The Sunni clashed with the Shia, and established new urban settlements such as Mogadishu. Both Shia and Sunni alike, however, continued to look upon Arabia as their homeland, and neither of them proselytized on any large scale. The third wave of Muslim colonists came from the Persian city of Shiraz. The Shirazis were also heterodox Muslims and likewise frequently clashed with the established Sunni. The successive waves of Arab and Persian

**Medieval Trading Ports
of the Indian Ocean**

------ Trade routes

immigrants to the East coast gradually produced a mixed Afro-Muslim community, not so much by means of armed conquest but by the slow process of intermarriage and of cultural interchange with black people.

Many townsmen adopted Islam, and high dignitaries used Arabic—sometimes in a rather garbled form—as their official language. It is impossible to say how widely Arabic was actually spoken. Nicknames and the play on words occurring in ancient documents suggest that the common speech of Kilwa, for instance, was something akin to Swahili. Recent archaeological finds—including bowls buried intact beneath flooring, a severed human skull, and possibly the litter of scattered bones—may indicate the survival of African animism and of human sacrifice, not merely among the common people but also among the rich merchants of Kilwa. The records of Zanzibar suggest cultural syncretism of a similar kind. It is clear that during the tenth century a Muslim dynasty reigned over the island. Trade was in Arab hands, but the country remained partly pagan, and the Muslims in turn became partly Africanized. The main cultural product of this union was the Swahili tongue, a Bantu language with Arabic words, which became the *lingua franca* of the coast, and which in time produced a vigorous literature of its own.

The coastal communities looked to Arabia and to India rather than the interior. Their ethos was maritime, and their commerce extended to distant places. They were in touch with Arabia and the Persian Gulf, with southern India, Ceylon, Java, Sumatra, and, probably indirectly, with China. Trade at times seems to have been accompanied by further settlement from the East. Some time in the beginning of the Middle Ages, there was perhaps a second Indonesian colonization in Madagascar. Evidence of Indonesian influence has also been found as far north as Somalia. Muslim culture, however, prevailed over all competitors, and during the thirteenth century the East Coast at last became integrally part of the Islamic world. Religious and cultural infiltration probably went hand in hand with growing commerce.

There was now an expanding market in Western Europe for luxury goods like ivory and gold. Muslim middlemen made good use of their opportunities, so that the first gold coins to be struck in London have, on assay, been found to be made of African gold. The Mongol conquests in the Near East may have given an additional impetus to these far-flung commercial contacts. In 1258 a Mongol army seized Baghdad and overthrew the Caliphate. But in Persia and Iraq alike the invaders adopted Islam. They safeguarded commerce as a matter of policy; they kept watch over the great roads that passed eastward from Caffa in the Crimea and from Tabriz; they opened new routes, so that by the late thirteenth century coins struck by the Mongol sultans of Tabriz have been found as far afield as Zanzibar.

The political history of the East African coast remains hard to disentangle for this period. The scattered chain of Muslim communities on the African shore of the Indian Ocean never coalesced into a confederacy. Sometimes in feud and sometimes in league with their neighbors, they each had their own rulers and probably their own commercial oligarchies, which were content to safegard local interests. Some time during the late twelfth century, Kilwa, for instance, may have gained control over the trade route that brought Rhodesian gold north from Sofala. Kilwa stood out as the most important commercial community in the south. Mogadishu was the biggest city in the north. But whatever the rivalries between these city states, their allies and clients were all of Muslim persuasion, and Islam gained a permanent foothold from which it was never subsequently dislodged.

NOTES

1. Nevill Barbour, ed., *A Survey of North West Africa (The Maghrib)* (London, 1962), pp. 15–19.

2. Gerster, *Nubien: Goldland am Nil, pp. 126–152.*

3. J. A. Ilbevare, *"Christianity in Nubia,"* *Tarikh,* vol. 2, no. 1 (1967), p. 60.

4. Ullendorf, *The Ethiopians* p. 59. This section is based on Ullendorf's excellent and most readable study.

5. Ullendorf, p. 62. The Abyssinian Church to this day retains many special features which bear witness to the manner in which Christianity managed to adapt itself to indigenous forms. Dances and the beating of drums enliven the liturgy on solemn occasions. On dedicating a new church, the faithful sacrifice an ox, a ewe, and a she-goat. The Abyssinians also observe a number of Jewish customs, including the Mosaic distinction between clean and unclean meat, that is, they reject the flesh of beasts that neither chew the cud nor have cloven hoofs.

6. See Mathew, "The East Africa Coast Until the Coming of the Portuguese," in Oliver and Mathew, eds., *History of East Africa,* vol. 1, pp. 94–127, especially pp. 114–117.

Wooden portrait statue of King Bom Bosh, Bushongo, Congo, ca. 1650–1660. The statue was intended to preserve the continuity of the royal power. 19¾ inches high. (Courtesy The Brooklyn Museum.)

196

Bronze head of a Queen Mother (Iyoba), Benin. 20 inches high. (Both by courtesy of the Federal Department of Antiquities, Lagos, Nigeria.)

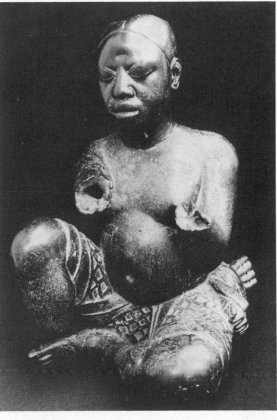

One of the greatest of the Ife bronzes, preserved *in situ* in the village of Tada, Nigeria. 20½ inches high.

Figure of a chief from the Tsoede group of Ife bronzes. 46 inches high. (By courtesy of the Federal Department of Antiquities, Lagos, Nigeria.)

Bronze plaque from the palace of the King (Oba) in Benin, Nigeria, capital city of the Bini empire. 20 inches high.

Iron Age terra cotta head from the Nok
culture of Nigeria. 14 inches high.

Esie, soapstone figure of a man, probably of Yoruba origin.

Mama, buffalo headdress mask used in dances to control the well-being of
the people. 24 inches long. (All pictures on this page by courtesy of the Federal
Department of Antiquities, Lagos, Nigeria.)

199

Yoruba mask from Nigeria and Dahomey. Used by the *Gelede* cult in dances to propitiate witches. (Collection of Mr. and Mrs. William Bascom.)

Ba-Luba face mask from the Congo (Kinshasa), worn in dances when a new chief or village head was appointed. (Buffalo Museum)

Bakongo face mask from the Congo (Kinshasa). Faceted face planes are rare in African art. (By courtesy of The Museum of Primitive Art, New York.)

Chapter 16

Some Early West and Central African Empires

A NOTE OF CAUTION

Medieval cartographers delighted in covering the African map with strange cities and fantastic animals. Progress in map making came only with the substitution of such colorful representations by blank spaces prosaically marked *terra incognita* or "unknown." Early African history is to some extent in the same state as African geography in the Middle Ages or the Renaissance. Scholars have accumulated a little knowledge. But an immense amount of additional information remains to be uncovered, and what we do know is liable to be reinterpreted again and again by successive generations of scholars. Historians of early Africa should never tire of pointing out the provisional nature of their findings. They should always stress that many of today's most cherished theories may tomorrow be discarded with the same impatience with which modern geographers dismiss ancient tales concerning the Mountains of the Moon. Grandiose concepts such as "waves of conquest," "state-building processes," "economic stimuli" are nothing but hypotheses liable to be broken down by more detailed accounts that will put specific information in place of generalities. Face to face with historical uncertainty, investigators of the African past find themselves in good company. England, to mention one example, forms part of a small island, easily accessible, thoroughly mapped, and studied by generations of brilliant scholars. Britain's Anglo-Saxon past is much better documented than the formative days of any African country. Yet modern students are still able to come up with revolutionary theories concerning the Germanic invasions. Thus the conventional "Anglo-Saxon" interpretation of early English history has recently been challenged by a new view, postulating the

202

Frankish origins of early Germanic society in southeastern England.[1]

Yet Africa's area of historical uncertainty is immensely vaster than England's. Antiquaries and historians have been at work in England for many centuries; African historiography is of recent origins. The huge African continent remains much more poorly supplied with scholarly institutions, archives, and libraries than a small European country like Great Britain. African history, moreover, makes immense demands on its votaries. Sources are scattered and hard to find. They are also hard to read. An Anglo-Saxon specialist can get by on a knowledge of Anglo-Saxon, medieval Latin, and Norman French. A modern scholar concentrating, say, on East Africa, should ideally know Arabic and Swahili—perhaps even Persian, Gujurati, and Amharic, as well as several Bantu languages, in addition to the modern European tongues that form the linguistic equipment of a conventional historian. An African historian, unlike his colleague in England, also needs to be an academic "maid of all work," familiar with subjects as diverse as plant biology and linguistics, physical and social anthropology, archaeology, the study of blood groups, and a host of other sciences. Scholars with such a comprehensive knowledge are hard to find—and despite the intellectual effort that has recently gone into the writing of African history, we are as yet far from any definitive account concerning the early history of any major African region. This caveat applies to West Africa as much as to any other portion of the continent, and the subsequent, as well as the preceding, chapters should be read with a good deal of caution.

MINERS AND NOMADS

For untold centuries West Africa was one of Europe's principal sources of gold. The miners and their country were known to the ancients as the Wangara, but the exact location of their country remained a well-kept trade secret of the middlemen. Modern research, however, has thrown a good deal of light on the subject.[2] The producers were chronically short of salt, and salt—available in large quantities in the Sahara—played a vital part in the gold trade of antiquity. The bulk of African gold presumably came from the western Sudan, from the regions between the upper Senegal and the Faleme rivers, and at the junction of the upper Niger with the Tinkisso. These were favorably placed in relation to river routes; they also lay within reach of the principal Sudanese markets where Barbary merchants gathered. The main sources of gold were almost certainly situated in the country of the Mandingo, a Negro people mixed with Berber and Arab strains. Besides being the name of a geographical area, Wangara was the term by which the Mandingo (also called Mande, Mandigans, Mandenga, or Mandinka), especially their Soninke branch were known in the western Sudan. The industry depended on mining from shallow pits and on alluvial workings. The fluctuating nature of this mining enterprise gave rise to the strangest tales. Gold supposedly grew in the sands of Wangara like corals, or like carrots; some even insisted that the precious metal derived from the nests of gigantic ants whose size equalled that of cats!

In addition, gold was probably exported northward from Lobi on the upper Volta further to the east. In this region ancient gold workings remained associated with stone constructions quite unlike any others found in West Africa. The builders' identity remains a problem, the solution of which would throw further light on the ancient trade. Whoever they were, they must have dug up a great deal of the precious metal. They were also more likely to have sold their wares to the Sudan than to the coast, their country being separated from the sea by dense forests. E. W. Bovill, the historian of the trade, thus concludes that the term Wangara must have referred collectively to all these auriferous regions, as well as to their inhabitants. It was the enterprise of these Wangara that created one of the most important extractive industries known to antiquity.

The miner's skill, however, would have been useless without the merchant's expertise or his willingness to take risks. The Mediterranean cities provided a market for precious metal; the problem was to get the product to the customer. From an economic geographer's point of view, the forest belt of the western Sudan is an "island," encircled by the ocean to the south and by the savannah and the desert to the north. The Sahara, like the sea, can be "navigated," but only by specialists inured to its perils. The nomadic Berbers of the interior—as we have seen in a previous chapter—thus came to occupy a key position as middlemen. Travelers from ancient times used bullocks and bullock carts for transporting goods and gold. Gold flowed northward in several main streams, especially from Gao to Fezzan and Tripoli in the east, and from the Niger to Sijilmasa (Morocco) in the west. During Roman times, the use of the camel spread to the desert races west of Siwa and gave an additional boost to long-distance trade. The employment of these hardy animals, able to eat plants that no other beast would touch, also influenced the nomads' way of life in other ways; in particular camelry revolutionized the art of desert warfare.

Nomads, bred to an arid environment, can survive only by making full use of their country's scanty water resources and by keeping on the move. The margin between plenty and starvation is always narrow; life remains precarious. Desert people must always be ready to defend their wells and pastures. They are skilled guides in the desert and are also apt to become enterprising merchants unafraid of risk or distance. The men of the desert have also traditionally turned to conquest. Whenever grazing fails, they tend to spill over their traditional boundaries in response to economic necessity. Seasonal migrations are extended in time and space. Migrations are accompanied by raids; raids may turn into permanent occupation; conquests in turn must be defended against new waves of desert-borne invaders. The nomads' courage, hardihood, communal discipline, and mobility on the battlefield make them dangerous neighbors. Even strongly centralized governments find difficulties in resisting elusive swarms of mounted warriors. Weaker communities of sedentary agriculturists usually found resistance impossible in open country where horsemen and camelry could operate without hindrance. Foot soldiers cannot normally beat such cavalry, unless they fight in disciplined phalanxes of spearmen or serried ranks of archers, from behind city walls, or in tsetse-ridden forest country, where the nomads' beasts die from disease and the riders are wiped out in ambushes. Generally speaking, desert-borne conquest in West Africa thus reached its limit at the edge of the forest, but mounted men usually prevailed in the savannah and always in the desert.

In addition to superiority in the market place and on the battlefield, the nomads also acquired a militant faith. In a previous section we have seen how in 642 A.D. Arab invaders began their first advance west from Egypt. In 678 the Muslims renewed their assault and marched through the Maghrib. They occupied Fezzan in the south and reached the oasis of Kawar, but turned back as they were on the point of discovering the grasslands of the Sudan. The Berbers offered ferocious resistance, and for a time even swept the invaders back into Egypt. Finally the Berbers became firmly converted to Islam, and the new creed conferred great benefits on the Maghrib. The Arabs brought a tradition of literature and learning, as well as a new breadth of outlook they had absorbed from the Hellenistic culture of the eastern Mediterranean. Islam also developed a new sense of unity among its votaries. As Bovill puts it: "Throughtout the length and breadth of Islam, the Muslim traveller was sure of a welcome wherever he went, and the same hospitality awaited him among isolated Muslim communities in infidel lands. There is no more striking example of the extraordinary breadth of the Muslim horizon than an incident in the life of that great traveller Ibn Battuta (1304–1377). While staying in Sijilmasa, in southern Morocco, he discovered that his host was the brother of a man whom he had met some years before in western China."[3] Another incentive to foreign travel was the Hadj or pilgrimage to Mecca. In obedience to religious duty, men of many nations annually gathered in the holy cities of Arabia, where they freely exchanged information about one another's lands. The Islamized races of the Sahara were linked to this great tradition, and this stood them in good stead when they stepped into places of power.

The blending of Islamic elements with the culture of the savannah contributed to the emergence of what J. S. Trimingham has called the "Sudanic state system." The states of the savannah, kingdoms such as Ghana, Mali, and Songhai, appear to have owed their origin to powerful lineages that managed to superimpose their authority over many outlying communities. The new rulers usually allowed the existing local dignitaries to continue in office. As Robert O. Collins, a modern historian, puts it, "the Sudanic kings ruled people, not land," and when their rule collapsed, life in the villages went on relatively undisturbed.[4] The new rulers widely practiced Islam as an imperial cult, but they did not try to Islamize the bulk of their subjects.

THE EMPIRES OF TEKROUR AND GHANA

One of the oldest West African states of which we have any records is the medieval state of Tekrour. It originated in the middle valley of the Senegal River, the age-old home of the Tokolor people. The Tokolor were able to raise fine crops of millet along the rich alluvial flood lands of the Senegal. They were also favorably placed for the long-distance gold trade. The Tokolor state probably originated several hundred years before the tenth century A.D. and its renown was such that its name became oynonomous with "Sudan" for interior West Africa. From the ninth to the tenth century, Tekrour was ruled by the Dya'ago dynasty which was probably proto-Fulani in origin. Sometime after 1000 A.D. War Dyabi, the king of Tekrour, and all his court were converted to Islam by the peaceful efforts of Arabo-Berbers from Mauritania.

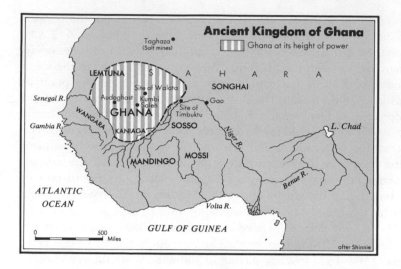

The upper strata of Tekrour completely identified themselves with Islam; indeed with the possible exception of the rulers of Kanem in the central Sudan, theirs was the earliest known conversion of a Negro kingdom to the Islamic religion.

The Tokolor state probably also included other races, such as Wolof, Serer, Fulani, and other minorities. In the eleventh century their country covered both banks of the Senegal River and extended inland to the south. Tekrour became one of the termini of the western routes traversing the Sahara and the Sudan from north to south and from east to west. But after the twelfth century pressure from the Moors forced the Tokolor to abandon much of the country on the right bank of the Senegal. This withdrawal, combined with the reorientation of the existing trade routes toward the west-central Sudan, may have caused the decay of its former greatness.

One of Tekrour's most powerful rivals was the kingdom of Ghana (not, of course, identical with the modern Republic of Ghana), another savannah state. Like Tekrour, Ghana may have derived its original impetus from the fruitful mingling of Negroid and Islamic cultural strains, and from the expansion of the trans-Saharan trade. During the eleventh century, at the height of its power, Ghana extended to the site of Timbuktu in the east, to the upper Niger in the southeast, to the Senegal in the south and southwest, and to the borders of Tekrour in the west. The northern limits of the empire at its zenith are less easy to define; but it probably extended at least over the southernmost Berber tribes.[5]

The beginnings of Ghana are shrouded in obscurity, but in all probability it originated in the settlement of Aukar, at that time inhabited by Mande-speaking Negroes, mainly the Soninke. According to Arab traditions, the first kings were "white" men, but the evidence is by no means clear. One school of thought holds that the founding dynasty was of "Judaeo-Syrian" origin. We do know that Jews and Berbers converted to Judaism played a part in trans-Saharan wars and trade, but the slender evidence does not seem to warrant a theory of Jewish origins. Alternatively, the early rulers of Ghana may have been Berbers. This seems a perfectly tenable assumption, since the adoption of the camel by North Africans would—as we have seen—enable desert-borne invaders to establish dominion over the Soninke. A third school of thought, represented by Raymond Mauny, suggests that the tradition of a white founding dynasty rests on a misconception and relates to later incursions. All authorities, however, agree that the people of Ghana were undoubtedly Negroes of Soninke stock, and that at the time of Ghana's greatest power and prosperity its rulers were black people of pagan faith. Ghana was certainly much affected by the north, although the remarkable feature was not the northerners' influence, but rather the Negroes' successful resistance to their advance and their success in turning the new order of things, especially the growing trans-Saharan trade, to their own advantage.[6]

Ghana's might seemed to have rested on its geographical position on the borders of the desert in the extreme north of the inhabitable part of the western Sudan. North African merchants settled in Ghana exchanged salt, copper, dried fruit, cowries, and other commodities for gold and slaves. Precious metal came from the lands of the Wangara, which seem to have been outside Ghana's political control. Trade and mining provided the kings of Ghana with ample revenue, enabling them to maintain an elaborate administration and also some form of economic controls designed to boost the price of gold. As Al Bakri, an eleventh century Arab geographer, put it: "From every donkey loaded with salt that enters the country, the king takes a duty of one golden dinar, and two dinars from every one that leaves. From a load of copper the duty to the king is five mithquals, and from a load of merchandise ten mithquals. The best gold found in the land comes from the town of Ghiyaro, which is eighteen travelling days from the city of the king, over a country inhabited by tribes of Negroes, their dwelling places being contiguous. The nuggets found in all the mines of the country are reserved for the king, only gold dust being left for the people. Without this precaution, the people would accumulate gold until it had lost its value. . . ."[7]

The Ghana empire relied heavily on the services of Muslim experts; according to Al Bakri, "the king's interpreter, the official in charge of his territory, and the majority of his ministers, are Muslims." The people, however, were pagans who practiced human sacrifice and offered successful resistance to the intrusion of Islam. The Muslims formed a separate community and lived in segregated quarters. "The city of Ghana consists of two towns lying in a plain. One town is inhabited by Muslims. It is large and possesses twelve mosques. . . . There are imams, muazzins, and salaried reciters of the Koran as well as jurists and learned men."[8] The wealthier people dwelt in houses of stone and acacia wood; the poorer folk presumably put up the pole-and-dagga huts characteristic of Africa as a whole. The king himself had a palace and a number of "dome-shaped dwellings," perhaps round huts. Archaeologists still dispute the exact location of his town, for the region contains many ancient ruins suggesting urban concentrations on a considerable scale. In all probability, however, the capital stood at Kumbi Saleh in what is now the modern Republic of Mauritania. Its stone-built ruins cover an area of about one square mile, and are surrounded by ancient cemeteries spreading over another two miles, so that the town must have been occupied for a considerable period. The finds dug up in the ruins suggest that the city was a rich medieval Muslim center destroyed at the height of its prosperity, though there is as yet no positive identification with pagan Ghana.

At the height of their power, the kings of Ghana were able to rule in an autocratic fashion, supported by their Muslim scribes and a host of pagan priests. "Around the king's town are domed buildings, woods and copses where live the sorcerers of these people, the men in charge of the religious cult. In these are also idols and the tombs of their kings. These woods are guarded and no unauthorized person can enter them, so that it is not known what is within them."[9] Al Bakri's description, however, clearly suggests that the Ghanaians, like most other Africans, venerated the spirits of their ancestors, especially those of their deceased kings. The king at the same time seems to have possessed a formidable machinery of coercion; his palace was surrounded by jails "and if anyone is imprisoned there, no more is ever heard of him." Ghana's military potential must have been equally impressive, even though Al Bakri's figure of 200,000 armed men, including 40,000 archers, belongs to the realm of rhetoric.

This centralized superstructure rested on village communities of peasant cultivators, administered by a hierarchy of officials, often recruited from pages, sons, or nephews of the great who had been educated at the royal court. The main concern of such administrations was the raising of tribute for the support of the king and of the semi-urbanized inhabitants of the capital. These included articles of consumption such as beer and foods, as well as merchandise for overseas trade, including ivory, skins, gold, copper, salt, and other commodities. Artists, craftsmen, and other specialists were located at the royal capital and were an important attribute of royal power.[10] Kings received tribute from outlying areas, but in turn redistributed some of this wealth to their followers, so that the royal revenue system must have acted in some ways as an internal exchange institution, designed to channel surplus goods to trusted followers and their clients. Most African monarchs appear to have acted as "distributor kings," and we shall meet this system again in many other contexts.

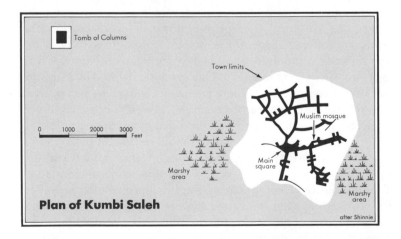

Plan of Kumbi Saleh

KINGSHIP HUMAN OR DIVINE?

The royal tombs of Ghana were objects of national veneration. As Al Bakri noted:

When their king dies, they build over the place where his tomb will be an enormous dome of *saj* wood. Then they bring him on a bed covered with a few carpets and cushions and put him inside the dome. At his side they place his ornaments, his weapons and his vessels from which he used to eat and drink, filled with various kinds of food and beverages. They also place there the men who had served his meals. They close the door of the dome and cover it with mats and materials, and then they assemble the people, who heap earth upon it until it becomes like a large mound. Then they dig a ditch around the mound so that it can be reached only at one place. They sacrifice victims for their dead and make offerings of intoxicating drinks.[11]

The parallel with ancient Egypt is obvious, and Professors Oliver and Fage have formulated an interesting theory to account for the similarity. They adhere to a diffusionist interpretation that places ancient Egypt in the center of the historical stage. According to their view, the formation of states in sub-Saharan and Bantu Africa rested on a fund of common ideas. The earliest lines of deployment run out in two long arms westward and southward from a common point of origin in the upper Nile Valley. Diffusion began in pre-Christian times; and the ideas of ancient Egypt, passing through the filter of ancient Meroë, thus formed the basic element of what they call the "Sudanic civilization."[12]

According to them, the diffusion of divine kingship ideas went with the spread of iron tools and weapons. According to this theory, refugees or adventurers from Meroë, or alternatively, Negroes from the Sahara who had previously been in touch with Egyptian civilizations, were thus responsible for founding the first great savannah states. Later on, conquerors armed with iron weapons supposedly moved southward into the forest belt, where they subdued the indigenous villagers and created new states.

These theories are fascinating, and there are many arguments in their favor. But they probably overestimate the impact of technology on politics. A knowledge of iron smelting does not necessarily lead to state-building. The Nok of Northern Nigeria, for instance, knew how to work iron by the third century A.D. But no great state emerged in Hausaland, the home of the Nok culture, until after the fourteenth century. The Ibo of southern Nigeria likewise had highly skilled smiths. But they never created any great states.[13]

Neither do we believe that divine kingship in Africa is necessarily of Egyptian origin. Divine kingship, for one thing, was found in other parts of the world, for instance among the Inca and the Aztecs, who had no contact whatever with Meroë. Oliver and Fage, moreover, do not give sufficient evidence to explain the individual steps that must have been involved in this process of culture transfusion. In explaining the emergence of great states in sub-Saharan Africa, they probably underestimate the impact of long-distance trade and the ambitions of powerful clans involved in such activities.

We thus incline toward the view that explains political structures by local needs, both human and ecological, and we prefer to explain divine kingship in sociological terms. Divine kingship also persists among some modern African peoples, including the Shilluk, a sedentary agricultural people who mainly inhabit the west bank of the Nile in the Sudan. Shilluk concepts of kingship came into being long after the Pharaoh's splendor had been forgotten. No historian has ever shown the existence of a direct link between the ancient Egyptians and the Shilluk to account for the supposed similarity of their political ideas. Shilluk social institutions had nothing to do with those of ancient Egypt. The Shilluk live in small settlements, each under its own chief, who inherits his position and is also confirmed by the king. The Shilluk feel themselves to be a nation under the leadership of their king, but the monarch has little control over their secular life. Kingship is identified with the general interests of all people, the fertility of men, cattle, and crops, and in the past success in war. The kingship is hallowed by association with *Nyikang,* who is the medium between God and men. Hence the graves of dead kings—formerly their capitals—become shrines of *Nyikang,* whose ritual power is distributed throughout the land. The kingship is thus greater than each individual incumbent of the throne. Such a scheme is well-adapted to a system in which the political segments are parts of a loosely organized structure, though the ritual and symbolism of kingship do not disappear even when there is a higher degree of centralized administration.

The Shilluk number little more than 100,000 people; but similar reasoning can probably be applied to larger states as well. Where conditions were propitious, ambitious rulers built up larger states by means of trade, alliances, and conquest. Once these larger states were well established, the prestige of kingship increased. Its ceremonial and ritual became more important, and the splendor of the court waxed in magnificence. Such kingdoms, however, contained an element of instability. The unifying influence of kingship might keep the disparate segments of the state united for many years. But internal dissensions could never be suppressed. Competition for the crown became keener between princes and their supporting chieftains and followers. Foreign conquest or civil war might upset the local balance of power, and in the end these great states always broke up. According to Gluckman, "Since the kingdom's segments were not dependent upon one another for specialized production of various goods, after periods whose limits I cannot fix, the state would fall apart, and there would be left many small chieftainships. Force at the centre, and ritual supremacy, seem to me insufficient to give permanent internal stability to such a state."[14]

Foreign trade was more likely to give power to the central government by providing rulers with revenue. According to Adu Boahen, a modern African historian, the first great sub-Saharan states were created by the long-distance trade.[15] But foreign commerce was only one of many factors which determined state building. Kings had to feed their warriors and courtiers. Rulers therefore set up markets and regulated trade. They adopted managed currencies—iron bars, gold dust, cowrie shells (the latter used as small change in several West African kingdoms by the fourteenth century at least). For the Sudanic economies as a whole, the importance of the long-distance traffic remained limited. Except for salt and metals, the caravans mainly brought luxury goods for the rich and powerful, not for the people. The conquered tribes each retained their distinctive customs and language. They were probably little concerned with the doings of the capital. They had little in common with each other, except their subjection to a central authority that always insisted on tribute and tax. The Sudanese empires and their kingship lasted only as long as the rulers maintained military supremacy. This was difficult, for communications were defective, and ambitious viceroys or disaffected tribal chiefs were likely to seize local power from an incompetent, slothful, or unsuccessful monarch.[16] None of the great West African empires succeeded in welding its subjects into a nation. None managed to create political and religious institutions of the kind which—despite many invasions and civil wars—kept the Nile Valley united under the Pharaohs' sway for centuries. The Sudanese empires and their kingship thus probably bore but small resemblance to the ancient Egyptian kingdom. Their fall was apt to be as swift as their rise, and the history of West Africa is punctuated by dramatic crashes from grandeur to insignificance.

THE RISE OF MALI

Ghana failed to solve the problem that had plagued so many civilized empires abutting on desert lands, that of holding in check the mounted nomads beyond its borders. The Ghanaians had to contend with the Sanhaja, the veiled Berbers living to the north, especially the Lemtuna and Goddala tribes, who dominated the trans-Saharan trade in salt. During the ninth and tenth centuries the Ghanaians successfully held their own, and by the end of the period, the people of Awdaghost, an important commercial center to the north, were actually paying tribute to Ghana. But the Sanhaja received new political and religious inspiration from the Almoravid movement, created by Abdullah Ibn Yasin, a Muslim divine.

Ibn Yasin, the advocate of a strict, fanatical, desert-borne puritanism, established a religious and military training center somewhere near the mouth of the Senegal. The Almoravid forces, subject to strict spiritual and secular discipline, outfought all their enemies and united many of the Saharan Berber tribes under their sway. The main body of the Almoravids went north to Marrakesh and subsequently imposed their lordship and creed on Morocco and on Spain. The southern branch, now comprising many of the Sanhaja communities, turned against Ghana. Ghana by this time had already passed the height of its greatness, and after several years of campaigning, the northern invaders in 1076 captured and pillaged Kumbi Saleh, the Ghanaian capital. The conquerors, as was the Muslims' wont, imposed a poll tax on their pagan subjects, exacted tribute, and induced many unbelievers to adopt Islam. The Sanhaja were, however, divided by tribal and factional quarrels; in 1087 Abu Bakr, the Almoravid leader, lost his life while suppressing a revolt, and shortly afterward the southern Almoravid empire broke up.[17]

The rulers of Ghana succeeded in regaining their independence, but not their former splendor. The Ghanaian writ ran only in Aukar and Bassikunu, and Soninke might decayed. Outlying provinces such as Diara and Kaniaga broke away from the empire, and Kaniaga instead became a contender for power in Ghana itself. The Sosso, a powerful community in Kaniaga, took the offensive, and in 1203 Sumanguru, a Sosso king, conquered Ghana. The country fell into a parlous state, and by 1224 we learn of traders deserting the kingdom for Walata, a new base in the western Sudan out of Sumanguru's reach. Sumanguru at the same time chose to challenge the growing might of Kangaba, a Mandingo state to the south. In 1235 Sumanguru was killed in battle. Sundiata, the Mandingo ruler, piled victory upon victory, and incorporated Sosso into what became the kingdom of Mali.

Sundiata appears to have been one of the greatest African rulers of all times, and his memory still lives in the epics of African *griots,* the bards and poets who have done so much to preserve the traditions of West Africa. Their tales are great heroic sagas. The hero was supposedly born of a strange and ugly sorceress; he suffered a sickly and miserable childhood, but grew up into a prodigy of strength and valor.[18] But above all, Sundiata—relying on the proceeds from trade and tribute—raised a professional army of mercenaries, far superior apparently to the temporary levies of his enemies. In this way he was able to build up an empire that, at the height of its power, controlled commerce throughout the western Sudan and stretched from the upper reaches of the Niger in the east to the mouths of the Senegal and the Gambia rivers in the west. In other words, a merchant making his journey from one end of the empire to the other would traverse something like 1800 miles, a distance about equal to that from New York to Wyoming, or from northern Scotland to Constantinople. Mali's sphere of influence far exceeded that of any medieval empire in Europe; yet foreigners like Ibn Battuta, a famed Muslim traveler and writer of the fourteenth century, were able to make trips in Mali with complete security, accompanied only by two or three companions.

Over most of this vast area, Mali's power was probably of an indirect rather than a direct kind. The kings levied tribute from local potentates and assured the safety of caravans, but could not directly rule the village communities. Mali nevertheless appears to have had a sophisticated system of administration by the standards of its time. Prosperity attracted not only Muslim merchants but also Muslim lawyers, scholars, and divines. This is how Leo Africanus, a great traveler to whom we shall make subsequent reference, described Melli, the capital, about 1513–14. "Heere are many artificers and merchants in all places: and yet the king honourably entertaineth all strangers. The inhabitants are rich, and haue plentie of wares. Heere are great stores of temples, priests, and professoures, which professours read their lectures onely in the temples, bicause they haue no colleges at all. The people of this region excell all other Negroes in witte, ciuilities, and industry; and were the first that embraced the law of Mahumet. . . ."[19] The bulk of the Mandingo continued to practice pagan cults, so that Islam remained the distinguishing mark of an elaborate court and a mercantile rather than a popular culture.

In 1307 one of the most famous of Mandingo kings, Mansa Musa, ascended the throne, and spread his kingdom's renown to the confines of the Mediterranean and beyond. Mali's reputation owed much to a spectacular pilgrimage which Mansa Musa made to Mecca. The king set out on his journey in 1324, surrounded by numerous followers and trains of camels loaded with precious gifts. The royal pilgrim, it is said, carried so much gold that his munificent gifts caused the price of the precious metal to fall in Egypt, and the pomp of his caravan remained a matter for wonder and gossip for many years. In Mecca, Mansa Musa met a poet and architect from Spain, called

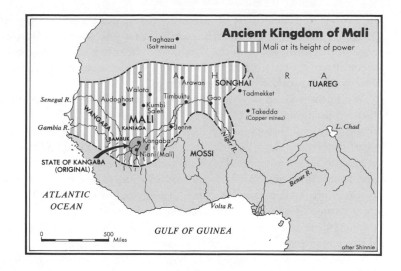

al-Sahili, and persuaded him to enter his service. Al-Sahili reputedly introduced burnt brick (the red brick now common in the Sudan) and put up numerous buildings, including the great mosques at Gao and at Timbuktu, as well as a palace for the king. When Mansa Musa died in 1332 he left behind him a remarkable empire, known even to map makers in northern Europe. Mansa Musa's successors, however, failed to control their enormous heritage. Timbuktu was lost to the Mossi, a fierce people from the upper Volta. The Songhai shook off Mandingo control; the desert Tuareg subsequently captured Walata. Caught between Berber pressure from the north and Mossi inroads from the south, exposed to the rising power of Songhai and riddled by internal dissensions, the Mali empire disintegrated. By the seventeenth century it was back to where it had started in Kangaba, the original Mandingo state.[20]

SONGHAI AT ITS ZENITH

The Songhai people dwelt on the banks of the middle Niger, where they made their living as farmers and fishermen. Probably in the ninth century, the Dia, a powerful dynasty, secured political control. The Dia subsequently developed the country's trade. In 1009 they removed their capital city to Gao (Gago) and at about the same time they became converts to Islam. Songhai had to resist onslaughts from all sides—from the Tuareg, the Mossi, the Mandingo—and in the first half of the fourteenth century became a tributary of Mali. About 1464 a new ruler, Sonni Ali, ascended the throne. Sonni Ali captured Timbuktu, and extended the boundaries of his kingdom over much of the middle and upper regions of the Niger, his military might resting apparently on the extensive use of cavalry. On Sonni Ali's death in 1492 the kingdom fell to one of the generals in the late king's employ, a usurper called Mohammed Touré who took the title of Askia. Askia Mohammed (1493–1538) proved an outstanding administrator who encouraged trade and learning and created the largest and wealthiest of all kingdoms in the Sudan. At the height of its power Songhai probably stretched from what is now the southern border of Algeria to the edge of the forest lands in the south, from near the shores of the Atlantic in the west to Agades in the east;[21] Songhai was even greater in territorial extent than Mali, which was wholly absorbed within its confines.

We know a good deal about this state through the reports of Leo Africanus, one of the most remarkable travelers of the Renaissance. Born a Moor, he was captured by pirates, and subsequently "given" to Leo XI as a present. The Pope, much impressed by the slave's knowledge, set him free and even permitted him, on baptism, to assume his own name—Leo. Leo's account describes Songhai as a highly stratified kingdom with a wealthy and cultured Muslim ruling class, dependent on trade and tribute, and concentrated in cities like Timbuktu and Gao. The kingdom became a great center of Muslim civilization in the Sudan.

The rulers' and the rich men's style of life, however, contrasted sharply with that of the pagan countryfolk, that is to say the great majority. The villagers' commerce was used by the king, for he had a royal right of pre-emption. "So soon as he heareth that any merchants are come to town with horses, he commandeth a certaine number to be brought before him, and chusing the best horse for himselfe, he payeth a most liberal price for him."[22] The king was served by royal officials, "his councellors and other officers, as namely his secretaries, treasurers, factors and auditors." The king acted as principal judge, but was assisted by specialized functionaries at the center, with judges, tax collectors, and market inspectors in the outlying provinces. Songhai carried on an extensive entrepôt trade, sending slaves, ivory, ostrich feathers, and of course gold to the markets of the Mediterranean, and importing salt as well as manufactured goods from the Mediterranean and Northern Europe. "Horses bought in Europe for ten ducates, are heere sold againe for fortie and sometimes for fiftie ducates a piece. There is not any cloth of Europe so course, which will not here be sold for fower ducates an ell, and if it be anything fine they will giue fifteene ducates for and ell: an an ell of the scarlet of Venice or of Turkie-cloath is here worth thirtie ducates. A sword is heere valued at three or fower crownes, and so likewise are spurs, bridles, with other like commodities, and spices also are sold at an high rate: but of al other commodities salt is most extremelie deere."[23]

Revenue from tribute and trade enabled the king to maintain a considerable urban intelligentsia. According to Leo Africanus "Here are a great store of doctors, judges, priests and other learned men, that are bountifully maintained at the king's cost and charges. And hither are brought diurs manuscripts or written bookes out of Barbarie, which are sold for more money than any other merchandize."[24] Sonni Ali and Mohammed Askia apparently established a greater degree of central control over the outlying provinces than had been exercised by the rulers of Ghana and Mali. Kings kept Gao under their own immediate surveillance and ruled the remoter regions through governors appointed from the ranks of their kinsmen or court favorites. These dignitaries in turn depended on extensive bureaucracies. Militarily, the monarchs depended on great squadrons of canoes that patrolled the Niger, the main riverine link between the far-flung parts of the empire. Songhai also had a consider-

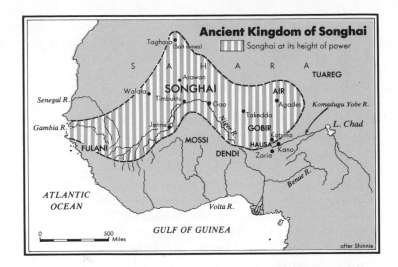

able army, including armored cavalry as well as footmen. The soldiers of Songhai, however, had no firearms. Hence they proved incapable of resisting Moroccan invaders who assaulted the kingdom at the end of the sixteenth century. The Songhai monarchy, like others of its kind, also suffered from severe internal weaknesses. Governance depended on a small minority; there was no sense of national unity. Songhai was riddled by many internal dissensions to which further reference will be made in a subsequent chapter, and its splendor therefore rested on a relatively precarious basis that was later shattered by foreign invasion.

KANEM-BORNU, THE HAUSA STATES, AND THE LIMITS OF ISLAM

The central Sudan provided somewhat different conditions. The lands adjoining Lake Chad in particular were fertile; nomads could easily move around with their beasts in a region devoid of natural boundaries, without mountains or tropical forests. The Lake Chad country thus attracted settled farming communities, who in turn were raided by nomadic pastoralists from the desert. The desert also served commerce, and from about eighth century onward, the Ibadi Berbers from Zawila controlled an important trade route passing from Lake Chad to the coast of what is now Libya. The early history of the Chad region is still in dispute, but about 800 A.D. the Kanuri emerged as a distinct community with their own dynasty east of the lake. Islamic influence came in from the north and, according to indigenous tradition, the first Muslim ruler mounted the throne in 1085. The Kanuri state, known as Kanem, soon grew in power and prosperity. The people learned how to build in red brick; they adopted Arabic script; they organized an extensive caravan trade. They also learned a great deal from the Muslims concerning military organization; they built up a powerful force of cavalry, and after the twelfth century began to equip their horsemen with chain mail and other elaborate accoutrements. But although Islamic influences contributed much to the arts of warfare and administration, they apparently had little effect on the ideology of power. Arabic feudal concepts did not strike root. The "divine" character of the monarchy persisted. The queen mother continued to wield extensive power, despite the subordinate role assigned to women by Islam. We may conclude, therefore, that Islam remained the religion of the ruling classes and was probably confined largely to the capital city, while traditional concepts of divine kingship helped to secure the obedience of the ordinary farmers, who stuck to the traditional culture and religion.[25] The country's government bore some resemblance to Songhai's, with a ruling dynasty loosely governing a number of tributary peoples. Under King Salma (1194–1221) Islam became established more firmly, and the kingdom came to comprise the whole of the Chad basin as well as the trade routes as far north as Fezzan. Kanem appears to have established friendly relations with the Hafsid dynasty of Tunis, and later on with the Turks, who corresponded with Bornu during the sixteenth century and supplied the hinterland kingdom with firearms. In addition Kanem inported horses and manufactured goods from the north, sending slaves in exchange.

The Kanuri kingdom was, however, as unstable as its western neighbors. There were many revolts, and there were dissensions within the royal house itself. At the end of the fourteenth century, Mai Omar, the ruler of Kanem, decided that he could no longer hold his lands, and moved west of Lake Chad. The new state, known as Bornu, was likewise governed by a warlike aristocracy, clad in chain mail, quilted armour, and iron helmets, wielding long lances, and capable of ranging far afield on their horses. Bornu reached the height of its power under Mai Ali (1476–1507). Mai Ali built a new capital at Birni Gazargamo on the river Yobe on the border of what is now the Republic of Niger and of Nigeria. Its impressive ruins still survive. The city was surrounded by an immense earth wall with five great entrances and a great defensive ditch outside. These fortifications surrounded an area of one and three-quarter miles across which contained the ruler's red brick palace, other substantial buildings, and countless huts fashioned either of sun-dried brick or reeds. Gazargamo may well have been one of the largest African towns of its time, full of mosques and having a considerable agricultural hinterland. Bornu carried on an extensive slave trade, and its general character resembled that of the western Sudanic states, with all their strengths and their weaknesses.[26]

Further west, Hausaland developed a unique civilization. Its origins are obscure, but it seems likely that the Hausa were originally a Saharan Negro people who colonized the savannah soon after 100 A.D., being forced southwards by the desiccation of the desert and by pressure from the Berbers. The Hausa never formed a united empire, but the Hausa's commercial acumen built up extensive trading connections throughout West Africa, and caused the Hausa tongue to become almost a *lingua franca*. The Hausa states proper were situated in the savannah, and each one centered on a capital city, fortified with huge mudwalls. The capital always constituted a permanent base for the local army, a focus of the arts and crafts, and a distribution center for the trade between the forest regions of West Africa and Tripoli. Kano and Katsina were great entrepôts where merchants of many nationalities purchased slaves, gold, ostrich feathers, ivory, kola nuts, and leather in exchange for goods from

Europe, North Africa, and the Middle East—Venetian glassware, Arabic paper and parchment, cloth, beads, weapons, armor, salt, and silver. Kano and Katsina also became cultural centers and during the seventeenth century began to produce scholars of their own, some of whose writings have survived to the present day. The impact of Islam, however, was not apparently as profound as in Bornu. Bornu had been subject to Muslim penetration for a much longer period of time. Bornu moreover was a united empire, while the states of Hausaland were engaged in internecine warfare. The progress of Islam was accordingly more uneven, and Islamic practices widely blended with indigenous cultural traditions.

For reasons not yet clear to historians, Islam made no impression on the Mossi, a group of peoples who dwelt in the parkland between the savannah and the rain forest south of Songhai. Mossi traditions seem to indicate that warlike Dagomba horsemen left their crowded homeland in what is now Ghana to seek new pastures for their cattle further north. Here they intermarried with the indigenous Busansi, and these unions gave rise to the Mossi people. The Mossi subdued various neighboring peoples and formed a group of powerful new states. The most important of these centered on Ougadougou (in what is now Upper Volta); it appears that Ougadougou became the permanent capital during the reign of Mogno Naba Sana, the fifteenth ruler of the dynasty. In addition, other Mossi dwelling further to the north also extended their territory. They advanced as far as the Niger bend, and at various times sacked cities such as Djenne and Timbuktu. Mossi power reached its apogee sometime during the fourteenth and fifteenth centuries—historians still dispute the exact period. In 1497, however, the Mossi suffered defeat at the hand of Askia the Great of Songhai, and were forced to withdraw into their heartland.

A long history of armed conquest apparently led to a considerable degree of social stratification. The most important political positions were restricted to those who could trace their origins to the founders of the Mossi nation. All heads of kingdoms, principalities, districts, and villages claimed to be descended from the royal line. In addition, however, there were other kinds of chiefs, including the descendants of

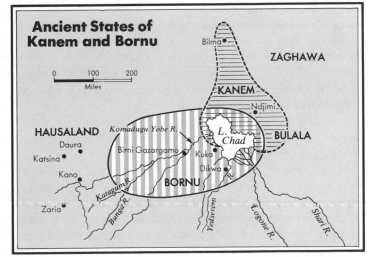

provincial ministers or of aboriginal chiefs, who were absorbed into the Mossi hierarchy. The lowliest dignitaries were the headmen of serf and slave villages, whose inhabitants made up the most subordinate element in Mossi society. Nevertheless, among the Mossi, as among their neighbors, there were strict limits on royal power. The villagers built their houses and cultivated their crops on land granted by the village chiefs to the respective lineages within the community. The Mossi rulers could extort tribute, but they did not own the land. Land was looked upon as a public good, whose proper utilization was in the best interests of rulers and subjects alike[27] and Mossi theories of property in this respect in no way differed from those current in most parts of Africa.

WEAKNESSES AND LIMITATIONS OF THE SUDANIC STATES

Modern historiography has shattered the myth of primeval African savagery. A new generation of scholars has acquainted mankind with the splendor of ancient kingdoms like Songhai, with the wealth and learning of its aristocracy, with the might of its armies and of its far-flung canoe fleets. These great states, however, were also subject to considerable limitations. The great mass of the common people had no part in Songhai's sophisticated culture. Many villagers probably looked on the royal tax-gatherers and soldiers with as much dread as they viewed foreign enemies. The king's army, composed of a standing force of cavalry and foot archers shooting poisoned arrows, "have often skirmishes with those that refuse to pay tribute, and so many as they take, they sell vnto the merchants of Tombuto."[28] The country folk presumably benefited from the monarch's ability to maintain peace throughout the land. But they remained subject to heavy burdens; they felt little loyalty to a distant government, and they derived no advantage from a commercial system that—except for salt—could distribute luxuries accessible only to a small ruling stratum. The cities sustained a sophisticated culture for a small minority. As Leo Africanus put it "The residue of this kingdome containeth nought but villages and hamlets inhabited by husbandmen and shepherds, who in winter couer their bodies with beasts skins; but in sommer they goe all naked saue their priuie members: and sometimes they weare vpon their feet certaine shooes made of camels leather. They are ignorant and rude people, and you shall scarce finde one learned man in the space of an hundred miles. They are continually burthened with grieuous exactions so that they haue scarce any thing remaining to liue vpon."[29]

Songhai, like its predecessors, could not overcome the handicaps of size, of regional and cultural diversity. None of these great tribute-gathering states solved the problem of unifying the Western Sudan.

Many Sudanic peoples, moreover, must have suffered seriously from the slave trade across the Sahara. The Arab invasions into West Africa and the Sahara inevitably gave a new stimulus to this commerce. Arab merchants repaired to the Fezzan to sell captives. Marauding Berbers and Arab nomads began to participate in the traffic. The medieval kingdoms of West Africa all became linked to a great slave-trading network. The capital of ancient Ghana, for instance, gained renown for its slave market. When

Ghana was overthrown by the Almoravids, the great city of Kumbi was sacked, and its people in turn were deported, to be sold in North Africa. The Mali aristocracy kept large numbers of captives. The Hausa states were extensively implicated in the traffic. The early expansion of Bornu-Kanem toward the region southeast of Lake Chad may have been partly occasioned by the desire to find new areas for the supply of Negro slaves to Egypt and North Africa.

As Joseph Anene, a modern African historian, puts it, slavery formed the very basis of these Islamized states. A great deal of the more unpleasant work was left to slaves. Slaves did much of the household chores; slaves tilled the fields; slave women served their masters as concubines; slave eunuchs took care of harems and guarded the palaces. Where trade extended, slaves might toil as beasts of burden or even be used as currency. The more land a Muslim lord owned, the more slaves he needed to cultivate his estates. The larger his household, the greater was his need of domestic attendants.[30]

Islamic slavery knew an infinite number of gradations, and some slaves might attain fame and even fortune. Slaves attached to the households of kings and aristocrats might be employed as scribes and secretaries. Some attained high political or military office, and often attained preferment over more highborn men.

This slave aristocracy, however, formed but a tiny proportion of the servile labor force. The bulk of the slaves formed a poverty-stricken proletariat. In Mecca for instance, the heaviest tasks, such as building and quarrying, were performed by black Nubians. Sudanese bondsmen were likewise set to labor with brick and mortar and to do other rough tasks. In their spare time, these men might seek employment as water carriers or day laborers. Other Negro slaves, better equipped by their education and background, served as domestic retainers or shop assistants. The more adaptable slaves became trusted assistants. Some were freed, for emancipation was regarded as a meritorious act, and manumission did not alter the familiar relationships between master and man. Practically no office was closed to such freedmen, and some of the most influential citizens in Mecca, owners of houses and shops, were former slaves.

Muslim Arabs never practiced the kind of racial exclusivism that was later developed in the plantations of the New World, with their insatiable demand for servile labor. Muslim sages argued that all true believers were equal in the sight of Allah. Muslim employers bought white slaves from the Balkan Peninsula as well as black slaves from the "land of Zanj." Pigmentation alone never became the badge of slavery as such. But from medieval times onward, white slaves became increasingly scarce; slavery and blackness became increasingly associated with one another in many Muslim minds. Even the great Ibn Khaldun held that Negroes naturally accepted slavery owing to their low degree of humanity and their proximity to the animal stage. Arab stereotypes concerning black people often resembled those later developed in the New World. Prejudice and discrimination were common in Muslim as well as in Christian lands.[31]

The impact of Islamic slavery on the Sudan is hard to assess. No one knows, for instance, how many people were abducted from Africa to the slave markets of the Muslim world. According to one estimate, Islamic slavers took over a million people across the great African desert belt during each century of the later Middle Ages.[32] This figure is certainly exaggerated. Caravan traffic presented great logistic difficulties. The market for captives, though great, was not unlimited. The Muslims, as we have seen, desired slaves as soldiers, domestic servants, concubines, craftsmen, and casual laborers. They also employed slaves as field hands. The Muslim states of North Africa did not, however, create plantation economies on the scale later developed by the Christians in the New World for the purpose of producing tropical crops for export, with an almost limitless demand for unskilled workmen. Islamic slavery, on the whole, was linked more to the needs of small-scale craft industries, to the desire for home comforts and sensual pleasures, to the needs for conspicuous consumption and war. Plantation slavery existed in various parts of the Islamic world, but never on the transatlantic scale. Hence the Muslim slave trade never reached the proportions attained by the Christian traffic from the seventeenth century onward.

The effects of the slave trade on the indigenous African people was uneven. Some communities might suffer severely; others might be wholly spared. The Islamic slave trade also labored under geographical limitations. Muslim merchants never succeeded in penetrating very far into the southern forest belt of the south. They drew the bulk of their supplies from the parkland and grassland belts of the Sudan. This vast region became a major source of captive manpower for the most civilized states of the Islamic world, just as Slavonic Europe for many centuries supplied its western neighbors with prisoners.

For all that has been said, the Islamic traffic was nevertheless stained with much blood. The principal method of obtaining captives was by raiding weaker neighbors. Ostensibly, such attacks were confined to pagan settlements. But the Muslims did not always live up to their own principles, and some did not scruple to harry Muslim villages within their own states.[33] Neighbor turned against neighbor in skirmishes that might produce many casualties. Countless slaves perished on the route to North Africa. There could be no sense of community between the raiders and the raided, and slavery may have added an element of instability to the great Islamic empires of the Sudan.

WEST AFRICA AND THE ZENITH OF ITS VISUAL ARTS

The forest lands of West Africa lay well beyond the ken of Arab travelers whose accounts have made such a great contribution to our knowledge of the ancient savannah states. In fact, so much mystery surrounded the more distant regions that the most fantastic stories kept circulating concerning the habits of the Negroes. There is, however, no doubt that the forest communities also made considerable progress in the arts of civilization. Leo Africanus's description of "Ghinea," which he placed "two hundred and fiftie miles along the riuer of Niger, and [which] bordereth vpon the Ocean sea in the same place, where the Niger falleth into the saide sea," has a ring of authenticity. The forest communities practiced a developed agriculture, and they supplemented their fare by hunting and fishing. They lacked the art of writing; there were no urban communities on the scale of, say, Timbuktu's; but there were "agro-towns" dependent mainly on farming, yet also containing craftsmen and merchants. The forest people were familiar with the arts of navigating canoes, weaving cotton, working metal, and other crafts. The forest lands exported considerable quantities of gold to the kingdoms of the savannah, and the forest economy clearly supported a group of specialists skilled in tribal lore and the arts of government.

We only have archaeological records and oral traditions to illustrate the more detailed history of the various forest communities. Much controversy persists, and we shall confine ourselves to a few illustrative examples. One of many powerful state builders were the Akan, who dwelt in what is now Ghana. The Akan, like many ruling peoples of their kind, have a long tradition of a journey from a distant origin. They had supposedly come from the north, from near the Niger, some 600 years ago. Having arrived in the new country, they founded Bono Mansu, their capital, some seventy-two miles north of where Kumasi now stands. The city lay in orchard bush, beyond the northern forest limit, and also grew rich on trade with the Sudanic states. Again it is possible that the legend refers to immigrants who settled among the established Akan speakers, perhaps some time during the fourteenth century. In the next century there may have been further movement from the north into the forest; a number of small Akan states grew up, though those in the north remained the strongest, the forest zone remaining strongly influenced by its Sudanic orientation. The most important and creative of the forest states were perhaps those of the Yoruba (living in what is now southwestern Nigeria). According to their own traditions, the Yoruba have sprung from Lamurudu, one of the kings of Mecca. Samuel Johnson, a noted African scholar, while discounting the story of a Meccan ancestry, had no doubt that the people must have come from the east.[34] If there was indeed any eastern immigration, it is more likely that it consisted of a more limited group of conquerors who subdued an indigenous farming population. But whatever the Yorubas' descent, they lived close to the northern edge of the forest, and maintained close contact with the savannah states.

A brilliant culture centered on Ife in what what is now southwestern Nigeria, just beyond the northern limit of the forest. Probably at some time during the twelfth and thirteenth centuries Ife craftsmen developed a unique style of bronze and brass sculptures. These artifacts are distinguished for their delicate and highly naturalistic styles and bear comparison with the best of Greek art.

The artists of Ife were possibly the greatest masters of sculpture who ever worked in Africa. The reasons for their excellence are hard to explain. All we can safely say is that they lived in societies that produced a considerable economic surplus, that allowed for a good deal of specialization, and that created complex states. Ife artists portrayed their rulers, probably for the purpose of ancestor worship; according to one interpretation, the heads may have been prepared as traps for the spirits of the deceased. Each sculpture bore an authentic, clearly distinguished likeness to the original. Harmonious and noble in expression, these productions were superior to anything of comparable character in twelfth century Europe. Art historians call the bronze casting technique employed the *cire-perdue* (lost wax) process, and it was possibly imported from the Mediterranean. The actual modelling was done with wax over an earthen core. Another layer of earth was firmly packed around the head. The

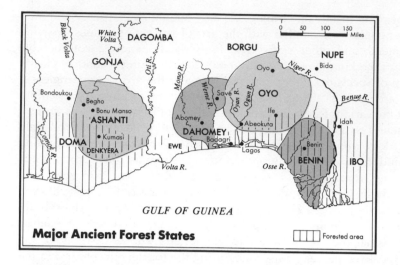

Major Ancient Forest States

GULF OF GUINEA

Forested area

whole was then heated to melt out the wax, and molten bronze was poured into the hollow form thus created. Ife in turn exerted a great influence on Benin. During the fourteenth century the people of Benin adopted Ife's bronze casting techniques, and Benin artists produced a profusion of masterpieces in metal, and also in wood and ivory. (The great age of Benin metalworking continued until the eighteenth century.) In addition to ancestor heads, Benin craftsmen turned out a great variety of works that had nothing to do with the spirit world but served to glorify the ruler and his court.

Most other African cultures gave much greater emphasis to geometrical patterns in their art. Some scholars explain this tendency toward abstract art as a result of the craftsmen's efforts to convey the "otherness" of the spirit world, and to divorce the supernatural from the mundane world of everyday appearances. This interpretation, however, still leaves unexplained the varying degrees of abstraction that may be encountered within the same artistic culture. H. W. Janson, an art historian, has given an interesting explanation. He argues that the increasingly abstract quality of sculptures, such as those fashioned successively by the Bakota of Gabon in West Africa, derives from endless repetition. Artists stuck to certain basic outlines in modelling, say, the guardian figures of their people, though successive craftsmen each introduced minor variations. Any shape that is endlessly repreated tends to lose its original character. It becomes "ground-down," simplified by a process of what Janson calls "abstraction by inbreeding."[35]

Artists in West Africa and many other parts of the continent also paid special attention to making masks for ritual dances. In Africa and many other similarly constituted societies in other parts of the world, acting-out ceremonials assumed a vast variety of patterns and purposes. The costumes, always with the mask as the center piece, became correspondingly elaborate. Masks, as H. W. Janson puts it, form by far the richest chapter in primitive art; the proliferation of shapes, materials and functions is almost limitless. Even the manner of wearing them varies surprisingly. Other masks were made to be displayed rather than worn, though their meaning is often hard to ascertain. The ceremonies used in placating the spirits usually contained elements of secrecy that were jealously guarded against the uninitiated, especially if the performers belonged to secret societies. This emphasis on the mysterious and spectacular in so much of African art not only heightened the dramatic impact of the ritual but also permitted the wearers of masks to strive for imaginative new effects, so that the masks generally were less subject to traditional restraints than other kinds of sculpture.

NOTES

1. Vera I. Nevinson, *The Fifth-Century Invasions South of the Thames* (London, 1965).

2. This account mainly comes from E. W. Bovill, *The Golden Trade of the Moors* (London, 1968), pp. 191–202.

3. Bovill, p. 59.

4. Robert O. Collins, ed., *Problems in African History* (New Jersey, 1968), p. 215.

5. John Donnelly Fage *An Introduction to the History of West Africa* (Cambridge, 1969), pp. 19–20.

6. John Donnelly Fage, "Ancient Ghana: A Review of the Evidence," *Transactions of the Historical Society of Ghana* (Achimota, 1957), vol. 3, part 2, pp. 89–90.

7. Quoted from Al Bakri's *Description of Northern Africa*, in Fage, "Ancient Ghana," pp. 80–82, especially p. 82.

8. Al Bakri, quoted by Fage, "Ancient Ghana," p. 82

9. All Bakri, quoted by Fage, "Ancient Ghana," p. 82.

10. Roland Oliver and John D. Fage, *A Short History of Africa* (Baltimore, 1962), p. 45.

11. Al Bakri, quoted by Fage, "Ancient Ghana," pp. 81–82.

12. Oliver and Fage, pp. 49–50.

13. Adu Boahen, "The History of Nigeria and Ghana," *Journal of African History*, vol. 8, no. 3 (1967), pp. 541–580.

14. Gluckman, *Politics, Law and Ritual in a Tribal Society*, pp. 130–144, especially p. 143.

15. Boahen, p. 544.

16. Fage, *An Introduction to the History of West Africa*, pp. 16–17.

17. See Fage, "Ancient Ghana," pp. 85–90.

18. See D. T. Niane, *Sundiata: An Epic of Old Mali*, trans. G. D. Picket (London, 1965).

19. Leo Africanus, *The History and Description of Africa and of the Notable Things Therein Contained . . . Done into English in the Year 160 by John Pory*, ed., Robert Brown (London, 1896) vol. 3, p. 823.

20. Shinnie, *Ancient African Kingdoms*, pp. 51–56.

21. Shinnie, pp. 56–63.

22. Leo Africanus, p. 825.

23. Leo Africanus, p. 827.

24. Leo Africanus, p. 827.

25. John E. Flint, *Nigeria and Ghana* (Englewood Cliffs, N.J., 1966), pp. 47–51.

26. Shinnie, pp. 67–70.

27. Elliot P. Skinner, *The Mossi of Upper Volta: The Political Development of a Sudanese People* (Stanford, 1964), pp. 7–30.

28. Leo Africanus, p. 825.

29. Leo Africanus, p. 827.

30. Joseph Anene, "Slavery and the Slave Trade," in Joseph Anene and Godfrey N. Brown, eds., *Africa in the Nineteenth and Twentieth Centuries* (New York, 1967), pp. 94–98.

31. Bernard Lewis, "Race and Colour in Islam," *Encounter* (August 1970), p. 18–36.

32. See for instance Anthony Luttrell "Slavery and Slaving in the Portuguese Atlantic (to about 1500)" in Centre of African Studies, University of Edinburgh, *The Transatlantic Slave Trade from West Africa* (Edinburgh, June 1965), p. 63.

33. Ronald Cohen, "Slavery Among the Kanuri," *Trans-Action,* January-February 1966, p. 48.

34. Samuel Johnson. *The History of the Yorubas from the Earliest Times to the Beginning of the British Protectorate* (Lagos, 1957), pp. 3–4.

35. H. W. Janson, *History of Art: A Survey of the Major Visual Arts from the Dawn of History to the Present Day* (New York, 1966), pp. 24–31.

Akan terra cotta funerary head from Ghana, placed on grave of
ancestor. 12⅜ inches high. (By courtesy of The Museum of Primitive
Art, New York.)

Hide-covered headpiece from the Ekoi, Nigeria. 31½ inches high.

Ifa cup from Yoruba, Nigeria, showing a chief on horseback with his attendants. 10¾ inches high. (Collection of Mr. and Mrs. William F. Kaiser.)

Mende helmet mask from Sierra Leone, used in women's secret society. 13¾ inches high. (Collection of Mr. and Mrs. S.I. Hayakawa.)

Mahongwe face mask from the Itumba region, border of Gabon and the Congo (Brazzaville). 14 inches high. (Collection, The Museum of Modern Art, New York.)

Nalu horned crocodile mask from Guinea. 52½ inches long.
(Courtesy of The Museum of Primitive Art, New York.)

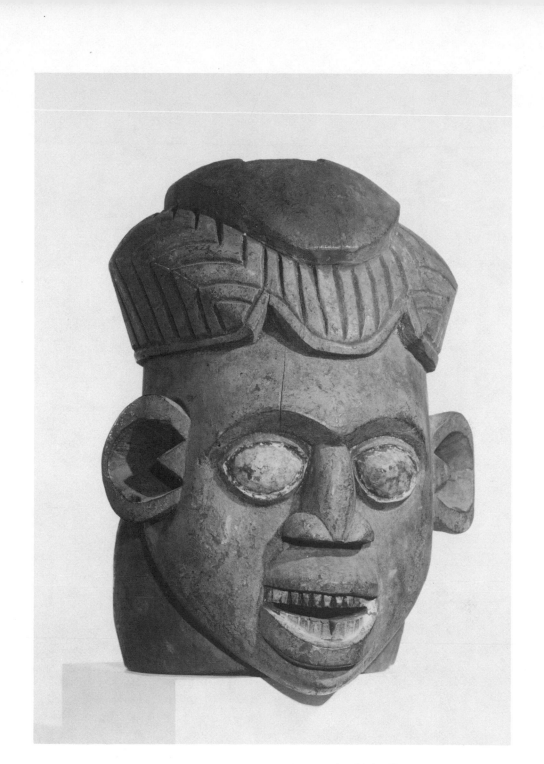

Nkom helmet mask from Cameroon. 17 inches high. (Courtesy of The Cleveland Museum of Art.)

Baga headdress mask from Guinea. Symbolic of the positive forces in nature. 46½ inches high. (Courtesy of The Museum of Primitive Art, New York.)

Chapter 17

East and Northeast Africa to the End of the Fifteenth Century

THE EAST AFRICAN COAST

The great states of the western Sudan—linked to the Mediterranean and Middle East by well-trodden caravan routes—made up the southern hinterland of the Muslim world. The cities of the East African coast, on the other hand, formed its furthermost maritime frontier in Africa. Coming to a great settlement like Mogadishu, in what is now Somalia, a pious Muslim traveler like Ibn Battuta would find himself perfectly at home. The local sultan, though not speaking much Arabic, would lodge the learned stranger in the city's student quarters, provide him with food, and make him at home in his palace. Further south lay Mombasa, another important community. Continuing his journey to Kilwa, in what is now southern Tanzania, Ibn Battuta found "a fine substantially built town and all its buildings are of wood." Its people were mainly of African origin; according to Ibn Battuta, "the majority . . . are Zanj, jet-black in colour, and with tattoo marks on their faces."[1] The Kilwans were constantly engaged in expeditions against the heathen "Zanj" on their borders. But the coastmen lacked cavalry. Animal disease prevented the large-scale use of four-footed animals. Even though the Muslims traded far into the interior—often through Bantu intermediaries —their direct political influence remained confined to the lands adjoining the seashore; hence Islam could never make the vast territorial conquests achieved in the savannahs of West Africa.

The coastmen rather looked outward to the countries abutting on the Indian Ocean and the Red Sea. According to Gervase Mathew, an historian of East Africa, their traffic in gold, ivory, and slaves from the mainland reached its greatest extent some-

231

time during the late fourteenth and early fifteenth centuries. This commercial expansion may have gone with the development of new trade routes in the Near East and the increasing prosperity of Europe. The international court culture that flourished in the West from the fourteenth century onward created new markets for luxury goods such as gold, ivory, and spices. This enterprise was joined to increasing traffic from east to west in the Indian Ocean. In 1368 the Ming dynasty gained control in China. The Chinese built a substantial navy, and during the fifteenth century Chinese squadrons sailed as far as East Africa. In Burma, the Mon dynasty created a great entrepôt at Martaban, and ceramic ware from China and Amman found its way right across the Indian Ocean. The fifteenth century also saw an expanding trade between Africa and Muslim India, whose merchants looked to the continent for ivory, gold, iron ore, probably copper, and certainly slaves, especially slave warriors.

The East African coastmen (or Swahilis) had a goodly share in this growing wealth. By the beginning of the sixteenth century, Kilwa—a wooden town in Ibn Battuta's days—consisted of:

very handsome houses of stone and lime, with many windows in our [the Portuguese] style, very well laid out, with many terraces; the doors are of wood very well wrought with beautiful joinery, around are many tanks of water, and orchards, and gardens with much fresh water. They have a Moorish king over them, and they trade with those of Sofala [an ancient port once situated in what is now Portuguese East Africa, south of Beira] from which place they brought much gold, which was spread hence through all Arabia Felix. . . . The Moors in it are some white, some black; they are sufficiently well dressed with many rich cloths of gold and silk and cotton, and the women also with much gold and silver in chains and bracelets which they wear on their feet and arms, and many jewels in their ears. . . .[2]

Archaeologists have reconstructed much of the Swahilis' material culture—the flat-roofed, semidetached houses with their elaborate sanitation, their narrow courts, and their women's quarters, and museum exhibits still show the coastmen's taste for beads and for costly Chinese porcelain.[3]

Swahili civilization thus attained considerable wealth, but it was a frontiersmen's creation whose intellectual culture could not compare with that of older Arab centers. In countries such as Spain, the Arabs not only preserved and passed on to their Christian enemies the legacy of Hellenism, they also made their own contribution to the literature, art, and science of the world.[4] The Swahilis were by no means intellectually unproductive, but Zanzibar and Kilwa could not rival Cordova, Toledo, or Seville in learning or letters. The East African city states were also relatively weak in war. They generally had little difficulty with the inland tribes, most of whom were too disunited for effective military action. The tribesmen were also too backward in their material culture to form an effective menace. The citizens of Mozambique, for instance, felt little fear about the heathen of the mainland "who go naked and covered all over with red clay, they have their loins wrapped in strips of blue cotton cloth, without any other covering, and they have their lips pierced with three holes."[5] But the Muslim cities did not form part of a united empire. Separated from one another by great stretches of the sea, their ruling commercial oligarchies were often locked in bitter rivalry with competing groups in control of other towns. The East Coast communities could no more fuse into a united commonwealth than the Greek city states of antiquity. Neither could any single city gain permanent supremacy over all the rest.

In the fourteenth century, for instance, Kilwa ruled the Mafia Island with two capitals at Kisimani and Kua. Malindi, in the north beyond Mombasa, appears to have been on friendly terms with Kilwa, for both were united in common hostility against Mombasa (on the coast of what is now Kenya). Mombasa was able to control much of the littoral traffic toward the Red Sea, to the Persian Gulf and India, and may also have become the headquarters of the Gujarat traders from India who settled on the East African shores. By the end of the fifteenth century, Mombasa was in the ascendant and Kilwa in the decline. But Mombasa could no more fuse the East Coast settlements into a larger league than could its rivals; hence Muslim internecine struggles proved a fatal weakness in the face of the subsequent irruption into the Indian Ocean on the part of the united Christian kingdom of Portugal from the Atlantic periphery of the Islamic world.

THE CONGO BASIN AND EAST AFRICA

The kingdom of the Kongo centered on the lower Congo basin, a region of dense forest. According to indigenous tradition, the son of a chief ruling over the small chiefdom of Bungu (near the present town of Boma on the Congo River) emigrated with some companions to the south of the Congo sometime in the fourteenth century. He conquered the plateau area of the Kongo, and the invaders allied themselves by marriage to the main lineages of the region. The Kongo state further extended its influence by incorporating existing states or by voluntary submission and became an important power. Other territories lying beyond the borders in the east, southeast, and south recognized the overlordship of Kongo, and irregulary sent tribute or presents to the Kongo ruler, who was known as the *mani kongo.*[6]

The Kongo kingdom was only one of many similar states that covered nearly the whole region south of the tropical Congo forest, west of Lake Tanganyika and north of the middle Zambezi and the lowlands of southern Angola. These comprised, among others, the Luba empire, which appears to have originated in the sixteenth century, and was situated between Lake Tanganyika and the upper Kasai. This state may have owed its origin to conquering hunters, whose prowess in the chase gave them obvious military advantages in the struggle for political power. Little is known about the political structure of the early Luba kingdom. But it may have differed in certain respects from the coastal states. Society was organized into patrilineages grouped into villages. Villages were subordinate to local chiefs; local chiefs in turn were responsible to provincial heads. Some chiefdoms and villages, however, depended directly on the king, who claimed supernatural powers and exercised very considerable authority within the country.

The full story of these states remains to be written. There is also a good deal of controversy concerning their origin. Most scholars today reject the assumption that the various African states of the Kongo and Luba kind derived from one single region. These states probably had their origin from several centers: one perhaps north of Stanley Pool, possibly one on the upper Tshuapa within the Congo forest, and one near the headwaters of the Zambezi.[7] Presumably there was much local invention, stimulated by outside contact, by the diffusion of ideas, and by the need to solve new local problems as they arose.

In all probability, these states were themselves but islands of political cohesion in a sea of smaller statelets whose fortunes remained in constant flux—like those of their larger neighbors. The existence of more powerful states depended on the conjunction of a number of favorable factors such as good communications, a relatively dense population and a fertile soil. Much of our existing knowledge as yet rests on guess-work. The bigger kingdoms and principalities in all likelihood were created by conquest on the part of better-organized immigrants who settled among and subdued the indigenous population. The newcomers may have excelled in military skill as hunters, in political ability as organizers, or in ritual knowledge as rainmakers and diviners. Whatever their origins, the various kingdoms tended to expand at their neighbors' expense. The larger states were surrounded by tributary states, gradually shading off into complete independence. Boundaries and spheres of influence kept fluctuating, though the nuclear states appear to have retained a certain measure of stability.

Conditions favorable to state-building were also found in Uganda, to the east of the main forest area, where fertile soil and good pastures were plentiful, and where rivers and great lakes afforded opportunities for the employment of canoe power. Between the thirteenth and fifteenth centuries, the Bachwezi (Chwezi), tall, brown-skinned cattle owners belonging to the Hima group, came in from the north and established their rule over the Bantu-speaking peoples who dwelt in the region between Lake Albert and Lake Victoria. The Bachwezi may have been the architects of the great fortified camps whose ruins are still found in the country. These fortifications were large enough to protect whole tribal groups, together with their cattle. They consisted of earthworks, surrounded by ditches, sometimes with a great mound in the center of the protected area. The trenches were cut into the rock underlying the surface, so that the builders must have wielded good tools and must have been capable of mobilizing a considerable labor force.

Sometime during the fifteenth century or thereabouts the region experienced yet another incursion from a Nilotic people collectively known as the Luo (Lwoo). The newcomers came from the southern Sudan, where they had developed a distinctive culture based on the herding of cattle. The Luo moved southward and imposed their rule upon the preexisting peoples of Bunyoro, Buganda, Toro, and Busoga. Historians still dispute the origin of these invaders, the details of their migration routes, and the form taken by their political rule. Some emphasize the military prowess of the new settlers. Others contend that their infiltration was more peaceful in character, that the interlacustrine peoples welcomed rather than opposed the Luo, because the Luo brought cattle to the country.[8]

All we can say with some certainty is that the Luo most have ended their dispersion as a tiny minority among their new subjects. They were extremely successful in spreading certain elements of their culture. But they were not necessarily more advanced than the people whom they subdued. In southern Uganda at any rate, the immigrants seem to have conquered people who were already more civilized than the conquerors. The newcomers apparently did, however, stand for a new principle of political organization. According to Roland Oliver, their advance marked the transition from kinship politics riddled by interminable blood feuds to more powerful territorial chieftainships where arbitration and compensation had more play.[9]

The details of this state-building process during the fourteenth and subsequent centuries are still hard to document. Geographical conditions, however, must have favored such a development. The great lakes allowed war bands and traders to move easily by canoe. The northwestern periphery of Lake Victoria was peculiarly fortunate in its climate. The banana plantain afforded the people an almost labor-free source of food and building material. The population was relatively dense. The farmers produced a food surplus sufficiently large to sustain a fairly elaborate state machinery. The Luo made good use of these opportunities, and became state-builders *par excellence.*

Further south, however, Hima dynasties managed to hold out in Ankole, Ruanda, Urundi, and Karagwe, that is to say the region comprised between Lake Kivu, the north end of Lake Tanganyika, and Lake Victoria. These states were subject to warlike, proud and rank-conscious aristocracies. Hence the Luo advance was eventually stemmed, and the southern kingdoms retained their peculiar character. Rwanda, for instance, fell under the domination of a series of clans collectively known as the Tutsi (Tuutsi), a cattle-keeping warrior people, who set up a rigidly stratified state. Rwanda subsequently developed into a centralized monarchy, which from the eighteenth century onward embarked upon far-flung wars of conquest.

SHONA AND THE MALAWI MONARCHIES

Southern Africa saw state-building on an equally significant scale. In a previous chapter we have seen how, perhaps sometime during the thirteenth century, the Karanga established a cohesive monarchy in what is now Rhodesia. The kingdom rested on the supremacy of the Rozwi, a powerful Karanga clan, who held their own against other invaders and in turn embarked on new conquests. The construction of Zimbabwe (near the modern township of Fort Victoria) was their most outstanding architectural achievement, and one of the greatest in sub-Saharan Africa.

The construction of the Zimbabwe complex took countless generations, and there is no time here to go into the vexed question of what Bantu groups built what, when.[10] Suffice it to say that local techniques of massive stone walling probably originated on Zimbabwe Hill, and by the middle of the fifteenth century the towering acropolis formed a safe retreat in wartime, a naturally powerful position reinforced with a network of great walls. Lookout posts could keep the surrounding countryside under observation, and the stronghold was almost impregnable to the assaults of warriors armed only with arrows, shields, daggers, and lances. Further down the valley, where aloes grow in fantastic shapes and kaffir blooms burst into magnificent red, stands the "Temple." This massive complex was probably the king's palace, its general layout showing remarkable resemblance to that of other Bantu royal head-quarters where stone was not employed, such as that built at a much later period by the Barotse paramount chief on the upper Zambezi. The king and his followers lived in huts made of pole and dagga, with floors of hardened earth. These were partitioned by walls, and the buildings now known as "Valley Ruins" probably also contained cattle kraals.

The Zimbabwe Ruins in Southern Rhodesia. Shown here is the Temple or Great Enclosure. (Courtesy Southern Rhodesia Department of Tourism.)

The Karanga traded in gold, and the port of Sofala (south of modern Beira in what is now Mozambique) became a major outlet for the gold trade to the interior. Arab merchants provided the Karanga with trade goods in return for precious metal, so that the Karanga king could pay his soldiers and retinue with cloth and other com-modities. In the fifteenth century the Karanga began to expand northward. Perhaps the Karanga wished to acquire more land for their growing population and more pastures for their cattle; perhaps they meant to develop new gold mines or new sources of salt, an ever-present need for an inland people who otherwise laboriously had to recover this precious substance from dung and reeds. According to indigenous tradition, Mutota, a great Rozwi chief, led a host northward, where the vanquished

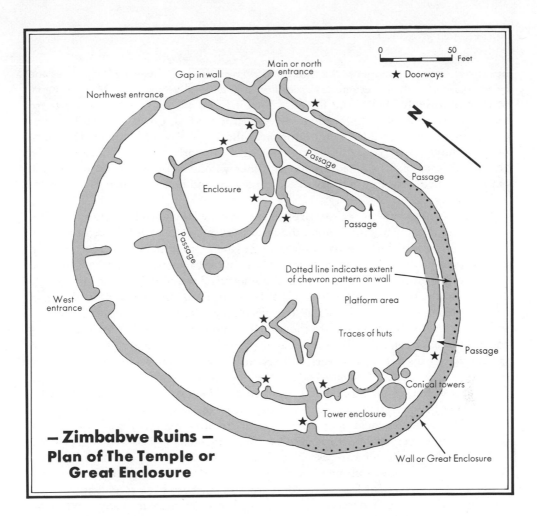

— Zimbabwe Ruins —
Plan of The Temple or
Great Enclosure

Labels within the plan:

- Northwest entrance
- Gap in wall
- Main or north entrance
- 0 ____ 50 Feet
- ★ Doorways
- N
- West entrance
- Enclosure
- Passage
- Passage
- Passage
- Passage
- Dotted line indicates extent of chevron pattern on wall
- Platform area
- Traces of huts
- Conical towers
- Tower enclosure
- Wall or Great Enclosure

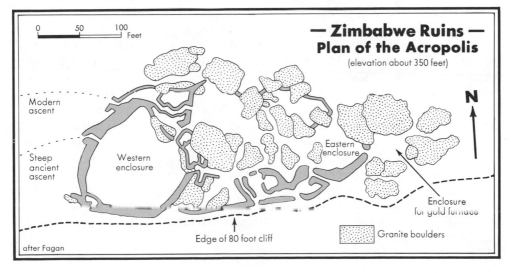

— Zimbabwe Ruins —
Plan of the Acropolis
(elevation about 350 feet)

Labels within the plan:

- 0 ____ 50 ____ 100 Feet
- N
- Modern ascent
- Steep ancient ascent
- Western enclosure
- Eastern enclosure
- Enclosure for gold furnace
- Edge of 80 foot cliff
- Granite boulders
- after Fagan

237

bestowed on their conqueror the title of "Mwene Mutapa," meaning "master of the ravaged land," which became a hereditary title generally known as Monomotapa. Mutota apparently shifted the focus of his kingdom to the newly won northern marches. He established his headquarters near the Chitako-Changonya Hill, east of Gota, and constructed a large stone fort near the Utete River for the protection of his household. Visitors can still see the remains of his work, consisting of stone walls, all built of granite slabs, piled upon each other without mortar, the main stockade being scalloped, probably in order to accomodate round huts with their walls adjoining the stockade.

Here, in the somewhat eerie escarpment country, where ghostly white fever trees and grotesque baobabs grow among the *mopane* bush, Mutota held court. In the end the southern area of the kingdom was reduced to mere provincial status. The northern portion became the most important of the Monomotapa's dominions, perhaps because of ease of access from the Zambezi, and numerous Arab merchants set up trading posts along the river. Tradition has it that later on in the fifteenth century Matope, another strong monarch, initiated a vigorous policy of further conquest which for a short time carried Karanga arms to the shores of the Indian Ocean.[11] Monomotapa's court, like that of all other Bantu monarchs, acted as the center of a vast system of tributary exchange. Subjects were obliged to forward tribute. In exchange they received gifts as well as protection against their enemies. A later Portuguese observer wrote that whenever the Monomotapa wanted gold he sent cattle to his people, who divided the beasts among themselves according to the labor accomplished.

The Monomotapas held sway over a great tribal confederacy whose economy rested on cattle keeping, hoe tillage, gold mining, and crafts such as weaving, pottery, and the production of ironware, as well as foreign trade in luxury goods such as ivory. As time went on, powerful men could afford richer clothes, finer ornaments, and better weapons than their followers, while warfare may also have accentuated incipient social differences. Monomotapa's state organization must, in many ways, have resembled that of the Kongo kingdom. The great nobles of the king's household formed the nucleus of the administration. The monarch also received assistance from a body of tribal intellectuals, part royal spirit mediums and part official historians, who were supposed to voice the will of the ancestral rulers and maintain the traditions of their race. There was also a host of office bearers, who held land and vassals, but who resided at the king's court. Local government remained in the hands of minor chiefs whose position depended on their ability to attract followers through gifts of food. As a subsequent Portuguese observer put it: "The greater part of this Kaffraria is governed by fumos and petty rulers, and though it has powerful kings whom it obeys, it has nevertheless these fumos and headmen by whom the people are governed. The fumos near Sena are Kaffirs, natives of the country, and very often the lowest are elected to this dignity. Most of them are forced against their will to accept the office, for when one has cows, millet, or naqueny which he can give them and spend, they elect him fumo, and his dignity lasts as long as he has anything to spend. When they have eaten up his property, they cast him out of the office, and pre-eminence is the most that they give him."[12]

The life of the ordinary people went on in much the same way as that of African communities in later days. Millet was the nation's staple food, as well as palm oil "which is a penance to those who are not accustomed to its use," but the Africans also liked to eat fowl and mutton, as well as game, which was then plentiful.

African society developed a material culture of its own; builders and smiths, weavers and potters acquired considerable skill; but the nation depended entirely on the spoken word to pass on its traditions and accumulated experience; writing remained unknown, and the African did not translate his thoughts into symbols engraved on stone or penned on papyrus. At the same time the villagers relied entirely on human muscle, their sole source of power. The use of the wheel was not known. No draught animals were used, neither were plows or carts, with the result that indigenous cultivators had to rely on hoes, and could produce but a limited surplus of food. The tribesmen could keep alive only by a rigidly laid out system of village cooperation; and religion and custom alike upheld a society where communal cohesion stood out as the supreme good. The whole tenor of society accordingly remained extremely conservative, and men looked askance at innovations. As Father Monclaro, a somewhat prejudiced Portuguese observer, said:

Their only houses are small straw huts plastered with clay, resembling round dove-cotes. The land is sterile for the most part, but its sterility does not equal their sloth, for even on the well watered plains, which they call *antevaras,* they sow very little, and if there is one among them who is more diligent and a better husbandman, and therefore reaps a fresh crop of millet and has a larger store of provisions, they immediately falsely accuse him of all kinds of crimes, as an excuse to take it from him and eat it, saying why should he have more millet than another, never attributing it to his greater industry and diligence; and very often they kill him and eat all his provisions. It is the same with cattle, and this is the cause of the scarcity. They are not provident, but quickly waste and consume the new crops in feasts and drinking.

They do not make use of any kind of animal for labour, and therefore many came to Sena, where we were, and showed much surprise and laughed heartily when they saw the oxen at the plough or drawing carts full of stones for the fort. They dig the earth with small hoes, and in the furrows and little trenches they throw the millet or other seed they are to sow and cover it lightly with earth; and it yields a good crop.[13]

African religion corresponded to this way of life. Bantu thinkers now recognized a supreme God; but there was no formalized theology, and tribal life was thought to be influenced rather by the ancestral spirits who might either help their descendants or punish them for their sins, and who kept up a never-ending interest in the affairs of the village.

There is some likelihood that Shona political predominance depended to a considerable degree on new and powerful religious concepts, for Zimbabwe and other centers had great ritual importance. They were especially concerned with rainmaking and above all, with Mwari, the supreme divinity of the Shona. Mwari could be approached only by tribal spirits called *mhondoro,* who expressed themselves through spirit mediums known as *svikiro.* The power of the Shona kings was apparently based on control of this religious apparatus; Shona religion may well have been the key to the political and social integration of the state. There were also other Shona states, including Barwe, Uteve, and Madanda. Each of these developed into autonomous kingdoms probably run on lines very similar to those of Monomotapa's state. We know very little about these countries as yet. It is, however, quite likely that during the seventeenth century each of these monarchies was as important as Monomotapa's.[14]

All we can say is that these Bantu states appear to have been subject to bitter internal dissensions, and that Monomotapa's monarchy must have suffered from many political weaknesses. These is some evidence that by the end of the fifteenth century the gold trade had begun to decline. The state had grown far too large; outlying areas could no longer be easily controlled, and there were constant disorders. Monomotapa's empire, like other Bantu states of its type, may also have suffered from the fact that the various provinces remained economically undifferentiated and therefore lacked economic ties to hold the kingdom together. To make matters worse, most of Matope's sons seem to have lacked their father's ability. However, a younger son, Changa, born of a lowly wife, assumed power over the central and southern provinces. Toward the end of the fifteenth century Changa further extended his power and in the end proclaimed himself king of the southern and central portion of the Karanga state, assuming the title of Changamire, and styling his new state Urozwi. The Monomotapas failed to re-establish their old authority; long drawn-out wars weakened both parties, and when Portuguese explorers arrived in the beginning of the sixteenth century, Monomotapa's empire had already passed the height of its power.

The regions comprised within the country north of the Zambezi, east of the Luangwa River and west of the Shire were inhabited by another group of Bantu-speaking peoples known as the Malawi. These people are today fragmented into

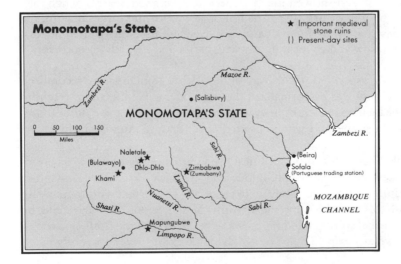

several different groups. All have a common tongue known as Nyanja. The ancestors of these different groups probably came from the Congo. They arrived in the country not as a monolithic bloc but in different groups who settled successively over a period of many centuries. They were certainly well established to the southwest of Lake Nyasa long before the Portuguese pioneers visited the country.

We know little about their early history. According to local traditions, the Malawi were led from the Congo into the region of Lake Nyasa by a chief whose title was Kalonga. According to Cewa lore, Kalonga sent out a number of junior royal relatives to establish suzerainty over the Cewa country. Other dignitaries assumed control in other areas. The Malawi depended on slash-and-burn agriculture; they also knew how to work iron, and they appear to have built up a considerable trade in ivory to the east coast. Kalonga's supremacy depended in part on his people's military prowess, partly on his control over foreign commerce, and partly perhaps on a national rain cult, which may have helped to weld the Malawi-speaking peoples into a cohesive community. During the seventeenth century Malawi developed into a powerful, though relatively short-lived empire; further reference to Malawi's period of greatness will be made in a subsequent chapter on the Portuguese impact.

ETHIOPIA'S MEDIEVAL SPLENDOR

From Monomotapa's kingdom and comparable forms of preliterate tribal confederacies, we pass to the empire of Ethiopia, a very different monarchy, with a developed African variety of feudalism and a much richer cultural tradition from the Mediterranean and the Near East. The restoration of the Solomonic dynasty by Yekuno Amlak about 1270, mentioned in a previous chapter, marked a decisive break in Abyssinia's checkered history. The country's center of gravity now rested firmly upon Amhara, the geographical heart of the great plateau, and Abyssinian policy aimed first of all at consolidating its position in the great central highland area.

Yekuno Amlak's grandson Amda Seyon, "the Pillar of Zion," 1314–1344, was a renowned warrior whose prowess in love was exceeded only by his valor in war. Amda Seyon, like his predecessors, carried on a series of bitter wars against the Muslim sultanates that circled Ethiopia along its eastern and southern fringe, especially Adal (Adel), Ethiopia's arch enemy on the Dankali and Somali coast. These Muslim states covered a much greater area than that controlled by the Christian Emperor, but Abyssinia, geographically a compact power, enjoyed the advantage of interior lines, while the Islamic peoples—spread in a vast semicircle without proper communications—lacked political cohesion. Amda Seyon thus managed to extend the borders of his kingdom, gaining the entire plateau down to the Awash River. During the course of the fifteenth century, Ethiopian arms gained even greater renown. In 1434, Zar'a Ya'qob, one of the greatest of Abyssinian monarchs (1434–1468), mounted the throne, and during his reign the country gained the summit of its power. Zar'a Ya'qob, a severe authoritarian ruler, carried through a comprehensive program of administrative and ecclesiastical reforms that determined the special character of the Abyssinian monophysite church once and for all; he was a great patron of letters and an outstanding soldier. In the long and merciless struggle against Adal, he consolidated the Abyssinian position in the Sidama country, and his victories gave Ethiopia a long breathing space before the Muslims were ready to strike again.[15]

Under the restored Solomonic dynasty, Ethiopia saw a great literary renascence that continued for something like five centuries. Hitherto, Abyssinian writing had been confined to translations from Greek. The new writers also rendered Coptic and Arab originals into Ge'ez, mainly choosing religious subjects, including hagiographies, hymns, prayers, and litanies. In addition, Abyssinian authors paid a great deal of attention to history. *Kebra Nagast* belongs to the beginning of the period; it tells how the Ethiopian kingdom originated and glorifies the newly restored line of Solomon. It was followed by translations concerned with the deeds of the ancient Jews, of Alexander the Great, and also of the *Universal History* written by John Nikiu, an Egyptian bishop who lived shortly after his country's conquest by the Arabs. In addition, the Abyssinians began to record their own past. For the early period we have only popular romances, generally of a hagiographic kind, and also bald lists of kings, so contradictory and confused as to be largely valueless. But from the fourteenth century on, Ethiopian scholars used the official annals kept by the monarch's scribe to compile the annals of their own times. These accounts have many gaps. From the beginning of the sixteenth century, however, begins a series of contemporary chronicles extending to modern times and giving to Abyssinian history a degree of documentation absent for most other African kingdoms.

Abyssinian power rested on a substantial economic basis. At the beginning of the sixteenth century, Alessandro Zorzi, a learned Venetian, compiled notes from authentic travel reports that tell us a good deal about the country. Zorzi made a deliberate attempt to break away from Ptolemy and the traditional geography of the Middle Ages and to use firsthand information from people who had actually traveled in distant lands. Zorzi's notes, derived from an Ethiopian as well as an Italian informant, refer to an extensive commerce in gold, jewels, pearls, spices, medicinal herbs, silk cloth, and other luxury products, and also in mules and horses. The Abyssinians traded with the Arabs on the coast, Hungarian and Venetian as well as Muslim coins serving as a widely accepted currency. Zeila, a Muslim port (south of the modern Djibouti), acted as an entrepôt for the far-flung trade between India, Arabia, and the Ethiopian interior.

Abyssinia also possessed great agricultural wealth:

. . . as in all the lands of Presta Jani [Prester John, the Ethiopian ruler]; there grow all fruits except chestnut, and there grow peas, beans, chick-peas, beans ("fasali"), and in the best and richest grounds there grow many trees and date-palms, but the dates are not as good as those of Cairo because they like sand. There grow lemons, citrons, oranges to full perfection. There grow not melons, but gourds and other things and herbs, flowers of different kinds, and roses (all very fragrant and of pleasant odour), honey, much sugar, countless domestic animals such as buffaloes, oxen, cows, sheep, goats, dromedaries, great store of fair horses, mules, assses, and very great dogs, stags, roe-bucks, hares, gazelles, countless elephants, lions, panthers, giraffes, lynxes. Item, many other forest animals, amongst which one that they call Aris, which is great as a cow but very bulky, of a tawny hue, with two horns on the head of one branch and curved, the one on the forehead curved backwards, the other between the ears curved forwards, with which it kills many men; it runs fast, and while running it breaks wind. . . . there are great serpents, e.g. serpents ('bise') . . . There is much silk, and cotton grows there, and they make clothes ('panni') of silk, wool and cotton, very fair and abundant, which they wear.[16]

Ethiopia was well provided with iron, and its soldiers were armed in much the same fashion as European early medieval soldiers. The country also impressed travelers by the people's skill in the arts and architecture and by the piety and learning of its churchmen. The Ethiopians, according to Zorzi,

are fine men and women, and wear their hair long as we do; and in battle they are well equipped and chiefly with cuirasses of mail and swords, spears and bows; and they have iron in great quantity that is mined in those mountains . . . a little way from Axon is a very good iron and steel mine, and that there are dug up colouring materials for the pictures in their religious buildings, but that they will not have sculpture, but their temples are of great worth and great and vaulted . . . , covered with lead, and in the same manner are their palaces and forts . . . , and many monks of every order and priests, canons, bishops and archbishops and excellent Christians; they do not commit perjury of blaspheme, but always bless God. Almoners have many manuscript books in their script. . . .[17]

The Abyssinian state organization was of a kind that would probably have been familiar to the administrators of Charlemagne (the greatest of Frankish kings, subsequently emperor of the West, 800–814). The kingdom had no fixed capital. The Abyssinian monarch was crowned at the ancient city of Axum, but spent much of his life traveling through his dominions and governing his subjects from a great moving camp. His army consisted of soldiers provided by the governors and sub-governors at their own expense. The troops, insofar as they did not live on the country, brought their own provisions, and Abyssinian forces thus had great difficulty in keeping the field for extended periods. The governors of all grades lived on the tribute of specific villages assigned for their maintenance. The great central officers of state were similarly endowed with fiefs granted to them by the king. The churches and monasteries were supported by other villages and lands; these were held in perpetuity and not, like the fiefs of secular lords, at the king's pleasure, so that the church was a powerful landholding corporation. The rest of the country belonged to the king. The monarch depended for his revenue on income from the crown lands, taxes paid by the people, royalties on all mines not worked by himself, tributes from his princes and governors, including both payments in kind, such as horses, oxen, cotton, and gold. The crown's only regular expense consisted in the maintenance of his own household and entourage. He was thus able to accumulate a considerable surplus and to make lavish gifts to his dignitaries.[18] The monarch also sent presents to neighboring heads of state, normally receiving as much as he sent, so that the Abyssinian king, may, in some ways, also have acted as a "distributor king," channelling and rechannelling part of the national wealth through an elaborate tributary network.

The Church played perhaps an even greater part in the structure of Abyssinian than of early Frankish feudalism. The Solomonic monarchy succeeded in effecting a well-nigh total fusion between Church and State. The kings founded a truly prodigious number of churches and monasteries, which, in proportion to the population, may have been even more numerous than in medieval Europe. Many of these were magnificent constructions, with stone sanctuaries, divided by stone pillars and arches into aisles and vaulted, their walls covered with splendid paintings. The Church played an essential part in royal governance and in the difficult task of assimilating conquered provinces into the Abyssinian form of Christianity and culture. Zar'a Ya'qob's zeal for Christianity led to vigorous attempts to suppress pagan and Judaic creeds by force, and there were all manner of inquisitions and persecutions.

Despite this imposing facade, the Abyssinian kingdom appears to have shared many of the weaknesses besetting the great savannah states of West Africa. The monarchs ruled over a great congerie of peoples, Christian, pagan, Muslim, or Judaic in persuasion, many of whom could not be integrated into the culture of the ruling class. Indeed many popular customs appear to have remained profoundly "African." The monarchs practiced polygamy as a form of national diplomacy. The people paid bride-wealth for their women "who are fair and marry without dowry; instead those men who would marry give money to their fathers that they may have them."[19] Despite attempts at rigorous centralization, the hereditary power of provincial rulers could not be eliminated; the influence of the great *Rases* (provincial governors, comparable in some ways to medieval German dukes) remained considerable and emphasized the kingdom's centrifugal tendencies. If we are to believe reports concerning the enormous wealth accumulated by the king, the burden of tribute and other exactions must have weighed heavily on the common people. As John Pory, a sixteenth-century compiler, put it, "Prete Ianni his government is very absolute, for he holdeth his subjects in the most base servitude, and no lesse the great noble and great, then those of meaner qvalite and condition, entreating them rather slaves, then subjects." Hence in Pory's estimation the masses "want that generositie of minde which maketh man ready to take up armes, & to be couragious in dãger."[20] The king's military potential remained limited. The Abyssinians lacked fortified cities to act as bases of resistance against the foreign invasions; they could not produce any firearms of their own and failed to establish a permanent military superiority over their Muslim opponents. Transport at the same time remained a major problem in a mountainous country, and the king's far-flung and variegated dominions could not be easily held together.

Much depended on the ruler's personality, and with the death of Zar'a Ya'qob, Ethiopia's might began to wane. Some of the most recently conquered provinces became restive. The feudal lords whom Zar'a Ya'qob had brought under submission reasserted their regional authority. The senior clergy relapsed into their former ways. Indeed the Church itself may have suffered from an organizational crisis.

The number of monks and priests apparently became so great that the endowments of churches and monasteries, huge though they were, could no longer support all these ecclesiastics. This applied particularly to the royal churches, which were served by a special order of married priests whose succession was strictly hereditary, every son of a canon becoming a canon himself. The staff of every royal church thus became, by natural increase, too numerous for its endowments (a difficulty only a celibate clergy, like that of Western Europe, was able to avoid). In order to relieve their difficulties, the kings continually founded new churches, but even so, the problem could not be solved, and the clergy, including monks, had to pursue secular avocations.[21]

Thus for all its imposing splendor, the kingdom's foundations were by no means secure. By the end of the fifteenth century, the Abyssinian state—like the Frankish dominions at Charlemagne's death—had outgrown its size. Islamic power remained firmly entrenched on the shores of the Red Sea, and during the sixteenth century the Ethiopian kingdom was destined to collapse under Muslim blows in a holocaust of misery and murder.

NOTES

1. Ibn Battuta, *Travels in Asia and Africa, 1325–1354,* trans. and ed., H. A. R. Gibb (London, 1929), pp. 110–112.

2. "Extracts from the Book Written by Duarte Barbosa," in Theal, *Records of South-Eastern Africa,* vol. 1, pp. 98–99.

3. Gervase Mathew, "The East African Coast until the Coming of the Portuguese," in Oliver and Mathew, *History of East Africa,* vol. 1, chap. 1, p. 122. This section is mainly based on the chapter cited.

4. Sir Reginald Coupland, *East Africa and Its Invaders* (Oxford, 1961).

5. "Extracts from the Book Written by Duarte Barbosa," in Theal, p. 98.

6. Jan Vansina, *Kingdoms of the Savanna* (Madison, 1960), pp. 38–40.

7. Vansina, Mauny, and Thomas, eds., *The Historian in Tropical Africa,* p. 96.

8. For details see Collins, *Problems in African History,* pp. 115–165.

9. Roland Oliver, "Discernible Developments in the Interior c. 1500–1840," in Oliver and Mathew, vol. 1, p. 179.

10. For a good popular summary, see Roger Summers, *Zimbabwe: A Rhodesian Mystery* (London, 1963).

11. For a general summary, based on the work of D. P. Abraham, R. Summers and others, see Lewis H. Gann, *A History of Southern Rhodesia: Early Days to 1934* (London, 1965), pp. 5–13.

12. Father Monclaro, "Account of the Journey Made by the Fathers of the Company of Jesus with Francisco Barreto in the Conquest of Monopotapa in the Year 1569," in Theal, ed., *Records of South-Eastern Africa,* vol. 3, p. 227.

13. Father Monclaro, p. 231.

14. Edward Alpers, "The Mutapa and Malawi Political Systems," in T. O. Ranger, ed., *Aspects of Central African History* (London, 1968), pp. 1–27.

15. Ullendorf, *The Ethiopians,* pp. 66–71.

16. O. G. S. Crawford, ed., *Ethiopian Itineraries circa 1400–1524; Including Those Collected*

by Alessandro Zorzi at Venice in the Years 1519–24 (Hakluyt Society, Second Series, No. CIX, Cambridge, 1958), p. 143

17. Crawford, p. 143.

18. A. H. M. Jones and Elizabeth Monroe, *A History of Ethiopia* (Oxford, 1955), pp. 63–76. For a more detailed account see John Pory, *A Briefe Relation Concerning the Dominions, Revenues, Forces and Manner of Gouernment of Sundry the Greatest Princes Either Inhabiting Within the Bounds of Africa, or at Least Possessing Some Parts Thereof . . . ,* in Robert Brown, ed., *The History and Description of Africa* (London, 1898), vol. 3. pp. 974–985.

19. Crawford, p. 171.

20. Pory, *A Briefe Relation,* pp. 977–980.

21. To this day the secular clergy in Abyssinia are not bound by any vows of celibacy and generally belong to families who exercise the ministry in an almost hereditary fashion.

Chapter 18

Africa by the End
of the Fifteenth Century

JEWISH, CHRISTIAN, ISLAMIC, AND INDONESIAN INFLUENCES

"That part of inhabited lande extending southward, which we call Africa . . . is one of the generall parts of the world knowen vnto our ancestors; which in very deed was not thoroughly by them discouered, both bicause the Inlands could not be trauailed in regard of huge deserts full of dangerous sands . . . and also by reason of the long and perilous navigation vpon the African coasts, for which cause it was by very few of ancient times compassed by nauigation, much less searched or intirely known . . ."[1]

Leo Africanus's introduction to his great *History and Description of Africa* applied not only to the Europeans and Arabs of his day but also to all the indigenous peoples of the continent. At the end of the fifteenth century even the most widely travelled merchants of Timbuktu, Axum, and Kilwa were acquainted only with a limited portion of the great continent. The vast majority of the African peoples—as indeed of people all over the inhabited globe—knew nothing but their own little world. Their lives normally centered on a village or, in the case of Bushmen, Hottentots, or Somalis, on their nomadic band. Yet, if their world was so much smaller than ours, the sheer difficulties of travel made it enormously larger. A caravan proceeding, say, from Timbuktu to Marrakesh, would cover what to the participants was a tremendous distance. A Bushman band looking for new hunting grounds a hundred miles away was engaged in a major enterprise. Thus the overwhelming majority of the people lived in small communities, isolated from the outside world.

247

We should not exaggerate the difference that existed between the Africans and many European peoples living at the end of the fifteenth century. Few African tribesmen ever lived in greater isolation than the inhabitants of Erris, a desolate tract in County Mayo, Ireland, many of whom—during the late 1840s—had never seen a living tree bigger than a shrub. Few Africans subsisted under more miserable conditions than Irish cabin dwellers, whose habitations were cut out of living bog, with entrances so low that the people had to crawl inside on all fours, with large families being confined in a space of eight to ten square feet, their state being described by contemporary British observers as lower than that of the Ashanti or the wild Indians.[2]

Neither should we make too much of Africa's isolation. As we have pointed out in previous chapters, large areas of the continent—especially in the north and east—had over the centuries become cultural melting pots, producing a variety of syncretic civilizations, many bearing the stamp of Islam. Among the most ancient, but the least successful, competitors in the spiritual scramble for Africa had been the Jews. From Biblical times onward, Hebrew emigrants had settled in Egypt, in other parts of northern Africa, as well as in Ethiopia, having come as merchants and mercenary soldiers, cultivators, and craftsmen. The extent of Jewish influence is difficult to document. Sixteenth century compilers like John Pory were still fond of postulating the existence of Hebrew kingdoms in "Certaine vnknowne mountaines, between the confines of Abassia, and Congo," or "on the banks of the river Zaire [Congo]." Evidence for such settlement is, however, scanty, and such stories are generally to be discounted.

Jews traveled far afield in northern and eastern Africa, but Judaism as a religion and culture did not catch on widely. The most important exception to this rule occurred in Abyssinia. Here Judaic and indigenous Agaw elements fused to produce the culture of the Falasha, a dark-skinned community, who knew only the Old Testament, stayed ignorant of subsequent Talmudic traditions, and remained strongly influenced by pagan lore. Much more important were the Jews in Egypt, where "in great, and in a manner in all the cities and townes thereof, they exercise mechanicall arts, and vse traffick and merchandize, as also take upon them the receit of taxes and customes."

Many other Hebrews dwelt in North Africa, especially in Morocco. These Jewish congregations were greatly reinforced by the expulsion of the Jews from Spain at the end of the fifteenth century. From Spain, "they passed one after an other into Africk and Mauritania, and dispersed themselues euen to the confines of Numidia, especiallie by meanes of traffick, and the profession of goldsmithes, the which . . . is utterly practised amongst them by the Iewes, as are likewise diuers other mechanicall crafts, but principallie that of black smithes." In addition, many Jewish refugees from Portugal "went ouer into the kingdomes of Fez and Morocco, and brought in thither the artes and professions of Europe vnknowne before . . ." Jewish influence extended far into the savannah belt where "they passe also by way of traffick euen to Tombuto [Timbuktu]."[3]

Christianity had also made an impact on Africa, though by the end of the fifteenth century most of its early conquests had been lost. North Africa, one of the bastions of early Christianity, had become largely Muslim in religion, and only small remnants of the original Christian population survived. These included the Copts of Egypt, who claimed that St. Mark, the first archbishop of Alexandria, had established their church. The Copts had embraced the Monophysite creed, and Catholics maliciously called them "Christians from the girdle vpward: for albeit they be baptized . . . yet they do circumcise themselues like to the Iewes: so as a man may say, their Christianitie comes no lower than the girdlestead."[4]

In earlier days, Coptic cultural influence had spread into Nubia, into what is now the southern part of the United Arab Republic and the Sudan. But these isolated enclaves could not hold out against the Muslim tide. By the end of the twelfth century, Dongola, for instance, was sunk in poverty; the people grew no more than a little millet and some dates; the king's palace was the only building not constructed of grass, and the monarch could not understand Arabic. According to Arkell, the culture of Christian Nubia did not spread far afield; there is said to be no evidence that its influences ever extended further west than the Wadi Muqaddam, some twenty miles west of Omdurman. The Dongolan kingdom in time became a tributary state, supplying oxen, rock salt, and emeralds to Cairo. In 1315 Egyptian troops occupied the country and carried away Kerenbes, its last Christian ruler. Kerenbes was reinstated for a time, but the fortunes of Dongola continued to decline. Muslim intruders invaded the country, and as the newcomers amalgamated with the riverine Nubians, Islam totally supplanted Christianity.[5]

Ethiopia remained the most powerful outpost of Christendom in Africa. As we have seen in previous chapters Coptic Christianity had fused with indigenous elements to produce a vigorous syncretic civilization with a great monastic tradition and distinctive literary, architectural, and religious achievements of its own. Ethiopia was largely though not wholly isolated from the West. There was, for instance, an Ethiopian community at Jerusalem, and in 1141 two Ethiopian delegates from that congregation attended an ecclesiastical council at Florence. The Italian city states, the popes, the kingdoms of Aragon and Portugal all had commercial or religious interests in the eastern Mediterranean and its African hinterland. Some looked to the far interior for trade; others thought of fantastic schemes for getting support from "Prester John" against the Muslims.

From the middle of the fifteenth century, European interest in Ethiopia increased steadily. A handful of Western merchants and churchmen made their way into the distant mountain kingdom whose foreign community contained, toward the end of the fourteenth century, a few immigrants from Naples, Venice, Genoa, Catalonia, and the Levant, including one Nicolo Branchalion, a Venetian painter who exercised his craft with conspicuous success. Ethiopia, however, remained geographically remote; Western influence was tenuous in character and Ethiopian Christianity and culture retained its distinctly "African" flavor.

Throughout North and East Africa, the Crescent occupied an infinitely more powerful position than the Cross.

The Mahumetan impietie, [Pory wrote, sadly but accurately] hath spred it selfe throughout Africa beyond measure. . . . The wicked walke roun about; according to thy greatness. . . . Where they could not come, nor giue no blow with armes; there they haue ingraffed themselues, by preaching and traffike. The heresie of Arrius [Arius, a Libyan theologian and Christian heresiarch, ca. 256–336 A.D., who denied that the Son was consubstantial with the Father] furthered their enterprize, wherewith the Vandals and Gothes then being inhabiters of [Northwest] Africa were infected. To further their designments they brought in the Arabicke language and letters. They founded Vniuersities and Studies, both for riches of reuenew [revenue], and magnificence of building most notable, epecially in Maroco and Fez. But there is nothing that hath greatlier furthered the progression of the Mahumetan sect, then perpetuitie of victorie & the greatness of conquests. . . . The Arabians not contented in Africa to haue subiugated with armes and with false doctrine to haue pestered Barbarie, Numidia, Lybia and the countrey of Negroes, they further on the other side assailed the lower Ethiopia . . . and . . . they erected the kingdomes of Mogdazo [Mogadishu], Melinde, Mombazza, Quiloa [Kilwa], Mozambique and . . . the kingdomes of Dangali [Dongali] and Adel. So that on the one side they haue spred their sect, from the Red sea to the Atlantike Ocean, and from the Mediterran sea to the riuer Niger, and farther: and on the other, haue taken into their hands all the easterne coast of Africk, from Suez to Cape Guardaf, and from this, euen to that of De los corrientes and the adjoining islands.[6]

North Africa, in other words, was now fully part of the Islamic world.

In addition, Islam spread to the southern termini of the great trans-Saharan trade routes. Muslim influence in time became supreme throughout most of the Sudanic savannah belt, where the ruling strata largely became assimilated into Muslim culture. In the eleventh century, for instance, the rulers of Tekrour, a commercial state straddling the Senegal River, were converted. In the same century the puritanical Almoravid movement made its appearance among the Berber tribes of southern Mauritania, and Mauritanian preachers later left a strong Muslim imprint on many regions south of the Senegal. The Mali empire also played a major role in spreading Islam, especially among the Mandingo people. When the Portuguese arrived on the West African shore at the end of the fifteenth century, they found Islam well established at most Senegambian courts.[7]

West African Islam drew much of its strength from *marabouts* or holy men who prayed for the chief and also handled the royal correspondence. As a reward for their services, they received land and were allowed to form villages. These in turn developed into solid Islamic communities whose people supported Koranic schools, kept the fast of Ramadan and formed part of a wider Muslim world. Although Islam first took hold among the followers of great chiefs, the new religion later found its most devoted supporters among the *jambur* or free peasants, while the aristocratic *tyeddo* or warrior class tended to remain hostile. Many other villagers occupied an intermediate position, mixing pagan beliefs with those of Islam.

Converts to the new faith were linked to fellow-believers in other countries through *tariqas* or religious brotherhoods. These fraternities had their origin in Sufism, an Islamic variety of mysticism. Sufism was part of a reaction against the coldness of orthodox theology; it was comparable in some respects to the Hasidic revolt against orthodox scholastic forms of Judaism during the eighteenth century.

Like Hasidism, Sufism appealed to the poor rather than to the highly educated. But Sufism also played an important part in adapting Islam to the needs of more backward tribal cultures. Among the Sufi, the pious men often congregated round a leader known for his piety or for his reputed ability as a miracle worker. Having been initiated, the disciple in turn went forth to spread his master's teachings. In this way networks of religious communities were built up, often extending from one end of the Islamic world to the other, linking the faithful in a loose form of organization particularly well adapted to the needs of an Oriental trading and craft economy.

In addition, Islam dominated the Red Sea as well as large stretches of the African East Coast, Islam's maritime hinterland in the far south. Islam, however, had failed to penetrate into the African forest belts; in East Africa its influence was confined to the coastal belt, so that the greatest part of the continent remained little affected or wholly untouched by the three great monotheistic religions of mankind.

Madagascar formed another cultural enclave, characterized by the fusion of African and Indonesian elements. Islam also had some influence on the island civilization. Indonesian immigrants continued to come as merchants, farmers, and warriors; some of these new arrivals seem to have become partly converted to Islam, either in Indonesia itself or in other regions adjoining the Indian Ocean. Islamic influence was not, however, very profound. Some Malgache communities abstained from pork and other impure food; they acquired some knowledge of Mohammed, of Biblical personages, and sometimes observed the month of Ramadan. Islamic traditions of magic spread into Madagascar; so did a specialized, Arab-derived vocabulary concerned with the lunar calendar, the names of days, weeks, and months, and with astrology and divination. The peoples of the northeast were familiar with the art of building in stone; they imported fine garments, pottery, and oriental jewelry and adopted various east coast customs. The people of the southeast coast, on the other hand, appear to have been largely isolated; they lacked regular maritime traffic and settled down to farming, especially the cultivation of rice. The new settlers, though small in number and soon submerged among the mass of Malgache peoples, appear to have introduced new political conceptions; these contributed to the building up of larger kingdoms. Malgache civilization probably had some impact on Africa by spreading new foodcrops; but lacking any kind of political cohesion, the islanders could not become conquerors, and failed to exercise any political influence on the mainland.[8]

AFRICAN STATE ORGANIZATIONS

By the end of the fifteenth century Africa had experienced countless migrations, and the majority of its indigenous peoples occupied much the same regions where they dwell today. The peoples of Africa had evolved a great number of political and social institutions. Diversity had become the keynote of the continent. There was now an enormous "spread," both in the people's material culture and in the scale and complexity of their constitutions. On the one end of the human spectrum were tribal communities of "wilde and lawless people, living (after the manner of the ancient Scythians and Nomades, and like the Tartars and Baduin-Arabians of these times) a vagrant kind of life, vnder cabbins and cottages in the open forests . . . of countenance most terrible, making lines vpon their cheekes with certain iron instruments . . . man eaters, and couragious in battaile. . . ." On the other end, there were sophisticated city states like Mombassa "peopled with Mahumetans: their houses . . . of many stories high, and beautified with pictures both grauen and painted . . ."9—whose livelihood depended on an elaborate exchange economy.

The most primitive nomadic communities, like those of the Bushmen, kept alive by gathering herbs and edible roots and by hunting. Living from hand to mouth, they were unable to build up any kind of surplus; there was no specialization of labor and life remained extremely precarious. Slash-and-burn cultivators, cattle keepers, and mixed farmers—including many Bantu communities—could draw on much ampler resources, and built up more developed institutions. Smiths, magicians and diviners had become recognized specialists.

Economic diversification of course did not necessarily lead to the creation of great kingdoms. The majority of Africans at this time were probably not organized into states in our sense of the word, but relied for help on kinsmen, on neighbors, or on members of the same age set. They looked for protection to bonds of reciprocity, to ritual institutions, or to other devices for maintaining public peace. In fact even the threat of blood feuds between different clans may have acted as a means of restraining the violent, for blood feuds involved whole kinship groups, and the clans did not lightly embark upon serious conflict. Some of these so-called stateless societies comprised only a handful of people. Others embraced much larger groups whose members lacked any centralized machinery of coercion, but dwelt in a condition of "regulated anarchy."10 Unfortunately we do not know much about the way in which these institutions worked in the remoter past. Tribal praise-singers and European chroniclers alike were more interested in the doings of great monarchs. Besides, our information about early stateless society largely derives from the reports of European or Arab travelers. These visitors were habituated to political constitutions of a very different kind; they commonly misunderstood what they saw; hence our historical reconstructions are largely based on informed guesswork.

In addition to these stateless societies, there were African kingdoms and principalities, many of them distinguished by considerable size and complexity. Again generalizations are hard to make, for our sources of information are deficient. All we can say for sure is that, even by the end of the fifteenth century, African political constitutions were probably as multifarious in kind as those of ancient Greece. Some of them are, however, better documented than others, and we may take the Kongo kingdom as an example of a more extensive tribal monarchy whose economy rested on slash-and-burn agriculture, on a fairly simple Iron Age technology, and on a rudimentary division of labor.

The basis of the political structure—and this was true of every sub-Saharan polity except the commercial cities of the east coast—was the village. In the kingdom of Kongo the village core appears to have been a localized matrilineage (that is to say, people descended from one ancestress). In other parts of Africa villages were organized on the patrilineal principle, but whatever the people's kinship structure, the majority of villagers were related to one another by bonds of blood, and all owed their primary loyalty to kinfolk. Villages were grouped into districts; these in turn were integrated into provinces. This hierarchical principle appears to have been characteristic of all larger African kingdoms, though there were great differences in the extent of centralization that kings were able to enforce and in the relationship between the center and the periphery. In the Kongo kingdom, the provinces were ruled by governors appointed by the king and removable at his pleasure. The keystone of the structure was the king, who was assisted by specialized officials such as the head of the royal quarters in the capital, the senior judge, and so forth. The government derived its income from taxation and labor services. Tribute was paid in raffia cloth, ivory, hides, and slaves. Tolls and judicial fines provided additional revenue. The military structure of the Kongo state was of a kind that would have been perfectly intelligible to, say, an Anglo-Saxon chieftain during the days of the English heptarchy.[11] The Kongo king had a permanent bodyguard attached to his household. These men were comparable to the Saxon *gesithas* or companions, who in peacetime shared the joys of the lord's banquet hall and fought for him in war. In case of need, territorial officials would mobilize a subsidiary force, composed of all the able-bodied men in their area. This general levy corresponded to the Saxon *fyrd,* and its military potential was limited. There were no military technicians; there was no knowledge of elaborate tactics or strategy; there was no commissariat; armies had to live off the land and could not keep the field for any length of time.

The Kongo and similar systems depended on the existence of vast unused land resources and on systems of agriculture where no one—be he king or commoner—could accumulate a vast surplus of food for trade. When we look at the Kongo state, we cannot therefore speak of feudalism in the Western European sense. True enough, there were already rudimentary class divisions. By the end of the fifteenth century the Kongo village probably contained already some slaves—criminals or prisoners of war—whose social status was inferior to the freemen's. Higher up in the social hierarchy stood the dignitaries of the provincial administrations and the central government, who between them formed an aristocracy.[12] The great title holders benefited from the royal bounty derived from tribute, labor service, or the spoils of war. They had a vested interest in maintaining the monarchy, though not necessarily in supporting the reigning king. In states of this kind, internecine struggles centered not on social conflicts but on competition between different aristocratic factions for control of the state machinery with its tributary network.

Subsequent Portuguese observers interpreted this system in terms of European feudalism and described the magnates of Kongo as counts and barons. The Kongo aristocrats did not, however, derive their power from hereditary fiefs granted by the suzerain to his tenants-in-chief, who in turn bestowed land on lesser vassals. The more developed forms of Western European feudalism grew up under conditions where the amount of available land was already restricted. In the Kongo kingdom, as in most other African states, the supply of land was, however, almost unlimited. The bush, which stretched out before the village like an endless sea, belonged to the community as a whole. Chiefs or headmen merely acted as trustees for the people, controlling the allocation of gardens, grazing grounds, and fishing sites. Methods of cultivation were extensive. These forms of socio-economic organization thus bore a marked resemblance to those of the Teutons described by Tacitus. The ancient Germans, according to Tacitus, "do not settle on one spot, but shift from place to place. The state or community takes possession of certain tracts proportioned to its numbers; allotments are afterwards made to individuals according to their rank and dignity. The ground is tilled one year, lies fallow the next, and a sufficient quantity remains." Chiefs, great or small, could neither store nor sell large quantities of food. Hence they "invested" their wealth in judicious gifts to relatives, friends, and clients. The road to power lay in a man's ability to secure a large following through generosity. Society, from top to bottom, was held together by an elaborate network of gifts. The king had to give away his wealth; as Tacitus wrote of the Teutons: "The chief must show his liberality, and the followers expect it. . . . The prince's table, however inelegant, must always be plentiful: it is the only pay of his followers." Even the humblest husbandman depended on his ability to secure the allegiance or support of his kinsmen, for "a numerous train of relatives is the comfort and honour of old age."[13]

The internal organizations of African states varied enormously. But they mostly had certain features in common. African rulers normally practiced polygamy—as did many of their subjects. Polygamous marriages, often contracted for political reasons, helped to tie states together by means of personal bonds between the rulers and other powerful families. Polygamous marriages, however, produced numerous offspring. Standardized rules of succession were hard to formulate and even harder to maintain. Hence rival branches of the royal lineage might become engaged in bitter disputes. African state-builders tried a variety of solutions to escape from these difficulties. We do not know a great deal about the social institutions of medieval states, but we can make reasonable inferences from societies of a more recent vintage. By the early nineteenth century, the Bariba of Dahomey in West Africa, for instance, had adopted a system whereby the equal right of all royal princes to succeed their monarch led to the practice of alternating the crown among different branches of the royal family. But at the same time the Bariba had developed a numerous nobility who lived by war and disdained peaceful pursuits.

The prevailing pattern of family life, by which young noblemen were distributed for education among paternal kinsmen, reinforced the struggles that occurred within the framework of so many a polygamous society. The regular practice of intermarriage with clients, drawn from the ranks of commoners, afforded contending half-brothers the support of different groups of maternal relatives. Moreover, the close association of territorial command with social status, and the noblemen's monopoly of all state appointments above that of village headman, made for conflict. While there were always many rivals at every level of political power, unsuccessful claimants had nowhere to go but back to the ranks of ordinary commoners.[14] Every ambitious nobleman would thus constantly jockey for power, and appeals to military force were commonplace. The only alternative was a career of conquest, and many unsuccessful princes would seek glory abroad to compensate for humiliation at home.

Generalizations, we must stress, are dangerous. Some states remained small and poor. But where conditions were favorable, slash-and-burn agriculture and an Iron Age technology could sustain much more elaborate institutions. The subjects of Monomotapa, as we have seen, exported gold on a large scale; they could build great stone fortifications and palaces; their monarchs depended on an extensive system of trade and tribute. The great West African savannah states and Ethiopia had gone much further still. They were no longer dependent—like the Bantu, for instance— on the strength of human muscle alone, but employed camel, donkey, and horse power for transportation and war. Their civilizations could sustain towns; they each had assimilated one or the other of the great Near Eastern monotheistic creeds to African conditions; they had literate priests and scribes, familiar respectively with the cultural heritage of Islam or Christianity; they had elaborate governmental institutions with considerable degree of administrative specialization of labor.

At the same time, the more advanced states began to professionalize war. Ordinarily defense was a part-time duty incumbent on all able-bodied men, or at least upon all free men. Among the Yoruba of West Africa, for instance, the recruitment and command of such levies was organized either through age-grade associations or through residential quarters and villages. But civilian specialization of labor also appears to have contributed to greater professionalism in war. For instance, blacksmiths who manufactured iron weapons assumed a peculiar military significance. Hence Ogun, the Yoruba god of iron, also became the god of war. In addition, hunters were apt to become regular soldiers. The chase provided an excellent training in courage, patience, persistence, and planning. In the absence of a standing army, or sometimes even of a royal bodyguard, hunters watched over the security of early Yoruba towns and trade routes; hunters thereby obtained considerable political power. Hunters also seem to have played an important role in the emergence of other states, such as those formed by the Lunda people in Central Africa.

Military professionalism finally was encouraged by the introduction of the horse into regions where the climate and topography allowed the employment of mounts in peace or war. Horses have to be cared for and trained. Cavalrymen cannot be improvised; they require considerable experience before they become useful in battle. Hence mounted warriors often became the nucleus of a standing army, not only in the savannah kingdoms proper, but also in Oyo, a Yoruba state where ecological conditions were suitable for horses. During a series of lengthy wars waged by Oyo against its neighbors during the sixteenth century, the military chiefs became a highly-organized group wielding a great deal of political influence.[15] Military professionalization appears to have gone with social differentiation; professional warriors usually managed to appropriate a larger share of worldly wealth for their use than the more peaceful tillers of the soil. Whatever the details of this process, the savannah states of the Sudan, as well as the more highly developed kingdoms of West Central Africa, developed elaborate distinctions of rank and status. Many of these states also carried out commerce on a considerable scale, and their rulers acquired command over considerable resources of wealth. But even in these states, the ruling strata did not apparently own the principal means of production, the land. Great dignitaries might have special claim to favored fishing sites, to trading monopolies, and other advantages. They could control the allocation of land to their followers. But in most parts of Africa the supply of land remained almost unlimited; the rulers could not directly appropriate their subjects' soil, even though they might enforce the payment of tribute.

Perhaps the only major exception to this rule may have been among some of the city states of the east coast, the only polities where land shortage may have become somewhat of a problem in certain places. Though infinitely smaller in territorial extent than the "trade and tribute" states of the savannah, the east coast towns probably had even more specialized economies. There were highly skilled craftsmen, well-to-do merchants, intrepid navigators whose knowledge and daring formed an intangible asset of great importance. The east coast cities had to rely on sea power; their vessels represented a considerable physical investment. Their maritime connections stretched far afield, and their economy presumably depended on commerce to a much larger extent than that of Songhai or of Ethiopia.

EUROPE AND AFRICA AT THE END OF THE FIFTEENTH CENTURY: A TENTATIVE COMPARISON

A comparison between Europe and Africa at the end of the fifteenth century is a bold, but not an impossible, undertaking. Both continents were characterized by immense internal differences. Indeed the more backward parts of Europe and of Africa had much more in common with one another than with the more progressive and urbanized portions of their respective continents. The inhabitants of Kilwa or Cairo would have looked with some disdain on the subjects of the Kongo king. A Lisbon merchant, for all his strong religious convictions and his hatred of Islam, would have found himself more at home in the house of a Mombassan businessman than in the rough cabin of a Montenegrin shepherd. A petty Galla chief would have been more comfortable in the company of Celtic clansmen from Ireland than in the presence of learned scribes from Axum. Under Celtic custom the clan or sept was the ultimate holder of the land. Celtic customs were those of a tribal society much on the move, especially in summer, when the whole people would migrate into the mountains together with their cattle. Ireland was a wild, war-torn country whose people were customarily described by prejudiced Englishmen as savages, whose "promiscuous generation of children, their neglect of lawful matrimony . . . , uncleanness in apparel, diet and lodging; and . . . contempt and scorn of all things necessary for the civil life of man" formed standard items in Elizabethan travel literature. An Irish chief like Con O'Neill, who made his submission to the English Court at the end of the sixteenth century, created as much astonishment in London as contemporary caciques from Brazil.[16]

The overwhelming majority of Africans lived—as they still do—on the land. Their life was hard and dangerous. Whenever the rains failed, when locusts made their appearance, or when enemies burned the crops, stole the cattle, took the women, and murdered the men, there was famine. An irregular or deficient diet commonly resulted in reduced powers of resistance. Malaria, hookworm, and other diseases formed a perpetual drain on the African's energy, and nothing would be further from the truth than to imagine African villagers as strong and lusty peasants abounding with health and vitality. Few if any tribal communities possessed the resources to tide themselves over prolonged periods of want; the population remained much smaller than it is now and increased only slowly, if at all. But the same, to a considerable extent, was true of Europe. The vast majority of white men also made their living from the soil. They too were familiar with hunger and disease. Their bodies were more stunted than our own; Siegfried, Beowulf, Roland, and other legendary heroes would have seemed small fry placed next to a professional American football team of the twentieth century. Famine continued to stalk the more ill-favored parts of Europe until the nineteenth century.

We have no record that any part of Africa ever experienced a human catastrophe comparable to the "Great Hunger" brought about by the failure of the Irish potato crop in the 1840s, when something like a million and a half people died of starvation and sickness. Malaria, to take another example, was widespread not only in Africa but also in many parts of southern Europe and even in the Rhine Valley. (To this very day the city of Mainz on the Rhine has a *Goldene Luft Gasse,* a "golden air lane," which derived its name from the fact that in the olden days it was reputedly free from malaria, this happy accident being ascribed to its "golden air".) Fifteenth century Europe produced great civilizations, but the wealth and splendor of the great Flemish, Rhenish, or Italian cities—like the magnificence of Songhai or Ethiopia—rested on strictly circumscribed minorities.

A highly-educated fifteenth-century traveler like Leo Africanus, familiar with the learning of the Islamic and the Christian world alike, thus conveyed an impression of Africa very different from that of a nineteenth-century explorer. Leo speaks both of backward and of highly-civilized African communities. But the great landmass was to him in no way a "Dark Continent" in the sense of being a ferocious land peopled by savages. The most developed cities of Africa were comparable with those of Portugal or Spain. African forms of feudalism at their highest bore some resemblance to those of medieval Europe. A medieval Sudanic army, "swinging tassels in the dust, harness brasses that glitter against quilted armour, long spears pennoned and pointed, brilliant cavaliers, all the creak and swing and clatter and pomp of an aristocratic army saddled for sack and loot,"[17] must have impressed the most sophisticated. The tribal frontiers that encompassed the hinterland of such civilization were indeed backward, but the people who dwelt there were not greatly different from the fierce clansmen of northern Scotland or Albania.

Nevertheless, there were major differences. The technology available to a Bantu kingdom did not basically differ from the technology employed by the ancient Teutons. During the early Middle Ages, however, Northern Europe had already managed to move ahead. By the ninth century Saxon and Danish farmers were familiar with a heavy plow, with the triennial rotation of crops, the use of animal manure, and water mills. Thirteenth-century European craftsmen used hydraulic power to run grain and hammer mills, and they had discovered the value of the spring and the treadle. By the fourteenth century gearing was highly developed; a century later European technologists employed complicated devices such as the crank, the connecting rod, and governors. Power was relatively plentiful, and long before European vessels set out for their great voyages of discovery, the more advanced European countries had developed a technology far superior to that of most communities in sub-Saharan Africa.

Europe, with its indented coastline, was much better served with communications than the great African landmass. European farmers were spared many tropical diseases that attacked their beasts. European farmers could produce a relatively large agricultural surplus that could feed town-bred specialists. The European continent thus had a much larger number of cities and a much richer tradition of urban life than any part of Africa, save certain portions of the Islamic north and the east coast. Europe, like Africa, had its tribal hinterland. But whereas in Europe, tribalism was confined to small, out-of-the-way mountain remnants, tribalism of some variety or other formed the characteristic mode of organization in most parts of Africa. Except for the Islamic north, the savannah regions, and Ethiopia, the overwhelming majority of African communities remained subject to the most stringent technological limitations and had to rely solely on the power of human muscle to make their living or to make war. Instead of plows, black villagers used hoes and axes to till the soil. They depended on the strength of their arms and backs to carry burdens, to fire missiles, or to row canoes. Yet even the backward Irish, who in the sixteenth century were still said by hostile Englishmen to "retain themselves in their sluttishness, in their uncleanliness, in their rudeness," had ox-drawn plows.[18]

The culture gap was beginning to widen even between the most advanced parts of Europe and Muslim Africa. It is true that during the fourteenth century many European countries had experienced a disastrous slump. But in contrast to the prolonged decline that had affected so many Islamic countries, the economic depression in Western Europe was temporary. The ravages of the Black Death, of conflicts such as the Hundred Years' War, were made good, and from about the middle of the fifteenth century, Western Europe saw new progress. The cities of Italy and Catalonia secured by far the greatest share of the maritime trade in the Mediterranean. Christian merchants and bankers became the main middlemen in international commerce. The development of mining, metallurgy, the textile industry, and other manufactures provided Europe with new products for export. European craftsmen made all sorts of technical advances. The best of European shipbuilders could turn out more powerfully armed vessels than their opposite numbers on the African east coast. European workshops could manufacture mechanical clocks and other marvels that could not be rivalled in Africa. European gunsmiths were generally superior to their Muslim competitors. European miners worked with new and superior kinds of equipment. Far from producing new developments in agriculture and industry, the North African states in fact experienced a progressive decline in their economic prosperity. A region that once had supplied southern Europe with grain found itself bereft of an export surplus. In the artistic and intellectual fields there was nothing to compare with the early European Renaissance, the rediscovery of classical antiquity, or the rise of national literatures.[19] No part of Africa shared in the heritage of the Catholic Church; no part of Africa shared in the new learning or the Reformation. By the fifteenth century the intellectual elite of Europe had developed a world view totally alien to that of tribal sages on the African continent. African seers were spirit mediums, basically similar to the Welsh augurs described by Giraldus Cambrensis, a medieval scholar who wrote:

There are certain persons in Cambria, whom you will find nowhere else, called Awenddyon, or people inspired; when consulted upon any doubtful event, they roar out violently, are rendered beside themselves, and become, as it were, possessed by a spirit. They do not deliver the answer to what is required in a connected manner; but the person who skilfully observes them, will find, after many preambles, and many nugatory and incoherent, though ornamented speeches, the desired explanation conveyed in some turn of a word: they are then roused from their ecstasy, as from a deep sleep, and as it were, by violence compelled to return to their proper senses. After having answered the questions, they do not recover till violently shaken by other people; nor can they remember the replies they have given. If consulted a second or third time upon the same point, they will make use of expressions totally different; perhaps they speak by the means of fanatic and ignorant spirits. These gifts are usually conferred upon them in dreams: some seem to have sweet milk or honey poured on their lips; others fancy that a written schedule is applied to their mouths, and on awaking they public declare that they have received this gift.[20]

Welsh and African seers alike considered themselves the mouthpiece of spirits, at one with the universe. The majority of European thinkers, on the other hand, made clear distinctions between the world of reason and the world of faith, natural law and revelation, matter and spirit. They envisaged the universe as the work of a rational creator whose secrets rational men need not divine, but which might be revealed to some extent by rational inquiry and experiment. There were similar differences in politics. No part of Africa experienced anything like the administrative and governmental reorganization affected in the stronger and better organized kingdoms of Western Europe. The economic, technological, political, and cultural gaps that existed between the most advanced European and the most advanced African communities were destined to widen. The resultant power differential came to dominate the future of the African continent.

NOTES

1. Leo Africanus, *The History and Description of Africa,* vol. 1, p. 12.
2. Cecil Woodham-Smith, *The Great Hunger: Ireland 1845–1849* (London, 1962), p. 311.
3. John Pory, "A Summarie Discourse of the Manifold Religions Professed in Africa," vol. 3, pp. 1004–1006.
4. Pory, p. 1023.
5. Anthony J. Arkell, *A History of the Sudan from the Earliest Times to 1821* (London, 1955), pp. 192, 197–199.
6. Pory, pp. 1018–1021.
7. For this and much of the following see Martin A. Klein, *Islam and Imperialism in Senegal: Sine-Saloum, 1847–1914* (Stanford, 1968), pp. 63–65., and the works of John S. Trimingham.
8. Hubert Deschamps, *Histoire de Madagascar* (Paris, 1960) pp. 54–59.
9. The quotations are from "Certaine Answeres of Don Francisco Aluarez (Who from the Yeere 1520 . . . Had Trauailed . . . in the Countrey of Prete Ianni . . . ," in Brown, ed., *The History and Description of Africa,* vol. 1, p. 61 and p. 56, respectively. It might be added in explanation that the practice of cannibalism, mentioned by Alvarez, was in fact not widespread.

10. The term derives from Christian Sigrist, *Regulierte Anarchie* (Olten and Freiburg im Breisgau, Walter-Verlag, 1968).

11. Heptarchy was the name given to the seven Anglo-Saxon kingdoms that flourished in England between the fifth and ninth centuries A.D.

12. Vansina, *Kingdoms of the Savanna*, pp. 41–45.

13. Tacitus, "A Treatise on the Situation, Manners, and People of Germany," in E. H. Blakeney, ed., *The History, Germania and Agricola* (London, 1927), pp. 321–328.

14. Jacques Lombard, *Structures de type "féodal" en Afrique noire: Etudes des dynamismes internes et des relations sociales chez les Bariba du Dahomey* (Paris, 1965).

15. J. F. Ajayi, "Professional Warriors in Nineteenth Century Yoruba Politics," *Tarikh,* vol. 1, no. 1 (1965), pp. 73–74.

16. A. L. Rowse, *The Expansion of Elizabethan England* (London, 1955), pp. 96 and 106.

17. Basil Davidson, *The Lost Cities of Africa* (Boston, 1959), p. 80.

18. Rowse, p. 105.

19. Muhsin Mahdi, *Ibn Khaldûn's Philosophy of History: A Study in the Philosophic Foundation of the Science of Culture* (Chicago, 1964), p. 26.

20. Giraldus Cambrensis, *The Itinerary through Wales and the Description of Wales,* intro W. Llewelyn Williams (London, 1930), p. 179.

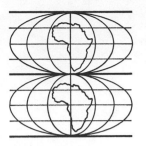

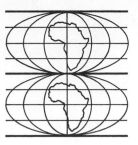

PART VI

AFRICA AND THE PORTUGUESE IMPACT: 1418 to 1600

Chapter 19

First Steps in Exploration: 1418–1482

ISLAM AND THE RISE OF PORTUGAL

In the fourteenth century Islam seemed to enjoy a decisive and world-wide superiority over Christianity. Muslim soldiers had repelled the Crusaders from the shores of Syria; successful Muslim offensives in Asia Minor had reduced the Byzantine dominions to insignificant proportions, confined entirely to European soil. In the extreme west the Muslim possessions in the Iberian Peninsula were shrinking. But conquests made by the Ottoman Turks and additional Muslim gains as far afield as the Sudan, Russia, India, and Indonesia, were so extensive that they appeared to dwarf Islamic losses in the West.

Internally, however, conditions were nothing like as impressive. Muslim India suffered cruelly from Mongol invaders; so did northern Persia and Iraq. Egypt remained a prosperous kingdom, but the region extending westward from Tripoli to Morocco shared little of Egypt's stability. The Muslim kingdom of Granada in southern Spain was decidedly the most prosperous and civilized portion of the Islamic world in the West, but Granada was subject to constant Christian pressure, and a century later—in 1492—Moorish power in Spain was finally extinguished. The Muslim states of the Maghrib suffered heavy depredations. Nomadic inroads injured the prosperity of agriculture and of industries based on farming, for which Tunisia and Tripolitania had especially been famous since Roman times. An independent dynasty ruled in eastern Algeria and adjacent Tunisia and Tripolitania, a second in western Algeria, a third in Morocco. All were weak, and spent much time fighting one another. The North African states lost control over large stretches of the interior, and had to cope with nomadic assaults from the south, and with pressure from the maritime Christian states of the north. In the West African interior, Mali—as we have seen—reached the peak of its renown in the beginning of the fourteenth century. But after the splendid reign of Mansa Musa, Mali began to decline, and Arawan, Timbuktu, and most of the north fell to the Tuareg tribes of the desert.

With a background such as this, Ibn Khaldun (1332–1406), a Berber and the greatest philosopher of history born on the African continent, developed a profoundly pessimistic interpretation of human development. Civilization, according to Ibn Khaldun, was essentially the product of large towns. Only great capital cities, with a resident court, a large population, a rational division of labor, and developed crafts and commerce, could create wealth and thereby opportunities for the arts and sciences. But urban culture in turn produced luxury and decay. The people's public spirit was rotted by luxury, bureaucratic exactions, and inequitable taxation. City civilizations would thus periodically succumb to the assaults of desert-borne conquerors, whose fierce courage, puritanical way of life, and social cohesion—all products of the harsh conditions and the clan loyalties of the desert—would prove invincible to urban folk. But the victors in turn would fall before the temptations of the town, and the grim cycle of corruption and conquest would start again.

Ibn Khaldun's interpretation is of profound significance for the history of the Arab world and the great savannah states of West Africa. His analysis, however, took no account of the rising civilization of Western and Southern Europe.[1] In countries such as Portugal, Aragon, and England, there were many cities whose economic life depended neither on courts nor on luxury expenditure alone. These urban communities developed new capital and a patrician class with a spirit of civic solidarity. The Islamic states of Africa had to contend with opponents of a new kind—Christian powers whose internal structure embodied alliances between the courts, the great landowners producing substantial surpluses for the market, and wealthy city merchants. The new powers developed a fairly elaborate technology and a brilliant literary tradition. They were not exposed to threats from nomadic tribesmen; they were held together by cohesive systems of administration, animated to some extent by a sense of national community, and endowed with relatively large economic resources. They accordingly presented a challenge much more dangerous than that from nomadic barbarians; even though the Islamic world partly managed to counter the threat, the old Muslim superiority became a thing of the past.

One of the most remarkable of the new Christian states was Portugal. The kingdom began an independent life in 1128 when Alfonso Henriques rejected the allegiance due to the king of Leon and Castile. In 1144 the ruler of Portugal placed himself under the vassalage of the Holy See, and called on the Papacy for protection against the ambitions of Castile. The Moors, who occupied the greater part of the country, were gradually driven out, and in 1249 the country attained national unity. The fourteenth century saw a new conflict with Castile when the Castilian king threatened to seize the Portuguese crown. But in 1385 the Portuguese candidate, Prince John of the House of Aviz, gained a decisive victory at the battle of Aljubarrota, and the Spaniards were driven back.

The Aviz dynasty gave many favors to the craft guilds and towns. It established a relatively centralized form of administration. During the whole of the fifteenth century Portugal was a united kingdom, virtually free of civil strife, whereas France was distracted by the closing stages of the Hundred Years' War and the rivalry with Burgundy; England was shaken by the struggle with France and the Wars of the Roses, and Spain and Italy were undergoing dynastic and other internal convulsions. Maritime expansion was the line of least resistance for a relatively small state, situated on Europe's westernmost Atlantic shore and incapable of attaining supremacy over the Iberian Peninsula. By the first half of the fifteenth century, Portugal may have had something like a million inhabitants and was well placed for overseas enterprise. Agriculture remained the chief source of wealth. Lisbon and Oporto became important maritime centers, and Portuguese merchants traded as far as Flanders and England.

After lengthy wars with Castile, hostilities were ended by a definite peace treaty in 1411, and Portugal became free to extend her power beyond the Mediterranean. The long struggle had drawn many men from their usual occupations and accustomed them to a life of fighting and plunder. The Portuguese king was eager to employ these adventurers, to satisfy the chivalric ideas of his sons, to check piracy, and to continue the Portuguese tradition of crusading against the Moors, that is to say, the Christian version of the *jihad,* the Muslims' holy war against the unbelievers. In 1415 the Portuguese captured Ceuta, a thriving commercial center and a bridgehead for further military enterprises across the Strait of Gibraltar. Ceuta was also one of the terminal ports for the trans-Saharan gold trade, though it is uncertain to what extent the Portuguese realized this before they took the city. But the occupation of Ceuta clearly enabled the Portuguese to obtain more information about the Negro lands of the upper Niger and Senegal rivers.[2]

By this time the art of navigation had made considerable progress. Compass, astrolabe, and timepiece were all in common use in the Mediterranean. European scholars, especially Italians, Jews, and Catalans, had made great advances in the art of map making. Earlier medieval cartographers had tried to illustrate the ideas of some classical author, of some learned prelate, or the legends and dreams of chivalrous deeds. But the *portolani,* or navigation manuals, drawn up with the aid of compasses from the middle of the thirteenth century onward, met the practical needs of mariners, showing the directions and distances between different ports and giving reasonably accurate outlines of the Mediterranean shores. Venetian scholars played a distinguished part in the new science of geography. So did learned Jews, particularly those from the island of Majorca. For instance, Abraham Cresques, a Majorcan, became Master of Maps and Compasses to the king of Aragon. His son Judah, a convert to Christianity, entered the Portuguese service under the name of Jacomo de Majorca and proved of great value to his employers. The Portuguese also benefited greatly from advances in the arts of gunnery and shipbuilding. The caravel, a three-masted sailing vessel with a roundish hull and high bows and stern, provided the Iberian nations with a seaworthy ship capable of undertaking long journeys, so that the Portuguese now commanded the technical means for transoceanic exploration.

The organizational drive was provided by Henry the Navigator (1394–1460), a Portuguese prince who had shown exceptional valor in the Ceuta campaign. Henry was not a seafaring man but a patron of scientific research and a statesman of exceptional ability. He settled on the Sagres Peninsula, in the extreme south of Portugal, and attracted some distinguished scholars into his employment. His ships made extensive use of the nearby port of Lagos and began to explore the Atlantic, not just as individual freebooters but as part of an organization with a wider purpose. Just what Henry's plans were at the start remains a matter of some dispute. Some have talked in terms of a grand design whereby the Portuguese meant to outflank the Muslim barrier in the Near East, gain direct access to the gold trade of the Sahara and the commerce of the Indies, combine with Prester John against the forces of Islam, spread the faith, and found a great Portuguese empire.

The reality was somewhat less dramatic. Henry indeed wished to spread the Catholic religion. But except in Morocco, with its implacably hostile Muslim population, he had no desire to make conquests by the sword. His first voyages were devoted to rediscovery and pioneering. Genoese, Breton, and Catalan sailors had all penetrated some way into the Atlantic. Henry meant to follow up these journeys, consolidate Portugal's geographical knowledge, and extend Portuguese trade, so that research would ultimately finance itself. His kingdom needed more revenue. Europe in general and Portugal in particular suffered from a severe gold shortage that threatened to become a famine. Europe drew most of its slender supplies of gold specie from the West African forest belt. Central Europe was a substantial producer of silver, but many of the European mines seem to have suffered a fall in production. Yet gold and silver coins were indispensable to purchase spices, silks, and other luxury goods from India and the Middle East. In Portugal the shortage, combined with past government policy of debasing the currency, had caused a scarcity of gold coins. The Portuguese could not easily escape from this economic strait jacket. They did carry out a certain amount of trade with the Near East, but they could not challenge the power of Venice in the Eastern Mediterranean; hence Atlantic enterprise seemed more promising. Henry at first thought in terms of limited goals and promoted what might be called short-range discoveries and rediscoveries, the peaceful conversion of pagans, and the colonization of uninhabited lands such as the Madeira Islands, until exploration in the end became both a payable proposition and a popular cause.

HENRY THE NAVIGATOR AND THE OPENING OF TROPICAL AFRICA

In 1418 João Gonçalves Zarco and Tristam Vaz Teixeira, two squires in Henry's household, sailed for the coast of Guinea. They were caught by a storm and driven to the island of Porto Santo in the Madeira group. Henry the Navigator was delighted at the news, and in the following year his two captains rediscovered Madeira itself, an island once found and forgotten by Genoese seafarers. Henry divided the land between the two pioneers on feudal terms, and settlers were dispatched with livestock to farm.[3] Madeira, an uninhabited land with fertile soil and a gentle climate, proved attractive to the colonists, and their exports—wine, sugar, and timber—acquired considerable importance in the Portuguese economy. In 1431 Gonçalo Velho Cabral, another Portuguese seaman, sailed to Formigas Rocks in the easternmost Azores, and the Portuguese later implanted other settlements. The island group proved most suitable for the cultivation of sugar cane, wine, oranges, and bananas, and subsequently attracted Flemish as well as Portuguese immigrants.

In addition, Henry pushed his sailors to penetrate beyond Cape Bojador (situated on the coast of what is now Spanish Sahara). The sailors' imagination endowed these distant seas with the terrors of hell; serpents, unicorns, and other horrific monsters were thought to lurk in these uncharted oceans; genies, fairies, and diabolical magicians supposedly lay in wait for any ship's crew bold or impious enough to venture into these regions. Henry, however, persevered, and in 1434 Gil Eanes rounded Cape Bojador, and dispelled whatever supernatural fears might have existed about the nature of the sea and coastlands beyond. In 1445 Dinis Dias landed near the mouth of the Senegal River and doubled Cape Verde, reaching part of Mali's commercial hinterland.

The Portuguese had at last gone beyond the land of the Moors and reached the true Negro country. They began to seize a certain number of slaves. The commerce in captives began on a very small scale as there was not much employment for slaves in Portugal itself, and the prisoners were looked upon at first as curiosities, as a source of information about their respective homelands, and as potential converts to Catholicism. Henry's own motives were not those of a slave dealer. He wanted to use manhunting as a means of Christianizing and civilizing the indigenous people, an object of supreme interest to the Papal Curia. In the eastern Mediterranean things were going badly for the Christian cause. The Byzantine Empire was under furious assault from the Turks (in 1453 Constantinople, its capital, fell to Sultan Suleiman the Magnificent). Cyprus and Rhodes, the two main Mediterranean strongholds of Christianity, were constantly being menaced, as was Hungary, another frontier bastion of Christianity. The Papacy thus threw all its support behind the cause of Portuguese naval expansion, and in 1452 the papal bull *Dum diversas* gave the Portuguese monarch ample power to wage war on the infidels and to reduce them to serfdom, with the aim of converting them to Christianity. A second bull, *Romanus Pontifex,* issued in 1454, read almost like a monopolistic charter in favor of the Portuguese. The pope gave them wide powers to rule the newly discovered provinces, islands, and seas. He bestowed on them the right to trade with the inhabitants, subject to an embargo on strategic goods like ships, iron, weapons, cords,—items that might be used by the infidels in their wars against Christendom. The pope finally commanded that none should presume to sail towards these distant seas without Portuguese royal permission, so that the Portuguese were confirmed in a policy of national monopoly, as opposed to older concepts of an all-Christian crusade.

The slave trade was accordingly regarded as morally justifiable, an essential component in a policy of religious expansion. Portuguese captains, however, did not usually aim that high. Kidnaping became a recognized industry, and soon bitter fighting broke out along some stretches of the Gambian coast. The traffic was as yet of small proportions. Once back in Portugal, the captives were usually treated with consideration;[4] there was no demand for plantation hands, so that the young men were taught trades; prisoners were allowed to acquire property, and many were set free. Henry's exploration nevertheless resulted in initiating the sea-borne slave trade of West Africa, an enterprise ultimately fraught with grim consequences for the African continent.

The Portuguese were, however, much more interested in gold, an imperishable commodity of small bulk and high intrinsic value. Henry's captains accordingly pushed further along the West African coast and brought back a good deal of information about the indigenous races of West Africa. Luigi da Cadamosto, a Venetian in Portuguese employ, pushed farther up the Senegal River than any European had done before, and after 250 miles up country reached the land of "Lord Budomel," a ruler "so honest that he might have been an example to any Christian." Budomel's kingdom was characteristic of many other small Negro states of the west coast. The king's subjects lived in villages comprising some forty or fifty huts, and carried on a certain amount of trade in millet, skins, palm leaves, vegetables, and gold. There was a rudimentary state organization of the kind we have encountered before. The monarch had a bodyguard of two hundred warriors; in addition, he had a large following made up of numerous children from polygamous wives. One group of the king's descendants always resided at court; a second group was scattered up and down the country as a kind of royal garrison. The death penalty was inflicted for the smallest infringements and, according to Cadamosto, the common people lived in great poverty. Negro society already possessed a rudimentary class structure; "ministers of religion" and great nobles enjoyed various privileges, and between them possessed the sole right of access to the "Mortal God," their chief.[5]

The last voyage of Henry's lifetime was undertaken by Diogo Gomes, who followed up Cadamosto's researches. Gomes travelled a considerable way up the Gambia River and:

went up the river as far as Cantor, which is a large town near the river-side. Farther than this the ships could not go, because of the thick growth of trees and underwood, but there I made it known that I had come to exchange merchandize, and the natives came to me in great number. When the news spread through the country that the Christians were in Cantor, they came from Tambucatu in the North, from Mount Gelu in the South, and from Quioquun, which is a great city, with a wall of baked tiles. Here, too, I was told, there is gold in plenty and caravans of camels cross over there with goods from Carthage, Tunis, Fez, Cairo and all the land of the Saracens. These are exchanged for gold, which comes from the mines on the other side of Sierra Leone . . . The parts to the East were full of gold mines but the men who went into the pits did not live long because of the foul air. The gold sand was given to women to wash the gold from it . . . [6]

When Henry the Navigator died in 1460 the Portuguese had made astonishing progress. They had broken down the wall of superstitious fear that impeded navigation beyond Cape Bojador. They had penetrated into the unknown south for a distance of nearly two thousand miles. They had gone some way toward finding the way to India. They had made a slight beginning in spreading their own faith and civilization; indeed a few Africans had been taken to Portugal and allowed to return home with news of the strange kingdom beyond the seas. Above all, they had taken the first step toward outflanking the land-borne trade to the gold-bearing regions of West Africa, and initiated the sea-borne commerce in gold and slaves. This was an achievement of far-reaching importance, for even the small caravels of the Portuguese were able to transport goods more cheaply to Europe than camel caravans could carry merchandise by land to North Africa. In the long run the Portuguese discoveries shifted the axis of trade for the West African forest belt away from the accustomed northern outlets to the savannah and North Africa toward the south and the Atlantic shore.

THE PORTUGUESE ON THE GOLD COAST

After Henry's death the Portuguese continued to make some progress in tropical Africa, but the pace of advance was at first slow. King Affonso V (1438–1481) was much occupied with extending his power in Morocco, even though the Christians were never able to make substantial headway in that country. Henry's demise had removed a powerful sponsor of exploration from the political scene, and Affonso for a time leased the whole of the Guinea coast to one Fernão Gomes, on condition that Gomes should pay to the Crown a yearly rental of 200,000 reis and explore 500 leagues beyond Sierra Leone. Gomes carried out the exploratory part of his bargain. His voyagers pushed eastward along the Guinea coast, and in 1471 João de Santarém and Pedro de Escobar discovered the island of São Tomé.

Meanwhile the trade had become somewhat more profitable. Portuguese navigators, penetrating southward to the coast of what is now Liberia, found a useful article of commerce in the peppery guinea grains: *Afromomum melegueta.* These sold well in Europe where spices were costly and played an important part in preserving the meat of animals that had to be slaughtered during the hardy winter seasons. Guinea grains ceased to be worth shipping only when the opening of a sea route to India reduced the price of real pepper to competitive levels and made the African *Ersatz* product harder to sell. The lands immediately beyond the "Grain Coast" proved difficult to exploit. The Atlantic littoral, with its mosquito-ridden swamps and lagoons, was hard of access. Only in 1470, when the Portuguese sailed onward, did they again encounter firm ground on a coast where a succession of headlands and bays provided sheltered anchorages in the vicinity of native farming and fishing communities. The local Africans had ivory and gold for barter. The country's auriferous resources seemed so immense that the Portuguese called the whole country "The Mine." (Later it became known as the Gold Coast, and is called Ghana today.) The Portuguese, however, overestimated the riches of the newfound country. Much of its stock of precious metals (most of it worked into ornaments) must have accumulated over countless generations. Indigenous methods of washing gold from rivers or of digging mines in the interior were subject to many technical limitations, and these put a limit to the scale of the industry.

Nevertheless there was gold, and the indigenous people were delighted to find a new market for their product. The Gold Coast lacked many natural resources that only the white strangers could supply. Apart from gold, the only metal worked in appreciable quantities was iron, obtained by smelting the hard concretions embedded in laterite soil, but the amount produced hardly seems to have met essential needs. Cotton could not be grown. The native sheep and goats were of the shorthaired variety, so that indigenous materials for clothing were limited to hides and bark cloth. The Portuguese were thus able to export shipload after shipload of brass vessels—often crudely described as pisspots in contemporary documents—basins and bracelets made of copper or brass, new and secondhand clothing, cloth, hatches, beads, wine, and many other novelties. The demand in fact proved almost insatiable, for the taste for the new imports spread from the landing sites to the interior. Trade between the coast and the inland peoples had existed already in remote times, when both parties in the commerce relied on stone implements. Now the volume of commerce began to increase. Coastal merchants made their way northward with porters through the tsetse-ridden hills behind the littoral, bringing European-made wares to the hinterland and returning with ivory and gold. In addition, they brought back slaves—prisoners of war, bondsmen, or poor wretches who had no means of making a living in a fairly simple agricultural economy.[7]

The Portuguese, however, soon had to deal with the problem of European interlopers. Even the king of England, an ally of Portugal, petitioned the pope that he might permit Englishmen "to pass over to any parts of Africa for traffic and the exchange of baser merchandise for nobler," on the grounds that "it is advantageous to the Christian religion that wealth and other things precious for natural excellence should be drawn into its power from the hands of the infidels."[8] The Portuguese had recourse to diplomacy and dissuaded the English from backing interlopers. The Spaniards also were a potential danger. For a time they contested the papal awards which granted a monopoly of the West African coastal trade to the Portuguese. Between 1475 and 1480 Spanish seafarers made a determined attempt to secure the lion's share of the Guinea trade.

Spanish adventurers, however, did not receive the same consistent and energetic support from their rulers as did the Portuguese from theirs. Moreover, Spain's financial and cereal problems were less acute than those of Portugal. Finally, the existence of the Moorish kingdom of Granada on Andalusian soil, the commitments of Aragon in the Mediterranean, and the need to strengthen the Crown of Castile against unruly vassals at home provided powerful distractions not present to the same extent in Portugal. In 1480 the Portuguese were able to conclude the treaty of Toledo with Spain. This instrument allotted the whole of Africa to the Portuguese sphere of influence, while the Spaniards contented themselves with the Canary Islands. The Portuguese attempted to enforce a policy of strict monopoly—very different from the ancient approach of an all-Christian crusade. Portuguese captains received orders to seize all foreign ships in African waters and to throw the captured sailors into the sea (an instruction not always carried out). The Portuguese also tried to keep their charts secret and spread all kinds of misleading rumors about Africa.

The Portuguese, however, still lacked an adequate base to enforce their monopoly. The trading post at Arguin, established in 1445 on an island by the southern fringe of the Sahara Desert, never became important and was geographically too remote for the defense of the Guinea trade. In 1482 the king of Portugal therefore initiated a system of commercial forts. The Portuguese began to construct the Castle of the Mine, the present Elmina Castle on the Gold Coast.[9] The castle stood on a favorable site in a part of the West African littoral where the relative abundance of gold and a dense population promised profits. It enabled the Portuguese to keep a naval and military force permanently stationed in West Africa. The Portuguese thus succeeded for a time in largely eliminating foreign competition. They also succeeded in rerouting much of the country's internal trade to the castle, where capacious storerooms were provided. A Portuguese ship no longer had to lie offshore for weeks or months on end while African traders dribbled in to barter their wares piecemeal. Instead goods were promptly discharged into the castle, and the cargo for the return voyage was loaded into the storerooms. The new method, subsequently copied by all other Europeans on the west coast, resulted in a speedier turnover of ships; it also reduced disease among the crews, who would commonly catch malaria during a long stay on a disease-ridden shore. Elmina also served as a central base for minor trading houses along other parts of the coast, and for the time being the Portuguese position seemed unchallengeable.

As time went on, Portuguese colonization produced a new kind of half-Lusitanized African society, clustering round Elmina and other forts. Along the coast between the Senegal and the Niger, the Europeans did not encounter any powerful empires but only small states centering on a single little town or on a town with dependent, semiautonomous settlements. These small states were often at war with one another, and African political fragmentation subsequently led to a dispersal of trading posts. The strangers had to look to their own protection; they also began to train African employees and slaves to perform various types of essential work. Retail trade was gradually left to the people of the surrounding settlement. Local contractors supplied food and timber, both for the regular inhabitants of the castle and for the ships that called there. Trading posts such as Elmina provided both a stationary and a moving, that is to say, a sea-borne, market, and the new forms of enterprise in time produced profound effects on the peoples of West Africa.

NOTES

1. H. R. Trevor-Roper, *Men and Events: Historical Essays* (New York, 1957), pp. 24–29.
2. C. R. Boxer, *Four Centuries of Portuguese Expansion, 1415–1825: A Succinct Survey* (Johannesburg, 1961), pp. 5–6.
3. For a general history of the period, see Charles E. Nowell, *A History of Portugal* (New York, 1952); and for Henry himself, C. Raymond Beazley, *Prince Henry the Navigator: The Hero of Portugal and of Modern Discovery 1394–1460 A.D.* (New York, 1897). A recent general history is Harold Victor Livermore, *A New History of Portugal* (Cambridge, 1966).
4. António da Silva Rego, *Portuguese Colonization in the Sixteenth Century: A Study of the Royal Ordinances (Regimentos)* (Johannesburg, 1959), pp. 15–18.
5. Beazley, *Prince Henry the Navigator*, pp. 273 277.
6. Beazley, p. 291.
7. The account is based mainly on A. W. Lawrence, *Trade Castles and Forts of West Africa* (Stanford, 1964), pp. 30–34.

8. Petition of King Edward IV of England to Pope Sixtus IV . . . 27 February 1481, in John William Blake, ed., *Europeans in West Africa 1450–1560* (London, 1942), p. 297.

9. Boxer, p. 9.

Chapter 20

Congo, Cape,
and Calicut: 1482–1515

TO THE CONGO AND THE CAPE

From the death of Henry the Navigator in 1460 to the accession of King João II in 1481, Portuguese exploration in Africa had suffered from lack of powerful sponsorship. The new monarch, however, proved one of the ablest men who ever occupied the Portuguese throne. The great feudal magnates, Portugal's "over-mighty subjects," were reduced to impotent submission at home. Abroad, the Guinea trade was protected through the construction of Elmina and other measures discussed in the previous chapter. In addition, João sent out another navigator, Diogo Cão (Cam), to carry the Portuguese royal standard yet further south. Cão sailed from Portugal in 1482 and during the same year reached the mouth of the Congo River, known to the Portuguese as Rio Poderoso, later called the Zaire. For the first time the Portuguese found themselves in touch with a relatively powerful Bantu state, the kingdom of Kongo. Nzinga Kuwu, the Kongo monarch, was only too anxious to establish contact with the strangers from the sea. There was an exchange of embassies, and the Portuguese initiated what was, for the time, an important missionary and technical assistance project. In 1490 Portuguese ships brought clerics, artisans, and soldiers to the Congo. The priests began to evangelize among the Kongo, and in 1491 the Kongo ruler, known as the *mani kongo,* himself accepted the Christian faith. German lay brothers set up a printing press; Portuguese men-at-arms helped the Kongo king to defeat a rebellious vassal. Cão's enterprise thus began an important chapter in the history of Luso-African cultural relations, to which more detailed reference will be made in a subsequent chapter.

273

After Cão's return, the Portuguese began preparations to follow up their maritime discoveries, and in 1487 yet another squadron left for the southern seas. The little armada was commanded by Bartolomeu Dias, the superintendent of the royal warehouses and a cavalier of the king's household. It consisted of two caravels, each displacing about 100 tons, and a small storeship. Dias proceeded southward, beyond the lands discovered by Cão. He finally reached the southeasternmost extension of the Indian Ocean, landing at Mossel Bay in what is now the Cape Province of South Africa. The Portuguese encountered a native party—probably Hottentots—but when the natives saw the strange apparitions from the sea, they fled with their flocks. As the herdsmen ran the Portuguese had time to observe that the natives had the same kind of fuzzy hair as the aborigines of Guinea. The tribesmen, however, soon regained their courage, and as the Europeans were taking water hard by the beach, a fierce bombardment of stones started from the hillside above. Dias, like the other explorers, had strict instructions not to cause any harm or "scandal" to the indigenous people. But he became so incensed at the unexpected attacks that he fired off his crossbow and killed one of the assailants, the first victim of white-black conflict to die in South Africa.

Dias continued on an eastward course, but by the time he had reached Algoa Bay or some adjacent stretch of the coast, his men had had enough. Weary of travel, worn out with scurvy, wary of the perils to come, they demanded to return home. Dias decided to compromise. The ships were to proceed for another two or three days, and if by that time nothing worth while was encountered, they should all sail back home. At the end of the stipulated period, the pioneers had reached a river, probably the Keiskama or the Kowie. (The Keiskama discharges its waters into the Indian Ocean at the Eastern Cape, somewhat to the southwest of what is now the port of East London.) The crews then held Dias to his agreement, and he reluctantly went back. On their return journey the Portuguese rounded Cape Agulhas, and it was probably in April 1488 that they saw for the first time the majestic spectacle offered by the Cape of Good Hope. The squadron then proceeded on its way home. Dias had at last established Africa's southernmost limit; he had decisively disproved older theories that envisaged the continent as a limitless landmass stretching to the South Pole. He had, however, not yet managed to reach the East and—as a sixteenth-century chronicler put it—Dias "saw the land of India, but, like Moses and the Promised Land, he was not allowed to enter therein."[1]

The Portuguese did not confine their efforts to maritime discovery but also determined to supplement existing information about India by a landward expedition. In 1487 Pedro da Covilhã, a Portuguese military officer and an experienced intelligence agent thoroughly conversant with Arabic, was dispatched to the Indian Ocean by way of Rhodes Island, Alexandria, Cairo, and Aden. The Portuguese wanted more data concerning the spice trade of the Orient and the Indian Ocean. They also wished to find out more about Prester John, the half-legendary king of Abyssinia, whom Christian strategists hoped to enlist as an ally in the struggle against the Muslims. Covilhã's exact itinerary is now hard to establish, but in all likelihood he visited not only India but also the East African coast, including Moçambique, Sofala, Kilwa, and Malindi, and he provided his master with valuable information concerning the trade and geography of the Indian Ocean. He subsequently travelled to Mecca, Aden, and Ormuz, and later embarked for Zeila, the main port for Abyssinia. At the court of the Ethiopian monarch he was well received, so hospitably, in fact, that the king would not let him go and it was in Abyssinia that Covilhã ultimately died.[2]

Covilhã's journey to the East was paralleled by the much vaster Spanish design of reaching the treasures of Asia from the west. Columbus, having unsuccessfully offered his services both to Portugal and to England, succeeded in obtaining a Spanish command, and in 1492 set out on his great journey across the Atlantic. He discovered Cuba and Haiti, both of which he imagined to be parts of Asia. Subsequent journeys added further substantial knowledge to the unexpected great land barrier between Europe and the East, the enormous regions which turned out to be an unsuspected New World. The pope supported Spanish enterprise by the grant of no less than five pontifical bulls, which, in Lisbon's eyes, seriously affected Portuguese rights of discovery. João II thus decided to shift the current diplomatic battle from Rome to a direct agreement with Spain. In 1494 he negotiated the treaty of Tordesillas, dividing the transmaritime world into a Spanish and a Portuguese half, the demarcation line between the two being much more favorable to Portugal than that drawn in a previous papal bull. The new African discoveries remained wholly within the Portuguese sphere; the Spaniards gave up all rights to the Cape route to the Indies—yet to be discovered. The two countries promised each other that neither would seek release from their compact by appealing to the pope or to anyone else, and the Portuguese accordingly gained a resounding diplomatic victory. When João died in 1495, his country stood at the threshold of its greatest period. The turbulent nobility at home had been effectively subdued. Portuguese navigation had made vast progress. Portuguese legal claims beyond the seas stood secure, and every preparation had been made for a great Portuguese empire.

VASCO DA GAMA AND THE QUEST FOR THE INDIES

Bartolomeu Dias returned to Portugal in 1488, but nine years elapsed before the Portuguese resumed their quest. The royal counsellors at Lisbon apparently showed much scepticism concerning the returns to be secured for the great outlay in men and money that had already been poured into the work of exploration. Year after year the monarch waited for news from Covilhã; worse still, in 1495 the ailing João died. Finally in 1497, Vasco da Gama, the younger son of a distinguished family, was dispatched with a small fleet of four vessels. After many adventures, the squadron rounded the Cape and sailed into the Indian Ocean. The vessels cast anchor at Moçambique, where Gama's highhandedness provoked the first of many bloody "incidents." The Portuguese then continued on their course to Mombasa, an ally of Moçambique. Here the Christians—according to information obtained by the Portuguese from prisoners under torture—were to be trapped inside the port, but the scheme miscarried, and the fleet went on to Malindi. At Malindi the "Franks" received a cordial welcome from the local Muslim authorities, possibly because of the longstanding enmity between Malindi and Mombasa. After a spot of blackmail, the

Portuguese at last obtained a pilot who could speak Italian and was able to guide the strangers across the Indian Ocean—an event of catastrophic significance to the Muslim world. As an Arab chronicler put it:

At the beginning of the tenth century of the Hegira [1495–1591], among the astounding and extraordinary occurrences of the age was the arrival in [West] India of the curst Portugals, one of the nations of the curst Franks. One of their bands had embarked in the straits of Ceuta, penetrated the [sea of] darkness and passed beyond the mountains of Al-Komr [the white mountains] within whose regions rises the Nile. They went east and passed through a place near the coast where [the sea] is narrow; on the one side [of this place, to the North] is a mountain; on the other [to the South] are crested waves of Darkness. . . .

[Before they had reached the West coast of Indian and whilst they were on the East cost of Africa], they continued seeking advice regarding this sea [of West India], till the moment when they used for a pilot a skilful mariner named Ahmad ibn Majid, with whom the chief of the Franks called Almilandi made acquaintance, and he became bewitched by the Portugal admiral. This mariner, being drunk, shewed the route to the admiral saying to the Portugals: Do not approach the coast at this place; make for the open sea; then approach the coast [of India] and you shall be sheltered from the waves. When they followed these indications a great number of the Portugal ships avoided shipwreck and numerous ships arrived in the sea of [West] India.[3]

On May 20, 1498, perhaps the most important date in Portuguese history, the seafarers finally dropped anchor at Calicut. When some astonished Tunisian traders asked what the devil had brought the Franks that far, Gama's men allegedly replied "Christians and spices." They had come to save souls, purchase pepper, find friends, but also to wage war.

It is true that the Portuguese lacked numbers and had to operate at a great distance from their metropolitan bases. However their technical equipment, fighting prowess, navigational skills, and morale stood unsurpassed, and in the absence of a strong Asian naval power, they were able to win mastery over the Indian Ocean with astonishing speed. The Chinese had by this time deliberately turned their backs on maritime expansion, favoring instead an isolationist policy. The trading cities of the African east coast carried on constant feuds with one another, and Malindi—as we have seen—threw in its lot with the Portuguese against Mombasa. There is indeed some evidence that by the time Christian fleets were gaining supremacy in the Indian Ocean, Swahili prosperity was already in decline, partly as the result of internecine fighting, partly because of disorders occasioned in may inland regions by the invasions of warlike Zimba and Galla communities. The coastal states of India were riddled by internal dissensions. The Muslim rulers of Egypt and Turkey were greatly hampered in their occasional efforts to build fleets for service in the Indian Ocean by the absence of timber on the shores of the Red Sea and the Persian Gulf. In 1509 the Portuguese inflicted a crushing defeat on an Egyptian armada at Diu; the Muslims for the time being could not repair this disaster, and Portuguese supremacy was not seriously challenged in the Indian Ocean until the appearance of Dutch and English vessels nearly a century later.

The Portuguese fortified their position by far-flung strategic bases. In 1505 they established themselves at Sofala. In 1507 they seized control over Moçambique, thereby laying the foundations for an East African empire. In 1510, Affonso de Albuquerque, one of Portugal's greatest empire builders, wrested Goa from the Muslim Sultan of Bijapur.[4] Goa became the main Portuguese headquarters in India. The capture of Malacca in 1511 secured to the Portuguese the main eastern emporium of the spice trade and the strategic key to the South China Sea. With the seizure of Ormuz in the Persian Gulf in 1515, the Portuguese acquired a stranglehold over a major trade route to the Levant, the Portuguese now being able to enter the Red Sea at will.[5] The Portuguese were thus able to gain a commanding position in the carrying trade of the Indian Ocean. Many of Portugal's Arab, Gujarati, or Swahili rivals were ousted altogether; others were brought under some form of control, and rigorous reprisals were taken against all sailors whom the Portuguese regarded as interlopers. As the aforementioned Arab chronicler saw it, the Franks had become a deadly peril: "Unceasingly, reinforcements came to them from Portugal; they began to cruise aginst the Mussulmans, taking prisoners and looting. They took every ship by force thereby causing great losses to the Mussulmans and, generally, to all seafarers."[6] The Portuguese were able to use sea power on a grand scale and thereby occasioned a decisive change in the world's balance of power.

NOTES

1. Quoted in Eric Axelson, *South-East Africa, 1488–1530* (London, 1940), pp. 12–22.
2. Axelson, pp. 23–30.
3. National Archives of Rhodesia and Nyasaland, and Centro de Estudos Históricos Ultramarinos, *Documents on the Portuguese in Mozambique and Central Africa, 1497–1840* (Lisbon, 1962), vol. 1, pp. 33–35, quoting an account from Kuth ad-din an-Nahrwali.
4. C. R. Boxer and C. de Azevedo, *Fort Jesus and the Portuguese in Mombasa, 1593–1729* (London, 1960).
5. Boxer, *Four Centuries of Portuguese Expansion*, pp. 13–16.
6. Quoted in *Documents on the Portuguese in Mozambique and Central Africa*, vol. 1, pp. 33–35.

Chapter 21

The Portuguese in East Africa

LUSO-KARANGAN RELATIONS IN THE SIXTEENTH AND EARLY SEVENTEENTH CENTURIES

"Pero d'Anhaya," laconically states an ancient Portuguese memorial, "set out for India on the 18th May [1505] as captain-major of six sails to cross to India and bring back the spice cargo, and the other three to remain with him on the coast of Sofala where, after his arrival, he built a fortress of timber. . . ."[1] In time the makeshift structure was replaced by a massive fort to dominate the gateway to the east. Sofala, Europe's first stronghold in southern Africa, now lies in ruins. The encroaching sea covers its crumbling stone walls. But when the tide goes out, remnants still stand out in sodden sand and mud against a low shore, about half a mile away. Pale green mangrove swamps and lofty coconut palms still make the same picture which Pero d'Anhaya saw on his arrival. Tourists can still prod among the rubble and unearth broken bits of pottery and, occasionally, a rusty cannon ball, before the tide returns and the visitor must hurry back.

Four and a half centuries ago the lonely post was a microcosm of Portuguese colonial society, comprising men-at-arms and clerks as well as Portuguese craftsmen, a physician, chaplains, convicts sent abroad for serious offenses committed in Portugal, a few white women, and slaves, some of whom served as building workers or as interpreters. Sofala was designed as a victualing station for ships going to the Indies, as well as a base for exploration and trade to the interior. The Portuguese, however, had a hard task. The garrison and fort were expensive to maintain, and even though Sofala played some part in the transoceanic commerce between Portugal, Africa, and the Indies, it never developed into a great center of the gold traffic, as the Portuguese had hoped it would. The transit trade remained largely in the hands of Muslim merchants, familiar with the bush paths, wise to the ways of Bantu chiefs, and endowed perhaps, over the centuries, with greater resistance to malaria and other tropical diseases than were Portuguese immigrants. Muslims continued to run up the Zambezi with their wares; they retained a powerful position at Monomotapa's court, while internecine struggles between Urozwi, the southern and central portion of Monomotapa's old kingdom, and the dominions of Monomotapa proper in the northern part of what is now Rhodesia weakened both parties and interfered with the gold trade. Indigenous miners, moreover, faced serious technical problems. Lacking pumps, they had no means of dealing with seepage of water, and their excavations rarely exceeded a hundred feet. African miners had no explosives; they could only heat the rock with open fires built against the face of the veins and then pour cold water over the heated stone to make it crack. The "Ancients" also faced serious difficulties regarding transport. Production in some cases was discouraged by Portuguese greed, and the gold trade never reached anything like the proportions the Portuguese had anticipated.

The Portuguese nevertheless established a tenuous sphere of influence in the interior, using both spiritual and secular weapons in fitful attempts to expand their influence. In the sixteenth century, Father Gonçalo da Silveira, a Portuguese Jesuit of noble birth, succeeded in converting Nogomo Mupunzagutu, the reigning Monomotapa, to Catholicism. But this alarmed the powerful Muslim party at the court, who rightly feared Christian penetration both on commercial and religious grounds. The stranger, they argued, was sent by the Portuguese to spy out the land, to destroy the nation by pouring water over the heads of its great men, and by uttering magic spells. These arguments proved only too convincing, and in 1561 Silveira was murdered, the first well-documented martyr to die for the Christian faith in south-central Africa. The death of Silveira provided the Portuguese with an excuse for war, and in 1569 a sizeable expedition sailed from Lisbon, amid prayers and the warlike blare of trumpets. In 1572 Francisco Barreto, the Portuguese commander, set out from Sena in the fever-stricken Zambezi Valley on the long trek into the interior, accompanied by some 560 men on foot, twenty-three horsemen, and a few pieces of artillery. His army was reduced by fever; the men were sweating in the tropical heat under the weight of their armor. Worse still, on this, as on all similar occasions, the unhealthy climate prevented the extensive employment of cavalry, which played such an important part in giving victory to the Spanish conquistadores over their Indian enemies in Central and South America. The lack of draft animals also made for difficult supply problems, a source of perennial difficulty for European forces operating under tropical African conditions. The Portuguese nevertheless gave an excellent account of themselves. They utterly crushed an army composed of Mongaze, a turbulent people living near the lower Zambezi who were at constant war with Monomotapa's Karanga people.

The Monomotapa decided to negotiate; Karanga policy aimed at manipulating the Portuguese in such a fashion as to use European arms against the Monomotapa's unruly vassals. In return the Karanga gave various trade and missionary privileges to the Portuguese, and in 1607 the reigning king promised to make over all the mines in his kingdom in return for military aid. At the same time the Monomotapa agreed that several of his sons should be brought up as Christians. The Portuguese thus rendered military assistance to the empire of Monomotapa. The white man's arquebus proved its superiority over lance and knobkerrie (a short club), and Portuguese intervention probably helped to prevent the complete disintegration of Monomotapa's kingdom, by now greatly reduced in power and territorial extent owing to much internal dissension.

Karanga foreign policy, subject to rival pressures from pro-Portuguese, pro-Muslim, and other regional factions was, however, subject to rapid changes. The Karanga were naturally determined to gain the maximum benefit from the whites for the minimum of concessions. The Portuguese, often headed by incompetent or tempestuous men, would often default on their financial or political obligations—faced as they were with the constant problem of distance, disease, and overheads. The Luso-Karanga alliance always remained unstable and subject to sudden ruptures. For all the Portuguese efforts, Monomotapa's kingdom could never be permanently made into a Portuguese satellite state. Portuguese policy makers also faced other handicaps. Between 1581 and 1640 Portugal came under Spanish sway. The kingdom was reduced to what Portuguese patriots called a "Babylonian captivity"; and Portuguese colonial interests were neglected at Spanish expense. Brazil proved a more attractive field for Portuguese colonization than the fever-ridden possessions of East Africa. The Portuguese could not easily control the interior, where power was widely held by holders of great landed estates, known as *prazos*, whose lords collected taxes, maintained their own private levies, and even waged war against one another.

Worse still, the Portuguese lost their naval monopoly. In the beginning of the seventeenth century the "Protestant peril" made its appearance in the Indian Ocean in the form of English and Dutch men-of-war, so that the Portuguese had little energy to spare for the far interior.

The Portuguese nevertheless made fitful attempts to enlarge their power. In 1629, for instance, a Portuguese force advanced into Karanga country, put the Monomotapa's troops to flight, and installed a new monarch by the name of Mavura Mhande, who promised to acknowledge Portuguese suzerainty, pay a regular tribute, expel all Arabs from the kingdom, and accept baptism. But the economic foundations of Portuguese power were cracking. Commerce languished in the interior, where powerful Portuguese or half-caste estate owners continued to maintain their own private armies, and exercise an independent jurisdiction. The local administration found itself without funds, and money even had to be sent from Goa to Moçambique.

Poor administration, the appointment of unsuitable officials, the absence of effective central control, and depredations from local Portuguese all seem to have contributed to a major African uprising. Nyambo Kaparavidze, the leader of the anti-Portuguese faction, effectively wiped out Lusitanian influence. Portuguese missionaries, traders, and their followers were slaughtered; some 300 to 400 white men and some 6000 Africans perished, the Christians suffering the greatest military disaster that had as yet struck them in southeast Africa. News of the rising reached Moçambique in 1631. The Portuguese reacted vigorously, and in 1632 a Portuguese force, consisting of some 300 arqubusiers strengthened by African levies, marched inland to avenge their losses. Kaparavidze's army were defeated; the trading centers were reopened and commerce was restored. The Portuguese even discussed a major European settlement scheme in the healthy, fertile uplands of the interior. But the reputed riches of the country could not be found; lack of manpower—a serious problem for a small country like Portugal—crippled Portuguese strength even in India itself, with the result that in 1637 the project had to be abandoned.[2]

THE DECAY OF PORTUGUESE POWER IN MONOMOTAPA'S COUNTRY

During the seventeenth century Portuguese ecclesiastics continued their attempts to spread Christianity in the far interior. Evangelization went hand in hand with a policy of political alliances, and the Christian preachers apparently concentrated their efforts on the royal lineage. Mavura Mhande, as we have seen, became a Catholic, and on his death in 1652 the Dominicans managed to get his son, Siti Kazurukumusapa, to accept baptism. News of the Monomotapa's change of faith caused great joy in Lisbon, and occasioned more conversions in the country itself. One of Monomotapa's sons entered the Dominican order under the name of Miguel; he "studied with application, and afterward occupied the teacher's chair with no less capacity, passing on to the conversion of the souls of those who lost him as a prince to find him as a Teacher. . . ."[3] In 1670 Miguel received a Diploma of Master in Theology, and finally ended his days in Goa as Vicar of Santa Barbara, one of the earliest of expatriate intellectuals from southern and southeastern Africa. The Portuguese found the task of evangelization somewhat easier among the Bantu than among the Muslims. Apart from members of the nobility, whose religious decisions were clearly influenced by considerations of diplomacy, the Dominicans also met with some success among Karanga women, "because of the pious affection they have for the law which obliges men to love and esteem their own wives, and makes them sole mistress of the house." The Dominicans also made some progress among the younger Africans whom the Fathers tried to seek out in their first years.

But despite the protracted nature of Luso-Karangan culture contacts, the Portuguese could apparently make no impact on Bantu social institutions. There was little demand for European goods, except firearms, cloth, and trinkets. Neither was there much interest in the white man's faith. Tribal beliefs appeared adequate to a people who possessed land in abundance and felt no need to change their accustomed way of life. Perhaps the white man's cast of mind, wont to categorize the spiritual and material aspects of life into fairly separate compartments, could not adjust to a people whose philosophy of life was so different. The Karanga, like the Portuguese, believed in a Supreme Deity, but their religious concepts otherwise had little in common with those of the whites; the missionaries could make no headway against ancestor worship, and failed to make many converts. The Karanga, in all probability, came to identify missionary with political penetration and determined to reject both. Portuguese mission, like Portuguese political enterprise, also suffered from serious internal dissensions and from lack of men and money, so that the Portuguese could not sustain their religious offensive on a larger scale.

The Portuguese found great difficulties in competing with the Muslims, either in the worldly or the religious sphere. In trade, Muslim merchants operated at lower overheads than their Portuguese competitors. Unlike the Portuguese, the Muslims do not seem to have set themselves up as landowners. Islamic religious penetration did not require an ecclesiastical organization but depended on the traders' precepts and preaching alone. Many Portuguese despised Africans and showed a good deal of race prejudice, in which hatred of the unbelievers and a sense of superiority curiously mingled with pride of blood, rank, caste, and color.[4] "White" Arabs were by no means devoid of similar sentiments. But Islam, unlike Christianity, recognized polygamous marriages, which played such a vital part in the structure of Bantu society. Hence "the Kaffirs imitate them [the Muhammedans] in all, catching contagion from their proximity, and what most attracts them and leads them astray is the liberty of having many wives."[5]

The Portuguese likewise encountered enormous political and administrative difficulties. Their administrative superstructure was topheavy. There were constant disagreements between the distant home government at Lisbon (which wished for friendly relations with Monomotapa and a liberal racial policy), the local governors, and the hard-fisted frontiersmen who did the actual job of opening the interior. Portuguese administrators always suffered from lack of men and money. Many officials engaged in illegal trade to supplement their incomes; many were unsuited to their positions, owing their appointments to favoritism. There were irregularities such as those committed by Ruy de Mello e Sampayo, a commander of Moçambique, who allegedly "robbed the natives, and did not pay the soldiers, having privately strangled some of them which caused a mutiny."[6] The Portuguese also produced soldiers of outstanding ability, heroic and self-sacrificing priests such as Luis do Espírito Santo, a martyr to the Christian faith, and learned linguists such as Francisco de Trinidade, a Bantu scholar of much ability. But men of such caliber could not make up for the general weakness of Portuguese administration. The kingdom as a whole, numbering little more than a million people, could not effectively govern its enormous empire, and the Portuguese were gradually forced to give up their position in the interior.

In Monomotapa's country, the Portuguese backed the wrong horse. They attempted to gain influence through controlling the Karanga kingship. But from the 1680s onward the Changamire dynasty began to expand its power northward from Urozwi, and the Portuguese suffered one blow after another. In 1693 Changamire's forces attacked the important trading center of Dambara. All Portuguese and Indian merchants were killed; the tribesmen disinterred the bones of the dead to grind them into a powerful medicine and flayed several Portuguese corpses, displaying the skins at the head of their army. Portuguese and Indian refugees retreated to a fort near Monomotapa's court, but soon had to abandon their stronghold, while Changamire's warriors overran the remainder of the Karanga county, raiding to the very gates of Tete. The Monomotapa was left with a sorry remnant of his empire, over which the Portuguese continued to wield some influence. Effective power largely remained with the Changamires, and Portuguese trade inland decayed. Portugal's political power remained largely confined to the lower Zambezi Valley. They also managed to exercise some control over various chiefs in Manica, but Christian power inland could not be effectively restored.

The Portuguese impact north of the Zambezi was even more limited. Portuguese pioneers visited Malawi, but there was no gold in the area and the Portuguese had little interest in direct intervention. The indirect effects of Portuguese interference may have been more considerable. According to a hypothesis formulated by Edward Alpers, a modern historian on whose researches we have based the present account, Portuguese attempts to evict the Muslim merchants from the Zambezi Valley may have seriously interfered with Malawi's ivory trade. Malawi political power was intimately linked to this traffic. Hence Portuguese intervention may have produced numerous disorders. According to Alpers, these commotions may have set off the migration of the Zimba, a fierce host who terrorized considerable stretches of southeast Africa. The term "Zimba" is a loose one; the word was often used for any bellicose group. But the people referred to as Zimba were probably the followers of Lundu, an important Malawi chief.

Kalonga at first could not cope with the ambitions of his "own-mighty subject." He therefore concluded an alliance with the Portuguese. Kalonga's forces assisted the Portuguese in suppressing some rebellious chiefs across the Zambezi who had challenged Monomotapa's authority, and thereby offended against Portuguese interests. In return, the Portuguese helped Kalonga against Lundu, who was defeated. By the middle of the seventeenth century the Malawi empire comprised not only Malawi proper but also the country stretching to the coast north of Moçambique Island.[7]

The creation of the Malawi empire resulted in the opening of a new overland route from the Zambezi to Moçambique Island. The main item of trade was ivory, and Malawi became an exporter of elephants' tusks. The Malawi state also had a national rain cult, but Malawi religious institutions may have been incapable of fully integrating the non-Malawi subjects into the state. The Malawi empire grew too large; thus the Malawi kings could not control the huge area and the multitude of different tribes under Kalonga's sway. The Malawi empire did not survive the seventeenth century. Much of the internal trade of the region fell into the hands of the Yao, a partly-Islamicized Bantu people from the east, who came to dominate the ivory traffic of Mozambique. The Kalongas continued to claim a vague form of sovereignty over Malawi proper, but they could not reassert their authority, and the empire broke up into various minor chieftainships that often warred against one another, leaving the Malawi people powerless against future invasions.

THE PORTUGUESE IMPACT EVALUATED

The Portuguese, though not very successful in the interior, obtained a stronger foothold along the shores of the Indian Ocean. The Swahili cities failed to collaborate against their Christian enemy, and during the early years of the sixteenth century Portuguese might seemed almost irresistible. City after city capitulated to the Western invader. Kilwa, Zanzibar, Malindi, and Lamu all accepted some form of Portuguese suzerainty for a time. Mombasa, a great Muslim center, was successively burned in 1505, 1529, and 1587, the sack of 1587 occasioned by Mombasa's temporary submission to the Ottomans. The center of Portuguese power in the Indian Ocean accordingly shifted northward, and the island of Moçambique soon took the place of Sofala as Portugal's principal *place d'armes* on the East African shore. In 1508 the Portuguese began to construct the massive stronghold of São Sebastião whose great hulk still stands today, towering above a low white coral reef. Within its walls there were quarters for a thousand men, a gigantic cistern, a chapel, and a hospital. By the end of the century, it contained some 400 Portuguese residents, whose numbers multiplied many times when a fleet wintered at the island before sailing on to India. The port prospered as a depot for men and goods, and became the center of an important local trade from which the Portuguese derived more profit than they did from the commerce between the metropole and the East. The factors at Moçambique shipped African gold and ivory to India. The Portuguese also found a market for captives on the Indian subcontinent, and during the sixteenth century they ousted the Muslims as the main suppliers of African slaves for unskilled or domestic employment in India.

It was from Moçambique that the Portuguese attempted to control or curtail Arab coastal shipping along the East African littoral to the imagined gain of Portugal.[8] The Portuguese were famed for their gunnery, their navigational and shipbuilding techniques, and these skills stood them in good stead against all their Muslim opponents in the Indian Ocean and the Red Sea. The Portuguese also secured control over extensive teak forests in India. From these they could find timber for their ships more easily than the Turks, who had to draw on the distant forests of the Lebanon and Anatolia for their raw material. The Portuguese thus gained maritime supremacy in the Indian Ocean, and Portuguese men-of-war struck terror into the hearts of their Muslim opponents far from Portugal's main bases. Portuguese ships even penetrated into the distant Red Sea. In 1580 the Portuguese also succeeded in capturing Muscat, capital of the Muslim state of Oman in southeast Arabia.

The effects of Portuguese rule have been assessed in very different fashions. The defenders of Portugal's record point to the humanitarian intentions of Portugal's government, expressed in the *regimentos* received by Portuguese fortress commanders. The *regimento* of Sofala, issued in 1530, thus enjoined the Portuguese to "favor" African natives. Those who were to receive the positive treatment of "favor" were generally Africans who had been more or less assimilated by the Portuguese, especially if they had been baptized. The priest in charge of the "factory" was to take special care about the instruction of converts, and the sick were to be tended with Christian charity. Muslims were not to be "ill treated," though the captain of Sofala was to "provoke" the conversion of unbelievers by all possible means.[9] Writers of the pro-Portuguese school admit that the struggle between Christian and Muslim was accompanied by many grim atrocities, but point out that the cruelties were by no means all on the Christian side; they also show that in the history of East Africa there are many instances of Portuguese-Arab collaboration, such as the longstanding alliance between Malindi and Portugal. Some historians go further still and propound the thesis of "Luso-tropical" civilization. According to this, the Portuguese—alone among Europeans—managed to implant their civilization in the tropics, and, being free of race prejudice, assimilated at least a part of the African population to Portuguese civilization.

The anti-colonial school of thought provides a very different interpretation, and sees the Portuguese role purely as a destructive one. The Portuguese, according to this view, disrupted the traditional trade of the area and largely ruined the prosperity of the east coast cities. The Portuguese had comparatively little to export; accordingly they used the conquered towns as bases for organizing trade rather than as commercial centers in the true sense. They never understood the Arabs or the role of Muslim entrepôt trade; by trying to grab too much, by attempting to liquidate all competitors, they upset the commercial framework of the East and ruined their own prosperity.[10] Portuguese influence had equally nefarious effects on the interior. They brought to Africa new and savage methods of waging war; their exactions ruined the kingdom of Monomotapa; Portuguese rapacity wrecked the gold-producing economy of Monomotapa's kingdom; Portuguese political intervention allowed Monomotapa's feudatories successfully to assert their independence against the central monarchy; the ordered power of the interior faltered and fell apart while the coastal cities disappeared beneath the veiling bush.[11]

In our opinion, the "Luso-tropical" thesis can hardly be sustained. The Portuguese did assimilate some Africans, and a handful of Bantu converts reached distinguished positions in the Portuguese hierarchy. Few Portuguese women, moreover, emigrated from their homeland; hence the overwhelming majority of Portuguese inevitably entered into regular or irregular unions with African women, producing numerous mulatto children who sometimes adopted their fathers' customs and their fathers' tongue. But the Portuguese were not without ethnic prejudice of their own, blended strangely of pride in caste, color, and religion. The Portuguese, above all, were deficient in number. At its peak, the Portuguese official establishment in late sixteenth-century East Africa never exceeded 900 people. The Portuguese colonial empire remained what it was, "a commercial and maritime organization cast in a military and clerical mould."[12] Its influence was mainly confined to a few trading stations on the coast and in the lower Zambezi Valley. Inland penetration in Mozambique depended largely on a small number of traders, fighters, and frontiersmen, who failed to leave much of a cultural imprint. The Portuguese authorities did not succeed in effectively controlling large slices of the interior. From the seventeenth century onwards they tried to solve this problem by granting vast estates to adventurers of their choice; but the owners of these *prazos* became semi-independent lords who ruled their subjects in the manner of African chiefs, waging wars and raising revenue on their own account, developing what might be called a crude form of bush feudalism.

Portuguese efforts to introduce a new civilization lacked the sustained impact of a large settler population. In contrast, the Swahili culture had become firmly embedded along wide stretches of the coast—the product of countless centuries of contact between the Muslim world and the African societies of East Africa. The Portuguese thus never succeeded in "Lusitanizing" the conquered Arab cities on the coasts of Tanganyika and Kenya, and today few traces remain of Portugal's past presence in the art, architecture, dress, or language of East Africa, except in Mozambique.

The anti-Portuguese school, in our opinion, similarly exaggerates its case. The argument that the Portuguese wiped out the Muslim seaborne trade rests on a fundamental misconception concerning the potentialities of sixteenth-century sea power. The fleets of Portugal, like those of Portugal's enemies, were small in number.

Portuguese caravels, like Arab dhows, were able to cruise but slowly; they depended on favorable winds and had to spend long periods in port. Naval power could be exercised in a spasmodic fashion only and, whatever Portugal's intentions, the task of imposing a watertight blockade on Muslim shipping along the immense East African shore was a task entirely beyond Portugal's naval capacity. (An assignment of such a kind would indeed still tax the resources of a great twentieth-century navy, provided with air support, radio communications, and all the other appurtenances of modern industrial technology.) The Portuguese could never put a stop to Muslim commerce, even though they might sink or capture some ships. Licensed or unlicensed Arab trade continued even within the immediate sphere of Portuguese influence. However unenlightened Portugal's mercantile approach, it is indeed probable that Portuguese trade and Arab trade were to some extent complementary. The Arabs brought in merchandise from the Near East. The Portuguese imported goods from Western Europe and the Mediterranean, including cloth from Flanders, France, and Brittany, beads from Venice, lambs from Oran, and mugs, knives, skins, barbers' basins, and brass vessels. Arab traders might handle Portuguese account books in the interior. Portuguese merchants for their part carried on an illegal as well as legal commerce with Muslims as well as pagans.

Neither do we share the pessimistic assessments of the impact on indigenous Bantu societies by the Portuguese in the interior made by historians such as Basil Davidson. The Portuguese did not wreck Monomotapa's empire; modern research seems to show that Monomotapa's kingdom had already overextended its power by the end of the fifteenth century, before the Portuguese had arrived on the scene.[13] The Portuguese impact had nothing to do with the southern "separatism" of Urowzi. The unenlightened nature of Portuguese economic policy may well have contributed to the decline of Karangan gold production. But technological factors probably played a more important part. Indigenous miners, lacking pumps and explosives, could not penetrate the soil to any great depth, so that miners were worked out much more quickly than they would be under modern conditions. The Portuguese certainly introduced the indigenous people of Africa to new methods of warfare. But African warfare could be savage enough without the arquebus. Sociologists have not as yet come up with really satisfactory explanations for the way in which some African societies degenerated into total militarism—specialization in warfare. But it is clear that migrant warrior people like the Zimba were able to do an enormous amount of damage, not only to indigenous communities but also to Muslim opponents. (The Zimba were first heard of in Portuguese history near the modern town of Sena.) Like the Ngoni some centuries later, the Zimba, a heterogeneous group of peoples, seem to have abandoned peaceful farming and a settled existence for a war economy of swift migration and plunder. The Zimba were responsible for bloodshed on a vast scale. Armed with nothing but the weapons of the Early Iron Age, they were dreadful opponents indeed and in 1587 even succeeded in sacking the rich city of Kilwa, largely exterminating its population. The Zimba invasions were not directly connected with the activities of Portugal; hence no "Euro-centric" explanation is required to account for the ferocity of internecine warfare on the East African littoral.

The fact remains that Portuguese colonization in eastern Africa belied its promises;

the Portuguese failed to make imperialism pay. Southeast Africa produced gold, but consignments of the precious metal were erratic in their arrival and variable in quality. At no time, for instance, was the supply of gold sufficient for the revenue of Sofala to balance Portuguese expenditures on the fortress and factory. The Portuguese strongholds in East Africa were situated on low-lying land near the sea, where rainwater accumulated and mosquitoes multiplied. Fever took a heavy toll of the garrisons; fresh water was often hard to get; grain and vegetables could be grown only with great difficulty, so that the Portuguese settlements remained dangerously dependent on the surrounding countryside. All too often the Arabs, antagonized by senseless brutalities, answered in kind, and thereby occasioned new outbursts of savage feuding. Portuguese mercantile policy sought shortsighted monopolies. The Portuguese also sought too intently after gold. In the latter half of the sixteenth century, however, the price of gold dropped, and had the Portuguese paid more attention to the commerce in ivory, their returns might have proved more attractive. As it was, individuals might make their fortunes out east, but Portugal's overall profits remained small, and the colonies occasioned a steady drain of manpower, which a small country like Portugal could ill afford.[14]

Worse still, from the Portuguese point of view, the Muslims—though politically divided—recovered their breath, once the first Portuguese impact had spent its force. There was heavy fighting, and the Portuguese decided to shift their power center further to the north. In 1593 they began to build a powerful fortress at Mombasa, known as Fort Jesus, a great, grim stronghold that still stands today. For a time the Portuguese managed to consolidate their hold on the coast of Kenya, but their resources—engaged as far afield as Brazil and India—were badly overextended. In 1650 the Omanis finally shook off the Portuguese yoke and immediately afterwards began to reassert their ancient power in East Africa. In 1669 they almost succeeded in taking Moçambique, but their main objective was the capture of Mombasa. In 1696 a powerful Muslim armada sailed against the city, and at the end of 1698 the Portuguese defense finally collapsed. When a Portuguese relieving fleet arrived at last, the Christian sailors found the red flag of Oman flying over the castle walls. Within a few years the remnants of Portuguese power were confined to the regions south of Cape Delgado, and despite some feeble attempts at retrieving their fortunes, the Portuguese never succeeded in permanently reasserting their influence beyond the Rovuma River.

ETHIOPIA, THE MUSLIM INVASIONS, AND THE PORTUGUESE

In a previous chapter we have seen how Zar'a Ya'qob, one of the greatest of Ethiopian rulers consolidated a great empire that comprised within its borders subjects of many ethnic groups. The Ethiopian state rested on an indigenous church, on loyalty to the person of the sovereign, and on an Afro-Christian civilization, strongly influenced also by Semitic influences from Southern Arabia. This civilization sharply differentiated the people from its Muslim neighbors. The country, however, remained subject to rebellions from within and military inroads from abroad. Its appearance of strength was but superficial. The Christians had to take up arms against the Muslims, and the initiative in the ensuing power struggle seems to have been linked to a social and political change within the Sultanate of Adal (later known as Harar). Adal's prosperity depended on trade through the Red Sea port of Zeila, and the more settled urban people had little interest in a war to the knife with the Christian highlanders. Adal, however, experienced a series of incursions from Afar (Dankali) and Somali tribesmen who stood for a nomadic way of life, for territorial expansion to enlarge their grazing grounds, and for a more fanatical form of Islam than the kind professed by the merchants of Adal. The invaders relegated the ruling dynasty to a position of impotence. Hostilities against Ethiopia were transformed into a *jihad* and bitter fighting followed. The Ethiopians at first resisted with some success. But the Muslims secured firearms from the Ottoman Turks through the Red Sea, and thereby temporarily overturned the existing military balance of power. The Muslims at the same time secured a leader of outstanding ability, Imam Ahmed Ibn Ibrahim al-Ghazi (nicknamed Gran, the "left-handed," by the Ethiopians). Gran's hordes overran the greater part of Ethiopia, leaving behind them a bloody trail of pillage, rapine, and murder. Many Ethiopians were converted to Islam at the point of the lance, and Lebna Dengel, their emperor, died a harried fugitive. Lebna Dengel's successor, Galaw-dewos or Claudius (1540–1559), was able to restore the situation by calling on Portuguese help. In 1541, 400 Portuguese soldiers armed with superior firearms landed at Massawa, and in the following year Gran sustained a serious defeat.

The Ethiopian war now formed part of a wider struggle between Christians and Muslims. Sultan Selim the Inflexible, head of the Turkish Ottoman state (1512–1520), had conquered the whole of Syria, obliged the Caliph of Cairo to surrender his jurisdiction, and finally annexed Egypt after defeating the Mamelukes in 1516. Under Selim's successor, Suleiman the Magnificent (1520–1566), the Turkish Otto-man empire attained the pinnacle of its power. In 1521 Suleiman captured Belgrade in distant Serbia, in 1522 he wrested Rhodes from the Knights of St. John, and in 1526 he inflicted an overwhelming defeat on the Hungarians. The Turks, in other words, dominated Syria, Egypt, Anatolia, and the bulk of the Balkan Peninsula, as well as the Arabian coasts, and succeeded in consolidating a large part of the Islamic cause. The Turks, however, suffered a number of serious checks. In 1535 Charles V (Holy Roman Emperor and King of Spain) seized Tunis, and Turkish naval power in the Western Mediterranean suffered a serious blow. The Turks also met with bitter resistance on their southern maritime frontier. When Turkish vessels penetrated into the Red Sea and the Indian Ocean, they already found the Portuguese strongly entrenched there. In 1538 the Turks failed to take the Portuguese bastion of Diu in Northwest India, and the Portuguese remained in command of the open waters of the Indian Ocean. The Portuguese in turn tried to oust the Turks from the Red Sea. In 1641, for instance, the Christians attacked the Turkish naval port of Suez, but the expedition failed in its main object.

The Turks were thus able to supply Gran with a force of 900 musketeers and ten cannon to subdue local Ethiopian resistance. Gran again took the offensive, and after a hard-fought encounter in the valley of the Wofla, the Christians were defeated. Dom Christovão da Gama, the Christian leader, a son of the famous explorer, was taken, tortured, and killed. Gran, however, overestimated his success, dismissed the Turkish contingent, and returned to his earlier headquarters at Lake Tana. Galawdewos joined with the remaining Portuguese and in 1542 gained a decisive victory at Wayna Daga near Lake Tana. Gran fell in battle, his army went to pieces, and Galawdewos was able to recapture all Christian territory without encountering effective opposition.

The Muslim invasions, however, had disastrously weakened both combatants. Ethiopia was ravaged and exhausted. Its people, though largely reconverted from Islam, were demoralized; fifteen years of Muslim rule had weakened traditional bonds of allegiance to Church and Crown. The Church itself had never betrayed its traditions but, emerging from a long period of desperate warfare, it remained isolationist and wedded to a policy of rigid conservatism. The effect of war on the Muslims was equally serious. As Trimingham puts it, Gran had gambled everything on the potentialities of the Afar and Somali nomadic regions. The gamble failed; the war of expansion failed as it would probably have done even without Portuguese intervention. The Muslims had to battle not only against Christian arms but also against the high altitudes and the harsh rainy seasons of the interior that sapped the morale of Gran's desert- and steppe-nurtured followers. Continuous warfare left the Muslim towns and nomadic communities exhausted. Famine and pestilence followed upon the marching columns. The coastal communities found themselves in a parlous state at the very time when a new group of invaders, the dreaded Galla, began to make their appearance on the local scene.

The Galla today occupy extensive portions of central and southern Ethiopia. They probably originated in Southern Arabia and crossed over about 1000 B.C. into northern Somalia and subsequently moved west and southward toward the barren country near Lake Rudolf. They were herdsmen who lived off their beasts and were constantly on the lookout for new pastures. Magnificent horsemen, they could attack swiftly and retreat with equal rapidity, leaving barren country behind them.[15] About the middle of the sixteenth century they turned to the north, toward the plateau, where the indigenous people had been left enfeebled by Gran's invasion. The Galla herdsmen tended to bypass heavily forested country, but succeeded in occupying extensive regions on the fertile uplands. They were never a united group, and they never succeeded in threatening the existence of the Ethiopian state. They did, however, manage to wrest large areas from Ethiopian control; by the beginning of the seventeenth century the territories south of Shoa were lost by the Christians, and the borders of the empire had to be withdrawn to the natural defenses of the Bay and Awash Rivers, with Galla groups inserted on the eastern spurs of the plateau. The Galla invasions inflicted even greater damage on the Muslim kingdom of Adal, now known as Harar.

Exhausted by Gran's campaigns, Harar was ill equipped to check the new invaders who pillaged far afield and imperiled Harar's vital links with the port of Zeila. Harar tried to reassert its power against Galla and Ethiopians alike, but the effort overtaxed its strength. In 1577 the Ethiopians inflicted a crushing defeat on them at the River Webi; the flower of Harar's nobility perished in battle, and Harar was permanently extinguished as a great military power. The seat of the Harar sultanate had to be transferred to the oasis of Aussa in the Dankali Desert. But the Galla continued to harry the country, and Aussa degenerated into a small nomadic community. Harar survived as a city state, but the vital force of Islam was gone, and the Muslims could no longer hope to challenge Christian power in Ethiopia by force of arms.

Portuguese political intervention provided the Catholic Church with an opportunity for religious evangelization. Rome entrusted the task of rescuing the Ethiopians from the Monophysite heresy to the Jesuits, and a number of missions departed for the mountain kingdom. The Jesuits adopted the same strategy in Ethiopia as in Monomotapa's kingdom; they wished to convert "from above," winning first the emperor and magnates to the Catholic faith before spreading their net in a more extensive fashion. For a time the Jesuits seemed near success. In 1603 Father Pedro Paez, a Spanish father of great charm and subtlety, and skill in languages and architecture, came to the Jesuit mission at Fremona near Aksum. Paez started a school for the sons of the nobility and succeeded in converting the emperor Za Dengel. The emperor sought military help from Spain, but the magnates revolted, and the apostate monarch died in battle. Za Dengel's successor, Susenyos (1607–1632), again adopted the new persuasion, but the Jesuits failed to make use of their chance. Paez was succeeded by Alfonso Mendes, who tried to force the new faith on the nation but only succeeded in alienating the people. The Jesuits apparently showed none of the flexibility that distinguished their work in many Asian countries. Mendes suppressed the Ethiopians' most cherished customs, rebaptized the people as though they were pagans, insisted on introducing the Latin rite and calendar, and prohibited deeply-rooted customs like circumcision and the observance of the Sabbath. The reaction against Latinization provoked great popular insurrections, and some chiefs declared that they would indeed prefer Muslim rule to the Portuguese yoke. At length Susenyos in 1632 restored the ancient religion, and subsequently abdicated in favor of his son Fasiladas (1632–1637). The Jesuits were expelled; Catholicism—identified by the Ethiopians with Portuguese imperialism and Western domination—was rooted out from the country.[16] As a popular song put it:

> "St. Mark and Cyril's doctrines have o'ercome
> The folly of the Church of Rome . . .
> . . . no more the Western wolves
> Our Ethiopia shall enthral."[17]

The state was thrown back on its slender spiritual resources. The empire, now centering on the city of Gondar in the Amhara country, stayed what it was—a small Monophysite enclave hidden in a remote mountain fortress. The Christian highlanders remained culturally and geographically isolated from the West. Scholars continued to compile hymns, histories and hagiographical works in Ge'ez, the traditional literary language. But Ethiopia had no share in the great religious, literary and cultural movements that changed the West.

Neither did the Ethiopian sovereigns manage to gain mastery over their "overmighty subjects." The Emperor Fasilidas (1632–1667) picked Gondar in the extreme north of his kingdom for his capital. He ceased to move with his court from place to place, and for the first time provided the government with a fixed headquarters situated in a region safe from Galla invasions. But the sovereign became unable to make his power felt outside the Amhara province. His writ ran only in a small area north of Lake Tana, occupying but a tiny portion of Ethiopia's present territory. The influx of Galla prisoners and Galla mercenary troops brought a further element of instability to the Ethiopian capital; the monarch could no longer control his great feudatories, and after the assassination in 1706 of Iyasu the Great (1682–1706), Ethiopia was plunged into a dark age of royal murders, palace revolts, and provincial dissensions.

NOTES

1. "Register of the Fleets 1515," *Documents on the Portuguese in Mozambique and Central Africa*, vol. 1, p. 160.

2. See Eric Axelson, *The Porguguese in South-East Africa, 1600–1700* (Johannesburg, 1960), and Axelson, *South-East Africa, 1488–1530*, as well as the work of D. P. Abraham, for instance, "The Early Political History of the Kingdom of Mwene Mutapa (850–1589), in *Historians in Tropical Africa; Proceedings of the Leverhulme Inter-Collegiate History Conference Held at the University College of Rhodesia and Nyasaland, September, 1960*, pp. 61–91.

3. "Extracts from the History of the Order of Saint Dominic . . . by Friar Luis Cacegas . . .," in Theal, *Records of South-Eastern Africa*, vol. 1, p. 404.

4. See C. R. Boxer, *Race Relations in the Portuguese Colonial Empire, 1415–1825* (Oxford, 1963).

5. "Extracts from the History of the Order of Saint Dominic," p. 402.

6. "Extracts from *Asia Portuguese* by Manuel de Faria e Sousa," in Theal, *Records of South-Eastern Africa*, vol. 1, p. 317.

7. Edward Alpers, "The Mutapa and Malawi Political Systems," in T. O. Ranger, ed., *Aspects of Central Africian History* (London, 1968), pp. 17–26.

8. James Duffy, *Portuguese Africa* (Cambridge, Mass., 1961), pp. 32–35.

9. Silva Rego, *Portuguese Colonization in the Sixteenth Century*, pp. 66–68.

10. Shinnie, *Ancient African Kingdoms*, pp. 110–111.

11. Davidson, *The Lost Cities of Africa*, pp. 328–329.

12. Boxer, *Four Centuries of Portuguese Expansion*, p. 63.

13. See Abraham, "The Early Political History of the Kingdom of Mwene Mutapa (850–1589)," pp. 61–91.

14. Axelson, *South-East Africa, 1488–1530*, pp. 161–163.

15. The standard work is George W. B. Huntingford, *The Galla of Ethiopia: The Kingdoms of Kafa and Janjero* (Ethnographic Survey of Africa: North-Eastern Africa; London, International African Institute, 1955).

16. Richard Greenfield, *Ethiopia: A New Political History* (London, 1965), pp. 59–62.

17. Quoted in Greenfield, p. 45, from a contemporary source.

Chapter 22

The Portuguese in West Africa

THE KINGDOM OF KONGO AND THE PORTUGUESE

During the sixteenth and early seventeenth centuries, the Portuguese—alone of European nations—made a deliberate attempt to spread their faith and culture in some of the great kingdoms of black Africa. As we have seen in previous chapters, they failed to acclimatize their civilization in Monomotapa's country, having to contend with long, uncertain lines of communication and with Muslim rivalry. They were equally unsuccessful in Ethiopia, where the Latin form of Christianity could not compete with a strongly entrenched Afro-Christian creed. In the kingdom of Kongo conditions seemed more favorable. The Kongo state was geographically more accessible to Lusitanian sea power than was Monomotapa's monarchy. There were no alien competitors on the cultural scene; the local rulers were anxious to acquire foreign skills and to expand their trade; hence the field seemed open to European penetration, and the Kongolese might perhaps be trained to supply Europe with tropical produce.

When Diogo Cão first established contact with the *mani kongo* in the 1480s, he found a great Bantu state with a well-established government. Its economy depended on a developed form of slash-and-burn agriculture, supplemented by hunting, fishing, and metal working. The Kongolese, unlike the Portuguese, had not mastered the arts of writing, navigation, or making firearms, but had not a great deal to learn from whites in most branches of the metallurgical and textile industries. The basic political unit, as in all other African states, was the village governed by local headmen drawn from the dominant local lineage. Villages were grouped into regions ruled either by royal officials or provincial governors removable at the king's pleasure. The keystone

292

of the structure was the king, who controlled a number of specialized officials at the capital, including dignitaries such as the controller of the royal quarters, the first judge, and so on. The military system was of the kind that would have been perfectly intelligible to the soldiers of an early Anglo-Saxon king in the days of the English heptarchy. The king had a permanent bodyguard of chosen warriors, mainly foreigners. In case of war he could also mobilize a general levy, comparable in many ways to the Anglo-Saxon *fyrd,* made up of all able-bodied villagers called out through the district officials and headmen. Protracted warfare was impossible on a large scale because armies had to live off the land and could not be maintained in the field for any length of time. The government derived its income from tribute and labor services which enabled the monarch to keep an impressive retinue of officials, pages, musicians, and soldiers. The king's power was enhanced by control over the royal fisheries at Luanda Island, which yielded *nzimbu* shells for the national treasury. These shells passed for money; they could not be found in any place besides the royal fisheries and thus provided the king with an instrument of power rare in Bantu Africa —absolute monopoly over the currency. As in other Bantu states, the ruler also acted as "distributor king," and his monetary monopoly gave him a position of peculiar strength in carrying out this function.

There was social stratification of a rudimentary kind. Slaves, including criminals and prisoners of war, stood at the bottom of the ladder. The bulk of the people consisted of free villagers. The highest rungs were occupied by princes, descended from polygamous royal marriages, and by the most important officeholders. These dignitaries formed a kind of aristocracy and between them wielded political power. Kings were chosen by an electoral college made up of the greatest magnates. There were, however, no clear rules for the succession to the throne; opposing factions were locked in a constant struggle; these conflicts involved all the great territorial commands, since monarchs would appoint their own relatives as provincial governors or district heads. The Portuguese imagined a likeness between the institutions of Kongo and those of late medieval Europe. But the kingdom of Kongo was not a truly feudal state. Land was plentiful; each villager was entitled to as many gardens as he could work with the help of his wives and dependents. The great nobles were not magnates in the European sense; their position depended on their kin connections and on their role in the state hierarchy rather than on the possession of hereditary fiefs. There was no national church with literate clerks to give a spiritual and administrative cohesion to the state, and the kingdom of Kongo remained what it was, a great tribal confederacy with a limited degree of political centralization.[1]

When the Portuguese first arrived at Kongo, the reigning sovereign Nzinga Kuwu (died 1506) welcomed the strangers and sent an embassy to Lisbon. In 1491 the Portuguese dispatched a substantial expedition containing missionaries as well as explorers and artisans to Kongo. Nzinga Kuwu accepted baptism under the name of João I but subsequently reverted to his ancestral gods. After a civil war, in which a faction claiming to be Catholic battled against one of pagan persuasion, Affonso, one of Nzinga Kuwu's sons, mounted the throne. Affonso (died about 1541) stood out as one of the greatest rulers in Kongo, and followed a determinedly pro-European policy. He sent young Kongolese overseas to be trained in Lisbon so as to build up an indigenous intelligentsia. He also obtained priests and technicians from Portugal. In 1512, for instance, the Portuguese dispatched a considerable mission to bring tools, domestic animals, and edible plants to the country. The expedition also contained artisans, and Simão da Silva, the Portuguese commander, received orders to build a multistoried house so that the Kongo monarch "might live in greater health and dignity, and that he might be instructed in the manners of the table and in all things, so that he might hold court as becomes a Christian."[2] Affonso's reforms were of a relatively cautious kind. He sensibly refused to take over the Portuguese legal code or to reorganize the law courts on Portuguese lines. He was, however, determined to destroy the "house of the great fetishes." As Vansina puts it, Affonso apparently wished to demolish the ritual objects of traditional kingship and thereby its whole spiritual basis. Henceforth the right of the king to rule was to be based on Christian rather than indigenous values. Affonso may possibly have tried to strengthen royal authority by this ideological shift. In Kongo, as in Ethiopia and Monomotapa's kingdom, evangelization was directed at the top layer of society. The Christian pastors hoped that once the new creed had been adopted by the aristocracy, the faith would percolate downward to the lower strata. One of Affonso's sons, Dom Henrique, was educated in Europe and in 1520 was ordained a bishop, becoming the first Catholic bishop derived of Bantu parentage. Henrique tried to build more schools and churches, but died soon after his return from Europe, and the lack of a qualified staff largely wrecked his policy. The number of Portuguese expatriates available was puny in relation to the country's vast size; immigrants lacked moral fiber or became absorbed in secular pursuits; the white man's mortality rate remained high. The foreign missionaries, moreover, were concentrated at the royal capital, and Christianity did not affect the population at large.

Affonso's death was followed by new disorders until Nkungi Mpudi, a Nzinga, mounted the throne as Diogo I. Diogo, reputedly a cruel and luxury loving sovereign, continued Affonso's pro-Catholic course, and in 1547 a Jesuit mission arrived in the kingdom. The Fathers opened a school; there were many baptisms, but again the work of conversion was superficial. Bitter quarrels broke out between the monarch and the Jesuits; by 1558 Kongo was again left with but a handful of secular priests, and the Christian impact remained small.

The reasons for Portugal's lack of success were manifold. Portugal's resources were evidently much too small for the gigantic work of acculturation involved in the conversion of Kongo. The Portuguese suffered heavily from tropical disease and many of them died. Then there was the element of time. Hundreds of years had passed before the barbarians of Western Europe truly accepted the Cross during the Dark Ages. The Portuguese effort largely exhausted its impetus within just over a century. Yet evangelization was no easier among Kongolese tribesmen than it had been, say, among the wild warriors of Norway. In addition, there were sociological factors. The Catholic Church would not accept polygamy or marriages between close relatives. Yet both institutions were apparently vital to the Kongo polity. Royal concubines were not only a sign of status and a source of pleasure, they also helped to cement all important political marriages in the country through affinal links to the king. Weddings between close relatives were a device whereby provincial rulers maintained close ties with their sovereign. Speaking in more general terms, Portuguese policy was perhaps one of too little or too much. Outright conquest and occupation might have led to some degree of cultural assimilation of the kind that occurred in the Scottish Highlands after the conquest of the clans at the hand of the Redcoats. But such a task was totally beyond the means of Portugal. The people of Kongo had no real incentive to abandon their accustomed institutions; the old gods successfully battled against the new religious dispensation. The impact of the Gospel remained slight, and resulted only in a certain amount of religious syncretism.[3]

Portugal's alternative was a policy of mutual respect and equality. But Portugal's approach was inconsistent. On the one hand, Lisbon policy makers tried to turn Kongo into a sovereign Christian nation. On the other hand, they tried to restrict Kongo sovereignty by preventing the *mani kongo* from having independent contacts with other European powers, including the Vatican. In the economic sphere, the Portuguese approach was plagued by similar contradiction. The Portuguese Crown attempted to maintain a monopoly of Kongo's foreign trade whereby all private intermediaries would be cut out. At the same time Portugal had a stake in the well-being of its colony at São Tomé, which competed with the royal trade monopolies. The Portuguese in Kongo accordingly split into two hostile factions, with the king's adherents on one side and the settlers of São Tomé—sworn enemies of metropolitan commercial monopolies—on the other. Portuguese factionalism only acerbated Kongolese internecine struggles and thereby made cultural penetration more difficult. Commercial development, moreover, was very limited. The Kongolese began to import all sorts of merchandise from Europe—firearms, cloth, and gunpowder, for example. But they had comparatively few goods for export, and the most profitable merchandise was manpower. The Kongolese thus began to export slaves to Portugal on a considerable scale, but the slave trade presented the Kongolese with new political problems. In King Affonso's own words, " 'They [the slave traders] bring ruin to the country. Every day people are enslaved and kidnapped, even nobles, even members of the king's own family.' "[4] The bush traders were hard to control. In some cases they encouraged the local chiefs to rebel against the king; in others they fomented internecine strife.

Worse disasters came when, from 1568, Jaga hordes invaded Kongo. The Jaga, probably related to the Lunda people of the interior, were formidable enemies. Their society, like that of the dreaded Zimba, was totally organized for warfare. The Jaga hosts, by a peculiar process of tribal militarization, would incorporate young captives of both sexes into their ranks. The Jaga hosts thus rapidly snowballed, so that each Jaga victory made further resistance more difficult. The Jaga devastated large areas of Kongo, and it was only Portuguese assistance which, between 1571 and 1573, enabled the Kongolese to chase the Jaga out of the country. The Kongo kings subsequently tried to consolidate their military position by forming a specialized, permanent military formation equipped with arquebuses, but Kongo power was left seriously weakened, and the original Portuguese acculturation program largely ended in failure.

THE PORTUGUESE IN ANGOLA AND THE KONGO BREAKDOWN

Portuguese empire building in Angola began as a by-product of penetration into Kongo and was linked with Lusitanian settlement in Brazil. The region between the Dande River and the Cuanza (both south of the Congo) was subject to the dynastic chief of the Kimbundu known as the *ngola*.[5] In 1519 the reigning *ngola*, anxious perhaps to expand his trade and to fortify his position against Kongo, his overlord, asked to receive Portuguese merchants and priests at his court. The first Portuguese mission did not achieve much. But subsequently Portuguese merchants—many of them from São Tomé—came to the *ngola*'s capital; the *ngola* waxed in strength and in 1556, after a successful campaign against Kongo, declared himself independent of his former sovereign. The next *ngola* confirmed his predecessor's request, and in 1560 a Portuguese mission, consisting of four Jesuits led by Paulo Dias de Novães, arrived in the country. The Jesuits, rebuffed already in their effort to proselytize in Kongo, failed to achieve much success. But Dias persisted in his plans. The difficulties besetting the Portuguese in Kongo, the martyrdom incurred by Father Silveira in Monomotapa's kingdom, and perhaps also internal divisions among the local tribes seemed to show that a policy of working through indigenous chiefs and of cautious evangelization would not suffice.

Angola was a potentially valuable source of slaves for Brazil, the principal Portuguese colony on the Atlantic. The Portuguese believed that silver and other precious ores would be found inland. They also looked for a highway into the interior of Africa and mistakenly imagined that the Cuanza River would serve as an artery for inland penetration. Hence colonial strategy in Angola was to differ greatly from the policy of indirect influence adopted in Kongo. Portuguese power was to be firmly based on the system of *donatárias* (territorial proprietorships) that already worked successfully in Brazil and that was attempted in a similar fashion through the *prazos* of Mozambique. The proprietors chosen by the Crown would settle, evangelize, and defend their lands. In return they would receive administrative and fiscal privileges over their respective territories, and recoup their expenses from imposts paid by the indigenous people. Dias accordingly received an extensive land grant, a salt monopoly, and other specified rights concerning the export of slaves. In 1576 Dias began the construction of São Paulo de Luanda on the mainland north of the Cuanza, the present capital of Angola. He erected a fort, a church, and a hospital, as always the triple pillars of Portuguese might. But the rumored silver mines of the interior turned out to be a mirage.

The Portuguese were divided between the Jesuits, who meant to set up local theocracies, and traders, soldiers, and officials who were busy buying slaves for the Brazilian markets or collecting head tax from their subjects. Dias penetrated some seventy miles up the Cuanza. But the Portuguese lost heavily from enemy spears and the equally deadly bite of the malaria mosquito; they had to rely more and more on African auxiliaries who were liable to defect to the enemy. The African tribes, though disunited and often at war with one another, bitterly resisted the Portuguese advance into the interior. Some Portuguese and half-breed frontiersmen and traders made their way far inland. The use of imported firearms gradually spread to other tribes.

But the Portuguese failed to occupy the country in depth. Portuguese colonization was essentially of the maritime kind; Luanda accordingly remained a tough frontier town, dependent mainly on the growing slave trade to the New World.

The Portuguese did, however, strengthen their hold on some other stretches of the coast. In 1617 Manuel Cerveira Pereira founded the town of São Filipe de Benguela. The settlement attracted a motley crew of renegades from Kongo, exiles and convicts from Portugal, criminals and frontiersmen from Brazil, who became the country's first genuine settlers. As Duffy puts it, "Frustrated in their search for mineral wealth and unable to compete at first with the slave marts of the north, they were driven to gain an existence from the soil and the sea. The settlement of Benguela was from an early date the home of traders, farmers, and fishermen, a strange contrast from the bustling mercantile center of Luanda."[6]

In the meantime, the Kongo kingdom gradually disengaged itself from Portuguese political influence. Portuguese armies had expelled the savage Jaga from the country, and for a time the Portuguese had a great say in the country. The Jaga wars produced vast hauls of captives, and the slave trade flourished. The Kongolese courtiers tried to follow the Portuguese example in clothing, food, and etiquette. About 1590 the Portuguese titulature came into use, and African magnates began to rejoice in European titles such as count, marquis, and duke, which, in Africa, acquired a significance very different from the one they had borne in feudal Europe. In external policy, however, Kongolese policy shifted from cooperation with the Portuguese to increasing hostility. In 1581 Álvaro I, the reigning Kongo monarch, still sent an army to help Dias in Angola. In 1590, however, his successor, Álvaro II, formed an alliance with Angolan chiefs against Portugal. Kongo instead turned for diplomatic support to the Vatican, and Rome's influence played some part in stemming Portuguese invasion attempts from Angola. Portuguese influence thus decayed.

But the Kongolese kingdom began to lose its cohesion, and when Álvaro II died in 1614, the country was in a parlous state. Vansina lists among possible reasons for the breakdown excessive taxation by the chiefs, the growing inability of the Kongo sovereigns to protect the people, the devaluation of the *nzimbu* shell currency, and the corruption of the courts. The alien slavers produced much unrest, and so did factional quarrels among the Portuguese themselves. At the capital, succession disputes continued with unabated bitterness; there were constant rebellions in the Kongo's far-flung domains. Subsequent Kongo monarchs made valiant attempts to repair the position—but in vain. A hundred years after Álvario II's death, the kingdom of Kongo had become something like the Holy Roman Empire during its decline: a host of petty chiefdoms recognized a distant and impotent ruler, but effective power had gone, and nothing survived but empty dreams of ancient greatness.[7]

Portuguese colonization never grew to great proportions, but the Portuguese in Angola, Congo, and elsewhere made a major cultural contribution by transmitting the agricultural achievements of the American Indian civilization to the African continent. Maize entered Central Africa in the second half of the sixteenth century, possibly via Kongo. Manioc was introduced about 1600; it may first have been cultivated near Luanda and on plantations north of the city.[8] Groundnuts and sweet potatoes were also brought in—probably from Brazil. The Portuguese likewise acclimatized the sugar cane. In all likelihood they imported the domestic pig and the domestic cat as well as tobacco and tomatoes and other forms of vegetable food; all these crops gradually spread inland along indigenous trade routes, and in time were cultivated by black farmers who had never even heard the name of Portugal.[9]

WEST AFRICA AND THE PORTUGUESE: ECONOMIC AND CULTURAL RELATIONS

When Portuguese vessels first sighted land on the Gulf of Guinea during the fifteenth century, the indigenous peoples of the forest belt had already developed variegated cultures of their own. As we have seen, they knew how to mine gold and other metals; they had mastered the art of working in iron, copper, bronze, and ivory; they had developed a variety of food crops; they had built walled agro-towns, some of them the centers of powerful states where kingship was sanctified by religious and magic means. These included forest states such as Benin, which vastly expanded its boundaries during the fifteenth century. For countless years the forest peoples had exported gold and other commodities to the savannah and beyond. Although the production of gold in Europe, notably Hungary, increased during the fourteenth century, consumption rose even more rapidly. European merchants increasingly looked to Africa for further supplies, and their expanding demand occasioned further economic activity in the Western Sudan during the later fourteenth century.

According to Ivor Wilks, a modern historian, Mande-speaking traders (Malinke-Bambara-Dyula and Soninke) from the upper Niger began to extend the commerce with the auriferous lands to the south, especially along the Jenne-lower Guinea Coast axis. (The movement of Mande-speakers into the Jenne area was probably part of a wider migration that also caused Muslim traders to penetrate into Hausa land, where they introduced their own faith to the indigenous peoples.) Mande traders founded posts such as Bobo-Dioulasso, some fifteen days' journey south of Jenne; they subsequently created settlements at Kong, Bouna, and other cities. These became staging posts where they might rest and change their pack-horses, asses, and bullocks for fresh animals. The southernmost limit of permanent Mande settlement was at Begho, just north of the dense forest in what is now the Brong-Ahafo region of Ghana. Begho was probably colonized about 1400 A.D., though subsequently other Mande-speakers penetrated even further south, where they made their homes in existing towns. Itinerant Mande traders were already in the El Mina area when the Portuguese first arrived there in 1471. The Mande were eager to do business with the Portuguese; they were particularly anxious to acquire fire arms in exchange for slaves from Benin and beyond. By the time the whites first came to West Africa, the coastal peoples had in all probability already developed a local maritime trade. It is possible, therefore, that the Portuguese were especially attracted to the El Mina region, not merely because of the available gold, but also because their great ships enabled them to operate in a competitive fashion as middlemen within a complex commercial system in existence at the time of their arrival.[10]

The Portuguese nevertheless made a considerable further impact on the coastal peoples. Their presence created new markets, stimulated commerce over wider areas,

[margin handwritten note: Trade with africa to gold mineraly began]

and created new needs. The development of the southern trade probably stimulated the growth of towns inland. Archaeological evidence from southern Ghana for instance points to increased urbanization in the sixteenth century, with settlement patterns quite distinct from those adopted by earlier Iron Age farmers.

The Portuguese thus linked West Africa with the maritime economy of Western Europe; they imported all kinds of new merchandise. Most indigenous rulers welcomed the white newcomers. The *oba* or king of Benin, for instance, was sufficiently cautious not to permit the Portuguese to build any fortifications in his territory. But he was glad to sell slaves and pepper to the white men. Benin expanded the trade in human beings and built a seaport at Gwato, where the Portuguese bought captives for shipment to São Tomé. The traffic in slaves in turn provided Benin with firearms and strengthened her in the long struggle for control of the inland trade routes. The Portuguese also enjoyed a powerful commercial position on the Gold Coast, where El Mina remained a major exporter of gold. In addition, they purchased pepper, ivory, and other luxury products from the west coast; they developed the rich fishing grounds off the Cape Verde archipelago; they gathered salt, and they also dealt in civet, palm oil, ambergris, hides, skins, rice, and other commodities. In return they sold cloth, beads, hardware, gunpowder, and firearms, providing the indigenous communities with new kinds of goods, and developing new wants in consequence.

The Portuguese were also the first Europeans to take their share in African interterritorial trade. Rice and slaves were transported from areas south of Senegambia to the regions in the north; Portuguese merchants bought slaves, cotton cloth, leopard skins, and palm oil at Benin to be carried by ship to El Mina and sold to African traders in return for gold. Portuguese colonization at the Cape Verde Islands, at São Tomé, and at Principe not only contributed to the expansion of their traffic with the mainland but also caused these islands to become new centers of enterprise off the African shores. Planters at São Tomé built up a prosperous sugar industry worked by African slave labor; São Tomé also produced fruits and vegetables for the El Mina market, as well as hides, skins, fats, and cotton for Portuguese customers at home.[11]

On the West Coast as in Kongo, the Portuguese likewise played an important role as agricultural middlemen. They diffused a host of new plants that improved the quality of the Africans' diet and allowed the indigenous people to multiply their numbers in subsequent centuries. Citrus fruits and melon were introduced from southern Europe. After the Portuguese had penetrated into the Indian Ocean, they brought back the coconut and the Asian yam to West Africa. They also played their part in transmitting to West Africa the familiar complex of American Indian food crops, including maize, pineapple, pawpaw, sweet potatoes, guavas, and tomatoes. Of all these plants, maize was the most important because it provided the farmers with a staple in addition to yams.[12]

The Portuguese also tried to make progress in the religious and cultural sphere. A church was built in Benin; Portuguese missionaries made a number of converts among Africans in Benin as well as on the Gold Coast; Portuguese spread widely as a spoken *lingua franca* along the coast, and some Africans were taken to Portugal to be educated for office in church or state. Portuguese evangelization, however, was no more successful on the West Coast than in the Congo. Traditional kingship was too firmly entwined with pagan sanctions and polygamy to be effectively Christianized. The Portuguese, unlike the Muslims in the northern savannahs, failed to transmit the art of reading and writing Portuguese to the Africans.

However the bulk of Portuguese visitors were themselves illiterate, unlike the Arab traders of the savannah, and the literate Portuguese governors and merchants had neither time nor inclination for teaching. Even the missionaries regarded oral catechism preparatory to baptism as more important than literacy. The Catholic faith was not a Bible-reading religion.[13] In addition, the time element once again played an important part. The Portuguese were deficient in manpower, and they did not persist in systematic evangelization for a sufficiently long period. Once the Portuguese had made extensive contact with India, the East Indies, and Brazil, they neglected the more limited opportunities of West Africa, and Portuguese mission work in West Africa decayed.

In fact, the developing culture contacts between white man and black were just as likely to assimilate white men to Africans as the other way round. Portuguese merchants from the Cape Verde Islands, for instance, traded far afield along the Senegal and Gambia rivers. Portuguese colonists of Cape Verde established agents at numberous points on the coast and on many creeks and rivers between the Senegal and Sierra Leone. Settlers on the islands of São Tomé and Principe in the Gulf of Guinea developed extensive sugar plantations and carried on commerce with Benin and other African countries. The Portuguese traders on the mainland, however, tended to settle down, marry African wives, and establish a half-caste society free from the more annoying restrictions of both European and African life. This society attracted a motley crew of fugitives and exiles from Portugal and other European countries. It exerted no Christian influence on the Africans, but instead adopted various African characteristics. Neither did the Luso-Mulattoes bear much loyalty to a European country most of them had never even seen. When, during the sixteenth century, merchants from other European states began to appear on the scene, the half-castes were quite willing to forget the interests of Portugal and serve as middlemen for other foreigners.[14]

However slight in the ideological and religious sphere, the Portuguese impact was of great importance in economics and politics. The Portuguese had pioneered the modern sea-borne trade of West Africa. The peoples of the forest zone thus found themselves in a better strategic position for the acquisition of trade goods and firearms than most of the savannah dwellers.

THE END OF SONGHAI AND THE RISE OF THE HAUSA STATES

Portuguese empire building affected the savannah in unexpected ways. For many decades Morocco had seen bitter fighting between Muslims and Christians. Portuguese conquests on the Moroccan coast produced a religious and popular resistance movement that found expression in a *jihad*. In 1578 the Portuguese embarked on a great gamble and sent a mighty army into Morocco, where two rivals were struggling for the throne. The Moroccans waited until the invaders had marched into arid hill country, and in 1578 suddenly gave battle at Alcazár Kebir. The Portuguese army was annihilated. Hundreds of Portuguese lords were taken prisoner, and had to be ransomed at tremendous expense. Morocco, under its Sultan Ahmad IV, "al-Mansūr," "the Victorious," emerged as a powerful state and was able to turn to southward expansion. The Songhai empire by this time was shaken by succession disputes, and Morocco decided to exploit Songhai's internal weakness in order to capture the gold and salt trade of the interior. In 1590 a Moroccan expedition set out from Marrakesh, led by Judar Pasha, a Spaniard in Muslim service who commanded a mixed force consisting mostly of Christian captives and renegades. The invaders had firearms such as had not been seen before in the Sudan, except in Bornu. The soldiers of Songhai could not resist their opponents' superior discipline and weapons, and the flower of Songhai's army perished at Tonbidi near Gao.

Songhai was soon confined to the small province of Dendi, but the Moroccans did not profit from their victory. True enough, they brought back slaves and much precious metal as the spoils of victory. Ahmad IV, famed already as a great builder and administrator, added new renown to his name, and became known as "al-Dhahbī," "the Golden." But the Moroccans could not capture the actual gold-producing lands of the south; weary and sick of tropical ailments, the northern soldiers were no match for black warriors fighting in the thick bush and forest of their own country. The Moroccan invasion was purely destructive in its effect. The victors smashed the power of Songhai, and disrupted the system of government on which so much of the gold trade depended. The Moroccans could do little more than hold Gao, Timbuktu, and Jenne. But operating at a great distance from their home base they were unable to preserve order over vast regions.[15] Fulani, Tambara, and Tuareg warriors looted and plundered in a once prosperous land. The gold trade of the moors contracted. Even at the best of times, camel-borne commerce could not have easily competed with ship-borne traffic, for even the small caravels of the sixteenth century could carry trade commodities more cheaply than pack animals going by land. Now widespread disorder made the Muslim merchants' task even more difficult, and West Africa's commercial axis generally tended to shift southward, toward the sea, and also eastward toward the land of the Hausa.

The Hausa, a dark-skinned people of mixed stock, may originally have come from the north, from the central Sahara, from where their ancestors may have been driven out by warlike Berber who themselves were pressed upon by Arab conquerors. All this is highly speculative. We do know, however, that the Hausa, even though politically disunited, became expert traders thoroughly experienced in the technique of the trans-Saharan commerce. They began to be converted to Islam during the thirteenth century as a result of mercantile and diplomatic contacts with Mali. The Hausa were forced to submit to the might of Songhai, but the various Hausa communities recovered their independence. After the Moroccan conquest of Gao in 1591 the Hausa entered upon a period of great prosperity. The bulk of the trans-Saharan trade shifted eastward. Katsina and Kano became great mercantile cities, and the Hausa became a highly civilized people. They developed the Arabic alphabet; they produced a literature of their own as well as a striking degree of unity, comparable in many respects to that of the nations of Europe in modern times.

NOTES

1. This chapter is largely based on Vansina's outstanding *Kingdoms of the Savanna,* pp. 37–69.

2. Quoted by Diedrich Westermann, *Geschichte Afrikas: Staatenbildungen südlich der Sahara* (Colonge, 1952), p. 393.

3. See, for instance, Georges Balandier, *La vie quotidienne au Royaume de Kongo du XVIe au XVIIIe siècle* (Paris, 1965), pp. 247–268.

4. Quoted in Vansina, *Kingdoms of the Savanna,* p. 52.

5. This section is based mainly on Duffy's standard work, *Portuguese Africa,* pp. 47–64. See also David Birmingham, *The Portuguese Conquest of Angola* (London, 1965).

6. Duffy, *Portuguese Africa,* p. 62.

7. Vansina, *Kingdoms of the Savanna,* pp. 152–153.

8. Vansina, p. 21.

9. Further reference to the subject of food crops will be made in a subsequent chapter.

10. Ivor Wilks, "A Medieval Trade-Route from the Niger to the Gulf of Guinea," *Journal of African History,* III, No. 2, (1962), pp. 337–341.

11. S. Daniel Neumark, *Foreign Trade and Economic Development in Africa: A Historical Perspective* (Stanford, 1964), pp. 37–38.

12. John E. Flint, *Nigeria and Ghana* (Englewood Cliffs, N.J., 1966), pp. 73–74. This is an excellent summary for the whole period.

13. Flint, pp. 74–75.

14. Fage, *An Introduction to the History of West Africa,* pp. 51–56.

15. Fage, pp. 28–31.

PART VII

SLAVES, SETTLERS, AND THE GUNPOWDER FRONTIER

Chapter 23

The Emergence of
the Northern Sea Powers
in the Seventeenth Century

THE DECLINE OF PORTUGAL AND THE RISE OF HOLLAND

The Portuguese pioneered European exploration in Africa. But even in the earlier period of Portuguese colonization they never quite had the field to themselves. For a time the Castilians proved troublesome rivals on the West African coast, until the energies of Spain were diverted to the New World. During the first half of the sixteenth century French pirates and privateers began to prey on Portuguese vessels off the coasts of Guinea and Brazil, seizing precious cargoes destined for the markets of Lisbon. In addition, French merchants also carried on some peaceful trade along the shores of Guinea and Senegambia. In time the Portuguese had to contend with the challenge of England's emergent sea power as Englishmen tried to take their cut of the West African trade. Anglo-African commerce began in a small way at the end of the fifteenth century and became somewhat more regular during the reign of Queen Mary. Then in 1530 Williams Hawkins the Elder, probably copying the French example, sent a ship to Guinea, thence to Brazil and home, repeating this notable triangular voyage in 1531 and 1532. After a subsequent lapse, the English ventured forth into West Africa once more and from 1551 started a regular traffic to the Barbary Coast and Guinea.[1] Like their competitors, the English bought slaves, gold, ivory, and pepper in exchange for a variety of goods, including firearms, cutlery, metal basins, and imitation pearls.

They faced, however, a difficult task. The Portuguese might sink their rivals' ships on sight. Alternatively they might try to organize anti-English boycotts among the African coastal populations. An English merchant captain might thus have to contend

305

with a "Portugals' brigandine, which followed us from place to place to give warning to the people of the countrey, that they should not deal with us." Finally, the newcomers from the North Sea would have to adapt their methods and merchandise to the fluctuating nature of African markets and to the demands of sophisticated customers. Indigenous chiefs struck hard bargains and turned out to be very different from the simple savages of legend: "The 16 day in the morning," thus sadly reported an English mariner,

. . . we went into the river with our skiffe, and tooke some of every sort of our marchandize with us, and shewed it to the negroes, but they esteemed it not, but made light of it, . . . for the basons they would have given us some graines, but to no purpose, so that this day wee tooke not by estimation above one hundreth pound waight of graines, by meanes of their captaine, who would suffer no man to sell anything but through his hands and at his price; he was so subtile that for a bason hee would not give 15 pound waight of graines, and sometimes would offer us small dishfuls, whereas before wee had baskets full; and when he saw that wee would not take them in contentment, the captaine departed. . . ."[2]

As time went on, Portugal's competitors, however, began to perfect their methods, and Portugal found increasing difficulties in maintaining her former position. During the fifteenth century the Portuguese monarchy, with its relatively large territorial base, was able to mobilize larger resources than the Italian city states that had once conducted such a large proportion of Europe's sea-borne commerce. But Portugal in turn was dwarfed by the larger powers of Western Europe—Spain, France, England, and the Netherlands. For a time Portugal, as we have previously seen, lost its independence. In 1580, Philip II annexed the country. Until 1640 Portugal became an adjunct to its more powerful neighbor, and the kingdom entered upon its "Babylonian captivity." The Spaniards used Portuguese revenue for the imperial designs of the House of Hapsburg; Portugal's military and naval strength was made to serve foreign purposes, and Portugal became embroiled in wars that did not effect the country's own vital interests. Philip II was determined to crush the political and religious revolt of his Netherlands subjects (begun in 1572, finally terminated by Spain's recognition of Netherlands independence in 1648). Philip also became involved in war against Protestant England; he took sides in the religious civil war of France, and Portugal thus needlessly acquired new enemies. In 1588 the Spaniards used Lisbon to assemble their great armada for an attack on England. A large Portuguese contingent sailed with this great fleet to the North Sea and was involved in its utter destruction. In 1594 Philip II tried economic pressure against the Dutch. Lisbon's valuable trade with the Netherlands largely came to an end, and the Portuguese lost a major market. In addition, the Dutch began to attack Portuguese possessions overseas. The Portuguese conducted a resolute resistance, and for a time generally managed to hold their own. In 1596, for instance, they repelled a Dutch attempt to seize Elmina. They likewise beat back repeated Dutch assaults on Mozambique.

But gradually Holland's superior resources began to tell. Seventeenth century

Holland was one of the most economically advanced countries in the world. Dutch agronomists led in the science of agriculture; Dutch engineers were the world's foremost dike builders and soil reclamationists. The Dutch built up great fisheries, a powerful merchant marine, and an immense carrying and entrepôt trade. Dutch sailors made a redoubtable name for themselves in every major maritime theater of war. The Dutch also created a powerful banking and credit system; the Netherlanders always kept faith with their creditors. They were in a position to mobilize large quantities of capital, and they turned Amsterdam into the greatest financial center of Europe. Worse still, from the Portuguese point of view, the Dutch decided to bypass Portugal and to open up direct communications with the East. In 1602 Dutch capitalists formed the Dutch East India Company, which received a monopoly of Dutch trade east of the Cape of Good Hope and west of the Strait of Magellan. In 1619 the Dutch built Batavia in Java, which soon outstripped the Portuguese possession of Goa in India, and the Portuguese were driven out of many of their eastern possessions. In 1621 the Dutch founded their West India Company with extensive trading rights in West Africa and the New World, where the Portuguese encountered yet another challenge. A year later the Portuguese met with further disaster. In 1622 Shah Abbas, the ruler of Persia, suddenly turned to an alliance with the English against Portugal. An Anglo-Persian expedition assaulted Ormuz, the Portuguese key base in the Persian Gulf. Rui de Andrade, Portugal's last great admiral in the East, conducted a magnificent defense, but was overwhelmed at last, and the 1620s ushered in a long period of progressive decline for Portugal.

THE LUSO-DUTCH STRUGGLES ON THE WEST AFRICAN COAST AND IN BRAZIL

In the sixteenth century Europe's most important import products were gold and spices—luxury goods of small bulk and great price. By 1640 a well-informed observer would probably still have classed bullion, cloves, pepper, and similar articles as the most important merchandise furnished by tropical countries to the west.[3] Gradually, however Europe became accustomed to a variety of tropical crops, to semi-luxury goods with a much wider market. Cocoa from America, and tea and coffee from Asia slowly acquired popularity as beverages for men of fashion. Despite the expostulation of moralists, tobacco won its way into popular esteem. Indigo from the East, dyewoods from Brazil and Central America were used to dye European fabrics. Above all, European housewives, who previously had no means of sweetening food except honey, slowly began to buy more sugar. In addition, syrup, left over from the refining of sugar cane, was distilled into rum, and added yet another item to the taverner's selection.

The Portuguese pioneered the cultivation of cane sugar in Madeira, and later in the Cape Verde Islands and São Tomé. But the demand for sugar and similar plantation-grown tropical products grew insatiable. The Portuguese and other Europeans thus began to experiment with different expedients. The Portuguese gave technical assistance to the Kongo kingdom to promote the cultivation of crops for the European market. They employed Indian slaves on great estates in Brazil. The British and

French subsequently set to work European convicts or contract laborers to cultivate land in the Lesser Antilles. But the most profitable combination was the plantation —located in tropical America, staffed by European managers, and worked by slaves from Africa. Slaves were sturdier and more reliable than West Indians. Above all, they were more resistant to tropical disease than white men.[4] Hence plantation slavery came to dominate a considerable part of the Atlantic economy. The tropical areas of the New World were to rely to a large extent on the transatlantic slave trade.

This profound social transformation was part of a wider revolution that, in different forms, affected many different parts of the world. As Robert C. Binkley, a modern historian, has put it, in places of the world where the expanding European economy touched land along its overseas fringe and its eastern land frontier, the rulers commonly encountered a labor problem they often met by imposing restraints on the free movement of workmen. This development was by no means limited to the tropical areas of the world. In sixteenth- and seventeenth-century Russia, for example, the frontier squires acquired new political duties as tax collectors over the free peasants. Then, to keep the free farmers from moving away, the tillers were bound to the soil. In the overseas colonies the rulers not merely had to hold labor power on the land, but in many cases they had to import their manpower in the first place. Convicts and indentured servants from Europe, as well as slaves from Africa, provided this bond of labor. When slave labor became associated with the plantation system geared to the production of goods for the European market, the resulting economic complex showed as much tenacity as the Russian system of serfdom. The bondage imposed upon the Russian peasant and colonial slavery rose together. They persisted for several hundred years—right down to the nineteenth century, and in the end, they both fell together.[5]

Brazil's economic mainstay became sugar. The cultivation of this crop required manpower from Africa. The transatlantic demand for manpower in turn created a well-defined "triangular" traffic between Europe, Africa, and America. Ships left Lisbon or Oporto for Luanda or Brazilian ports, laden with manufactured goods from Europe and also with Chinese and Indian wares imported from Goa. Portugal's own industrial production could not supply the demands of her own South Atlantic empire; hence a large proportion of the outward-bound cargoes consisted of goods purchased from other European countries, especially England. Merchants would dispose of their loads in Angola and purchase slaves and ivory in exchange for textiles, rum, sugar cane, brandy, and tobacco. On reaching Brazil, the slaves were usually sold for sugar or tobacco, which was then sent back to Portugal in annual fleets. Profits from these sales in Lisbon went to the purchase of European or Asian goods for re-export to Angola or Brazil, including wigs, ribands, silk stockings, and other luxuries for wealthy planters, traders, or officials, as well as necessities like wine, olives, codfish, wheaten flour, and textiles. This triangular trade might be carried on in any direction. A Lisbon dealer could, for instance, dispatch goods for sale to Brazil and invest his gains in slaves from Angola. Similarly, a planter or trader in Brazil could send sugar, tobacco, or dyewood to Lisbon and receive the return in European manufactures. Alternatively he could send tobacco, brandy, or rum to Angola and purchase "black" or "white" ivory in payment.[6] Angola became both the hinterland and an economic dependency of Brazil.

The Dutch, having already won enormous success with their Dutch East India Company, decided to break into this Atlantic triangle and seize the sugar trade of Brazil and the slave traffic from West Africa as well as the commerce in spices from the East. In 1621 the Dutch formed the West India Company and embarked on an aggressive strategy in the South Atlantic.

As regards sheer numbers, Holland—with perhaps 1¼ million people—had no advantage over the Portuguese. But Holland's economic and financial resources were immeasurably superior to Portugal's. Holland, unlike Portugal, was able to make extensive use of foreign mercenaries; the Dutch fleet was considerably larger than Portugal's, and the Dutch generally had also a much better understanding of how sea power should be employed strategically. But considering their disabilities, the Portuguese defended their possessions with astonishing vigor. True enough, the Portuguese failed in the East, where the Dutch seized Malacca in 1641 and Jaffna, the last Portuguese stronghold in Ceylon, seventeen years later. The major portion of Portugal's eastern empire crumbled; the Dutch gained control of the cloves, mace, and nutmegs of the Moluccas, the cinnamon of Ceylon, and the pepper of Malabar as well as the lion's share in the carrying trade of the Asian waters. The Dutch were similarly successful in West Africa. At first they failed disastrously when in 1625 they tried to take Elmina and suffered a crushing defeat at the hands of a combined Luso-African force. Subsequently, however, they resumed their attack, and in 1637 gained possession of Elmina. When hostilities ended, the Dutch were the supreme European naval and trading power on the Gold, the Slave, and the Ivory Coasts.[7]

The Portuguese, however, put up a stout defense in East Africa and kept their hold on Mozambique. Worse still, from the Dutch point of view, the Netherlanders could not destroy Portugal's Angola-Brazil axis in the South Atlantic. In 1641 the Dutch occupied the coast of Angola, and established friendly relations with both the Kongolese and the Jaga. For a time Portuguese power was confined to a few strongholds in the Cuanza Valley, and by 1648 the combined forces of the Dutch, the Jaga, and the Kongo kingdom were on the point of extinguishing Portuguese power altogether in the country.

But the Portuguese position was restored by intervention from the New World. Between 1635 and 1644 the Dutch had managed to occupy the northern, that is to say, the richer, part of Brazil. In 1645, however, the people of Pernambuco rebelled against the Protestant invaders. The Portuguese were able to rally wider popular support than the Dutch; indeed the bulk of the Portuguese forces consisted of mulattoes, Negroes, Amerindians, and half-breeds of various hues, while the most outstanding Portuguese leader, João Fernandes Vieira, was the son of a Madeira gentleman and a mulatto prostitute. The Dutch suffered defeat after defeat until the last Dutch stronghold in Brazil had to capitulate in 1654. Victory in Brazil enabled the Portuguese to save Brazil's economic hinterland on the African shore. In 1648 a Luso-Brazilian expedition from Rio de Janeiro recaptured Luanda; the Dutch had to leave the country, and the Portuguese once more retained command of the now highly profitable slave markets in Angola. The Dutch were also unsuccessful in the cultural field. By the time the Netherlanders made their supreme effort in Angola and Brazil, the Portuguese had succeeded in implanting their speech or Africanized forms of Portuguese along wide stretches of the African coast. The Dutch never succeeded in imposing their own tongue either in Brazil, Kongo, or Angola, and Portuguese or Portuguese-derived African dialects for long remained the most widely known *lingua franca* throughout most of West Africa and Southeast Africa.

THE FOUNDING OF CAPE COLONY: 1652–1677

The Dutch empire, like the Portuguese, was built upon trade. The security of its commerce rested on sea power and on well-chosen naval stations along the main routes of maritime traffic. European merchant ships traveled southward into the Atlantic to the vicinity of Sierra Leone, then southwest along the coast of Brazil; from there they followed the prevailing wind to the Cape. Thence, the great, creaking three–masters might make their way through the Mozambique channel to East Africa and India. Alternatively they might run far out towards the shores of Australia and then, on a southeaster, to the Spice Islands. The Cape was the one point where vessels, coming or going, might conveniently make landfall.[8] The Cape had other advantages. Sailors on their six month journey from Western Europe to the East Indies required fresh water and fruit, fresh meat and vegetables to fight scurvy, the mariners' greatest scourge next to storms. The Cape, with its pleasant climate and fertile soil, was eminently suited as a refreshment station. Yet nearly a century and a half passed after its discovery by the Portuguese until white men made permanent homes for themselves at the Cape. They wanted spices and precious metals; but Bushmen hunters and Hottentot herdsmen had neither gold nor pepper to sell. Storms and, above all, perilous tides and offshore currents rendered the Cape dangerous to navigators, and many a merchantman was wrecked at its shores. At long last, however, the Dutch decided to act. They had failed to capture Mozambique from the Portuguese and therefore lacked a base of their own in southeast Africa; they were determined to forestall their English rivals who had also begun to take an interest in the area. The task of founding a station at the Cape was entrusted by the Dutch East India Company to Jan van Riebeeck, a thick-set, weather-beaten surgeon with much seagoing experience. Van Riebeeck received instructions to build a fort, secure a good water supply, plant gardens, and keep on good terms with the indigenous people for the sake of buying cattle. In 1652 van Riebeeck's small squadron dropped anchor at the Cape, and the Dutch built their first simple fort of earth and timber on a site close to Cape Town's present main railroad station.

The new settlement, a glorified market garden, counted for little compared with such splendid Dutch possessions as the Moluccas or Java. Yet, by a curious historical irony, the Cape was Holland's only colony where Dutch, and subsequently a derivative of Dutch, survived permanently as a spoken language. The Dutch aimed at trade rather than colonization, but as an afterthought they permitted a handful of free burghers, married men of Dutch or German descent, to take up land to breed cattle, plant vines, and grow corn. The farmers sold their crops to the local garrison and, more important, to the ships on their way to the Indies, the "floating market" of the Cape. The Company's administrators wanted a small, compact settlement, easily defensible and not likely to involve the Dutch in expensive native wars. The Dutch government tried to impose all kinds of controls, but the lure of the frontier proved too strong. The Hottentots wanted to acquire hardware, trinkets, and tobacco; the burghers were anxious to acquire cattle; there was also some demand for luxury goods such as ivory, rhino horns, feathers, and ostrich eggs, so that the aborigines' and the settlers' economy became to some extent supplementary. Traders and hunters made their way inland, and the backwoods in time produced their own breed of frontiers-men, comparable in certain ways to the Portuguese and mulatto "wilderness special-ists" of Angola and Brazil.

The European settlers were few in number; there were more skilled jobs than workmen, and from 1657 onward the Dutch tried to solve their manpower problem by importing slaves, mainly from the East. The European settlers, helped by their bondsmen, in turn pressed upon the Hottentots' herding grounds. The Hottentots, divided into small kinship units, could make no effective resistance, and their society broke under the triple impact of white settlement, white military power, and white-imported disease. The Hottentot communities splintered, roughly speaking, into three different groups—clans that kept in touch with the whites, but still kept some-thing of their traditional organizations, communities that saved their cohesion by withdrawing into the interior, and detribalized, partly Europeanized people in and about the colony. Some Hottentots became converts to Christianity; a handful even married Europeans. But as a body the Hottentots were not readily assimilable into white society, while the Europeans generally looked down upon the dark people as depraved and dirty heathen. In 1672 the Dutch claimed the whole of the small Cape Peninsula as "justly won by the sword." Two years later, a white commando (raiding party), assisted by Hottentot "friendlies," took the field against hostile clans. A few years later, in 1677, a joint force of Dutch troopers, burghers, and Hottentots embarked on an armed expedition against the Bushmen in the eastern borderlands.

The commando achieved little success against their elusive foes. But the enterprise was significant in other ways. Henceforth the Europeans met with little further resistance from the Hottentots. Instead, the two cattle-owning peoples often worked against their common enemy, the Bushmen. These aboriginal hunters objected to foreign intrusions into their accustomed hunting grounds; they regarded the strangers' cattle as a lawful prey; they could hardly be assimilated into European society, except occasionally as stockmen and trackers. Their fate was grim, and their bands were decimated.

The Cape thus produced a colonial society very different from the Euro-African societies that developed in the vicinity of white settlements on the west coast. The temperate climate of the Cape enabled white women to settle in the country and to raise healthy children. The presence of white women discouraged, though it did not at first wholly prevent the colonists from marrying dark-skinned wives. Irregular unions between white men and brown continued, but their offspring bore the double badge of illegitimacy and racial contempt. Slavery further accustomed the colonists to despise persons of color, by associating a dark complexion with menial labor and permanent bondage. Greater still, perhaps, was the impact of the frontier, the home of "the heathen, the sons of Amalek." The frontier was a permanent meeting ground of different races and cultures. The frontier did not always occasion hostility between the races. White hunters and traders might establish amiable relations with aboriginal communities. White farmers, however, commonly clashed with their neighbors in struggles for springs, pastures and fertile acres. In the course of these battles, cultural and national differences became forever identified in men's mind with the uniform of color.

As the tide of European conquest rolled on, the whites appear to have become increasingly color-conscious. Certainly, by the end of the eighteenth century the sacrament of baptism no longer sufficed to make a half-breed the equal of a white man in the civic sense. A Cape burgher now had to be born free, of free-born white parents, to be accepted as a fully qualified citizen. The colonists, whose early ancestors had included immigrants as varied as Hollanders and Frenchmen, Germans and Sephardic Jews, a few Christian Malays, even a handful of Hottentots, had evolved into a separate caste-nation, whose membership was defined by color, as much as by economic interest, language, culture, and religion.[9]

ENGLAND AND FRANCE IN WEST AFRICA

The English were late-comers in the colonial field. But once they had started their career of empire building they soon outstripped their competitors. As against Holland, England had many advantages. England had a larger population and a much more extensive territorial base. England had made vast advances in iron-smelting, mining, cloth manufacturing, and other enterprises, so that England's power was sustained by a much broader industrial foundation than Holland's. English sailors and shipbuilders could rival the Dutchmen in skill; at the same time England enjoyed a more favorable geographic and strategic position than any of her continental rivals.

England and Holland were sometimes in alliance and sometimes at war. The Dutch fought with great stubbornness, and during the two Anglo-Dutch wars (1652–1654 and again, 1664–1667) English admirals were equally matched by the formidable Netherlanders. In the long run England's superior resources told against the Dutch, and by the second half of the seventeenth century, the English had acquired a far-flung empire that included a great chain of settlement colonies stretching all the way from Maine to the Carolinas, a West Indian island empire, footholds on the Persian Gulf and on the coast of India (including Madras, founded in 1639, and Bombay, acquired from Portugal in 1661 as part of a royal marriage alliance).

In West Africa, the English gained their first permanent footing in 1608 when they erected a fort on James Island, not far from the mouth of the Gambia, to gain a share of the river trade to the interior. They subsequently extended their operations on the West African coast, where they dealt both in gold and slaves. As the plantation economy of the West Indies and North America expanded, the demand for slaves always tended to exceed the supply, and from about 1650 onward the traffic in "black ivory" became highly competitive. In addition to English, Dutch, Portuguese, and French slave traders, merchants of smaller countries such as Denmark, Brandenburg, and Courland tried to gain a footing in the business. Unlike England and France, the smaller countries, however, lacked great plantation colonies of their own. They could therefore make money only as middlemen, by selling slaves to the planters of other nations, and they could never seriously compete with the English. The English economy, on the other hand, was much more broadly based; the English participated in the African trade through the sale of English manufactures, the purchase and export of slaves, and the production of tropical crops in the New World; hence the English gradually ousted their Dutch rivals.

As the Dutch gradually ceased to be England's main enemy, their place was taken by the French. At the end of the seventeenth century, France was the most powerful state on the European continent. Her population was about three times that of England. Her armies were regarded as the finest in the world; her maritime power was formidable; her trade was extensive. The French had acquired extensive overseas dominions, with Martinique (occupied in 1635) and other valuable possessions in the West Indies, colonies in North America, and footholds in India. The French also had an interest in Africa. They made their first settlement in Senegal sometime about 1626, and secured the island of St. Louis, conveniently situated at the mouth of the river route to the interior. They subsequently captured numerous stations south of St. Louis from the Dutch, and the Peace of Nijmwegen (1678) confirmed the French in the possession of the former Dutch trading posts of Rufisque, Portudal, Joal, and Gorée. The French developed a valuable trade in gum, wax, ivory, hides, and slaves. But their profits were insufficient to sustain their interests over so great an area. The French West African companies were also incapable of securing sufficient slaves for the French West Indian plantations. The African population near the mouth of the Senegal was small, while the further the French penetrated up the river, the more they met with opposition from inland people engaged in the trans-Saharan trade. The French were thus forced to seek elsewhere for most of their slaves. In 1687 they established themselves at Assini on the Ivory Coast, but for various social and geographical reasons the Ivory Coast could never compete with the neighboring Gold Coast as a center of trade.[10]

The various European powers tried to restrict the transatlantic traffic to a monopolistic corporation, for only large and powerful companies could afford to build and maintain the forts deemed essential for the conduct of the slave trade on the West African coast during the seventeenth century. The European merchants bought their slaves from African middlemen who obtained the bulk of their captives in the interior, and the Europeans accordingly had to set up depots where stocks of slaves and trade goods could be kept. During the seventeenth century these depots had to be fortified to ensure their defense against foreign rivals. The first effective English company, the Company of Royal Adventurers into Africa, was thus chartered in 1660 (and succeeded in 1672 by the Royal African Company). In 1664 the English captured Carolusborg, a Gold Coast fort previously taken by the Dutch from the Swedes during the long and confusing struggle for African trade bases. In 1674 the English rebuilt the fort, known now as Cape Coast Castle, as the headquarters of the Royal African Company, Cape Coast Castle was an impressive sight:

with handsome staircases on the outside at certain distances on each front, for a communication between the lodgings of the garrison; and under the balconies are several shops. Next the agent-general's apartment is a large stately hall. There are also spacious store-houses and counting-houses for the factors and other officers; some of which rooms were not quite finished in the year 1682. The then agent Greenhill, my very good friend was diligently employed in finishing them.

The garrison and other company soldiers amount to about a hundred Whites, and near the number of Gromettoes [African mercenaries], with their respective officers all clothed in red, and in the pay of the Royal African Company.

They are supplied with water in time of scarcity from a large cistern which holds above three hundred tun of rain, gathered in the wet season from the tops and leads of the houses in the castle.

The gardens belonging to the agent and other officers of the castle, are at some distance from it, towards the strand, and full of orange and lemon trees; but have very few plants and herbs. In the midst of them is a square summerhouse for their diversion. Another place, much like a garden, but all planted with coco-trees, is the common burying ground for the garrison and officers.[11]

Fortifications like Cape Coast Castle developed into important centers of local European influence. But European power was restricted to a few islands, a few coastal forts, or to indirect control of other lands within sight of deep water and within the range of naval guns. West Africa was too unhealthy for large-scale European settlement, while indigenous farmers already utilized the cultivable ground near the forts. The few large-scale plantations initiated by white men on the Gulf of Guinea were soon abandoned as the promoters died of tropical disease, became involved in local wars, or exhausted the soil. For conquest there was little opportunity and, for long, little inducement. Inland were great African empires and confederacies. But on or near the coast, between the Senegal and the Niger, the sea-borne invaders found a patchwork of small states, centering on a town, comprising sometimes a few dependent towns. The various African states were often at war with their neighbors, and political fragmentation among Africans led to a corresponding dispersal of white trading posts. Each European country or company aimed at securing a trade monopoly, and could often obtain it within the limits of some particular kingdom in return for an alliance. The Africans who permitted a fort to be built on their territory looked for imported muskets and ammunition; they desired white protection against their local enemies and if necessary looked to finding refuge under the protection of foreign cannons. As a rule, however, the coastal communities became more or less subject to the fort; alliances tended to develop into undefined protectorates of varying effectiveness. The commander of a large garrison could exact obedience from the citizens of a small state, whereas a weak company was liable to be used as a cat's-paw in intertribal politics, to the point of getting drawn into war, not only against Africans but also against other Europeans. On some parts of the west coast one white nation or another succeeded in eliminating a rival by purchase or conquest. But elsewhere the forts of different countries remained interspersed in a crazy quilt, and this arrangement often continued into the nineteenth century.[12]

NOTES

1. Blake, *Europeans in West Africa, 1450–1560,* p. 389.

2. "William Towerson's First Voyage to Guinea 1555–6," in Blake, p. 367.

3. Shepard Bancroft Clough and Charles Woolsey Cole, *Economic History of Europe* (Boston, 1952), p. 122.

4. See Philip D. Curtin, "Epidemiology and the Slave Trade," *Political Science Quarterly,* LXXXIII, 2 (June 1968), pp. 190–216.

5. Robert C. Binkley, *Realism and Nationalism 1852–1871* (New York, 1935), pp. 88–89.

6. C. R. Boxer, *The Golden Age of Brazil, 1695–1750: Growing Pains of a Colonial Society* (Berkeley and Los Angeles, 1962), pp. 25–27.

7. This section is taken from Boxer, *Four Centuries of Portuguese Expansion, 1415–1825,* the best short survey relating to the subject. For more details, see C. R. Boxer, *The Dutch in Brazil, 1624–1654* (Oxford, 1957).

8. This section is based on Eric A. Walker, *A History of Southern Africa* (London, 1957), pp. 29–47. Walker's book is the most comprehensive history of South Africa in English.

9. For a valuable though somewhat controversial interpretation, see I. D. MacCrone, *Race Attitudes in South Africa: Historical, Experimental and Psychological Studies.* (Johannesburg, 1957), p. 1–136.

10. Fage, *Introduction to the History of West Africa,* p. 68.

11. Lawrence, *Trade Castles and Forts of West Africa,* pp. 185–186, quoted from a seventeenth-century account.

12. Lawrence, pp. 26–27.

Chapter 24

The Development of the Transatlantic Slave Trade

SLAVERY AND THE SLAVE TRADE IN THEIR AFRICAN CONTEXT

The origin of slavery in Africa dates from remote antiquity, and the slave traffic may have been Africa's earliest form of labor migration. Ancient Egyptians brought slaves from Nubia; Carthaginians used slaves from the Sudan to work on their plantations and fight in their armies. In more recent times East Africa had became an important supplier of captives for Asia long before the transatlantic slave trade came into being. From East Africa human merchandise was sent to Turkey, Arabia, Persia, India, Indonesia, and even China. Records of this trade are scattered in different parts of the world and uneven in quality, but occasionally some of the documents are very telling. For instance, there was a great revolt of African slaves in ninth-century Persia that continued for fifteen years. The Arab invasion of North Africa and the subsequent Arabic conquests inland occasioned a substantial increase in the trans-Saharan slave trade; this traffic in turn gave considerable wealth to many of the medieval kingdoms and empires of West Africa; it also accounted in part for the growth and prosperity of the Hausa city states.

On the whole, however, neither the Arabs nor the Afro-Islamic societies of Africa developed huge plantations with an unlimited demand for unskilled manpower. There were occasional exceptions; nineteenth-century Zanzibaris, for instance, profited from clove plantations worked by servile hands. But Muslim slavery in general depended on the requirements of small-scale craft industries, on the need for soldiers and domestic servants, on the desire for conspicuous consumption, and the luxuries of the harem. The rich men of Bornu, for example, bought slaves as concubines, as eunuchs for their harems, as palace retainers, as wrestlers, and as craftsmen, as well as field hands. But they did not employ labor gangs on a huge scale to work large estates dependent on export industries.

Islamic like indigenous African slavery knew an infinite number of social gradations. Slaves were attached to great households, and their status would vary enormously according to their masters' standing. The eunuchs who attended a monarch might act as royal secretaries. In some states important offices were reserved to people of servile descent, who were prevented by their status and their lack of kin connections from building up a personal influence independent of the sovereign's pleasure. In minor households bondsmen might act as housekeepers and factors. Some might even become slave owners on their own account.

Slavery also existed among many of the non-Muslim African societies. Free men could lose their liberty by being captured in war, as a result of being convicted for crimes, or by becoming the victims of political intrigues. There were even certain voluntary kinds of slavery. Among the Ibo, for instance, a man might pawn his person for debt, or offer himself as a cult slave to a local deity.[1] Captives or criminals might even be sacrificed to the gods. The fortunes of a slave were subject to immense variations. In some societies his fate might be of the harshest. In others the slave was practically absorbed into the owner's family. Among the coastal communities of Nigeria, for example, slaves were usually assigned to the house of an owner's polygamous wife. These women became the "mothers" of the slaves and treated them with much kindness. The "house" system welded slaves and freemen into closely knit trading corporations in which slaves had opportunities to acquire wealth and improve their social status.[2] Slaves might fare equally well among pastoralists such as the Ila in what is now Zambia. The Ila had no rigid social barriers. Children—free or slave —would play together, herd the cattle, run errands, and perform similar tasks. Adult bondsmen had to do the more unpleasant kinds of menial labor, but they were allowed to own cattle, like freemen.[3] African systems of slavery need not be idealized. Once the colonial powers abolished the system, few former bondsmen ever lobbied for the restoration of their previous condition. But African slavery was distinguished by a number of gradations, and among many societies the difference between bondsmen and citizens was one of degree rather than kind.

In all probability, however, the development of foreign trade and of mining caused domestic slavery to be put to new use, and may thereby have helped to worsen the captives' lot. The people of Monomotapa employed slaves, including women, in the gold mines of ancient Rhodesia. So did the Ashanti in what is now Ghana. In Ashanti there were also strict barriers on the bondsmen's economic progress. Slaves were apparently excluded from skilled crafts. These were endowed with religious significance and could only be practiced by adherents of the national cult. [4]

Some African slaves came to be employed on the land. Thus John Matthews, an English naval officer sent to Sierra Leone in 1785, noted that Mandingo notables in the highlands often owned from seven hundred to a thousand slaves apiece. Many of these bondsmen had to work in the fields. Among the Mandingo (as among West Indian and American slaves) the farm laborers suffered more brutal treatment than the domestic servants, and there were even rural insurrections. In early nineteenth-century Dahomey, the foreign demand for palm oil caused Dahomeans to employ domestic slaves on estates. Prisoners not required for this purpose were sold abroad.

West Africa, however, never developed an indigenous plantation economy on a large scale. Until the advent of peasant-grown crops such as peanuts and cocoa in the later nineteenth century, West Africa's agricultural exports remained limited in size, and confined to certain specialized goods such as palm oil, or to luxuries like kola nuts (chewed as a pleasant stimulant). Backward methods of production and transport, lack of technical knowledge and capital probably prevented the West African notables from building up plantation economies on anything remotely resembling the transatlantic scale.

Africans in the remoter parts of the continent found themselves in even greater difficulties. Wherever tribesmen came in contact with foreign traders, they increasingly became accustomed to the use of imported cloth, knives, hatchets, beads, guns, and the like. All too often, such commodities either could not be turned out at all with existing methods of production; or they could not be made as cheaply or as well as foreign manufactures. It is likely that the industrial revolution in Europe, especially in Great Britain, may have further stimulated Africa's demand for inexpensive foreign goods. These imports, however, had to be paid for. To some extent, Africans were able to meet their obligations by selling ivory or gold. But the riches of nature were not inexhaustible. Elephants might be exterminated in the ruthless search for tusks. Alluvial gold supplies were liable to be worked out. Many impediments stood in the way of expanding agricultural exports. Many African communities thus were beset by what one might call a perennial balance of payments problem. Accordingly, they were encouraged to sell men, their most precious asset, and the slave traffic in time became Africa's most extensive export industry.

THE GROWTH OF THE TRANSATLANTIC SLAVE ECONOMIES

The pioneers of the Christian slave trade in Africa were the Portuguese, and during the latter part of the fifteenth and the early portion of the sixteenth centuries, there was a considerable rise in the export of slaves. But in all likelihood the Muslims remained the main slave dealers in Africa. From the seventeenth century onward, however, crucial changes took place in the extent and organization of the maritime slave traffic. The Northern European powers, especially the Dutch, forced their way into the slaving business. The overseas commerce of Europe, moreover, experienced profound modifications. The purchase of luxury goods for the few was replaced by the importation of consumption goods for an increasingly large number of customers. The reasons for this transformation are complex, and can be only briefly alluded to in this chapter. Improvements in agricultural techniques, for instance, allowed more European housewives to buy fresh meat all the year round and thereby diminished the importance of spices. Western Europe built up new industries; living standards went up and Europeans began to buy tropical plantation products on a much larger scale. Commerce with the tropics thus grew both in bulk and in value, becoming concerned with necessities more than luxuries.

Tobacco importing, for example, received a tremendous impetus as the habit of smoking and taking snuff spread to all classes. Coffee, tea, and chocolate began to be widely drunk. The consumption of these beverages in turn stimulated the demand for cane sugar, leading to what some historians have called the "sugar revolution." Molasses or sugar could also be distilled into rum, and this heavy liquor proved as popular with Red Indian braves and Benin warriors as with British tars. Similarly, the growing British and French textile industries depended on large-scale imports of cotton and of dyes like indigo, brazilwood, and cochineal—all indispensable to manufacturers before the advent of chemical dyes.[5]

All these commodities were supplied by plantations in what might be called Europe's agricultural periphery in the New World. Before the days of mechanized farming these plantations required a vast army of cheap and preferably docile laborers inured to the heat of the tropics. Increasingly the plantation owners came to rely on the manpower reservoir of sub-Saharan Africa. The far-flung partnership between European shippers, merchants, and manufacturers, and transatlantic land owners and African slave-trading chiefs produced one of the most extensive and brutal systems of forced labor known to history. Reduced to its simplest dimensions, this system depended on a triangle of trade, whereby European work-shops shipped their products to West Africa; Africans sold their captives to the plantations of the New World, which in turn dispatched their crops to Europe. Hence from a cold economic point of view, the history of transatlantic slavery can be written in terms of sugar, tobacco, cotton, rum, and similar commodities.

The main beneficiaries of this trade were not—as is sometimes assumed—the territories now comprised within the United States. The thirteen colonies imported few slaves before the eighteenth century. Even thereafter, between 1700 and the American Revolution they received only about 20 percent of the British slave trade. Philip Curtin, an outstanding modern historian, has reassessed past estimates of the traffic in a pioneer study.[6] The Old World was but little affected by the huge *Völkerwanderung* brought about by the commerce in slaves. Only something like 1.8 percent of all the captives were taken to Europe. North America received no more than 6.8 percent of all the slaves, 4.5 percent being sent into the territory of what is now the United States. Subtropical and tropical America, extending from Brazil to the Caribbean, employed something like 90 percent of all the Africans taken to the New World. Important as slavery became in the history of North America, the main development of plantation slavery took place in the West Indies and in Latin America. These statistical facts have been obscured since by the high growth rate of the Afro-American population in the United States, as against the low survival rate of slaves in Brazil. These figures cast doubt on the theory propounded by some scholars that Mediterranean-derived institutions helped to protect the slaves against their masters.

The first great plantation country was Brazil. Unlike Spanish America which was developed initially for its mineral wealth, Brazil began as an agricultural colony from the very start. Sugar was by far the most important Brazilian cash crop, and slave labor formed the economic base of the great sugar industry that grew up during the sixteenth and seventeenth centuries in the northwest, in Pernambuco and the region of Bahia. During the eighteenth century the Bahia planters turned to tobacco, but the cultivation of this crop required just as many field hands as cane sugar; hence the demand for black slaves continued. There were also other customers for Africa's "black ivory." From the end of the seventeenth century, for instance, Brazilian pioneers began to open up the wealth of the Minas Gerais, and during the eighteenth century Brazilian gold miners began to purchase slaves on an extensive scale. The Portuguese Crown at first attempted to restrict the number of Negro slaves entering the Minas Gerais. But all these prohibitions proved futile. Unable to buy sufficient slaves from Angola, the Brazilians began to import captives from Guinea.[7] Slaves also worked as domestic servants, as artisans, and in many other capacities, so that Brazilian slave society assumed a highly variegated pattern, as it did in Spanish America.

The economic history of the West Indies in many ways resembled Brazil's. In 1605 the English laid claims to Barbados, their first possession in the Caribbean. The first English settlers cultivated their own small holdings and raised many different crops, including tobacco, cotton, indigo, and ginger. Later they were joined by royalist refugees from the Cival War in England who brought along indentured white laborers, mostly Scottish and Irish prisoners of war. By this time, however, the extensive cultivation of sugar began to revolutionize the island's economy, and Barbados was rapidly transformed. Sugar was not well suited to be a small man's crop. To yield profits in a highly competitive market, the cane had to be grown on a large scale, and most small holdings were gradually absorbed into large plantations. Even before the intensive cultivation of sugar began to exhaust the soil of Barbados, the plantation system spread to other islands, including Jamaica, captured from Spain in 1655.[8] England's rivals in the West Indies built up agricultural island economies of a similar kind. The Spaniards, for instance, extensively cultivated slave-grown sugar in Cuba, while the French turned Martinique, and Haiti into great tropical exporters dependent on vast slave armies.

Speaking in general terms, these plantation systems usually had a proclivity toward expansion. The growing demand for sugar and other tropical crops caused entrepreneurs to step up production. Increasing monoculture production with unskilled and unwilling workmen, generally based on methods ill-designed to preserve the fertility of the land, commonly led to soil erosion. The planters tried to open up new acres on which they raised more crops, which in turn furnished the profits to purchase additional slaves. By and large, however, the supply of servile labor born in the West Indies did not keep pace with the demand. The planters were, therefore, often under pressure to overwork their laborers. Overwork, poor living conditions, and ill treatment of field hands entailed heavy mortality rates and thereby gave yet another stimulus to the Atlantic slave trade.

In the subtropical regions of North America large-scale slavery became an established institution only after a considerable time lag. In 1619 the North American colonies received their first consignment of African slaves. During the rest of the seventeenth century, however, the increase in slaves was small. For a variety of economic and geographical reasons the plantation economy of the South grew at a slow pace; the colonists preferred to use white indentured laborers, who were ultimately assimilated into the community. Most early Americans at first opposed the introduction of Africans, and colonial legislatures passed a series of acts designed to prevent or hinder the importation of black men.

The appearance of rice and indigo culture in South Carolina and the concurrent expanison of tobacco production in Virginia from about 1680 onward led, however, to an economic and social revolution of vast consequences. By the early eighteenth century the days of a largely self-sufficient agriculture were at an end. South Carolina planters began to make large profits from rice and indigo grown in the marshy lands of the sea-coast and along the rivers. In Virginia the cultivation of tobacco expanded, and the small, independent farmers gave way to the lordly proprietors of hundreds, even thousands, of acres. Virginia and Maryland became the tobacco colonies. South Carolina and later Georgia were the rice colonies. Their labor requirements could not be met—even partially—by white redemptioners and convicts. The southern colonies became increasingly dependent on African labor, South Carolina and Virginia remaining the major customers. Large–scale slavery, broadly speaking, found its limit at the borders of the temperate zones, where the cultivation of tropical crops proved impracticable. But the slave trade was also important for the economy of the northern colonies whose mercantile houses, shipping firms, and incipient manufacturing establishments likewise participated in the slave trade.[9]

Slavery in North America received yet another great stimulus with the invention of the cotton gin in 1793. By this time British textile manufactures were being increasingly mechanized, and British factory owners cried out for more raw material. The cotton gin allowed American planters to meet this demand. Previously the customary process of seeding cotton lint by hand had been so slow as to prevent cotton from becoming a great American export. The cotton gin, however, enabled unskilled black workmen to seed lint on a vastly expanded scale. The new device thereby changed a by-product of southern agriculture into a staple crop, raised the price of slaves, increased the size of plantations, and firmly convinced the southern landowners that slaves were indispensable for raising cotton. Plantation slavery, therefore, formed the backbone of the transatlantic slave trade and profoundly affected the fortunes of the African continent.[10]

THE MIDDLEMEN

The development of the transatlantic plantation economy gave tremendous opportunities to European and African merchants alike. But after the Dutch had broken the supremacy of the Portuguese on the African west coast during the seventeenth century, no European state was able to attain a monopoly of the African commerce. Dutchmen, Englishmen, Frenchmen, Portuguese, and Brazilians all took part in the West African slave trade, but no single power was able to dominate the region. The Europeans' direct influence did not extend much beyond the range of the guns mounted on their forts and their men of war. Throughout the seventeenth century, moreover, the greater part of the West African shore remained innocent of European trade. There were permanent posts from the Senegal River down to the Sherbro, on the Gold Coast, and in Angola. But except on the Gold Coast, where the factories of different European powers jostled in profusion, such settlements were few and far between. The influence a European power could wield in West Africa depended, in the last instance, not on brick and mortar but on the number of warships it could allocate to the region. There was a good deal of fighting between local white competitors; but gradually a policy of live and let live came to prevail among the white powers, so that even a number of smaller powers, including Sweden, Denmark, Brandenburg, and Courland, were able to obtain more or less temporary footholds.

The growth of the transatlantic trade stimulated the formation of European companies sufficiently wealthy to maintain forts and factories on the West African coast and sufficiently powerful to negotiate agreements with African rulers. In 1672, for instance, the French founded the Compagnie du Sénégal, which did not, however, prosper financially. In the same year English entrepreneurs created the Royal African Company as a joint stock venture with extensive privileges.

During the eighteenth century, however, the organization of the commerce underwent considerable changes. The War of the Spanish Succession (terminated by the Treaty of Utrecht in 1713) resulted in major British successes over the French and left Great Britain the world's leading naval power. European, especially British, manufactures became cheaper and played a growing part in the indigenous economies of West Africa. Coastal Africans became ever more eager to exchange their goods for British goods and castles on the littoral lost a good deal of their previous importance. The Royal African Company was unable to maintain a monopoly against interlopers. Having to maintain the local forts, it could not compete effectively with separate traders in the slaving business and, as the historian of the company puts it, "free trade was given its chance by one of the least ideological of all revolutions."[11] In 1752 the Royal African Company finally terminated its career, and control over the forts was transferred to a committee of British merchants assisted by a government subsidy.

At the same time, the center of the British slave trade moved from the south to the north of England, where most of the kingdom's new manufacturing industries came to be located. Up to the end of the seventeenth century, London, the headquarters of the Royal African Company, was England's principal slaving port. After the trade was thrown open to independent traders, Bristol outstripped London, but Bristol in turn was outdistanced by Liverpool. Liverpool was geographically much closer to the source of goods for the Guinea trade than her rivals. Manufacturers in the Midlands, Lancashire, and Yorkshire preferred to ship their textiles, iron bars, copper pans, glass beads, cutlery, and muskets to West Africa via Liverpool, and by 1797 the port was reported to control five-eighths of Great Britain's African trade, and three-sevenths of the African commerce with the whole of Europe.[12] Other great European cities such as Bordeaux and Amsterdam also played their part in the African trade and so did many coastal towns of New England. New Englanders, for instance, would ship food stuffs, lumber, and manufactured products to the West Indies in exchange for rum. The captains would proceed to Africa, barter their liquor for slaves, who were then transported to the West Indies. In exchange, Americans bought sugar and molasses, which were carried to New England to be distilled into rum. Alternatively, Yankee mariners would take rum, trinkets, bar iron, beads, and cloth directly to Africa, where they bought Negroes with the proceeds. No nation, however, could rival England's mercantile position in Africa, and the English became the chief European promoters of the African slave trade.

The white foreigners, almost without exception, depended on indigenous suppliers and middlemen for the supply of their merchandise. In a discussion of the African side of the slave trade, two cautions should be kept in mind. First of all the commerce in human beings and also the more spectacular caravan traffic in luxury goods over long distances formed but a small proportion of African commerce. As Dr. Colin Newbury shows from his researches, the bulk of West Africa's local trade hinged on the exchange of surplus food between pastoralists, grain growers, fishermen, and root croppers. This exchange in turn depended on a huge number of small, unspectacular transactions. Secondly, the organization of the slave trade differed as widely as did the political structures and the customary forms of servitude found among the African communities involved in the traffic.

Speaking in general terms, however, foreign trade was more important from the political point of view than local commerce. Powerful rulers could establish monopolies more easily over the traffic in ivory and slaves than over the far-flung exchange in local food. Foreign trade, moreover, enabled monarchs to acquire imported weapons and thereby provided participants in the traffic with an immediate military advantage. The kingdom of Dahomey, a highly centralized monarchy to which we shall refer in subsequent pages, ran the slave trade as a state enterprise. Early in the eighteenth century Dahomey seized the port of Whydah and the neighboring trading centers. The king then instituted a royal monopoly on exports and certain imports, levied fixed duties, and closed down, as far as possible, all rival outlets betwen Grand Popo in the west and toward Badagri in the east. Dahomey was unable to attain a complete corner in the local commerce because of competition from ports protected by the Yoruba,[13] but Dahomey's traffic in slaves nevertheless reached vast proportions. Dahomey, for instance, carried on an extensive commerce with Brazil through Porto Novo, opened in the eighteenth century by João de Oliveira, a Brazilian. Oliveira in fact was himself a freed slave. But he was so well adjusted to the Brazilian way of life that he returned to Africa in order to buy human merchandise for the markets of Bahia and Pernambuco, and having made his fortune, retired to Bahia.[14]

The trade of Dahomey and of similar kingdoms depended on powerful monarchs. In the Niger Delta, on the other hand, the traffic was conducted by a multitude of "Houses," which might be described as cooperatives of leading merchants, assisted by their kinsmen and slaves. Between them these "Houses" made up many of West Africa's minor city states and, in certain respects, combined tribal with capitalist modes of social organization. Among the Nembe of Nigeria, for instance, the members of each "House" might reside in a particular quarter of the city. Petty chiefs might own parts of a smaller town, farms, or fishing villages. The "House" acted as a trading corporation, but its members might also fish and farm. They likewise operated as military units, each "House" being required to equip at least one war canoe for the navy of its respective city.[15]

In addition, many inland kingdoms began to participate in the slave trade as caravans penetrated ever more deeply into the interior, creating new wants, supplying a kind of "moving market" that furnished favored communities with firearms and other goods. By the eighteenth century, for instance, even the distant Lunda kingdom of Chief Kazembe (situated in what is now northeastern Zambia) traded with the coast of Loango (on the Atlantic, north of the Congo River).[16]

The slave trade thus involved a good deal of shunting and the organization of a large-scale transport network. Both in East and in West Africa the coastal peoples seldom supplied slaves from their own ranks. They purchased captured prisoners from the peoples in their hinterland. These in turn, while delivering some captives from their own regions, looked for their main supply to other peoples still farther in the interior. Long-distance traffic by land, however, posed enormous logistic problems; these set certain limits to the amount of shunting that could be done. The bulk of the slaves were drawn from a belt of territory that reached inland from the coast for several hundred miles, but seldom very much further. The West Coast Africans, the principal dealers, drew their regular supplies from the relatively abundant peoples of the forest belt and to a lesser extent from the sparser populations of the grassland beyond the forest.[17]

The Bantu kingdoms of the southern savannah appear to have dealt over longer distances, through regions whose transport problems may not have been quite as difficult as those of the dense woodland of West Africa. But the southern Bantu never played as great a part in this commerce as the West African Negroes. West Africans thus remained both the principal beneficiaries and the chief victims of the transatlantic slave trade.

THE VICTIMS

The story of the slave trade is a tale of horrors. Slaves might or might not be well treated once they reached their destination. But untold numbers perished in battle or died of starvation as a result of internecine wars waged for slaves.

Vast numbers of slaves expired on the march to the ports. Many died of exhaustion or despair; others became the victim of all manner of atrocities. The Muslims, for instance, inflicted surgical castration on those of their victims whom they deemed to be useful as harem attendants, and only a tiny percentage survived this ordeal. The Christians did not indulge in this particular atrocity, but invented many of their own. Slaves who sought for death on the dreaded "Middle Passage" across the Atlantic by refusing food were flogged. Lest beating should prove ineffective, every Guineaman was provided with a special instrument called *speculum oris.* It looked like a pair of dividers with notched legs and a thumbscrew at the blunt end. The legs were closed and the notches were hammered in between the slave's teeth. When the thumbscrew tightened, the legs of the instrument separated, forcing open the slave's mouth; then food was poured into it through a funnel.[18]

More destructive of human life than individual horrors were the living conditions inflicted on the human merchandise in transit. Countless men and women died on the long trek from the Sudan to the slave markets of North Africa. Even more people must have perished on the over-crowded, disease-ridden hell ships that took the

Female slaves as seen in a
nineteenth-century print.

captives across the Atlantic. There were two schools of thought among the Guinea
captains, the "loose packers" and the "tight packers." The former argued that by
giving the slaves a little more room, with better food and a certain amount of liberty,
the slavers could reduce the mortality among their victims and receive better prices
for each slave in the West Indies. The "tight packers" answered that although the loss
of life might be greater on each voyage by cramming a vessel to capacity, so too were
the net receipts from a larger cargo. The argument between the two schools continued as long as the trade itself, but for many years after 1750 the "tight packers"
were in the ascendant.[19]

The white soldiers and sailors who were involved—directly or indirectly—in the
traffic suffered almost as much as their victims. The military garrisons at the African
forts were subjected to a ruthless discipline in an effort to keep them from going
completely to pieces under the combined effect of cheap liquor and women, bad
climate and food. In 1782 a private who had deserted from Cape Coast Castle was
blown from the muzzle of a gun. The sailors who manned the Guineamen suffered
almost as badly as the wretched slaves in the holds. Some were even treated worse,
for while the slaves at least represented a capital investment, the sailors (often re-

cruited by methods that differed little from kidnapping blacks) did not. Eighteenth-century Englishmen, who flogged their own children and apprentices, thought nothing of inflicting even worse punishments on soldiers and sailors often drawn from the dregs of society. The loss of life on board ship was accordingly heavy. In addition, many captives perished on arrival in the West Indies.

No one will ever know how many people were abducted or killed through the slave trade. All we can say is that the number was tremendously high. Anthony Benezet, an eighteenth-century abolitionist, calculated that during the middle of the century—when the traffic was at its height—British slavers brought something like 100,000 Negroes a year from Africa to the New World. In addition, other European nations carried their burden of responsibility, especially the French, the Portuguese, and the Dutch.[20] The figures varied considerably from year to year, and the evidence is contradictory. According to the calculations of Robert Kuczynski, one of the world's most prominent population experts, something like 15,000,000 people were taken from Africa to the New World between the sixteenth and the nineteenth centuries, though the total may well have been larger.[21] Basil Davidson, another British writer, opts for an even higher figure. Bearing in mind the loss of life caused by slave wars as well as slave sales, he concluded that "before and after embarcation, the Atlantic slave trade must have cost Africa at least 50,000,000 souls" over several centuries.[22]

The most recent researches into the subject have seriously modified these figures. Present investigations suggest that the figures customarily accepted owe more to abolitionist passion than statistical knowledge. Philip D. Curtin, an American scholar, suggests that the total number of slaves shipped across the Atlantic during the four centuries of the trade did not exceed some 9,000,000 and that the figure may well have been rather less. Curtin doubts whether the Europeans had enough shipping space to transport more people over such huge distances. He also considers that the losses incurred by the captives en route could not have amounted to more than about 16 percent. This indeed would still be a high figure, equivalent to that suffered by an army in battle. Nevertheless, if his estimates are correct, the total number of men and women taken from Africa during the entire period of the slave trade could not have exceeded some 11,000,000 people.[23]

For all its bloody inhumanity, the traffic in West Africa as a whole presumably did not diminish the total number of people. Even during the eighteenth century, when the traffic was at its peak, the trade merely tended to check the natural population growth. For the other centuries, the effects of the trade would have been relatively slight. Certainly, densely populated regions like the Akan states, the Yoruba and the Benin kingdoms, were also most deeply implicated in the trade. In the New World, on the other hand, many black communities must have increased their numbers by natural growth rather than by forcible transplantation. (This must have been particularly true of the black people in the United States, who experienced a phenomenal expansion of their numbers from the end of the eighteenth century to the present.)

In the absence of truly reliable statistics, these questions can never be fully resolved. All we can say for certain is that the slave trade—for all the abolitionists' exaggerations—occasioned human misery on an unimaginable scale, and that it must have been very destructive of human life. Certain areas suffered severely; others were little affected or even derived economic benefit from the growing commerce. The traffic cannot, moreover, be understood in isolation; it went with a more extensive process of African state building. The traffic partly Africanized portions of the New World; it permitted the rise of tropical plantation economies and brought about a transatlantic variety of hereditary serfdom in which bondsmen came to be distinguished by the color of their skin. The transatlantic traffic represented the greatest forcible transplantation of human beings known to history until the mass deportations and expulsions initiated by the totalitarian regimes of the twentieth century. Muslim traders in North and East Africa played their part in the traffic—together with their African associates. But the main culprits were the kings and merchants, the slavers and their Afro-European partner who supplied the transatlantic slave owners' insatiable demand for cheap manpower.

THE PROFITS

The economic effects of the slave trade have been assessed in very different fashions. Marx considered what he called the "transformation of Africa into a game reservation for the commercialized hunting of black skins" as part of the original process of capital accumulation. According to Marx, the traffic in slaves together with the exploitation of the mineral riches of the New World, the conquest and spoliation of the East Indies, and similar early colonial enterprises signified the "rosy dawn" that ushered in the age of capitalist production.[24] Eric Williams, a modern West Indian politician and statesman, has developed this theme in considerably greater detail:

The triangular trade thereby gave a triple stimulus to British industry. The Negroes were purchased with British manufactures; transported to the plantations, they produced sugar, cotton, indigo, molasses and other tropical products, the processing of which created new industries in England; while the maintenance of the Negroes and their owners on the plantations provided another market for British industry, New England agriculture and the Newfoundland fisheries. By 1750 there was hardly a trading or a manufacturing town in England which was not in some way connected with the triangular or direct colonial trade. The profits obtained provided one of the main streams of that accumulation of capital in England which financed the Industrial Revolution.

The West Indian islands became the hub of the British Empire, of immense importance to the grandeur and prosperity of England. It was the Negro slaves who made these sugar colonies the most precious colonies ever recorded in the whole annals of imperialism.[25]

Williams shows how the slave trade influenced the development of shipping and shipbuilding, the growth of the great British seaport towns, the manufacture of goods used in the traffic, including textiles, sugar refining, rum distillation, the manufacture of knicknacks known as "pacotille," the metallurgical industries, banking, insurance, and numerous other enterprises. French historians have demonstrated the importance

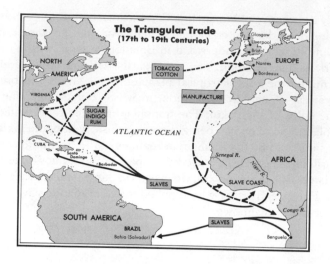

of the African trade for the commerce of the French Atlantic ports and of the various commercial and industrial interests associated with these cities. American writers have come to similar conclusions about the role of the slave trade for their own country. The slave trade did not merely help to create the plantation economies of the Deep South. It also played a major part in the economy of the northern colonies. In Rhode Island, for instance, the African trade gave employment to a large number of artisans —woodsmen, blacksmiths, cord- and sail-makers, to mention only a few. The economic benefits of the traffic also extended to the owners and sailors of small coasting boats that delivered materials to Rhode Island, and of course also to the distilleries, which produced huge quantities of strong drink to be exchanged on the African coast for men and women. New England fishermen were concerned with salt and dried fish; these were important articles of commerce with the West Indies and the southern colonies because they were used as food for the slaves. Landowners were likely to profit from the sale of timber from his woodlot or forest land, and so on. Indeed "the financial ramifications of the trade with Africa extended deeply into all elements of American society"[26]

The complexities of the traffic were such that no one will ever be able to draw up an exact balance sheet of profits and losses. The difficulty of striking a balance is increased by the fact that the commerce in human beings was so inextricably intertwined with "legitimate" trade in commodities that the various trends of the triangular trade can hardly be disentangled. There is not the slightest doubt that slavery played a great role. Without this massive importation of labor the plantation economies of the New World could not have developed in the way they did. Sugar, tobacco, and similar crops could all have been grown by free workmen or by indentured white laborers. But during the seventeenth and eighteenth centuries, before the extensive development of agricultural machinery, small farmers could never have rivalled the immense production figures obtained on slave-run plantations. There is no doubt that the American, Brazilian, or West Indian planter owed his very existence to the transatlantic slave trade. Similarly, the traffic gave a stimulus to European trade and manufactures.

But the tale of unlimited profits can easily be exaggerated, and recent research has done much to modify the reputation of the African trade for immense gains. The commerce in slaves was subject to serious internal weaknesses that subsequently played an important part in bringing about its abolition. The traffic involved little capital outlay to the African slave hunters and middlemen who supplied the human "raw material." But European participants had to invest an immense amount of capital to make their business pay. They had to outfit vessels for long journeys. They had to meet the cost of cargoes made up of goods as varied as cloth, firearms, gunpowder, knives, brass and iron ware, pewter, and rum. They had to supply food and drink to their crews and garrisons, pay salaries, maintain forts and factories, and incur all manner of miscellaneous expenditure. They stood to suffer immense losses from fire, tempests, or pirates. A great concern such as the Royal African Company thus failed to make ends meet and finally had to be wound up. Smaller independent traders subsequently seem to have done better, but for them too the slave trade represented a gamble. As K. G. Davies, the historian of the Royal African Company, puts it: "While all seaborne trade in the eighteenth century was risky, the slave trade must have been among the riskiest. The alternations of war and peace in some remote African kingdom could determine the scarcity or glut of Negroes. The local demand for European goods in Africa was liable to fluctuate sharply from year to year and from region to region. Sudden changes in world prices for sugar or rum could make or mar a whole voyage. An outbreak of disease on the dreaded "Middle Passage" could wipe out a fortune in a few days."[27] Finally there was the ever-present threat from competition. Traders from Portugal, Holland, France, England, and even smaller countries tried to outbid one another, so that lesser competitors such as Brandenburg had little chance from the outset. Lastly, it is very difficult to separate the money made in the slave trade from the gains obtained through the purchase of other African goods such as gold, ivory, beeswax, and pepper. In crediting all receipts from sales of the inward cargo to the sale of slaves, many abolitionist writers in the nineteenth century tended to exaggerate the profits from the slave trade. S. Daniel Neumark, an economist, thus concludes that "probably, on balance, the direct returns to the European economy that can be credited to the slave trade *alone* were barely sufficient to cover all costs."[28] Similarly, the importance of the colonial trade to the European economy as a whole can easily be overestimated. Overseas trade accounted for but a fraction of Britain's total commerce. During the eighteenth century, when the slave trade (a highly speculative enterprise), had reached its zenith, the bulk of British trade was carried on with Europe, especially with the countries geographically closest to the British Isles. "Compared with this, the traffic with India, the West Indies and North America was small, and that with Africa insignificant."[29]

Finally we must touch on Marx's theory of primitive accumulation, which raises issues much wider than those connected with the slave trade. Marx, like those early advocates of the slave trade who had praised the traffic as the mainstay of British wealth, was overly preoccupied with the spectacular forms of long-distance commerce. But England's industrial revolution was linked even more closely with im-

vements in technological skills, entrepreneurial expertise, and agricultural pro-
ctivity. The origins of British industrial capital in the eighteenth century were of
e most variegated kinds. (Earlier financiers comprised merchants. But many others
began their respective careers as goldsmiths, corn dealers, or even cattle drovers.)
Many European merchants, planters, and cutthroats made fortunes from the exploitation of the slave traffic, the transatlantic plantations, or the South American gold and
silver mines. Some of this capital certainly helped to finance other economic pursuits.
But the questions remain: how large a share of this "primitive" capital was reinvested
into industry? How much was channelled into unproductive expenditure devoted to
conspicuous consumption and war? How much of this enterprise may actually have
represented a misdirection of economic effort? The Marxian theory does not explain
why some countries, such as Portugal and Spain—not to speak of the slave-trading
states of the Sudan—could not make this primitive accumulation derived from slaving, gold mining, the entrepôt trade, and similar activities fructify into industrial
capital. Instead it was precisely these states which suffered from economic stagnation
while their competitors prospered. At the same time, regions like Rhenish Prussia and
Bohemia, which had never participated in the colonial trade to any extent whatsoever,
managed to build up factories at a remarkable pace during the nineteenth century.

The debate may never be fully resolved. But on balance we believe that the slave
trade and its associated economic interests primarily benefited the transatlantic landowners and a limited section of the commercial bourgeoisie. It also indirectly influenced other economic pressure groups, but it played only a limited part in the
immense industrial and agricultural development that brought about the vast technological and economic superiority attained by Northern Europe over the rest of the
world between the seventeenth and the nineteenth centuries.

NOTES

1. Ronald Cohen, "Slavery in Africa," *Trans-Action,* January to February 1967, p. 45.
2. J. C. Anene "Slavery and the Slave Trade," in Anene and Brown, eds., *Africa in the Nineteenth and Twentieth Centuries,* p. 95.
3. Arthur Tuden "Ila Slavery: Zambia," *Trans-Action,* January to February 1967, pp. 51–52.
4. David McCall, "Slavery in Ashanti: Ghana," *Trans-Action,* January to February, 1967, pp. 55–56.
5. Clough and Cole, *Economic History of Europe,* pp. 259–262.
6. Philip D. Curtin, *The Atlantic Slave Trade: A Census* (Madison, University of Wisconsin Press, 1969).
7. Boxer, *The Golden Age of Brazil,* pp. 43–46.
8. Daniel P. Mannix and Malcolm Cowley, *Black Cargoes: A History of the Atlantic Slave Trade 1518–1865* (New York, 1962), pp. 50–51. See also Philip D. Curtin, *The Image of Africa: British Ideas and Action, 1780–1850* (Madison, 1964).
9. Peter Duignan and Clarence Clendenen, *The United States and the African Slave Trade 1619–1862* (Stanford, 1963), pp. 1–5.
10. Will D. Weatherford and Charles S. Johnson, *Race Relations: Adjustment of Whites and Negroes in the United States* (Boston, 1934), pp. 124–125.

11. K. G. Davies, *The Royal African Company* (London, 1957), p. 152.

12. Mannix and Cowley, *Black Cargoes*, p. 71.

13. C. W. Newbury, "The Slave Coast and the Niger Delta," in Sir Richard Burton, *A Mission to Gelele King of Dahome*, ed., C. W. Newbury (New York, 1966), p. 4.

14. Pierre Verger, *Bahia and the West Coast Trade (1549–1851)* (Ibadan, 1964), p. 24.

15. Ebiegberi Joe Alagoa, *The Small Brave City State: A History of Nembe Brass in the Niger Delta* (Madison, 1964), pp. 11–13. See also the major work of Kenneth Onwuka Dike, *Trade and Politics in the Niger Delta, 1830–1855: An Introduction to the Economic and Political History of Nigeria* (Oxford, 1956).

16. David Birmingham, *Trade and Conflict in Angola: the Mbundu and Their Neighbours under the Influence of the Portuguese, 1483–1790* (Oxford 1966), pp. 156–157.

17. Basil Davidson, *Black Mother: The Years of the African Slave Trade* (Boston, 1961), p. 106.

18. Mannix and Cowley, *Black Cargoes*, p. 119.

19. Mannix and Cowley, pp. 105–106.

20. According to one estimate, the British in 1790, carried 38,000 slaves to America, the French 20,000, the Portuguese 10,000, the Dutch 4000, and the Danes 2000.

21. His estimates are as follows:

16th century: nearly	900,000
17th century	2,750,000
18th century:	7,000,000
19th century: over	4,000,000

See Robert Kuczynski, *Population Movements* (Oxford, 1936), pp. 8–15, quoted by Robert O. Collins, ed., *Problems in African History* (Englewood Cliffs, 1967), pp. 350–352.

22. Davidson, *Black Mother*, p. 80.

23. See the important article by J. D. Fage, "Slavery and the Slave Trade in the Context of West African History," *Journal of African History*, vol. 10, no. 3 (1969), pp. 394–404. This discusses Philip D. Curtin, *The Atlantic Slave Trade: A Census* (Madison, 1969), now the major work on the subject.

24. Karl Marx, *Das Kapital: Kritik der politischen Ökonomie* (Berlin, 1932), p. 694.

25. Eric Williams, *Capitalism and Slavery* (London, 1966), p. 52

26. Duignan and Clendenen, p. 10.

27. Davies, pp. 348–349.

28. S. Daniel Neumark, *Foreign Trade and the Economic Development in Africa: A Historical Perspective* (Stanford, 1964), p. 57.

29. T. S. Ashton, *The Industrial Revolution 1760–1830* (London, 1948), p. 47).

Chapter 25

The Effects of the Slave Trade

THE BLACK IMPACT ON THE NEW WORLD

The record of the slave trade is one of cruelties rarely exceeded in the annals of the world. But the transatlantic migration also helped to enrich the Americas with a vigorous new racial strain and to develop that vast region. The transplanted Negroes were as numerous as a great contemporary European nation.[1] The majority of the black people settled in the West Indies and the tropical parts of Latin America, as we have seen earlier in this chapter.

These immigrants, for the most part, came from the more advanced regions of Africa. The captives comprised within their ranks not only backward people from, say, the remote interior of Angola, but also Mandingo, Yoruba, Hausa, and others possessed of considerable culture. Even the field hands who labored in the plantations were far from being unskilled. They came from societies with a culture considerably more elaborate than that of, say, the Indian aborigines in Brazil or North America. Being skilled farmers, the African slaves were better adjusted to the needs of tropical agriculture than the Indians. They also supplied the New World with all manner of specialized skills. Brazilians for instance, obtained from Africa "mistresses of the house," technicians for their mines, experienced herdsmen for their ranches, and also members of more specialized professions including cloth and soap merchants, schoolmasters, and even priests or men learned in the Koranic traditions.[2] The composition and background of the slave population in the various parts of the New World differed a great deal. Some colonists deliberately mixed the various black races whom they had subjugated in order to prevent concerted risings. Others worried less, and in 1837 a British visitor to Bahia observed that the local blacks: ". . . are the most handsome to be seen in the country; tall men and women, well built, usually intelligent, some of them even being proficient in the Arabic tongue. They have nearly all been imported from the Mina Coast; and not only because of their greater physical and intellectual sturdiness, but also because they are more united among themselves, they show themselves more inclined to movements of revolt than the mixed races of other provinces."[3]

Many slaves, indeed, never became reconciled to their fate, and where circumstances proved favorable they would escape and set up independent communities in the vastness of mountain or jungle country. As early as the sixteenth century, the Spaniards had to cope with these so-called maroons, who ranged up and down the tropical rain forest of Panama and helped any European power willing to fight the Spaniards. Sir Francis Drake, the greatest English seafarer and raider of the time, received invaluable assistance from the maroons, without whose knowledge of the country and of bushcraft he could not have operated in the interior of Panama. The maroons, unlike the whites, became completely adjusted to life in the jungle (helped perhaps by a greater hereditary resistance against tropical disease). The maroons blended African with European culture traits. They hunted game with bow and arrow; they knew the wild fruit of the jungle. They dwelt in well-built settlements protected by ditches and high mudwalls and divided into streets. But they also wore clothes in the Spanish fashion and held the cross in veneration, even though they had no priests and were easily persuaded by Drake to become "Protestants."[4]

Other maroon communities sprang up in the more inaccessible parts of the Caribbean, where escaped Negroes set up independent village communities of their own, sometimes fought the whites and sometimes concluded formal treaties with the Europeans. The so-called "Bush Negroes" in Dutch and French Guiana shook off the slave owners' yoke and established small, independent polities in the inaccessible interior. So did the maroons of Jamaica, who fought long and desperate guerrilla wars against the British. In 1738 they finally managed to conclude a treaty whereby the Crown recognized their de facto independence in the inhospitable mountains of the hinterland. In Mexico the captive blacks, who mostly dwelt in the coastal lowlands, frequently rebelled against their masters. The Negroes, unlike the Indian, could not hope for the king's protection, and the more active spirits among them took recourse to self-help. The best known rising took place during the eighteenth century, near Orizaba. The insurgents fought so well that they obtained their freedom, and were allowed to found their own village, called San Lourenzo de los Negros, under their own rule.[5]

The history of these Negro revolutionary movements in the New World as yet remains to be written. They range all the way from minor outbreaks among maroons to the great slave rising of Haiti in the beginning of the last century. This led to the establishment of an independent black republic in 1804, to which further reference will be made later in the book. The African rebel could make headway in areas where the terrain was exceptionally favorable to guerrillas, or where the climate proved insalubrious to white soldiers at a time when Europeans had no effective remedies to cure malaria and yellow fever. In addition, numbers played an essential role. North

America, for instance, never experienced a successful slave rising because the blacks were too few and the whites too many. In Haiti numbers favored the blacks against the mulattoes and the French. In Brazil the Portuguese maintained their supremacy; but the struggle was hard, and the story is worth telling in some detail.

Brazilians began to import slaves from the sixteenth century onwards. Black people attained such importance that the Portuguese, during the seventeenth century, were able to expel the Dutch from Brazil only by means of a joint Luso-African effort in which the Black Regiment of Henriques Dias won martial fame. The subsequent development of Brazil is no less a story of Euro-African enterprise. African resistance, however, was a permanent factor in Brazilian colonial life. Fugitive slaves established their own settlements, known as *quilombos,* where Africans attempted to recreate their own societies on American soil. The most important of these communities was the Negro republic of Palmares in Pernambuco, which maintained its independence throughout most of the seventeenth century. The Africans had their own monarch known as the *Ganga-Zumba,* who kept court in a great royal enclave, assisted by numerous officers. After bitter fighting, the state of Palmares was finally wiped out (1694). Its destruction marked a milestone in Brazilian history. Had Palmares continued to exist, the Portuguese might well have been confined to the coast, facing not one but a number of independent African states in the backlands of Brazil. The destruction of the Palmares monarchy may have prevented the breakup of Brazil into distinct ethnic components.[6]

Once separatism had failed, black Brazilians on numerous occasions resorted to armed insurrections. The Muslims of Bahia, for instance, proved to be particularly militant men. Blacks also participated in risings that sought neither escape nor aimed at a seizure of power but sought to improve intolerable conditions. During the early nineteenth century black and mulatto people also took part in the various wars of independence that freed Spanish America from the rule of Madrid. In addition, soldiers of color fought in numerous civil wars; indeed many of the struggles that shook Latin America can be hardly understood unless the African factor is taken into consideration.

The man who responded with knife and musket to slavery made one kind of cultural response. But there were others of a more subtle kind. The African impact on the New World helped to produce a host of syncretic cultures that differed widely, not merely from one country to the next but also within different regions of the same territory. In North America, for instance, a Negro's life was very different on the rice plantations of the Carolina coast or in the cotton country of Alabama, from the existence of, say, a Negro employed in a turpentine factory or on a small upland farm.[7]

The rate of acculturation differed in a similar fashion. A field hand on a large plantation usually led a harsh life (though not necessarily a worse one than that of, say, a white redemptioner or a white sailor press ganged into the British navy). Field hands had little opportunity for learning new skills; in this respect there was no difference between a serf exploited on a great estate in Brazil or on a similar establishment in, say, Hispaniola. (Modern research has modified the once widely held belief that slavery in Brazil was essentially milder in nature than elsewhere and that Portuguese people in general were more tolerant of slaves than Northern Europeans.) But in Brazil, where white women were scarce, miscegenation took place on an even greater scale than it did in the French, Spanish, and English colonies. Miscegenation entailed a considerable degree of cultural reciprocity; African influences made a profounder impact on the social and economic institutions of Brazil than on those of English-speaking North America, where Negroes remained in a minority and had to compete with a considerable class of white artisans and small white farmers. But whatever their nationality, all European colonists made use of both skilled and un-skilled Negro labor in their tropical and subtropical possessions. The whites made extensive use of the Negroes' experience; the whites likewise passed on some of their own culture to the slaves.

In addition, all the transatlantic colonies, English as well as Portuguese and Span-ish, gradually acquired a class of free Negroes, former redemptioners whose contracts had expired, blacks legally manumitted by their masters, or even free immigrants from other territories. This group varied greatly in numbers, attainments, and pur-suits, depending on local circumstances. Some became soldiers or frontiersmen; some acquired estates and even slaves of their own. Others became traders, artisans, or even members of the liberal professions. Many of them proved highly adaptable, and their life stories reveal a great deal of personal initiative. Olaudah Equiano, an Ibo enslaved in Africa at a tender age during the eighteenth century and subsequently freed in the New World, thus became proficient in all manner of jobs. He knew something of seamanship; he could work as a barber; he knew how to distill liquor and run a store. He acquired an excellent command of English and compiled what is still a highly readable autobiography in his adopted tongue. He also became a convinced abolition-ist and helped to interpret the cultural heritage of his own people for the benefit of his English readers.[8]

The less tangible effects of the Negro's forcible transplantation into the New World are harder to assess. Discussion is bedevilled by two opposing stereotypes. The oldfashioned view sees the Negro immigrants as a mass of faceless men, stripped of all tradition or individuality, mere human raw material to be shaped at the will of their master. A more recent school of thought tries to make up for these failings by putting special stress on the Negro's personality. In doing so, it sometimes—though not always—descends into a murky mixture of philanthropy and romanticism. A history of limitless suffering, age-old aboriginal contact with nature, a special sense for the numinous and for the deeper rhythms of life have supposedly given black people a more profound and intuitive understanding of nature than is available to white men bred in the materialistic and mechanistic tradition of the West. This interpretation sometimes also assumes that black men have a richer sexuality and a deeper feeling for the rhythm of life than white folk.[9]

We strongly disagree with both interpretations. We regard the "faceless man" school of slavery, according to which black captives were like so many bricks, to be placed into a white-designed structure, as a piece of fantasy. We equally disagree with the folk-soul interpretation, which reminds us of nothing so much as the musings of many German romantics in the nineteenth and twentieth centuries. These theoreti-cians (who never worked the land themselves) nevertheless extolled the virtues of the German peasantry and the beauties of the German soil. They contrasted Germanic spirituality with the shallow, soulless materialism supposedly characteristic of Frenchmen, Jews, and other aliens. We regard this as mystical mishmash. We likewise can make nothing of what strikes us as sexual obscurantism. We merely note in passing than men will often, but quite erroneously, ascribe heightened sexual powers to "outgroups" of any colors whom they hate or fear.

But we are fully persuaded that different Negro cultures did indeed make their impact on the New World. This impact differed greatly in intensity, being greatest in Brazil and the West Indies, but being found wherever Negroes were forced to settle. To prove our point, we should like to give a few illustrative examples.

Africans, for instance, considerably enriched the diet of the New World. Edible plants such as the kidney bean, the banana, and the okra were transferred from Africa to America. Negro cooks taught their masters how to prepare all kinds of new dishes; they also introduced palm oil and malaguetta pepper to the New World.[10] American English to this day reflects the economic impact made by the Negro migration across the Atlantic in African-descended words such as goober (peanut), gumbo (okra), yam (sweet potato), and so forth.

The African also brought with him his music. Music, like dancing, easily crosses linguistic boundaries, and Negro strains have had a profound impact on the musical heritage of the world. As Hubert Herring, a modern specialist on Latin America puts it, "the subtle rhythms that haunt so much of typically Brazilian music today, the simple short melodic line, the repetition of phrases, derive in large part from the chants in the religious rituals of the Sudanese, and from the songs of every occasion of daily life that were so much part of the African tradition." Brazilian composers have drawn heavily on African themes; Brazilian musicians have adapted African percussion instruments to their use; José Mauricio, a Negro priest in the colonial period, was the founder of Brazil's first real school of music.[11] The African cultural heritage had an equally profound effect on the music of North America. American spirituals probably came into being through a blending of European Protestant and African music. Jazz, the most distinctive North American contribution to the world's music, derives its inspiration from the rhythm of African drums, with its vigor and infinite variety.[12]

African slaves likewise carried their dances across the Atlantic. The samba, the national dance of Brazil, derives from the *quizomba,* a wedding dance from Angola, and from the Angola-Congolese dance called the *batuque.* The Cuban rumba is African in its spirit; so are many other Latin American as well as North American dances, such as the "Charleston." the "Blackbottom," the "Buzzard Lope," and the "Ring Shout," some of which are used in present-day gospel movements. Even a well-known American song like Stephen Foster's "Camp-Town Races" has been traced back to a Yoruba tune.

Black men also left their mark on the literature and folklore of the New World. The popular tales and legends of Brazil are, in large part, of African origin. Most North American children are familiar with the tales concerning Uncle Remus or Br'er Rabbit (whose French West Indian cousin goes by the name of *Pé Lapin*). West Indians entertained their youngsters with tales like the Spider stories from Ashanti, which gloried in the Spider's cleverness. They cast their folk wisdom in pithy proverbs of the kind that warned the tactless not to speak of long ears in the donkey's house.

An account either of the folk literature or the more sophisticated literary works produced by Afro-American writers in English, French, Spanish, or Portuguese would fill many volumes. So would an account of black influence on the European languages spoken in the New World. Such a survey would have to range all the way from the creation of independent French and English *patois* in the West Indies to the infiltration of the individual words into English, terms like "tote" (to carry) or "juke" as in "juke box." The musical quality, the tonality, the cadence of American Negro speech is reflected in southern white dialects. The African influence on southern American English was apparently of much greater significance than the Bantu impact on Afrikaans in South Africa.

Negroes similarly played their part in the visual arts. Yoruba artists, for example, decorated the temples of Bahia in Brazil with wooden figures; the churches of Brazil are full of images and other sacred objects fashioned by black artists out of wood, clay, or metal. In the colonial period of Brazil a whole school developed round the mulatto Aleijadinho, a church designer and sculptor of rare ability, while Sebastião, a Negro, received wide acclaim for the manner in which he painted the ceilings of numerous churches in Rio de Janeiro.

Finally, Africans brought their religious beliefs into the New World, where they blended with both Catholic and Protestant traditions. In Brazil the masters often gave official recognition to different ethnic communities among the slaves. Within these "nations," religious fraternities grew up that also played a secular role. The immigrants practised various syncretic cults in which Catholic saints might be worshipped alongside Yoruba deities and Catholic and Yoruba ritual might mingle. A similar process occurred in Haiti, where African folk beliefs were embodied in voodoo practices together with European elements. The fusion of the two apparently resulted in the creation of a new religion of a distinctive national type.[13]

The slave trade, in other words, had the unintended effect of Africanizing the West Indies and parts of the mainland, and in the course of this process many African gods emigrated to the New World, together with their votaries. In parts of the West Indies, Shango (a Yoruba deity, the god of lightning) continued to be propitiated by the sacrifice of a black or white cock or of pigeons. Oshun, mistress of the ocean, received female goats or hens. Dreams, visions, and spirit possession went on to play an important part in the people's life. The spirit world was real to the uneducated. Spirits intervened in real life, so much so that if a man failed in business or incurred a similar misfortune, supernatural trickery on a neighbor's part might be invoked as an explanation. But the sense of supernatural powers also produced protest, and there was a close link between slave rituals and slave risings.[14]

In Protestant America some Negro churches seem to have continued certain African traditions, albeit curiously blended with white Protestant revivalist strains. In the Catholic countries the Negro impact may have been more profound than in the Protestant regions, though this remains a matter of some dispute. Clearly the white impact was bound to be greater in North America, where the blacks were in a minority than, say, in Haiti, where Africans came to form the great majority of the population. According to Roger Bastide, the French scholar quoted above, the impact of Catholic Christianity was also somewhat different in kind. Afro-Catholicism emphasized ritual and collective participation more than mystic beliefs; the inculcation of Christian doctrines was on the whole more superficial than in the Protestant countries. The slaves in North America, on the other hand, acquired a much greater familiarity with the Bible than their brethren in the Latin countries; the Negroes were also quick to see real or assumed parallels between their own situation and that of the Jews in the Old Testament—as demonstrated by their spirituals. The details of this cultural and religious debate remain to be resolved. It is, however, clear that cultural assimilation was a two-way process and that Negro strains have decidedly influenced many of the emergent cultures of the New World.

ECONOMIC AND SOCIAL EFFECTS ON AFRICA

"Our common goods here for a prime slave . . . up the river Sharbrow in the year 1755 . . . stands thus" recorded an English slave dealer in his journal, "4 guns, 2 kegs powder, 1 piece blew baft (a coarse cotton material from the East Indies), 1 kettle, 2 brass pans, 1 duzn. knives, 2 basons, 2 iron bars, 1 head beads, 50 flints. 1 silk handk."[15] Commodities such as these were imported into Africa in large quantities and helped to occasion considerable changes in many indigenous economies. Guns and gunpowder were of value not only in war but in the chase. Hunters equipped with firearms could shoot "for the pot" more easily than their ancestors had been able to do with bows and lances. In regions where elephants were liable to trample over the crops, villagers with guns could drive away these great animals with less peril and trouble than their more old-fashioned neighbors who depended on fiery torches and spears. Knives and hatchets proved a boon to artisans and cultivators alike. Textiles supplied a valuable article of everyday use. Iron bars supplied smiths with the raw material for their craft. Imported salt provided an indispensible article of cookery. In many parts of Africa the indigenous people were therefore enmeshed—however tenuously—into a world-wide network of trade. Many of the so-called "traditional" economies, which anthropologists described in later generations, had for a long time been affected by foreign intercourse and had benefited to some extent from international exchange and the operation of the market.

Foreign contacts also enriched the Africans' larder. West Africa was not well supplied with native fruits and green vegetables. The European garrisons stationed in West Africa had to supply these deficiencies. Every fort maintained a large garden to grow European salad plants, cabbages, and cauliflowers from imported seed, as well as fruit trees introduced mainly from tropical Asia and America. Many of these crops can first be traced to the Portuguese, though some appear to have been introduced later, chiefly by the Dutch. Among the earliest of these plants were the lemon, the sugar cane, and melons, which could be obtained in the Mediterranean. They were probably brought to Africa via the Portuguese-owned islands of Madeira and São Tomé. The orange, tamarind, banana, and coconut came from the Indian Ocean. The pineapple, pawpaw (papaya), and guava derived from the Americas. Europeans acclimatized these crops in their gardens and helped to pass them on to their African neighbors.[16]

Danish cultivators, among others, made deliberate attempts to create agricultural plantations in their West African possessions. In this respect the Danes appear to have been more successful than either the British farther west on the Gold Coast or the French in Senegal. In 1809 Christian Schionning, a Dane, had 40,000 coffee shrubs on his estate at the foot of the Akwapim Scarp, and a further 100,000 plants in an adjoining nursery.[17] The dissemination of such crops was a slow process. This may be inferred from the fact that in 1692 a coconut grove near Accra formed a landmark to seamen who called it the "Spanish cavalry." Palms also seem to have been rare on other parts of the coast now fringed with them. Also, the mango, avocado, and other fruits that have become quite common since seem to have been unknown until the nineteenth century.[18]

The Europeans (and possibly also the Arabs) likewise carried essential subsistence crops to Africa, most of them of American Indian origin. These included maize, now an article of major importance to Africa. Apparently maize did not quickly become a popular food. As late as 1784 the Fanti grew it only for sale to Europeans or to Africans living near the forts. In contrast, the groundnut or peanut, of American derivation, soon became widespread. Cassava or manioc, the present staple food of many African communities, was probably introduced to Africa by the Portuguese, who brought it from Brazil to their stations in Africa, all the way from Elmina in present-day Ghana to Mogadishu in Somalia. The plant was first acclimatized around the mouth of the Congo and from there spread all over Central Africa. Manioc was probably taken to the upper Guinea coast at the same time it was taken to the Congo, but it became established in indigenous agriculture there much more slowly than in the south. It was almost certainly brought to the Portuguese stations in East Africa at a later time than to the west.[19]

Other plants owing their spread to the transoceanic trade included the prickly pear or Indian fig, sisal, and aloe, as well as tobacco; all these were first developed in America and formed part of the great agricultural heritage that the Indians bequeathed to the rest of the world.

These gains were bought at a terrible price, and no balance sheet can ever present the full debt account of the slave traffic. Some historians have ascribed the relative cultural backwardness of sub-Saharan Africa to the ravages of the traffic. The commerce, according to their argument, deprived Africa of countless able-bodied workers; it perverted or disrupted indigenous societies; it also created an atmosphere of violence, debauchery, and uncertainty that militated against all economic progress. As Anthony Benezet, an eighteenth-century writer, puts it in the forceful language characteristic of the abolitionist literature of his time:

Instead of making use of the superior knowledge, with which the Almighty, the common parent of mankind, had favoured them, to strengthen the principle of peace and good will in the breasts of the incautios Negroes; the Europeans have, by their bad example, led them into excess of drunkenness, debauchery and avarice; whereby every passion of corrupt nature being inflamed, they have been easily prevailed upon to make war, and captivate one another; as well to furnish means for the excess they had been habituated to, as to satisfy the greedy desire of gain in their profligate employers; who to this intent have furnished them with prodigious quantities of arms and amunition. Thus they have been hurried into confusion, disstress and all the extremities of temporal misery.[20]

Benezet's description contained some truth. But not all African communities were equally affected. The chief sufferers were the weaker and more scattered tribes, often those not yet supplied with muskets. As the gunpowder frontier gradually moved inland, the erstwhile victims would, however, acquire firearms and in turn prey on their neighbors, so that the impact of the traffic was very uneven. The slave trade helped to strengthen the great West African states such as Oyo and Dahomey. Indeed, the most impressive development of the seventeenth and eighteenth centuries was the growth of African states just inland from the coastlands and the shift of West Africa's economic center of gravity away from the Sudan toward the Atlantic shore.[21]

In a previous section we have already referred to the biological losses Africans sustained as a result of the transatlantic slave trade. The traffic must have inflicted tremendous casualties on its unfortunate victims. But the total social effects of these casualties are not easy to assess. The ravages of the transatlantic commerce extended over some four centuries. Their incidence was uneven. They did not lead to wholesale depopulation. As J. D. Fage points out, nearly 80 percent of the slaves exported in the 1780s derived from the region between the Gold Coast to the Cameroons. If the Atlantic slave trade had caused serious depopulation, the loss of manpower should have been most clearly evident in this region. But the available figures do not show any such results. On the contrary, these West African lands are as thickly settled as any in Africa.[22]

Economists have arrived at similar conclusions. S. Daniel Neumark calculates that even if the population of West Africa amounted to no more than 20,000,000 at the height of the traffic—a very conservative estimate—the average annual loss was at the most 0.5 percent. The slave trade must have reduced population densities in some areas. But it is still not certain that a higher level of economic development would have been attained in the absence of the traffic. What may be an optimum population under one set of technological and economic conditions may be either above or below the optimum under another.[23] Migration, one might add, does not necessarily impede development. During the nineteenth century, for instance, some 19,000,000 people left Great Britain; but this was a period of unparalleled economic growth in the United Kingdom. In Africa population densities may also have been kept down by unfavorable geographical and climatic conditions, as well as by political instability that had nothing to do with the commerce and that also plagued regions unaffected by the trade (such as early nineteenth-century Zululand). Some authorities have accordingly even speculated whether the ghastly commerce did not at times play the role of more peaceful migration to happier lands, relieving pressure on scanty means of subsistence for those who remained.

Such theorizing is highly problematical. But we can be certain that the *absence* of the traffic did not necessarily make for a greater degree of economic development or cultural maturity. The kingdom of the Barotse (Lozi) in what is now Zambia was not much involved in the slave trade. The Lozi were geographically far removed from the main centers of the trade, and they were anxious to bring people into the fertile Zambezi Valley, rather than to export their manpower. But Barotseland's cultural attainments were inferior to those of the great West African kingdoms that played such a dominant part in the commerce. Similarly, the Matabele of southern Africa did not deal in slaves. They raided their neighbors but preferred to assimilate their captives within their own community rather than sell them abroad. But the Matabele did not succeed in progressing beyond a fairly simple pastoral economy, while their victims suffered as much or more than they would have done had they been exposed to the depredations of slave commerce. We consider, therefore, that writers like Benezet seriously overstated their case. Their conclusions may well have been valid for the more backward and less populated parts of Africa, including Angola, and later on many regions of East Africa. Their findings are not, however, generally to be applied to the bulk of West Africa which—in purely *economic* terms—probably gained as much as it lost from the transatlantic trade.

The wider social effects of the traffic are even harder to assess. The commerce certainly altered the traditional balance of power in many indigenous communities, especially perhaps among matrilineal peoples. Among matrilineal peoples such as the Yao of what is now Malawi, the husband exercised little authority over his wife and his children. Married women and their offspring were subject, above all, to the discipline exerted by the wife's elder brother. Under traditional arrangements, the system made for social equality. The eldest living brother would try to build up power by looking after his sisters and their offspring. But younger brothers and maternal nephews would compete with the eldest living brother for followers, and villages would break up into smaller communities. The slave trade introduced an entirely new factor. An ambitious chief who acquired slave wives by purchase or raiding upset the accustomed ways. His mates lacked a recognized social status in their master's village. The concubine and her offspring were totally dependent on their lord. Slave owners acquired direct authority over their slave children, who came to address their master as *ambuje* or grandfather. Slave owners, in other words, were thus able to strengthen their immediate following in a way that would have been impossible under the older dispensation. Villages tended to grow in size, and among the Yao the slave traffic clearly contributed to the emergence of greater territorial chiefdoms.[24]

We have drawn this example from Central Africa, a region exposed to the Muslim rather than to the Christian slave trade. But the Atlantic slave trade is likely to have occasioned similar effects among matrilineal peoples in other parts of Africa. Foreign exchange—the point bears repeating—supplied rulers with new revenue, no matter whether the chiefs dealt with Arabs, Englishmen, or Portuguese. Many African potentates either took part in the traffic directly or they benefited from the commerce through levies, customs, duties, and other imposts. Local dignitaries on the West African coast also charged rent from white men for the right to trade. This income provided black lords with a means to increase their power. The black monarchs remained "distributor kings." They might control the wealth of their respective countries; but they could not accumulate riches to any very great extent. By and large they continued to give their surplus to their followers; they invested their revenue in political power rather than in more productive enterprises.

The slave trade did not, therefore, give rise to new methods of production in Africa. African craftsmen in any case could not easily compete with European factory workers. African technicians could not rival the skills of their more advanced contemporaries in Europe. African smiths could not outsell goods made in Birmingham, England. African weavers could not undercut the cotton goods of Lancashire. Indeed, the only West African communities that exported manufactures on any considerable scale were the cities of Hausaland on the western flank of Bornu. The artisans of Katsina, Kano, and Zaria, for instance, were renowned for their skills in weaving, dyeing, leatherwork, glass making, and fashioning metal. The Sudanic towns, however, looked northward, to the great caravan routes that radiated across the Sahara to Tripoli and Ghadames, and then on to Tunis.[25] They exerted but little influence on the Negro states of the southern forest belt. Indeed, the slave trade, as we have seen, helped to shift West Africa's center of economic gravity from the Sudanic interior to the littoral, and the transatlantic commerce possibly helped to diminish the relative importance of traditional craft industries.

The states of the woodland belt involved in the Christian slave trade developed what might be called a proto-middle class, including African slave vendors as well as indigenous agents of European firms (many of them mulattoes). Nevertheless, there was no bourgeoisie in the European sense. Wealth meant the ownership of consumer goods. Slaves were generally the most profitable form of investment, and all they bought in return were more consumer goods. Chiefs and wealthy commoners alike used their riches in conspicuous consumption or as a means to gain more clients and added status. Hence there was no capital formation in the Western meaning of the term.

The members of the proto-middle class tended to be reabsorbed again into traditional society, even those who had been sent to Europe for their education. The only exception was to be found in the city states of the Niger Delta, where traders acquired great political power as heads of "Houses" (a type of social organization discussed in previous sections). Even so, the "House" system was largely based on the customary structure of political organization. Far from collapsing, the system proved resilient and adaptive enough to prevent the formation of a modern bourgeoisie.[26]

THE POLITICAL EFFECTS OF THE TRANSATLANTIC SLAVE TRADE: THE KONGO, LUBA, LUNDA, AND BEMBA

The impact of the slave trade varied a good deal from region to region. Many parts of African were little affected by the transatlantic commerce; the customers of the New World mainly derived their human merchandise from the west coast, from the Gambia to the Bight of Benin, and from the regions north and south of the Congo mouth. During the nineteenth century the main focus of the trade shifted to the Slave Coast and the Niger delta, so that not all parts of West Africa suffered equally at the same time. In addition, a third but much smaller source of slaves was found on the east coast south of Cape Delgado, from where captives were shipped round the Cape of Good Hope to America. Exact statistics are, however, hard to come by and even harder to evaluate; hence a great deal of additional work remains to be done in the field.

The effects of the slave trade on the African societies involved in the traffic are even more difficult to assess. Much depended on the internal cohesion of the participant communities. Well-organized peoples could, so to speak, take the strain, while weaker ones succumbed. Equally important was the policy of the local white partners in the commerce. The commandants of European forts on the west coast had small ambitions and scantier resources. The Portuguese in Angola, on the other hand, commanded a relatively large military establishment supplemented by great forces of black auxiliaries. They were the only whites who took an active part in the business of catching slaves as well as buying them. They accordingly carried out a much more aggressive policy than the British, Dutch, and Frenchmen on the Guinea coast, and Angola was in some ways like a great African slave-dealing kingdom.

In addition, geographical factors counted a great deal. The states of the interior were shielded from direct pressure on the part of the Europeans but benefited from the trade as suppliers or middlemen. Distance, however, might involve a law of diminishing returns. Tribes that were geographically too remote or politically too weak to take their share in the gun trade suffered great military disadvantages. They tended to become the victims of their better–armed neighbors, or at any rate to experience a decline in their relative influence.

The impact of the slave trade on the indigenous states of Africa remains a matter of dispute. One school of historians attributes tremendous importance to the traffic in human beings in the creation of the great forest states of West Africa. According to their interpretation, the arms and revenue derived from the trade enabled Benin or Dahomey to expand at their neighbor's expense and build up powerful empires. Similarly, the destruction of these states is ascribed to moral decay from within and to destruction of the slave trade by pressure from without.

Recently other historians have challenged some of these conclusions. They have argued that the wide-spread, but little documented exchange of food between hunters, cultivators, and fisherman has been of greater importance to African economic history than the more spectacular long-distance traffic in slaves and gold. Some also believe that the effects of slave wars have been exaggerated by European missionary and humanitarian opinion, that European imperialists had a natural interest in painting a dark picture of precolonial Africa and that conflicts such as the Yoruba wars of the nineteenth century did not produce a general holocaust. Wars between African states, moreover, did not necessarily derive from disputes about commerce, though such disagreements may have further envenomed diplomatic relations between hostile communities.

Even in so far as the slave trade nourished wars by providing soldiers with imported guns and ammunition, the commerce in human merchandise did not by itself necessarily create the political issues that had created the need for foreign-made weapons in the first place. In all probability, the traffic in guns allowed traditional chiefs, or even upstart warlords, to arm their retinue with more effective weapons, giving them considerable advantages over the ordinary villagers. Common peasants could still fashion their own bows and lances. But they could not manufacture muskets to rival the weapons of more professional soldiers. Among the Yoruba, for example, military specialization was encouraged not only by the challenge of troubled times but by the changing nature of warfare. From an army consisting of mounted men and levies armed with homemade arms, the Yoruba forces gradually turned into infantry armed mainly with muskets. Cavalry declined as Fulani conquerors in the savannah belt cut off the supply of horses from the north. The Yoruba warriors learned how to fire their guns accurately; they developed new tactics of war, and they taught these skills to young recruits through a process of apprenticeship. Every successful war chief built up his own clientage of followers in search of booty and fame. The war leaders became increasingly important in Yoruba politics and often clashed with the traditional civil authorities.[27] The importation of fire arms thus gave an impetus to military specialization of labor, whereby rulers with an adequate surplus surrounded themselves with a professional or semiprofessional class of privileged warriors. The musket did not, however, initiate this process, which seems to have begun in many of the more advanced African states long before the introduction of the pistol and the blunderbuss.

On the basis of the existing literature, we ourselves do not as yet feel qualified to arrive at a definitive conclusion in this matter. We surmise that the slave trade tended to benefit the strong and to injure the weak and that it always accelerated existing social trends. Thus kingdoms already in the ascendant derived further benefit from foreign commerce. States suffering from internal dissensions were wrecked. Space prevents us from documenting the effects of the traffic for each part of Africa. We shall select two specific areas, the kingdom of the Kongo and the regions to the south, and the forest states of the west.

THE KONGO

The Kongo monarchy, it seems, was largely wrecked after an initial period of prosperity. It was situated south of the Congo estuary, in a region strategically vulnerable to Portuguese pressure. As we have seen in a previous section, the Kongo monarchs could not cope with internal instability, and when they took up arms against the Portuguese they were unable to prevail. In the early 1660s war broke out with Portugal over the possession of reputed gold mines situated in a province over which the Kongo king had little control. In 1665 a mixed Portuguese-African force encountered the army of Kongo, which, for its part, also contained a white Portuguese contingent. The Kongolese were defeated and António I, their sovereign, was wounded, captured, and slain.[28] The Kongo state, already in a weakened condition, never recovered from this defeat. Its subsequent history is a confused tale of struggles between rival claimants to the throne and between warring provinces.

In the sixteenth century the Kongo had been a united kingdom that raided slaves among the petty states of Mbundu in Angola. But when the kingdom decayed the wheel came full circle. Angola was now held together by a strong colonial administration, and it was the Kongo that became a raiding ground for slave raiders from the south.

Portuguese pressure accelerated the breakdown of the kingdom, for when the Portuguese wanted slaves, they made war. But the disintegration of the Kongo was not caused by Portuguese influence alone and had already started long before António's death. The Kongolese had black as well as white enemies. During the latter part of the sixteenth century the country had already been ravaged by Jaga raiders, and the *mani kongo* had relied on Portuguese aid. But above all, the people of the Kongo were incapable of coping with internal factionalism. By 1700 the various princes descended from the numerous polygamous marriages within the royal line had become so numerous that they formed a social class of their own, the *infantes,* who struggled between one another for appointments and power. The royal house, once closely knit, split into small factions, each led by strong personalities supported by their kinsmen and armed followers. Every group fought against every other; alliances would be formed against a common enemy, but these soon broke up, to be replaced by yet another shifting constellation.[29] Internal strife did not cease with a simple victory of one group over another; royal power was not reconsolidated, and there was chronic instability. In this respect Kongo resembled earlier African kingdoms that had not been involved in the slave trade, but had both outgrown their size, and failed to solve the problem of how to settle disputes over succession to the crown within the framework of a polygamous kinship system.

The breakup of the Kongo state contributed to the rise of the first Afro-Christian revolutionary creed recorded in modern history. A young woman of aristocratic descent, known as Donna Beatrice to the Portuguese and as Kimpa Vita to the Kongolese, founded a popular church that appears already to have had the characteristics of subsequent millenarian protest movements of the nineteenth and twentieth centuries.

We shall make further reference to Kimpa Vita's doctrines in the last chapter of this work when we discuss millenarian prophecy. Suffice it to say at this point that Kimpa Vita believed herself to be inspired by St. Anthony. (She may well have been a spirit medium, familiar with apparitions from an early age.) According to Kimpa Vita, Jesus had been born a black man; Kongo was the Holy Land, and the ancient Kongo monarchy would one day be restored in all its glory. She foresaw a Messianic Age, when the earth would change into gold and when the true believers would inherit the white man's riches. She tried to Africanize Christianity and set up a popular church, which acquired great political influence. Kimpa Vita, however, backed the wrong horse in the dynastic struggles of the Kongo. King Pedro, the reigning monarch, received support from Capuchin missionaries against the pretender backed by Kimpa Vita. "The prophetess was captured, condemned and burnt as a heretic."[30] Vita Kimpa stood for a revolutionary creed of blackness, but she put her trust in some miraculous cataclysm that never occured. Some popular millenarian traditions survived in the Congo, but "Antonism" never became a political force of permanent consequence.

LUBA, LUNDA, AND BEMBA

In the more distant interior, the effects of the trade in slaves and muskets was of a different kind. The old order did not collapse. There was no talk of prophets or salvation. Instead the importation of guns seems to have given an impetus to traditional empire building. Muskets provided monarchs with weapons that were usually more efficient than the arms manufactured by their subjects. Trade enabled successful chiefs to reward their followers with goods as well as political office and thereby contributed to the consolidation of stronger kingdoms.

In the Congolese hinterland, for instance, the advent of foreign commerce caused considerable political change. During the sixteenth century—or perhaps even earlier —invaders known as the *Balopwe* had entered the vast region of the upper Lualaba and north of the Katanga lakes. Here they founded an empire known as the Luba kingdom. Luba emigrants subsequently penetrated further west and established their rule over the Lunda people. The Lunda in turn made further conquests, and in doing so they may have been helped by firearms brought in by Umbundu traders in exchange for slaves. The possession of guns and the expanding commerce with the west coast probably strengthened the Lunda rulers (known by the title of Mwata Yamvo), who built up a powerful state machinery, complete with an elaborate hierarchy of officials and a complex ritual.

Not all the princes of the royal blood, however, could find suitable offices.[31] Many of these dignitaries thus set out with their followers to found new dependencies. These states gradually became independent of Mwata Yamvo's direct control as the conquerors intermarried with their subjects and the links with Katanga weakened. The Mwata Yamvo, however, generally retained a kind of ritual suzerainty, and the Lunda between them continued to represent a powerful political force.

One of the most important of these new states was the kingdom of Kazembe on the Luapula River, founded by Lunda invaders sometime during the eighteenth century. The Lunda had acquired blunderbusses from foreign traders; they were also knowledgeable in the art of building field fortifications. Hence they enjoyed a decisive military superiority over the various indigenous peoples and founded a powerful new monarchy. Kazembe traded with the Portuguese on the west coast through African intermediaries. He also established commercial contacts with the Muslims on the east coast and later with the Portuguese in Mozambique. Kazembe's might rested on his command over the fertile Luapula Valley and on his strategic position in the inland trade. Kazembe ruled over a great stockaded agro-town on the Luapula. He trafficked with the Portuguese in Angola through the good offices of Mwato Yamvo. Also, by the end of the eighteenth century, Yao traders kept him in touch with the Arabs in Zanzibar. Kazembe was able to exercise a very autocratic rule; his kingdom greatly impressed foreign visitors like Dr. F. J. M. de Lacerda e Almeida, a Brazilian scholar and administrator of note who managed to make his way into the interior in the late 1790s.[32]

A kindred people to the Lunda were the warlike Bemba, of Luba origin. Bemba tradition states that the tribe became separated from the Lunda and Bisa people, when Chitimukulu (Kitimukulu), the Bemba captain, was killed by the Bisa with a poisoned arrow. The Bemba then avenged their chief's death upon his slayers and extended their power at the expense of the Bisa and other Bantu tribes, such as the Mambwe in what is now the dry bushland of northeastern Zambia. An early Portuguese account, dating from the beginning of the nineteenth century, states that "they live by pillage and the chase . . . The weapons they use are bows, arrows, axes, and some have spears, but these are not often used. In their wars they always procure a surprise attack, but this is put in without discipline and without any particular tactics . . . I saw no manufactures among them, and the instruments and tools which they use are either pillaged or bought from other tribes. . . ."[33] Later on, however, the Bemba acquired firearms from abroad (including discarded British army muskets). The Bemba were thus in a position to raid their neighbors for slaves; they sold their captives in exchange for guns, gunpowder, and cloth; their main suppliers were Muslims from the east rather than the Portuguese. The states of northeastern Zambia, in other words, formed a kind of commercial crossroad, where the advancing gunpowder frontiers from the east and west coasts of Africa merged into a single trading system.

THE POLITICAL EFFECTS OF THE TRANSATLANTIC SLAVE TRADE: WEST AFRICA

THE FOREST STATES OF WEST AFRICA

The effects on the forest states of West Africa were equally complex. The West African rain forest zone produced a civilization of its own, distinguished by a number of peculiar features. The peoples of Oyo, Benin, Dahomey, and Ashanti all had a similar cultural background. They practiced ancestor worship and these cults were used by each of the original immigrant groups as a means to bind many separate tribal groups into united nations. The authority of the rulers derived to a considerable extent from their position as spiritual heirs of the original conquerors, who were revered as the founding fathers of the nation. The forest zone as a whole yielded a considerable surplus of food; there was a good deal of labor specialization, and all the four nations mentioned above attained a high degree of skill in the plastic arts, especially the casting of figures in bronze and brass.

According to the historical school represented by Professor Fage, the slave trade made a profound impact on these countries. The European demand for slaves caused Benin, Dahomey, and Ashanti to become powers comparable in military strength, organization, and extent of territory with the great savannah states of the western Sudan. The slave trade was also an element of some importance in the expansion of Oyo. In the long run, however, the traffic tended to bring about the corruption and ultimate decay of these countries.[34] Life became cheap, and in many African kingdoms the ruling classes were probably demoralized. Human sacrifice had of course been practiced in West Africa long before any Europeans made their way to the shores of Africa. But the enormous growth of the commerce provided increasing numbers of victims, and kingdoms like Benin and Dahomey became increasingly wedded to fierce and bloodthirsty rituals that were intended to strengthen the religious cohesion of the state. At the same time the traffic in human beings generally tended to solidify monarchical power. Slaves brought profits to distributor kings. Profits—runs the argument—enabled the sovereign to purchase more muskets, raise more soldiers, and acquire more followers. Larger armies allowed the sovereign to gain control of additional trade routes, seize more territory, and engage in even more extensive campaigns. The vicious circle of war thus continued, until the gunpowder state outgrew its optimum size, or until it encountered a stronger or better-placed opponent.

This interpretation is being either supplemented or challenged by historians who place less emphasis on the importance of foreign trade in the creation of these African kingdoms. These scholars argue that the process of state building in the West African forest zone had begun long before the first Portuguese galleon had cast anchor on the shores of West Africa. They are concerned with the role of domestic exchange, the part played by varying systems of kinship, by the development of specialized ritual, military, and governmental skills. They point out how more powerful rulers created markets, devised currencies, managed trade, levied tolls, tribute and other imposts, in return for protection against the real and imagined dangers of the present world and the hereafter. African empires would have continued to grow, even if no European sailor had ever set foot on the African littoral.[35]

We do not consider ourselves competent to give an all-embracing answer to these questions. We are convinced, however, that there can be no unitary explanation for so complex a process as the creation of African states. Conditions differed greatly from age to age and place to place. Probably these kingdoms did not originate through trade alone, but they tended to enhance their power by commerce and conquest abroad.

BENIN AND THE NIGER DELTA STATES.

One of the most powerful states on the west coast was Benin in what is now Nigeria. Benin owed its origin to settlers from Ife to which previous reference has already been made. Sometime in the fifteenth century Benin became independent from Ife, and the extent of the empire was markedly enlarged under a series of great rulers, including Ewuare the Great (ca. 1440–1473), Ozolua (ca. 1481–1504) and Esigie (ca. 1504–1550). Benin built up a considerable seaport at Gwato on the Atlantic shore, an entrepôt for the slave traffic. During the seventeenth century, Benin armies fanned out both eastward and westward to secure control of as much of the coast line as they could. Benin, though a littoral state, was powerful enough to avoid the fate of the Kongo monarchy, though territorial expansion perforce led to a considerable degree of decentralization. Benin boatbuilders constructed huge canoes fitted with imported European cannon, and these provided a means for extending Benin's power inland and northward up the Niger River. Benin influence finally extended as far as Idah, now in the northern region of Nigeria. The Ibo of the interior were raided periodically, often from hilltop fortresses; the captives were then taken to the nearest river station, packed into canoes, sold and resold by numerous middlemen before reaching the holds of European ships.[36]

According to this interpretation, the slave trade thus "made" the Benin empire. John D. Graham, a revisionist historian, has reassessed the evidence, however, and come to different conclusions. He points out that the expansion of Benin began long before white people ever sold muskets on the Guinea coast. According to his interpretation, the Binis made war on their neighbor in order to extort tribute. In his view, moreover, the slave trade in Benin proper was never large in absolute numbers. The Binis exported gold, pepper, and ivory, as well as dyed cotton cloth, jasper stones, leopard skins, palm oil, and other products. The wider area known as "Benin" (that is to say the territory between Bonny and Lagos), should be distinguished sharply from Benin proper (a limited area at present demarcated by the Benin divisional boundary within Nigeria). The peoples of Benin were often at war with one another; there were numerous struggles between rival claimants to the throne, between neighboring communities, or between the *oba* (the Bini overlord) and recalcitrant subjects unwilling to pay the required tribute. None of these conflicts was necessarily linked to the slave traffic; moreover, the extent of depopulation brought about by these clashes has been much exaggerated by traditional historians.[37]

Whatever the extent of the slave trade, its influence was never sufficiently great to enable the monarchs of Benin to obtain a monopoly of firearms or to set up a highly centralized state. Swamps and jungles impeded communications between the capital and the more distant regions. The outlying areas in time reinforced their economic position by trading directly with the whites. They refused to pay further tolls and tributes to Benin, and the might of the *obas* began to wane.

One of the first lands to fall away from Benin was the Niger delta. Much of the land was covered by mangrove swamps. The country could not support an extensive agriculture, and many of its people turned to fishing and salt panning, eking out a precarious living by trading their surplus with the Ibo farmers of the forest area. The arrival of the Europeans provided new commercial opportunities. The fishing villages developed into city states each with its own squadrons of monster canoes armed with imported brass cannon. The delta towns developed an extensive trading network, but no one community ever succeeded in unifying the whole coast under a single government. There were numerous wars, especially between New Calabar and Bonny, but these conflicts did not seriously diminish their prosperity. By the end of the eighteenth century, their ruling classes imported all manner of goods from Europe: liquor, mirrors, pictures, silver, cutlery, china, silk, prefabricated houses from Britain, as well as huge quantities of muskets, powder, and cannon. As Professor Flint puts it, "unlike Benin, the city-states of the delta did not eventually collapse under the impact of the trade which made them rich. In this respect they were unique, and the explanation lies in their extraordinary adaptability and willingness to come to terms with new conditions. Even when the slave trade was finally abolished . . . they rapidly adapted their commercial supremacy to the new conditions of the nineteenth century."[38]

THE YORUBA, DAHOMEY, AND ASHANTI

The development of these states left the older Yoruba empire of Oyo in an unfavorable position. Oyo's center of gravity was situated on the edge of the savannah where its formidable cavalry could operate with ease. Oyo at first looked northward to the Hausa trade and the commerce of the Sahara. From the sixteenth century, however, Oyo armies also began to march southward. By the end of the seventeenth century Oyo had reduced the seaport of Porto Novo to tributary status, and by the eighteenth century the Oyo king, known as the *alafin,* ruled over a great Yoruba empire that linked, so to speak, the forest to the savannah zone. The expansion of Oyo primarily depended on military means; imported guns further strengthened Oyo's might, but again the slave trade was probably a contributory more than a primary factor in Oyo's military supremacy.

Oyo, like Benin, however, overextended its military resources, and provincial chiefs began to defy the power of the monarch. From the beginning of the eighteenth century, moreover, the might of Oyo was increasingly challenged by the rise of Dahomey. The people of Dahomey, like those of the smaller states of Whydah (Ouida, Hueda) and Allada (Ardra) spoke languages belonging to the Twi branch of Kwa. These various communities were in no sense a united people. The western group (known today as Ewe) never developed kingdoms of any size. The eastern group however, seems to have been influenced by Yoruba notions of governance. In addition they began to engage in overseas trade, so that the various Twi states developed on very different lines.

The most powerful Twi state was Dahomey, whose capital was situated about fifty miles north of the port of Whydah. By the end of the seventeenth century Whydah and Allada alike had begun to deal with the whites, and European merchants who set up posts at Whydah. Dahomey at first had to conduct its traffic with the coast through middlemen. By the time of King Agaja (1708–1727), the rulers of Dahomey realized that they could make even greater profits by selling their captives directly to the white men at the coast; Dahomey secured control over Whydah as well as Porto Novo, and thereby successfully overcame the disadvantages of its inland position.

The kings of Dahomey were regarded as of divine origin. They also occupied a central place in the economy.[39] They received tribute from his subjects and foreign traders. This revenue was redistributed among the high officials in the form of presents. The subordinate dignitaries in turn gave presents to their followers, so that the nations as a whole had a stake in the economic activities of the monarchy. The power of the state rested on formidable armed hosts, including a professional corps of amazons. The military forces engaged in regular slave wars, so that the army, so to speak, paid for its own upkeep. The king also controlled extensive agricultural holdings. Every high official was a plantation owner, and the monarchy attempted to control the production of crops in accordance with the presumed national needs. The redistributive system of the palace economy depended on an extensive administrative and planning apparatus. A count was taken of the population and of the number of workers in each occupational category. There was even a census of livestock and other resources. These censuses enabled the king to maintain a comprehensive system of taxation.

Dahomey used its income to equip its armies with firearms from the south. The Dahomeans gradually acquired thereby a decisive military superiority over the cavalrymen of Oyo and succeeded in freeing their country from Oyo's overlordship. Dahomey also attempted to expand its power to the coast. Historians still differ in their interpretation of Dahomean foreign policy. According to one school, the Dahomean's "drive to the south" was designed to cut out the middlemen and enable Dahomeans to participate more effectively in the slave trade. I. A. Akinjogbin, an African historian, has recently put forward a different interpretation. According to Akinjogbin, outstanding Dahomey rulers like King Agaja in fact wanted to discourage the slave trade, a fickle export business on which no permanent prosperity could be built. Agaja would apparently have preferred commerce in tropical cash crops. It was the Europeans' increasing demand for "black ivory" and also Oyo ambitions to dominate the slave coast that obliged Agaja to sanction slave trading. Even then, he contrived to make slaving a state monopoly, not merely to maintain his own revenue but to prevent the worst abuses of the traffic.[40]

Be that as it may, Dahomey attained a considerable degree of political cohesion. The monarchies became more powerful than hitherto; chiefs were appointed to high office by reason of their ability rather than their ancestry. Loyalty to the throne took precedence over loyalty to the extended family or to other local bonds.

Dahomey became totally independent from Oyo about 1818, by which time the empire of Oyo had fallen into a sorry state. The growth of trade with the Atlantic littoral tended to strengthen the coastal communities which became ever more anxious to assert their independence. The rise of Fulani power in the north presented an even greater menace to Oyo. Disaster occurred when an Oyo general called in the Fulani to strengthen his own position against his suzerain. The Fulani duly came, but quickly thrust aside the rebel, and established a new emirate centering on Ilorin. By the middle of the nineteenth century, Dahomey was a powerful military state. But the Yoruba nation, which had taken so important a part in the slave trade, was in a state of complete disarray, a victim of its lack of unity and of the ravages occasioned by the traffic.

Further west on the Gold Coast, the political effects of the transatlantic trade were equally profound. The coastal region was divided between a large number of small states, all of which struggled against one another for control of the commercial routes. Some of the fishing villages on the Atlantic coast developed into thriving ports like Sekondi, Kommenda, and Kormantin, and by the seventeenth century they possessed a class of skilled workers employed by white men as carpenters, builders, and cask makers, as well as many indigenous merchants. No coastal state was able to dominate its neighbors.

In the interior, political development followed a different course. The forest region of what is now Ghana contained a number of small states peopled by the Akan (members of a group of people collectively known as Kwa, who range from the Kru of what is now Liberia to the Ibo of what is now eastern Nigeria). The Akan communities developed a profitable trade in gold and also in kola nuts and other rain forest products. They dealt with Mande and Hausa merchants from the north; in addition the Akan expanded their trade to the Atlantic coast, where the Dutch sold great quantities of firearms to their customers.

During the latter part of the seventeenth century Osei Tutu, king of Kumasi, an Akan state, built up a powerful monarchy. Osei Tutu, apparently one of the most brilliant of African kings, strengthened Kumasi's army. He also convinced his followers that his throne, the "Golden Stool" had descended from heaven, that the Golden

Stool contained the soul of the Ashanti people, and that its occupant, the Asantehene, should be recognised as a divinely ordained overlord. The new monarchy waged numerous wars of conquest, Ashanti became the paramount power of the interior. Ashanti did not, however, succeed in dominating the coast. In response to Ashanti pressure, the Fante, another Akan people dwelling to the south of Ashanti, built up a tribal confederacy. The Fante could not maintain a united front, but at least they managed to stabilize their trading position. They also enjoyed support from the British against the Dutch-backed Ashanti, and English language and culture thus increasingly influenced the Fante coast lands.

In conclusion, the slave trade affected the indigenous states of Africa in many different and contradictory ways. Much depended on the volume of the commerce, the existing social and political institutions of the peoples involved, and their ability to make use of the new military and commercial opportunities afforded by the traffic. The commerce caused an almost unprecedented amount of suffering, and occasioned one of the great transatlantic migrations of history. But it also had its positive side; the traffic in human beings went with the exchange of ordinary merchandise; the transatlantic exchange thereby introduced a great quantity of new food crops and of foreign-made goods such as muskets, hatchets, cloth, and beads to African peoples only too anxious to acquire some of this new food and merchandise.

The trade did not, as had often been asserted, bring about Africa's relative cultural backwardness in the eighteenth century. On the contrary, it was precisely kingdoms such as Dahomey, Benin, and Oyo that both played a major part in the traffic and also attained a considerable degree of civilization. On the other hand, many Central African communities, shielded from the trade by sheer distance, did not make anything like the material progress effected in West Africa.

From the political point of view, the trade on the whole appears to have made the strong stronger, while the weak were driven to the wall. It did not by itself start the process of state-building in Africa; it did, however, give an additional impetus to the consolidation of more powerful kingdoms. The traffic probably gave an advantage to those African chiefs and merchants who knew how to turn Western weapons and trade goods to their own advantage; the commerce may thus have helped to speed up social stratification within the more highly developed kingdoms involved in the traffic. But nowhere did the trade produce a bourgeoisie of the Western type; even the new monarchies of the forest zone appear to have retained the traditional patterns of tribal politics, with its emphasis on status and its restrictions on the accumulation of capital.[41]

NOTES

1. In 1750 Voltaire estimated the population of Great Britain (including Ireland) at about 10,000,000; of European Russia at 10,000,000; Poland at 6,000,000; European Turkey, Sweden, Denmark and Holland at about 3,000,000 each. The total number of Negroes in the New World may have numbered between 5,000,000 to 6,000,000. These figures are highly speculative.

2. Gilberto Freyre, *The Masters and the Slaves: A Study in the Development of Brazilian Civilization* (New York, 1956), pp. 180 and 311.

3. Cited by Verger, *Bahia and the West Coast*, p. 32.

4. David Howarth, *Panama: 400 Years of Dreams and Cruelty* (New York, 1966), p. 71.

5. Victor Alba, *The Mexicans: The Making of a Nation* (New York, 1967), p. 30.

6. Raymond R. Kent, "Palmares: An African State in Brazil," *Journal of African History*, vol. 6, no. 2 (1965), pp. 161–175.

7. Melville J. Herskovits, *The Myth of the Negro Past* (Boston, 1958), p. 112. Herskovits's, like Freyre's work, is still essential reading on the subject.

8. See Paul Edwards, ed., *Equiano's Travels: His Autobiography: The Interesting Narrative of the Life of Olaudah Equiano or Gustavus Vasa, the African* (London, 1967) and Philip D. Curtin, ed. *Africa Remembered: Narratives by West Africans from the Era of the Slave Trade* (Madison, 1967).

9. For interpretations of this kind see for instance the work of Léopold Sédar Senghor and the French West Indian poet, Aimé Césaire. Part of Senghor's work has been translated into English. See specially Léopold Sédar Senghor, *On African Socialism*, translated and with an introduction by Mercer Cook (New York, 1964), especially pp. 72–74. For an analysis of German historical thought see George G. Iggers, *The German Conception of History: The National Tradition of Historical Thought from Herder to the Present.* (Middleton, Conn., 1968). Senghor, interestingly enough, has always been conscious of the debt he owed to German romanticism, as well as to those French scholars who extolled the peculiar local virtues of specific French regions.

10. Freyre, *The Masters and the Slaves*, pp. 459–60.

11. Hubert Herring, *A History of Latin America from the Beginnings to the Present* (New York, 1961), pp. 111–113.

12. For a more detailed evaluation of the whole subject see John A. Davis, "The Influence of Africans on American Culture," *The Annals of the American Academy of Political and Social Science*, July 1964, pp. 75–83.

13. Roger Bastide, *Les Amériques noires: les civilisations Africaines dans le nouveau monde* (Paris, 1967).

14. Philip Sherlock, *West Indies* (New York, z966), pp. 126–8.

15. The full list from which these items have been abstracted is printed in Eveline Martin, ed., *Nicholas Owen, Journal of a Slave Dealer: A View of Some Remarkable Axcedents in the Life of Nics. Owen on the Coast of Africa and America from the Year 1746 to the Year 1757* (London, 1930), p. 46.

16. Lawrence, *Trade Castles and Forts of West Africa*, p. 37.

17. Georg Nøregaard, *Danish Settlements in West Africa 1658–1850* (Boston, 1966), passim.

18. Lawrence, *Trade Castles and Forts of West Africa*, p. 38.

19. William O. Jones, *Manioc In Africa* (Stanford, 1959), p. 60.

20. Anthony Benezet, *Some Historical Account of Guinea* (New York, 1968), p. 97.

21. Oliver and Fage, *A Short History of Africa*, p. 122.

22. Fage, "Slavery and the Slave Trade in the Context of West African History," p. 400.

23. Neumark, *Foreign Trade and Economic Development*, pp. 51–52.

24. Edward A. Alpers, "Trade, State and Society among the Yao in the Nineteenth Century," *Journal of African History*, vol. 10, no. 3 (1969), pp. 405–420.

25. Roland Oliver and Anthony Atmore, *Africa Since 1800* (Cambridge, 1967), p. 10.

26. Christopher Fyfe, "The Impact of the Slave Trade on West Africa", in University of Edinburgh, Center of African Studies, *The Transatlantic Slave Trade from West Africa* (Edinburgh, 1965), pp. 81–88.

27. J. F. Ajayi "Professional Warriors in Nineteenth Century Yoruba Politics," *Tarikh,* vol. 1, no. 1 (1965), pp. 72–81.

28. Birmingham, *Trade and Conflict in Angola,* pp. 121–123.

29. Vansina, *Kingdoms of the Savanna,* p. 153.

30. Balandier, *La vie quotidienne au royaume de Kongo,* pp. 261–268.

31. Victor W. Turner, *Schism and Continuity in an African Society; a Study of Ndembu Village Life* (Manchester, 1957), p. 2.

32. See F. J. M. de Lacerda e Almeida, *The Lands of Cazembe: Lacerda's Journey to Cazembe in 1798,* translated and annotated by R. F. Burton (London, 1873).

33. A. C. P. Gamitto, *King Kazembe and the Marave, Cheva, Bisa, Bemba, Lunda and Other Peoples of Southern Africa . . . ,* trans., Ian Cunnison (Lisbon, 1960), p. 159.

34. Fage, *An Introduction to the History of West Africa,* p. 87.

35. This emergent controversy has interesting parallels in the historiography of other countries. Jesse D. Clarkson, writing of the thirteenth century state of Kiev in Russia, explains that the bulk of Kiev's population in medieval times depended on subsistence agriculture. "The higher level, which gave the towns their economic *raison d'être* was foreign trade. The commodities of this trade were acquired by the urban population, not through economic services rendered by the town to the countryside, but by the use of the political authority *(vlast)* of the town to extract from the rural inhabitants of the town's provinces *(volost)* surplus forest products in demand at Constantinople or at Baghdad or in the Baltic ports. Which of these two levels should be taken as the essential characteristic of Kievan Rus is the whole substance of the controversy between [Vasili O.] Kliuchevski [a great Russian historian who lived from 1841 to 1911], who stressed the foreign trade, and of the neo-Marxist [Boris D.] Grekov [1882–1953], who stressed sustenance agriculture." See Jesse D. Clarkson, *A History of Russia,* (New York, 1963), p. 41.

36. This and the subsequent section has been taken from Flint, *Nigeria and Ghana,* pp. 80–97, which contains a brilliant summary.

37. James D. Graham, "The Slave Trade, Depopulation and Human Sacrifice in Benin History," *Cahiers d'etudes Africaines,* vol. 5, no. 18 (Paris, 1965), pp. 317–334.

38. Flint, *Nigeria and Ghana,* p. 85.

39. For a detailed discussion see Karl Polanyi, *Dahomey and the Slave Trade: An Analysis of an Archaic Economy,* in collaboration with Abraham Rotstein, (Seattle, 1966).

40. I. A. Akinjogbin, *Dahomey and its Neighbours: 1708–1818* (New York, 1967).

41. The effects of the various economic policies pursued by precolonial states in Africa remain to be investigated. Powerful kings may have assisted economic development by protecting merchants and cultivators alike against raiders and bandits. The subjects of many indigenous kings may have paid an excessively high economic price for the services which they received. Potentates such as the rulers of Dahomey probably impeded economic growth by diverting a large proportion of the national wealth into the pockets of courtiers, warriors, and priests. For instance, the rulers of Dahomey levied heavy taxes; they deliberately restricted the production of certain commodities such as salt for the purpose of raising revenue. Their use of a managed currency based on cowrie shells prevented credit transactions and thereby impeded the accumulation of capital. Their sustained policy of official wage and price fixing may have had similar effects. For a brilliant analysis see Karl Polanyi, *Dahomey and the Slave Trade: An Analysis of an Archaic Economy.* Polanyi places special stress on the deleterious effects of the Dahomey religious establishment which not only exacted a high price in human sacrifice, but whose exactions caused the Dahomean kinship groups to be "decapitalized by a permanent ecclesiastical draining."

PART
VIII

THE NEW COURSE

Chapter 26

Abolitionism
and its Aftermath

THE EVANGELICAL REVIVAL: IDEOLOGICAL, POLITICAL, AND ECONOMIC IMPULSES

The first pioneers of the Gospel in sub-Saharan Africa were the Portuguese, who conducted evangelization as part of their established state policy. The Catholic Church employed religious orders as its main instrument for conversion, including Dominicans, Jesuits, and other groups. These orders comprised Catholics from many different nations—Spaniards, Frenchmen, Italians, Germans, as well as Portuguese— and all made valiant attempts to carry the Gospel to a few selected parts of the African interior. By and large, however, their religious impact remained small, and by the eighteenth century the Catholic missionary impulse had lost much of its original strength. The Englightment and secular rationalism put traditional Christianity on the defensive, and the Catholic Church itself was subject to bitter differences on matters affecting both religious philosophy and secular policy. The cause of evangelization in Africa suffered yet another blow when, between 1759 and 1760, the Marquis of Pombal, a radical reformer, caused the Jesuits to be expelled from Portugal and its empire.

The missionary initiative thus slowly passed to northern European Protestants. The Protestants entered the evangelical field only after a considerable delay. English ecclesiastics were originally more interested in the spiritual welfare of their own settlers than in the salvation of the heathen. In 1649 the English Parliament passed an act for the purpose of setting up "A Corporation for Promoting and Propagating the Gospel of Jesus Christ in New England." Later on, missionary work received a

357

further impetus when religious societies were created in England to combat the "infamous clubs of Atheists, Deists and Socinians," whose doctrines were considered dangerous to church and state alike.

In the eighteenth century these societies greatly increased in strength. There was a series of great religious revivals, emotional rather than intellectual in character, devoted to spirituality more than doctrine, popular rather than hierarchic in nature. Many believers discovered an intense kind of religiosity that affected thought throughout many lands. In Germany the so-called Pietists objected to what they considered the rule of arid dogma in the Lutheran Church. They did not secede from Lutheranism but stressed the importance of individual religion and practical piety. The missionary impulse found an early object among the German Jews, especially vagrants without a recognized domicile, unemployed teachers and disappointed millenarians. Under the influence of Pietism, Christian missionaries sought a more sympathetic understanding of Jewish religion and a more objective knowledge of Jewish customs than they had possessed in the past. They also made some deliberate attempts to integrate their converts into Christian society at large. This domestic impulse soon spilled over into foreign lands.

In Poland and the Ukraine there was a spiritual revolution of another kind. Jewish Hasidim, mainly drawn from the ranks of the poverty-stricken masses, rebelled against the predominance of the learned and the wealthy. They tried to break with what they regarded as the dry scholasticism of the rabbis. Instead they stressed personal commitment, purity of life, and the religious values of popular music and dancing. In England the Methodists wished to bring a more emotional element and a deeper personal religiosity into the Anglican Church. The more detailed history of all these movements does not concern us here. We must, however, mention the *Unitas Fratrum* or Brethren's Congregation, which pioneered the new missionary movement. The Brethren had their origin in Bohemia, one of the bastions of revolutionary Protestantism in postmedieval Europe, and the homeland of John Huss (1373–1415), one of the earliest of the great Protestant reformers. In 1720s Christian David, a German carpenter professing the radical doctrines of the Brethren, crossed the Bohemian border into Saxony, accompanied by some of his followers. The refugees settled on the estate of Count Zinzendorf, and with his permission built the town of Herrenhuth. Zinzendorf was a fervent Lutheran of the Pietist persuasion. Under his direction the democratic ecclesiastical tradition of the Brethren fused with Lutheranism of a more conservative type. The Brethren built settlements on the lands of other nobles sympathetic to their cause, and practiced a quiet, inward-looking religiosity.

Their number remained small, but their spiritual influence was quite out of proportion to their numerical strength. The Brethren, unlike earlier Protestant sects, put enormous stress on the Christian duty of converting the pagans abroad and in 1732 launched a missionary movement overseas with far-reaching effects for the future. Peter Boehler, a Moravian, converted John Wesley (1703–1791) and his brother Charles (1707–1788), who later became the leaders of British Methodism. Moravians also had a share in England's wider evangelical revival.

In Great Britain this movement was closely linked to industrialization. The Methodists and others of their kind, including "Evangelicals" within the established Anglican Church, were ready to preach the gospel both in the countryside and in the new factory towns that were so often neglected by the older churches. They were determined to appeal to the masses and taught the forgiveness of Christ, but also the virtues of thrift, sobriety, and hard work. Their converts experienced an intense sense of personal sin. Equiano, an Ibo convert to their cause, put it,

> Like some poor pris'ner at the bar
> Conscious of guilt, of sin and fear
> Arraign'd, and self-condemned I stood—
> Lost in the world, and in my blood.[1]

But sin would be overcome by the love of Christ, and Christ meant his followers to lead a life of intense personal commitment. This creed had profound secular as well as spiritual consequences. Poverty, the preacher believed, was neither a holy nor an inevitable state. But the way to deal with the problems of society was not by means of armed revolution. Instead the faithful should work within the existing framework of society, make full use of the new opportunities afforded by the workshops, factories, and counting houses of England, and develop their God-given talents in their appointed sphere of life. Society, however, was capable of peaceful transformation. The Christians, indeed, owed a special obligation to children, sick people, madmen, prisoners, and slaves—all those who could not look after themselves in the hurly-burly of the new free enterprise economic system.

From helping the poor at home, it was but a short step to converting the heathen abroad, and many European movements of social reform thus spilled into the colonies. The first Protestant mission school in sub-Saharan Africa was set up by the Dutch at Elmina on the Gold Coast in 1644. In 1722 the Danes followed suit by setting up an educational establishment at Christiansborg (Accra), and some Ashanti chiefs later sent their children to be educated under European auspices. The main European mission effort, however, came from Great Britain. By 1776 Evangelicals within the Anglican Church, drawing much of their enthusiasm from Methodism and the new dissenters, founded the Society for Missions in Africa and the East (later known as the Church Missionary Society). In 1787 the British Methodists set up a regular system of foreign missions, and in 1792 the Baptists followed their example. In 1795 the London Missionary Society came into existence under Congregationalist inspiration. British as well as foreign (especially German) missionaries started to preach the Gospel in many parts of a world made more accessible by the steady expansion of West European trade. Their activity owed nothing to the ecclesiastical state monopolies of earlier periods. It depended on the private enterprise of competing private societies, financed by voluntary contributions from pious merchants, manufacturers, aristocratic wellwishers, and some of the better off artisans as well as the small donations of poorer church goers.

The growth of missionary and mercantile interest in Africa was paralleled by the development of scientific interest in Africa. In 1788 Sir Joseph Banks, a British naturalist, founded the Association for Promoting the Discovery of the Interior Parts of Africa (commonly known as the African Association), which soon sent out travelers to the interior of Africa to report on geography, ethnography, and natural history. The African Association and similar bodies worked as distinct pressure groups, informing as well as influencing British policy.[2]

By and large the supporters of these organizations believed in freedom of trade, of conscience, and of wage contracts. They had no patience with the slave trade, which they considered to be contrary both to the word of God and to individual human dignity and to what they regarded as man's God-given right to dispose of his labor to his best advantage. They launched a campaign against the slave trade. The abolitionists received much support from adherents of the older British dissenting sects, including many Baptists and Quakers. In addition they obtained a great deal of backing from Socinians, rationalists, and deists. Reforming nonconformity thus entered into a working alliance with secular humanism. In the United States especially, the abolitionist movement rested on a close association between the adherents of "natural religion," like Benjamin Franklin and Thomas Paine, and the American Quakers, who were much more opposed to the traffic than the bulk of their English coreligionists.

Abolitionist doctrines also seemed to make economic as well as moral sense. The slave trade was inextricably intertwined with what British economic historians call the Old Colonial System. This rested on a complicated set of commercial preferences. These, broadly speaking, were designed to turn Great Britain into a hive of industry, capable of supplying the colonies with manufactures and shipping facilities in exchange for agricultural commodities such as sugar and timber. The northern colonies in America never quite fitted into this system, and—except for Canada—the North American colonies broke with the British connection. But the system also met with strong opposition in Great Britain itself. According to Adam Smith (1723–1790), Britain's greatest economist, it benefited only a limited section of the British bourgeoisie, including the merchants and shipowners involved in the slave trade, as well as the West Indian planter aristocracy. But the nation at large obtained no benefits. Tariffs designed to protect West Indian sugar and similar commodites increased the cost of living for British consumers. The system impeded the free flow both of labor and capital, thereby injuring national prosperity. According to the abolitionists, the West Indian "interest," a powerful coalition of slave owners and their hangers-on, formed an iniquitous pressure group within the British political system that had to be liquidated in order to promote much-needed social and political reforms. Slavery in the end entailed economic loss. As H. C. Carey, a nineteenth-century writer, explained, the passage of man from the condition of a freeman to that of a slave meant that "he has steadily less to sell, and can therefore purchase less; and . . . thus the only effect of a policy which compels the impoverishment of land (through soil erosion) and its owners is to destroy the customer, who under a different system of policy might become a larger purchaser from year to year."[3] The commerce in slaves also stood in the way of legitimate trade in Africa by disrupting markets, impeding the production of cash crops such as palm oil, and by encouraging the killing or kidnapping of possible customers. The joint interests of religion and profits alike thus required the abolition of the slave trade. As Equiano, an anglicized African, put it:

May the blessing of the Lord be upon the heads of all those who commiserated the cases of the oppressed negroes, and the fear of God prolong their days; and may their expectations be filled with gladness! The liberal devise liberal things, and by liberal things shall he stand,' Isaiah xxx11.8 . . .

As the inhuman traffic of slavery is to be taken into the consideration of the British legislature, I doubt not, if a system of commerce was established in Africa, the demand for manufactures would most rapidly augment, as the native inhabitants will insensibly adopt the British fashions, manners, customers etc. In proportion to the civilization, so will the consumption of British manufactures.[4]

The abolitionists thus began a widespread campaign that pioneered many modern lobbying techniques. Their agitation began at a favorable time, after the American War of Independence had delivered a smashing blow to the existing British imperial system. The abolitionists skillfully organized propaganda committees, court actions, public meetings, and petitions; they circulated pamphlets widely; they used the pulpit. They brought the matter before the British Parliament and gained the sympathy of William Pitt the Younger (1759–1806), the leading British statesman of the time. The French Revolution temporarily postponed their triumph, for the abolition of the slave trade was identified with total emancipation of the slaves, and emancipation in turn with Jacobinism, bloodshed, and social upheaval.

The revolutionary French Convention seriously compromised the friends of the Negroes with the British public when it conferred honorary French citizenship on William Wilberforce (1759–1833), a British parliamentarian and philanthropist, as well as champion of the abolitionist cause.[5] The abolitionists, however, did not relent, and embarked on a series of more limited campaigns with far-reaching effects for the future.

THE FIRST ATTACKS ON THE SLAVE TRADE: THE DANISH AND BRITISH INITIATIVES

The initial impact of abolitionism should not be overestimated. Serfdom or slavery seemed part and parcel of life throughout most parts of the world and was accepted as such. To give just one example: in the early eighteenth century Job ben Salomon, a Fula prince, was tricked into slavery and sold to a Maryland tobacco farmer. Job was put to rigorous field work, and, after attempting to escape, succeeded in contacting some distinguished philanthropists in England. The former captive, a Muslim who could write Arabic, was redeemed, invited to London, and lionized in British high society before being shipped back to his native Gambia. Job's story now seems strange. There is an incongruous element in the tale of an ex-slave who mingled on terms of social equality with the Governor of the Royal Africa Company, the Duke of Montagu, and was presented at the Court of St. James as a distinguished stranger. But the story did not strike either Job or his hosts in this fashion. Both parties believed in the mysterious working of Divine Providence. Muslim Fula and most Christian Englishmen both considered slavery or some other variety of servile status as a normal part of human existence. Job himself did not deplore slavery as such; on the contrary, he dealt in slaves himself.[6] British patriots extolled their country as freedom's chosen bastion. But they saw nothing wrong in pressganging white sailors into the Royal Navy under conditions scarcely, if at all, better than slavery, in purchasing mercenaries from petty German princelings, or in flogging their own soldiers with incredible brutality.

In the latter part of the eighteenth century, however, there was a slow and gradual change in what might be called the European climate of opinion. The institution of slavery especially came increasingly under intellectual attack. This assault owed little to African initiative, except for the protests of a few black expatriates who adopted Western values. The antislavery campaign was part of a wider European movement, of an upsurge against hereditary class and kin privileges that affected the whole of Western Europe and many parts of Central and Eastern Europe and also had profound consequence for the West Indies and Africa. Slave traders, plantation owners, and many great landed *seigneurs* in Europe all had a stake in a social order that allotted a subordinate hereditary status to certain groups of farm workers—white or black. Whether a field hand was well treated or badly, he could not escape from his station in life without his master's consent. Even if he did, his social mobility remained extremely limited. From the end of the eighteenth century onward, however, the whole of Western and Central Europe was shaken by a profound social transformation in which old seignorial claims were suppressed, serfdom disappeared in all of its many forms, and labor became free to seek its own price.[7] The French revolutionary governments played an essential part in this process, but, quite independently of the French example, major reforms were also pioneered by Denmark, a small power. Denmark, indeed, was the world's first country to abolish the slave trade and thereby had an influence on world history quite out of proportion to the size of the country.

Denmark enjoyed a favorable geographical situation between the Baltic and the North Sea. In the eighteenth century Danish entrepreneurs made good their opportunities and greatly expanded their country's trade and banking. At the same time Danish agriculturists multiplied their crops and their cattle. The kingdom's economic development, however, placed an intolerable strain on the traditional institution of villeinage and resulted in bitter political conflict. In the end the innovators won the day, and in 1788 Count Reventlow (1748–1827), a great Danish statesman, abolished the *Stavnsbaand,* the instrument that laid down the terms of Danish serfdom. Further reforms followed, and in 1799 a royal ordinance put an end to all remaining labor obligations of the feudal kind. Denmark experienced a peaceful land reform; many peasants received plots of their own, and Denmark successfully moved from villeinage to a system of fairly widespread freehold ownership.

The campaign against Danish feudal privileges did not stop at home, but spilled over into the colonies. In addition to pioneering European land reform, the Danes were also the first people to abolish the slave trade. In 1792, four years after the suppression of the *Stavnsbaand,* the Danish king issued an edict prohibiting the traffic. This prohibition came into force in 1803, thereby leaving time to Danish colonists in the West Indies, in St. Thomas, St. John, and St. Croix, to purchase sufficient workmen for their needs. The Danish reformers were also fortunate in that they did not have to contend with a powerful colonial lobby. The Danish possessions were small. Danish plantation owners could no longer expand their acreage. The local black population in the Danish possessions was gaining in numbers owing to relatively good treatment and a high birth rate. The Danish estate owners could thereby make do without large additional imports, and the reformers did not have to battle against a powerful but desperate pressure group. Neither was there much to fear from Danish shipping interests. Denmark was mainly an agricultural country. Danish Guinea merchants thus found considerable difficulties in competing against British traders with their cheap manufactures. Despite state aid, the Danish Baltic and Guinean Trading Company kept incurring losses, and the abolition of the slave trade was accomplished without serious internal friction.[8]

The Danish initiative had far-reaching consequences. The slave traders' front broke at its weakest link. By the end of the eighteenth century the Danish slave trade was open to the flag of all nations. Foreign, especially British, merchants had managed to gain the lion's share of the Danish slave traffic. Denmark's prohibition of the commerce in slaves destroyed Britain's best foreign market for black captives, and thereby delivered a serious blow to the British slave trade. The British now faced a major decision. Their policy, backed by the country's overwhelming naval might, would decide the course of Europe and the world at large.

The British political climate had by this time become increasingly favorable to the abolitionists' cause. In the early part of the eighteenth century abolitionism had been advocated primarily by a few "Negrophilist" intellectuals. Later on missionary and other ecclesiastical groups began to play their part in the abolitionist campaign. Toward the latter part of the century the abolitionists formed political groups that transcended sectarian boundaries. Finally, the abolitionists—many of them Quakers —began to exert pressure on Parliament itself, and their cause became a major political issue.

At the same time there was a profound transformation within the structure of British politics. The "West India Interest," powerfully represented in the unreformed House of Commons before the Reform Bill of 1832, largely rested on the strength of the great sugar producers in the Caribbean. By the end of the eighteenth century, however, these powerful landowners were facing extraordinary difficulties. Much of the good land in the British West Indies had been exhausted by wasteful methods of production. There was competition from Santo Domingo. New competitions arose in the East Indies, where the British East India Company took up sugar production in 1789. (Later on, yet another rival appeared on the scene when European tillers learned how to grow beet sugar.) In addition, the American War of Independence delivered a smashing blow to the "Old Colonial System." Trade between independent America and Great Britain rapidly increased, thereby helping to discredit accustomed mercantilist orthodoxies. The war also brought about political changes. The British faced renewed unrest in Ireland, and in 1800 the British Parliament passed an Act for the Union of Great Britain and Ireland in order to cement the imperial structure. British abolitionists at Westminster now obtained an unforeseen but welcome advantage in the shape of Irish members who lacked a direct economic stake in the traffic. Finally, the abolitionists benefited from internal political change in Great Britain itself. In 1806 Lord Grenville and Charles James Fox, an enthusiastic advocate of freedom for Negro slaves and one of the fathers of British parliamentarian radicalism, formed the short-lived "Ministry of all the Talents." In 1806 the new government put a Slave Importation Restriction Act on the statute book, forbidding British subjects from participating in the foreign slave trade. A year later, in 1807, shortly after Fox's death, the British legislature finally passed the momentous Act for the Abolition of the Slave Trade.

Once the British had put a stop to their own traffic they had a natural interest in preventing foreigners from engaging in a trade that the British themselves had forsaken and that went counter to the aspirations of British and foreign humanitarians alike. British statesmen became the foremost advocates of abolitionism on the international plane. Great Britain used her enormous naval, financial, and diplomatic resources to wipe out the commerce altogether. In 1807 the United States followed the British lead. In 1814 Holland formally terminated the traffic; Sweden made it illegal in 1815, and France outlawed the trade in the early 1820s.

Legal prohibition did not put an immediate end to the slavers' depredations. Captives continued to be exported on a large scale from Africa to the New World and to many parts of the Near East. But the concert of Europe, in theory at least, would no longer countenance slave dealing. In 1815 the Congress of Vienna, under British pressure, pronounced the slave trade to be contrary to the principles of civilization and human rights. It thereby asserted for the first time a rudimentary doctrine of international trusteeship. Subsequently the western Christian fleets, above all the Royal Navy, waged a long and costly maritime campaign, involving the ships of many nations—American as well as European. The British decision to outlaw the commerce thus marked a decisive event.

Abolitionism had strong humanitarian motives. But it also implied a new kind of inequality between white and black. The old-time slave dealers had dealt with their African partners on a basis of equality. The abolitionists, on the other hand, were determined to force their own ideas upon Africa and to assert the cultural superiority of Europe. Abolitionism implied intervention by sea; in time the new humanitarian policy would involve European intervention in Africa itself. The British decision to outlaw the commerce thus marked a historical break. It may conceivably have prevented the gradual Africanization of extensive stretches of the New World. It helped to lay the groundwork of white empires; it played its part in inaugurating a social revolution fraught with profound consequences for the peoples of Africa as well as for the black diaspora in the New World.

THE ABOLITION OF SLAVERY AND THE STRUGGLE AGAINST THE TRANSATLANTIC SLAVE TRADE

THE METROPOLITAN POWERS OF EUROPE

Great Britian, as we have seen, took a peculiarly active part in the abolition of the slave trade. The British also took a major share in persuading other nations to follow their example. Great Britain, where the antislavery cause was sustained by a powerful domestic lobby, was also the only country to shoulder extensive foreign financial commitments to secure its object. The British government for the first time initiated a kind of international aid in pursuance of a policy that sought to combine humanitarian and economic aims in equal measure. In 1815 Portugal agreed to the abolition of the slave traffic and received £ 300,000 from the British taxpayer in compensation. Spain forbade the commerce after 1820 in return for £ 400,000. The British also disbursed considerable sums to patrol the coasts of Africa and thereby showed themselves willing to back their ideals with hard cash.

These payments and promises did not at first stop the trade. On the Niger delta, for instance, the abolition of the traffic merely allowed private Portuguese and especially private Brazilian shippers to take the place of their Liverpool competitors. Brazil and Cuba required more captives for their expanding sugar and coffee plantations. The American cotton economy was expanding westward; hence entrepreneurs of many nationalities stepped in to supply this new demand. In many cases the business became even more horrible than it had been in the past. Unscrupulous captains made up for increasing risks by cramming more blacks into their ships. In 1824 the British imposed the death penalty on slave traffickers. Fearful of being hanged, the slave traders became all the more willing to throw their compromising cargo overboard at the first sight of a British frigate in the distance.

The story was, however, not one of unrelieved evil. The treatment of slaves in the British West Indies seem to have gradually improved, but British public opinion was wrought-up and tended to judge all the planters by the worst examples. At the same time the planters came to be looked upon as an economic liability. Sugar from Brazil, Cuba, and Mauritius gained an increasing share of the British market. The West Indians produced too much sugar and could sell their surplus only in Europe in competition with cheaper Brazilian or Cuban sugar. This could only be done by subsidies and bounties. Hence "the West Indian sugar planters were being paid . . . to compete with people who . . . were some of Britain's best customers."[9] At the same time British consumers had to pay more for protected West Indian sugar than they would have paid on an open market. The slave question thus became a great crusading cause, one on which British landed noblemen, factory owners and workers, Christians, and secular humanitarians could all agree. The slave owner came to be looked upon as a villain whose assumed depravity lost nothing in the telling. "I am here," complained a Jamaican planter in 1823, "in a state of banishment and gliding fast into ruin; and while thus weighed down with misery, without one ray of hope to illuminate the dreary prospect before me, I am with the rest of the colonists, depicted by the Saints, the Methodists, the Quakers and the Man of Beer, and at their instigation by three-fourths of the people of Great Britain, as a hard-hearted, inhuman monster. . . ."[10]

West Indians had a case, but the political tide was strongly running against them. In 1832 Great Britain effected a major scheme of parliamentary reform that enfranchised the British urban middle class, gave representation to the new factory towns, and also had the incidental effect of destroying the old West Indian interest in the British legislature. There was a spurt of social reform legislation from which the British slaves benefited in the same way as English children in factories and other depressed groups within the British body politic. In 1833 the British Parliament passed the decisive Act for the Emancipation of Slaves. All slaves were to receive their freedom within twelve months. Domestic slaves would be apprenticed to their former masters until 1838, and slaves engaged in agricultural work until 1840. The slave owners were allowed £ 20,000,000 compensation, while friends of the slaves persuaded the House to make the payment a free gift and not a loan to be repaid by the freed slaves.[11]

The abolition of slavery applied to all British possessions, to the British territories in South Africa as well as to the West Indies. Emancipation thereby had profound consequences in the history of the Cape; these will be discussed at greater length in a subsequent section. All we can make at this point are certain broad generalizations. The British managed to abolish slavery a generation before the Americans were able to do so in the Southern states. The British were able to avoid armed risings on the part of aggrieved slave-owners by a combination of armed strength and financial generosity. The West Indian "plantocracy"—unlike the much more numerous and powerful slave-owning class in the American South—could never attempt to assert their independence against the overwhelming might of the Royal Navy. In the Cape, on the other side of the globe, discontended Afrikaans-speaking farmers preferred to trek beyond the frontiers of the British dominated Cape Colony, rather than challenge the British Redcoats musket in hand. Instead the erstwhile slave owners of whatever nationality preferred to pocket whatever they received in the way of compensation, however much they might justly grumble at the manner in which substantial amounts of money earmarked for compensation found its way into the bank accounts of British bankers and financial agents. The former slaves, unlike the freed serfs in many parts of nineteenth-century Europe, were not burdened with a great load of debt. The British decision to compensate the slave owners at the British taxpayer's expense was therefore an investment in social stability. The abolition of slavery in the British Empire was brought about without the suffering, the bloodshed, and the intense hatred entailed by the American Civil War.

Emancipation did produce, however, vast social changes in many parts of the Empire. It helped to start the Great Trek in South Africa, a vast movement of Afrikaner emigration that carried white rule all the way from the borders of the Cape to the banks of the Limpopo. In the West Indies, emancipation contributed to the elimination of a long-established planter economy and the manifold interest groups dependent on this peculiar form of enterprise. Emancipation was the greatest step ever taken on the way towards a fully capitalist society based on free wage labor, free trade, and a free market economy.

The abolition of slavery was thus followed by the progressive disruption of British preferential tariffs. In 1846, the British legislature abolished the corn laws designed to protect her agricultural producers. Three years later the navigation acts disappeared from the statute book, and from 1854 onward both colonial and foreign-grown sugar were admitted on equal terms. Great Britain, the foremost industrial power of the world, was firmly wedded to free trade. The belief in free trade commonly went with an impassioned denunciation of empire as the plaything of the well-born and the tool of tyranny: "We venture to say," wrote Macaulay, "that Colonial empire has been one of the greatest curses of modern Europe. What nation has it ever strengthened? What nation has it ever enriched? What have been its fruits? Wars of frequent occurrence and immense cost, fettered trade, lavish expenditure, clashing jurisdiction, corruption in governments, and indigence among the people."[12]

But the belief in free trade often also went with an impassioned conviction that Britain's task was to help the oppressed, be they victims of foreign tyranny, slavish superstition, the darkness of paganism, or the brutality of slave traders. This humanitarian inspiration was thus apt to have contradictory consequences. What if foreigners or savages were to interfere with the natural flow of commerce? Britain, according to some, might then have occasion to intervene in a good cause. British idealists also felt a moral obligation to intervene on behalf of the downtrodden "aborigines," be they oppressed Kaffirs in South Africa, Maori in New Zealand, or Indians groaning under oppressive systems of land ownership. Yet, by a strange paradox, these convictions could also go with the belief that the aborigines in need of protection were innately inferior to whites and might have to be justly controlled for their own protection, so that abolitionism at times was apt to beget a new doctrine of paternal imperialism.

In France, on the other hand, the abolition of slavery and the campaign for free trade never became popular issues, capable of evoking crusading fervor, as in England. Abolitionist sentiments were strong among French Protestants, but they were too few in number to make much of an impact on the mass of the people. The Abbé Grégoire, a bishop of the French "Constitutional" (that is to say prorevolutionary, anti-Papal, and secessionist) Church, strongly advocated the abolition of slavery, the elimination of civic disabilities for Jews, and similar measures. But Grégoire's efforts never had the same popular response as those made by nonconformist preachers in Great Britain. Bodies such as the Société des Amis des Noirs gained support from distinguished men like Condorcet, Mirabeau, and Lafayette, but they failed to acquire the influence exercised by abolitionist lobbies in England. Slavery was legally abolished for a time in 1794, during the revolutionary period in France, but this reform had little immediate effect on Africa.

French slavery, however, suffered a serious blow when the slaves of Haiti (in the western part of the island of Santo Domingo) rose against their masters under the leadership of Pierre Dominique Toussaint l'Ouverture (1744–1803), one of the greatest of all black West Indians. Toussaint l'Ouverture, a contemporary of Napoleon and himself a Napoleonic figure, was the son of a West African chief. Captured by slave traders and brought to Haiti, he acquired a good education, and achieved great prestige among the rebels owing to his western education as well as his reputation as a magician. Toussaint l'Ouverture freed the island, fought against the Spaniards under the tricolor banner of the French Republic, and subsequently beat the British, who had intervened on the side of the planters. The Haitians worked out an impressive system of military tactics that made good use of massed formations, cover, and surprise. They were able to resist the ravages of the climate where white soldiers perished of fever, and became a power in their own right. Napoleon then inveigled Toussaint l'Ouverture into negotiations; the Haitian was forcibly put on board a French warship and taken to France, where he was left to die neglected in a jail. The French could not, however, recover their former possession.

In 1804 Haiti formally declared its independence. The remaining whites were expelled and the plantation economy largely collapsed. Haiti became a land of peasants who mainly labored to sustain their own families, but who also developed a small export trade in commodities such as coffee and cocoa, logwood and mahagony. The Haitians continued to speak a French *patois;* French remained the language of the educated. Independent Haiti, however, was beset by savage civil wars, by bloody faction fights both between blacks and mulattoes, and between the blacks themselves. Economic progress was impeded, by wide-spread financial peculation, by heavy foreign debts contracted by impecunious leaders, and also by conflicts between the Haitians and their Spanish-speaking neighbors in Santo Domingo to the east. The peasantry remained the lowest stratum in the state. (There was indeed a law that no peasant might enter a city except on market day, or to fulfill his military service.) Hence Haiti became a byword for political corruption, and its very existence often came to be used as an argument by white men against granting civil rights even to Westernized blacks.[13]

The Haitian example showed that blacks, if driven too far, might well become a military danger. But Haiti remained too weak to become a revolutionary force of its own. Neither did the Haitian uprising seriously affect the fortunes of the French empire elsewhere.

The French legally abolished the slave trade in 1815, but abolition of slavery as such was rather the incidental result of a great metropolitan upheaval, the revolution of 1848. The new Republican government asserted the equality of its citizens before the law and the rights of man. Its first act was to proclaim universal suffrage. Next it abolished at one stroke slavery throughout the French possessions, thus freeing about half a million slaves. It was a belated reform, introduced for ideological reasons without any preparation or precautions and brought immediate disaster to the French slave colonies.[14]

At the same time the Second Republic, in the tradition of Jacobin assimilationism, attempted to grant all persons born in a French colony, black or white, the same civil and political rights as French citizens. The ideologists of the revolution never quite understood the immense difficulties in the way of such a policy, and equality largely remained a paper right. But Senegal did gain the right to elect a deputy to the French National Assembly at Paris. Nearly 5,000 votes were enrolled, and in November 1848 the territory returned a Negro representative to the French legislature. The Second Empire under Louis Napoleon subsequently revoked this concession. But Gallicized mulatto and African traders continued to look to the French authorities for the protection of their commerce against the Muslim lords of the interior; they also considered France their cultural home; hence this small Europeanized minority later made an important contribution to what French historians have called "Senegalese imperialism," that is, to the expansion of French rule into the interior.

THE INDEPENDENT STATES OF THE NEW WORLD

The abolition of slavery in the United States is a subject familiar to American readers, and only a few salient features need to be pointed out in this work. Emancipation came very late in American history (later, indeed, than the emancipation of the serfs in Russia, who were freed in 1861). The emancipation struggle involved profound differences of political philosophy. Most Southerners imagined that their whole way of life was bound up with slavery. For many Northerners abolitionism became almost an article of religious faith. Many Northern theorists, like their English *confreres,* knew little of the real conditions on the plantations but took their stand on broad principles of humanitarianism, social responsibility, and democratic reform. The intellectual advocates of abolitionism had contacts with like-minded men in other countries, in France, Great Britain, and Brazil, and from the 1830s to the 1860s there was indeed something like an "abolitionist internationale."[15]

The clash between the abolitionists and their opponents was embittered by differences over economic policy. The southern states depended on the export of tropical crops, especially cotton. Much of their trade was conducted with Great Britain; hence the farmers had a natural interest in free trade, which would enable them to sell their crops in exchange for cheap manufactured British goods. Many northern states, for their part, were beginning to develop industries, and many manufacturers accordingly looked to protective tariffs. But above all abolition was a political question, one intimately linked to the future of the American West. The problem of whether slavery should be transplanted to the western frontier raised wider issues of political power within the Union and of states' rights versus Federal rights. Compromise proved impossible, and in 1861 war broke out between the two opposing blocs. President Lincoln issued his famous Emancipation Proclamation in September 1862 chiefly as a declaration of policy designed—among other things—to gain more support from Great Britain. The Emancipation Proclamation did not by any means free all the slaves, even in the North. But the question was finally settled by the capitulation of the Southern states in 1865, and abolitionist principles at last found effective legislative expression in instruments such as the Thirteenth Amendment to the United States Constitution.

Slavery survived longest in the New World in Cuba and Brazil. In Cuba slavery was inextricably intertwined with the sugar industry, and Cuban planters continued to make profits after the British estate owners in the West Indies had lost their convenient source of servile labor. Under pressure from Cuban reformers, however, the Spanish authorities on the island decided to introduce various reforms. These included emancipation of the slaves, who finally gained their freedom in 1886.

Slavery's last great bastion in the New World was Brazil, the largest Latin American country, with trade links of ancient standing to West Africa. British pressure dictated the abolition of the slave trade in Brazil (1829). But the law was not at first effectively enforced. On the contrary, British free trade policies opened up new markets for sugar produced by slave labor in Brazil and Cuba; hence Portuguese and Brazilian ship captains transported even more captives across the Atlantic than before, and the illegal importation of slaves came to an end only in 1851. British interference, through offending Brazilian national pride, seems to have contributed to the abolition of slavery proper.

The great *fazendeiros* generally believed at first that the ending of slavery would ruin their estates and wreck the national economy. But these gloomy forecasts proved unfounded. From the 1850s onward, Brazil experienced a period of great prosperity. Many European immigrants came into the country with official encouragement. The railway system greatly expanded, and the country's center of economic gravity began to shift to the south. The southern cattle herds multiplied, and São Paulo's coffee became an important export crop. Brazil began to develop some indigenous industries of its own, and these new enterprises depended on free labor—not on slaves. Slavery was now opposed by the majority of the townsmen, by secular and clerical humanitarians, and by the Brazilian monarchy itself. When in 1866, for instance, the Benedictine Order in Rio de Janeiro freed sixteen hundred slaves, Emperor Pedro II made a personal call on the Benedictines to congratulate them. The *fazendeiros,* often softened by the pleasures of Rio de Janeiro and Paris, slowly began to lose their hold, and the slave owners' position was further weakened by the victory of the northern states in the American Civil War.

In 1871 a movement led by the liberal Nabuco de Aráujo and the conservative Viscount Rio Branco took action and partially abolished slavery in the country. This legislation, affecting something like 1,700,000 slaves, was received with popular enthusiasm. The Brazilian antislavery societies—by local action in various provinces and resistance on the slave owners' part—gradually disintegrated. In 1888 accumulated pressure from the abolitionists led to further action from the Brazilian legislature, and in 1888 the last seven hundred thousand slaves were freed without compensation to the owners.[16] The Brazilians, unlike the North Americans, thereby succeeded in ridding their country of slavery without a great civil war. Abolitionism secured its final victory in the New World.

At the same time the navies of the Western maritime powers, above all the British fleet, embarked on vigorous action to disrupt the transatlantic slave trade. This was a difficult undertaking, for European powers as yet controlled but a small portion of the African coast. Slavers could flit in and out of lonely ports without being observed. Captains resorted to all kinds of deception. The navies of the world still depended in the main on windpower; they lacked as yet telegraphic communications, and the sailors all too easily fell victim to tropical diseases. The assault on the slave traders occasioned disagreements between the western powers themselves over the right of search. In addition Brazilians and Portuguese, Americans and Frenchmen often accused the British of conducting the anti-slavery campaign for purely selfish reasons. By the end of the 1830s, however, Spain, Brazil, Portugal, the Netherlands, France, Denmark, and the German Hanseatic cities had all conceded to Great Britain the right to stop and search merchant ships.

For a time the United States remained almost the only power unwilling to allow this privilege to the British. But the Americans themselves took an active share in suppressing the slave trade, and in 1842 the United States and Great Britain agreed to maintain a permanent American naval force on the African west coast to help put down the traffic. The American ships did not operate in East Africa, and some

American slave ships began to appear in East Africa. Indeed the 1850s saw a revival of the American slave trade, and New York became the center of some illicit traffic. In addition a few British subjects continued to engage in slave dealing. From the 1860s, however, the long, bitter maritime guerrilla warfare began to go in favor of the antislavery squadrons. In 1862 the Americans withdrew their squadrons from Africa so that their vessels might participate in the blockade of the Confederate States. The Americans accordingly gave to the British the right to search and seize American slavers both on the African and the Cuban shores and the slave trade was finally ended.[17]

British diplomacy, backed by overwhelming seapower, played a major part in Africa itself. In 1873, for instance, the Sultan of Zanzibar bowed to British pressure and forbade the transoceanic slave trade in his dominion. Improvements in naval engineering and tropical medicine also played their part, and by the third quarter of the nineteenth century the seaborne slave trade had largely disappeared from history.

ECONOMIC IMPLICATIONS OF ABOLITION: A HISTORICAL CONTROVERSY

Apart from the great slave rising in Haiti, the abolitionist transformation was, in a way, a revolution from above, comparable in certain respects to the government-sponsored elimination of serfdom in countries such as Denmark, Prussia, and Austria. Historians have accordingly interpreted the British initiative in many different ways. For British historiography of the traditional kind, "the unweary, unostentatious, and inglorious crusade of England against slavery may probably be regarded as among the three or four perfectly virtuous pages comprised in the history of nations."[18] Critics of the British imperial record, including both Marxists and German nationalists of the pre-World War I variety, have arrived at very different conclusions and have emphasized the element of economic self-interest in British policy.

The most convincing case comes from the pen of Franz Hochstetter, a German historian whom we have quoted in the previous section, and whose writings are now largely forgotten. Hochstetter argues that the loss of the American colonies led to a severe crisis in Britain's West Indian possessions. The West Indian islands needed the American market. Once war broke out between Great Britain and her American subjects, the British were, however, compelled to prohibit trade between the West Indies and the rebellious colonies, with serious consequences to the West Indian slave owners' prosperity. After the end of hostilities, the British tried to restrict the American trade of the British West Indies to British vessels, and again the British planters suffered great loss. They also had to contend with bitter competition from French and Spanish colonists in the West Indies, who enjoyed numerous natural advantages. Many foreign-owned islands suffered less from soil erosion than the British sugar islands. Foreign plantation owners in many cases had more unused land at their disposal than their British rivals; hence the British faced a serious outside threat.

The British plantation owners faced other difficulties. Many were absentee landlords, great agrarian capitalists, who worked their land through local overseers specializing on a single crop. A large number of Spanish and French planters, on the other hand, lived on their estates; their capital investments and administrative overheads were smaller; they often went in for more diversified forms of farming; they did not labor under the same fiscal burdens as their British rivals. The foreign plantation owners also derived considerable benefits from the disruption of Britain's American trade. British experts, therefore, began to argue that the French challenge could be overcome only by a different system of culture, run at less expense, and based on the labor of free Negroes. The breakdown of the British mercantilist system at the same time helped to associate abolitionism with the growing movement for free trade because British consumers resented having to pay higher prices for British West Indian produce than they would have had to disburse in a free market economy. In addition British economists became convinced that the slave trade primarily benefited Britain's foreign competitors in the West Indies.[19]

The British slave trade threatened to become an economic liability. What was the point of allowing British slavers to supply French plantation owners with cheap labor if British shippers thereby strengthened the Frenchmen's economic position? The British plantation owners, of course, also wanted slaves. But they gradually discovered that they were no longer as dependent on labor imports as in the past. Toward the end of the eighteenth century, the black death rate in the British West Indian possessions started to diminish. The black population gained from natural increase, and the supply of slaves began to exceed the local demand. In many cases the British land owners had less need of imported hands than the French and Spaniards, who had more unused land at their disposal than the majority of their British rivals.

The abolitionists also pointed to the increasing losses incurred by British slave traders on the coast of Africa itself. Even at the best of times the commerce had been highly speculative. It became even more so as foreign competition increased, as more and more European and American goods were sold on the African west coast, and as black African dealers were able to charge higher prices for their wares. In the non-British colonies British slave traders began to meet increasing discrimination from foreign governments, especially from the Spanish and French authorities. The traffic in slaves became "a losing commerce."

Fortunately there was a possible alternative. If profits could no longer be made from slaves, British merchants might recoup their losses through "legitimate trade" in manufactured goods. Toward the end of the eighteenth century, Western European living standards slowly began to rise. For instance, there was a growing demand for better illumination at night as well as a greater vogue for personal cleanliness. West Africa was a potential supplier of palm oil and palm kernels needed by European soap and candle manufacturers. "Legitimate trade" was preferable to the slave traffic for purely maritime purposes. The slave trade was disastrous, not merely to the well being of African captives, but also to the health of British sailors. Mortality among British seamen on slaving vessels was high. Some ships lost as much as one-fifth or even one-fourth of their white crews owing to sickness and ill treatment on the long journey; hence many abolitionists justly described the slave trade as the "grave" rather than the "nursery" of British mariners.

The abolitionist campaign, according to Hochstetter, suffered a severe check when in 1793 the British once more became involved in war against France. The French temporarily lost most of their West Indian possessions. The black slaves in Santo Domingo took up arms and established a revolutionary dictatorship under Toussaint l'Ouverture (1774–1803). Toussaint was subsequently captured by treachery and died in a French jail, but the French could not reestablish their rule in the new Negro republic. The British navy maintained an effective maritime supremacy, and British colonial producers once again competed successfully on the world market. British West Indian prosperity, however, was short-lived. The temporary peace treaty concluded with France at Lunéville in 1802 was highly unfavorable to the British. Great Britain had to restore most of her conquests, including Martinique, and the British thereby lost not only a great deal of territory, but also extensive capital investments. At the same time French-American trade began to revive. British West Indian producers had to meet growing competition from the Indies, where free laborers produced sugar and coffee more cheaply than West Indian slaves. Neutral powers, including the United States and the German Hanseatic cities garnered a goodly share of the colonial trade. Napoleon's continental blockade (a grand scheme to exclude all British goods from the European continent) was in no way completely effective, but it did inflict further damage on British trade and thereby worsened the problem of overproduction in colonial sugar.

The British slaving lobby weakened further as a result of internal economic conflicts among the British slave owners themselves. Trinidad (taken from the Spaniards in 1797 and finally ceded in 1802) was a fertile island with great economic potentialities. The plantation lords of Trinidad thus presented a serious threat to their competitors in the older British possessions who could no longer expand their production at the same rate as the Trinidadians. By a strangely ironic twist, many sugar producers in the older British islands themselves began to attack the slave trade as immoral and demanded that further imports into Trinidad and Guiana be restricted. The British imperial authorities, however, could hardly consent to such discrimination, even if only for technical and legal reasons. They also faced the "Danish problem" occasioned by Denmark's abolition of the slave trade in 1803. In addition terrible slave risings in Haiti and Guadeloupe as well as serious black unrest in various British possessions pointed to possible military dangers if the slave population was allowed to increase further. The British accordingly decided to make a clean sweep and in 1807 prohibited the slave trade once and for all.

Eric Williams, a West Indian historian influenced by Marxist arguments, developed an economic interpretation essentially similar to Hochstetter's. Williams argued, like the German, that the traditional role of the West Indies as a supplier of tropical produce, especially of sugar, was increasingly questioned from the time of the American independence struggle. During the Napoleonic wars there was overproduction. The British sugar lords also faced increasing competition from foreign rivals such as Brazil, Cuba, and Mauritius. Free traders, representing the cause of consumers and manufacturers, attacked discrimination against foreign sugar, while the traditional allies of the old protectionist system began to desert the West Indian interest. The slave owners' position further worsened when Napoleonic policies gave the first impetus to the cultivation of beet sugar on the European continent. Most British West Indian sugar producers came to grow their crops at a loss. Williams also emphasized, like Hochstetter, the conflict between the "saturated planters," that is to say, the plantation lords in the older colonies, and "the planters on the make," that is to say, those in the newly acquired West Indian possessions. He also argued that war and Napoleon's continental blockade made abolition imperative if the older colonies were to survive and thereby provided a convincing explanation of British policy.[20]

We ourselves take a point of view about halfway between the older humanitarian explanation and the economic interpretation provided by Hochstetter and Williams. We agree with Roger Anstey, a British historian, that the economic argument is persuasive in so far as it shows that the decline of mercantilism made action against the slave trade much easier. Anstey, however, points to some serious flaws in a purely economic interpretation. British policy makers did not point only to the distress caused to West Indian planters by overproduction. They also pleaded, like Lord Grenville, that Great Britain must do justice to the slaves as well as their owners and that the "detestable traffic" could not be allowed to continue, even if it brought profits to the landlords of Jamaica and Trinidad. Overproduction, in Anstey's view, was not a sufficient reason to abolish the slave trade altogether. British politicians would not have met a problem, occasioned by the special circumstances of wartime, with a measure which—in their view—would also have permanently limited output in peace-time. Anstey notes, moreover, that the British parliamentary committee set up to inquire into the grave economic condition of the West Indies reported only *after* the decisive step of abolition had been taken. The sugar crisis, Anstey agrees, certainly played a part, but the West Indies had seen severe depressions before, and the sugar planters had always been in debt. There was, moreover, no direct relation between the profitability of sugar and the British parliamentary vote—rather the other way around. (For instance, in 1796, a boom year for the West Indies, a British parliamentary majority favored abolition. 1804 was likewise a fairly good year for sugar, and again a majority of parliamentarians favored abolition.)

John Hargreaves, another British historian, lends further weight to Anstey's critique of the Williams thesis. He demonstrates that the slave-supported trade (which amounted to one-seventh of Britain's foreign commerce) did diminish in importance later on. The decisive change occurred after the wars. Historians cannot, therefore, infer that economic change already required the new policies during the period from 1783 to 1807.

The advocates of the economic school fail to produce adequate evidence to show how the selfish considerations that allegedly motivated British policy were actually translated into ministerial decisions and parliamentary votes. Politicians in the early nineteenth century had no reason to hide their "real" economic motives in private letters to one another. But neither Hochstetter nor Williams adequately buttress his case through evidence from such sources. Hargreaves shows that Williams did not fully grasp the political balance of power within the British parliament. According to Williams, the emergence of the Lancashire cotton interest in parliament strengthened the abolitionist cause, for the new capitalists necessarily advocated laissez faire rather than monopoly. In fact, however, the "Cottontots" were by no means united; some of them petitioned for abolition and others petitioned against it. Williams also paid inadequate attention to the views of county members in the British parliament. Yet abolition in fact seems to have been precisely the sort of question on which independent country gentlemen were liable to be influenced by a well-organized moral appeal. Williams, according to Hargreaves, also erred on several other minor points. (For instance, Williams exaggerated the scale of the East India Company's involvement in sugar plantations; sugar imports from East India greatly increased between 1791 and 1833, but even at the best of times these imports were still less than those derived from the declining island of Antigua.)

We conclude that changing economic circumstances did profoundly change the climate of opinion and the balance of political forces in Great Britain and elsewhere. Commerical expansion and the breakdown of the "Old Colonial System" had transformed the British economy to such an extent as to *permit* the abolition of the slave trade. But abolition had not as yet become an economic necessity, and the abolitionist movement cannot be explained in terms of trade balances and commercial preferences alone. Abolitionism went with profound changes within the "political nation" —a world where, above all, landed property, mercantile capital, and great hereditary or semiheriditary "connections" dominated the country. But abolitionism also formed part of a wider humanitarian movement that owed a profound debt to Christian and secular thinkers alike.[21]

The abolition of the slave trade indirectly linked Africa to the great revolution that steadily disrupted many hereditary privileges, social distinctions, and economic privileges throughout a large part of Europe, wiping out all manner of hereditary bondage, and seignorial and caste prerogatives. As Heinrich Heine, one of Germany's greatest poets, and a man of profound intuitive sense, put the matter a few years before the British abolished slavery, "What is the great task of our age? It is emancipation. Not only the emancipation of Irishmen and Greeks, of Frankfort Jews and West Indian Blacks, but the emancipation of the entire world, especially of Europe, which has become of age, and now breaks away from the iron leading string of the privileged . . . the aristocracy."[22]

Europeans were well aware of the connexion between the various forms of white and black bondage. *Uncle Tom's Cabin,* an influential antislavery novel, was translated into Russian, for instance, and abolitionist ideas influenced the extinction of serfdom. The Abbé Grégoire, a militant opponent of slavery in France, also advocated civic equality for the Jews. Heine, a bitter critic of Prussian aristocracy, lampooned the Dutch slave traders, who prided themselves on their Christian virtue. Negro insurgents, such as Toussaint l' Ouverture, who ended Negro slavery in Haiti, took a small but heroic part in this wider campaign against social and economic contraints. So did a handful of Western-educated people like Equiano. But abolitionism owed little to the indigenous people of Africa and mainly derived from Europe. Indeed, if the slave trade was to be destroyed, the European maritime powers would have to exert an increasing influence on the African continent itself in order to crush black African and brown Swahili as well as white beneficiaries of the traffic. The abolitionist campaign thus marked the end of what might be called the transatlantic plantation period of African history and marks the beginning of a new epoch—the age of paternalist imperialism.

NOTES

1. Edwards, *Equiano's Travels*, p. 172.

2. Philip D. Curtin, *The Image of Africa: British Ideas and Action, 1780–1850* (Madison, 1964), pp. 17–18.

3. H. C. Carey, *The Slave Trade, Domestic and Foreign: Why it Exists and How it may be Extinguished* (Philadelphia, 1856), p. 70.

4. Edwards, *Equiano's Travels*, p. 158.

5. Élie Halévy, *A History of the English People in 1815* (Harmondsworth, Middlesex, 1938), pp. 79–82.

6. Douglas Grant, *The Fortunate Slave: An Illustration of African Slavery in the Early Eighteenth Century* (London, 1968). See also the review article by J. H. Plumb, "Royal Slave," *Spectator* (London), September 20, 1968, p. 402.

7. In 1793 the French Revolution put an end to all seignorial claims and restrictions in France. In Belgium and the Netherlands the remaining seignorial dues were suppressed during the period of French domination (1795–1814). Later Prussia and Austria also introduced extensive reforms.

8. Franz Hochstetter, "Die wirtschaftlichen und politischen Motive für die Abschaffung des britischen Sklavenhandels im Jahre 1806/1807," in *Staats- und Sozialwissenschaftliche Forschungen*, (Leipzig, 1905), vol. 25, part 1, pp. 99–102.

9. Eric Williams *Capitalism and Slavery* (London, 1964), passim.

10. L. Burns, *The British West Indies* (London, 1951), p. 113.

11. E. L. Woodward, *The Age of Reform 1815–1870* (Oxford, 1949), p. 356.

12. Thomas Babington Macaulay, "The West Indies," in *Critical, Historical and Miscellaneous Essays* (Boston, 1886), vol. 6, appendix, p. 324

13. Sir Spenser St. John, *Hayti or the Black Republic* (New York, 1889), p. 137.

14. Alfred Cobban, *A History of Modern France, vol. 2: 1799–1945.* (Baltimore, Maryland, 1963), p. 135.

15. The phrase is Professor George Shepperson's, of Edinburgh University.

16. Hubert Herring, *A History of Latin America from the Beginnings to the Present* (New York 1961) p. 744, and Herman G. James and Percy A. Martin, *The Republics of Latin America: Their History, Governments and Economic Conditions* (New York, 1923), p. 124.

17. Duignan and Clendenen, *The United States and the African Slave Trade*, pp. 24–53.

18. William Edward Hartpole Lecky, *A History of European Morals from Augustus to Charlemagne* (London, 1884), vol. 1, p. 153.

19. According to British statistics quoted by Hochstetter, something like three-fifths of British slave exports went to foreign colonies by the end of the 1780s.

20. Williams, *Capitalism and Slavery.*

21. For details of this discussion see Roger T. Anstey, "Capitalism and Slavery: A Critique," *The Economic History Review*, Second Series, vol. 1, no. 2 (1968), pp. 307–320, as well as John Hargreaves, "Synopsis of a Critique of Eric Williams' *Capitalism and Slavery*," in *University of Edinburgh: Center of African Studies, "The Transatlantic Slave Trade from West Africa"* (1965), pp. 30–43.

22. Heinrich Heine, "Italien," *Werke.* (Hamburg: 1956 ed.), p. 315. Written in 1828.

Chapter 27

The Emergent Afro-European Societies on the West Coast

THE HUMANITARIAN FRONTIER IN WEST AFRICA

THE BRITISH AND THE FOUNDATION OF SIERRA LEONE

The British abolitionists could not destroy the slave trade right away. But they faced a serious problem right on their own doorstep. Eighteenth-century England contained something like 50,000 black people, including domestics brought in from the West Indies, sailors, and even a few well-educated people. After the American War the number of black poor increased owing to the influx of black American servicemen who had fought on the British side. All these immigrants were legally free, the British judiciary having decided that the law did not countenance slavery in Great Britain. But jobs were hard to find; there was a great deal of misery among destitute Africans, and Granville Sharp, a leading abolitionist, decided to take up their case.

The British government was persuaded to give free passage to a handful of black volunteers bound for Sierra Leone, where Sharp proposed to found the "Province of Freedom," a self-governing African community. The first settlers arrived in 1787 and were granted land by the local Temne chiefs, but they were soon beset by all kinds of misfortunes. The immigrants had come too late in the year to plant crops and heavy rains washed everything out of the ground. They suffered from disease; there was peculation of stores. Many colonists left and some even traded in slaves on their own account. To make matters worse, the newcomers became involved in quarrels with the neighboring Temne, who drove them out and burned their town.

Sharp could not afford to start the colony again, and the British government would not do so for reasons of economy. British well wishers thus founded a commercial corporation, later incorporated as the Sierra Leone Company. The new concern wished to combine philanthropy with profits. The promoters hoped to recuperate their outlay from quit rents on the settlers' lands, from trade, and from revenue derived from the company's own holdings; they also vowed not to deal in slaves but to confine themselves to legitimate commerce. The company brought back some of the earlier settlers, but their principal recruits were black loyalists who had fought for the King in the American War of Independence, had received promises of land in Nova Scotia, but had failed to get their fair share. The Nova Scotians were Christians, with their own churches and pastors.[1] Their language was English and so were many of their customs. They derived their political philosophy from current ideals concerning the rights of man, Anglo-Saxon liberties, Christian freedom, and American slogans rejecting taxation without representation. They had an intense yearning for social equality with white men, feelings that sometimes turned into blancophobia, the unreasoning hatred of all whites. As P. E. H. Hair, a modern historian, puts it, "they were politically conscious, politically opinionated and politically active. They were almost the first black Africans anywhere, and surely the first within Africa, to echo the sentiments and slogans of the modern world."[2]

The newcomers made many complaints concerning taxation; they publicly demanded more land, and privately grumbled at the British refusal to sanction the local slave trade. They also suffered from all the difficulties that immigrants may expect to encounter in tropical countries. Sierra Leone was far from being the land of lush tropical fertility imagined by the planners. Most of its coastlines and creeks are lined by unhealthy mangrove swamps. Large areas of the interior are covered by brushwood and forest. Disease conspired with climate to make the colonist's life exceptionally hard. Sierra Leone's hot moist coastal climate turned the settlement into a white man's grave and a black man's purgatory. American blacks were no more immune to African diseases than Europeans, and sickness took a grim toll. Farmers faced torrential rain falls; these were followed by a long dry season, punctuated sometimes by tornadoes or by desiccating northeast winds carrying clouds of fine Sahara dust.

The cultivators also met many economic difficulties. They lacked markets for their produce. They bore a heavy burden of rent. The company, itself an under-capitalized concern, charged too much for the use of the land, for the directors greatly overestimated the resources of the soil, failing to realize that unimproved bushland cannot be made valuable simply by charging a great deal of money for its use. To make matters worse, war broke out in 1793 between Great Britain and France. French men-of-war captured a good many of the company's ships, and in 1794 a French squadron sacked Freetown, the colony's diminutive capital.

The settlers' sufferings, their spirit of independence, and their grievances against the company combined to produce political turmoil, and in 1800 dissident black people, led by Isaac Anderson, a free Negro, set up their own government. The rebels established a rudimentary system of price control, imposed their own fines for economic as well as moral transgressions, and insisted that "the Governor and Council (appointed by the company) shall not have anything to do with the Colony no farther than the company's affairs . . ." The British put down the rising with a strong hand, hanged Anderson, and banished some of the ringleaders.

The condition of the colony improved only after 1807, when the bankrupt colony was wound up, and the British government began to administer the territory as a crown colony. Missionaries established a rudimentary system of education, and English—or a modified form of English—became the local *lingua franca.* The country was found unsuited to the production of export crops or to plantation agriculture. There was, however, some scope for peasant farmers laboring mainly for their own subsistence. Some colonists gradually became acclimatized, cleared farms, traded with the inland tribes, and settled down to the life of a typical pioneer community.

Encouraged by this success, the British authorities from 1809 onward began to settle freed slaves in Sierra Leone, and the Nova Scotians soon were heavily outnumbered by a great mass of less sophisticated immigrants from many parts of West Africa. The British tried to settle the newcomers into villages where they would be taught market gardening and crafts. Most of these villages, with English names like Gloucester and Kent, did not fulfil the hopes of their missionary friends and benefactors. The most enterprising black people turned to trade, and some became substantial businessmen on their own account.

Economic development led to considerable social change. By the early 1820s society at Freetown was composed of four main classes: the indigenous inhabitants of the area, including the Temne people, the newly arrived "liberated Africans," that is to say, freed captives taken from slave ships, including people of the most variegated ethnic background, the anglicized black settlers, and the British officials at the top of the social hierarchy.[3]

The black colonists gradually overcame the hardships occasioned by the difficulties of climate and geography, and the country attained a modest degree of prosperity. Freetown, with its splendid harbor, became a center for the trade in palm oil and peanuts, as well as an important naval station for British operations against the slave trade. The port also attracted immigrants from many other parts of West Africa, including Wolof from the Senegal, Fulani from the interior, and Kru from what is now Liberia.

Above all, Sierra Leone acquired great importance as a British missionary base. British teachers and clergymen built up a relatively well-developed system of education. In 1827 the Church Missionary Society (an Anglican body) set up Fourah Bay College (subsequently affiliated to the University of Durham, England). Fourah Bay became the first and, for the time being, the only institution of higher learning on the West African coast, and Sierra Leoneians were quick to benefit from these educational advantages. The Sierra Leone Creoles, English-speaking Africans, pushed outward along the coast and inward into the hinterland as missionaries, teachers, traders, clerks, government employees, and sometimes even as farmers; in doing so they became—so to speak—middlemen of western civilization in Africa. By the late 1850s, the Creoles—the colony-born descendants of Nova Scotians, black poor, Maroons, liberated Africans—had emerged as a distinct cultural group. Their values were, above all, those of middle-class Victorian England; yet they were Africans more than Afro-Britons. In addition they had a taste for certain things American, and the Creole community provided a small but profitable market for American merchants. Yankee shipmasters also made their way to other parts of West Africa. American rum, tobacco, flour, and lumber acquired a well-deserved reputation all along the coast. The British gradually abandoned their restrictive practices against foreign competitors, and American commerce became so important that in 1852 a British order-in-council declared American money to be legal tender in Sierra Leone, along with British coinage.[4]

THE BRITISH IMPACT: GAMBIA AND THE GOLD COAST

In addition to Sierra Leone the British also held a few scattered possessions elsewhere on the West African shore. One of these was Gambia, where the British first built a fort on the mouth of the great river in 1651. Merchants traded up and down the Gambia River. In addition, Gambia benefited from contact with the New World. In the 1820s black veterans from the Royal African Corps and the West India Regiment settled in the colony. So did a handful of black pioneers from the United States, including Thomas Joiner, an ex-slave of Mandingo extraction who became a substantial merchant and ship owner in Gambia.[5] The British West African colonies, like their French counterpart in Senegal, thus developed a Europeanized or semi-Europeanized indigenous elite; these men often had a material interest in the extension of imperial rule for the purpose of securing their trade, of obtaining employment in government, or of participating in missionary enterprise.

The British also continued to control a few posts along the Gold Coast. As the nineteenth century opened, these factories were under the control of a privately chartered company of merchants. In 1821 the governor of Sierra Leone became directly responsible for these possessions as well. But the expense of maintaining the forts proved too great; in 1827 the British government withdrew its officials from the Gold Coast, and private traders once more took over the management of the forts. Their administration was headed by George Maclean, a young army officer, who arrived at the Gold Coast in 1830. Maclean succeeded in negotiating a peace treaty between the coastal people and the British on the one hand, and the warlike Ashanti on the other. The Ashanti renounced their claims to the Atlantic shore and promised freedom of trade in the interior. Maclean's diplomacy and the activities of European and of Afro-British merchants spread British influence farther afield, and in 1843 the new administration concluded an agreement with various Fante communities embodying the humanitarian and commercial aspirations of the time. The African rulers agreed to protect the strangers' persons and property; they declared their willingness to abolish "human sacrifice and other barbarous customs"; the chiefs also permitted British courts to exercise jurisdiction over certain crimes originating in the territories surrounding the forts.

The advance of trade also encouraged European mission enterprise. As early as 1722 Danish pioneers had opened a school at Christiansborg (Accra) on the Gold Coast. In 1820 emissaries of the Basel Missionary Society, a vigorous Swiss body, took over the local teaching work. The Swiss were followed by missionaries from the British and Foreign Bible Society, and the Bremen Mission, a German Protestant body. One of the most outstanding of these evangelists was the Rev. Thomas Birch Freeman, the son of an African father and an English mother, who from 1837 tried to spread Wesleyan doctrines to the Cape Coast. A few stations were also set up further inland. In 1844, for instance, the Church Missionary Society, established a mission at Abeokuta, among several hundred Yoruba who had been removed from the holds of slave ships, settled in Sierra Leone, but had subsequently decided to return to their own country.

The influence of the missions should not be overestimated. Their impact was limited to a few regions; hence the new educated elite mainly derived from a small number of unusually favored communities. Mission work nevertheless affected secular as well as spiritual life in Africa. The emissaries of the gospel not only preached Christianity they also spread literacy and other secular skills; they tried to promote the cultivation of cash crops, the use of new tools, the employment of more efficient building methods, and so forth. Missionaries, white and black, determined to change indigenous society as well as indigenous thought. The evangelist always saw himself as an agent of social change as well as a spokesman of Christianity. The humanitarian, the missionary, and the mercantile frontier thus advanced in concert; between them they gradually initiated a far-reaching social transformation in West Africa.

LIBERIA

The abolitionist movement had wide-spread repercussions in the United States. In addition the Sierra Leonian experiment at colonization found admirers in the United States. Contrary to a widely held belief, some of the earliest settlers in North America included free Negroes as well as slaves. Free Negroes had a share in the American commerce with Africa; free Negroes also helped to colonize the West. The number of freemen of color gradually increased by manumission, but free blacks were never truly absorbed into American society. Some American Negroes, including a handful of ex-slaves, thus sought to better their condition by emigrating to Africa. One of these pioneers was Thomas Joiner, an American slave of Mandingo origins, who acquired his freedom in the New World and later settled in Gambia, where he became a substantial merchant and shipowner. Other Afro-Americans began to consider plans for colonization of a more systematic kind. In 1788 a group of educated black people in Newport, Rhode Island, proposed a plan for settling black Americans on their ancestral continent. The Newport group included Paul Cuffee, a merchant, who in 1811 sailed his own ship *The Traveler* to Sierra Leone with thirty-eight Afro-Americans aboard. In 1817 American humanitarians founded the American Colonization Society for the purpose of settling free black people in West Africa.

The project at first aroused a good deal of controversy. Governor Charles Macarthy of Sierra Leone, for instance, suspected that the society was a mere cloak for the purpose of establishing an American colony to injure British interests. Macarthy actually requested permission from London to seize the island of Sherbro and thereby forestall the suspected American peril. The British government did not back its proconsul over this matter, but even in the United States the American Colonization Society met with a good deal of hostility. Many abolitionists believed that the emigration of free Afro-Americans would simply strengthen slavery in the South. The great majority of American Negroes, for their part, had little interest in the scheme, and no more wanted to leave for Africa than the Pennsylvania Dutch desired to return to their ancestral villages in western Germany.

But the Colonization Society also had powerful friends. President Monroe expressed sympathy for the Society's aims; so did numerous Northern "Negrophilists." Many Southern slave owners likewise supported the society on the grounds that freed slaves could not be absorbed by the American people and that their very presence on American soil formed a potential danger to the established social order. Discontented black Americans had their own reasons for an African solution. Their case makes eloquent reading. Black people in the United States, they said, were exposed to the most severe forms of political, economic, and social discrimination; they were debarred from civil office and from participation in government; they had been reduced to a separate and distinct class, inferior even to white foreigners; black complaints were left unattended; black hopes for an improvement in their condition had become extinguished.

These pessimistic conclusions seemed to be borne out by the facts of American economic life. The invention of the cotton gin and the expansion of the textile industry in Great Britain, Belgium, and other countries introduced profound changes in the economic condition of the South. Cotton became king. It required a great labor force; hence the price of slaves rose, manumissions diminished in number, and the chance of abolishing slavery seemed to disappear. Americans, moreover, had to find a home for black captives found on board slave ships intercepted on the Atlantic run. In 1821 the American Colonization Society, with official help, purchased a small tract of land on the coast of what is now Liberia. In addition a number of independent bodies set up a few settlements of their own, unconnected with the older centers of the American Colonization Society.

The settlers had to cope with difficulties of the harshest kind. There were conflicts with indigenous tribes, who not only resented the loss of their land but also feared the newcomers' interference with the slave trade. The colonists had to face a harsh tropical country; they were unfamiliar with local agricultural conditions; they suffered from all manner of hardship and disease. Gradually, however, the settlers' fortunes improved. In 1826 Jehudi Ashmun, a remarkable white man, assumed charge of the main colony at Cape Mesurado, already called Liberia. Liberian and American forces cooperated in wiping out a notorious local center of the slave traffic, known as Trade Town. The local chiefs were compelled to abstain from the commerce in human beings and the colony's fortunes greatly improved.

But Liberia's greatest statesman was perhaps Joseph Jenkins Roberts, a Virginian of mixed white and black ancestry. A successful businessman ambitious for learning, Roberts subsequently studied at various times under Edward Blyden, a black West Indian scholar and an early black nationalist. Roberts above all was a man of action. Lighter in complexion than many Europeans, tall and erect, with a heavy moustache, he had a military look which gave him an impressive appearance. Having made his mark as a merchant in the United States, he emigrated to Liberia in 1829. A year later he was elected to the office of sheriff, and soon embarked on a spectacular political career. By this time the majority of the immigrants demanded to control their own affairs, and called upon the American Colonization Society to relinquish its power. Roberts sided with the antigovernment men, and soon acquired great influence.

In 1838 the scattered Libero-American colonies on the west coast united in a Commonwealth; all positions of power passed into the hands of the colonists, except the right to elect their governor. Thomas Buchanan, the first and only white governor, wisely appointed Roberts as his lieutenant, and Roberts turned out to be a brilliant choice. He quelled various indigenous risings, battled against foreign slave traders, conducted punitive expeditions against Africans unwilling to pay their debts to the government, and acquired additional territory by making treaties with local chiefs.

Upon Buchanan's death in 1841, Roberts succeeded to the governorship, and guided his country through one of the most difficult phases of its existence. The Libero-Americans remained a small minority. Their country was in financial straits; the colony's international position was in doubt; there were disputes centering on the question whether the colony should break all links with the Colonization Society.

Liberia, moreover, was rent by various social divisions. The more conservative element, many of them adherents of the American Colonization Society, largely consisted of mulattoes, some of them prominent traders and ship owners. The mulattoes were better educated than their darker-skinned neighbors. Some had inherited property from their white fathers; they regarded themselves as a social elite and considered themselves to be entitled to the better jobs in commerce and government. They looked to new immigrants from the United States to replenish their numbers; they feared the danger of "mobocracy," and they subsequently tried to defend their political interests by founding the True Liberian Party (later known as the Republican Party).

The mulattoes were opposed by darker-skinned settlers who mainly composed the less affluent element of the population. The darker-complexioned people were assigned land outside Monrovia, the main settlement, and often accused the Colonization Society's white agent of discriminating on the mulattoes' behalf in the allocation of town lots. The darker-skinned later formed the True Whig Party; they called for the unification of all tribes and classes in the country, and professed a more democratic outlook than the rival party. Nearly all Libero-Americans in turn made a sharp distinction between themselves, the "civilized," and the aboriginal communities, with whom at various times they competed for land or fought pitched battles.

Despite these divisions the greater part of the settlers gradually became converts to the cause of independence, especially after they received inadequate support from the United States in Liberian disputes with the British. Only independence, Roberts argued, would relieve the Liberians of future embarrassment and settle the objections raised by Great Britain concerning Liberia's sovereignty. In the end the matter was put to a popular vote. Only two-thirds of the tiny Americo-Liberian electorate, including a few hundred African aborigines, cast their votes. But of these a majority backed Roberts on the independence issue, and in 1847 a constitutional convention assembled to work out a new instrument of government, largely on the American model.

On July 26, 1847, Liberia formally declared its independence, the first modern black state in Africa, and Roberts became its first president.

Roberts successfully negotiated with the American Colonization Society, which agreed to cede all public lands within the limits of Liberia to the new government. More important still, Roberts set out on a diplomatic visit to Great Britain, where he received a splendid welcome. Great Britain was the first nation to accord international recognition to Liberia. (The United States did not follow suit until the Civil War because of the racial issues in America.) Above all, Roberts, despite his conservative leanings, demanded that "the whole aboriginal population of the Republic should be drawn as rapidly as possible within the circle of civilization and be fitted by suitable educational training for all the duties and social life; . . . (so that) we too shall be exerting a hallowed influence upon the tribes of our far interior."[6]

Roberts's assimilationist doctrines bore much similarity to those formulated by British missionaries and also by the French. Liberian, like French assimilation remained a matter of theory rather than practice for the time being. Liberia's tiny "civilized" population lacked both the men and the means to anglicize vigorous indigenous communities such as the Kru. Assimilation stood even less chance with the powerful Mandingo of the interior, who professed the Islamic faith. The military forces at Roberts' command remained puny. The Liberian administration was weak and often inept. Many of the indigenous tribes nominally under Liberian sovereignty were probably quite unaware of their supposed subordination to Monrovia. The immigrants had come as colonists, and Roberts in many ways had to act in a manner not very dissimilar from, say, a British administrator in Africa. (From 1843 onward, for instance, Roberts called together unification councils over which he presided in order to settle tribal disputes or arbitrate between opposing interests.)

At the time of independence his difficulties were many. The Libero-American ruling stratum numbered no more than 3000 people, who tended to remain a small, self-conscious minority. There were bitter disputes among the colonists; there was a good deal of graft and incompetence in public life; there was all too little enterprise and less money. The American Civil War emancipated the American Negro slave, and thereby lessened Liberia's attraction for black North Americans. Spanish- and Portuguese-speaking black people had no incentive and no opportunity to seek a new home in a country where English was the official language. Liberia was a hard country in which to make one's fortune; the free black—for all his disabilities—usually had greater opportunities on the American continent. Liberia had no religious significance for black Americans, comparable to that which the Holy Land possessed for the Jews and which was later channelled into Zionism. The black diaspora in the New World also lacked the cohesion, the financial resources, and the ideological incentives to build Liberia into an economically prosperous and military powerful country like modern Israel.

But for all its weaknesses, Liberia held together. Its internal politics never reached the turbulence of Haiti's; the ruling Libero-American oligarchy secured a certain degree of stability, and the country developed a syncretic Anglo-African culture of its own. There was plenty of social and political discrimination; but discrimination could never harden into a rigid color bar of the South African variety. Roberts' ideal of national unification remained a long-term political goal that—for all the current abuses—the more enlightened Liberians expected to reach in the distant future.

THE PORTUGUESE AND FRENCH IMPACT ON WEST AFRICA

The anglicized Africans on the west coast found their counterpart in Africans of mulatto origin who adopted a modified form of Portuguese or French as their native tongue. Many Portuguese immigrants, for instance, were settled on the Cape Verde Islands, from where they traded with the African mainland. The Portuguese also held a number of fortified posts, including Bissau, situated in a swampy archipelago in what is now Portuguese Guinea. A few white merchants settled permanently on the west coast, took African wives or concubines, and taught Portuguese or a modified form of Portuguese to their children. These people of mixed ancestry traded far and wide along the coast. Some penetrated far up the rivers and creeks between the Senegal River and Sierra Leone, becoming middlemen of both Portuguese commerce and culture.

The Portuguese played an important part in the transatlantic slave trade, and Angola especially became an important supplier for the plantations of Brazil. Angola, in some ways, became as much of a dependency of Brazil as of Portugal, and the tenor of life in Luanda, Angola's chief city, followed that of Brazil. The settlers cooked their meals in the Brazilian fashion; they adopted some of the particularities of Brazilian architecture and often spoke a Brazilian form of Portuguese. Fashionable ladies perambulated through the streets accompanied by a train of slaves; educated men read pamphlets about Brazil's separation from the Portuguese mother country in 1822. Farther south, at Benguela, an influential party even instigated a brief rising in favor of a federal union with Brazil, and some Brazilian emigrants settled in Angola.

The Portuguese, however, never settled in large numbers. The bulk of Portugal's emigrants preferred Brazil to the scattered and disease-ridden possessions in Africa. In 1836 the Portuguese government officially abolished the slave trade and tried to replace the accustomed revenue from the traffic by profits from "legitimate" commerce. Reforms, however, were hard to enforce in practice; Portuguese attempts to strengthen the postabolition economy by a vigorous policy of territorial expansion to capture additional trade had only limited success. Africa's Portuguese-speaking population remained small. By the 1840s the entire colony of Luanda numbered less than 2000 whites and less than 6000 mixed breeds.

Perhaps the most important European colony in West Africa at the time was French, centering on the port of St. Louis. Already by the end of the eighteenth century this French colonial city supposedly numbered something like 10,000 people, including several hundred whites. The majority of the inhabitants at that time consisted of household slaves, many of them Bambara. Domestic bondsmen, however, were rarely sold, and in effect became part of the Senegalese community. Most Frenchmen also took permanent African mistresses, known as *signares,* and saw to it that their children obtained a French education. Indeed in all but legal status the *signares* were wives, and their marriages were celebrated with all the pomp of normal weddings.[7] Many *signares* were formidable women, with a substantial stake in commerce, and their descendants were assimilated to some degree into French culture. Many Senegalese accepted Catholicism; others practiced cults in which Christianity strangely mingled with Islam and even paganism. Christian Negroes served in the French armed forces. They made a living as craftsmen, interpreters, and captains of river boats, as well as salaried employees of European merchants. Senegal carried on an important traffic in gum, and the more shrewd and skillful African agents set themselves up in business on their own account. Assimilation also meant that some black people consciously adopted French standards and values. In the main these were confined to the towns, but in all probability Gallicized Wolofs and other immigrants remained in touch with their rural kinfolk so that a small measure of French urban influence also filtered into the countryside.[8]

The habitants included a small number of cultured people of wide interests and attainments. One of their most outstanding representatives was the Abbé P. D. Boilat, a young African, who was sent to France in the early nineteenth century to prepare for the priesthood and who later made his name as a historian, as an ethnographer, and as a vigorous advocate of French civilization. The habitants also began to take an active interest in politics. In 1789 on the eve of the French revolution, a meeting at St. Louis, chaired by the mulatto mayor, Charles Cornier, drafted a *cahier* calling on the Estates General in Paris to abolish the commercial monopoly of the Senegal Company as an odious privilege, contrary to the law of reason and nature. These and other demands met with a good deal of sympathy in Paris. For a long time brilliant philosophers such as Montesquieu had denounced what they considered unjustified privileges, the undue concentration of landed property in a few hands, and also the institution of slavery. An influential school of economists, known as physiocrats, asserted that true wealth derived from the land. They demanded freedom of commerce and competition, freedom from feudal and servile bonds, and freedom from guild regulations and monopolistic restraints on the grounds that such institutions were incompatible with human dignity as well as economic prosperity. In France the anti-slavery cause gained much support from outstanding intellectuals and politicians such as Condorcet, Mirabeau, Sièyes, Lafayette and Brissot, all of whom were members of a Negrophile body known as the Société des Amis des Noirs.

The French antislavery cause, however, never became a great popular crusade with a strong moralistic flavor, as it did in England. The reformers' ideological inspiration did not derive from Protestantism, with its great network of dissident popular churches, but from a more secular-minded faith in the "natural religion" and the rights of man. The rights of man, however, were also asserted by plantation owners dissatisfied with Bourbon government, and slave owners were present in the revolutionary assemblies. Colonial reforms were determined by French metropolitan needs, and to a lesser extent West Indian, rather than by African needs and interests. In 1790 the French legislature, however, enunciated the revolutionary principle that the colonies formed an integral part of France, a concept intimately linked to the centralizing policy pursued by the revolutionaries at home. In 1791 colored men who were the sons of a free father and a free mother received the vote on the same terms as white men. In 1793 the French convention voted to abolish the slave trade, and a year later, for the abolition of slavery itself.

These concessions did not at first mean a great deal in practice. In 1802, under Napoleon's authoritarian regime, slavery once again became legal, and during the same year the French put down a rising of Africans and mulattoes in Senegal. Worse still, from the French point of view, the overseas empire suffered a series of devastating blows. Revolutionary France lost command of the seas. Haiti, one of the greatest slave colonies in the French Indies, obtained its independence after a bloody and protracted revolutionary war. Slavery and the French presence were alike wiped out from the island, and the country became a black peasant state, subject to the unstable rule of successive dictators. Louisiana had to be sold to the Americans. Senegal's prosperity suffered severely. The colony experienced a British naval blockade; its trade was disrupted, and between 1809 and 1816 the British temporarily occupied the country. But when the French returned, things could never be the same again. France had accepted, at any rate in theory, the revolutionary principle of assimilation for a minority, and French-speaking mulattoes and Africans remained a force to be reckoned with in the commercial and cultural life of the French possessions in West Africa.

NOTES

1. This section is based on Christopher Fyfe, *Sierra Leone Inheritance* (London, 1964), especially pp. 6, 114, 124–25. See also the same author's massive *A History of Sierra Leone* (London, 1962).

2. P. E. H. Hair, "Africanism: the Freetown Contribution," *Journal of Modern African Studies,* vol. 5, no. 4 (December 1967), pp. 521–539.

3. A. T. Porter, "Family Histories and West African Social Development: The Role of the Creole in Nineteenth Century Sierra Leone," in *Historians in Tropical Africa: Proceedings of the Leverhulme Inter-Collegiate History Conference,* pp. 305–315.

4. Clarence C. Clendenen and Peter Duignan, *Americans in Black Africa up to 1865* (Stanford, 1964), p. 9.

5. Florence K. Mahoney, "African Leadership in Bathurst in the Nineteenth Century," *Tarikh,* vol. 2, no. 2 (1968), pp. 25–38.

6. Quoted from Abeodu B. Jones, "Joseph Jenkins Roberts: First President of Liberia," *Tarikh,* vol. 1, no. 4 (1967), pp. 41–54, see also Clendenen and Duignan, *Americans in Black Africa,* pp. 44–88, on which much of this chapter has been based.

7. Michael Crowder, *Senegal: A Study in French Assimilation Policy.* (London, 1962), p. 8.

8. John D. Hargreaves, *West Africa: The Former French States.* (Englewood Cliffs: N. J., 1967), pp. 67–76.

Chapter 28

South and
South Central Africa

BANTU, BOER AND BRITON AT THE CAPE

In a previous chapter we have outlined the process whereby, within a generation, the Dutch settlement at the Cape developed from a transit station to the Indies to a white settlement colony. German, Dutch, and other newcomers came to the Cape. The Europeans in South Africa, like those on the west coast, took women of color as their mistresses and, occasionally, as their lawfully-wedded spouses. These unions produced many offspring and the Cape—like Senegal—saw the emergence of a racially-mixed people with the blood of Europeans, Malays, Hottentots, and Bushmen in their veins, whose descendants are now known in South Africa as "Coloureds." The climate at the Cape was, however, much healthier than that of West Africa. Most settlers accordingly were able to marry women of their own race, and the Cape produced a self-consciously white society that sharply marked itself off from outsiders, first by religion and then by race.

The Europeans received reinforcements when, in 1685, Louis XIV revoked the Edict of Nantes, which had hitherto guaranteed religious toleration for French Protestants. As a result countless industrious people left France. A few hundred of these refugees took advantage of an offer made by the Dutch East India Company and accepted a free passage to the Cape as well as free land in the new country. The newcomers soon intermarried with other Europeans, and many South Africans today bear French names such as Marais, du Toit, Le Roux, de Villiers, and so forth, though the French language completely disappeared among them. The immigrants made excellent settlers and brought with them an expert knowledge of viticulture as well as other skills. They built up the wine-making industry of the Cape, one of the country's most valuable economic pursuits, and supplied Cape Town with wine, grain, and other crops. The wealthier European landowners could afford stately farm houses, constructed in the Cape Dutch style, some of which are still tourist attractions to this day.

The white population at the Cape also comprised townsmen, including merchants, artisans, company officials, and others. By 1806 the Cape supposedly contained a population of just under 27,000 whites. Of these, some 6000 lived at Cape Town, the main city, so that by contemporary standards the Europeans in South Africa were already a relatively highly urbanized people. Neither the townsmen nor the farmers at the western Cape had to contend with the menace of a tribal frontier, and their outlook on life came to differ greatly from that of the white pioneers in the interior.

Educated men in the cities looked to the Netherlands and, to a lesser extent, to France and Great Britain for new ideas, and a small minority of colonists was influenced to some extent by the ideas of the Enlightenment that trickled in from overseas. The trekkers on the frontier (to whom we shall make further reference in subsequent sections) were a very different breed. In the interior there was insufficient rainfall for intensive arable farming. Stock rearing, supplemented by the cultivation of a little maize, by hunting, by transport riding, and a few rural crafts thus became the most profitable occupation inland, and the white frontier society became sharply distinct from European colonial societies in the older settled regions.

Frontier farming required an immense amount of grazing land and depended on continuous territorial expansion. The extension of the white man's pastoral frontier often had grim consequences for the aboriginal people of the Cape. The Bushmen's resistance to the encroachment of alien pastoralists of whatever color usually took the form of stock lifting. The white men's domesticated beasts offered an irresistible attraction for Stone Age hunters. The Boers, seeing their livelihood endangered, took savage reprisals to protect their herds, and well-organized commandos systematically hunted down the aborigines. Some Bushmen became sufficiently "tame" to be employed as trackers, stockmen, and domestic servants in Boer households; but the Bushmen people largely became extinct, and Bushmen survived only as independent clans in a few inaccessible, arid regions.

The Hottentots did not fare much better. The Hottentots had cattle and fat-tailed sheep, but unlike the Boers or the Bantu they had no knowledge of arable farming, and they never seem to have been organized in political units larger than extended clans. The Hottentots could offer little resistance to the trekkers. Drink, smallpox, and musket balls took a heavy toll, and by the beginning of the nineteenth century free Hottentot "captaincies" had largely disappeared. Some Hottentots escaped beyond the shifting borders of the colony. They mingled with runaway slaves and indigenous Koranna people, as well as with a handful of white pioneers and outcasts. Their offspring formed nomadic bands of mounted cattle keepers who pursued a roving existence in the neighborhood of the Orange River, the more advanced "Bastards" (people of mixed Afro-European origin) living in many ways rather like white trekkers. But the mass of the Hottentots were reduced to complete dependence on the whites. They could not legally own land, there were no native reserves for them, and the bulk of the Hottentots became vagrants and poverty-stricken farmhands whose economic status did not differ much from serfdom. By 1806 there were supposed to be just over 17,000 within the borders of the Cape Colony. These, together with the 29,000 persons returned as slaves, including Malays, black people, and mixed breeds, formed the lowest stratum of Cape society. The descendants of the original Hottentots and the people of mixed origin generally adopted Afrikaans as their native tongue, so that South Africa produced its own variety of a half-Europeanized *métis* society.[1]

The farmers on the eastern frontier met opponents very different from the Hottentots. They encountered Bantu communities who knew how to smelt iron, herd cattle, and plant crops, and who were also skilled in war. The Fish River region became a boundary zone, and it was no longer safe for mere families to push into "Kaffirland." The Bantu competed with the Boers for grazing grounds and succeeded to some extent in diverting Boer expansion from the coastal belt into the northern interior. The Bantu could not, however, impose a permanent check on the Afrikaners, and the government of the Dutch East India Company soon had a perennial problem on its hands. The settlers clamored for military protection; the financial authorities called for economy. The Company, having no stomach for new territorial responsibilities, tried to stop all intercourse between black and white so as to prevent friction and consequent expenditure on armaments. Company regulations could not, however, be enforced. Whites continued to travel inland in order to hunt game, trade or steal domestic animals, or seek new pastures. Bantu people made their way into the European settlements for all kind of reasons: to buy and sell, to accept temporary employment, and often to rustle cattle. The Bantu acquired a taste for certain kinds of European goods, and the contact between whites and blacks created a new economic network that could not be broken by mere regulations. In addition there was a good deal of violence. The Company could not effectively enforce law and order; thefts begot reprisals as the aggrieved of either race took to arms, and the frontier became a land of intermittent fighting.

In 1778 Governor van Plettenberg visited the disputed area and concluded a treaty with the "Kaffirs," that solemnly fixed the Fish River as the dividing line between the Colony and the Bantu territories. But Plettenberg's plan of territorial separation did not work and neither did similar projects hatched in subsequent years. In the first place, the treaty seems to have been concluded without reference to the great Xhosa chiefs further inland. Secondly, the governor and the African negotiators probably interpreted the agreement in very different fashions. The whites thought in terms of private property in land and of political annexation, with exclusive rights of control up to the frontier. Bantu custom, however, knew only usufructuary rights in land, and the tribesmen presumably believed that their traditional claims would still be safeguarded. The Fish River, moreover, was not a good frontier in the geographical sense. Except when the watercourse is flooded it does not form a barrier at all but can easily be traversed along its greater part. There was also a certain vagueness about what was meant by the Fish River line. For about forty miles from the coast inland the river might serve as a boundary of a kind. But from above the point where Fort Beaufort now stands the main stream runs parallel to the coast almost at right angles to any natural dividing line between Colony and "Kaffirs." To follow the river to where it bent back to the southwest meant, in effect, making a full right turn, which cut out of the Bantu territory some of its most valuable lands.

The Fish River could never become a boundary of effective white occupation. There were Africans to the west and Europeans to the east of it, and the colonists' attempts to clear their side of Bantu tribesmen were never successful. The Bantu were periodically expelled but in wide, almost trackless bush country forcible population transfers were quite impracticable. In fact white settlement may, in some cases, even have encouraged the immigration of black people. Fighting, therefore, continued between Boer commandos and Bantu hosts, and the frontiersmen learned how to rely on their own strength more than on assistance from the distant government.[2]

The failure of the Dutch government to afford effective armed support to the frontiersmen and to govern its dependencies effectively had far-reaching consequences. In 1795 the Boers at Graaff-Reinet seized the magistracy and elected their own officials. A few months later the farmers at Swellendam set up a short-lived republic. At the same time, Holland was drawn into the wars of the French Revolution, with disastrous consequences for its position overseas. The motherland was occupied by the French, who turned the country into the Batavian Republic, a French revolutionary satellite. Holland's ruler, the Prince of Orange, fled to England, and in 1795 the British occupied the Cape in the prince's name. During their temporary occupation the British rescinded the Company's restrictions on trade, but on the conclusion of a peace treaty with France the country was restored to Holland. Between 1803 and 1806 a liberal Dutch administration tried to effect various reforms, but war broke out again. In 1805 the British smashed the allied French and Spanish navies at Trafalgar, and in the following year they once again seized the Cape—this time for good.

In the beginning the British did not greatly affect the country's tenor of life. Broadly speaking, the British initially administered the country as lackadaisically as had the Dutch. They had no use for South Africa's vast hinterland; they were primarily concerned with the Cape as a strategic bastion; their administrative machinery was weak, and their administrators were always in financial trouble. The British occupation nevertheless had profound long-term consequences. The British hold on the Cape provided the Royal Navy with a vital strong point on the road to the Indies and transformed the strategic pattern in the southern Atlantic. The British made many unsuccessful attempts to anglify the Dutch but thereby only strengthened the Afrikaners' feeling of ethnic identity.

The British conquerors, like their Dutch predecessors, found themselves encumbered with unwanted responsibility and unwanted expense in the interior. They could not avoid spending money and employing troops in the hinterland. The latest conflict between an economy-minded central government, more often than not willing to live at peace with the "Kaffirs," and the frontiersmen assumed new forms. The struggle was embittered by differences of language, of internal social stratification, and culture. The rural Dutch trekkers, for their part, could no longer deal with a weak Company or Dutch metropolitan authority, but with the world's most powerful maritime state, a country that was beginning to be strongly influenced by the evangelical and humanitarian ideals of its Protestant urban middle classes at home.

South Africa, moreover, became part of Western Europe's missionary frontier. The first to come had been the Moravian Bretheren who, in 1792, had established the earliest mission station in South Africa. In 1799 the London Missionary Society sent out its emissaries to South Africa. The society was dominated by the Rev. Dr. Johannes Theodorus Vanderkemp, a typical representative of missionary Protestantism. A Hollander by birth, he had served for sixteen years in the Army where he held the ranks of Captain of Horse and Lieutenant of Dragoon Guards. He had studied medicine in Edinburgh and obtained the M.D. degree of that university. He was also the author of books that were described as being of "terrifying prolixity." After a terrible tragedy, in which he lost his wife and only child, he underwent a transforming spiritual experience and at the age of nearly fifty offered his services to the London Missionary Society, to become one of the great missionary statesman of the nineteenth century.[3]

Failing to establish itself in "Kaffirland," the Society, under Vanderkemp's direction, set up a station known as Bethelsdorp. Its object was to convert and civilize the Hottentots, turn them into "useful" producers, and improve their civil status, with the ultimate object of building up a native church with native pastors. The missionaries looked to the central government to ameliorate the position of the indigenous races; South Africa in time became a battleground between two opposing concepts —imperial-minded missionary humanitarianism on the one hand, and the trekkers' frontier philosophy on the other.[4]

SLAVES, HOTTENTOTS, AND "COLOURED" (EURAFRICAN) PEOPLE

The early Cape, like Zanzibar, the West Indies, and the southern states of the United States, were founded upon servile labor. In the Cape as elsewhere slavery, however, entailed many different forms of bondage. Slaves worked in domestic service, a major form of employment in little-developed economies. Slaves, particularly those of Malay origin, also made their living as builders, painters, masons, bakers, and such. According to contemporary observers, labor conditions at the Cape appear to have been rather better than those prevailing in the West Indies. South Africa had no plantations of the American kind. The wine farmers of the western Cape, the wealthiest and most cultured land owners in the country, required a considerable number of workmen. But elsewhere the number of slaves was limited. Boer pastoralists required only a relatively small number of herdsmen. Slaves indeed formed but a small portion of the Colored (Eurafrican) population at the Cape. (In this respect the country was quite unlike the West Indies, where almost the entire non-European population was enslaved.)

The British, having occupied the Cape, introduced a number of reforms. They abolished the rack and the wheel; they limited the number of lashes to a figure that must have moved British soldiers and sailors of the time to bitter envy! Above all they not only legally abolished the slave trade, but made their prohibition effective. The price of slaves began to rise, and owners were given an additional economic incentive to treat their slaves with greater humanity.

Even at best, however, slavery was a brutal system. Slave families could be split up and their members sold separately. Masters continued to impose harsh punishments on slaves, if they felt so inclined. Slavery also profoundly influenced race relations in a more general fashion. The senior officials of the Dutch East India Company had brought white servants to South Africa. But in time the Dutch *knecht* also became a master. Menial labor was associated in the settler's mind with slavery; slavery, in turn, became indissolubly linked with a dark skin. The slave wore what Hilda Kuper, a modern anthropologist, has called "the uniform of color;" so did the poor man, the Hottentot vagrant without land, and the fierce Bantu tribesman beyond the border, a potential raider or cattle thief, in the settler's eyes. Above all, slavery was economically inefficient. As the Rev. Dr. John Philip, a British missionary in South Africa, wrote in 1819:

The slave system as it is carried on in the Colony is injurious to morals, to industry, to wealth and comfort. Half a dozen of good English servants could do more work than twenty slaves. In the Lange Kloof you may find from twenty to fifty slaves and Hottentots on one farm and under one roof. From such a retinue of servants it might be expected that the farmer should cultivate much land. This is not however the case; he does not seem to think of more than is necessary to supply his family and servants with food and enable his wife and daughters to appear fine when they go to church . . .[5]

The prohibition of the slave trade forced upon the colonists by the British authorities induced many European masters to look for additional farm hands among the indigenous Hottentots. These were by now in a sorry state. European settlers continuously pressed upon the land; the aborigines' nomadic pastoral system proved incompatible with settled administration. By 1801, wrote a British missionary, "the whole nation [was] in the most degraded and miserable condition, without lands, without liberty (slaves), without property, without knowledge, without clothing, except the sheepskin, without education, without religion."[6] They had to work for white farmers; or they had to trek beyond the borders of the colony, turn to banditry, or become vagrants, eking out a miserable living as best they might. The British authorities both tried to meet the colonist demand for labor and to protect the Hottentots. The remains of tribal law were abolished, and the aborigines were placed under colonial law. Circuit judges were instructed to receive their complaints. But at the same time the Hottentots were forced to carry passes; they could no longer freely move about the country. Hottentot children born to couples in service with white men were apprenticed to their parents' master. "Vagrants" became liable to arrest. The bulk of the Hottentots were thus reduced to economic dependency on the European farmers.

The Hottentots found their most impassioned defenders among British missionaries, especially among the London Missionary Society. Perhaps the most outstanding of these missionary-politicians was the Rev. John Philip, a Scottish weaver's son, one of the many poor boys who during the nineteenth century made a name for themselves in public life and the world of letters by entering the missionary professions. Philip, an admirer of Adam Smith, wished to protect the Hottentots against forced labor; he thought that they should be considered as potential consumers, not only as unskilled laborers. Above all, they needed land, laws, and schools of their own, so that they might ultimately attain a condition of equality with the whites. Philip, in the best humanitarian tradition of the time, was also a convinced segregationist. He opposed the indiscriminate mixing of the races, which, in his opinion, must follow from the dispersion of the Hottentots on the farms. The Hottentots required missionary protection; hence Philip pressed for additional land grants to mission stations where Hottentots might live in reserves of their own and improve their economic as well as their spiritual condition.

The philanthropists attained their greatest success over the question of improving the legal condition of the non-Europeans. Philip formed an alliance with Thomas Fowell Buxton of antislavery fame and with the "Clapham Sect," an influential evangelical group ably represented in the British House of Commons. He also obtained some support at the Cape, including that from liberal-minded Afrikaners like Captain Andries Stockenström, a distinguished administrator. In 1828 the British authorities at the Cape promulgated the much quoted Fiftieth Ordinance which revolutionized the position of "Hottentots and other free persons of colour." Forced labor was abolished; Hottentots were enabled to own land and also benefited from various other reforms. The Ordinance did not place the Hottentots on a footing of complete equality with the whites; there was no provision for giving land to the landless. Few Hottentots, moreover, were able to buy farms of their own or emerge from their proletarian condition.

Missionary attempts at settling Hottentots in "Institutions" met with no permanent success. The missionaries tried to teach crafts to their charges. But as a contemporary British missionary put it: "In a thinly scattered country like this, where almost everyone is his own smith and carpenter, where is the demand for such tradesmen? Hence the attempt to establish a woollen cloth manufactory; but the evident impossibility of taking that leap over the middle age of a nation's civilization, and turning a pastoral race into a manufacturing population will sufficiently explain the failure of this scheme."[7] Agriculture and cattle grazing were the only alternatives available to the Hottentots, but these occupations required more land than was available to the "Institutions." Hence their inhabitants often had to subsist on living standards inferior to those of farm laborers in white employment. In the words of the missionary observer: "We have located on a spot where twenty families could not live two hundred or more who might perhaps otherwise by being distributed among the farmers had had abundance of wholesome food and many of the comforts of life."[8]

Emancipation of the Hottentots did, however, enable them to sell their labor to the highest bidder and thus indirectly better their condition. The new legislation probably accelerated the drift of Coloured people to the towns and villages, where life was more interesting and where conditions of employment were often superior to those found in the backwoods.

The ending of slavery brought about comparable changes. In 1833, as we have seen in a previous chapter, the British Parliament decreed the abolition of slavery throughout the Empire. The slave owners at the same time received some compensation. The direct financial cost of emancipation was thrown on the British taxpayer—not on the local slave owning societies. The freedmen were spared a crushing financial burden. The former masters were not likely to revolt in anger or despair. Admittedly, they had many justified complaints concerning the fashion in which compensation was paid, and the manner in which British bankers and financial agents benefited from the complicated transactions involved. But a substantial amount of money did pass from Great Britain to South Africa. In some parts of the country, the influx of British funds indeed appears to have contributed to a boom and a rise in land prices during the late 1830s. The emancipated slaves, however, were in no position to purchase any of the more highly priced real estate, and most of the former slaves continued to remain landless laborers. The freeing of the Hottentots and the slaves thus tended to produce a composite people, later known as the Coloreds. The Coloreds generally professed Christianity, more or less followed the way of life customary among the more indigent white settlers, and ultimately—for all practical purposes—became an indigenous, Afrikaans-speaking proletariat.

SOUTH AFRICA'S NORTHERN FRONTIER

The white dominated society at the Cape had an inbuilt bias in favor of territorial expansion. The desire for new land did not derive from government policy. The Dutch East India Company had no desire to assume new responsibilities or shoulder additional expenses in the interior. In 1707 the authorities abolished the existing system of giving free passages to European colonists, a clear indication that the Company had by now achieved its limited objective of creating a naval base and an "ocean tavern" on the road to the Indies. The Company would have liked to confine European settlement to a limited region easily controlled by the government. But the authorities reckoned without the country's geography. The pioneers who made their way into the western Cape found a fertile country, where wheat and wine flourished and where there were no warlike Bantu tribes to trouble the settlers' peace. The newcomers created a stable agricultural society, centering on fine farm houses built in the Cape Dutch style, and dependent on Colored labor. In the older Western districts, the mixed breeds descending from unions between Hottentots, Malays, and white men adopted a form of Cape Dutch as their mother tongue. The western Cape became mainly Afrikaans-speaking. It was the only part of Africa where European settlers spoke the same language as their non-European neighbors. In the western Cape whites and non-whites were probably fairly evenly balanced, so that numbers favored the Europeans to a greater degree than in any other part of Africa.

Only a small part of South Africa receives regular winter rains. Most parts of the interior are less favored. The Karroo, the high plateau of the interior, has good soil, but its annual rainfall is low, and even modern farmers need something between ten and twenty acres of land to graze a single sheep. Geographic conditions alone forced dispersion upon the colonists. The only alternative was to push out along the south coast, between the Indian Ocean and the Karroo escarpment, running roughly parallel to it most of the way. But here too the colonists faced many obstacles. Much of the soil is poor; the rains are often irregular in their onset and deficient in quantity. The frontier farmers inevitably came to depend mainly on cattle and adopted a very extensive system of agriculture. Their herds required vast grazing grounds. Fencing to conserve the pastures was unknown, and would in any case have been uneconomic under conditions where markets were small, capital and skilled labor scarce, and where only land was plentiful. Hence the pioneers came to accept units of 3000 or 4000 *morgen* (some ten square miles) as the minimum required for a single farm in all the outer districts.

A variety of factors combined to produce the trekker, the characteristic frontiersman of South Africa. From the early days of Dutch settlement, adventurers used to push inland in order to hunt game and buy cattle from the Hottentots. Gradually these expeditions went further and further afield. The men who participated in these ventures were predominantly bachelors, some of them respectable folk, some of them criminals more apt to loot than to barter. But whatever their background, these seminomadic people became, so to speak, the pathfinders of white settlement. According to one school of thought, population pressure gave the main push to subsequent expansion. This pressure derived not so much from a lack of natural resources as from the immediate scarcity of capital, skill, and economic opportunities. Sons of prolific Boer families could not work in Cape Town as craftsmen alongside Malay slaves; neither could they find sufficient room on their fathers' farms, unless their fathers had enough money and drive to subdivide their properties and develop them more intensively. Some farmers no doubt were doing this; but the majority lacked the required capital and the necessary economic opportunities. Hence extensive land use remained the predominant pattern of rural life among the Boers.

Trekking, as Sir Keith Hancock notes in an excellent summary, therefore became "a movement from higher to lower land values, or—to put it more bluntly—from land that had to be paid for to land that could be had for nothing or next to nothing."[9] The frontier tended to attract poor people. Richer men by and large preferred to stay at home rather than risk their capital in the interior, where farmers had to cope with long distances, high transport costs, droughts, and animal diseases, where children could not easily get an education, and where men might have to battle for their lives against Hottentot or Bantu tribesmen. Poor farmers, on the other hand, could make do with relatively little. A span of oxen, a wagon, a few tools, some firearms, some animals of his own—these were a sufficient stock of capital. For labor he had his own family, landless Hottentots, and later, in some districts, landless Bantu. A substantial percentage of the Boers in the early nineteenth century had no legal title to their land. It was not lack of opportunity but lack of individual motive that created this class of men. In Hancock's words, a "farm on wheels" was less troublesome to manage than an established property. To settle as a *bywoner* on another man's land was a respectable thing to do. As long as frontier conditions survived, *bywoners* were in much demand as a reinforcement to the security of the white community. *Bywoners* and farm owners both usually had large families, and the growth of population occasioned new treks. Close neighbors meant close competition for pasture and water; in time the land began to suffer as a result of overstocking, and once again trekkers began to move further inland.

The trekkers, however, also reacted to other economic motives. The frontiersmen were never self-sufficient. As time went on, even the pioneers on the extreme edge of the settlement became increasingly dependent on imported articles such as guns, tea, coffee, and cloth. The best means of paying for this merchandise was by driving cattle to market, for the town was now a long way off and cattle possessed the great advantage that the beasts could walk to the market on their own feet. There were a few goods of small bulk and high value such as soap, candles, beeswax, and ivory that could be transported to the coast on wagons. First the farmers supplied the Cape market; later new ports—Port Elizabeth, East London, and Durban—were opened up on the east coast and in turn became advanced points of departure for inland expansion. Overland migration was made easier when itinerant traders (smouse) supplied the frontier with a moving market, so that farmers no longer had to waste their time taking their wares to town.[10]

In time the Boers of the interior became a new nation, no longer speaking Dutch, but speaking Afrikaans, a South African derivative from Dutch that began to assume something like its present shape during the eighteenth century. The trek-boer became one of Africa's foremost wilderness specialists. Rough and illiterate as he often was, he adjusted to frontier conditions that would have completely baffled his ancestor. He knew how to handle a span of oxen in the most rugged country; he became knowledgeable as a "soil prospector," wise to the ways of finding the best farm land in the wilderness. He learned how to make astonishingly good use of the military potential characterizing a pastoral backwoods economy. Boer tactics depended on the employment of wagons. These served both as a means of transport and—when formed into closed circles defended by accurate rifle fire—as pivots of mobile defense. The use of these laagers was combined with the employment of mounted sharpshooters, whose superior mobility and firepower generally proved irresistible to indigenous tribesmen fighting on foot. The Boer frontiersman thus turned out to be a formidable fighter, an expert huntsman, and a natural-born sniper whose exploits still exert an irresistible fascination on white South Africans today.

In discussing the story of the South African frontier, we should, however, remember two central though half-forgotten facts of history. First of all, trekking was not confined to white men alone. The frontier attracted men of every race who sought land, liberty, or loot in the interior. Some Hottentots, for instance, escaped beyond the shifting borders of the Cape Colony in search of greater economic opportunities. Here they mixed with runaway slaves, with indigenous tribesmen, and also with white pioneers, refugees, or criminals. The offspring of such unions formed seminomadic groups of Griquas (or "Bastards" in earlier Afrikaans terminology). Some of these, such as the inhabitants of Griquatown, came under missionary influence. Many of these mixed breeds lived in a manner very much like that of the white trekkers; they pastured cattle; they acquired horses and guns and fought fierce battles against Bushmen and other indigenous people. The Griquas produced some able chiefs such as Adam Kok and later, Andries Waterboer. By and large, however, the mixed breeds were the weakest and most poverty-stricken element among the frontiersmen. They were subject to constant pressure from white trekkers having greater military resources, superior numbers, and political cohesion. In the long run the Griqua communities could not maintain their separate identity and generally merged into the mass of the Colored proletariat.

More important still, all the Boers did not trek; the frontier absorbed only a part of the Cape population. We have seen earlier—and the point is worth repeating—that, by compory standards, the Europeans in South Africa were already a relatively highly urbanized people. In 1806 some 6000 whites lived at Cape Town, out of a total European population of 27,000 in the Cape as a whole. Few of these townsmen wished to leave their homes for the uncertain chances of the frontiers. Neither did the wealthy wine farmers of the western Cape show much desire to emigrate. Many Boers became deeply rooted in the soil. As Sir Keith Hancock points out, members of the great Smuts family dwelt continuously, for a century and a half, in the wheat and vine country of the Swartland. Lastly, the frontier was not all of a piece. The story still remains to be told of the slow social and economic change behind the trekker's frontier, as the raw pastoral frontier gradually turned into "old settlement," as little towns grew up to buy the farmer's produce and to supply rural householders with their goods.

Frontier society was by no means homogeneous. There were many kinds of frontiers, depending on varying geographical and political circumstances. The settlers differed in the way in which they responded to frontier conditions. Some made their living above all as hunters and traders, and often managed to fit well into the African societies with which they came into contact. Most were poor; some were men of property; a few managed to acquire substantial wealth. Some "went native." The great majority tried to maintain their accustomed way of life, but still had to make all kinds of adjustments to local conditions. The pioneers often clashed with their African neighbors over the right of access to pasturage and water holes, over quarrels concerning stock thefts and so forth. But the legend notwithstanding, war was by no means the universal condition of the frontier, and many a trekker managed to live on amicable terms with his African neighbors. Settlement, indeed, would often lead to a good deal of economic interchange between different societies that were suddenly thrown into contact with one another.

Finally, we should not make the mistake of regarding the trekkers simply as "primitives," as quasi-Biblical herdsmen lost in the wilds of Africa. Despite all vicissitudes, the Boers remained largely a literate people, firmly grounded in their Bible and Catechism. Distances might be formidable; frontier conditions militated against regular schools; teaching, therefore, devolved to wandering scholars of sorts and on the Church. Quarterly journeys to the nearest village for the purpose of taking communion were prolonged to allow for Bible classes as well as for business and social activities.

Many Boers took a good deal of trouble to educate their children. Immigrant Calvinist clergymen from Scotland and Holland helped to provide the colony with educated men, and their offspring usually became assimilated into the Afrikaner nation. The Dutch Reformed Church naturally remained somewhat isolated from European intellectual impulses. The shortage of itinerant preachers meant that the trekkers suffered from a want of education, especially those families who had moved farthest into the interior. The Dutch Reformed Church, despite valiant attempts to maintain literacy and religious practice, met with extreme difficulty. It had little share in the evangelical revival of the early nineteenth century. It did in the first instance try to respect the equality of all believers within the church, irrespective of color.

During the first two centuries of Dutch settlement at the Cape, the Church insisted on common church membership and on common worship for white and nonwhite alike. Many Coloureds became converts to Christianity; they spoke the local Dutch *patois* as their mother tongue. Cultural assimilation was not, however, an easy matter. Toward the end of the eighteenth century the clerical authorities began to hold separate weekday services in simplified language to enable Coloreds to follow the ordinary Sunday services held in High Dutch.

Afrikaner congregations often resisted the principle of common church services, but up to the middle of the last century the church generally withstood all attempts on the part of frontier congregations to segregate white and nonwhite members. In 1857, however, the church at last succumbed to popular pressure, and a stormy synodal meeting at last sanctioned the practice of separate ministration for white and nonwhite believers. The resolution emphasized that the new policy was not rooted in principle but was occasioned by "the weakness of some." Failure to respect white sentiment, the argument ran, would alienate many church members. Separation would in fact benefit the Coloreds, who would feel more comfortable in their own congregations and would have a better chance of participating in church government. Coloreds (and latterly black people) would rather be deacons in their own congregations than occupy the back pews of an integrated church.

The decision of 1857 thus became a watershed in the racial policy of the Dutch Reformed Church, the single most influential force within the Afrikaner community. The decision made by the church not only settled the question of status for non-European members; it unwittingly provided the blueprint for what Afrikaners now call *eiensoortige ontwikkeling,* or group development along indigenous lines. The Afrikaners refused to assimilate non-Europeans, even Afrikaans-speaking Coloreds, into their community, and the decision made by the church synod of 1857 still influences South Africa today.[11]

NOTES

1. William M. Macmillan, *The Cape Colour Question: A Historical Survey* (London, 1927), pp. 26–36.

2. William M. Macmillan, *Bantu, Boer and Briton: The Making of the South African Native Problem* (London, 1929), pp. 25–30.

3. Desmond K. Clinton, *The South African Melting Pot: A Vindication of Missionary Policy, 1799–1836* (London, 1937), pp. 8–52.

4. The standard work in English on South Africa's past is Eric A. Walker, *A History of Southern Africa* (London, 1957). This has now been supplemented, and in some ways superseded by Monica Wilson and Leonard Thompson, eds., *The Oxford History of South Africa* (Oxford, 1969), vol. 1.

5. Cited by Macmillan, *The Cape Colour Question: A Historical Survey,* p. 76.

6. Dr. van der Kemp, quoted by Macmillan, *The Cape Colour Question,* p. 271.

7. Quoted by Macmillan, p. 275.

8. Macmillan, p. 274.

9. W. K. Hancock, "Trek," *The Economic History Review,* Second Series, vol. 10, no. 3 (1958), p. 334. The standard work in Afrikaans is P. J. van der Merwe, *Studies oor die Mobiliteit van die Pioniers-bevolking aan die Kaap* (Cape Town, 1945), Hancock's discussion has been very fully used here.

10. See S. Daniel Neumark, *Economic Influences on the South African Frontier, 1652–1836* (Standford, 1957).

11. Susan Rennie Ritner, "The Dutch Reformed Church and Apartheid," *Journal of Contemporary History,* vol. 2, no. 4 (1967), pp. 22–37.

Chapter 29

The Frontier Moves Inland

EASTERN CAPE AND THE GREAT TREK

In 1834 a British traveler visited Afrikaner emigrants who had made their homes by the Orange River. He got into conversation with a dignified patriarch highly thought of among the Boers and asked him when the farmers would cease trekking and live like civilized people. "When they reach the sea—the old man replied—let them trek; they must trek as Abraham, Isaac and Jacob did before them. . . . On pointing out the totally different circumstances of the Israelites . . . and pressing the old man . . . to say *how far* the Boers were to trek? He raised his hand so as to indicate a great distance northward and said in a loud decisive tone, *'Tot ander kant uit'*—till out on the other side."[1]

In their northward drift the Boers at first experienced little effective resistance, either from Bushmen or Hottentots. The dry country north and west of the Cape at first attracted but a sprinkling of settlers. The main body of the colonists preferred to seek new land near the east coast, along the line of greater rainfall. Here for the first time they met with serious resistance on the part of Bantu tribes who were moving southward in search of additional pastures. From the latter part of the eighteenth century, the two competing groups of pastoralists, black and white, began to clash, and the year 1779 stands out in conventional South African history books as the first of many "Kaffir Wars."

On the face of it there was a good deal of similarity between the South African and the North American frontier during the eighteenth century. In both cases European settlers and indigenous tribesmen coveted the same land. But, as Professor W. M. Macmillan points out, a real parallel would require prerevolutionary America to have consisted of just one colony, with a total white population perhaps equal to that of Rhode Island, spread out over the whole of New England and first meeting with Indian resistance in the Great Lakes region in the later years of King George II! The Cape colonists were numerically much weaker than the New Englanders; they were much more dependent on cattle farming, and they were far less strongly based, having but one distant seaport behind them.

The opposing Bantu communities, on the other hand, were much less redoubtable foes than the Indians of the forest even though they were relatively closely massed against the white men, on a comparatively narrow front. True they had attained a higher level of material civilization than most North American Indians. They knew how to smelt iron; they combined hunting and slash-and-burn agriculture with pastoralism. Owning cattle, they were probably better fed than the Indians. Being normally well provided with beer from millet, they did not crave the white man's liquor with the same intensity as the Indians. They proved a hardy people, resistant to disease, capable not only of vigorous exertion but also of intelligent adaption. Even later in the nineteenth century, when the white settlement frontier was much further extended, their main bases in the eastern Cape and Natal were outflanked more than penetrated, and they were never fully dispersed. Hence there was never much likelihood of a North American "solution" of the problems occasioned by the clash of such unevenly equipped peoples.[2]

The government of the Dutch East India Company was weak. The Dutch authorities had little money to spend on frontier defense; especially in the last phase of Dutch rule, various Dutch officials tried to conciliate the Bantu in a manner designed to infuriate the white frontier farmers. Their British successors found themselves with a difficult legacy on their hands. At first the British tried to temporize. In 1812 they decided in favor of a strong policy, and tried systematically to expel the Bantu from the hilly Zuurveld country on the colonial side of the traditionally accepted Fish River boundary separating Bantu from white men. To protect the border, they set up a new fort called Grahamstown (1819). Next year, in 1820, the authorities introduced some 5000 British-born settlers to people Grahamstown and to strengthen the British hold on the frontier districts. Many of the newcomers were not suited to farming under frontier conditions. Many of them came from cities like London and Edinburgh. Many others had been brought up in partly-industrialised counties like Middlesex and Lancashire. These pioneers were no paupers. Even a short perusal of the emigrants' lists showed that the newcomers included a large number of well-educated people— schoolmasters and surgeons, ministers and "master mariners." The colonists also supplied South Africa with a great number of scarce skills. The newcomers comprised blacksmiths, wheelwrights, carpenters, cabinet makers, and such like.[3] There were merchants. There were also farmers and market gardeners. But even these agriculturists did not necessarily prosper in South Africa. Englishmen who would do well on a holding in say, rural Devonshire, with its lush meadows and manicured countryside, were not necessarily suited to make a living on the Cape, where much of their previous experience was useless, and at times worse than useless. Moreover holdings commonly proved inadequate in size. Many colonists made their way to the towns, where they provided a considerable stimulus to economic development, and where they—and subsequent immigrants—helped to give a curiously English imprint to much of South Africa's urban life. Others stuck it out on the land, adjusted themselves to local ways of farming, and acquired a great deal in common with their Boer neighbors.[4]

Immigrants from different European countries brought in a variety of professional and technical skills. There was an increasing demand for education, and in 1829 a small college opened its doors at Cape Town, the nucleus of South Africa's first university. The new institution was designed to give instruction, not only in classical subjects, but also "in the higher and abstruser branches, elucidating the constitution, structure and properties of natural objects generally." Despite its ambitious purpose, it suffered from a great many initial troubles: "The collegiate principle, under which scholastic matters, including discipline, were entrusted to a senate, worked badly . . . Unruly boys were sentenced to confinement on bread and water, and lesser culprits to 'marks of degradation' within the building. Flogging was nominally forbidden, and in 1832, the senate had to fall back on petitioning council to erect six new cells."[5] Nevertheless, the college attracted some distinguished scholars, and soon extended its reputation. In addition more private as well as "free" government schools came into being. In the first generation of British rule at the Cape there was no radical objection to the presence of Colored, and even of slave children at these institutions, provided they were "decently clad and free from disease." Racial segregation in the schools only developed gradually. (Especially at the mission schools in the backwoods, poor white pupils continued to attend classes alongside Colored children until the end of the nineteenth century, when separation became complete.)

Settlers from different parts of northern Europe also introduced new economic techniques and new export crops. These pioneers comprised a good many Germans, including colonists like Maximilian Thalwitzer, a Jewish merchant converted to the Dutch Reformed Church, who played a major part in creating the South African merino wool industry. Newcomers from Europe also helped to extend the South African network of trade. Local banks and other credit institutions came into being, which in turn brought about major changes in the country's economy.

South Africa's incipient economic revolution required political stability; stability in turn depended on a secure border. British policy makers assumed at first that settlers and tribesmen could be segregated by a defended frontier zone. The country between the Fish River and the Keiskama to the east was declared to be a neutral belt. Troops were posted in forts and blockhouses to keep the peace. Segregation, however, proved impossible to enforce in difficult, broken country where white men and black often competed for the same pastures. Besides, Europeans and Africans became increasingly dependent on one another. Many farmers wished to buy cattle from the Bantu; many Africans desired to buy goods from the whites or to work in return for merchandise or money. The British themselves began to encroach on the neutral belt and tried to expel the blacks from forbidden regions so as to make the frontier more secure. The whites thereby increasingly deprived the border tribes of land and freedom to maneuver; they did not, however, succeed in driving the Bantu back into the hinterland. Wherever they could, the tribesmen crept back to their accustomed abodes and rustled cattle from the whites. The colonists retaliated by organizing raids to recover their losses, so that frontier life became increasingly insecure. In 1834 the warlike Xhosa tribes again went on the war path; a powerful African force invaded the eastern part of the Cape, ravaging the country from Algoa Bay to Somerset East. The British counterattacked, and after confused and bitter fighting (known to South African history as the Sixth Kaffir War) annexed all the country between the Kat and the Kei rivers, under the name of Queen Adelaide Province. In theory the Kaffirs were to be driven from the land, but the British soon realized that this was impossible. Missionaries and humanitarians bitterly attacked the policy of expulsion; London was notoriously reluctant to shoulder new financial or territorial responsibilities; Britain's machinery of government at the Cape was of the weakest, and in the end the British decided to restore the conquered region to the Xhosa.

For many Dutch frontier farmers, the British withdrawal from Queen Adelaide Province was the last straw. It seemed to dash all hopes of relieving the farmers' land hunger in the eastern province; it appeared to symbolize British unwillingness to give adequate protection to the pioneers on the fringe of white settlement. The Afrikaners also had many other grievances. English was the only official language of the government and the law courts. Afrikaans, the language of the backwoodsmen, had to battle against unsuccessful attempts at anglifying the Boers. (In addition the Afrikaans tongue had to struggle against Dutch, the speech of educated burghers who hoped to maintain Hollands as a literary language, and who had as little respect for the speech of the rural white people as the English.) The Boers also objected to British missionary interference. They resented the interference with their labor supply brought about by the emancipation of the Hottentots. Anglo-Dutch relations were further embittered by the abolition of slavery at the Cape, and by the inadequate way in which many former slave owners were compensated for the loss of their property. Slavery was not, however, the main issue. The pastoral Boer economy required, after all, only a very limited number of bondsmen. The dispute between the British authorities and the Boers involved two totally different sets of beliefs, customs, and political ideals. The British wished to introduce their own legal and administrative institutions; they insisted that English should be the only official language in the Cape, and they insisted on freedom of contract and of equality before the law between white men and colored. The Afrikaner frontiersmen, including many English-speaking sympathizers, for their part would accept neither interference from overseas nor equality with non-Europeans at home. Piet Retief, one of the most prominent trekkers wrote:

Despair of saving the colony from those evils which threaten it by the turbulent and dishonest conduct of vagrants who are allowed to infest the country. . . . We complain of the severe losses which we have been forced to sustain by the emancipation of our slaves and the vexatious laws which have been enacted respecting them. We complain of the continued system of plunder which we have for years endured from the Kaffirs and other coloured classes . . . We complained of the unjustifiable odium which has been cast upon us by interested and dishonest persons under the name of religion, whose testimony is believed in England to the exclusion of all other evidence in our favour, and we can foresee as a result of their prejudice nothing but the total ruin of the country. . . . We quit this country under the full assurance that the English Government has nothing more to require of us and will allow us to govern ourselves without its interference in future. . . .[6]

The pattern of Afrikaner migration was profoundly influenced by Bantu politics. The Xhosa remained a formidable opponent. Hence the whites were prevented from advancing further along the line of highest rainfall. The Afrikaners also skirted the heavily populated territory ruled by Mosheshwe (Moshesh), the creator of the Sotho (Basuto) nation. Instead the trekkers began to make their way into the sparsely populated regions of Natal and the Transvaal. Much of this country had been thrown into a state of turmoil occasioned by the rise of a great Zulu warrior kingdom in Natal, to which further reference will be made in a subsequent chapter. Zulu raiders set neighbor against neighbor and in turn occasioned large-scale Bantu migrations. The trekkers met with little effective resistance on the open veld. Great columns of ox wagons, heavily laden with household goods, slowly lumbered inland, and by the end of 1837 something like 5000 Boers had crossed the Orange River. Some settled in what later became the Orange Free State; others made their way into the territory subsequently known as the Transvaal. A group of Boers also tried to set up a republic in Natal. In 1838 the Afrikaners inflicted a smashing defeat on the Zulu at the battle of Blood River; but the Boer occupation of Natal merely precipitated the country's annexation by the British. The Boer emigrants thus once again set out on their travels and found new homes beyond the Vaal River.

The Great Trek was the frontiersmen's Declaration of Independence. Admittedly, its immediate effects should not be exaggerated. A large number of Afrikaners did not leave the Cape. The Dutch Reformed Church looked askance at the trekkers; so did most of the wealthy wine farmers of the western Cape. Nevertheless, the Afrikaners' national center of gravity began to swing northward, and South Africa's strategic position became revolutionized. The main body of the Bantu in the Eastern Cape and Natal were—so to speak—outflanked by the Afrikaner offensive on the high plateau of the interior. At the same time the area of black-white contact was immensely enlarged. The customary disorders on the narrow 100-mile front along the Eastern Cape had been a sore embarrassment to the successive British governors. Now the frontier stretched indeterminately for 500 miles or more in almost every direction; the Afrikaners were spread out thinly over immense new regions and competed with Bantu tribes for vast stretches of the interior.

The Great Trek also brought about new complications in Anglo-Boer relations. The imperial authorities at first claimed that the immigrants were still British subjects, but they could not in fact effectively control the far north. Acting partly under the influence of missionaries anxious to protect black men and Griqua against Boer encroachment, the British concluded treaties with various indigenous potentates. In 1847 they also annexed all the land up to the River Kei on the Eastern Cape under the name of British Kaffraria. British interference inland, however, proved expensive and therefore unpopular with metropolitan tax payers. Many British reformers insisted on white self-government; many denounced the missionaries; quixotic philanthropy, said the critics, was no solution.

In 1852 a disillusioned British government, by the Sand River Convention formally allowed the immigrant farmers beyond the Vaal to manage their own affairs. The Transvaalers promised to abstain from slavery; the British assured them of access to firearms and disclaimed any kind of alliance with the Bantu tribes inland. Two years later a similar treaty admitted the independence of the Orange Free State. Two thinly-settled white frontier states—each saddled with extensive "native problems" —now held sway over the interior. The British, on the other hand, firmly held onto the Cape and to Natal. In 1853 they promulgated a constitution that gave the Cape a bicameral legislature elected on a color-blind franchise conceding the vote to any qualified person, white, brown, or black, who met the required qualifications. In practice the franchise largely remained confined to the propertied whites, but racial equality was admitted, at any rate in principle. The Transvaalers for their part proceeded on a very different line. They worked out their own *Grondwet,* or constitution, and in 1858 solemnly declared that "the people will have no equality between colored people and the white inhabitants either in Church or State." According to the Transvaalers' point of view, a standpoint shared by most British settlers, the indigenous Bantu peoples might coexist with the whites but could never be culturally or politically assimilated into the dominant white community. The "Great South African Schism" was complete.

However, some Africans benefited from the new economic and intellectual opportunities brought about by European penetration, the creation of new markets, the development of new skills, the establishment of missions, and the ending of intertribal warfare. In 1841, for instance, Protestant missionaries supported financially by the Free Church of Scotland set up a training institution at Lovedale. Lovedale served both black and white pupils. It provided instruction not only in reading and writing but also in trades urgently needed on the frontier, like wagon-making, black-smithing, masonry, printing, and bookbinding. The students included Africans from many different ethnic groups. In addition girls began to attend. Institutions like Lovedale received support from the local British administration, which was anxious to spread saleable skills and expand commercial opportunities. Hence Lovedale and other mission stations began to train a new kind of African: teachers, evangelists, and craftsmen, who made a major contribution to the economy of the Cape. Missionaries and administrators also encouraged settled farming by Africans. Plows and irrigation furrows first made their appearance on mission stations; subsequently the authorities encouraged their adoption among African farmers. Charles Brownlee, a noteworthy British official, even bought sheep for the Xhosa at his own expense, for he believed sheep owners would be less mobile than cattle owners and therefore less inclined for war. Whatever the merits of his sociological assumptions, his initiative helped to diversify the indigenous economy—as did the efforts of missionaries and the example of white farmers. The European impact was therefore double-edged in its effect, destructive and constructive at the same time.

The Bantu reacted in various different fashions. As long as the white man could be kept at arm's length, the Bantu communities were satisfied to trade, and even occasionally to work for wages in European employment. European contacts were ambiguous in their effects. The colonists created new markets for African cattle and African crops, so that some Africans benefited from new opportunities. Missionaries began to set up schools. (By the 1850s, something like 9000 African youngsters were receiving some type of scholastic education in the Cape Colony.) Educated Africans began to read books, and by the middle of the nineteenth century, mission presses were already publishing material in vernacular tongues. On the other hand, white pressure tended to become more severe on the frontier.

African tribesmen would fight. Sometimes the blacks won, but usually the Europeans' superior mobility and firepower would decide in the white man's favor. A common animist reaction to military defeat, loss of land, the growing demand for new acres brought about by a rising population, and the spiritual challenge posed by Christian churches and schools was to seek supernatural aid. The Xhosa thus listened to diviners or prophets who urged purification from witchcraft and sacrifices to the shades of the departed. In the war of 1819, Makanda, a diviner, thus assumed command of the Xhosa. In the 1840s a young man, Mlanjeni, built up a reputation as a witchfinder and urged men to abandon sorcery. He also commanded the sacrifice of all dun- and cream-colored cattle in the Xhosa country. He convinced his warriors that he could fill the white men's guns with water and make the black fighters invincible. This flight into the irrational became even more serious in the 1850s, when a Xhosa prophetess was inspired by reports of the Crimean War that the Russians would help the blacks to drive the English from Africa. The Xhosa, however, would have to pay a price. They would have to slaughter *all* their cattle, destroy their grain and refrain from sowing. Then all the dead heroes would rise, the black people would inherit riches beyond the dreams of avarice, and a great wind would sweep the English into the sea. Needless to say, these and similar prophesies proved disastrous to the believers. The Xhosa slaughtered their herds; by 1857 the countryside was starving, and the power of the chiefs never quite recovered from this disaster. The cattle-killing episode was clearly in one respect a resistance movement, whereby the people wished to drive out the whites. It was also a Messianic movement involving purification from witchcraft. It was likewise a fusion of old religious ideas, of revelation through diviners and ancestor worship, with Christian teachings concerning the apolcalypse.[7]

NATION BUILDING AMONG THE SOUTHERN BANTU

The regions now comprised within the South African province of Natal make up some of the most pleasant, the most fertile, and the best-watered lands of southern Africa. The green hills of Natal attracted immigrants of various kinds, including the so-called Nguni peoples. The Nguni probably entered the county in several distinct streams of migration ending about the fifteenth century. They were not a united nation, but probably comprised many clusters of clans, each with its own history and customs. Some of these newcomers may have been farmers pure and simple. Many others, however, owned great herds of cattle; they also cultivated millet, pumpkin, and other crops; they hunted; they knew how to work iron and generally followed a way of life that had much in common with that of the ancient Teutons as described by the Roman historian Tacitus.

The Bantu, like the Boers, required a great deal of land to sustain their herds and to practice slash-and-burn agriculture. As Professor M. Gluckman suggests, the continuous growth of population may possibly have led to harsher competition for pastures; quarrels over grazing lands resulted in more sustained fighting; warfare in turn necessitated more centralized political institutions and new ways of organizing armies.

In all likelihood Zulu society was influenced also by an increase of foreign trade; in all probability European merchants, especially Portuguese traders, brought in more European-made goods through Delagoa Bay. From the second part of the eighteenth century foreign traffic increased considerably. The Nguni, like the trek Boers of the interior, seem to have become more dependent on imported merchandise than they had been in the past. The development of the east coast ports may have played a part in causing the Boers to trek further inland. Similarly, the expansion of the Delagoa Bay trade may have become a factor in creating the Nguni military states that crashed into the interior with such devastating effects. The struggle for local commercial monopolies may have put a premium on military efficiency. Control over foreign exchange transactions may have strengthened the power of local chiefs.[8]

Whatever the reason, there were profound changes in Zulu society. The Bantu kingdoms had originally been small, as the Bantu communities had tended to segment into lesser states that contended for grazing lands. The "Bantu Backwash," however, seems to have been associated with a social revolution whereby weak kingdoms became associated into more powerful military states instead of breaking up into lesser principalities. Whatever the explanation, Bantu political organization underwent a profound change. By about 1810 three larger states, Mthethwa, Ndwandwe and Quabe, dominated the rest. The traditional age-sets of the Nguni, composed of men who had been circumcised at the same time and who were bound to assist one another in various ways, completely changed in character.[9] Age-sets were formed into military regiments, each led by a nominee of the king, and soldiering became a more highly skilled occupation.

The regiments were armed with long-handled throwing spears, the traditional weapon for hunting as well as war. Warriors who had thrown their missile had to retire from the fighting line; they could not operate in close formations; casualties remained relatively light, and decisive results were hard to obtain. The Nguni revolutionized traditional ways of warfare and learned how to use the military potential of a pastoral economy to its utmost limit. Shaka and other great Zulu captains trained their forces to fight in close order, to advance in crescent-shaped formations behind the cover of closely linked oxhide shields, and to charge home with heavy jabbing spears, while keeping a tactical reserve for a decisive thrust. Historians used to attribute this change to the genius of one great man, Shaka, a Zulu of Napoleonic grandeur and of barbaric ruthlessness. William F. Lye, a modern American scholar, shows that the change in political and military organization came about more slowly, as the result of competition between different Zulu communities and also by reason

A young Zulu as seen by a nineteenth-century artist. (National Archives of Rhodesia.)

of Zulu contact with the Sotho. But Shaka, like Napoleon, fully utilized the military reforms conceived by his predecessors; he further improved his military instrument and became one of South Africa's most outstanding generals. Shaka had no use for limited wars; he believed in a strategy of rapid movements and of annihilation, allowing his enemies no time for recovery.[10] The new way of fighting needed careful and prolonged drill. Shaka kept his forces permanently on active service and raised them to heights of military efficiency unparalleled in the annals of Bantu warfare.

The three Nguni states soon clashed with one another. The first major struggle occurred between the followers of Sobhuza, a powerful Ngwane chief, and the subjects of Zwide, head of the Ndwandwe tribe. Sobhuza's people were defeated and retired into the mountains of Swaziland, where Sobhuza laid the foundations of the present Swazi nation. Zwide subsequently crushed Dingiswayo, Shaka's overlord, and then turned his attention to Shaka's forces. After a brilliant campaign, Shaka annihilated his enemy; the Ndwandwe kingdom broke up, and from 1819 onward Shaka's people, the Zulu, became the dominant military power in Natal.

The militarization of the Nguni peoples had far-reaching results. Zulu armies periodically raided their neighbors for cattle and captives. The looted beasts augmented the Zulu herds and provided the Zulu warriors with extra food at their neighbors' expense. The women were given to the victors; the captured men and boys were incorporated into the Zulu regiments. War thus served to strengthen both Zulu numbers and Zulu fighting power. The Zulu kingdom became what John Barnes, a modern British anthropologist, has called a "snow-ball state." The Zulu state was probably not the first of its kind in African history. Presumably the constitution of the Zimba and of other ancient conquerors had a good many parallels with that of the Zulu and kindred peoples. Not only the Zulu but the ancient Hebrews, another cattle-keeping warrior people, took captured women for their spoils; the code of Moses as employed against the vanquished Midianites was indeed even harsher than the practice of Shaka. Nevertheless, Zulu warfare was extremely destructive, and the Zulu turned out to be peculiarly efficient in the art of winning battles. The regiments were stationed in military towns where they drilled and danced together under the authority of officers appointed by the king. During their period of service the men were not allowed to marry. They fed on the produce of the royal herds; they drank the king's beer; they received their weapons from the royal stores. They came to think of themselves first and foremost as followers of the king, and the monarch acquired far greater power than had ever been held by the Nguni kings of old.

Shaka took care to keep on good terms with the British. He traded with the whites, and under Shaka's reign the Zulu never tried to fight the redcoats. But military specialization made the Zulu irresistible to their immediate neighbors, and Shaka made full use of his superiority. A bloodthirsty tyrant, he nevertheless proved as able an organizer as he was a tactical innovator and field commander. When he was assassinated in 1828 his kingdom did not disintegrate. Instead the Zulu state continued to play an important part in South African history until the Zulu host was overwhelmed by the British in 1879. To this day the Zulu survive as a people with a sense of nationhood.

Outside Zululand proper, the effects of Shaka's campaigns were equally far-reaching. The Zulu raids not only caused a great deal of immediate destruction; they also forced other tribes to flee from the Zulu reach and thereby carried terror far beyond the original center of disturbance. When Shaka perished, much of the country now comprised within the modern Orange Free State, the Transvaal, and Natal had been devastated or at least thrown into the utmost confusion. This disaster occurred at the very time when the Boer immigrants were looking for new homes further north. Hence the Zulu raids had the unintended effect of facilitating in some respects subsequent Afrikaner expansion beyond the Orange River.

Nguni militarism also forced other tribes to strengthen their state organization for the sake of survival. In 1840 Mswazi, one of the great rulers of his time, became king of Swaziland; he further extended his territory, assimilated numerous petty Sotho clans into his people, strengthened his military forces, and consolidated the Swazi state with its highly stratified society. [11]

The Nguni impact was even greater on the Southern Sotho, another Bantu-speaking people of mixed farmers. The Sotho at one time occupied an extensive region, including the northern and western fringes of Basutoland, where land was more plentiful than on the narrow coastal belt. Perhaps for this reason the problem of land shortage did not become as acute among the Sotho as it did in Zululand, and the Sotho were not forced into building a powerful military monarchy. Whatever the reason, the Sotho could not at first compete with the Nguni and suffered terribly from Nguni attacks. Their fortunes began to improve only after Mosheshwe (Moshesh), one of the greatest nation-builders of South African history, led his people into the rugged mountains of central Basutoland. Here Mosheshwe settled on Thaba Bosiu, a natural stronghold with easily defended slopes, with a top large enough to accommodate many people and their horned beasts, and surrounded by fertile pastures in the valley, where the people could graze their animals in peacetime.[12] The king successfully rallied the remnants of many broken tribes and welded them into the Sotho (Basuto) nation.

Having to deal with so many disparate elements, Mosheshwe was in no position to impose the Zulu military system upon his people. Instead his kingdom grew rather by peaceful attraction, by diplomacy and conciliation. The Sotho, moreover, were ready to learn from others. When mounted Griqua freebooters swooped down upon the Sotho cattle, Mosheshwe encouraged his people to acquire guns and horses. Within a brief period of time the Sotho became a nation of mounted warriors, with their own tough breed of ponies, one of the few Bantu tribes capable of raising irregular cavalry like the Boers. Mosheshwe also called in French Protestant missionaries. Thus Sotho converts learned how to read and write, so that the Sotho had a relatively early start in the subsequent race for literacy. Sotho evangelists participated in European mission work in many parts of southern Africa. The white clergymen provided the Sotho with diplomatic advisers wise in the European's ways and with a lobby capable of rousing philanthropic opinion in Europe on the king's behalf. Mosheshwe sought to gain British backing against the Boers, but this policy proved difficult to implement when the British recognized the independence of the two Boer republics. The Sotho had to prove their mettle not only against the Orange Free State burghers but also against the British. In the end the Sotho lost a good deal of their most fertile acres to the Orange Free State, but like the Swazi they survived as a nation, and retained a viable territorial base. The Sotho displayed a good deal of skill in playing off the burghers of the Orange Free State. In 1868 the Sotho secured formal British protection, a considerable diplomatic victory for Basutoland at the time, and the Sotho thus prevented their country from being wholly absorbed by the white settler's frontier.

BANTU BACKWASH

THE GREAT VÖLKERWANDERUNG

For untold centuries Bantu peoples had migrated in a general direction from north to south. The European northward advance did not reverse this perennial tide. European conquest, for instance, did not prevent Bantu immigrants from peacefully finding new homes for themselves in parts of the Cape Province. But the Bantu could no longer make large-scale armed conquests on their southern frontier. The Nguni campaigns successively set in motion other groups who in turn pressed upon *their* neighbors. None of their warlords chose the road to the south. Instead they looked northward. In the end a number of great hosts fought their way as far afield as the upper Zambezi Valley or the Tanzanian plateau. These great hordes were looking for physical security and for new pastures. They were accompanied by their women, their children, and their captives; they pillaged where they could, and they swept new peoples into their train. They all had cattle which, so to speak, provided these moving warrior states with a mobile supply of food, and thereby vastly added to their range of action.

One of these migrations was led by Mzilikazi, one of Shaka's generals. Mzilikazi was accused of holding back horned beasts that by custom should have been delivered to the monarch. This was a deadly charge, for the king's economic power among the Zulu largely depended on his ability to control the allocation of the nation's cattle. Realizing that Shaka would assuredly put him to death, Mzilikazi fled with his followers across the Drakensberg Mountains and laid waste immense tracts to the north. For a time he found new pasture grounds for his people near Zeerust, on the borders of what is now Botswana. Mzilikazi's subjects, known as the Ndebele (Matabele), successfully defended themselves against Griqua raiders and other indigenous enemies; their assault parties ranged far afield to despoil local tribes of women and cattle; but the Ndebele could not easily resist mounted Boer commandoes. After several hard-fought engagements against the Afrikaners, Mzilikazi decided to trek once again, and sometime about 1840 his people settled in what is now Matabeleland in Rhodesia. From here they raided westward into Bechuanaland (Botswana) and eastward into Mashonaland, where many of the indigenous people had already suffered great depredations at the hands of a second group of invaders from the south.

This host, known as the Ngoni, was led by Zwangendaba, at one time a subchief of the Ndwandwe. About 1821 Zwangendaba led a party of refugees into the region west of Delagoa Bay. Here they met Shoshangane, another Ndwandwe refugee from Shaka's power, and both hosts raided the indigenous Tsonga people. Shoshangane's people subsequently clashed with the Portuguese, inflicted several defeats on them, and settled in the interior of what is now Portuguese East Africa (Mozambique), becoming known as the Gaza. Zwangendaba's people, for their part, first of all marched into Rhodesia and hurled themselves on the remnants of the Rozwi state.

At the time of the great southern invasions the Rozwi dynasty of Changamire still had a semblance of its former power. The Rozwi overlord, known as the Mambo, and his supporters continued to occupy the great stone enclosure of Zimbabwe. His Shona subjects had elaborated a fairly diversified form of agriculture; they continued to produce some gold, and they traded with the Portuguese settlements on the Zambezi. Shona smiths, Shona potters, and other craftsmen were renowned for their skills, and the Mambo's overlordship extended over what is much of present-day Rhodesia. The Rozwi sovereigns apparently worked in close alliance with the priests of Mwari, the Shona high god. Shona priests maintained a great network of sacred shrines near all the major centers of the Rozwi state. Local representatives of the cult apparently paid regular visits to the central shrines in order to bring gifts and to return with commands and advice from the deity.[13] The Shona political system was, however, ill-equipped to meet the new barbarian menace. The Shona lacked centralized military institutions; on the contrary, various Shona chiefs were apt to fight against their neighbors. According to some local traditions, even the Mambo's religious power may possibly have decayed; by the time of the Ngoni invasions, the Mambo had ceased to make the traditional obeisance to the deity. Whatever the details of the story, Shona power collapsed before the invaders. The Mambo was caught and skinned alive. His sovereignty disintegrated, though some traditions of the Mambo's former greatness persisted to inspire the remnants of his people.

Zwangendaba's host then continued on its way to the north, and crossed the Zambezi River in 1835 (the exact date has been identified by an eclipse of the sun). The great horde reached the vicinity of Lake Tanganyika about 1845 and subsequently split up. Some settled west of Lake Tanganyika, where they became known as the Watuta. Others found homes for themselves in parts of what is now Malawi. A further group led by Mpeseni proceeded to the west. Mpeseni's decision was an unfortunate one, for about 1856 the Ngoni encountered the Bemba. The Bemba were well-known raiders on their own account who were supplied with muskets received from Arab traders in exchange for slaves and ivory. Mpeseni therefore retreated to the south and finally settled in what is now northeastern Zambia.

The repercussions of the Ngoni wars were also felt as far afield as the upper Zambezi Valley. The Kololo (Makololo), a group of cattle-keeping Bantu people with a Sotho core, marched northward, crossed the Vaal River, made their way through Bechuanaland, crossed the Zambezi River sometime about 1840, and for a time settled in the Tonga country of what is now southern Zambia. The Ndebele, however, continued to press upon them, and the Kololo, led by their great chief Sebitwuane, moved into the upper Zambezi Valley, where Sebitwuane made himself ruler and once more consolidated the Barotse (Lozi) kingdom.

PATTERNS OF BANTU CONQUEST

These great migrations may well rank with the most famous marches of history—the wanderings of the Israelites through the desert, or the retreat of the ten thousand, Greek soliders recounted by Xenophon in the *Anabasis.* In terms of sheer distance alone the exploits of a people like the Kololo were stupendous. All in all, the core of the Kololo host must have moved on foot for something like a thousand miles—as far as from New York to the southern tip of Florida or from London to the plains of Hungary. For the Ngoni, the Gaza, and the Ndebele alike this was a heroic period. The Ngoni flourished—they were successful brigands on the march.[14] But the brigands in turn became rulers who had to solve the question of how to exercise permanent power. The Kololo on the one hand, and the Ndebele, Ngoni, and Gaza on the other, varied sharply in their response to the new challenge.

The Kololo took over an existing empire; they became the ruling people in the Zambezi Valley, with its fertile mounds, its rich fishing grounds, and luscious cattle pastures. The people of Sotho stock formed the core of the ruling aristocracy. Apparently one or two Kololo families lived in each village to supervise local affairs; villages were grouped into larger administrative units under the control of great Kololo chiefs. The vanquished were forced to render various services and to cultivate the land. The subject tribes continued to pay annual tributes of grain, nuts, spears, hoes, ivory, prepared skins, and so forth. The king, like his Lozi predecessors, redistributed these goods among his followers, reserving only a small proportion for himself.

In the end, however, the Kololo fell on evil days. The highlanders came from a country where malaria was little known, and they had little resistance against the deadly fevers prevalent in the river valley. Sebitwuane's successors lacked his abilities. The Kololo fell prey to bitter dissensions and failed to keep their grip on the country. The Kololo had never succeeded in subduing the whole of the old Lozi empire, so that the flame of resistance was never quite extinguished. In 1864 the Lozi and Batoka simultaneously rose in order to cast off the alien yoke. The Kololo put up little effective resistance; their men were slain and their women were forcibly incorporated into the Lozi community.[15]

The conquerors of Zulu and related origin, on the other hand, formed entirely new states whose ruling strata had nothing to fear from the wrath of the conquered. These states rested on raiding and pastoral agriculture; they were largely oriented toward war. The most powerful of them was the Ndebele monarchy, which, at the height of its power, could perhaps mobilize something like 20,000 men. The regimental system caused the army to remain at a high pitch of military efficiency; it also provided the nation with a means of assimilating new captives.

Robert Moffat, a British missionary, wrote:

The Matabele take from the conquered tribes boys and girls, the boys of course acquire the language and the habits and customs of their captors and are reared for soldiers, so that by far the greatest majority of that people are composed of such tribes. At each town of any consequence of these people there is generally a Matabele officer and some soldiers to receive tribute, and to such natives Moselekatse (Mzilikazi) in general gives over a number of cattle to be taken charge of. In conversing with such I have observed that there is nothing they deplore so much as their children being taken from them just at a time when they become useful to their parents. It is therefore quite common to see a soldier having a boy or youth, whom he calls his servant, whom he has taken in the above manner to rear up for war.[16]

Mzilikazi at the same time strengthened his military and political position through skillful "cattle diplomacy"; conquered chiefs who submitted to Ndebele rule received herds on loan for their people's use; Mzilikazi in fact acted as a distributor king in the accustomed fashion. The Ndebele monarch kept a particularly tight hold over the ivory trade, which was steadily growing in importance. Wrote Moffat, "Moselikatse is the only one with whom barter can be effected. Every tusk of ivory is his, and no one dare dispose of one but himself, and from what I have seen he is a hard merchant to deal with. He can ask what he likes, knowing that there is no one else in his extensive dominions that can undersell him."[17]

These "Black Spartans" were not immovable monoliths. All were affected to some extent by the forces of change that impinged upon them from without, as well as by the cultural and religious ideas of the people whom they conquered. The Ngoni who settled in northern Malawi, for instance, began to subjugate neighboring tribes as political units, not simply as individuals. Their army ceased to be a simple aggregation of age-sets, but also included quasi-professional fighters armed with guns supplied by Mwase Kasungu, a neighboring Chewa chief. The Ngoni groups in Tanganyika became involved in the slave trade to the coast. Even the Ndebele, who kept aloof from the slave traffic, could not adhere for long to their original policy of splendid isolation. In 1853 they concluded a treaty with the Transvaalers, permitting Boer hunters to visit the country. The Ndebele also paid some attention to the religious ideas of their subjects, especially those of the Shona. The native priests of Mwari, the Kalonga high god, continued to practice their rites in the Matopo hills and received gifts from Mzilikazi, who would periodically consult them on affairs of state. In addition there were social changes within the ruling group itself. After the occupation of Matabeleland, the Sotho captives from the south, now considered old members of the nation, rose in status. The Sotho or *Abenhla,* the "people from upcountry," admittedly did not attain full equality with the *Abezansi,* the privileged Ngoni aristocracy, but the Sotho did manage to rise to responsible posts, while *Abenhla* and *Abezansi* looked down with undisguised contempt on the *Amaholi,* the Shona subjects, who formed the lowest stratum within the community.

But for all these changes the various Nguni or Zulu states remained basically conservative in their outlook, overspecialized toward war, and generally little suited to successful adaptation even in the purely military sphere. The Ndebele, for instance, did not carry on much foreign trade; hence they could not easily buy imported rifles. Ndebele aristocrats were too proud to work for Europeans to acquire guns in exchange. When they did acquire modern firearms Ndebele herdsmen and warriors lacked the mechanical skills to maintain their weapons. Unlike the Southern Sotho

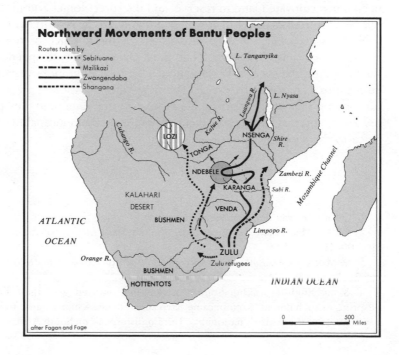

and the Tswana, the Ndebele failed to switch over from spears to firearms. Instead they remained wedded to traditional shock tactics and a suicidal cult of "cold steel"; they devoted more attention to the ceremonial aspects of military life than to tactical innovations. Once the Ndebele, the Ngoni, or the Gaza clashed with better-armed white men, the collapse of these "spear kingdoms" turned out to be as spectacular as their original rise to power.

In addition the new raiding states suffered from economic contradictions. To some extent they were parasites living off their neighbors. Explorers and missionaries may have exaggerated when they spoke of massive depopulation in entire regions by reason of foreign raids. Nevertheless, the margin of survival in a backward rural society was necessarily small. When the herds were looted, the seed grain stolen, and the men folk killed in battle, the survivors might starve. Raiding also had deleterious consequences of an indirect kind. Weaker communities would have to choose village sites with an eye to the defensive rather than to the agricultural potential of their location. Raiding might therefore impede the best use of the available soil, and victorious raiders would thereby impoverish their neighbors. The raiders, in the long run, may sometimes have also impoverished themselves. The Fort Jameson Ngoni in northeastern Zambia, for instance, dwelt in large villages. The high density of their population was appropriate only to a victorious kingdom relying for part of its subsistence on crops and cattle raided beyong the country's borders. According to an estimate by John Barnes, the Fort Jameson Ngoni were settled in precolonial times at a density in excess even of the critical land-carrying capacity attained during the 1940s (by which time much land had been alienated to whites). "There cannot have been much cultivated land in reserve, and the [precolonial Ngoni] State was exhausting the wealth of its own soil as well as drawing on the resources of its neighbours."[18]

Such estimates are hard to substantiate in the absence of reliable statistics, but certain conclusions do emerge. The great Bantu backwash speeded up a process of state-building and social differentiation. The great migration further complicated the ethnic mosaic of southern Africa. The new states occasioned a good deal of destruction among their more peaceful neighbors. At the same time they became subject to unforseen internal weaknesses that later on made them incapable of prolonged resistance to the superior arms of white men.

NOTES

1. Quoted in van der Merwe, *Trek*, p. 299.

2. W. M. Macmillan, *The Road to Self-Rule: A Study in Colonial Evolution* (London, 1959), pp. 100–101.

3. E. Morse Jones, *Roll of the Settlers in South Africa Part I up to 1826* (Cape Town, 1969), pp. 22–72

4. Some English-speaking South Africans intermarried with their Boer neighbors; the offspring of such unions often became Afrikaners; hence a man's name today no longer forms a sure guide to the bearer's nationality. But English-speaking South Africans as a whole became

a distinct community of their own, marked off by a peculiar accent. This is apparently influenced by Cockney, Scots, and Afrikaner sound-patterns; it is spotted as easily as Canadian or Australian English, and marks off English-speaking South Africans as a separate group.

5. Alan F. Hatterseley, *An Illustrated Social History of South Africa* (Cape Town, 1969) pp. 133–134.

6. Quoted by L. C. A. Knowles and C. M. Knowles, *The Economic Development of the British Overseas Empire: The Union of South Africa* (London, 1936), vol. 3, p. 25, from *Mr. Rudolph's Reminiscences of South African Pioneers,* ed., E. V. Bambrick (Natal, 1905)

7. Monica Wilson, "Co-Operation and Conflict: The Eastern Cape Frontier," in Monica Wilson and Leonard Thompson, eds., *The Oxford History of South Africa,* vol. 1, pp. 256–60.

8. See Alan Smith, "The Trade of Delagoa Bay as a Factor in Nguni Politics" in Leonard Thompson, ed., *African Societies in Southern Africa: Historical Studies* (New York, 1969), pp. 171–189.

9. John A. Barnes, *Politics in a Changing Society: A Political History of the Fort Jameson Ngoni* (Cape Town, 1954), pp. 4–7.

10. The best accounts are to be found in Leonard Thompson's two chapters entitled respectively "Co-operation and Conflict: The Zulu Kingdom and Natal" and "Co-Operation and Conflict: The High Veld" in Wilson and Thompson, *The Oxford History of South Africa,* vol. 1, pp. 334–404; and also J. D. Omer-Cooper, *The Zulu Aftermath: A Nineteenth-Century Revolution in Bantu Africa* (Evanston, 1966). A readable, popular book is E. A. Ritter, *Shaka Zulu: The Rise of the Zulu Empire* (London, 1955).

11. For a detailed analysis of the Swazi see Hilda Kuper, *An African Aristocracy: Rank Among the Swazi* (London, 1947).

12. For a succinct account of his carrer, see J. D. Omer-Cooper, "Moshesh and the Creation of the Basuto Nation—the First Phase," *Tarikh,* vol. 1, no. 1 (1965), pp. 42–52, and, by the same author, "Moshesh and the Survival of the Basuto Nation—the Second Phase," *Tarikh,* vol. 1, no. 2, 1966, pp. 1–13.

13. Terence O. Ranger, "The Nineteenth Century in Southern Rhodesia," in Terence O. Ranger, ed., *Aspects of Central African History* (London, 1968), p. 115.

14. Barnes, *Politics in a Changing Society,* p. 63.

15. M. Mainga, "The Lozi Kingdom," in Brian M. Fagan, ed., *A Short History of Zambia* (Nairobi, 1966), p. 124.

16. *The Matabele Journals of Robert Moffat, 1829–1860,* ed., J. P. R. Wallis (London, 1945), vol. 1, p. 319.

17. *The Matabele Journals of Robert Moffat, 1829–1860,* p. 325.

18. Barnes, p. 104.

PART
IX

MUSLIM
AND AFRO-CHRISTIAN
CIVILIZATIONS

Chapter 30

The Muslim Impact

ISLAM IN THE WESTERN SUDAN

The eighteenth century witnessed a series of great popular revivals affecting adherents of all the great monotheistic religions in different parts of the world. In Galicia in eastern Europe, Baal-Shem-Tov (Israel ben Eliezer, 1700–1760) preached a creed that appealed to poor, unlettered Jews and that went counter to the scholasticism of the rabbis. In England, John Wesley (1703–1791) set himself to spread "scriptural holiness over the land." Almost an exact contemporary was Muhammad ibn 'Abd al-Wahhab (1702–1792), a native of Najd in central Arabia whose objectives were in certain respects comparable to Wesley's. Ibn 'Abd al-Wahhab determined to return to the purity of original Islam. He meant to wipe out those syncretic deviations in Islam that, in his view, sinfully linked persons and things with a God who, in a common Muslim phrase, "has no associates." All these movements met a popular religious need. But they operated in totally different environments. Baal-Shem appealed to poverty-stricken hawkers, innkeepers, and day laborers who eked out a scanty living in countries primarily dependent on a backward agrarian economy. His followers could not possibly aspire to political or social power and sought salvation in a religion that emphasized joy in the Lord and personal repentance. Wesley, on the other hand, labored among the poor in what was then the most advanced industrial country in the world. He stood for conservatism in politics, but stressed the virtues of thrift, hard work, temperance, and organization, the very qualities that would make for personal advancement within a developed and highly competitive Western country. Ibn 'Abd al-Wahhab, on the other hand, worked among a warlike

421

people dependent mainly on pastoralism and oasis agriculture. He was a puritan in arms and soon became convinced that peaceful persuasion was not enough. The sword must aid the word. A *jihad* must be waged against the synthesists. By the end of the eighteenth century, Wahhabism had spread over most of the Arab Peninsula.[1] Its influence extended far beyond the boundaries of Arabia into other parts of Asia and Africa.

There was a spiritual resurgence in parts of the Sudan. The Moroccan invasion of 1591 had caused the Songhai state to break up and had helped to produce a state of general political disintegration. Even at the best of times Islam had never made much of an impact on the villages. In empires such as Mali, Songhai, and Bornu, the kings, and the great civil and military dignitaries as well as the merchants professed the religion of Muhammed, but most villagers remained pagans. The rulers themselves upheld the traditional rituals and taboos that their subjects regarded as essential for ensuring the welfare of the community.[2] Even the towns were not fully Islamized. Many Sudanic cities were agglomerations of villages, and a considerable proportion of their people was engaged in agriculture. Members of the same ethnic group commonly congregated in adjacent settlements, practicing their own customs under their own chiefs. Foreign traders visited the cities to do business, but they too dwelt in their own suburbs. Islam was the creed of the richer and the more educated, but even among the upper strata the practice of Islam did not succeed in unifying the Sudanic kingdoms.

From the believers' point of view, the state of religion, as it existed in many parts of the Sudan, further deteriorated after the breakup of the Songhai empire. A few "islands" of purity remained. Kanem-Bornu, for instance, was still a powerful and civilized state that carried on extensive trans-Saharan commerce and was ruled according to Islamic law by pious rulers. Elsewhere the practice of religion deteriorated or Islam accomodated its practices to pagan customs. Some territories, formerly under Muslim rule, reverted to pagan governance. This fate, for instance, overtook the Bambara communities of Segu and Kaarta. Even where Islam was able to maintain itself, as in the Hausa cities west of Kanem-Bornu, the enforcement of Koranic law and practice often became lax according to the standards of the orthodox. Many of these commercial towns to the west fell into serious economic straits. Much of the overland trade appears to have been diverted to the eastern routes terminating in Bornu and Hausaland, and Muslims in the decaying western settlements were careless in their observance of the faith. Many nominally Muslim rulers such as the Hausa condoned paganism; Muslims also accomodated themselves to pagan society under pagan rulers governing pagan peoples like the Mossi and the Bambara.

The existence of a great Muslim diaspora, consisting of Tukulor, Fulani, Soninke, Hausa, and other ethnic groups widely dispersed among unbelievers, raised serious problems for the faithful. A Muslim subject to a pagan lord might have to pay uncanonical forms of tribute, or he might have to fight for a Muslim ruler who adhered to Islam in only a nominal fashion. Pious men could easily demonstrate on religious grounds that political or social subordination to unbelievers should not be tolerated. There was a clear canonical obligation not only of flight from pagan lands, but also of a *jihad* against the heathen lords who oppressed the righteous. The

Muslims, with their knowledge of Arabic and their ability to read and write, enjoyed great intellectual advantages. They formed part of a universal culture, a great network of religion and trade. They also had a formidable fighting record. Provided the Muslim minorities could find an able leader capable of inculcating religious and military discipline in his followers, they might easily take up arms. Once a Muslim rebellion succeeded, the victors might continue the battle in order to make more conquests, garner tribute from newly-conquered lands, and strengthen their own numbers by converting the pagans abroad.[3]

Militant Islam made a special appeal to the Fula (Fulani or *Peuls*) a pastoral people of mixed Negroid and Berber descent. During the sixteenth and seventeenth centuries, the Fula of Futa Toro on the south bank of the lower Senegal, went over to Islam. One particular group were known as the Torodbe. Historians of an older vintage have tended to describe them simply as Fula. More recent research suggests that the Torodbe contained believers of Fula but also of other ethnic origins. These men were often former bards or former artisans, people from a relatively low station in life, who rallied under the banner of Islam. The Torodbe became the spiritual guides of Muslim militants, supplying the Fula with migrant intellectuals who devoted their lives wholly to the practice of religion. These teachers trained small bands of followers who were organized into confraternities (called *turuq* or *tariqah*). These had an ancient tradition in Islam, and there were brotherhoods of many kinds. Their members sought a special state of mental concentration through which they would reach mystic communion with God. They also became adept in Islamic scriptural and legal traditions. Their wandering manner of life made them peculiarly suited to act as religious guides for nomadic people, and their mode of worship provided them with a particularly efficacious form of spiritual discipline.

Islam of the militant kind found a refuge in the Futa Toro south of the Senegal River. During the early part of the eighteenth century, missionaries from the Futa Toro converted the Fula of the Futa Jallon, a hilly region in the central part of what is now the Republic of Guinea. The Fula clashed with the ruling Jalonke, a branch of the Susu people, who had apparently become nominal adherents of Islam but who retained many pagan practices. The Fula found allies among other ethnic groups, including the Mandingo and the Susu. Islam, unlike western Christianity, permitted polygamy. The Islamic religion, born of the desert, was adjusted to the ways of nomadic peoples and did not require an elaborate and costly organization. With its unified system of religion and law and its great literary traditions, it offered both intellectual and spiritual attractions; it gave comfort to men who had suffered much from the confusion of the times; it also provided a means of overcoming many internal rivalries. Hence the Muslims gradually overcame their opponents.

The victorious Fula founded a new kind of state, the Imamate of Futa Jallon. Political and military power alike was placed into the hands of a religious leader, the almamy. The country was divided into provinces and districts. The almamy, an elected officer, tried to rule the state according to strict Islamic precepts. Practice did not quite conform to theory. The Imamate retained many features of traditional West African life; the country subsequently suffered a good deal from internal instability, and the office of almamy came to be monopolized by two ruling families. But Futa

Jallon retained its cohesion and survived more or less intact until the French invasion at the end of the nineteenth century.[4]

The Futa Jallon became a center of Islamic influence, and students from abroad visited the country to perfect their religious knowledge. One of these was Sheykh Sulayman Bal, a famous *marabout* or traveling preacher. Sulayman took advantage of the bitter tension that had long existed in the Futa Toro between the Torodbe and the ruling class of Fulani known as Denyankobe. Life in the country had become insecure as the result of internal quarrels between the Fulani clans and Moorish raids from the Senegal Valley. Sulayman began a *jihad,* and in 1775 the ruling dynasty was replaced by a new line of imams.[5]

The new states could not rival the ancient empires in size, power, or splendor. Neither could they reverse the shift of West Africa's commercial center of gravity from the Sahara and North Africa toward the southern coast and the Atlantic. They did, however, convert many of their pagan subjects to Islam. They spread the legal and ethical concepts of their religion as well as diluted traces of Islamic cosmopolitanism. They also paid a good deal of attention to education, a subject dear to the Muslim intellectuals who had so important a share in the Muslim resurgence. The first European visitors to Futa Jallon noted in 1794 that the local people strictly attended to their religious duties; they were also impressed by the number of Koranic schools to be found in the country. The Fula, the most important ethnic component of the new ruling strata, had an economic stake in urban occupations, in crafts and commerce, as well as in pastoralism. They were therefore anxious to protect the caravan traffic, so that the Futa Jallon, for instance, became an important meeting place for traders from the forest and the savannah alike. European visitors found the Muslim towns impressive settlements, larger than the pagan villages, with spacious houses made of sun-baked brick and protected by city walls or stockades. Traders assisted the outward spread of Islam. Individual Fula agents in the service of French traders carried their faith as far as the shores of Sierra Leone. The prestige of the victorious Muslims also spread further afield, to the Wolofs of Senegal and to the Hausa country in the territories comprised within the modern states of Niger and Nigeria.[6]

THE FULANI EMPIRE, THE YORUBA, AND BORNU

When the Fula *jihads* began in the western Sudan, the vast region now comprised within the confines of Northern Nigeria remained subject to the sway of Hausa rulers. From the fifteenth century onward, the Hausa had been influenced by Islamic scholars and traders from North Africa and from great empires like Songhai to the west. The Hausa kings dwelt in fortified cities. Their people prospered from commerce and from craft industries, specially from weaving, dyeing, and the manufacture of leather; they also dealt in slaves. The Hausa kings and courtiers, the noblemen and great merchants professed the Muslim religion. Islam, however, never spread to the masses, and even the Hausa lords made many religious concessions to indigenous practices.

The Hausa rulers also faced many other difficulties. The Hausa never united into a single empire; they were divided by bitter internecine struggles. Katsina and Kano,

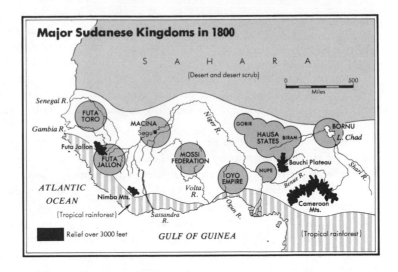

for instance, two powerful savannah states, battled over control of the northern trade routes. Another rival for power was Gobir, which became the most formidable of these Hausa states during the second part of the eighteenth century. The Hausa were threatened from the east by Tuareg raiders who had established themselves on the left bank of the Niger near Gao and who boldly ranged beyond the river. More dangerous still was the threat from the Fulani, who had infiltrated the Hausa states for several centuries.

The Fulani, had become divided into two groups. Some remained herdsmen in the country. Others established themselves in the towns, intermarried with the Hausa, and made their name in many urban professions. Many of these town-bred Fulani reached high political office under the Hausa. In addition, many Fulani scholars and divines acquired a reputation for the purity of their lives and the soundness of their Islamic doctrine.

One of these groups were the Toronkawa clan of Fulani who resided in Gobir and who became famous for their missionary fervor. In the 1770s a young Toronkawa, Usman dan Fodio (1754–1817), began his career as a reforming preacher. Usman at first confined himself to matters of faith; he attacked indigenous practices of magic and witchcraft and also began to distribute manuscripts in Arabic throughout the Hausa states. Usman's religious campaign, however, also had political overtones. He attacked the Hausa rulers for perverting Islamic law and for levying taxes not sanctioned by the Koran. In 1795 Usman announced to his followers that a heavenly vision had instructed him to arm his followers. In 1802 he left Gobir with his adherents and established his headquarters outside Gobir territory. This was a significant step which Usman likened to Muhammed's famed *Hegira*.

In 1804 Usman's forces routed the Gobir army at Tabkin Kwotto, and a new *jihad* began in earnest. As John Flint, a modern British historian, put it, the movement assumed an essentially revolutionary character. Fulani herdsmen flocked to Usman's standards, seeking loot or liberty. Hausa peasants joined Usman's armies, anxious to rid themselves of tax gatherers. The revolutionaries succeeded in unifying the bulk of northern Nigeria, and by 1812 Fulani emirs were ruling over most parts of this great region. Usman dan Fodio then retired from political life to devote himself to writing and meditation. He divided the empire into two parts. The western half centered on Gwandu with his brother Abdullahi as suzerain. The eastern section consisted of Sokoto and the surrounding regions, with his son Muhammed Bello as Sultan.

The new overlords had no traditional claims to loyalty. They were denied the rights of divine kingship by Islam. Their authority rested on the precepts of the Koran, the oaths sworn by subordinates, and—above all—on the well-disciplined cavalry.[7] The traditional checks that had limited the power of the ancient Hausa rulers disappeared. The tax gatherers continued their exactions, and the peasants paid tribute as before. Many of the old ways continued as the new Fulani ruling class mingled with the old Hausa oligarchy. Hausa remained the main spoken tongue and Hausa culture continued. But the political and religious life of the region was refurbished, with Arabic as its written language. The Fulani also succeeded in a major political task where their Hausa predecessors had failed. Internal wars among the Hausa communities largely came to an end. The Fulani greatly reduced local raiding; they brought security to the trade routes, so that merchants from Kano and other great centers could travel in peace, and the urban Fulani, at any rate, derived some benefit from the changing order of society.

The Fulani extended their power further to the south, into regions where the older Hausa rulers had never held sway. In 1806 the Fulani established a new emirate centering on Yola, the farthest point of navigability on the Benue. Further downstream they set up the emirate of Muri. The native pagans put up a stout guerrilla warfare in the hills but in turn were raided by Fulani slave traders. The Fulani likewise gained much influence over Nupe, an indigenous kingdom that straddled the Niger.

The Fulani also intervened in the affairs of the decaying Oyo empire. Oyo, a great Yoruba state, had begun to show signs of weakness, and Dahomey repudiated its tributary status. The Egba asserted their independence, and the Fulani were presented with new opportunities. In 1817 Oyo tried to discipline Ilorin, a rebellious province southwest of Nupe where Fulani had already made great inroads. Ilorin called in Fulani aid; Oyo was defeated, and Ilorin was subsequently absorbed into the Fulani empire. The defection of Ilorin hastened the disintegration of the Oyo empire. The remaining Yoruba towns ceased to obey Oyo's rule. Yorubaland fell into an almost permanent state of internecine warfare.

The effects of the Fulani *jihads* extended even to the New World, to distant Bahia in Brazil, where Muslim slaves of Hausa and Yoruba origin rallied both against their masters and against Christian and pagan slaves in a series of risings that extended from 1807 to 1835.[8] From the military standpoint these insurrections all proved failures. But they helped to bring about a change in Brazilian public opinion on the question of slave trading. Many Brazilians began to advocate the abolition of the traffic, not only because it was inhuman and uneconomic, but also because it seemed to entail so many dangers to the country's social and political stability.

Despite the far-reaching effects of their campaigns and despite their military successes, the Fulani, however, never succeeded in their declared ambition of "dipping the Koran into the Atlantic." Fulani horsemen were hard to defeat in the open savannah country. Cavalry, however, could not easily penetrate into the rain forests, where the horses died from disease and where the Fulani squadrons were easily ambushed. The Yoruba, moreover, increasingly began to rely on firearms from the south, whereas the horsemen of the grassland became skilled in the use of guns only toward the end of the last century. The Fulani, moreover, could not easily cope with fortified cities.

In 1829 a mixed party of Yoruba refugees established a new town at Ibadan on an excellent defensive position. Ibadan was an agrotown; most of its people depended on farming rather than trade. Ibadan, however, developed into an important military power; in 1840 the army of Ibadan obtained a decisive victory over Ilorin, and the Fulani thereafter were never able to advance further into Yorubaland.

The Fulani empire was equally incapable of conquering Bornu. During the eighteenth century the empire of Bornu had fallen into decay. In 1808 Fulani forces invaded Bornu and forced the reigning *mai* to flee. The unfortunate monarch appealed for help from the Kanembu who dwelt east of Lake Chad. Bornu then found a new savior in El Kanemi, a devout Muslim and a great warrior who began his career as the leader of a private army. El Kanemi reduced the reigning *mais* to puppets; he repelled the Fulani threat and later extended Bornu's sway to include Kanem and Braghirmi to the east, so that Bornu recovered much of its medieval power. In 1846 El Kanemi's son, Sheik Omar, abolished the *mai*-ship altogether and thereby ended one of the most ancient dynasties in Africa.

THE EAST COAST AND ITS HINTERLAND

The militant puritanical movements were born of the savannah and the desert. They exerted no influence on the southern maritime frontier of the Muslim world. The cities on the African east coast were Muslim oligarchies that depended on trade, looked toward the Indian Ocean for their profits, and stood for a way of life very different from that of the Sudanic interior. East coast civilization fused cultural elements from South Arabia and Persia with those brought in by Bantu immigrants from the mainlands, and there was a distinctive unity in language, commerce, and culture. Swahili gradually replaced Arabic, not only as the language of the people, but also as the ordinary language of the educated. For instance, the official history of Kilwa, commissioned by the local Sultans, was begun in Arabic. But by the end of the eighteenth or the beginning of the nineteenth century, the chronicler charged with compiling the official history of Mombasa preferred to use Swahili, a hybrid *lingua franca* not understood in the Arabic homeland.[9]

East coast society was further influenced by immigrants from India who had settled on the coast for many centuries. Much of the ocean shipping was owned and manned by Indians. Indians played a major part in banking and money lending. They controlled much of the local trade, either as businessmen on their own account, as financiers, or as managers for wealthy land-owning magnates. Indians thereby rendered an essential service to the community. But at the same time they steadily increased their economic power vis à vis the old Arab or partly Arab families whose income depended increasingly on revenue from land or high political office. Besides the great Muslim land owners and Indian merchants there were poorer Arabs, as well as a growing population of mixed Afro-Arabic origin whose ranks were further swelled by African newcomers from the mainland. Last but not least in numbers came the African slaves who worked in the houses, gardens, and plantations of the rich, and who served as caravan-porters, soldiers, and unskilled laborers. Sometimes slaves were also employed as commercial agents. Some even managed to acquire a good deal of wealth of their own, for east coast slavery allowed for an infinite number of gradations from extreme misery to comparative affluence. As one British observer put it in the latter part of the nineteenth century: "that gaily dressed man with riches of cloth for exchange is a slave, and that poor woman who has brought her basket of meal into the market to sell looks at him in awe and envy with her companion who carries her ware and who is her slave."[10]

This highly variegated society looked primarily to trade. Slaves were exported to India, Arabia, and Persia. (No figures are available until relatively recent times, but the numbers involved must have been considerable, for by 1835 the slaves in Oman were said to constitute no less than one-third of the population.) The east coast merchants also dealt in ivory, ambergris, coconut oil, and wax from Africa, as well as in manufactured goods, including cloth, metal work, and beads from India, Persia, and Arabia. They manufactured some cloth of their own, but local industries rarely served the overseas market. Land owners cultivated oranges, palms, sorghum, millet, and beans; they bred cattle, goats, and sheep, but all these were for local consumption and not for sale abroad. Even the commercial position of these towns deteriorated. When the Portuguese had first come to the Indian Ocean the east coast cities were still a power to be taken into account, and their wealth had taken the Christians by surprise. But what startled European visitors in subsequent centuries were the signs of decay—ruined mosques and crumbling stone walls. The east coast cities had suffered from Portuguese control of the Indian Ocean. They sustained commercial loss from internecine rivalry. Worse still were the effects of tribal migrations on the mainland. In 1587 marauding hordes of Zimba had massacred the inhabitants of Kilwa, a disaster from which the town never fully recovered. The northern part of the coast was affected by the advance of the Galla. Between 1600 and 1650, for instance, Galla invaders destroyed the towns of Ozi and Kilifi, and reduced Malindi to a heap of ruins. All this led to the impoverishment of the older Shirazi culture from Persia and prepared the way for the overwhelming predominance of Southern Arabia.[11] By the end of the eighteenth century there were still some wealthy people; there was still some trade, but its range had narrowed, and Swahili sea power had ceased to be a formidable threat to foreigners. The east coast cities lay in a backwater, aloof from Europe and little affected even by the great tidal waves occasioned by the Napoleonic Wars.

In culture and politics the east coast cities were in an equally unhappy position. Skilled artisans still built some fine houses or fashioned tasteful carvings from wood.

There were also a few learned men who wrote literary or historical works. But the east coast towns had always been more interested in commerce than in scholarship. They never knew anything of the intense intellectual life that had once distinguished great Muslim centers such as Cordova or Baghdad.[12] Neither had they anything of the harsh religiosity of the desert, and they experienced no revivals of faith comparable with those of Arabia and the Western Sudan. Politically, the east coast cities were divided, and unable to present a common front to foreign invaders. The Portuguese, having lost Mombasa to an expeditionary force from Oman in 1698, made some subsequent attempts to reassert their influence in the north. These endeavors all came to nought, but resistance centered on Oman, and not on the cities themselves. In 1740 Ahmed ibn Said, scion of the Albusaid dynasty and founder of a new line of Omani rulers, freed his countrymen from Persian control, and from then onward Oman was a stronger sea power in East Africa than Portugal. The Portuguese abandoned all hope of reconquering the lands north of the Rovuma River, and the Arabs for their part were content to leave the Christians undisturbed in the south.

The Omanis, however, still faced the difficult problem of establishing effective political control over the east coast cities. Most of the settlements on the African littoral wanted to manage their own affairs, and Oman was too preoccupied with its internal troubles to assert its authority. In 1741 the Omani Governor of Mombasa, Muhammad ibn Uthman al-Mazrui, declared his independence from Oman, and the house of Mazrui became the ruling dynasty of Mombasa. Mombasan forces subsequently intervened in the island of Pemba, which was later partitioned between Mombasa and the Sultanate of Pate, another east coast state. Failing to maintain their hold over Mombasa, the Omanis tried to consolidate their hold over Zanzibar and Kilwa, and later on, in the nineteenth century, they shifted their center of gravity to Zanzibar. At the same time there was renewed Arab immigration. Many Arabs, recruited as mercenaries to fight the Portuguese, had settled down in the decayed coastal towns. Entire Afro-Arab families came into Zanzibar from other settlements. But above all newcomers from Southern Arabia, especially Hadramaut (west of Oman), made their home on the East African coast, and it was this element that remolded Swahili culture and imprinted it with the dominant stamp it bears today.[13]

During the eighteenth century some east coast cities, especially Kilwa, gained new customers in the French. In the beginning of the eighteenth century the French had occupied ths islands of Mauritius (known to the French as Île–de-France) and Réunion in the Indian Ocean. In 1735 they sent to Mauritius its most famous governor, Mahé de la Bourdonnais, who founded Port-Louis, built new roads and fortifications, established cotton and indigo factories, introduced manioc from Brazil, and extended the cultivation of the sugar cane, first brought into the country by the Dutch. Many French immigrants made their homes in the island. Mauritius became like a West Indian sugar island whose plantations depended on imported slave labor. By the end of the eighteenth century there were over 100,000 slaves in the two islands, as against less than 20,000 whites and mulattoes.[14] But la Bourdonnais was primarily interested in the strategic value of Mauritius, and the island became an important naval base against the British. French sea power, was, however, inadequate to sustain French maritime traditions. During the Napoleonic Wars the British effectively intervened in Egypt, Persia, and along the Red Sea littoral. In 1810 an expedition from India captured Mauritius itself. By the time Napoleon had fallen from power, the Royal Navy wielded absolute and undisputed supremacy in the Indian Ocean.

The British subsequently tried to suppress the seaborne slave traffic. But this was a very lengthy process, and throughout the first three quarters of the nineteenth century the inland traffic in human merchandise kept growing, and the Muslim traders' frontier continued to expand inland. By the eighteenth century this process had not yet gone very far, and direct Islamic influence was confined to the coast. A certain amount of business was, however, done in the interior through African middlemen, especially Nyamwezi in what is now Tanzania, Yao west of Lake Nyasa, and Bisa in what is now northeastern Zambia. Omani intervention on the east coast may well have given a new impetus to such dealings by increasing the demand for goods from the interior. Buganda tradition, for instance, relates that during the latter part of the eighteenth century, cups, plates, coarse blue Indian calico, cowries, and copper bracelets began to be imported from the coast, so that even the most distant regions of Africa were tenuously linked to the world economy.

THE SULTANATE OF ZANZIBAR

The great maritime conflict between Great Britain and France had disastrous effects on the prosperity of the Muslim monarchy at Oman. When the British seized Mauritius in 1810, the French flag disappeared from the Indian Ocean. The Arabs lost their opportunities of making quick profits by trading with the French. The principal Indian firms returned from Muscat to British India. Indian firms successfully competed for the commerce of the Red Sea while British naval squadrons suppressed Arab piracy. Within a short space of time, the Omani Arabs dropped from the heights of prosperity to the depths of poverty, as their ports became full of discontented and jobless soldiers. Conditions were no better on the east coast of Africa itself. The Muslim communities were riddled by internal dissensions as the dominant Busaidi dynasty of Oman struggled for pre-eminence with the ruling Mazrui family of Mombasa. To make matters worse for the Arabs, the British, during the 1820s and 1830s, gradually extended their sphere of influence on the Persian Gulf. Subsequently they pushed into the Red Sea, and in 1839 they annexed Aden in Southern Arabia.[15]

The Omanis, no longer able to engage freely in war or politics on the gulf, began to emigrate in increasing numbers to East Africa. Sultan Seyyid Said (1804–1856), the ruler of Oman, finally decided to follow their example. In 1840 he removed his own residence from Oman to Zanzibar. Zanzibar was strategically well placed to isolate Mombasa through the use of superior sea power. The city had a numerous Muslim population well disposed toward Oman; it stood upon an island and was safe from the depredations of warring tribes from the mainland. Zanzibar, moreover, occupied an important position with regard to the trade in slaves and ivory from the African mainland, and Zanzibari merchants sent their wares as far as India. Sustained in part by Indian merchant capital, Zanzibar became the center of a far-flung empire;

it continued to hold this position until Seyyid Said died and the African and Arab portions of his kingdom became separate political entities.

Seyyid Said's first problem was to assert his power against the great Arab families of the coast. The Arab magnates owned great estates, derived a considerable revenue from commerce and the cultivation of cash crops for the Indian Ocean trade, and each controlled his own retinue drawn from armed followers and slaves. The sultan, however, enjoyed many advantages over these great lords. His opponents were disunited; their military and financial resources were much smaller than the Sultan's. Seyyid Said's contacts in Oman and other coastal cities enabled him to recruit a corps of administrators personally loyal to the Crown and reasonably well trained for their task. By encouraging immigration from Oman the Sultan was able to build up a large popular following within the Arab community. His government offered many advantages to the magnates themselves. The sultan's army served as a shield against social unrest, a serious danger in a state that depended so heavily on slavery. (In 1840, for instance, Zanzibar experienced a slave rising so serious that the insurgents could be suppressed only after reinforcements were called in from Oman.) The sultan's soldiers provided backing for the expansion of Arab land settlement at the expense of the indigenous African population. His navy gave protection to Zanzibari merchants in other coastal cities. The sultan himself took an active part in trade. His own interest in the middlemen's and carrier business, as well as the sense of security engendered by his authority along the coast gave a stimulus to inland commerce.

More important still, Seyyid Said provided his country with a new cash crop— cloves. Till the end of the eighteenth century cloves had been known to prosper only in the Moluccas in the Dutch East Indies. Later on cloves were carried to Île-de-France. No one knows who first introduced cloves to Zanzibar, but Seyyid Said fully understood their importance and decided to make clove culture the primary industry of Zanzibar. Setting an example on his own plantations, he insisted that all land owners should plant cloves either instead of or in greater numbers than coconut palms. He did the same thing in the twin island of Pemba, and his efforts were crowned with astonishing success. By the end of the sultan's reign the plantations, which twenty years earlier had still been in their infancy, produced an average annual crop worth about seven million pounds, and the value of cloves exported every year came next to that of ivory and slaves.[16]

But as time went on the trade in slaves and cloves brought in so much revenue that the character of the Arab settlement became completely transformed. There was a vast increase in the number of European and American merchantmen casting anchor at Zanzibar. At the same time Zanzibar traffic to the interior greatly increased. Caravans bearing the sultan's flag penetrated deep into the East African interior beyond the great lakes. The larger caravans were well protected and generally possessed a clear military superiority over the local upland communities, so that Arab penetration came to be the first great invasion from the coast. Arab merchants set up trading centers and fortified stockades along the caravan routes; some even became petty sovereigns on their own account. On the basis of the Arab presence inland, the sultan began to claim sovereignty over most of East Africa. Generally speaking these claims were empty. The sultan's writ ran no further than the main towns, and there was no continuous effective Arab occupation of the countryside. But Arab commercial influence was considerable, and Muslim traders also propagated their religion and language (Swahili) in the interior. The revenue derived from Zanzibar's far-flung trading empire enabled the sultan to support his own army and navy, a judicature, a revenue department, and a civil service of sorts. Zanzibar became capable of conducting its own foreign policy and, unlike the chieftainships of the interior, became recognized by the European powers as a quasi-legitimate state, admitted to some extent into the comity of nations.

Internally, the Zanzibari state was sharply stratified. The ruling strata consisted of Muslim landowners of Arab or Afro-Arab descent. Arabs occupied the top positions in government and administraton. In addition many Arabs traded far into the interior, hoping ultimately to retire to Zanzibar with the money earned from the traffic in ivory and slaves. Early European explorers told marvelous stories concerning the Muslim traders' ease and splendor, but recent research does not support these accounts. Large fortunes from the ivory trade were uncommon, and the majority of Arab people in the Sultanate, be they traders, soldiers, or artisans, apparently lived in modest circumstances.

Zanzibar also contained a numerous Indian population. Indians played a major part in Zanzibari commerce; they acted as bankers, financed clove plantations and slave trading caravans, and even managed the sultan's own ivory and opal trade in the interior. The Indian merchants at Zanzibar were usually the agents of Bombay houses; the wealthy Indian traders had their homes in Sind, Karachi, Kathiawar, and Bombay; they spent most of their lives in East Africa, but their families usually resided in India.[17] In addition Indians worked in the sultan's financial and other administrative departments, where they did most of the technical, clerical, and auditing work. Nothing, however, would be more mistaken than to picture all Asians as merchant princes or well-placed civil servants. Many Indians eked out a bare living as commercial employees; many others tried their luck as petty traders in the interior.

The vast majority of Zanzibar's population consisted of Africans.[18] By the time Seyyid Said moved his capital to Zanzibar, the African inhabitants of Zanzibar and Pemba had coalesced into three main tribal groupings, the Pemba, the Tumbatu, and the Hadimu. Of these three peoples, the Hadimu alone sustained the full impact of Arab immigration. A lengthy process of land alientation left the Arabs in possession of roughly the western half of Zanzibar Island, and the Hadimu on the eastern half. The Arabs came to own the most fertile soils and thereby acquired a virtual monopoly of intensive clove and coconut cultivation. The steady emigration of Hadimu to the eastern part of the island created a de facto native reserve where fishing and labor migration supplemented the peasants' meager livelihood. In Pemba, on the other hand, arable land was far more plentiful; Arab land alienation did not result in a rigid pattern of racial segregation based on land ownership, and many African as well as Arab land owners began to profit from clove cultivation.

This plural society rested on slavery. Slaves worked on the wharfs and as doormen; slaves labored in the clove plantations; slaves were shipped to the markets of Southern Arabia and Persia as concubines; slaves were exported to the sugar estates of Réunion; slaves apparently accounted for the greater part of Zanzibar's trade. Zanzibari slave society was highly diversified; there was no rigid color bar, and there were many gradations that allowed an intelligent or lucky bondsman to rise in the social sphere. However brutally or sadistically a slave might be treated on the march from the kraal to the coast, he does not seem to have been treated with undue severity by his master. Toward the end of the century a high British official opined that a slave would prefer to remain with his old owner rather than be liberated and be put in the charge of a Christian mission. According to the Englishman, the Arab's "tolerable form of servitude" was more agreeable than "the tutelage of a Christian mission, with its regular hours of work, its plain diet, severe chastity and absence of exhilarating orgies."[19] The fact remains that Zanzibar became essentially a servile society, and by about the middle of the century something like two-thirds of its population consisted of slaves, and the various social strata of Zanzibari society were sharply split.

On the face of it, this multiethnic state—for a time the most powerful in East Africa —had little in common with Ethiopia, the only other East African kingdom with a literary tradition of its own. Zanzibar was a maritime and Ethiopia a highland state. The rulers of Zanzibar were Muslim, those of Ethiopia Christian. The former depended mainly on trade, on plantation culture, and on high government positions; the latter derived their power from the imperial court or from their positions as feudal magnates and warlords. Both states, however, derived their cohesion from minority races; neither managed to coalesce into a truly national society.

THE EAST COAST TRADE IN SLAVES AND IVORY

Nineteenth-century free traders and humanitarians used to maintain that the abolition of the African slave trade must necessarily go with the development of legitimate commerce. From about the middle of the last century onward, the economic history of West Africa generally justified this confidence. In the peak years of the early nineteenth century, exporters of many nationalities may have been shipping something like 100,000 slaves per annum across the Atlantic. But from then onward British naval interference with the traffic became increasingly effective. At the same time West African cultivators delivered ever-increasing quantities of palm oil and peanuts for sale, and the slave trade rapidly declined along the West African shores north of the equator.

From the humanitarian point of view, the position of the slave trade was equally encouraging in South Africa. The British suppressed slavery by law. In any case there was no longer a market for captives. Warlike African communities like the Zulu or the Matabele preferred to assimilate their captives rather than sell them. The white cattle farmers of the interior, unlike the plantation owners of Brazil, did not require a great many servile hands. The wine-grape growers of the Western Cape were able to make do with free labor. Transport riders with their ox wagons could move bulky goods much more efficiently than slave porters. As the South African economy expanded during the second part of the century, European entrepreneurs became even more hostile to the slave trade in all its forms. White mining managers and railway entrepreneurs needed African labor, but they did not want to own Africans or keep them till their dying days. They did not require women or children. They desired adult workers for limited periods, bound to their employers by wage contracts. The European mining firms were willing and able to recruit free labor and pay cash. Wages, with the indirect pressure of taxation, the lure of new goods, and—as time went on—the facilities of efficient recruiting organizatons combined to produce the required hands. The slave trade conflicted with British moral ideals. As a senior British police officer put it, the traffic also entailed "an iniquitous abduction of valuable labour." It stood for a "rival kind of civilization to that of the white man" in Southern Africa, and the British suppressed it where they could.[20]

East Africa, however, was in a very different position. Neither the Arabs nor the Indian or Goanese settlers in the region had a part in the humanitarian heritage. They still regarded slavery as Britons had considered it in the seventeenth and early eighteenth century, as an institution hallowed by religion, custom, and economic necessity alike. East Africa's economic and geographic condition, moreover, differed greatly from that of West or South Africa. The region lacked convenient waterways such as the Senegal, the Gambia, or the Niger rivers. Technical skills were scarce. Inland traders could make profits only by exporting goods of small bulk and high value, that is to say, slaves capable of traveling on their own feet, or ivory, a produce of exceptional worth. Ethiopia produced some coffee. Traders on the East African coast did some business in palm oil. But until white farmers introduced new crops such as coffee, sisal, and pyrethrum and until white entrepreneurs construced railways, the bulk of the region remained economically backward. The greater part of East Africa lacked export crops that might serve as a satisfactory substitute for slaves and did not require servile labor for their cultivation. The most profitable merchandise was cloves, widely used in cookery and confectionery. But clove cultivation needed a good deal of cheap and unskilled labor. The Zanzibaris apparently lacked sufficient manpower on the spot to perform all the required tasks. They did not command the financial or administrative resources to organize a system of free labor migration. Hence they employed slaves and resorted to manhunts. Slaves also served as an article of export for the markets of Southern Arabia, Persia, and the islands of Réunion. In addition Portuguese half-caste raiders from Mozambique took part in the traffic. Mozambique exported slaves as far as Brazil. But in addition Mozambique dealers also raided for slaves to supply a domestic demand. In Livingstone's days the so-called "Mambari" were already conducting their traffic far up the Zambezi, and subsequently they penetrated into the Luangwa Valley of what is now Zambia, where they caused great devastation. These southern invaders never attempted to set up permanent political authority. The Zambezi Valley was their home. It was here that their great estates, called *prazos,* were situated. Their living in the main depended on the exploitation of these land holdings, and catching slaves was a convenient way of increasing the number of retainers on their fiefs.

Even more significant than the commerce in slaves was the traffic in ivory. During the nineteenth century the uses of ivory were wide and novel. In some ways it played the same part as do plastics in the twentieth, and as the European luxury industries expanded their demand for ivory steadily went up. Ivory was fashioned into billiard balls, piano keys, cutlery handles, and all those knicknacks with which Victorians used to cram their parlors. At the same time India, known to merchants as the "backbone of the trade," purchased enormous quantities of ivory rings left over from the turning of billiard balls; these were sold in bazaars as women's bangles. Indian craftsmen also used ivory for carving toys and ornaments. All these producers preferred African to Indian tusks, so that by about 1870 Africa was estimated to supply about 85 percent of the world's ivory.

The onslaught on the ivory resources of the interior took the form of a three-way thrust. White and half-caste frontiersmen made their way inland from South Africa. The hunter was often a kind of entrepreneur whose capital included horses, wagons, and firearms; he employed African servants, who themselves were armed with muskets. Wherever they could, the white pioneers hunted on horseback. But gradually the elephants retreated into remote tsetse-infested areas, and a few of the older hunters adapted themselves to hunting on foot, which was even more toilsome and dangerous than shooting from the saddle. By the late 1870s the ivory resources south of the Zambezi were largely exhausted. The hunters turned to providing specimens and trophies for museums and guiding prospectors and tourists (the characteristic expedients of all professional hunters in the days of a closing frontier), and elephant hunting generally became more of a sport than a livelihood.

East Africa was more important still as a source of ivory, and throughout most of the nineteenth century the region appears to have ranked as the world's foremost supplier. At first Portuguese half-caste as well as Swahili merchants and hunters exhausted the resources along the coast. As elephants became scarcer, the hunters pushed further inland, cutting out some of the intermediate traders. Seyyid Said vigorously encouraged this policy, and by the second part of the century a number of well-defined routes led from the coast to Lakes Nyasa, Tanganyika, and Victoria. Unyanyembe (Tabora) and Ujiji in what is now Tanzania became great inland markets where Arabs settled down to a manner of life customary in Zanzibar.[21] Merchants from the coast brought in vast quantities of foreign cloth, especially *merikani,* an inexpensive white cotton first introduced by Americans, as well as beads and other trinkets, tools, and firearms, including many discarded British army muskets.

The third thrust came from the north, as Egyptian and Sudanese adventurers pushed southward from Khartoum squeezing out the European adventurers. Khartoum became an important center for the trade in ivory and slaves. The local merchant magnates, mostly Egyptians with a sprinkling of Greeks and Italians, never amounted to more than about a dozen or so, but they wielded tremendous influence. They were allotted monopolistic control over whole districts by Egyptian officials and farmed these for ivory. Some of the larger firms had as many as 2000 men each in their pay, terrorizing the countryside. The Khartoum traders would also back penniless adventurers, many of them criminals from Egypt, who were sent up the Nile in special vessels. On reaching their destination, these cutthroats captured slaves and cattle, whom they ransomed for ivory. The Zanzibari traders, however ruthless, at any rate brought in goods; the Sudanese, on the other hand, seem to have largely depended on a purely predatory economy. By the early 1870s traders from the Sudan had got as far as Lake Albert in Uganda, and from then onward the various hunting and slaving frontiers gradually began to merge.

Traditional historiography used to see an inseparable connection between the ivory and the slave trade. The traffic in elephant tusks, runs the argument, depended on slave porterage. Slaves bore the ivory from the mainland to the coast, supplying in their persons both the only means of transport available at the time and also a valuable piece of merchandise at the expiration of their work. But the main slave and ivory routes did not always coincide. Ivory porterage, moreover, was a skilled job that could hardly be left to starving and demoralized captives. Much of the porterage fell to free tribesman such as the Nyamwezi, who specialized in the difficult task of carrying big and valuable tusks to their destination and who also took loads from the coast inland on their return journeys. Nevertheless there was a link between the traffic in tusks and slaves. The quest for elephants' teeth lured traders further and further inland. Africans who wanted to buy goods but had no ivory in exchange would use slaves to pay for their purchases. The slave trade, in other words, might be a symptom of a balance of payments problem facing a backward tribal economy anxious to acquire manufactured goods such as cloth and muskets. Again penniless thugs lacking merchandise for sale might abduct prisoners for sale abroad or for ransom against ivory, thereby making up for lack of capital by the use of violence. As the commerce in ivory became ever more competitive and as more and more African communities acquired firearms, violence apparently increased apace, and the effects of the traffic became ever more serious.

The long term economic effects of the East African slave and ivory trade are hard to assess. Harsh as it was, the commerce did promote the importation of new products —textiles, guns, knives, pots and pans, and beads and trinkets, and thereby increased local consumption by linking backward tribesmen to a wider world economy. But a hunting and a man-catching economy ultimately depended on wasting assets. It could not provide the basis for lasting prosperity. Even the promoters of the ivory trade rarely built up large fortunes. White elephant hunters such as William Finaughty, an early Rhodesian pioneer whose hunting enterprise was run as a well-managed business, did not acquire vast riches. The wonderful stories told by many European explorers concerning the east coast Arabs' luxury were heavily overdrawn. Gross profits of the ivory trade must have been high; but against these the entrepreneur had to set the high cost of porterage, the enormous interest on borrowed capital— sometimes as high as 100 percent—the wastage of time, as well as the risk of total loss. Ivory prices, moreover, were liable to fluctuate sharply (for instance, the effects of the Russo-Turkish war of 1877 to 1878 were felt by ivory hunters in the wilds of Central Africa, who suffered from a fall in prices for ivory).

For all the hustle and bustle in the markets of Ujiji and Zanzibar, the total value of East Africa's trade remained much smaller than West Africa's, and for the most part East Africa remained, relatively speaking, an economic backwater.

INDIGENOUS RESPONSES TO MUSLIM TRADE IN EAST AND CENTRAL AFRICA

The indigenous African peoples reacted in very different ways to the new challenge posed by the trade in slaves and ivory. Practically all of them were interested in foreign commerce of some kind. But some were reluctant to traffic in slaves, not so much from humanitarian motives as from general social motives. The Tutsi kingdom of Rwanda, a highly stratified warrior aristocracy, would not admit strangers within its frontiers, probably for fear of domestic subversion. The kingdom of the Barotse, situated in the fertile flood plain of the Upper Zambezi, was interested in foreign trade, but was little concerned with slave dealing. The Barotse had a highly diversified system of agriculture; they had cattle; they caught fish and water fowl, and while they extorted tribute from their subjects, they gave them cattle and other products in exchange. Indeed their economy needed men with many different skills. Instead of exporting labor, the Barotse tried to increase their manpower, either by raiding their neighbors, by enforcing tribute on children, or by encouraging voluntary immigration. In any case the Barotse had some merchandise such as ivory, wild rubber, beeswax, and curios for legitimate trade with the Portuguese from the west and with half-caste, Griqua, and British traders from the south. Despite some lapses, there was always a good deal of Barotse opposition to the slave trade, and the traffic did not seriously affect the country. Similarly the Ngoni and Ndebele, warlike cattle keeping tribes from the south generally preferred to assimilate their captives rather than sell them abroad.

Many other Central African tribes, however, became deeply implicated in the trade, though not always in the same fashion. The southern trade routes from the coast to the interior came to be largely dominated by the Yao. The Yao were a Bantu people who, according to their own tradition, had come from the Lujenda and Rovuma rivers east of Lake Nyasa. During the eighteenth century they had carried out a flourishing trade with the Arabs of Zanzibar and with the Bisa, another inland Bantu tribe famous for its commercial ability. Gradually the Yao drifted into what is now southern Malawi, coming not as a great, unified army but as small groups of settlers in search of land. The Yao, like so many of the indigenous people of East Africa, lacked a central state organization. Minor chiefs and headmen competed with one another for power. This power they could acquire only by getting followers; and one of the means of obtaining a sizeable retinue was the slave hunt. The captured women became junior wives, while the men were set to farming, building, basket making, and other recognized male occupations. Chiefs' sons, who were not in the recognized matrilineal line of succession, were encouraged to make their names as war leaders. The greater chiefs had an additional political incentive for engaging in the trade. Traffic in slaves and ivory would bring them gunpowder. The possession of gunpowder in turn gave them both some kind of control over their turbulent minor vassals and an appreciable military superiority over the indigenous Nyanja-speaking peoples of southern Malawi, many of whom were gradually subdued.

Further to the north, the Nyamwezi people on the high plateau of what is now central Tanzania occupied an equally important position in the commerce. The Nyamwezi, like the Yao or the Bisa, lacked powerful chiefs of their own. Their power derived from commerce, and by the beginning of the last century they had already become famous as long-distance traders, having utilized their strategic position to create a network of trade routes radiating in all directions from their homeland. To the north they trafficked with the Baganda and to the west with the ivory hunters around Lake Tanganyika. From the south they carried copper from the mines of Katanga, and from the east they brought goods from the coast. Skill in trading and porterage became status symbols among the Nyamwezi, titles being conferred chiefly in recognition of unusual abilities in either. Between 1825 and 1850 a few adventurous Arabs made their way to the plateau, and the Nyamwezi so much welcomed these new partners that in 1839 they concluded a treaty of alliance with Seyyid Said. The Nyamwezi guaranteed safe passage to the sultan's caravans and exempted them from tolls. Trade continued to increase, but slowly friction grew between the Arabs and the Nyamwezi. The caravans became larger and frequently placed a heavy strain upon the food resources of the clans through whose areas they passed. Lacking a central authority, the Nyamwezi found great difficulties in adhering to the treaty as disputes concerning tolls and other matters grew increasingly violent. The Arabs finally won control of the route to the Lake Tanganyika ivory grounds and became a major political force.[22]

Arab traders and settlers likewise acquired a strong position in what is now Malawi. A typical incident in this story of penetration, repeated with variations elsewhere, was the occupation of Marimba on the western shore of Lake Nyasa. First of all a trader came from Zanzibar with a large caravan. He settled at Kota Kota by the lake, living at first on friendly terms with the local Nyanja chief. Later, however, friction arose. The Arabs then subdued their former host, reducing him to the status of a headman. Later on other chiefs came in with their people to settle under the new ruler. The new paramount gave offices impartially to local men, to Yao and Bemba retainers, and to Zanzibaris, refusing special advantages to his original followers. He protected his people against other raiders. Like any native chief, he raised revenue by collecting grain from local headmen, levying tribute from other caravans, and insisting on a share in all the ivory gathered in his dominions. He also sold rice to passing caravans, and by these means he managed to make politics pay and also acquired a firm base for his own trading operations.[23]

In addition, Muslim slave traders pushed southward from Egypt into the Sudan and beyond. In an earlier chapter we have seen how Muhammad Ali, responding to western pressure, began to modernize his country's institutions and to increase the number of Egyptian rulers abroad. The rulers of Egypt (many of whom were of Macedonian, Albanian, Circassian, or Turkish descent, having little in common with the Egyptians of today) first of all turned to the regions south of Aswan. Between 1820 and 1822 they subjugated all the little chieftaincies along the Nile from Dongola to Sennar. In 1824 the Egyptians founded Khartoum, at the junction of the White Nile and the Blue Nile, and Khartoum in turn became a base for further expansion. The Egyptians tried to settle farmers around Sennar in the Gezira, an enormous plain lying between the Blue and White Nile; they also bought camels and other domestic animals from the nomadic tribes to the east and west of the river. But above all they wanted gold, ivory and slaves. Between 1839 and 1841 Salim, a Turkish sea captain in the Egyptian service proved the White Nile to be navigable for a thousand miles south of Khartoum, and Egyptian trade made immense progress.

The Egyptian dreams of gold did not come true. But Egyptian hunters discovered immense areas of splendid elephant country, and many made their fortunes from selling ivory. As the great beasts were shot out in one region, the hunters had to look for new supplies and the hunter's frontier thus steadily moved inland.

At first the forces at the disposal of the traders and the local inhabitants were fairly easily balanced. The Muslims with their armed sailing boats were superior on the river. The local inhabitants had the advantage on land. While these conditions lasted, the exchange of goods was peaceful enough. There came a time, however, when the supply of elephants near the river bank was exhausted and when the local demand for beads and trinkets was satisfied. The traders thus had to leave the river banks and penetrate into the distant interior. They responded to the new conditions by bringing up bands of armed Arab followers, who were placed into armed encampments spread over the whole back country of the White Nile and the *Bahr al-Ghazal.* There was little surplus food; the newcomers had to raid villages to feed themselves, and the traders gradually degenerated into raiders pure and simple.[24]

At the same time Egyptian territorial expansion became a menace even to Ethiopians. In 1838 the Egyptians raided Abyssinian territory from the east and threw Gondar into a panic. The French and British brought pressure to bear on Egypt to abstain from further conquests, but the Egyptians consolidated their sphere of influence, and the potential danger remained. In addition the Egyptians strengthened their hold on the Red Sea. In 1846 the Turks leased the port of Massawa (on the shores of what is now Eritrea) to Egypt. The extension of Egyptian power by land and sea thus threatened Ethiopia with possible encirclement and complete disruption.

Generally speaking, the trade in slaves, ivory, and firearms increased the power of local potentates, and encouraged the emergence of stronger political authorities among many of the stateless peoples of East Africa. The rulers of more centralized kingdoms in their turn grew more powerful. For instance, Arab caravans from Tanzania made their way via Tabora northward into the kingdom of Buganda, a highly centralized state. Their enterprise enabled the local kings to build up their stock of cloth and guns, thereby enabling them to arm and pay for more efficient armies, which in turn harried the Basoga to the east and the Bahaya to the south. The Lunda-Luba kingdoms of southeast Central Africa likewise greatly benefited from the traffic to the coast. In what is now northeastern Zambia, the most powerful participants were the Bemba, a Bantu people probably of Congo origin and Luba descent, who had set up a centralized military monarchy in their present country some time during the early eighteenth century. With their centralized military organization they managed to defeat all their opponents, including the warlike Ngoni invaders from the south. They possessed, however, no cattle; their country was infertile; hence they were unable to engage in trade with their neighbors, the Tabwa salt makers, the Fipa iron smelters, the cotton growing people on Lake Rukwa, or the Lungu cattle breeders. Instead the Bemba raided their neighbors, relying on their organization and the weight of numbers. They killed all men, and the status of a Bemba warrior depended on the number of heads he had taken. Some of the slaves taken lived with their masters like indigent relatives. The Bemba country, however, was too poor to support captives in large numbers. Hence many prisoners were sold to the Arabs in exchange for guns, especially "Tower" muskets, which the British Army discarded after the Crimean War. Arab traders similarly dealt with Kazembe, the paramount of the eastern Lunda on the Luapula River. In the eighteenth century the Lunda were already dealing in slaves through Bisa middlemen. They also trafficked with Angola through the Congo kingdom of Mwato Yamvo, whom Kazembe recognized as his "father." Kazembe's commercial position rested on his monopoly of ivory, which he exchanged for cloth and guns and which in turn helped to build up his political power.

The weaker communities, those exposed to slave raids, however, suffered a great deal. Richard Burton, the British explorer, estimated that in order to capture fifty-five women, the merchandise carried by just one caravan, at least ten villages had been destroyed, each having a population of one or two hundred souls, the greater part of whom were exterminated or died of starvation. The bestialities of the trade defied description:

If they (the slaves) lagged by the way or lay down, worn out with exhaustion, their throats were cut or they were shot. Often before reaching the coast the Arabs would stop at some settlement and roughly castrate a number of young boys so that they might be sold as eunuchs. Some died straightaway from the operation, other lingered a little longer and eventually perished from hernia induced by this operation. Those who survived usually had an extremely comfortable and prosperous afterlife in the harem of some Turk, Arab or Persian. The mortality among the children was terrible: the Arab slave drivers do not appear to have been actuated by motives of commercial expediency . . . They seem on the contrary to have been inspired by something more like devilish cruelty in the reckless way in which they would expose their slaves to suffering and exhaustion, and then barbarously kill them.[25]

The trade in slaves thus must have constituted a considerable drain on the population of Central Africa and been a source of terrible human misery. The traffic helped to push the "gunpowder frontier" inland from the coast, and thereby probably helped to make wars more destructive than in the past. Nevertheless the effects of the coastal commerce as a whole were not entirely negative. The importation of firearms helped to speed up the consolidation of indigenous states, great and small. It provided the indigenous people with a host of new goods. It also promoted the spread of Swahili as a *lingua franca* throughout much of what is now Tanzania and through parts of the territories now comprised within Malawi, Kenya, and Uganda. The caravan leaders also spread the religion of Islam in the interior, and thus helped to prise many East African communities from their accustomed intellectual isolation.

NOTES

1. George Rentz, "The Wahhabis," in A. J. Arberry, ed., *Religion and the Middle East: Three Religions in Concord and Conflict* (London, 1967), vol. 2, pp. 270–284.

2. J. Spencer Trimingham, *Islam in West Africa* (Oxford, 1959), p. 139.

3. H. F. C. Smith, "A Neglected Theme of West African History: The Islamic Revolutions of the 19th Century," in *Historians in Tropical Africa: Proceedings of the Leverhulme Inter-Collegiate Conference*, pp. 145–158.

4. Basil Davidson, *A History of West Africa to the Nineteenth Century* (New York, 1966), pp. 272–274.

5. Smith, p. 147.

6. Hargreaves, *West Africa*, pp. 51–53.

7. See Flint, *Nigeria and Ghana*, pp. 99–109, especially pp. 102–103. This account is mainly a summary of Flint's work.

8. Verger, *Bahia and the West Coast*, p. 34.

9. G. S. P. Freeman-Grenville, "The East African Coast 1498–1840," in Oliver and Mathew, *History of East Africa*, vol. 1, p. 162.

10. E. C. Hore, *Tanganyika, Eleven Years in Central Africa* (London, 1892), p. 73.

11. Trimingham p. 20.

12. Sir Reginald Coupland, *East Africa and Its Invaders From the Earliest Times to the Death of Seyyid Said in 1856* (Oxford 1938), pp. 36–39.

13. Trimingham, p. 22.

14. Coupland, *East Africa and its Invaders*, p. 74.

15. R. J. Garvin, "Sayyid Said," *Tarikh*, vol. 1, no. 1 (November 1965), pp. 16–29.

16. Coupland, *East Africa and Its Invaders*, p. 314.

17. R. W. Beachey, "The East African Ivory Trade in the Nineteenth Century," *Journal of African History*, vol. 8, no. 2 (1967), pp. 269–290.

18. By the middle of the nineteenth century the combined population of Pemba and Zanzibar supposedly amounted to 400,000.

19. Sir Harry Johnston quoted in Lewis H. Gann, "The End of the Slave Trade in British Central Africa: 1889–1912," *Rhodes-Livingstone Journal*, no. 16 (1954), p. 41.

20. Quoted in Gann, p. 41.

21. Beachey, "The East African Ivory Trade in the Nineteenth Century," pp. 269–290.

22. J. B. Webster, "Mirambo and Nyamwezi Unification," *Tarikh*, vol. 1, no. 1 (1965), pp. 64–71.

23. Gann, "The End of the Slave Trade," p. 30.

24. Oliver and Atmore, *Africa Since 1800*, p. 83.

25. H. H. Johnston, *Central Africa* (London, 1897), p. 158.

Chapter 31

The Civilizations
of Africa: A Review

THE LITERATE CIVILIZATIONS: MUSLIM AND ETHIOPIAN

In the days of the European Renaissance, the countries of the Mediterranean had constituted the heartland of Europe. Within the Mediterranean basin, the Islamic countries had played a leading role. The Ottoman Empire once rivaled the might of the Christian states, and as late as 1683 an Ottoman army was still able to threaten Vienna, the Austrian capital in the very heart of Central Europe. The great cities of North Africa were likewise important centers of culture and commerce, and their influence radiated deep into the Sudan. By the beginning of the nineteenth century, all this had changed. Europe's center of gravity had shifted to the north, and the majority of Mediterranean lands had become economic backwaters. This was true both of Christian realms such as Portugal or the Kingdom of the Two Sicilies, and of the Islamic states of North Africa and the Near East, all of which lagged behind the northern European countries in the arts of peace and war alike.

The most powerful of these North African states was Egypt, nominally a vassal of the Ottoman monarchy. Egypt was ruled by Muhammad Ali (1805–1849), a semi-independent viceroy who attempted to modernize his country according to western, especially French, lines. Himself of European Macedonian birth, Muhammad Ali relied to a considerable extent upon men of foreign origin, on soldiers from Albania, on advisers from many Levantine countries, and on military experts from France and the United States, so that his system of governance might be described in certain ways as rule by internal colonization. Muhammad Ali achieved many successes. He promoted western education; he reorganized the Egyptian army and fleet; he encouraged the cultivation of agricultural export crops; he gave military assistance to the Turks in Arabia, and he pacified the Red Sea, where seaborne trade once more revived. He also embarked on a policy of territorial expansion into the Sudan, a valuable source of slaves, ivory, and domestic animals.

The Egyptian colonizers founded Khartoum, strategically placed at the junction of the Blue and the White Nile. Egyptian sailing vessels commanded the Nile route to the south, and Egyptian expeditions regularly marched southward and eastward from their Sudanic strongholds in search of captives. The Egyptian state, however, rested on a very narrow social and economic basis. The Egyptian armed forces, though a match for those of the Turks, could not compete with those of Europe. Egypt's overambitious foreign policy bore no relation to Egypt's slender military potential. When the Egyptians tried to assert their power in Europe itself by assisting the Turkish Sultan against his rebellious Greek subjects, the European powers intervened, and in 1827 the Egyptian fleet was blown out of the water at Navarino by the combined squadrons of Great Britain, France, and Russia.

Tripoli, to the west of Egypt, was ruled by a hereditary pasha, Yusuf Karamanli, who relied on British support in maintaining his freedom from Ottoman control. He extended his authority over the Fezzan and established close relations with Bornu and Sokoto in the Sudan. Bornu received huge consignments of firearms in exchange for slaves, with the result that the city of Tripoli became the greatest slave market of the Mediterranean. The rulers of Tunis similarly lived on terms of amity with Great Britain and thereby secured almost complete independence from the Ottoman Empire, their nominal suzerain. Algiers, in contrast, was linked with France. During the Napoleonic Wars Algeria supplied grain to the French forces, and France thereby incurred considerable debts to the local bey. After Napoleon's defeat, the new Bourbon government in Paris refused to honor French financial commitments and thereby worsened relations between the two countries.[1] In addition the Algerian coast harbored many corsairs, whose depredations excited the Frenchmen's wrath. By the early nineteenth century, however, the growing technical superiority of the European and American squadrons had already greatly reduced the profits made by privateers on the Barbary Coast, and by 1830 the number of European captives in Algiers had declined to a mere hundred. Algiers, with its agricultural resources and its extensive trade connections, stood out as one of the most advanced Islamic states in the region. The bey's effective authority did not, however, extend far into the interior. The Berber and Arab tribes inhabiting the plateau behind the coastal plain could not be easily subdued, and mounted warriors from the dry inland regions sometimes carried their attacks to the very outskirts of the cities on the Mediterranean shore.

Morocco faced difficulties of a similar kind. In Morocco, as in Algeria, tribal groups from the high Atlas and the desert fringes penetrated the settled regions and extorted tribute from the peasants of the plains. The difficult nature of the country and the logistic problems faced the Moroccan armies with almost insuperable difficulties, and the Moroccan sultans could not effectively control the warring clans in the more inaccessible parts of the country. Nevertheless, Morocco still carried on a considerable trade to the south. The Moroccans exported vast quantities of salt in exchange for gold from the upper Senegal-Niger regions. They imported slaves as well as leatherwork and other luxury goods from the Sudan. Moroccan merchants also sold extensive quantities of European manufactured goods, especially British ones, to the communities in the interior, and Moroccan commercial and cultural influence extended all over the western edge of the Sahara down to the banks of the Senegal. The Moroccan university of Fez was an important religious center, and Moroccan influence played an important part in the formation of militant Muslim brotherhoods in the western Sudan.

As we have seen in a previous section, an earlier Muslim revival on the western Sudan had led to the creation of militant Islamic states in the Futa Jallon and the Futa Tora. But Islamic zeal was far from having exhausted its impetus. The early nineteenth century saw the beginnings of yet another great Fula *jihad,* headed by Usman dan Fodio. Fodio's combative and puritanical form of Islam appealed alike to Muslim intellectuals, to educated Muslim Fula townsmen discontented with the real or supposed corruption of the older Hausa ruling families, and also to many Hausa resentful of their overlords. The reformers also gained support from the pastoral Fulani of the countryside. Hence they were able to rely on a broad-based class alliance with revolutionary implications. There was fighting on an extensive scale, resulting in vast political changes, while Islam began to spread beyond the towns far into the villages.

The states of the savannah comprised some of the most extensive and stable political units of sub-Saharan Africa. Farmers in the savannah zone could often till their fields over many years; they combined animal husbandry with arable agriculture and accordingly produced food surpluses sufficiently large to maintain great states. The rulers of the savannah could build up extensive administrative and military establishments. They were able to mobilize considerable armies, mounted on horses or camels and supplied with firearms, which could control vast areas. They also made good use of Islamic religious, legal, and administrative knowledge to strengthen their position. The Fulani kingdoms, for instance, skillfully blended Islamic with traditional elements. Overlords of Futa Jallon were thus first of all installed, according to Muslim custom, in front of a mosque. When this ceremony was over, the new monarch followed the corresponding pagan ritual. He returned to his house and remained in seclusion for seven days. To ensure prosperity to the new reign, the people scattered grains of rice, millet, and fonio. By rolling naked over the seeds, the king impregnated them with the fertilizing virtues he had supposedly acquired during the appropriate ceremony and thereby conformed to ancient custom. At the same time the Fulani overlords employed a host of Islamic scholars, scribes, and judges who administered Islamic law.

But military considerations overshadowed all others. Power rested on conquest; conquests in turn provided the revenue needed to make yet further conquests. There were taxes on agricultural produce; there was a land tax payable by all free non-Fulani, and an additional head tax on pagans. Rulers obtained wealth from the sale of offices, from death duties, market dues, slave raids, and from the employment of servile labor on large estates attached to various state offices, and from a tax on live stock, the only tax paid by nomadic Fulani.[2] As in so many other parts of Africa, the impact of taxation varied widely, and it is hard to generalize about the general impact of Fulani rule. On the one hand, commerce benefited from the imposition of stable authority. But all too often arbitrary methods of assessment and extortionate methods of collection interfered with economic progress and may sometimes even have led to stagnation.

Except for Muslim Africa, Ethiopia represented perhaps the most advanced form of civilization attained by any indigenous African state at the beginning of the nineteenth century. Politically, the Ethiopian monarchy had fallen on evil days, and the country was divided into a number of quasi-independent regions. But Ethiopia had an asset unknown to every other indigenous African state: an ancient literary tradition and a national church that acted as a repository of the people's national culture. Churchmen preserved a sense of national unity at a time when the power of the Crown had decayed and when the great magnates were able to do what was right in their own eyes. Even the Church had many weaknesses. Its theology was progressing; but its organization was inadequate. Its membership, however, comprised the bulk of the Amhara.

The Christian Amhara, a ruling race composed of farmers and warriors, subjected their Muslim subjects to harshly discriminatory legislation. The so-called Jabarti Muslims in the highlands were debarred from owning land. The Muslims were thus forced even more rigidly into commerce than before, and increasingly engrossed the country's trade. On their travels, Muslim merchants made many proselytes among the subject peoples of the Amhara, who often looked upon Islam as a bulwark against the religion of their Amharic overlords. Islam was not associated with the culture and creed of the highland conquerors who ruled the Church. Islam also acquired powerful allies from without. Galla invaders penetrated into the very highlands. Galla settlers interposed a solid corridor between Shoa and the remainder of Ethiopia; a Galla praetorian guard dominated the monarchy itself. Worse still, immigrant Galla adopted Islam, and but for the internal dissensions of the warlike Galla tribes, the Ethiopian monarchy might well have disappeared from history.[3]

PRELITERATE CIVILIZATIONS OF WEST AFRICA

The woodland and forest states south of the Sudanic belt developed cultures of a very different kind. Few people, if any, knew how to read or write. Knowledge was therefore hard to store; kings depended on the memory of praise-singers and diviners; ideas could be transmitted only by the spoken word. The impact of Christianity or Islam remained insignificant, and the people of sub-Saharan Africa largely adhered to pagan creeds. The peoples of the West African forest zone now looked to the south, to the Atlantic, rather than to the northern savannah for their foreign trade. Much of their overseas commerce still depended on the sale of slaves, though the slave traffic sometimes went with a limited export of tropical crops such as palm oil. Foreign trade, however, accounted for only a small proportion of the total number of goods exchanged. Parts of West Africa had developed a considerable exchange of locally produced agricultural products and luxury goods. In many parts of West Africa there was a relatively dense population, and there were some large towns, capable of supporting specialized crafts and complex political institutions. The rulers were no longer personal leaders in close touch with their followers. They had instead become remote beings, screened from the common people behind their palace walls. Titles and offices proliferated; the people were divided according to rank and status. Political and commercial development favored the emergence of larger, more centralized states with a considerable degree of social differentiation.

Within these limits, West African forms of political organization differed enormously. An African Aristotle, interested in studying the different kinds of political institutions to be found on the continent, would have found as many varieties as did his namesake in ancient Greece. Dahomey was the prime example of a despotic monarchy. Royal power had grown for several centuries while Dahomey acquired a dominant position on the trade routes to the west of the Yoruba country. In nineteenth century Dahomey, the king-in-council exercised supreme authority, but the king rather than the council held the reins of government. Lineages had lost their claim to provide the holders of state offices and retained only the right to administer their own internal affairs insofar as they did not conflict with public law or the interests of the state. The king controlled appointments to office throughout the land. He was served by a well-developed spy system. The standing army and the militia were officered by the king, and depended upon the monarch for their promotion. The king

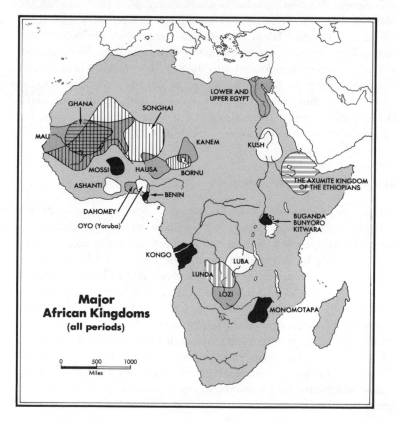

Major African Kingdoms (all periods)

was assisted by an elaborate court and by an extensive staff of civil officials. His revenues were supplemented by fines and confiscations, by the spoils of war, and by trading profits that fell to the king by virtue of his function as controller of foreign trade. No secret societies were permitted, lest they might subvert the king's authority, and the mass of ordinary citizens thus had much less influence than they did under the Ashanti dispensation. The priesthoods of the established cults were likewise subject to royal power, but took much of the national revenue.[4]

In Ashanti the process of centralization had not gone as far as in Dahomey. Ashanti was a confederation of towns whose power extended over a large part of what is now Ghana. During the eighteenth century, under the rule of Opoku Ware, Ashanti had coalesced into a powerful territorial empire. Its control extended far to the north, along the trade routes to Jenne, Timbuktu, Gonja, and Hausaland. In addition, the Ashanti expanded to the Atlantic Ocean in the south; but they never succeeded in permanently controlling the whole coast line, where they met with bitter resistance from the local Fante.

At the height of its power the Ashanti state was a confederacy of autonomous towns. Each town was ruled by a council comprising representatives from the great local lineages. Each town also had a Young Men's Association, composed of those who held no official position. The Young Men could demand the deposition of the ruler and the appointment of a successor; they could also influence other council decisions to some extent. The confederacy was headed by the Asantehene, lord of Kumasi. Kumasi and its ruler enjoyed ritual precedence over the other towns; the vassal cities accepted Kumasi's direction in certain matters, and they supplied the central government with troops as well as various goods and services. The central government alone had the right to inflict the death penalty. During the nineteenth century Kumasi succeeded in establishing yet greater control over the confederacy and acquired a standing army. The Ashanti confederacy nevertheless remained a decentralized commonwealth. The town governments retained a considerable degree of local autonomy; they appointed their own officials, and Kumasi could approach the local citizens only through their town councils.

The Yoruba, on the other hand, were unable to maintain a centralized commonwealth. The ancient empire of Oyo gradually disintegrated. Fula religious preachers penetrated into the northern provinces, which asserted their independence in 1817 and became a base for the further spread of Islam among the Yoruba. Soon afterward the majority of Oyo's people moved away. Some founded a new town (also named Oyo) on the edge of the forest. Others settled at Ibadan, which grew to be the greatest Yoruba city in the forest belt, a region where cavalry from the savannah could not easily operate. The various provinces of the Oyo empire became independent of central rule and fought each other for the control of territory and trade routes. There were bitter internecine struggles; many Yoruba lost their liberty and were exported as slaves. Yorubaland became a major supplier of human merchandise while Lagos and Badagry developed into the greatest slaving ports of West Africa. The principal profiteers inland were the Egba, who in 1830 founded a new capital at Abeokuta.

But no single state was able to dominate its neighbors, and even within each state power was widely dispersed. Most nineteenth-century Yoruba cities were ruled by kings; a few were governed by councils. But even where a monarch held sway, his powers were circumscribed by a council representing the major craft guilds, and the local trade associations, and controlled mainly by great lineages. The king had only a limited say in the selection of council members or even of minor officials; most office holders derived their revenue from fees attached to their offices or from their own lineages. It was these office holders who recruited armies and controlled their employment. In some Yoruba states great power was also wielded by secret societies whose senior officials might hold high government office. Such societies also exercised certain legislative powers and maintained a police force to maintain order.

Along the coast, especially along the Oil Rivers of Nigeria, there were numerous small independent towns. They depended on trade, and their merchants acted as middlemen between the Europeans and the people of the hinterland. The so-called "Houses," which made up many West African city states, formed semiautonomous communities, composed of a chief, his relatives, his followers, and slaves. The members of each House might reside in a particular quarter of the city. Petty chiefs might govern parts of a smaller town or a fishing village. The House acted as a trading corporation; in addition its members might fish or farm. Houses likewise acted as military units, each being required to equip at least one war canoe for the navy of its respective city. Houses also acted as associations for the maintenance of law and order; they played an important ritual role, and each House provided some form of social security for its members. Their sailors were famed for their skill in navigating the intricate network of rivers and channels of the Niger Delta, and their "canoe power" played an important part in local wars. These city states might in some ways be compared to the oligarchies of ancient Greece, but they were interested primarily in trade, and they never produced a literary culture.

To sum up, the savannah and forest zones were in many ways the most developed parts of "Black Africa." Great office holders and merchants began to accumulate property; class differences began to solidify. There was trade; there were regular markets. There was specialization of labor; craft guilds and trade associations flourished. There was a great variety of political organization, ranging all the way from highly centralized monarchies to small city states.

The kingdoms of the savannah could raise formidable cavalry units armed with lances or firearms. The forest states primarily relied on infantry equipped with muskets or more traditional weapons. Perhaps the highest form of African military technology was the great West African war canoe, which carried a brass cannon. Cannons and muskets, however, had to be acquired abroad. Even the most developed African state was unable to build an up-to-date armament or civilian industry, or rival even a backward Western European state such as Portugal in any other aspect of technology, science, or learning.

PRELITERATE BANTU AFRICA

By comparison with the more important states of West Africa, the Bantu monarchies of central and southeast Africa were relatively weak. They could not compare

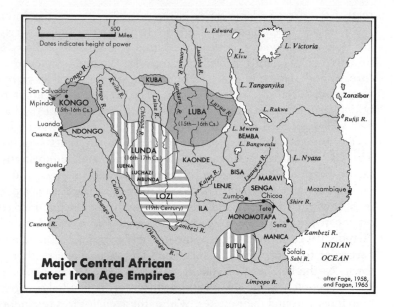

Major Central African Later Iron Age Empires

in population or resources with great kingdoms such as Dahomey. The inland states were less favorably placed for trade than those on the west coast. Some of them had to contend with barbarian invaders from abroad. Others fell prey to internal dissensions. The power of the Kongo kings was but a hazy memory. In the interior, the most powerful states were the Lunda kingdom governed by Mwato Yamvo, the Lunda kingdom of Kazembe on the Luapula, the kingdom of the Luba, the Bemba monarchy in what is now northeastern Zambia, and the Barotse (Lozi monarchy) on the upper Zambezi. All were centralized states whose rulers engaged in foreign trade, acted as distributor kings (gift-givers), and controlled a fairly elaborate centralized state machinery. They governed their provinces through a hierarchy of officials, but provincial governors were hard to control, and the authority of the central government tended to grow weaker toward the periphery of each state.

The lands bordering on the eastern edge of the Congo forest and extending along Lake Albert, Lake Victoria, and the northern shore of Lake Tanganyika also witnessed the emergence of important kingdoms. The region contained much fertile and well-watered soil. Skilled canoe-men could use the inland waters for the purposes of peace and war alike. The interior therefore attracted numerous conquerors, who mainly seem to have come from the southern borderlands of Ethiopia and from the plains and swamps of the Nile and its tributaries in the southern Sudan.

The newcomers were physically and culturally distinct from the Bantu; they were skilled in cattle-keeping and war, and their influence profoundly affected the culture of the region as a whole. By the end of the eighteenth century six large neighboring states had come into existence—Buganda, Bunyoro, Ankole, Karagwe, Rwanda, and Burundi. All of them were ruled by kings who received divine honor and governed their peoples through an elaborate hierarchy of court officials and provincial chiefs. All of them were well ordered, though their population was nothing like as large as that of the great Sudanic states in the northern part of the continent.[5]

In the seventeenth century Bunyoro had been the most powerful kingdom of them all. Bunyoro, however, overreached itself in disastrous military adventures, and the initiative subsequently passed to Buganda. Buganda achieved a highly centralized form of government in which all but the most ancient offices were held by administrators appoined at the king's pleasure. The Buganda monarchs built up a powerful bodyguard; Buganda war canoes dominated large stretches of Lake Victoria. Buganda's soil was famed for its fertility, and its agriculture was highly productive.

The Buganda thus developed a great agro-town, the *kibuga,* as their tribal capital. The *kibuga* was the royal seat, the nation's ritual and administrative center where the sacred fires and the drums were kept, and where matters of dispute were brought before the court of appeal. The *kibuga* formed an impressive agglomeration of buildings, constructed of cane and rattan, divided by well-maintained streets, and centered on the royal palace. Agro-towns, such as the *kibuga* or Kazembe's capital on the Luapula River, formed perhaps the greatest economic achievement attainable by this particular form of social organization. The *kibuga* was neither quite a village or a town. At the height of its splendor, the capital may have contained something like 40,000 people, but the city dwellers still largely depended on agriculture. Chiefs built high fences around their estates. Within these enclosures retainers cultivated gardens, but urban crops had to be supplemented by food brought in from country estates.[6]

The monarchs controlled a considerable agricultural surplus. They were therefore in a position to maintain a considerable bureaucracy and to control their country through an elaborate administrative service. The kings also employed their own hunters to shoot elephants. Long-distance trade, especially the commerce in ivory, became a royal monopoly, and the growing traffic helped to strengthen royal power. The rulers were able to reward their followers with imported merchandise, as well as land; hence the monarchs could carry political centralization to new lengths.[7] The development of long-distance trade also created new motives for territorial expansion. From the beginning of the nineteenth century onward, Buganda thus pressed further on its neighbors and became the greatest power in the region.

These great kingdoms nevertheless were subject to considerable limitations. Apart from a few unusually favored and densely settled regions, including certain areas along adjoining Lake Victoria, the Luapula Valley, and the upper Zambezi Valley, land was in practically unlimited supply. Indigenous farmers largely depended on shifting cultivation. They had neither motives nor opportunities for developing more intensive forms of agriculture. They could not easily build up large food surpluses, and they could not usually pay tribute on the West African scale. Hence most Bantu kings were unable to support courts as elaborate as those of West Africa. The Bantu monarchs likewise could not reward their followers by grants of land in the same way as medieval princes in Western Europe. Allotments of landed property in return for military and civil office were made only in a few parts of Bantu Africa, for instance among the Lozi of the upper Zambezi, or the Ganda. West African states such as Dahomey or Nupe had an even more highly differentiated economy, with slave labor and large-scale foreign trade. There were great landed magnates owning town and country houses, just as in Buganda. There were aristocratic factions that vied with one another for the support of the common people. This type of civil constitution might broadly be called Afro-feudalism: it bore certain similarities to its European proto-type; it did not, however, characterize Bantu Africa at large.

The majority of Africans lived in societies of a very different kind. The average Bantu tribesman considered that he had a right to be allocated gardens simply by virtue of belonging to a specific community. There was indeed plenty of land to go around. Kings and great dignitaries might acquire special privileges concerning the use of specially favored fishing sites and other advantages, but they could not become land owners in the western sense. Monarchs could reward their followers by political office, by a share in the tribute, gifts of imported merchandise or of loot taken from the enemy, or by similar favors. Among pastoral peoples, monarchs and other great men might also grant estates in cattle to their dependents. They acted as distributor kings. They tried to strengthen their position by gaining a monopoly of foreign trade in guns, ivory, and similar commodities. Sometimes they tried to build up a perma-nent force of retainers, equipped with firearms.

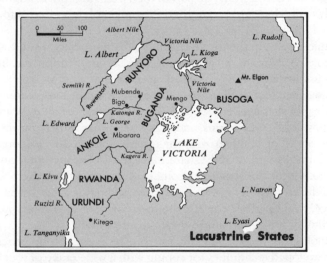

Stronger communities might appropriate their neighbors' cattle, or levy imposts in kind on conquered communities. Some chiefs got their people to work for them over short periods, but villeinage of the feudal king remained unknown and differ-ences in living standards between kings and commoners were not yet great.

Societies of this kind would differ greatly in their political constitution. Some were fairly egalitarian. Others, like the kingdom of the Bemba in what is now northeastern Zambia, were rigidly centralized, and the rulers enforced their authority by means of extreme severity:

In every village—wrote a late nineteenth century observer—are to be seen men and women whose eyes have been gouged out; the removal of one eye and one hand is hardly worthy of remark. Men and women are seen whose ears, nose and lips have been sliced off and both hands amputated. The cutting off of breasts of women has

been extensively practised as a punishment for adultery but . . . some of the victims
. . . are mere children . . . Indeed these mutilations were inflicted with the utmost
callousness; every chief for instance has a retinue of good singers and drummers who
invariably have their eyes gouged out to prevent them running away.[8]

Additionally, most Africans remained technologically more backward than, say,
the countrymen of King Stephen in twelfth-century England. The Bantu could neither
read nor write. Hence knowledge was hard to find and even harder to increase. The
Bantu kings faced similar difficulties in the economic sphere. Bantu monarchs tried
to distribute regional surpluses through gifts; but they could not easily stockpile food
to tide their subjects over bad seasons. Ancient rulers could float grain along the Nile
to Pharaoh's repositories. But even powerful rulers such as the medieval Monomotapas lacked such a transportation system. Even had they solved the problem of constructing and administering a network of warehouses, and of preventing their
contents from being spoiled or eaten by insects, they could not have conveyed large
quantities of corn or cassava from one part of their vast kingdom to another. Salt could
be traded fairly easily; but cattle comprised the only mobile source of food that could
be easily shifted in bulk.

The economic surplus at the disposal of any African society was usually subject to
severe limitations. A drought, a swarm of locusts, or an invasion was liable to cause
disaster. It is possible that even the more advanced Bantu kingdoms may have suffered
from a perennial manpower shortage: there were simply not enough people to
complete all the jobs that needed doing. The vast majority of all African peoples had
to rely on the power of a man's arms, and legs—on human muscle power. There were
exceptions: the Sotho of South Africa, for instance, learned to use ponies. But few
African communities south of the Sahara managed to harness draft animals to pull
plows and wagons until European newcomers introduced these methods of traction
in the nineteenth and twentieth century. African technology, unlike European medieval technology, could neither convert the force of wind into rotary motion for the
purpose of grinding grain nor utilize water to run a mill.

These technological weaknesses did not preclude change or progress. African
agriculturists developed techniques for coping with a wide range of soils and climates,
techniques that were efficient for their purpose and that yet required little physical
capital. They domesticated various wild plants and successfully naturalized imported
food crops such as cassava, maize, and sweet potatoes. In Abyssinia, in the eastern
highlands of Rhodesia, and in Kenya, some farming communities astonished posterity
by complicated terrace works that conserved the soil on stony hill sides. Africans in
a few favored areas such as the upper Zambezi developed intensive forms of riverine
farming. But throughout most parts of the continent cultivators stuck to simple kinds
of slash-and-burn cultivation. Hence even the greatest Bantu kings could wield only
a very limited degree of power.

Many Africans, perhaps even the majority, were not organized into states at all,
but solely depended on the help of their kinsmen and neighbors. In such societies
there was little inequality. Some men might enjoy special respect because of their
religious knowledge and ritual functions. Others might suffer the misfortune of

becoming prisoners of war and losing their liberty. But the land, the basis of all wealth, did not belong to any particular individual or to any particular kin group. This is not to say that society was communistic. Each family worked its own land and kept its crops, subject to certain social obligations. Kinship groups had cattle of their own. There was no community of private property. Hoes and axes, fishing nets and bows —important means of production in their own right—belonged to individual people, though they might be bequeathed to others as part of a well-defined system of mutual obligation. Some owned more cattle or commanded more followers than their neighbors. But the land was open to all, and in stateless societies great differences in power or property were unlikely. Amorphous polities, moreover, were ill-adapted to war, since they had no organization capable of mobilizing numerous warriors for defense, and thereby became easy victims to foreign aggression. Weaker still from the political point of view were the roving bands of Bushmen hunters and foodgatherers, who were still found in isolated parts of southern Africa, and whose communities represented one of the most rudimentary forms of social organization known to man.

NOTES

1. This is based mainly on the excellent summary contained in Oliver and Atmore, *Africa Since 1800,* pp. 1–103.

2. Trimingham, *Islam in West Africa,* p. 146.

3. J. Spencer Trimingham, *Islam in Ethiopia* (London, 1952), pp. 100–108.

4. See Elizabeth Colson, "African Society at the Time of the Scramble," in L. H. Gann and Peter Duignan, eds., *Colonialism in Africa 1870–1960,* vol. 1, *The History and Politics of Colonialism 1870–1914* (Cambridge, 1969), pp. 27–65.

5. Oliver and Atmore, *Africa Since 1800,* pp. 18–19.

6. Peter C. W. Gutkind, *The Royal Capital of Buganda: A Study of Internal Conflict and External Ambiguity* (The Hague, 1963), pp. 9–21.

7. Roland Oliver, "Discernible Developments in the Interior ca. 1500–1840," in Oliver and Mathew, *History of East Africa,* vol. 1, pp. 189–191.

8. Robert Codrington, "Report of the Administrator of Northeastern Rhodesia for Two Years Ending March 31st 1900," in *British South Africa Company: Reports on the Administration of Rhodesia, 1898–1900* (n.p., n.d.), p. 68.

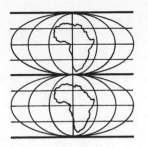

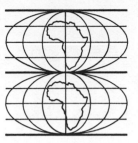

PART X

THE NEW
WESTERN CHALLENGE

Chapter 32

The White Man's Quest for Knowledge in Africa

THE SECULAR PIONEERS

The gradual liquidation of slavery in the New World and the suppression of the seaborne slave trade completely altered the place of Africa in the Atlantic economy. In the decades after 1815 no European nation made any serious attempt to recreate a wholly self-sufficient empire of trade and plantations on strictly mercantilist principles. Only France retained a few fragments of its former empire in the New World. The Spanish and Portuguese empires in South America disappeared as the Latin American countries gained their independence. Britain became wedded to the doctrines of free trade and completely dominated the Atlantic economy. British textile manufacturers were by far the most important customers for American cotton; British refineries bought sugar from the West Indies and Brazil. British factory owners supplied the bulk of the manufactured products destined for the tropics. Nevertheless, the South Atlantic accounted for no more than about 10 percent of British exports, and British commerce and investments flowed into much broader channels. The place of West Africa in the British system was insignificant; for instance, between 1847 and 1852 the whole of West Africa purchased no more than 0.89 percent of all British goods sent abroad.[1]

Despite Africa's modest place in the world economy, the dream of an African El Dorado, of a land immensely rich in minerals and fertile soil, remained alive. The African frontier stimulated the gold-seeker's imagination in much the same way as the American frontier. Untold riches were always supposed to lie beyond the horizon.

In the 1860s, for instance, Carl Mauch, an adventurous German school master, discovered what were in fact only a few modest gold deposits in what is now Rhodesia. Mauch, however, described his finds in lyrical strains, and his astonishing stories made a profound impression. The *Natal Witness,* a South African journal of the day, only gave expression of a widespread mood when it almost broke into song by publishing an article headed "I Speak of Africa and Golden Joys." The editor explained that the desire to prospect arose from man's obedience to God's first commandment. Writing like Karl Marx turned into a company promoter, he insisted that "the power of the precious metal . . . has transcended the influence of all morality, philosophy, jurisprudence, legislation or government ever known," and hoped that new cities would spring forth at the miner's magic touch. This interpretation might be called the "tropical treasure-house" theory of Africa. It received further support from erroneous assumptions concerning the fantastic fertility of Africa's tropical soils and verdant forests, where nature was somehow more bountiful and prolific than in the prosaic regions of the Northern Hemisphere. These theories often contained a modicum of good sense. There were precious minerals in Africa, if only they could be exploited. Africa could and did supply tropical commodities such as palm oil. Africa, moreover, was a possible source of cotton. For the British especially, the potential availability of cotton was an important consideration, for British manufacturers were becoming more and more concerned about their dependence on the United States for this key raw material. Their apprehensions turned out to be only too justified when the American Civil War disrupted British cotton supplies and occasioned serious distress among the mill hands of Lancashire.

The economic interests of Europe thus provided an incentive for the exploration of Africa, but the economic motive was only one of many. The late eighteenth and the nineteenth century witnessed immense advances in man's knowledge of the universe. The combined labors of naturalists, antiquaries, geologists, and archaeologists vastly lengthened the known span of history and brought about a revolution in our awareness of time. European and American scholars likewise extended man's knowledge of space, both on the geographical and the astronomical plane. Africa became a new explorer's frontier, where young scholars could still make great discoveries and gain fame in the world of learning. Much of this work depended on organized research, and in this the British played a leading part. In 1788 British scholars formed the Association for Promoting the Discovery of the Interior Parts of Africa, commonly known as the African Association. Its object was to send travelers to the interior to report on the geography, ethnography, and natural history of the continent. The Association also collaborated with mercantile, missionary, and humanitarian bodies, and acted as a distinct pressure group that tried to promote trade and exploration. During the nineteenth century new organizations came into being. In 1821 French Scholars founded the Société de Géographie de France, in 1831 the British established the Royal Geographical Society, and in 1863 the Germans set up a body known characteristically as the Centralverein für Handels-geographie (Central League for Commercial Geography), all of which took a great interest in African exploration.

The broadening of geographical knowledge went with extensive advances in the study of man. Western men of science in the nineteenth century have often been justly criticized for an unduly ethnocentric bias or for the real or assumed racist implications of their research. But, perhaps more than any other conquerors in the world's history, Europeans and Americans also took a sustained and systematic interest in the races with whom they traded or whom they subdued, in their way of life, their institutions, and their past. Egypt, for instance, had known countless conquerors. But Napoleon made history when, on his expedition to Egypt in 1798, he took with him a group of distinguished men of learning who compiled the *Description de l'Egypte* and laid the foundations of scientific Egyptology. Cecil John Rhodes, to give another example, subsidized research into the antiquities of Rhodesia at the end of the nineteenth century—the desire for new data concerning the country's gold resources and for academic knowledge blending strangely in the British empire builder's mind.

Scholars came to an interest in the cultures of Africa from many different backgrounds. As Professor Philip Curtin has shown, the strongest influence was that of the biological sciences, which happened to predominate in the sciences at the time. J. C. Pritchard, a British anthropologist, established a precedent by annexing ethnography to the study of man's physical nature. The first anthropological societies came into being through a further merger of Pritchard's biological orientation with the political concerns of humanitarians. The occasion arose in 1837 while a British parliamentary committee on the aborigines was in session. Dr. Thomas Hodgkin, a Quaker humanitarian, a friend of Pritchard's, and a professor at Guy's Hospital, London, began to supply the committee with ethnological data. He then formed a permanent organization with a dual purpose. One object was to save the aborigines in the British settlement colonies from extinction as a result of European immigration. The other was to study the native people in question. The new society, known as the Aborigines Protection Society, was thus partly a political pressure group and partly a scientific body. In France the order was reversed. In 1838 French scholars formed the Société Ethnologique. This was the first purely ethnographic society, and the preservation of the aborigines was its secondary objective.[2]

The scholars most interested in the peoples of Africa were explorers who studied the indigenous peoples as part of their wider researches in geography, the natural sciences, and related subjects. Or they were chair-borne students who laboriously pieced together accounts from travelers, ship captains, soldiers, and traders telling of strange customs practices by outlandish tribes. These accounts were analyzed, and all too often the various social systems were pieced together according to some preconceived scheme of evolution. Bushmen usually came at the bottom—Bradford businessmen came out on top. The Europeans, so to speak, looked at African societies from above and from outside. The notion that a scholar should study tribal communities through field work on the spot, by actually living among the "natives," was still exceptional. Traders or administrators might dwell in the midst of African communities for many years, but their main purpose, their interests and background, were not academic in nature.

THE MISSIONARY PIONEERS

In the religious history of Europe the nineteenth century was an age of paradox. On the one hand the era saw a concentric assault on all established religious creeds, one more thoroughgoing and better conceived than any launched in the past. Scepticism or atheism became an accepted part of the ideological scene. Many secular thinkers proclaimed the optimistic creed that either the whole of mankind, or a particular section of it—the proletariat, the Nordics, or some other elite—were fundamentally good, and did not need the creaking crutches of religion in order to lead humanity to a higher stage of development. Yet at a time when so many prophets foresaw that religion was on its way out, Christianity gained an almost unparalleled access of new strength. Theologians of various schools tried to reformulate their creeds in light of current scientific and philosophic challenges. Many churches embarked on a world-wide crusade that promised to make up for their losses in Europe by new conquests overseas, or that linked what the Germans called *Innere Mission,* (mission work at home), with the evangelization of the heathen abroad.

Missionary endeavor commonly represented an "overspill" of a wider movement for individual and improvement in the metropolitan countries. The missionary movement also managed to tap hidden sources of spiritual strength that sceptics in Europe often failed to understand. The age that sent white prospectors, traders, and soldiers of fortune to the remotest corners of the world also witnessed a similar movement of ecclesiastical pioneering, and Africa appeared as an enormous virgin continent where countless souls might as yet be saved.

Mission work in the old Portuguese and Spanish empires had depended on an alliance between throne and altar, on a missionary monopoly bestowed on the Catholic Church, on the initiative of the mighty. The new missionary endeavor owed much less to the power of the state; it was indebted above all to the private enterprise of the laity who subscribed to mission journals and put money into missionary collection boxes. The mission supporters differed considerably in their political outlook. By and large, however, they all wished to eschew violent political revolutions, while promoting a profoundly individualistic religiosity as well as social reforms. Missionary benefactors included men from many different strata, cobblers as well as counts. But the missionary movement made a peculiar appeal to the middle and the lower middle classes. It derived in the first place from Protestants in northern Europe and North America. And despite numerous disagreements between the various evangelizing bodies, one might almost speak of a "missionary internationale."

Perhaps the most influential pioneers in the field of ideology were the German Pietists who wished to rouse Lutherans from their apparent religious lethargy. During the eighteenth century for instance, the University of Hall became an important center for missionary work. Pietist thought also inspired the Moravian Brethren, a dissident Protestant sect who in 1731 sent out their first missionaries beyond the Atlantic. The spirit of the Moravian Brethren profoundly influenced John Wesley, the founder of Methodism.

In 1787 British Methodists formed the first of the great modern missionary societies. Soon the Baptists followed suit. In 1795 Congregationalist merchants in London formed the London Missionary Society, which began work in many different parts of the world, including the Cape. The evangelical revival also affected the established Anglican [Episcopalian] Church. Many Anglicans, conservative at heart, were at first suspicious of the evangelicals with their meddlesome zeal. Nevertheless, in 1799 a small group of Anglican enthusiasts formed the Church Missionary Society, destined to play an important role in the missionary history of Africa.

The British example in turn reacted on continental Christianity. In 1815, for instance, the Basel Missionary Society came into being, deriving support from southern Germany as well as Switzerland. Later on German Protestants created a host of other bodies, including the Berlin, the Rhenish, the Leipzig and the Bremen societies. German intellectuals also played a major part in working out a systematic body of theory which became known as *Missionswissenschaft,* and which paralleled contemporary German achievements in the fields of history, philosophy, and ethnographic studies. The religious revival also spread to France, where it benefited from the post-revolutionary reaction against scepticism and atheism. In 1828 French Protestants created the Paris Evangelical Missionary Society, an important link in the missionary internationale, with supporters spread as far afield as Italy and Scotland.

In the United States the missionary impulse was connected with the anti-slavery movement and with the movement to settle black freedmen on the soil of Africa. American evangelical endeavors also had a distinctively black national component. In 1816 Richard Allen, a former slave, founded the African Methodist Episcopal Church; this was free from white control, and at the same time did much work in West Africa. White Christians, who had much more extensive resources than the blacks, came to take an even greater part in the missionary campaign. American Protestants thus founded the American Board of Commissioners for Foreign Missions, which operated on an inter-denominational basis. The Board resolved that Africans should above all be trained to convert their own people, and in 1834 they sent out their first mission party to Liberia to accomplish this purpose.

The Catholic Church was at first slower in taking up missionary work overseas. During the eighteenth century, the Church had experienced doctrinal dissensions. Catholic missionary work had also severely suffered, when the major Catholic countries had expelled the Jesuit Order from their respective dominions for political reasons. Subsequently the Catholic Church had to face new challenges from the French Revolution which, for a time, seemed to endanger its very existence. The Catholic Church, however, emerged from the Napoleonic Wars with new-found strength. Catholic mission work revived, and the Sacred Congregation for the Propagation of the Faith began to initiate new campaigns. In this endeavor the Catholics began to draw financial support from the laity. In 1822, for example, the Institute for the Propagation of the Faith was founded at Lyons for the purpose of raising funds for missionary work. Similar bodies soon came into being in other cities and other countries. In addition, the Catholic Church came to form new religious orders specifically designed to preach the Gospel to the pagans.

However much the new bodies might disagree among themselves concerning discipline and doctrine, their strategy was necessarily determined to a considerable extent by maritime logistics. The white missionaries came to Africa by sea. They consequently depended on an expanding network of transoceanic trade. The thrust of missionary expansion into Africa was thus determined by the strategic location of certain ports. Two of the most important relay points for transatlantic exchange in West Africa were the city of Freetown in Sierra Leone, and the island of Fernando Po, a Spanish colony in the Bight of Biafra. In South Africa the bulk of missionary traffic at first passed through Cape Town. In East Africa, Zanzibar—the main island entrepôt for the seaborne commerce—served as point of departure for missions to the mainland. Trade, evangelization and scientific research would all complement one another in the creation of a new Africa.

These assumptions, we should stress, formed part of an almost universally accepted set of European beliefs. David Livingstone, the committed evangelist, and Karl Marx, the committed revolutionary, were equally convinced that savages should be civilized for their own good. Both shared what might be called the same "steam power optimism." In writing of India, Marx consistently argued that British entrepreneurs, railway builders, and engineers were performing a progressive function in destroying outmoded forms of society. British administration would promote Indian progress. "Modern industry, resulting from the railway system, will dissolve the hereditary distinction of labour upon which rest the Indian castes, those decisive impediments to Indian progress and Indian power."[3]

Also, Marx—like the sternest of missionaries—thundered forth against what he considered the abominations of primitive paganism. "We must not forget," he wrote in discussing the problems of contemporary India, that the Indian village communities confined man to an "undignified, stagnatory and vegetative life." Marx believed, as firmly as any priest or pastor, that Indian idolaters

. . . subjugated man to external circumstances instead of elevating man to be the sovereign of circumstances, that they transformed a self-developing social state into a never changing natural destiny, and thus brought about a brutalizing worship of nature, exhibiting its degradation in the fact that man, the sovereign of nature, fell down on his knees in adoration of Hanumam, the monkey, and Sabbala, the cow.[4]

Missionary enthusiasm, had also academic, as well as religious and economic implications. In the nineteenth century, the learned and what might be called the welfare professions were not anything like as diversified as in the twentieth. The missionary calling therefore attracted many people who in a subsequent epoch might have chosen academic secular welfare jobs in Africa. Many churches, moreover, provided a relatively inexpensive training for their ministers which enabled poor men to get an education of sorts. The missionary profession thus sometimes became a haven for an intellectual elite drawn from the less affluent strata of society, particularly the lower middle class. But above all the missionaries were able to draw on the funds of the faithful and they had a ready-made audience among their backers. In the English-speaking world especially, the great body of missionary literature formed acceptable reading matter during the long Victorian Sabbaths when evangelical Christians shunned lighter reading matter. The missionaries' first concern was with the salvation of the heathen. But European and American evangelists, or at any rate some of them, soon found that they also needed to study the history, language, and customs of their flock. Hence articles and books about mission work became an important source for the study of the Africans.

Many ecclesiastical designs undertaken by these pioneers had an oddly unworldly air, but many missionary theories of evangelization displayed an economically oriented quality. David Livingstone (1813–1873), one of the most outstanding Christian explorers in the nineteenth century, was only expressing a widely-held belief when he explained that "Christianity and commerce" must march together. Christianity, in Livingstone's belief, would not strike roots unless accompanied by a great social and economic revolution in Africa. "Legitimate trade" in tropical raw materials should replace the iniquitous traffic in human beings that depopulated the continent, and kept its people in misery. Railways and steam-driven ships would one day open up the African interior, thus doing away with the need for slave porters and making possible the cultivation of cash crops such as cotton. In return for its primary products, Africa would import manufactured goods from Europe—not just gunpowder and muskets —so that whites and blacks alike would benefit from a new economic partnership. According to Livingstone, development needed pioneers, and he therefore keenly favored European settlement in Central Africa, hoping that white colonists would teach new techniques of production to the indigenous people. Pioneering, however, required solid knowledge of tropical medicine, ethnography, and geography.

Many of these works now make heavy going. They repel modern readers by their unctuous style and their narrow, parish-magazine outlook. Often the missionary's accounts lacked realism. Evangelical labor, for one thing, depended wholly on financial support from private well-wishers in the metropolitan countries. Missionary writers, like their secular successors, the philanthropic organizations of today, were under constant pressure to report success stories and to minimize their failures. Many ecclesiastical pioneers described the victories of the gospel in terms more glowing than the facts would justify.

Unlike contemporary traders and explorers, the early pioneers of the gospel risked not only their own lives, but often the lives of their families. Only men of an unyielding cast of mind would risk the ever-present perils of malaria and blackwater fever. Only absolute faith in the values of the missionary's own society and of his religious message could justify such sacrifices. Early evangelists did not go to analyze, synthesize, or apologize; they went to fight Satan and all his works. The depredations of intertribal warfare or armed clashes within the various African communities were to them present reality, not a historical reconstruction worked out in the safety of the Pax Britannica or the Pax Gallica. Many, though by no means all, of the old-fashioned missionaries believed that African society was riddled with vice and that evil brooked no compromise. A preacher like François Coillard, a great missionary statesman in nineteenth century Basutoland and Barotseland, saw himself as the chosen Micah of the Lozi king. Coillard's account of the monarch and his people form a running commentary on the cruelty, thievery, lying, fornication, and superstition which—in Coillard's view—dominated Lozi life and threatened the people with eternal perdition.

Modern scholars do not make the same kind of value judgments. On the contrary, many features of African life that used to disgust so many white clergymen, such as drumming, dancing, and beer drinking, appear attractive amusements. Some academics defend hemp-smoking and female circumcision because they are seduced by a cult of the folksy and the primitive. Others are interested in the psychiatric aspects of African healing methods, therapeutic or supposedly therapeutic techniques that missionaires commonly denounced as heathen witchcraft. Modern investigators who use missionary sources must make allowance for the missionaries' prejudices and ethnocentric proclivities. Research workers must likewise examine their own assumptions and become conscious of their own acknowledged or unacknowledged values. But when these allowances are made, the missionary commonly turns out to have had a considerable knowledge of local history and local life. He stayed with "his" people over long periods of time, cut off from regular contacts with Europe. He shared in the vicissitudes of African life. He had, moreover, certain standards of anthropological comparison. Clerical training placed a tremendous emphasis on the manners, laws, and customs of at least one ancient, nomadic, cattle-keeping people—the Hebrews. Missionaries knew Leviticus inside out, and some of them applied this knowledge in a surprisingly modern manner. Ecclesiastical contact with preliterate people was also a two-way traffic. The Christians converted many pagans; but heathen example sometimes aroused doubts in missionary minds. The records of the London Missionary Society, for instance, contain material relating to the Reverend David Picton Jones, a clergyman working in what is now the northeastern corner of Zambia towards the end of the last century. Jones came to disbelieve in the divine inspiration of the Old Testament on the grounds that the Hebrews resembled the people around Fwambo station and that ancient Jewish folklore was probably no more reliable than its modern Bantu equivalent.

The outlook of old-time ecclesiastical pioneers was also shaped by other and more general factors. Men like Dr. Robert Moffat, one of the great evangelical pioneers of Bechuanaland and Matabeleland, were forced to depend on their own efforts in the "Far Interior." He had to be carpenter, farmer, teacher, and preacher, and sometimes even trader, judge, or soldier. This way of life had both negative and positive effects on the missionary's point of view. He usually had little time and scant opportunity for reading. He was an intellectual amateur who enjoyed none of the advantages that accrue to a modern academic through professional division of labor. On the other hand, the old-time missionary sometimes had a broader and more practical outlook on life. A former gardener turned clergyman like Moffat could not take refuge in an intellectual ivory tower, and he did not isolate himself behind the barrier of a highly technical terminology; he was also much better acquainted with the material base of society than many a modern research worker, whose sole training is academic. Missionary judgments therefore often displayed considerable insight and probably should command greater respect than they enjoy today.

Missionaries also made a major contribution to linguistic work in Africa. The white evangelist's first need was to make himself understood. He had to learn indigenous tongues; he compiled word lists and, in many cases, grammars and dictionaries. Learned Catholics pioneered linguistic work. Protestant missionaries followed suit. They especially came as the "People of the Book." They believed that the Scriptures contained everything needful to salvation. Translation work thus assumed tremendous importance in their eyes. The various mission societies in Africa produced scores and scores of Martin Luthers, unknown for the most part, who rendered the Bible, the shorter Catechism, or other religious works into indigenous tongues. Missionaries were usually the first to reduce various types of Bantu speech to writing, and thereby they laid the foundation of new literary languages. Their translations to some extent form a sociological as well as a linguistic record, and the trained student may find much of value in a detailed analysis of this linguistic material.[5]

To sum up, economic, humanitarian, academic, medical, and missionary motives combined to give a tremendous stimulus to the exploration of Africa and to the study of its peoples. There was an intellectual scramble for Africa that continued right through the nineteenth century and, in some ways, is far from having exhausted its impetus today.

AFRICAN EXPLORATION IN THE FIRST HALF OF THE NINETEENTH CENTURY

WEST AFRICA

At the beginning of the last century, Africa—in the eyes of Europe—was a continent of outposts. The British controlled Cape Colony in the south and a few stretches on the Gold Coast and along the shores of Sierra Leone and Gambia. The French had a foothold on the Senegal. The Portuguese held a few scattered possessions along the littoral of Guinea, at Cabinda near the mouth of the Congo, in the northern part of what is now Angola, along the coast of present-day Mozambique and on the lower Zambezi Valley. (The greatest foreign colonial power on paper was Turkey, which exercised a vague supremacy over the Muslim states of Tunis, Tripoli, Algiers, and Egypt.) The bulk of Africa, however, had no political links with the world overseas, and a kind of Baedeker to these polities, as they functioned at the beginning of the nineteenth century, will be provided in a subsequent section.

European cartographers had little knowledge of the African interior. They could draw an accurate outline of the African shore. They were fairly familiar with the lands adjoining the Mediterranean and the Cape. They knew about the Congo, usually called the Zaire, but they had no idea of its vast extent or of its many tributaries. Geographers believed that the Niger flowed westward, not eastward, and that it carried its water into the Atlantic through two main branches, the rivers Senegal and Gambia. There were all kinds of speculations concerning the source of the Nile. Many maps stated that it had its origin in a mysterious land known as the Mountains of the Moon somewhere near the Equator. Only vague rumors had filtered to the coast concerning the Great Lakes region, including "Lake Maravi" in what is now Malawi, but the interlacustrine region proper was unknown, and so was the course of the upper Zambezi. European libraries provided some information concerning a few great African empires such as Ethiopia, now in complete decay. But most of this information was inadequate, some was outdated, some was garbled, and in many instances there was no reliable data at all.

Often a harsh climate stood in the way of progress. So did natural barriers like the

Sahara Desert, or obstacles in the way of river traffic such as sandbars on the coast, swamp and forest deltas, or inland cataracts. Some African political authorities such as the trading states of the west coast discouraged inland penetration for fear of losing local monopolies to interlopers. But above all there was the threat of disease. No doctor, however highly qualified, knew how to cope with malaria, blackwater fever, yellow fever, or similar scourges. "Beware and take care of the Gulf of Benin, Where few come out, though many go in" ran a sailors jingle, and Africa's reputation as the white man's grave took a long time to die. Even at the very end of the nineteenth century, Harry Johnston, an outstanding expert, could still publish a map showing the whole of Africa's vast middle belt, stretching all the way from the Zambezi to Khartoum and from Benguela to Timbuktu as "unhealthy" or "extremely unhealthy," except for a few mountain strongholds in East Africa and Ethiopia.[6]

The peoples of Africa themselves—be they Boer hunters familiar with the inland haunts of elephants, Bisa or Umbundu merchants accustomed to traveling great distances, or Niger rivermen skilled in the navigation of the interior—had an acquaintance with their own region infinitely superior to the most learned scholar's. But their knowledge was confined to specific areas; it was not systematized or published in maps or manuals, and rarely was it communicated to outsiders.

European geographers thus faced a major task, and in order to solve it many scholars concentrated on elucidating the course of Africa's great rivers. If legitimate commerce was to be fostered, merchants had to find a means of bringing trade to the interior in areas where fly-borne diseases prevented horse-drawn or ox-drawn wheeled traffic. Once European explorers gained some knowledge of the savannah belt in the African interior, they often told wildly exaggerated tales concerning the potential value of inland Africa. In the savannah belt white explorers found political organizations more similar to those of Europe than to those of the coast. The centralized states of the savannah, their standing armies, their Islamic religion, their literacy and their systems of taxation were all recognizable by Europeans as "civilized." The savannah people, moreover, wore voluminous cotton robes, and here was a splendid oppotunity for Lancashire cotton exports. As Dr. John Flint puts it, "the picture began to emerge of a benighted and barbarous coast, shutting off the civilized interior."[7]

One of the first river riddles to be solved was the source of the Niger. In 1795 Mungo Park (1771–1806), a young Scottish doctor acting under the auspices of the African Association, set sail for the Gambia in quest of the Niger. In 1796 he succeeded in reaching Segou, a Bambara town on the Niger, and learned that the river proceeded northeast beyond Timbuktu. Park tried to go on, but weakened and without means, he finally collapsed with fever and was forced to turn back, having traced the course of the river for something like 300 miles and having disproved the older theories concerning the direction of the river. In 1805 he embarked on a much more ambitious venture, navigated down the Niger for hundreds of miles, but finally perished at Bussa.

Subsequent explorers secured new information concerning the Niger, and in 1830 Richard Lemond Lander (1804–1834) was sent by the British government to explore the Oil Rivers. Lander and his brother John journeyed on foot to Bussa, and then made their way down to the Bight of Benin by canoe, proving that the Niger and

Oil rivers were indeed the same. The British now had high hopes that the Niger might be turned into a commercial route, accessible to steam power. In 1832 two small steam vessels chugged up the river to its confluence with the Benue under Lander's guidance. In the following year the British managed to struggle yet further up into the interior, but to no avail. Most of the Europeans involved in the enterprise, including Richard, died of fever. McGregor Laird, a British shipbuilder who had backed the venture, suffered financial ruin. Undeterred by these disasters, the British persisted in their design. The abolitionists tried to further their cause by establishing a colony of freed slaves on the Niger, where commercial posts would promote legitimate trade and a model farm would encourage agricultural production. In 1841 another large expedition left for the river. Once more the pioneers suffered heavy loss of life from sickness, and in 1842 the venture had to be abandoned.

Clearly, the interior would always remain inaccessible until the danger from disease could be surmounted. Medical men as yet remained unaware of the connection between the mosquito and malaria, one of West Africa's most terrible scourges. From empirical evidence they found that malaria could be fought by means of the chinchona bark. Really effective chinchona prophylaxis had to wait until chemists developed a cheap, palatable, and more reliable derivative. Quinine was first isolated in 1820. By the 1830s its price had dropped sufficiently to allow its general use, so that the development of British chemical industries indirectly stimulated the opening of Africa. Dr. T. R. H. Thomson, a little known pioneer, worked out a regime of quinine prophylaxis that entailed a regular intake of sufficient pills. The Royal Navy accordingly switched over to the new treatment. Its final mark of success came in 1854 when Dr. William Blaikie took the steamship *Pleiad* up the Niger and the Benue. Baikie's expedition returned without a single fatality.[8] In the southern part of Africa, Livingstone likewise proved the prophylactic value of quinine, and the cause of European exploration in Africa thereby secured a decisive victory.

At the same time European explorers made a determined attempt to secure more information concerning the great Muslim states of the interior by using the trans-Saharan route from the north. In 1822, for instance, three English travelers, Dr. Walter Oudney (who was actually appointed British Political Agent to Bornu before that country was explored), and Lieutenant Hugh Clapperton and Major Dixon Denham, set out for the south. In 1823 the expedition reached Lake Chad, and its members were the first Europeans to see its waters. Subsequently they visited Bornu and the Hausa state of Kano, where Oudney died. Hugh Clapperton (1788–1827) subsequently proceeded to Sokoto, and might have succeeded in making his way down the Niger to the sea, had he not been stopped by the sultan of Sokoto. Clapperton later embarked on yet another venture to the interior. He landed at Badagri in what is now Nigeria, made his way to the Yoruba country, struck the Niger at Bussa, continued to Nupe, Kano, and Sokoto, but was prevented by a Sokoto-Bornu war from making further progress. Worn out by fever and disappointment, Clapperton died at Sokoto in 1827. Lander, his servant, a former page, footman, and valet, subsequently continued Clapperton's work, and, as we have previously seen, succeeded in navigating down the Niger.

The most outstanding of West African explorers was Heinrich Barth (1821–

1865), a German scholar who had already made his name in the Near East. In 1849 Barth secured a post with a British expedition, one of the many Germans to be associated with British geographical and missionary ventures at a time when there was a considerable migration of German men of science, entreprenuers, artists, and mission workers to Britain, then the industrial heartland of the world. The expedition, originally commanded by James Richardson, reached Bornu without difficulty, but Richardson died soon afterward, and Barth then took charge of the enterprise. He journeyed from Lake Chad across northern Hausaland to the Niger at Say. From Say he cut across the bend of the Niger to Timbuktu, descended the river back to Say, and thence to Sokoto, from which he made his way to Bornu. Barth also discovered the upper Benue River. In 1855 Barth finally returned to England, having unearthed an immense amount of information concerning the history, culture, and geography of the region, as well as many precious Islamic manuscripts. He received a somewhat grudging reward for his services. After some delay he was created a Companion of the Order of the Bath. From then onward his existence was ignored by a British government which, as Sir Harry Johnston caustically put it, thought Barth infinitely less worthy of remembrance than a Chargé d'Affaires at the Grand Ducal Court of Pumpernickel. Barth's massive work *Reisen und Entdeckungen in Nord- und Zentralafrika (Travels and Discovery in North and Central Africa)* remains a classic to this day. It helped to gain Barth a well-earned chair of Geography at the University of Berlin, where he made an important contribution, not only to the study of African civilizations but also to the science of linguistics.

EAST AND CENTRAL AFRICA

Throughout the eighteenth and the first part of the nineteenth century, West Africa was on the whole more easily accessible to European traders and explorers than East and Central Africa. Before the opening of the Suez Canal in 1869, European merchant vessels could approach East Africa only via the Cape, and East Africa was not as important to Western commerce as the west coast. Nevertheless, European travelers also supplemented the work done in earlier generations by Portuguese and Arab travelers in East Africa.

German savants and clergymen played a particularly noteworthy part. In 1835 the Church Missionary Society, an Anglican body, sent some emissaries to Ethiopia, including Johann Krapf and Johann Rebmann, two Germans who crossed the channel as part of the contemporary German "brain-drain" to England. The Church Missionary Society representatives, unable to stay in Ethiopia, subsequently moved to the east coast of Africa and in 1844 established its local headquarters in Mombassa. From there Krapf and Rebmann made some remarkable journeys inland. In 1848 Rebmann saw Mount Kilimanjaro—the first European to do so. In 1849 Krapf pushed further north still and caught a glimpse of Mount Kenya. The two Germans sent back astonishing reports of great lakes and snow-covered peaks in the midst of tropical Africa. At first they met with a good deal of scepticism from arm-chair geographers in Europe, but at the same time their work inspired others to continue the exploration of the interior.

The most outstanding of their successors were two Englishmen, Richard Francis Burton (1821–1890) and John Hanning Speke (1827–1864). Burton, an Oxford man, had served in the Indian Army, where he studied numerous oriental languages. He later made his name by an extraordinary pilgrimage to Mecca, disguised as an Indian Pathan, and a journey to the mysterious city of Harar in Ethiopia. In 1858 he and Speke discovered Lake Tanganyika, where he mapped out the northern shore. Burton was not only a brilliant linguist but also an accomplished writer, unusually prolific like so many of his Victorian contemporaries. His works include a great many books outlining his discoveries, and a translation of the *Arabian Nights* as well as of Camões' *Lusiads,* the Portuguese national epic. Speke also served in the Indian army, a body which contributed a great many soldiers, explorers, and administrators to the British imperial effort in Africa. Speke was the first white man to visit Lake Victoria Nyanza. In 1862 he returned to Lake Victoria Nyanza and proved it to be the source of the Nile River.

French travelers took a particularly noteworthy part in Ethiopian exploration and scholarship. Antoine d'Abbadie (1810–1897) spent a great many years in the country, together with his brother Arnaud. He surveyed Lake Tana, visited the ancient city of Lalibela with its great rock-hewn churches, and also carried out extensive studies in the Gojjam Province. D'Abbadie was interested alike in the languages, the history, the culture, and the geography of Ethiopia, and he himself catalogued the numerous Ethiopian manuscripts he managed to acquire in the country. French explorers also included Th. Lefèbvre, a highly cultured naval officer, Rochet d'Héricourt, and many others whose work helped to give France a commanding position in Ethiopian studies. Their discoveries were utilized by scholars working in the seclusion of their libraries in Europe. The greatest of these was August Dillmann (1823–1894), the refounder of Abyssinian studies. Dillmann wrote three works which are still indispensable to students of classical Ethiopia: a detailed grammar, a monumental dictionary of Ge'ez, and a great compendium based on his vast reading of Ethiopian literature.[9]

In addition the Europeans became interested in the upper course of the Nile, where a Catholic mission was established in 1848 with support from the Austrian government. Among these missionaries was Dr. Ignatius Knoblecher, who in 1849 explored the White Nile. Other explorations were carried out by Italians, including Giovanni Beltrame and Giovanni Miani, who visited the White Nile region and was later the first European to traverse the Nyamnyam country.

The most famous explorer, however, was David Livingstone. Livingstone's work in many ways came to symbolize the Victorian exploratory effort in Africa at large, and we therefore feel justified in devoting more space to his career than to others whose records were equally illustrious. He started life as an ordinary workman in a cotton mill, but managed to study medicine, and joined the London Missionary Society as a doctor. He arrived in Cape Town in 1841, subsequently traveled north and explored the interior of Bechuanaland. Here he discovered Lake Ngami, in 1849. In the following year he reached the upper Zambezi, and subsequently he made his way to the Angolan coast. In 1854 he arrived in Luanda on the Atlantic shore. But he realized that the west coast route would not be suitable for providing adequate supplies to mission stations that might be set up at some future time in the Zambezi Valley. The west coast outlet would prove equally unsatisfactory for the purpose of stimulating Barotse commerce. Livingstone determined on the hair-raising venture of following the Zambezi right to its mouth. He traversed the whole of Africa from west to east, and in 1856 reached Quelimane in Mozambique. He thus completed an amazing feat of endurance that won immediate recognition.

In evaluating his work, we should make a number of reservations. Livingstone was neither a very effective missionary nor administrator. As a geographer Livingstone displayed some remarkable flashes of insight; he formulated an interesting theory about the direction of the trade winds in relation to the earth's rotation; he understood the difficult hydrological problems of the upper Zambezi; and he saw that the central plateau of Africa was in some ways like a huge saucer, with slight rises inside, and a rim of higher hills outside, the rivers breaking through the rim in cascades and waterfalls. On the other hand, Livingstone made a good many mistakes. Sometimes these were caused by false information from others; sometimes clouds would impede the readings of his instruments or his scientific instruments would get damaged or lost. Lastly, Livingstone had an obsessional streak that made him sometimes misconstrue his own evidence, such as in the description of the lower Zambezi, which he firmly believed must be navigable, or his stubbornly held conviction that he would find the source of the Nile in the Lake Bangweulu region.[10]

But when all is said and done, Livingstone still stands out as one of the greatest figures in the history of African exploration. Livingstone had a methodical mind; his books supplied his contemporaries with an incredible wealth of geographical, ethnographic, medical, botanical, geological, and other information, in most minute detail. Livingstone, after all, was a doctor, trained to observe with accuracy, and his insistence on precision added much to the value of his work even on nonmedical subjects. This can be seen, for instance, in his anthropological observations, which are still of value to scholars today. In the days of Livingstone medicine had only just abandoned the metaphysical and even mystical cast of old and begun preferring empirical observation to a priori reasoning.[11]

Most ethnographic observations made by contemporary missionaries were still cast in an ethical form. The average missionary work on African customs tended to be an essay on the depravity of native ways rather than a clinical exposition. Livingstone, on the other hand, was more concerned with recording and analyzing facts, and this trait enabled him to play a major role in the elucidation of Africa's problems.

Equally important were Livingstone's purely medical achievements. We have already mentioned the importance of the prophylactic properties possessed by quinine in protecting human beings against malaria. Livingstone played an important part in popularizing the drug. As a doctor Livingstone also had other claims to prominence. He was one of the first to make extensive use of the clinical thermometer, the first to use arsenic on animals with sleeping sickness, and the first to link relapsing fever with ticks. In an age when medical men knew little about the impact of nutritional deficiencies on health, Livingstone noted that there was a connection between an ill-balanced manioc diet and night blindness. Livingstone also added to the knowledge of tropical medicine, then in a rudimentary state, by accurately describing and diagnosing some of the diseases he encountered in Africa, such as blackwater fever, syphilis, scurvy, bilharzia, and the now fortunately rare aberation of earth-eating.[12]

But above all, Livingstone made a deep impression on his contemporaries because his life was one of the great success stories of England, the story of a man who had worked his way up from poverty to fame through sheer hard work, through invincible strength of character, and a profound faith in the truths of Protestant Christianity. His appeal, moreover, seemed to transcend the interest of particular social classes. To working men he was a former millhand who had "made good." To employers he was a theoretician of social reconciliation at home, of commercial expansion abroad, and of rational reform and Christian endeavor all around. His life work symbolized that curious blend of philanthropy, scientific interest, and outgoing enterprise—no matter whether humanitarian, economic, or missionary—that characterized so much of Europe's exploratory work on the African continent during the nineteenth century.

In assessing the importance of all this geographical, ethnographic, and related work, many modern writers have rightly emphasized that these Victorian discoveries could not have been effective without the assistance of Africans. (Livingstone's journey to the west coast, for instance, was supported by the Barotse monarch on the upper Zambezi, who was also interested in finding a new trading route to the west coast.) Some recent scholars have tried subtly to downgrade the importance of the Victorian journeys by using the irony of inverted commas in referring to white "discoveries." They feel justified in taking this position on the grounds that all the regions thus traversed by white men have previously been known to Africans and, in many cases, to Arab traders. This reasoning is justified insofar as they point out that white pioneers—contrary to the prevailing contemporary stereotype—rarely hacked their way through untrodden jungles. In reality, the white explorers built on a great deal of existing African knowledge. They rarely made their way through virgin country. More often they used existing, albeit rudimentary, communication systems consisting of village paths, caravan routes, and canoe routes. Their greatness consisted above all in their methodical and scientific spirit, their trained intelligence, their ability to systematize their hard-gained knowledge, and their willingness to make it available to others rather than keep it as a trade secret. In this respect they differed from the indigenous travelers of Africa, whose knowledge remained restricted knowledge, and it was the white explorers' enterprise that now began to put the African interior on the world's map.

NOTES

1. Curtin, *The Image of Africa: British Ideas and Action, 1780–1850,* pp. 432–435. According to Curtin, the British West Indies during this period took 3.14 percent of British exports, Cuba and the foreign West Indies purchased 2.18 percent and Brazil 4.16 percent.

2. Curtin, pp. 329–330.

3. Karl Marx, "The Future Results of British Rule in India", *New York Daily Tribune,* Aug. 8, 1953," in S. Avineri, ed., *Karl Marx on Colonialism: His Despatches and Other Writings on China, India, Mexico, the Middle East and North Africa* (New York, 1968), p. 129.

4. Karl Marx, "The Government of India Bill", *New York Daily Tribune,* July 1, 1853, in S. Avineri, *Karl Marx on Colonialism,* p. 89.

5. L. H. Gann, "The Neglected Missionaries," *Africana Newsletter,* vol. 2, no. 3 (1964), pp. 8–12.

6. Sir Harry H. Johnston, *A History of the Colonization of Africa by Alien Races* (Cambridge, 1899), facing p. 275.

7. Flint, *Nigeria and Ghana,* p. 112.

8. Curtin, *The Image of Africa,* pp. 355–357.

9. Ullendorf, *The Ethiopians,* p. 20.

10. See Debenham, *The Way to Ilala: David Livingstone's Pilgrimage.*

11. Lewis H. Gann, *A History of Northern Rhodesia: Early Days to 1953* (London, 1964), pp. 29–31.

12. Michael Gelfand, *Livingstone the Doctor; His Life and Travels: A Study in Medical History* (Oxford, 1957).

Chapter 33

African
Intellectual Responses
to the Western Challenge

PROPHECY

From the European point of view, Africa throughout the eighteenth and early nineteenth centuries remained a continent of outposts. Direct trading contacts were largely confined to the coast. White inland penetration on a larger scale started only in the 1830s, first on the southern and then on the northern extremities of the continent. During the late 1830s, Boer trekkers made their way across the Orange and Vaal rivers, and southward again into Natal. In 1830 the last French Bourbon king, seeking to restore the tarnished glory of his dynasty, ordered French troops to occupy Algiers. The French adventure led to an unexpectedly long war, but between 1837 and 1847 the French gradually crushed Muslim resistance in most parts of Algeria. White colonists—Frenchmen, Spaniards, and Italians—followed in the wake of the conquering regiments, and Algeria became a French outpost on the southern shore of the Mediterranean.

In sub-Saharan Africa as a whole, however, the Christian powers as yet counted for little. British warships could intimidate the rulers of coastal states, but ships of the line could not penetrate inland. Portuguese attempts at evangelization in the Congo and elsewhere had not achieved much permanent success. The Protestant missions likewise had as yet made only a relatively small impact, and their activities were confined mainly to a few portions of West and South Africa. Islamic preachers and conquerors controlled fields immensely vaster than those held by their Christian counterparts. Islam appeared a more powerful challenge to traditional African ways than Christianity or any other western creed.

The West nevertheless had begun to make an impact on Africa, not merely economically and politically, but also in the realm of ideas. African contacts with the outer world led to the creation of what might be called a new mental universe—varied and beset by many internal contradictions, but full of promise for the future. Europeans had come to Africa. A handful of Africans had also visited both Europe and the New World as ambassadors or as explorers. (During the eighteenth and early nineteenth centuries, for instance, the kings of Dahomey sent several royal envoys to Lisbon and Bahia.) Afro-Americans came to their ancestral land as traders or settlers; Europeans and mulattoes speaking various Western tongues, as well as a handful of missionaries acted as intellectual middlemen between Africa and the West.

Broadly speaking, the African intellectual response to the new challenges was of three kinds—millenarian prophecy (based on Biblical inspiration and local prophetic traditions); the selective adaptation of Western institutions by ruling black minorities; and finally the cultural assimilation of individual Africans to western ways, so that the converts sometimes came to consider themselves as black Frenchmen, Portuguese, or Englishmen. We have mentioned cultural assimilation on the west coast. There was also a certain degree of anglicization at the Cape, where Christian communities separated themselves from their pagan neighbors and looked to the Imperial power for protection against the local colonists.

Generalizations of this kind of course always leave much to be desired. Real life does not know the clear-cut distinctions made in history books. The Africans whom we have styled prophets often wished to adapt certain features of Western life. The so-called "adaptationists," that is to say the Christian converts, commonly wished to preserve a good deal of their pagan heritage. Some of them even wished to retain the institution of polygamy, and white missionaries would accuse such deviationists of backsliding. Even the most Europeanized Africans were apt to praise many aspects of African life, however much they longed to reorganize African tribal society in their own image. Despite this overlapping, we cannot altogether avoid historical categories, and the responses mentioned differed sufficiently from one another to warrant separate treatment.

Perhaps the earliest recorded instance of Afro-Christian prophecy comes from the Congo. In previous chapters we have discussed the inability of the Portuguese to westernize the Congolese, the impact of the slave trade and the decline of the Kongo monarchy. By the beginning of the eighteenth century, the kingdom had indeed fallen on evil days. There was constant civil strife between differing contenders for the throne; there was misery and much popular discontent. The people at large had failed to accept Christianity, but some of the missionaries' doctrines were adapted by African prophets to new purposes. The most famous of these seers was Kimpa Vita, known to the Portuguese as Donna Anna. Kimpa Vita, whom we have previously mentioned in the section on the decline of the Kongo, had once been a pagan priestess, perhaps a spirit medium. Later she adopted various Christian tenets, but infused these doctrines with a strong anti-white content. She believed that she was in touch with Heaven, that she periodically died to be reborn into this world, and that she could perform miracles. She told the faithful that St. Antony had appeared to her and foretold the restoration of the Kongo monarchy. She foresaw a Messianic age, when the true believers would inherit all the white man's riches. Salvation would come through her son, who—like Jesus—had been begotten by the Holy Spirit. According to Kimpa Vita, Kongo was the Holy Land, San Salvador (the capital of Kongo) was Bethlehem, and Nsundi was Nazareth. Jesus had been born a black man. The whites—in her view—had grievously sinned by monopolizing for their own use both the Christian revelation and the secret for gaining wealth.

Kimpa Vita accordingly tried to Africanize Christianity. She identified the spirits with Catholic saints; she believed in spirit possession; she legalized polygamy; she adapted parts of the Catholic liturgy to African usage, but shed most Catholic doctrines of the traditional kind. She organized an independent popular church, complete with its own hierarchy and propagandists. She herself claimed to be the intermediary between the people and God, charged with the dual commission of restoring both Kongo's might and of leading her followers to salvation. Kimpa Vita thus attained great political influence. The faithful flocked to San Salvador to hear the new saint, and for a time the two principal dynastic contenders both tried to use the Antonine movement for their own ends. But Kimpa Vita could not remake the Kongo. She had to operate within the framework of a tribal state, and she finally backed a loser. She seems to have given support to the Kimpanzu faction, which was trying to wrest the crown from the ruling Ki-Mulaza line. King Pedro, the reigning monarch, was supported by Capuchin missionaries, who condemned the heretic.[1] In 1706 Kimpa Vita and her child were arrested and executed. Many of the Kimpa's followers believed that the saint had only died in one of her many forms; millenarian traditions of a similar kind appear to have survived in the Congo ever since.

Kimpa Vita's doctrines in many ways were not peculiar to Africans. German Anabaptists in the sixteenth century and English "Fifth Monarchy Men" in the seventeenth century shared some of her ideas. But Kimpa Vita operated within a different social context from that familiar to European prophets. Kimpa Vita not only put her trust into some Messianic miracle, she insisted in condemning what the Portuguese called "fetishes" with the same fervor as white missionaries. She also assumed that the Europeans' prosperity was rooted in some secret revelation that the whites had kept to themselves. Antonism thus represented a political form of escapism, and the Antonists—like their ideological successors in other parts of Africa—were never in a position to seize political power.

ASSIMILATION: REVOLUTIONARY AND CONFORMIST

By the beginning of the nineteenth century European influence in the Congo was slight, and the grandeur of Portugal was but a memory. Western penetration was of a more thoroughgoing kind in Egypt, South Africa, and later, in Sierra Leone. The Western cultural impact was symbolized by the simultaneous appearance, in 1800, of locally printed government gazettes in Cairo, Cape Town, and Freetown. The Cairo press, as P. E. H. Hair explains, was the product of Napoleon Bonaparte's invasion of Egypt. Napoleon's temporary conquest of Egypt had far-reaching cultural effects, both in spreading the French language and in encouraging French scholars to study

Egypt's ancient past. The second press, operating at Cape Town, at first did no more than print parish notices for a minor outpost of Holland in the South Atlantic. Even the Boers in the interior took little notice of such proclamations, and the black people were as yet hardly affected by Western thought.

The English-speaking settlements at Sierra Leone, the American quasi-colony of Liberia, as well as the French possessions in Senegal, on the other hand, came to assume far greater immediate importance in the cultural history of black Africa. The population of this region included some Europeanized and Americanized mulattoes and black people, as well as pagans. A handful of these Anglophone and Francophone Africans maintained contact with black expatriates in Great Britain and with Negroes in the West Indies and America. A tiny minority of French-speaking Africans in Senegal kept some links with France. A few Portuguese-speaking Africans in Guinea and Angola were quite well informed with respect to events in Lisbon and Rio de Janeiro. These people, unlike Kimpa Vita, knew how to read and write; they were the product of a syncretic culture blending many different elements, and some of them tried to find new ways of expressing their cultural identity.

The most radical-minded among them included Afro-American ex-soldiers who had fought on the British side in the American War of Independence because they detested American slavery. After the war these veterans had emigrated to Nova Scotia, where they once more fell foul of the local whites, and had therefore decided to seek a new home in Sierra Leone. Having suffered much at white hands they commonly displayed a bitter dislike of Europeans—so much so that in 1796 black colonists willing to vote for a white man on the local council were threatened with violence. The British governor reported with surprise this unique example of "making a white face a civil disqualification."[2] In 1800 a number of these Afro-American settlers took up arms against the British officials, at a time when the blacks of Haiti were in revolt against the French, and when a slave rising had broken out in Virginia. The insurrection derived its organizational framework from independent black churches whose very existence signified an anti-European protest. But the rebels' object was secular rather than religious, and their ideas owed much to current beliefs concerning the rights of man and the principles of the American constitution. The *Putsch* never got very far. But as P. E. H. Hair said, "the incoherent, unsystematic, and sometimes unreasonable complaints of the Nova Scotia settlers at Freetown were the beginning of African political nationalism, of Negritude in Africa—in sum of conscious Africanism."[3]

The ideals of the Afro-American insurgents bore certain curious resemblances to those expressed by discontented Afrikaners at the Cape. Some white frontier farmers also picked up revolutionary ideas concerning the rights of man, by which they meant the rights of white men. The Boers' widespread distaste for Bantu and Hottentots paralleled the hatred of whites by some Afro-Americans'. The white colonists shared the black settlers' dislike of being ruled by expatriate British officials. Stirred up by Jan Woyer, an ardent Jacobin, a group of Afrikaans-speaking farmers at Graaf Reinet in the eastern part of the Cape thus refused to give unconditional obedience to the newly installed British authorities at Cape Town. The settlers rallied round Marthinus Prinsloo, a countryman who styled himslef "Protector of the People's Voice." They agreed to accept a British appointed magistrate, but insisted that the occupying power must accept the locally elected *heemrad* (county court). The British prepared to use force, and Graaf Reinet submitted. But however ineffective, settler radicalism continued and played its part in the future of South Africa.

The insurrectionary response contrasted with what might be called revolutionary loyalism. When the French Revolution broke out in 1789 Senegal already contained a small number of mulatto and African merchants engaged in the up-country trade. Gallicized Africans welcomed the French declarations in favor of liberty, equality, and fraternity. The habitants of Gorée and St. Louis were proud to receive French citizenship from the young republic, and they joyfully subscribed for a contribution to help in the defense of France. Soon the birth registers announced the births of young Scipios and Robespierres, sons of Mamadou, Abdoulaye, or Moctar.[4] The revolution failed to keep its initial promises. The revolutionary government in France, acting under pressure from the French West Indian planters' lobby at Paris, soon restricted the privileges given to black people, and when Napoleon came to power the movement toward equality came to an abrupt end. The French restored slavery and the slave trade for the time being. Men of color were denied entry into France, and the French civil code forbade mixed marriages.

The colored trading community responded in a vigorous fashion. Gabriel Pellegrin, a Negro trader, helped to start an insurrection that appealed to the ideals of Robespierre and the Convention. The local French governor, who had installed an arbitrary trade monopoly, was removed from power, and the French took no action against the mutineers. Pellegrin subsequently cooperated with the British when they temporarily seized the colony during the Napoleonic Wars, but Pellegrin in the end became a loyal French citizen, convinced of the merits of assimilation. In 1817 the French regained control of the colony. The mulattoes were recognized as an influential group; mulattoes assumed senior positions in the administration, and Pellegrin shortly afterwards became mayor of St. Louis. The government of Louis Philippe (installed at Paris in 1830) further restated the principles of the French Revolution. In 1833 all freemen in Senegal were accorded French citizenship; the mulattoes became fully assimilated into French culture and continued to intermarry with white people.

Gallicization left the mass of urban and rural Africans untouched. However, a tiny minority of black people also managed to learn French and acquire a European education. Their ambitions found intellectual expression in the work of the Abbé D. Boilat who wrote a Senegalese ethnography. Boilat, like most British-educated black pastors of his time, felt that only Christianity and commerce, European art, religion, and morality could save Africa from all the "gross, if not dishonourable ways, known as the custom of the country, those absurd superstitions born of that silly deplorable gullibility. . . ."[5] British colonization produced its own variety of cultural assimilation. One of the most eminent of anglicized Africans was Surgeon-Major Africanus Horton, a black Sierra Leonian, distinguished alike as a physician, a soldier, and a writer on ethnography and political economy. Horton was what might be called an Afro-Victorian. Like David Livingstone, with whom he had certain features in common, he was born in lowly circumstances. By dint of hard study and hard work, he acquired a medical training as well as a broad general education. He was commissioned in the British army, served the British Empire in various positions and, like Livingstone, combined an ardent belief in Great Britain's civilizing mission with an indomitable faith in the future of the Africans. Horton firmly rejected the view "that the existence of British rule was a curse to this part of the [West] Coast; that the country was infinitely superior, commerce much more advanced, and life and property safer in the hands of the superseded native government than under the sovereignty of Great Britain."[6] On the contrary, he considered British governance a blessing to Africa, and in many ways he was an outspoken British imperialist. Yet he would have no truck with those who asserted the hereditary inferiority of the blacks. He gloried in the African past, and held high hopes for the future of his continent. Horton, like so many other British mid-Victorian imperialists, saw no contradiction between imperial power and local home rule. He had very clear notions of how self government should be achieved. In a self-governing Sierra Leone, for instance, the language of government would necessarily have to be English. There should be a bicameral legislature and a popularly elected monarch. On of the king's principal objects should be "to annexe the neighbouring territory as an integral part of his kingdom, and to endeavour to give protection and support to the merchants trading in it; this will in every way improve his growing revenue, which it should be his utmost endeavour to increase."[7] Just as many Franco-African merchants in Senegal stood for a "Senegalese imperialism," designed to protect the traders' interests under the French Tricolor, Horton and men of his class advocated an Afro-British variety of empire-building.

Other black theorists came to very different conclusions. Perhaps the most prominent of them all was Edward W. Blyden, a West Indian born at St. Thomas in 1832. Blyden tried to study in the United States, but racial prejudice prevented him from gaining admission to an appropriate institution. In 1851 he emigrated to Liberia, where he made his name as a scholar and statesman and where he served periodically as tutor to Joseph Jenkins Roberts, one of the most distinguished of Liberian presidents. Blyden believed that each race, including the black race, had its own cultural contribution to make to the advancement of humanity. He spoke, perhaps for the first time, of the "African personality," which he believed to be endowed with a unique form of spirituality, a special proclivity for cooperation and for sympathetic communion with nature. Africans, in Blyden's view, had a more pronounced sense of the numinous than Europeans. The great religions of the world had all originated in Africa, he claimed. The ancient Egyptians and Ethiopians had been of the black race. Africans should therefore look with pride upon their golden age, develop their own racial genius, and avoid miscegenation or contamination by alien thought.[8]

On the face of it, few men had less in common than Boilat, the Francophile from Senegal, Horton, the loyal British field officer, and Blyden, the eloquent spokesman of an expatriate's black nationalism. Yet Blyden was also an assimilationist of a kind. His doctrines were in no wise peculiarly African. They bore a curious resemblance, for instance, to the teachings of German romantics who extolled the simple virtues of the folk and contrasted the assumed spirituality of the Teutonic racial soul with the shallow rationalism that supposedly characterized the Western nations. Blyden was a child of his times; his beliefs in ethnicity were much like those of Benjamin Disraeli, whose novel *Tancred,* published in 1847, propounded the maxim "all is race; there is no other truth." Blyden's diffusionist view of history was a commonplace of his age. His idealization of the African past was in no wise different from that of European "antiquarians of profound learning and easy faith" who used to trace the origins of civilization to their own particular country. "Of these judicious critics," wrote Gibbon with his magnificent irony, "was Olaus Rudbeck, professor in the university of Upsal. Whatever is celebrated either in history or fable, this zealous patriot ascribes to his country. From Sweden (which formed so considerable a part of ancient Germany) the Greeks themselves derived their alphabetical characters, their astronomy, and their religion."[9]

Blyden's political ideals were equally assimilationist. He believed that Liberia, as an independent African state, was in a position to demonstrate to a sceptical world that Africans could create a new civilization. But the new civilization was to be built with Western tools by western-educated men. Blyden therefore put his trust into Afro-American immigrants. He hoped that experienced farmers, mechanics, teachers, and doctors from the New World would replace paganism by Christianity in West Africa, that they would introduce Western science, turn English into a *lingua franca,* and ultimately solve Africa's problems on Western terms. Blyden rejected accomodationist solutions such as those put forward by Booker T. Washington, the Afro-American educator; Blyden looked askance even at mulattoes; he would have nothing to do with gradualism. Blyden, however, was not a revolutionary in the insurrectionary sense; he did not preach war against the whites and ultimately eulogized the British administration at Lagos in Nigeria, for instance, in terms that might make convinced empire-builders blush with embarrassment.[10]

SELECTIVE ASSIMILATION

The experience of Basutoland (now called Lesotho) in the first half of the nineteenth century differed profoundly both from that of the Kongo kingdom and that of Liberia or Sierra Leone. Basutoland was not founded by Anglicized black people but by black tribesman forced to respond to military challenges from outside in a new way. The kingdom owed its very existence to Moshesh, one of the great nation builders of Africa, who fused a variety of scattered and sometimes demoralized groups into a nation. The Sotho kingdom, unlike the Kongolese state, was thus a relatively recent creation. Even Moshesh, of course, did not begin with a *tabula rasa.* The various components of the new Sotho nation also had traditions of their own. But the new Basuto state probably had a greater degree of plasticity than the Kongo, with its long-established institutions that had worked effectively long before the Portuguese had arrived on the West African shores.

The white agents of westernization in Basutoland also differed considerably from the Portuguese in the Kongo. During the early 1830s, members of the Paris Missionary Society settled in Basutoland in order to teach both the Gospel and worldly skills. The Society consisted of Protestants, a minority in their own country, connected neither to the French "establishment" of the time, nor to the British, nor to the Boers.

Most Portuguese priests in Kongo had naturally sympathized with the Portuguese monarchy. The Paris missionaries, on the other hand, had no national links with the other white communities of South Africa; instead the missionaries tried to identify themselves with the Sotho. The French were generally men of high intellectual and moral caliber; they were also determined to make Africa their home. They sought not only to win converts but to develop the national life of the Sotho on Biblical principles. In doing so they wished to use the New Testament as their guide in the task of evangelization and the Old Testament as a handbook for the purpose of social transformation. Some of their ideas sound unrealistic by present-day standards. Nevertheless, the missionaries' thorough knowledge of the Bible and their consequent familiarity with the customs of the ancient Hebrews, a warlike, patrilineal, cattle-herding people, comparable in certain respects to the Sotho, was not a bad preparation for work in the Basuto highlands.

The French did not simply try to turn the Sotho into Europeans. They also shared the troubles of the common people insofar as they could. For instance, when the victorious Boers imposed cattle-fines on the Sotho, the missionaries always gave their quota, even though they had no share in the original provocation or plunder that had given rise to these disputes. At times, the Boers even accused the French of taking up arms on the Sotho side, a charge not founded on fact. Nevertheless, in one of the many conflicts between Boers and Sotho, Orange Free State troops sacked Beersheba, one of the French mission stations.

The French thus gained a good deal of popular sympathy among the Sotho. In addition to these psychological advantages, the missionaries also enjoyed an unexpected climatic boon. The mountains of Basutoland were much less subject to tropical disease than the tropical forest belt of the Kongo; this epidemiological factor probably made some contribution to the French success.

The Sotho, for their part, were determined to learn European skills, and the French met with a favorable reception from the start. Moshesh sent his sons to a mission school; so did many other Sotho aristocrats. Literate Sotho loved reading, and as soon as the missionaries had reduced the Sotho tongue to writing, they supplied the Sotho with printed literature from the mission press. Knowledge of Christianity spread fast. The Sotho Church itself took part in the evangelization of southern Africa. Sotho evangelists, for instance, subsequently penetrated into distant Barotseland, where they assisted other French missionaries to preach the Gospel. Sotho evangelical activism seems to have satisfied both the national and the religious ambitions of the people, who took pride in Sotho successes obtained on foreign mission fields. The French also taught secular skills; they gave instruction in building methods, and they acclimatized various kinds of fruit trees, vegetables, and root crops in Basutoland and thereby enriched the people's diet.

The missionaries also satisfied certain psychic needs—a point that may all too easily be overlooked. Moshesh himself felt convinced that men must make a spiritual effort at belief. The king himself exhorted his chiefs as follows: "You say that you will not believe what you do not understand. Look at an egg. If a man break it, there comes only water and a yellow substance out of it, but if it be put under the wing of a fowl there comes a living being from it. This is incomprehensible to us, and yet we cannot deny the fact. Let us do like the hen. Let us place these truths in our hearts, as the hen does the egg under her wings, let us sit upon them and take the same pains, and something new will come out of them."[11]

The successes of white missionary work should not be exaggerated. The missionaries determined to civilize as well as to Christianize the people. The rigid Protestants especially would under no circumstances relax the rules of their faith. They condemned not only polygamy, but a host of African customs the missionaries believed would lead their converts to hell everlasting. In this respect there was little difference in the way in which British missionaries condemned African peasants and the manner in which many European clergymen deplored the customs of Welsh, Irish, and Portuguese peasants. (Nonconformist missionary journals especially contained the most lurid accounts of evils in European villages, accounts that were frequently as intemperate as any written with regard to brown and black villagers beyond the seas.) In the mission field the white evangelists created a small group of profoundly committed Christians, some of whom died for their faith in the manner of the ancient martyrs. But, as a modern African writer put it:

The African intellectual who came out of the missionary school was not only literate, but also he was a changed being. He looked about himself and saw nothing but evil. He saw his "heathen" brothers singing and dancing and drinking and loving in pursuit, as they thought of the Good Life, and he shook his head in pity. For suddenly these things had become ugly and sinful. No wonder, for, in his school days, this Black intellectual was subjected to teaching materials chosen or prepared with an eye to making them effective instruments for the continuous absorption of the Christian religion. Not only that, but in reading lessons, for example, while the ways of life of the peoples of Western countries were praised in glowing terms, and suitable tribute paid to their national heroes, selections from the oral traditions of the Africans were mostly ones that painted their past black, and the moral, always strongly implied or even overtly stated, was that they must be grateful for the coming of the White man who has led them out of their dark, dangerous, vile and sinful past. The process of alienation had begun. . . .[12]

Christianity, moreover, owed much of its impact to the prestige of white arms and white skills. In 1851 the British suffered a minor but humiliating defeat at the hand of Sotho warriors. This reverse wrecked Britain's local military reputation for the time being. The Sotho success also checked the advance of Christianity. Many Sotho including the bulk of the aristocracy, reverted to paganism, and the French made good their losses at a slow pace. Nevertheless, the Sotho benefited a good deal from missionary contact. A fair number of Sotho learned reading and writing and other skills. The Sotho rulers effectively used the Paris Mission Society as a propaganda agency to plead the Sotho cause abroad. The chiefs employed French missionaries as interpreters, secretaries, and as diplomatic advisers. To speak—as some have done—of a Christian Revolution may perhaps be overstating the missionaries' success. But the Sotho response to the Western challenge did represent a successful instance of selective adaptation, a solution fraught with profound consequences for the future of sub-Saharan Africa.

NOTES

1. Balandier, *La Vie Quotidienne au Congo*, pp. 261–268.
2. Hair, "Africanism: The Freetown Contribution," especially pp. 524–526.
3. Hair, p. 524–526.
4. Robert W. July, *The Origins of Modern African Thought: Its Development in West Africa During the Nineteenth and Twentieth Centuries* (New York, 1967), p. 71. This is the standard work on the subject from which the following has largely been drawn.
5. Quoted by July, *The Origins of Modern African Thought*, p. 160.
6. David Nicol *ed., Black Nationalism in Africa 1867: Extracts from the Political, Educational, Scientific and Medical Writings of Africanus Horton* (New York, 1969), p. 33.
7. Nicol, p. 46–47.
8. Edward W. Blyden, *Christiantiy, Islam and the Negro Race* (London, 1887). See also the excellent biography by Hollis R. Lynch, *Edward Wilmot Blyden, Pan African Negro Patriot, 1832–1912* (London, 1967).
9. Edward Gibbon, *The History of the Decline and Fall of the Roman Empire,* ed., J. B. Bury (New York, 1946), vol. 1, p. 170.
10. See Robert W. July "Nineteenth Century Negritude: Edward W. Blyden," *Journal of African History,* vol. 5 no. 1 (1964), pp. 73–86.
11. Cited in Catherine W. Mackintosh, *Coillard of the Zambesi: The Lives of François and Christina Coillard, of the Paris Missionary Society, in South and Central Africa (1858–1904)* (London, 1909), p. 46.
12. Daniel P. Kunene "Deculturation: The African Writer's Response," *Africa Today,* vol. 5, no. 4 (Aug.-Sept. 1966), p. 20.

Chapter 34

Africa at the Beginning of the Nineteenth Century: A Summing Up and an Epilogue

PROBLEMS OF PERIODIZATION

History, wrote a bored sceptic, is just one damn thing after another! We can easily sympathize with him for nothing is harder to comprehend than an endless stream of events, full of cross currents and intermingling eddies. But in order to make themselves intelligible, historians have to tell a story. Hence they must—so to speak—divide a gushing stream into little pools; they split their books into chapters, delimit more or less arbitrarily selected periods in order to make their tale more effective and emphasize striking developments.

Periodization unfortunately becomes progressively more difficult as historians have to deal with more extensive periods in time, larger regions in space, and less reliable data in the realm of ideas. Historians of Africa have not managed to remain exempt from these troubles. But they have managed to work out quite satisfactory systems of regional periodization. No writer has as yet worked out a universally accepted scheme, applicable to the subcontinent as a whole.

Marxist historiography postulates a general scheme that diffeitiates between tribalism, feudalism, and capitalism. This division, drawn from the European past, unfortunately raises as many problems as it answers. Were the people of Barotseland subjects of a feudal kingdom? There is no easy reply. Barotseland under the Kololo monarchs, for instance, had a clearly defined ruling stratum made up of warlike invaders from the south. There was sharp social differentiation. There was an elaborate system of rule, of ranks and grades, and of national councils that reminded early British district commissioners in later years of their own kingship, their House of Commons and

483

their House of Lords in London. Nevertheless there were many differences. The Barotse slaves were not like English villeins; Barotse land rights had little in common with feudal tenure in Europe. In Barotseland there were no knights in armor, no literate clergymen, no landless folk comparable to the mercenaries, wage laborers, or wandering scholars of medieval Europe.

The so-called "Houses" which made up many states in the Niger delta present similar difficulties to Marxist periodizers. The "Houses" acted as trading corporations; they accumulated capital; they made profits. In this sense the "House" might be described as an example of incipient capitalism, but it had traditional functions, and in some ways resembled a medieval guild. It helped to maintain law and order; it played a ritual role; each provided some form of social security for its members; each acted as a burial society; each operated also as a military unit, being required to equip at least one war canoe for the navy of its respective city.[1] A Nigerian "House," in this sense, was quite unlike a capitalist firm, and we cannot neatly arrange African institutions into convenient pigeonholes labelled tribalist, feudalist, capitalist.

Basil Davidson, a British writer, has worked out a different system of periodization. His cycle begins with the Early Iron Age, which started in Africa at Meröe during the fourth century B.C. and ended about 1000 A.D. By this time two great empires—Ghana and Kanem-Bornu—had come into existence in the Western Sudan, each with great market centers and incipient cities. The Early Iron Age, according to Davidson, was succeeded by an "Intermediate Period" lasting roughly from 1000 to 1300. Then came the "Mature Iron Age," during which Africa experienced the peak of its pre-European development. This era came to an end, roughly speaking, about 1600, though there were considerable regional variations. The period from 1600 to the present Davidson calls the "Age of Transition." During these long centuries Iron Age Africa grappled with new difficulties and developed new political solutions, but nevertheless increasingly fell behind the Euro-American world that moved rapidly into an age of science, mechanical invention, and industrialization. Late in the eighteenth century the Atlantic slave trade became sufficiently important to shape much of West Africa's development. During the nineteenth century the greatest part of Africa plunged ever more deeply into a crisis that derived partly from the inability of Iron Age ideologies and modes of action to cope with problems of foreign pressure and future growth.[2]

Davidson's system of periodization has a clear ideological purpose. He is determined to finish once and for all "with the ideological servitudes of our racialist past," and he considers the colonial period as "a prolonged interlude of destructive subjection and foreign occupation whose main achievement was not to carry Africa into a new world . . . but merely to complete the dismantlement of the old."[3] The colonial epoch is not therefore regarded as of sufficient importance to be alloted a period of its own. It becomes no more than the tail end for the "Age of Transition."

We ourselves do not share Davidson's assessment of colonialism. Neither do we find much utility in his fourfold division of African history, which merely obscures the complexities of Africa's past. Stone-age cultures, to give one example, continued to exist during the Iron Age. The Benin bronzes rank among the masterpieces of world sculpture and give evidence of remarkable technical and artistic achievement. Yet the finest of these sculptures were probably cast some time around the twelfth century or even earlier. According to Davidson's scheme, they would fall into the "Intermediate Period," not into the "Mature Iron Age," where they would properly seem to belong. The terms "Age of Transition" or "Intermediate Period" are both question-begging and vague. All ages in history are ages of transition. The word "transition," moreover, raises the question: transition from what?

Much of Africa's chronology remains uncertain, except for the more recent past. No single set of periods fits the whole of Africa. Historians of each region, conscious of Africa's immense ethnic diversity, would therefore be better advised to design their own frameworks of time division capable of fitting local circumstances. We have not attempted to construct a chronology applicable to the whole subcontinent, and the chapter headings used in this book were worked out for the sake of convenience rather than for the purpose of laying down a groundwork of universal applicability. Instead, we now propose to borrow from the anthropologists and group African societies in terms of size and function, rather than timespans.

AFRICAN STATELESS SOCIETIES

The keynote of political organization in precolonial Africa was diversity. Nothing is more mistaken than the conventional European view that regarded the Africans of old as an undifferentiated mass of savages, subject to the rule of bloodthirsty chiefs and superstitious witchdoctors. Cruelty and bloodshed there was indeed. It is a mistake to romanticize the "good old days," in Africa or anywhere else. But as Elizabeth Colson, an American anthropologist, states, "the assumed uniformity of savage life is but a foreign myth."[4] An African Aristotle intent on studying the political institutions extant on his continent at the beginning of the last century would have found as many varieties as his Greek namesake.

The simplest form was perhaps the band whose members made their living from hunting and the collection of food. By the beginning of the last century this form of organization had become relatively unimportant. In the remoter regions of South Africa and the Rift Valley small groups of people still roamed through the bush in search of game and edible wild plants. The band provided for common action on the part of groups large enough to maintain the daily round of subsistence. The main decisions of a band revolved round the questions of how to exploit local resources to their best advantage and how to plan a common itinerary. Bands within one region might form alliances; their members were likely to be linked by kinship ties enabling men and women to move fairly easily from one band to another. There were no formal longterm links between bands, and the headman of each group wielded only very limited powers. Occasionally, one band would fight another in order to defend its hunting grounds or in order to encroach on the territory of another, but such localized conflicts did not lead to large scale conflict or to the development of larger polities.

Much more important than such bands were the neighborhood groups described by Colson as "non-centralized political systems." Stateless societies of this kind were to be found among a great number of Iron Age people, both hoe farmers and herdsmen. No one knows the precise figures, but it seems likely that at the beginning of the last century a considerable proportion of Africans did not heed the word of permanent chiefs, but lived in communities where power remained temporary and dispersed. The most loosely organized societies consisted of amorphous polities of the kind to be found among the Tonga in what is now southern Zambia. The Tonga had no permanent political offices. There were no great distinctions of wealth. Richer and more successful men would wield a certain amount of influence, but there was no way of mobilizing an army. Hence amorphous societies could be conquered fairly easily by more powerful strangers.

Other stateless societies were organized in descent groups. Anthropologists refer to "lineages" consisting of people who trace their relationship to one another through descent from a common ancestor. "Segmentary lineages," on the other hand, are composed of groups who use the ideology of kinship in dealing with each other. Lineages often became responsible for protecting their kind and exacting vengeance from offenders who had caused harm to a lineage member. Systems of this kind were found in many parts of Africa, for instance in the southern Sudan, in northern Uganda, in northern Kenya, in Somalia, in central Nigeria, and elsewhere. Local communities might quarrel among themselves. But as soon as disputes arose with outsiders, the community would temporarily unite. Leaders might take over to repel an enemy assault or direct a raid. Such chiefs, however, had no permanent power. As soon as the emergency ended the people's precarious unity would disappear, and a man who had spoken for a hundred thousand yesterday might represent no more than a few hundred on the day after.

Age-sets provided for a somewhat higher degree of political organization. Age-sets consisted of men born at about the same time, who were formally initiated into a kind of all male corporation. Each age-set had its own name, insignia, songs, and dances. The members residing in one particular district formed a local chapter. Men remained in the same age-set throughout their lives, but graduated successively from initiate to warrior, and finally from warrior to elder. The chapters regulated most day-to-day activities, and the chapters in turn formed part of a wider hierarchy of age grades. The younger warriors raided cattle from hostile neighbors and also provided a readily available reserve for defense. The senior men acted as the executive arm of the elders. The elders in turn exercised ritual powers, adjudicated in difficult matters, and decided on general policy. Under the age-set system political office, so to speak, was collectivized. There were political distinctions, but each man would rise successively from a relatively lowly station to the position of elder, together with his age-mates. Social life was thus strictly regulated; the community could mobilize relatively large military forces; but no man had a hereditary claim to rank or office, and none could call himself a ruler.

AFRICAN STATE ORGANIZATIONS

African state organizations differed even more widely in their origin and forms of governance than stateless societes. Some states rested solely upon armed conquest. Warlike bands with specialized military techniques, such as the Ndebele and the Ngoni from southern Africa, thus terrorized great stretches of land now comprised within the borders of Rhodesia, Zambia, Malawi, Tanzania, and Mozambique. The invaders fashioned their own polities with spear, shield, knobkerry, and gun. They rustled their neighbors' cattle and captured their boys and women, who were incorporated into the conquering host. The communities on the march rapidly snow-balled, and their captains faced the problem of how to maintain political cohesion. Many of these warlords founded new territorial kingdoms that depended on farming and war. In addition, trading bands sometimes staked out their own principalities, either by slow infiltration or by outright conquest. Traders were particularly well placed for political aggrandizement in regions where they alone had firearms and where the indigenous backwoodsmen wielded only lances and bows. Early in the nineteenth century, Chokwe bands from Angola overran much of the Lunda country in the interior, trading or raiding, whichever yielded most profit. Later on, Yao adventurers from eastern Tanzania extended their sway into northern Mozambique and eastern Malawi. Swahili-speaking merchants armed with muskets and rifles likewise established themselves as lords over the littoral of Lake Nyasa and elsewhere, extorting tribute over their subjects and establishing local mercantile monopolies.

Kingdoms and principalities of whatever size suffered, however, from many weaknesses. In most parts of east, central, and southern Africa the court was not tied to a permanent site. As long as there was plenty of land and as long as the tribesmen could make their living by shifting agriculture, rulers could not easily reward officials and followers by gifts of landed estate. Landed estates attached to particular offices appear to have existed only in the Ganda and the Lozi kingdoms, where special conditions encouraged generations of men to till the same fields. In most parts of Africa, however, slash-and-burn agriculture prevailed. Many rulers would disperse their wives and children through a number of royal villages, and migrate with their personal retinue from one residence to another, as Charlemagne, in the medieval Frankish empire, had moved from one *Pfalz* (fortified royal residence) to another.

The material culture of the people varied a great deal. In most parts of Africa, the tillers lacked wagons and plows; fighting men did not wear armor; village intellectuals could not store their knowledge in the form of books. Government, generally speaking, was as unspecialized as the farming economy, and the agricultural surplus available to rulers was limited. Kings might reward supporters by particular favors. Among cattle-keeping peoples, the gift or loan or herds might help to cement the allegiance of powerful followers. Elsewhere particular groups might acquire special rights regarding fishing sites, or other privileges. By and large, however, officials depended on their share in the tribute paid by the subjects or in the wealth derived from small labor dues. Kings might establish monopolies in trading ivory, guns, copper, and other commodities suitable for long-distance commerce. They also served as the linchpin in complex systems of tributary exchange. Nevertheless their mode of life did not differ greatly from that of their subjects. Capital might be accumulated in the shape of increasing herds, but otherwise there were few opportunities for storing wealth, and generosity was adjudged a king's supreme virtue. Under such conditions, boundaries would fluctuate greatly; polygamous institutions tended to multiply claimants to the royal throne and thereby perhaps contributed to political instability; territorial magnates were always liable to assert their power against distant rulers; even at best, governments found great difficulty in enforcing more than a token allegiance from communities living at a great distance from the center of power.

In West Africa, on the other hand, there were many more complex kingdoms. In the savannah country farmers could combine animal husbandry with agriculture and cultivators were able to till their ancestral fields over long periods. Residential stability was encouraged in many areas by the development of economic tree crops like the kola nut and the oil palm. Tillers produced sufficient food to sustain cities dependent on trade and specialized craft industries, as well as farming. There were elaborate guild and trade associations with political and ritual as well as economic functions. There were regulated market and managed currencies. Local products were traded on a large scale; in addition caravans carried slaves, gold, and other commodities over long distances. The population in many parts of West Africa was fairly dense. In some areas good arable land was becoming in short supply, so that rulers could reward important followers with valuable estates in return for loyal service.

The impact of trade and of more developed modes of agricultural production produced a great variety of responses and resulted in a great diversity of state organizations. The Ashanti state in the middle portion of what is now Ghana was a confederacy of towns under the leadership of the Asantehene, the lord of Kumasi. Each town was governed by a council with representatives from all great lineages within its confines. Conciliar rule was subject to a great many checks and balances and commoners had well defined rights. Kumasi's over-lordship in turn was limited in many different ways. The Asantehene could call on his subjects for support in foreign wars; he received subsidies from the various states, but could neither enforce direct taxation nor appoint the various officials in the towns.

In Dahomey, on the other hand, power had congealed into nearly absolute rule. The king appointed the more important officials throughout the state. He enforced his authority through a network of informers, a well-drilled standing army, and bands of executioners. There was an elaborate court, maintained by fines, by confiscations, by the spoils of trade and of war, which accrued to him in his role as chief merchant. The monarch of Dahomey maintained a rigid control over the economy. He used his power to maintain traditional social differentiations. The exercise of royal sovereignty in some ways served as a break on production. Under a dignitary such as King Gezo, sugar, coffee, rice, and tobacco could not be cultivated around Whydah. There was a strict sumptuary legislation of the kind customary in medieval Europe: "A caboceer may not alter his house, wear European shoes, employ a spitoon-holder, carry an umbrella without leave, spread over his bed a counterpane, which comfort is confined to princes, mount a hammock, or use a chair in his own home. . . ."[5] The Dahomey ruling strata derived power from commerce and tribute; new conquests would add to both sources of revenue. But unlike a modern administrative bourgeoisie in present-day Africa, the lords of Dahomey could call on supernatural sanctions, which in turn were strengthened by human sacrifice; hence kings like Gezo aroused the ire of European missionaries for religious, humanitarian, and economic reasons alike.

The most powerful kingdoms, however, were found in the savannah belt, where horses and camels could be used alike for trade and war. By the early nineteenth century most of the older states in the western savannah had fallen under the sway of various Fulani overlords. The loose union of Fulani states subject to the rulers of Sokoto formed the largest territorial state found in sub-Saharan Africa during this period. The Fulani states were important centers of Islamic culture; there were learned divines; there were literate officials, so that in many ways a nineteenth century European would have found himself quite at home in a state like Sokoto.

Despite these great varieties in the political order, most African societies had certain basic institutions that continued to function whatever fate might befall the rulers. The vast majority of Africans made their living from the land, and depended on the help of their kinsmen. As Colson puts it: "Kingdoms might rise and fall, but lineages or other kin groups continued to care for their members in illness or distress. They provided protection against enemies and a measure of internal discipline. Where overall political organization was weak, lineages might assume important political functions. Where overall political organization was strong, lineages might continue as corporations controlling property rights in land, stock, or political and religious office."[6]

THE WIDENING CULTURE GAP

African societies gave a measure of security to their recognized members. Their members could meet a great variety of challenges and live meaningful lives. All indigenous societies nevertheless suffered from serious weaknesses that subsequently prevented them from stemming the European inrush. By the beginning of the nineteenth century even the most developed and complex African states had been left behind European developments. Africa, Muslim or pagan, had no part in any of the great movements that revolutionized European thought—the Renaissance, the Reformation, the Enlightenment, the scientific discoveries, the great eras of Western music, literature, and philosophy. No African kingdom had any share in the industrial and agricultural changes that completely altered the structure of European life during the eighteenth and nineteenth centuries.

Worse still, from the African's point of view, the industrial and military gap between Africa and the Euro-American world was rapidly widening. In the sixteenth century a sailing vessel from Mombasa or Kilwa could still make a respectable showing compared with a Portuguese caravel. By the start of the last century, however, the finest Zanzibari-built dhow looked puny when compared with one of Nelson's massive three-deckers, with its complicated sailing tackle and its massed guns. By the 1860s most advanced naval designers in Europe and America were creating armored, steam driven vessels having no equal anywhere else in the world, and depending on an elaborate technology and a great scientific tradition that no African state could match.

The more powerful African empires, moreover, were devoid of any sense of national unity. Whatever their degree of economic development, "rigid stratification marked by jural and social exclusion of various types . . . (was) widespread in traditional polities established and maintained by the forcible domination of one ethnic stock over others . . . Imperial states inevitably . . . (magnified) these structural and cultural differences and segregations of rulers and ruled. . . ."[7] Nothing indeed would be more mistaken than to speak of "primitive" communism or human equality in the precolonial African states. Such constructions are no more than a nostalgia for a mythical past, "organic, agrarian, instinctual," variously located by its votaries in "18th century England, the Middle Ages or primitive tribal life, but usually having overtones of the Biblical paradise."[8] On the contrary, a large number of precolonial African societies were marked by inter-ethnic and social division, by rigid segregation between the rulers and the ruled, by coercion in its rawest form. In this respect there was no distinction between technologically backward and more advanced people.

For instance, the Ndebele (Matabele) who depended on a fairly primitive form of agriculture, largely oriented their society toward war. They incorporated their prisoners and their subjects in a common framework of age regiments, so that victory in battle in turn strengthened the conquering host. Ndebele society was organized in a rigid hierarchy of endogamous castes in which the ruling Zansi comprised perhaps 15 percent of the people; the Enlha, an intermediate group composed of Sotho and Tswana, may have numbered about 25 percent; and the subjugated indigenous people in what is now the western part of Rhodesia, the Holi, embraced possibly some 60 percent. Intermarriage was forbidden. Most of the military officers and political heads were derived from the Zansi caste, which looked with disdain upon their subordinates. In Ruanda, the Tutsi conquerors established an equally stratified regime. The Bantu-speaking Hutu labored as serfs; they could neither marry into the ruling groups nor hold any important office. The more advanced Islamic states of the Sudan were marked by similar divisions. Even revolutionary regimes in time merely reproduced the inequalities of old. When the Fulani conquered the older Hausa states of Katsina, Kano, and Zaria in the first decade of the last century, the new rulers simply replaced the existing aristocracies, and in turn imposed severe labor dues, taxes, and levies on their subjects.

Africa was not only poorly equipped in a technological sense and politically divided, the peoples of Africa were also incapable of resisting the ravages of the slave trade. The traffic in human beings arose, so to speak, from Africa's perennial balance of payments problem. As Africans had grown more used to imported goods such as muskets, gunpowder, cloth, beads, knives, and hatchets, they stepped up the export of homegrown products. Ivory and gold, however, could not be produced in sufficient quantities to pay for all the commodities Africans desired from foreigners overseas, be they Muslim or Christian. Cash crops like Guinea pepper, kola nuts, and palm oil could not be produced on a sufficiently large scale to meet the demand for imported wares. Africans thus exported black manpower.

The abolition of the slave trade owed little or nothing to indigenous potentates.

The initiative came almost entirely from the Christian world. Western abolitionists, acting for a variety of humanitarian, political, economic, and religious motives, gradually put pressure on their respective governments to abolish the slave trade and later on to put an end to the contraband in human beings. Humanitarian intervention, however, foreshadowed colonialism of the paternalist variety. Western paternalism partly derived from the Africans' inability to cope with the problems occasioned by the slave trade and by the remorseless advance of the gunpowder frontier from the coastal to the inland regions of Africa. Western humanitarians meant to replace the commerce in slaves by legitimate trade. But many white and also many Europeanized black dealers, such as the French- English- and Portuguese-speaking creoles on the west coast of Africa, looked to the imperial power to defend their interests. The development of Western commerce therefore foreshadowed subsequent colonial regimes. So did the advance of the missionary frontier, for an educated black African was more likely to gain a position as a clerk, as a teacher, or as an evangelist under European than under indigenous auspices. In certain respects, the imperial powers tended to level down customary distinctions of rank within the territories under their sway. Imperial rule thus appealed to literate black Christians of lowly origins, and black people with a white schooling commonly became the allies of particular European powers.

EUROPE IN AFRICA BY THE FIRST HALF OF THE NINETEENTH CENTURY

By the first half of the nineteenth century, Africa was still a continent of outposts from the white man's point of view. European doctors did not as yet know the causes of malaria, sleeping sicknesses, yellow fever, and other diseases. Much of the interior remained inaccessible, a land of mystery. Nevertheless, the whites had penetrated to some degree into the temperate zones of Africa, and the pace of advance steadily increased. In 1830, French soldiers first planted the tricolor on Algerian soil. Muslim guerrillas waged a bitter fight against the Christian invaders, but the number of European settlers was beginning to increase. In 1837, the French appointed Thomas-Robert Bugeaud, a onetime grenadier in Napoleon's army, to command their forces in Algeria. Bugeaud turned out to be a brilliant soldier, and after ten years of bitter clashes, Abd-el Kader, the greatest of Algerian leaders, finally surrendered. By that time, 100,000 whites had already made their homes in Algeria, where European colonization was destined to bring about a social revolution of far-reaching consequences.

In West Africa, French power centered on the settlements in Senegal. Senegal, like West Africa as a whole, proved unsuitable for white farmers. The country formed part of the soldier's and merchant's frontier, where European firms and French-speaking mulattos dominated the economic scene. The colony began to acquire some economic importance during the middle of the nineteenth century, when peanuts became a profitable crop. African farmers successfully adjusted their production to the new demand, and exports of peanuts expanded in a phenomenal fashion. But the colony suffered from serious political problems. French governors found many difficulties in protecting traders up river along the Senegal against the exactions of Moorish people such as the Brakna and the Trarza. The French had to cope with the problems occasioned by a turbulent frontier, an extensive border zone where conflict prevailed. The ambitions of French soldiers avid for glory and the desire for security expressed by French and Franco-African merchants trading in the interior combined with pressure exerted on the French by Muslim lords to impel the French into a vigorously expansionist policy.

British power in West Africa was likewise largely confined to a few ports and to a navigable river route. By 1857, the Union Jack fluttered over the entire navigable portion of the Gambia, but malaria infected the river valley, and the colony exported little, except some peanuts. Further south, the British held Sierra Leone, with the magnificent port of Freetown, an important base for the operations carried on by the Royal Navy against the slave trade, as well as a center for trade in palm oil and peanuts. Freetown, with its shops and newspaper offices, became one of the few places where a modified form of the British Victorian tradition struck root in Africa. Its economy slowly expanded; Sierra Leone Creoles, English-speaking Africans of mixed origin, pushed outward along the coast and inward into the hinterland. They came as traders, clerks, government employees, mission teachers, sometimes even as farmers—but always as conscious or unconscious agents of British expansion.

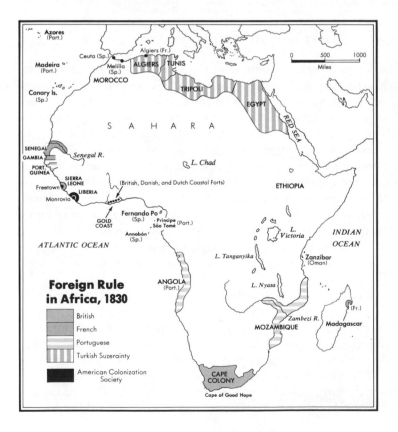

Foreign Rule in Africa, 1830

British
French
Portuguese
Turkish Suzerainty
American Colonization Society

The bulk of Britain's West African commerce, however, centered on lower Guinea. Along the Gold Coast the British supported the Fanti of the littoral against the Ashanti of the interior. The Ashanti, however, were formidable fighters. For a time the forest belt proved almost as effective a barrier against British redcoats, as it did against the Muslim cavalry from the savannah in the north. Sir Charles Macarthy, a British governor, was slain on the field of battle, and his skull ended as a royal drinking cup at the royal court of Ashanti. In the long run, however, British power was in the ascendant. The British merchants in control of the coastal fort found a governor of exceptional ability in the person of George Maclean, who steadily built up British influence on the coast. He succeeded so well that in 1843 the British Colonial Office decided to resume control of the coastal forts which for the previous fifteen years had been left to the administration of British traders.

Further east, the British carried on a considerable commerce in palm oil and other tropical products with the small African city states along the Niger Delta. In 1851, a British naval force captured Lagos, British sailors suppressed the traffic in slaves, and British merchants settled to conduct "legitimate trade." By the middle of the nineteenth century, the British slave squadrons, assisted by American and French men-of-war, had accomplished much of its task. Slavers now dreaded the sight of the White Ensign (the British naval flag) on the horizon; but humanitarian endeavor, combined with commercial interests, created its own form of expansionism, and a turbulent maritime frontier encouraged the British to extend their influence.

Portuguese power in West Africa was largely confined to a few possessions in what is now Angola. Here Brazilian influence was strong. In Luanda, the most important Portuguese city in Angola, the settlers lived very much like Brazilians. They cooked in the Brazilian manner, built in the Brazilian way, and sometimes even talked of uniting Angola with Brazil. The Portuguese settlers, however, remained too weak to cut their connections with Portugal. Portugal, in turn, was too poor to govern effectively the vast areas that it claimed. Portuguese power in Angola thus was confined largely to a few ports and trading posts, surrounded by ill-defined zones of influence. A few bold frontiersmen travelled far into the interior, but the bulk of the inland trade remained in the hands of indigenous black or Luso-African merchants.

While the Portuguese colonists in Africa remained numerically weak, and politically dependent on the mother country, South Africa had become the home of a vigorous white community, the largest on the African continent. Britons and Boers alike pressed upon the Bantu-speaking tribes along the turbulent frontier of white settlement. English and Afrikaans-speaking whites both quarreled, or cooperated with the British imperial government. By the middle of the nineteenth century, the Union Jack fluttered over the Cape Colony and Natal. But the process of devolving power to the local whites had already gone a long way. The lands beyond the Orange and Vaal rivers were largely controlled by emigrant Boers. The British had become convinced that they could no longer control these trekkers; and in 1852, the imperial government, by the Sand River Convention, formally guaranteed to the Transvaalers the right to run their own affairs.

In the same year, London issued an Order in Council which gave to the Cape Colony its own legislature. On paper, the British and the Boers greatly differed in their approach to the "native" franchise. The Transvaal constitution specifically stated that there should be no equality in church or state as between whites and blacks. The more liberal franchise adopted in the Cape was "color blind," in that there were no racial qualifications for the suffrage. In actual practice, however, the balance of power in the Cape, in the autonomous Boer republics of the Orange Free State and Transvaal, as well as in Natal, came to rest with the indigenous whites. Outside purely African areas such as Basutoland and Swaziland, the colonists' local supremacy became unchallenged.

In East Africa, again, the white men's territorial stakes as yet remained small. The Portuguese held a number of scattered forts and settlements on the coast and along the lower Zambezi Valley. They had, however, failed in their endeavor to control the fortunes of the hinterland through great *prazos*, or estates occupied by white land owners. The *prazos* were by now commonly held by Goanese, or by Portuguese-speaking half-breeds, whose governance differed little from that of indigenous chiefs. By the middle of the nineteenth century, the force of Portuguese colonialism seemed exhausted. Some Portuguese indeed suggested that the empire might have to be liquidated altogether. Nevertheless, the Portuguese tenaciously maintained their claims. Portugal recovered some of its previous prosperity, and schemes for partitioning the Portuguese empire, later put forward by Portugal's European rivals, all came to nought.

North of the Portuguese sphere, Arab influence remained supreme. By the middle of the nineteenth century, the Sultanate of Zanzibar carried on an extensive commerce in slaves, cloves, and ivory. Muslim merchants penetrated inland to Lake Nyasa where they spread a modified form of their faith, as well as a knowledge of the Swahili tongue. Zanzibari power, however, rested on slender foundations. Militarily the country was in no position to resist pressure from the British navy or the growing demand for the abolition of the traffic in slaves. Politically, Zanzibar became more and more dependent on Great Britain. London would have liked to do business with a stable self-governing sultanate, wedded to free trade and leaving the British free of direct administrative responsibilities. In practice, however, the British were forced to interfere to an ever-increasing extent with the country's affairs in order to wipe out the slave trade.

Militarily and economically, there was an ever-widening gap between the major European powers on the one hand, and even the most powerful black kingdoms on the other. There was growing tension on the turbulent frontiers along the fringes of white colonization in Africa. Missionaries and merchants in various parts of Africa kept calling for protection from the real or supposed exactions of indigenous potentates. Finally, there was the apparently irresistible pressure for what might be called "humanitarian imperialism," for intervention against slave traders and robber chieftains. The first outlines of Africa's colonial regimes were beginning to take shape. In time the whites would dominate the continent.

NOTES

1. For a detailed description see Ebiegberi Joe Alagoa, *The Small Brave City State: A History of the Nembe-Brass in the Niger Delta* (Madison, 1964), especially pp. 11–13.

2. Basil Davidson, *Can We Write African History?* African Studies Center, University of California, Los Angeles. Occasional Paper No. 1, November 1965.

3. Davidson, pp. 18–19.

4. This summary is largely based on Elizabeth Colson, "African Society at the Time of the Scramble," in Gann and Duignan, *Colonialism in Africa, 1870–1960*, vol. 1, pp. 27–65.

5. Sir Richard F. Burton, *A Mission to Gelele, King of Dahome* (London, 1893) vol. 1, p. 119.

6. Colson, "African Society at the Time of the Scramble," p. 53.

7. M. G. Smith "Pluralism in Precolonial African Societies," in Leo Kuper and M. G. Smith, eds., *Pluralism in Africa* (Berkeley, 1969) p. 128. This essay is the most detailed and authoritative study on the subject.

8. David Lodge, "Utopia and Criticism: The Radical Longing for Paradise," *Encounter*, April 1969, p. 74.

Bibliography

Abir, Mordechai. *Ethiopia The Era of Princes: The Challenge of Islam and the Re-Unification of the Christian Empire, 1769–1855.* New York, 1968.

Adloff, Richard. *West Africa: The French-speaking Nations Yesterday and Today.* New York, 1965.

Ajayi, J. F. A. *Christian Missions in Nigeria, 1841–1891: The Making of a New Elite.* London, 1965.

Ajayi, J. F. A. and Ian Espie, eds. *A Thousand Years of West African History: A Handbook for Teachers and Students.* Ibadan, 1965.

Ajayi, J. F. A. and Robert S. Smith. *Yoruba Warfare in the Nineteenth Century.* Cambridge, Eng., 1964.

Akindélé, Adolphe and C. Aguessy. *Contribution à l'Étude de l'Histoire de l'Ancien Royaume de Porto Novo.* Dakar, 1953.

Akinjogbin, I. A. *Dahomey and Its Neighbors, 1708–1818.* Cambridge, 1967.

Alagoa, Ebiegberi Joe. *The Small Brave City-State; a History of Nembe-Brass in the Niger Delta.* Madison, Wisc. 1964.

al-Bakri. *Description de l'Afrique Septentrionale.* Alger, 1913.

Alberto, Manuel Simoes and Francisco A. Toscano. *O Oriente Africano Português: Síntese Cronológica da História de Moçambique.* Lourenço Marques, 1942.

Alexandre, Pierre. *Langues et Langage en Afrique Noire.* Paris, 1967.

Alimen, Henriette. *The Prehistory of Africa.* (Translated by Alan Houghton.) London, 1957.

al-Kati, Mahmud. *El-Fettach Tarikh.* (Translated by Octave Houdas and Maurice Delafosse.) Paris, 1913.

Allan, William. *The African Husbandman.* New York, 1965.

Allan, William. *Studies in African Land Usage in Northern Rhodesia.* Cape Town, 1949.

Alldridge, Thomas J. *A Transformed Colony: Sierra Leone, As It Was, and As It Is, Its Progress, Peoples, Native Customs, and Undeveloped Wealth.* London, 1910.

497

Anene, Joseph C. and Godfrey N. Brown, eds. *African in the Nineteenth and Twentieth Centuries* . . . Ibadan, 1967.

Anstey, Roger. *Britain and the Congo in the Nineteenth Century.* Oxford, 1962.

Arberry, A. J., ed. *Religion and the Middle East: Three Religions in Concord and Conflict.* London, 1969.

Arcin, André. *Histoire de la Guinée Française.* Paris, 1911.

Ardrey, Robert. *African Genesis: A Personal Investigation into the Animal Origins and Nature of Man.* New York, 1967.

Argyle, William Johnson. *The Fon of Dahomey: A History and Ethnography of the Old Kingdom.* Oxford, 1966.

Arkell, Anthony J. *A History of the Sudan from the Earliest Times to 1821.* London, 1955.

Ashton, T. S. *The Industrial Revolution 1760–1830.* London, 1948.

Atger, Paul. *La France en Côte d'Ivoire de 1843 à 1893: Cinquante Ans d'Hésitations Politiques et Commerciales.* Dakar, 1962.

Axelson, Eric Victor. *Portuguese in South-east Africa, 1600–1700.* Johannesburg, 1960.

Axelson, Eric Victor. *South-east Africa, 1488–1530.* London, 1940.

Ayandele, Emmanuel A. *The Missionary Impact on Modern Nigeria, 1842–1914: A Political and Social Analysis.* London, 1966.

Ba, Amadou Hampaté and Jacques Daget. *L'Empire Peul du Maçina, 1818–1853.* Paris, 1962.

Bacon, Sir Reginald H. S. *Benin: The City of Blood.* New York, 1897.

Baikie, W. B. *Narrative of an Exploring Voyage up the Rivers Kwora and Binue (commonly known as the Niger and Tsadda) in 1854.* London, 1856.

Balandier, Georges. *La Vie Quotidienne au Royaume de Kongo du XVIe au XVIIIe Siècle.* Paris, 1965.

Balmer, William Turnbull. *A History of the Akan Peoples of the Gold Coast.* London, 1925.

Barbour, Nevill, ed. *A Survey of North West Africa (The Maghrib).* London, 1962.

Barnes, John A. *Politics in a Changing Society: A Political History of the Fort Jameson Ngoni.* London, 1954.

Barth, Heinrich. *Travels and Discoveries in North and Central Africa* . . . *1849–1855.* London, 1857–1858, 5 vols.

Bastide, Roger. *Les Amériques Noires: Les Civilisations Africaines dans le Nouveau* Monde. Paris, 1967.

Baumann, Herman and D. Westermann. *Les Peuples et les Civilisations de L'Afrique.* (Translated by L. Homburger). Paris, 1948.

Beazley, C. Raymond. *Prince Henry the Navigator: The Hero of Portugal and of Modern Discovery, 1394–1460 A.D.* New York, 1897.

Beckingham, Charles F. and G. W. B. Huntingford (trans. and eds.). *Some Records of Ethiopia, 1593–1646.* London, 1954.

Beier, Ulli, ed. *Introduction to African Literature: An Anthology of Critical Writing from "Black Orpheus."* Evanston, Ill., 1967.

Beier, Ulli and Gerald Moore, eds. *Modern Poetry from Africa.* Baltimore, 1963.

Bell, Sir H. H. J. *The History, Trade, Resources and Present Condition of the Gold Coast Settlement.* Liverpool, 1893.

Berbain, Simone. *Études sur la Traite des Noirs au Golfe de Guinée: le Comptoir Français de Juda (Ouidah) au XVIIIe Siecle.* Paris, 1942.

Biobaku, S. O. *The Egba and Their Neighbours, 1842–1872.* Oxford, 1957.

Birmingham, David. *The Portuguese Conquest of Angola.* London, 1965.

Birmingham, David. *Trade and Conflict in Angola: The Mbundu and Their Neighbours under the Influence of the Portuguese, 1483–1790.* Oxford, 1966.

Bishop, W. A. and J. D. Clark, eds. *Background to Evolution in Africa.* Chicago, 1967.

Blake, John William. *European Beginnings in West Africa, 1454–1578: A Survey of the First Century of White Enterprise in West Africa, with Special Emphasis upon the Rivalry of the Great Powers.* London, 1937.

Blake, John William. *Europeans in West Africa, 1450–1560: Documents . . .* London, 1942.

Blet, Henri. *Histoire de la Colonisation Française.* Grenoble, 1946–1950. 3 vols.

Blyden, Edward Wilmot. *Christianity, Islam and the Negro Race.* Edinburgh, 1967.

Boahen, A. Adu. *Britain, the Sahara, and the Western Sudan, 1788–1861.* Oxford, 1964.

Boahen, A. Adu. *Topics in West African History.* London, 1966.

Bodrogi, Tibor. *Afrikanische Kunst.* Vienna, 1967.

Bohannan, Paul. *Africa and Africans.* Garden City, N. Y., 1964.

Bovill, E. W. *The Golden Trade of the Moors.* London, 1968.

Bovill, E. W. ed. *Missions to the Niger: The Journal of Friedrich Hornemann's Travels . . . [and] the Letters of Major Alexander Gordon Laing.* Cambridge, 1964.

Bovill, E. W. *The Niger Explored.* London, 1968.

Bowdich, Thomas Edward. *Mission from Cape Coast Castle to Ashantee, with a Statistical Account of the Kingdom, and Geographical Notices of Other Parts of the Interior of Africa.* London, 1819.

Boxer, Charles, R. *Four Centuries of Portuguese Expansion, 1415–1825: A Succinct Survey.* Johannesburg, 1961.

Boxer, Charles R. *The Golden Age of Brazil: 1695–1750. Growing Pains of a Colonial Society.* Berkeley, 1962.

Boxer, Charles R. *The Portuguese Seaborne Empire, 1415–1825.* London, 1969.

Boxer, Charles R. *Race Relations in the Portuguese Colonial Empire, 1415–1825.* Oxford, 1963.

Boxer, Charles R. *Salvador de Sá and the Struggle for Brazil and Angola, 1602–1686.* London, 1952.

Boxer, Charles R. and Carlos de Azevedo. *Fort Jesus and the Portuguese in Mombasa, 1593–1729.* London, 1960.

Bradbury, R. E. and P. C. Lloyd. *The Benin Kingdom and the Edo-speaking Peoples of South-western Nigeria . . .* London, 1957.

Brelsford, William Vernon, ed. *Handbook to the Federation of Rhodesia and Nyasaland.* London, 1960.

Brunschwig, Henri. *L'Expansion Allemande Outre-mer du XVe Siècle à Nos Jours.* Paris, 1957.

Budge, Ernest Alfred Wallis. *A History of Ethiopia, Nubia and Abyssinia According to the Hieroglyphic Inscriptions of Egypt and Nubia, and the Ethiopian Chronicles.* London, 1928.

Burgt, J. M. van der. *Un Grand Peuple de l'Afrique Equatoriale.* Bois de Duc, Holland, 1903.

Burns, Sir Allen. *History of Nigeria.* Hartford, Eng., 1969.

Burns, L. *The British West Indies.* London, 1951.

Burton, Sir Richard F. *A Mission to Gelele, King of Dahome; with Notices of the So-Called "Amazons", the Grand Customs, the yearly Customs, the Human Sacrifices, the Present State of the Slave Trade, and the Negro's Place in Nature.* London, 1893. Abridged edition ed. and with an introd. by C. W. Newbury. New York, 1966.

Burton, Sir Richard F. *Zanzibar, City, Island and Coast.* London, 1872. 2 vols.

Busia, Kofi A. *Africa in Search of Democracy.* New York, 1967.

Caillié, René. *Travels Through Central Africa to Timbuctoo, and Across the Great Desert to Morocco; Performed in the Years 1824 1828.* London, 1830. 2 vols.

Cairns, H. A. C. *The Clash of Cultures: Early Race Relations in Central Africa.* New York, 1965.

The Cambridge History of the British Empire, Vol. VIII; South Africa. Cambridge, 1936.

Carey, Henry C. *The Slave Trade, Domestic and Foreign: Why it Exists and How It May Be Extinguished.* Philadelphia, 1856.

Cary, Mac Otto and Eric H. Warmington. *The Ancient Explorers.* London, 1929.

Caton-Thompson, Gertrude. *The Zimbabwe Culture: Ruins and Reactions.* Oxford, 1931.

Centre of African Studies. *The Transatlantic Slave Trade from West Africa.* Edinburgh, 1965.

Charpy, Jacques. *La Fondation de Dakar, 1845–1857–1869.* Paris, 1958.

Chittick, H. Neville. *A Guide to the Ruins of Kilwa. With Some Notes on Other Antiquities in the Region.* Dar es Salaam, 1965.

Chittick, H. Neville. *Kisimani Mafia: Excavation at an Islamic Settlement on the East African Coast.* Dar es Salaam, 1961.

Clapperton, Hugh. *Journal of a Second Expedition into the Interior of Africa from the Bight of Benin to Soccatoo.* London, 1829.

Claridge, William W. *A History of the Gold Coast and Ashanti from the Earliest Times to the Commencement of the Twentieth Century.* London, 1915. 2 vols. 2nd ed., 1964.

Clark, John Desmond. *The Prehistory of Africa.* New York, 1970.

Clark, John Desmond. *Prehistory of Southern Africa,* Harmondsworth, England, 1959.

Clark, John Desmond, ed. *Atlas of African Prehistory.* Chicago, 1967.

Clarkson, Thomas. *The History of the Rise, Progress and Accomplishment of the Abolition of the African Slave Trade by the British Parliament.* Philadelphia, 1808, 2 vols.

Clendenen, Clarence C. and Peter Duignan. *Americans in Black Africa up to 1865.* Stanford, 1964.

Clinton, Desmond K. *The South African Melting Pot: A Vindication of Missionary Policy, 1799–1836.* London, 1937.

Cobban, Alfred. *A History of Modern France.* Baltimore, 1962. 2 vols.

Cohen, Ronald. *The Kanuri of Bornu.* New York, 1967.

Coillard, François. *On the Threshold of Central Africa. A Record of Twenty Years' Pioneering among the Barotsi of the Upper Zambesi.* Trans. and ed. by C. W. Mackintosh. London, 1897.

Cole, Sonia. *The Prehistory of East Africa.* Harmondsworth, England, 1954.

Collins, Robert O., ed. *Problems in African History.* Englewood Cliffs, N. J., 1968.

Collins, Robert O. and Robert L. Tignor. *Egypt and the Sudan.* Englewood Cliffs, N. J., 1967.

Coquery, Catherine. *La Découverte de l'Afrique.* Paris, 1965.

Colson, Elizabeth and Max Gluckman, eds. *Seven Tribes of British Central Africa.* London, 1951.

Cornevin, Robert. *Histoire de l'Afrique.* Paris, 1964.

Cornevin, Robert. *Histoire des Peuples de l'Afrique Noire.* Paris, 1960.

Cornevin, Robert. *Histoire du Congo, Léopoldville-Kinshasa: Des Origines Préhistoriques à la République Démocratique du Congo.* Paris, 1966. 2nd. ed. rev. and enl.

Cornevin, Robert. *Histoire du Dahomey.* Paris, 1962.

Cornevin, Robert. *Histoire du Togo.* 2nd. ed. Paris, 1962.

Coupland, Sir Reginald. *The British Anti-Slavery Movement.* . . . London, 1964.

Coupland, Sir Reginald. *East Africa and Its Invaders: From the Earliest Times to the Death of Seyyid Said in 1856.* Oxford, 1938.

Coupland, Sir Reginald. *The Exploitation of East Africa, 1856–1890: The Slave Trade and the Scramble.* London, 1939.

Crowder, Michael. *Senegal: A Study in French Assimilation Policy.* London, 1962.

Crowder, Michael. *A Short History of Nigeria.* Rev and enl. ed. New York, 1966.

Crowfoot, J. W. *The Island of Meroë . . . and Meroitic Inscriptions.* London, 1911, 4 vols.

Cruickshank, Brodie. *Eighteen Years on the Gold Coast of Africa.* . . . London, 1966. 2 vols.

Cunnison, Ian. *History on the Luapula.* Cape Town, 1951.

Cunnison, Ian. *The Luapula Peoples of Northern Rhodesia.* Manchester, 1959.

Curtin, Philip D. *African History.* New York, 1964.

Curtin, Philip D. *The Atlantic Slave Trade: A Census,* Madison, Wisc., 1969.

Curtin, Philip D. *The Image of Africa: British Ideas and Action, 1780–1850.* Madison, Wisc., 1964.

Curtin, Philip D. and others, eds. *Africa Remembered: Narratives by West Africans from the Era of the Slave Trade.* Madison, Wisc., 1967.

Dalton, K. G. *A Geography of Sierra Leone.* Cambridge, Eng., 1965.

Davidson, Basil. *Africa: History of a Continent.* New York, 1966.

Davidson, Basil. *The African Past: Chronciles from Antiquity to Modern Times.* Boston, 1967.

Davidson, Basil. *Black Mother: The Years of the African Slave Trade.* Boston, 1961.

Davidson, Basil. *The Lost Cities of Africa.* Boston, 1959.

Davidson, Basil, and F. K. Buah. *A History of West Africa to the Nineteenth Century.* Garden City, N. Y., 1966.

Davies, Kenneth Gordon. *The Royal African Company.* London, 1957.

Davies, O. *West Africa before the Europeans: Archaeology and Prehistory.* London, 1967.

Debenham, Frank. *Nyasaland, the Land of the Lake.* London, 1955.

Debenham, Frank. *The Way to Ilala: David Livingstone's Pilgrimage.* London, 1955.

De Graft-Johnson, John Coleman. *African Glory: The Story of Vanished Negro Civilizations.* London, 1954.

De Kiewiet, Cornelius William. *A History of South Africa, Social and Economic.* London, 1941.

Delafosse, Maurice. *Esquissee Générale des Langues de l'Afrique. . . .* Paris, 1914.

Delafosse, Maurice. *Haut-Sénégal-Niger, . . . le Pays, les Peuples, les Langues, l'histoire, les Civilisations.* Paris, 1911. 3 vols.

Delcourt, André. *La France et les Ètablissements Francais au Sénégal entre 1713 et 1763.* Dakar, 1952.

Denham, Dixon, Hugh Clapperton and Walter Oudney. *Narrative of Travels and Discoveries in Northern and Central Africa in the Years 1822, 1823, and 1824.* London, 1826.

Deschamps, Hubert J. *Histoire de Madagascar.* Paris, 1960.

Deschamps, Hubert J. *Le Sénégal et la Gambie.* Paris, 1968.

Deschamps, Hubert J. *Traditions Orales et Archives au Gabon: Contribution à l'Ethno-histoire.* Paris, 1962.

Deschamps, Hubert J. Raymond Decary and André Ménard. *Côte des Somalis, Réunion, Inde.* Paris, 1948.

Dike, Kenneth Onwuka. *Trade and Politics in the Niger Delta, 1830–1885: An Introduction to the Economic and Political History of Nigeria.* Oxford, 1956.

Diop, Cheikh Anta. *L'Afrique Noire Précoloniale; Etude Comparée des Systémes Politiques et Sociaux de l'Europe et de l'Afrique Noire. . . .* Paris, 1960.

Diop, Cheikh Anta, *Antériorité des Civilisations Négres: Mythe ou Vérité Historique?.* Paris, 1967.

Donnan, Elizabeth, ed. *Documents Illustrative of the History of the Slave Trade to America.* New York, 1965. 4 vols.

Dow, George Francis, ed. *Slave Trade and Slaving.* Salem, 1927.

Driessler, Heinrich. *Die Rheinische Mission in Südwestafrika.* Gütersloh, 1932.

Du Bois, W. E. Burghardt. *The Suppression of the African Slave Trade to the United States of America, 1638–1870.* Cambridge, Mass., 1896.

Duffy, James. *Portugal in Africa.* Cambridge, Mass., 1962.

Duffy, James. *Portuguese Africa.* Cambridge, Mass., 1959.

Duignan, Peter, and Clarence Clendenen. *The United States and the African Slave Trade, 1619–1862.* Stanford, 1963.

Dunham, Dows. *Royal Cemeteries of Kush.* Cambridge, Mass., 1950–1963. 5 vols.

Du Plessis, Johannes. *A History of Christian Missions in South Africa.* London, 1911.

Du Plessis, Johannes. *The Evangelisation of Pagan Africa: A History of Christian Missions to the Pagan Tribes of Central Africa.* Cape Town, 1930.

Edwards, Paul, ed. *Equiano's Travels: The Interesting Narrative of the Life of Olaudah Equiano or Gustavus Vassa, the African.* New York, 1967.

Egharevba, Jacob U. *A Short History of Benin.* Ibadan, 1960.

Ellis, Alfred Bindon. *A History of the Gold Coast of West Africa.* London, 1893.

Fabumni, L. A. *The Sudan in Anglo-Egyptian Relations: A Case Study in Power Politics, 1800–1956.* London, 1960.

Fagan, Brian M. *Iron Age Cultures in Zambia (Kalomo and Kangila).* London, 1967.

Fagan, Brian M., ed. *A Short History of Zambia from the Earliest Times to 1900.* Nairobi, 1966.

Fagan, Brian M. *Southern Africa during the Iron Age.* New York, 1966.

Fage, John Donnelly. *Africa Discovers Her Past.* New York, 1969.

Fage, John Donnelly. *An Atlas of African History.* Rev. ed. London, 1963.

Fage, John Donnelly. *Ghana: A Historical Interpretation.* Madison, Wisc., 1961.

Fage, John Donnelly. *A History of West Africa: An Introductory Survey.* Cambridge, 1969.

Fagg, William Buller. *African Tribal Sculptures.* London, 1967. 2 vols.

Fagg, William Buller. *The Art of Central Africa: Tribal Masks and Sculptures.* New York, 1967.

Fagg, William Buller. *The Art of Western Africa; Tribal Masks and Sculptures.* London, 1967.

Fagg, William Buller. *Nigerian Images: The Splendor of African Sculpture.* New York, 1963.

Faidherbe, Louis Léon César. *Le Sénégal: La France dans l'Afrique Occidentale,* Paris, 1889.

Fairservis, Walter A. *The Ancient Kingdoms of the Nile and the Doomed Monuments of Nubia.* New York, 1962.

Faure, Claude. *Histoire de la Presquîle du Cap-Vert et des Origines de Dakar.* Paris, 1914.

Fieldhouse, D. K. *The Colonial Empires: A Comparative Survey from the Eighteenth Century.* London, 1966.

Fitzgerald, Walter. *Africa: A Social, Economic and Political Geography of Its Major Regions.* London, 1967. 10th rev. ed.

Flint, John E. *Nigeria and Ghana.* Englewood Cliffs, N. J., 1966.

Forde, Cyril Daryll, ed. *Efik Traders of Old Calabar, Containing the Dairy of Antera Duke, an Efik Slave Trading Chief.* London, 1956.

Forde, Cyril Daryll. *The Yoruba-Speaking Peoples of South-western Nigeria.* London, 1951.

Forde, Daryll, and Phyllis M. Kaberry, eds. *West African Kingdoms in the Nineteenth Century.* London, 1967.

Fortes, Meyer. *The Dynamics of Clanship among the Tallensi.* London, 1945.

Fortes, Meyer and E. E. Evans-Pritchard, eds. *African Political Systems.* London, 1950.

Freeman-Grenville, Greville S. P. *The French at Kilwa Island: An Episode in Eighteenth-Century East African History.* Oxford, 1965.

Freeman-Grenville, Greville S. P. *The Medieval History of the Coast of Tanganyika.* . . . London, 1962.

Freeman-Grenville, Greville S. P., ed. *The East African Coast; Select Documents from the First to the Earlier Nineteenth Century.* Oxford, 1962.

Freyre, Gilberto. *The Masters and the Slaves: A Study in the Development of Brazilian Civilization.* New York, 1956.

Freyre, Gilberto. *Portuguese Integration in the Tropics.* . . . Lisbon, 1961.

Fyfe, Christopher A. *A History of Sierra Leone.* London, 1962.

Fyfe, Christopher A. *Sierra Leone Inheritance.* London, 1964.

Gabel, Creighton, and Norman R. Bennett, eds. *Reconstructing African Culture History.* Boston, 1967.

Gailey, Harry A. *History of Africa to 1800*. New York, 1970.

Gailey, Harry A. *A History of the Gambia*. London, 1964.

Galbraith, John S. *Reluctant Empire: British Policy on the South African Frontier, 1834–1854*. Berkeley, 1963.

Gamitto, A. C. P. *King Kazembe and the Marave, Cheva, Bisa, Bemba, Lunda and Other Peoples of Southern Africa: Being the Diary of the Portuguese Expedition to That Potentate in the Years 1831 and 1832*. Translated by Ian Cunnison. Lisbon, 1960.

Gann, Lewis H. *The Birth of a Plural Society: The Development of Northern Rhodesia under the British South Africa Company, 1894–1914*. Manchester, 1958.

Gann, Lewis H. *A History of Northern Rhodesia: Early Days to 1953*. London, 1964.

Gann, Lewis H. *A History of Southern Rhodesia: Early Days to 1934*. London, 1965.

Gann, Lewis H. and Peter Duignan. *Burden of Empire: An Appraisal of Western Colonialism in Africa South of the Sahara*. New York, 1967.

Gann, Lewis H. and Peter Duignan, eds. *Colonialism in Africa 1870–1960, Vol. 1, The History and Politics of Colonialism 1870–1914*. Cambridge, 1969.

Gelfand, Michael. *Livingstone the Doctor, His Life and Travels: A Study in Medical History*. Oxford, 1957.

Gelfand, Michael. *Medicine and Magic of the Mashona*. Cape Town, 1956.

Gelfand, Michael. *Shona Ritual: With Special Reference to the Chaminuka Cult*. Cape Town, 1959.

Gerster, Georg. *Nubien: Goldland am Nil*. Zurich, 1964.

Gertainy, Alfred G. *Mauritania*. New York, 1967.

Gibbs, James L., Jr., ed. *Peoples of Africa*. New York, 1965.

Gluckman, Max. *Custom and Conflict in Africa*. Oxford, 1955.

Gluckman, Max. *The Economy of the Central Barotse Plain*. London, 1941.

Gluckman, Max. *Essay on Lozi Land and Royal Property*. London, 1943.

Gluckman, Max. *The Judicial Process among the Barotse of Northern Rhodesia*. Manchester, 1955.

Gluckman, Max. *Order and Rebellion in Tribal Africa. . . .* London, 1963.

Gluckman, Max. *Politics, Law and Ritual in Tribal Society*. Oxford, 1965.

Gorju, Joseph. *Face au Royaume Hamite du Ruanda*. Brussels, 1938.

Gray, John Milner. *A History of the Gambia*. Cambridge, 1940.

Gray, John Milner, *History of Zanzibar from the Middle Ages to 1856*. London, 1962.

Gray, John Richard. *A History of the Southern Sudan, 1839–1889*. London, 1961.

Greenberg, Joseph H. *The Languages of Africa*. Bloomington, Ind., 1963.

Greenberg, Joseph H. *Studies in African Linguistic Classification*. Branford, Conn., 1955.

Greenfield, Richard. *Ethiopia: A New Political History*. London, 1965.

Groves, Charles Pelham. *The Planting of Christianity in Africa*. London, 1948–58. 4 vols.

Guillain, Charles, ed. *Documents sur l'Histoire, la Géographie et le Commerce de l'Afrique Orientale*. Paris, 1856. 3 vols.

Gutkind, Peter C. W. *The Royal Capital of Buganda: A Study of Internal Conflict and External Ambiguity*. The Hague, 1963.

Haden-Guest, Stephen, John K. Wright and Eileen M. Teclaff, eds. *A World Geography of Forest Resources*. New York, 1956.

Hailey, William Malcolm, 1st baron. *An African Survey: A Study of the Problems Arising in Africa South of the Sahara*. Rev. ed. London, 1957.

Hallett, Robin. *Africa to 1875: A Modern History*. Ann Arbor, 1970.

Hallett, Robin. *The Penetration of Africa: European Penetration in North and West Africa to 1815*. New York, 1965.

Hallett, Robin, ed. *Records of the African Association, 1788–1831*. London, 1964.

Hammond, Richard J. *Portugal and Africa, 1815–1910: A Study in Uneconomic Imperialism*.

Stanford, Cal., 1966.

Hance, William A. *The Geography of Modern Africa.* New York, 1964.

Hardy, Georges. *L'Art Nègre. L'Art Animiste des Noirs d'Afrique.* Paris, 1927.

Hardy, Georges. *L'Enseignement au Sénégal de 1817 à 1954.* Paris, 1920.

Hardy, Georges. *La Mise en Valeur du Sénégal de 1817 à 1854.* Paris, 1921.

Hargreaves, John D. *Prelude to the Partition of West Africa.* London, 1963.

Hargreaves, John D. *West Africa: the Former French States.* Englewood Cliffs, N. J. 1967.

Harlow, Vincent, and E. M. Chilver, eds., assisted by Alison Smith. *History of East Africa, Vol. II.* Oxford, 1965.

Hediger, H. *Wild Animals in Captivity.* New York, 1964.

Herring, Hubert. *A History of Latin America from the Beginnings to the Present.* New York. 1963.

Herskovits, Melville J. *Dahomey, an Ancient West African Kingdom.* New York, 1938.

Herskovits, Melville J. *The Myth of the Negro Past.* Boston, 1964.

Hodgkin, Thomas Lionel. *Nigerian Perspectives. An Historical Anthology.* London, 1960.

Hogben, Sidney John. *The Muhammadan Emirates of Nigeria.* London, 1930.

Hore, Edward C. *Tanganyika, Eleven Years in Central Africa.* London, 1892.

Horton, James Africanus Beale. *West African Countries and Peoples, British and Natives, with the Requirements Necessary for Establishing That Self Government Recommended by the Committee of the House of Commons, 1865, and a Vindication of the African Race.* London, 1868.

Huntingford, George W. B. *The Galla of Ethiopia: The Kingdoms of Kafa and Janjero.* London, 1955.

Hutchinson, Edward. *The Slave Trade in East Africa.* London, 1874.

Huxley, Elspeth. *Four Guineas: A Journey Through West Africa.* London, 1954.

Huxley, Elspeth. *White Man's Country: Lord Delamere and the Making of Kenya.* London, 1953. 2 vols.

Ibn Battuta, *Textes et Documents Relatifs à l'Histoire de l'Afrique. . . .* Ed. and trans. by Raymond Mauny. Dakar, 1966.

Ibn Battuta, *Travels in Asia and Africa, 1325–1354.* Translated and Selected by H. A. R. Gibb. London, 1929.

Ibn Khaldun, 'Abd al-Rahman, *Histoire des Berbères et des Dynasties Musulmanes de l'Afrique Septentrionale.* Trans. by MacGuckin de Slane. Alger, 1852–56. 4 vols.

Ingham, Ernest Graham. *Sierra Leone after a Hundred Years.* London, 1894.

Ingham, Kenneth. *A History of East Africa.* 2nd ed. London, 1963.

Jackson-Haight, Mabel V. *European Powers and South-East Africa: A Study of International Relations on the South-east Coast of Africa, 1796–1856.* Rev. ed. New York, 1967.

James, Cyril Lionel Robert. *The Black Jacobins: Toussaint l'Ouverture and the San Domingo Revolution.* 2nd rev. ed. New York, 1963.

Janson, Horst W. *History of Art: A Survey of the Major Visual Arts from the Dawn of History to the Present Day.* New York, 1962.

James, Herman G. and Percy A. Martin. *The Republics of Latin America: Their History, Governments and Economic Conditions.* New York, 1923.

Johnson, Samuel. *History of the Yorubas from the Earliest Times to the Beginning of the British Protectorate.* Lagos, 1956.

Johnston, H. A. S. *The Fulani Empire of Sokoto.* London, 1967.

Johnston, Sir Harry H. *British Central Africa.* London, 1897.

Johnston, Sir Harry H. *A History of the Colonization of Africa by Alien Races.* London, 1899.

Jones, Arnold Hugh Martin and Elizabeth Monroe. *A History of Ethiopia.* Oxford, 1955.

Jones, G. I. *The Trading States of the Oil Rivers: A Study of Political Development in Eastern Nigeria.* London, 1963.

Jones, William O. *Manioc in Africa.* Stanford, 1959.

July, Robert W. *A History of the African People.* New York, 1970.

July, Robert W. *The Origins of Modern African Thought: Its Development in West Africa during the Nineteenth and Twentieth Centuries.* New York, 1967.

Kaberry, Phyllis M. and Mary Douglas, eds. *Man in Africa.* London, 1969.

Kent, Raymond. *Early Kingdoms in Madagascar, 1500–1700.* New York, 1970.

Kimble, George Herbert Tinley. *Tropical Africa: Vol. I, Land and Livelihood; Vol. II, Society and Polity.* Garden City, N. Y., 1962.

Kingsley, Mary H. *Travels in West Africa: Congo Français, Corisco and Cameroons.* London, 1897.

Kingsley, Mary H. *West African Studies.* London, 1899.

Kirkman, James S. *Men and Monuments of the East African Coast.* New York, 1966.

Kirkman, James S. *Ungwana on the Tana.* The Hague, 1966.

Kirkwood, Kenneth. *Britain in Africa.* Baltimore, 1965.

Klein, Martin A. *Islam and Imperialism in Senegal: Sine-Saloum, 1847–1914.* Stanford, 1968.

Knowles, L. C. A. and C. M. Knowles. *The Economic Development of the British Overseas Empire. Vol. 3: The Union of South Africa.* London, 1936.

Kohn, Hans, and Wallace Sokolovsky. *African Nationalism in the Twentieth Century.* Princeton, 1965.

Kollmann, Karl Paul. *Victoria Nyanza: The Land, the Race and Their Customs.* London, 1899.

Kopytoff, Jean Herskovits. *A Preface to Modern Nigeria: the "Sierra Leonians" in Yoruba, 1830–1890.* Madison, 1965.

Krapf, Ludwig. *Travels, Researches, and Missionary Labors in Eastern Africa and Abyssina.* London, 1867.

Kup, A. Peter. *A History of Sierra Leone, 1400–1787.* Cambridge, Eng., 1961.

Kuper, Hilda. *An African Aristocracy: Rank among the Swazi.* London, 1947.

Kuper, Hilda. *The Swazi.* London, 1952.

Kuper, Leo, and M. G. Smith, eds. *Pluralism in Africa.* Berkeley, 1969.

Lacerda e Almeida, F. J. M. de. *The Lands of Cazembe: Lacerda's Journey to Cazembe in 1798.* Translated and annotated by R. F. Burton. London, 1873.

Laird, Macgregor, and Richard A. K. Oldfield. *Narrative of an Expedition into the Interior of Africa by the River Niger in the Steam Vessels Quorra and Alburkah in 1832, 1833, and 1834.* London, 1837. 2 vols.

Lander, Richard and John Lander. *Journal of an Expedition to Explore the Course and Termination of the Niger.* London, 1832. 3 vols.

Lander, Richard and John Lander. *The Niger Journal of Richard and John Lander.* Edited by Robin Hallett. New York, 1965.

Last, Murray. *The Sokoto Caliphate.* New York, 1967.

Lawrence, Arnold Walter. *Trade Castles and Forts of West Africa.* Stanford, 1964.

Leakey, L. S. B. *The Progress and Evolution of Man in Africa.* London, 1961.

Leakey, L. S. B. *The Stone Age Races of Kenya.* Oosterhout N. B., 1970.

Leakey, L. S. B. and others. *Olduvai Gorge, 1951–1961.* Cambridge, 1965–1967. 2 vols.

Leakey, L. S. B. and Vanne Morris Goodall. *Unveiling Man's Origins; Ten Decades of Thought about Human Evolution.* Cambridge, 1969.

Leiris, Michel, and Jacqueline Delange. *Afrique Noire: La Création Plastique.* Paris, 1967.

Leo (Johannes) Africanus. *History and Description of Africa . . . Done into English in the Year 1600 by J. Pory and Now Edited by Dr. Robert Brown.* London, 1896.

Levine, Donald N. *Wax and Gold: Tradition and Innovation in Ethiopian Culture.* Chicago, 1965.

Levtzion, Nehemia. *Muslims and Chiefs in West Africa: A Study of Islam in the Middle Volta Basin in the Pre-Colonial Period.* Oxford, 1968.

Levy, Reuben. *The Social Structure of Islam.* Cambridge, 1957.

Lewis, I. M. *The Modern History of Somaliland from Nation to State.* New York, 1965.

Lewis, I. M., ed. *Islam in Tropical Africa.* New York, 1966.

Livermore, Harold Victor. *A New History of Portugal.* Cambridge, 1966.

Livingstone, David. *Livingstone's African Journal, 1853–1856,* ed I. Shapera. London, 1963.

Livingstone, David. *Livingstone's Missionary Correspondence, 1841–1856,* ed. I. Shapera. London, 1961.

Livingstone, David. *Missionary Travels and Researches in South Africa, Including a Sketch of Sixteen Years' Residence in the Interior of Africa . . .* London, 1957.

Livingstone, David. *The Zambezi Expedition of David Livingstone 1858–1863,* ed. J. P. R. Wallis. London, 1956.

Livingstone, David and Charles Livingstone. *Narrative of an Expedition to the Zambesi and Its Tributaries and of the Discovery of Lakes Shirwa and Nyasa, 1858–1864.* London, 1965.

Lofchie, Michael F. *Zanzibar: Background to Revolution.* Princeton, 1965.

Lombard, Jacques. *Structures de Type "Féodal" en Afrique Noire: Etudes des Dynamismes Internes et des Relations Sociales chez les Bariba du Dahomey.* Paris, 1965.

Lynch, Hollis R. *Edward Wilmot Blyden: Pan-Negro Patriot, 1832–1912.* London, 1967.

MacCrone, Ian Douglas. *Race Attitudes in South Africa: Historical, Experimental and Psychological Studies.* London, 1937.

McEwan, Peter J. M., ed. *Africa from Early Times to 1800.* London, 1968.

McEwan, Peter J. M., ed. *Nineteenth-Century Africa.* London, 1968.

MacMichael, Harold A. trans. and ed. *A History of the Arabs in the Sudan and of the Tribes Inhabiting Darfur.* Cambridge, Eng., 1922. 2 vols.

Macmillan, William M. *Bantu, Boer and Briton: The Making of the South African Native Problem.* Rev. & ed., Oxford, 1963.

Macmillan, William M. *The Cape Colour Question: A Historical Survey.* London, 1927.

Macmillan, William M. *The Road to Self-Rule: A Study in Colonial Evolution.* New York, 1960.

MacPhee, A. Marshall. *Kenya.* New York, 1968.

McCall, Daniel F. *Africa in Time-Perspective: A Discussion of Historical Reconstruction from Unwritten Sources.* New York, 1969.

Mahdi, Muhsin. *Ibn Khaldûn's Philosophy of History: A Study in the Philosophic Foundation of the Science of Culture.* Chicago, 1964.

Mair, Lucy. *Primitive Government.* Baltimore, Md., 1966.

Mannix, Daniel P. and Malcolm Cowley. *Black Cargoes: A History of the Atlantic Slave Trade, 1518–1865.* New York, 1962.

Martin, Eveline C. *The British West African Settlements, 1750–1821; A Study in Local Administration.* London, 1927.

Marty, Paul. *Etudes sur l'Islam et les Tribus du Soudan.* Paris, 1920–21, 4 vols.

Mauny, Raymond A. *Les Navigations Medievales sur les Côtes Sahariennes Antérieures à la Decouverte Portugaise.* Lisbon, 1960.

Mauny, Raymond A. *Tableau Géographique de l'Ouest Africain au Moyen Age d'après les Sources Ecrites, la Tradition, et l'Archéologie.* Dakar, 1961.

Metcalfe, George Edgar. *Maclean of the Gold Coast: The Life and Times of George Maclean, 1801–1847.* London, 1962.

Metcalfe, George Edgar, ed. *Great Britain and Ghana: Documents of Ghana History, 1807–1957.* London, 1964.

Mitchell, J. Clyde. *The Yao Village: A Study in the Social Structure of a Nyasaland Tribe.* Manchester, 1956.

Morris, Donald R. *The Washing of the Spears: A History of the Rise of the Zulu Nation under Shaka and Its Fall in the Zulu War of 1879.* New York, 1965.

Morris, H. F. *The Heroic Recitations of the Bahima of Ankole.* Oxford, 1964.

Murdock, George Peter. *Africa: Its Peoples and Their Culture History.* New York, 1959.

Nadel, S. F. *A Black Byzantium: The Kingdom of Nupe in Nigeria.* London, 1942.

National Archives of Rhodesia and Nyasaland, and Centro de Estudos Históricos Ultramarinos. *Documents on the Portuguese in Mozambique and Central Africa, 1497–1840.* Lisbon, 1962—.

Neumark, S. Daniel, *Economic Influences on the South African Frontier, 1652–1836.* Stanford, 1957.

Neumark, S. Daniel, *Foreign Trade and Economic Development in Africa: A Historical Perspective.* Stanford, 1964.

Newbury, Colin W. *The Western Slave Coast and Its Rulers . . .* Oxford, 1961.

Newbury, Colin W., ed. *British Policy Towards West Africa: Select Documents, 1766–1874.* New York, 1965.

Niane, Djibril Tamsir. *Sundiata: An Epic of Old Mali.* Translated by G. D. Picket. London, 1965.

Niane, Djibril Tamsir and J. Suret-Canale, *Histoire de l'Afrique Occidentale.* Conakry, 1960.

Nicol, Davidson, ed. *Black Nationalism in Africa 1867, Extracts from the . . . Writings of Africanus Horton.* New York, 1969.

Nørregaard, Georg, *Danish Settlements in West Africa, 1658–1850.* Translated by Sigurd Mammen. Boston, 1966.

Nowell, Charles E. *A History of Portugal.* New York, 1952.

Ojo, G. J. Afolabi, *Yoruba Culture: A Geographical Analysis.* London, 1967.

Ogot, B. A. and J. A. Kieran, eds. *Zamani—A Survey of East African History.* New York, 1968.

Oliver, Roland, ed. *The Dawn of African History.* London, 1968.

Oliver, Roland, ed. *The Middle Age of African History.* London, 1967.

Oliver, Roland and Anthony Atmore, *Africa Since 1800.* New York, 1967.

Oliver, Roland and Gervase Mathew, eds. *History of East Africa,* vol. I. Oxford, 1963.

Oliver, Roland and John D. Fage. *A Short History of Africa.* Baltimore, Md., 1962.

Oliver, Samuel Pasfield. *Madagascar and the Malagasy.* London, 1866.

Omer-Cooper, J. D. *The Zulu Aftermath: A Nineteenth-Century Revolution in Bantu Africa.* Evanston, Ill., 1966.

Ottenberg, Simon and Phoebe Ottenberg, eds. *Cultures and Societies of Africa.* New York, 1960.

Owen, Nicholas. *Journal of a Slave Dealer: A View of Some Remarkable Axcedents in the Life of Nics. Owen on the Coast of Africa and America from the Year 1746 to the Year 1757,* ed. E. Martin. London, 1930.

Palmer, Herbert Richmond. *The Bornu, Sahara and Sudan.* London, 1936.

Pankhurst, Estelle Sylvia. *Ethiopia: A Cultural History.* Woodford Green, Eng. 1955.

Pankhurst, Richard. *An Introduction to the Economic History of Ethiopia from Early Times to 1800.* London, 1961.

Parrinder, Edward Geoffrey. *African Traditional Religion.* Rev. ed., London, 1962.

Parrinder, Edward Geoffrey. *Religion in Africa* Baltimore, 1969.

Parrinder, Edward Geoffrey. *Witchcraft: European and African.* London, 1965.

Polanyi, Karl and Abraham Rotstein. *Dahomey and the Slave Trade: An Analysis of an Archaic Economy.* Seattle, 1966.

Posnansky, Merrick, ed. *Prelude to East African History . . .* London, 1966.

Prestage, Edgar. *The Portuguese Pioneers.* London, 1933.

Prins, Adriaan Hendrik Johan. *The Swahili-speaking Peoples of Zanzibar and the East African Coast: Arabs, Shirazi and Swahili.* London, 1961.

Radcliffe-Brown, A. R. and Daryll Forde, eds. *African Systems of Kinship and Marriage.* London, 1950.

Randles, W. G. L. *L'Ancien Royaume du Congo des Origines à la Fin du XIXe Siècle.* Paris, 1968.

Ranger, Terence O., ed. *Aspects of Central African History.* London, 1968.

Ranger, Terence O. *Revolt in Southern Rhodesia, 1896–7: A Study in African Resistance.* Evanston, Ill., 1967.

Rattray, Robert Sutherland. *Ashanti.* Oxford, 1923.

Rattray, Robert Sutherland. *The Tribes of the Ashanti Hinterland.* Oxford, 1932.

Read, Margaret. *The Ngoni of Nyasaland.* London, 1956.

Richards, Charles Granston and James Place. *East African Explorers . . .* Rev. Ed., Nairobi, 1967.

Ritter, E. A. *Shaka Zulu: the Rise of the Zulu Empire.* London, 1955.

Roberts, Andrew, ed. *Tanzania Before 1900.* Nairobi, 1968.

Rodney, Walter. *A History of the Upper Guinea Coast, 1545–1800.* Oxford, 1970.

Rodney, Walter. *Africa and the Atlantic Slave Trade.* Nairobi, 1967.

Rotberg, Robert I. *A Political History of Tropical Africa.* New York, 1965.

Rouch, Jean. *Contribution á l'Histoire des Songhay.* Dakar, 1953.

Rouch, Jean. *Les Songhays.* Paris, 1954.

Sabatie, Alexandre Camille. *Le Sénégal: Sa Conquête et Son Organisation, 1364–1925.* Saint-Louis, Senegal, 1926.

Schnapper, Bernard. *La Politique et le Commerce Français dans le Golfe de Guinée de 1838 à 1871.* Paris, 1961.

Seligman, Charles, G. *Races of Africa.* 3rd ed. London, 1957.

Senghor, Léopold Sédar. *On African Socialism.* Translated by Mercer Cook. New York, 1964.

Shinnie, Margaret. *Ancient African Kingdoms.* New York, 1965.

Shinnie, P. L. *Meroë: A Civilization of the Sudan.* New York, 1967.

Silva Rego, António da. *Portuguese Colonization in the Sixteenth Century: A Study of the Royal Ordinances—Regimentos.* Johannesburg, 1959.

Skinner, Elliott P. *The Mossi of the Upper Volta: The Political Development of a Sudanese People.* Stanford, 1964.

Smith, Edwin William. *African Ideas of God.* London, 1950.

Smith, Edwin William and Captain Andrew Murray Dale. *The Ila-Speaking Peoples of Northern Rhodesia.* London, 1920, 2 vols.

Smith, Michael G. *Government in Zazzau, 1880–1950.* London, 1960.

Smith, Robert, S. *Kingdoms of the Yoruba: Studies in African History.* London, 1969.

Speke, J. H. *Journal of the Discovery of the Nile . . .* London, 1863.

St. John, Sir Spenser. *Hayti or the Black Republic.* New York, 1889.

Stamp, Sir Lawrence Dudley. *Africa: A Study in Tropical Development.* 2nd ed. New York, 1964.

Staudenraus, P. J. *The African Colonization Movement, 1816–1865.* New York, 1961.

Stern, Henry A. *Wanderings among the Falashas in Abyssinia.* London, 1862.

Strandes, Justus. *The Portuguese Period in East Africa.* Nairobi, 1961.

Stokes, Eric and Richard Brown, eds. *The Zambesian Past: Studies in Central African History.* Manchester, 1966.

Summers, Roger, et al. *Inyanga: Prehistoric Settlements in Southern Rhodesia.* Cambridge, 1958.

Summers, Roger. *Zimbabwe; A Rhodesian Mystery.* Johannesburg, 1963.

Summers, Roger, K. R. Robinson and Anthony Whitty. *Zimbabwe Excavations 1958.* Salisbury, 1961.

Suret-Canale, Jean. *Afrique Noire, Occidentale et Central.* Paris, 1958–64. 2 vols.

Talbot, Percy Amaury. *Peoples of Southern Nigeria.* London, 1926. 4 vols.

Tempels, Placide. *Bantu Philosophy.* Translated by Colin King. Paris, 1959.

Theal, George McCall. *Ehnography and Condition of South Africa Before* A.D. *1505 . . .* 2nd rev. ed. London, 1919.

Theal, George McCall. *History and Ethnography of South Africa South of the Zambezi, from the Settlement of the Portuguese at Sofala . . . 1505 to . . . 1795 . . .* London, 1907–10. 3 vols.

Theal, George McCall. *The Portuguese in South Africa. With a Description of the Native Races between the River Zambesi and the Cape of Good Hope during the Sixteenth Century.* London, 1896.

Theal, George McCall. *Records of the Cape Colony.* London, 1897–1905. 36 vols.

Theal, George McCall, ed. *Records of South-eastern Africa.* Cape Town, 1898–1903. 9 vols.

Thompson, Leonard, ed. *African Societies in Southern Africa: Historical Studies.* New York, 1969.

Trimingham, John Spencer. *A History of Islam in West Africa.* London, 1965.

Trimingham, John Spencer. *The Influence of Islam upon Africa.* New York, 1968.

Trimingham, John Spencer. *Islam in East Africa.* Oxford, 1964.

Trimingham, John Spencer. *Islam in Ethiopia.* London, 1952.

Trimingham, John Spencer. *Islam in the Sudan.* New York, 1965.

Trimingham, John Spencer, *Islam in West Africa.* Oxford, 1961.

Tucker, Charlotte Maria. *Abbeokuta, or Sunrise within the Tropics: an Outline of the Origin and Progress of the Yoruba Mission.* London, 1853.

Turner, Victor W. *Schism and Continuity in an African Society: A Study of Ndembu Village Life.* Manchester, 1957.

Uchendu, Victor Chikezio. *The Igbo of Southeast Nigeria.* New York, 1965.

Ullendorf, Edward. *The Ethiopians: An Introduction to Country and People.* 2nd ed. London, 1960.

Urvoy, Yves, *Histoire de l'Empire du Bornou.* Paris, 1949.

Urvoy, Yves, *Histoire des Populations du Soudan Central . . .* Paris, 1936.

Van der Merwe, Pieter J. *Trek; Studies oor die Mobiliteit van die Pioniersbevolking aan die Kaap.* Cape Town, 1945.

Vansina, Jan. *L'Evolution du Royaume Rwanda des Origines à 1900.* Brussels, 1962.

Vansina, Jan. *Kingdoms of the Savanna.* Madison, Wis., 1966.

Vansina, Jan. *The Oral Tradition: A Study in Historical Methodology.* Chicago, 1964.

Vansina, Jan, R. Mauny, and L. V. Thomas, eds. *The Historian in Tropical Africa: Studies Presented and Discussed at the Fourth International Seminar at the University of Dakar, Senegal, 1961.* London, 1964.

Vedder, Heinrich. *The Native Tribes of South West Africa.* Cape Town, 1928.

Vedder, Henrich. *South West Africa in Early Times . . . up to . . . 1890.* Trans. and ed. Cyril G. Hall. New York, 1966.

Verger, Pierre. *Bahia and the West Coast Trade, 1549–1851.* Ibadan, 1964.

Verger, Pierre. *Dieux d'Afrique. Culte des Orishas et Vodons à l'Ancienne Coté des Esclaves en Afrique et à Bahia, la Baie de Tous les Saints au Brésil.* Paris, 1954.

Verger, Pierre. *Flux et Reflux de la Traite des Negres entre le Golfe de Bénin at Bahia de Todos os Santos du XVIIe au XIXe Siècle.* Paris, 1968.

Villard, André. *Histoire du Sénégal.* Dakar, 1943.

Wallis, J. P. R., ed. *The Matabele Journals of Robert Moffat, 1829–1860.* London, 1945.

Walker, Eric A. *A History of Southern Africa,* London, 1957.

Ward, William Ernest Frank. *A History of Ghana.* 2nd. rev. ed. London, 1958.

Ward, William Ernest Frank. *The Royal Navy and the Slavers: The Suppression of the Atlantic Slave Trade.* London, 1969.

Weatherford, Willis D. and Charles S. Johnson. *Race Relations: Adjustment of Whites and Negroes in the United States.* Boston, 1934.

Webster, J. D., A. A. Boahen, and H. O. Idowu. *History of West Africa. The Revolutionary Years —1815 to Independence.* New York 1970.

Westermann, Diedrich. *Geschichte Afrikas; Staatenbildungen südlich der Sahara.* Cologne, 1952.

Whiteley, Wilfred, ed. *A Selection of African Prose: Traditional Oral Texts.* Oxford, 1964.

Wiedner, Donald Lawrence. *A History of Africa South of the Sahara.* New York, 1962.

Wilks, Ivor. *The Northern Factor in Ashanti History.* Legon, 1961.

Willett, Frank. *Ife in the History of West African Sculpture.* New York, 1967.

Williams, Eric. *Capitalism and Slavery.* London, 1944.

Wills, A. J. *An Introduction to the History of Central Africa.* London, 1967.

Wilson, Monica and Leonard Thompson, eds. *The Oxford History of South Africa, Vol. I, South Africa to 1870.* Oxford, 1969.

Wolfson, Freda. *Pageant of Ghana.* London, 1958.

Woodward, E. L. *The Age of Reform 1815–1870.* Oxford, 1949.

Index

511